DATE DUE

DEMCO 38-296

Dance on Camera
A Guide to Dance Films and Videos

Edited by
LOUISE SPAIN

Foreword by
JACQUES D' AMBOISE

The Scarecrow Press, Inc.
Lanham, Md., & London
and
Neal-Schuman Publishers, Inc.
New York
1998

SCARECROW PRESS, INC.

Published in the United States of America
by Scarecrow Press, Inc.
4720 Boston Way
Lanham, Maryland 20706

4 Pleydell Gardens, Folkestone
Kent CT20 2DN, England

Copyright © 1998 by Dance Films Association, Inc.
This is a revised edition of *The Dance Film and Video Guide*
published in 1991 by the Dance Films Association

British Cataloguing-in-Publication Information Available

Library of Congress Cataloging-in-Publication Data

Dance on camera : a guide to dance films and videos / edited by Louise Spain.
      p.   cm.
1. Dance—film catalogs.   2. Dance—Video catalogs.   I. Title.
GV1595.D342   1997
792.8/0216 21   96-053236
                                                              CIP

ISBN 0-8108-3303-4 (cloth : alk.paper)

For Susan Braun, Founder and first Executive Director of Dance Films Association, who died too young at 79 to see her dream for a new edition of this guide to dance films and videos become a reality, but old enough to have seen the unique organization she founded in 1956 become a major contributor to its field, and survive to and beyond its 40th birthday.

For my parents, Harold M. Browner (1907–1996) and Molly Browner (1908–1996).

And for Victor Lipari (1945–1997), DFA's Executive Director from 1995 to 1997, an eminent contributor to the field of dance on camera.

Contents

Foreword

Jacques d'Amboise

Jacques d'Amboise was a principal dancer and choreographer for the New York City Ballet for over 30 years, and appeared in such films as Seven Brides for Seven Brothers and Carousel. He now heads the National Dance Institute, which teaches dance to thousands of inner city school children, many of whom perform at his annual "Event of the Year" in New York City.

Since ancient times the visual arts, including painting, architecture, and sculpture, have tried to communicate the impression or perception of movement. The huffing, puffing, and teeming animals rendered by early artists in the caves of Altimira and Lascaux, as well as the fabulous friezes of the Parthenon, are examples of how brilliantly art has attempted to recreate movement.

Flip books also achieve an illusion of movement by the rapid flipping of a series of figures, thus allowing each unit to have a slight change of position. This early attempt to capture movement eventually evolved into the freeze frames of the cinema. Whether on celluloid, videotape, computer-generated (or some future technological development), the moving picture is a comparatively recent art form. It is one that incorporates other arts such as music, dance, drama, and story-telling. Any form of communication that can be conceived is used by cinematography and, perhaps most importantly, choreography.

In the field of architecture, many arts and crafts are called into play to collaborate. The final collaborators are the users, the occupants of the building and their interaction with it. Similarly, in cinematography, collaboration by many artists and specialists realize the end product. With the capabilities of home editing and interactive technology, the final collaborator is the viewer, the user, who will perforce be a choreographer, ordering the sequence of images and their place in space, time, and action.

In dance and choreography it is invaluable to have the opportunity to view what has been done in the past, what is being done in the present, and to give support and encouragement to those artists who are in the forefront of experimentation, especially with film and video. Like building cathedrals and pyramids, cinematography is an expensive collaboration, and the complexity and cost of the tools keep growing. Artists in the field deserve all the support we can give. The *Dance on Camera* guide is an important and much needed resource to add to this support.

Preface

You hold in your hands a new edition of the one and only catalog of dance on camera published in the United States. This reference guide to dance films and videos aims to serve all those dance educators, librarians, curators, programmers, students, parents of aspiring ballerinas, living room or professional dancers, producers and directors, who are searching for information about, or names of distributors of, dance on film and video. It tries to anticipate every need and answer every research question with an abundance of data on each title and multiple indexes for cross-referencing.

This edition is an updated and revised version of the *Dance Film and Video Guide* published in 1991. Several features of that edition have been expanded, corrected, or changed, and some new features have been added. Due to the magic of computer technology, the supplementary indexes provide vastly more complete cross-referencing of all of the credits available in the Title Index, (choreographers, composers, dancers, dance companies, and directors). Each of these indexes is alphabetical by name, followed by a list of the titles in which that artist's work appears. Since more of these credits were added to the database and consequently retrieved by the computer program, these indexes are now approximately double the size of the previous edition. The guide also includes many new subject headings, and provides more indexes than before to expand your search, including ones for Excerpts (by the name of the excerpt), Awards (by the name of the award), and Series (by the series title).

Myriad corrections were made to the data, which was extensively rechecked and verified to be as accurate and reliable as possible. About one-third of the entries are new to this edition—either recently produced titles, older titles not previously included, or oldtime musical/dance feature films now available on home video.

The Title Index is an alphabetical list of over 1,400 entries which cover the full range of dance from around the world. Though thumbnail sketches are available in most distributors' catalogs, this guide combines such information in one place, and amplifies it by including, wherever possible, credit information on and indexes to: director, choreographer, principal dancers, dance company, and composer. Also listed are distributors, producers, date, running time, format, and whether black and white or color. A brief description following the credits in the Title Index gives a summary of the content, names of excerpts or full-length dances included in the film, and titles of any other related films.

In the Category Index, any one title may appear under two or three different subject headings. For example, if you are studying African dance you may search the Category Index under Africa, Folk Dance, or Religious/Ritual and peruse all the titles on the subject of dance in Africa. Then by turning back to the Title Index, you will find the film credits, annotation, and the name of the distributor or distributors who have the rights of rental or sale.

If you are making a documentary on a certain composer, dancer or choreographer, you can immediately find all the titles featuring works by that artist by looking by name in the Composer, Dancer or Choreographer Index. If your class is studying the dance of the 18th century and you wish to see sample dances of that time, you can scan the Category Index under Dance History. To find instructional material for beginners, look under Children, Instructional, or the particular style of dance (e.g. Tap, Ballet). Avant-garde films appear under Cinedance and Experimental.

To put the film or video in your own hands, a list of distributors at the back of the book has addresses and phone numbers, and provides a comprehensive guide to vendors who distribute titles numbering from one to a few hundred on the subject of dance. A guide to Resources (dance film and video collections, archives and festivals both in the United States and all over the world) is another feature of this book. These lists have been greatly expanded, since many more distributors of dance films and re-releases in video format have come onto the market, and new resources were identified and added. Fax numbers are a new feature of these listings.

The editor has also commissioned essays by scholars and dance professionals to give planning ideas, insight into the history of dance on film, and personal testimonies from notable artists. We hope to introduce you to the vast world of dance on camera—glorious performances preserved on film, provocative collaborations between dancers and filmmakers, fascinating documentaries, as well as the classic movie musicals.

For the dance teacher looking for curriculum material, the historian looking for vintage footage of legendary stars, the parent looking for beginning ballet instruction on video, the ethnographer looking for dance culture and customs, the producer looking for examples of avant-garde and experimental work, the programmer looking for a vital excerpt or specialized subjects such as Circus Arts or Ice Dance, the home video buyer looking for a popular Astaire film, the dancer/choreographer looking for a record of a performance—for one and all, there is a wealth of reference material and resources to be found in this new edition.

—Louise Spain

Acknowledgments

Many people and organizations deserve recognition for their contributions to this new compilation. First and foremost Ms. Susan Braun, Founder and President of Dance Films Association, who ceaselessly poured time, resources and energy into the promotion of dance on camera ever since she founded her organization in 1956. Regrettably, Ms. Braun died in October, 1995 at the age of 79. Though she did not live to see the new guide in print, she was actively involved in every facet of its production and considered it the culmination of one of her most cherished visions.

The late Victor Lipari, Executive Director from 1995–97, and many members of the Board of Directors—Vice President Deirdre Towers, Treasurer Debra Wakefield, Secretary Penny Ward, Virginia Brooks, Elizabeth McMahon, and former members John David Burkholder, Louise Bedichek and Leslie Shampaine—were all valued and helpful contributors and supporters. Mr. Lipari was an invaluable source of information and willing assistance. Ms. Towers' work of collecting the data for and compiling the 1991 edition was the essential foundation for this current effort. She also researched and submitted many of the 1996 titles.

Long-time friends and Advisory Committee members of DFA, William Claiborne, Emily Jones, and Pauline Tish offered untiring advice and support. Fred Rowley was the computer genius who devised the original and unique "Mediamix" database for this project, and provided ever-willing expertise and support, particularly in compiling the indexes.

Antonia Austin was the invaluable computer consultant and expert who reorganized, reassembled, and converted the database into its present form, and tirelessly helped to get it ready for publication. Evann Siebens served as a hard-working and dedicated research assistant, helping primarily to collect and verify data. The assistance of LaGuardia College's Nancy Schoppner, who lent an able hand with fact-checking, typing, and proofreading, was greatly valued and appreciated.

The City University of New York and a grant from the Professional Staff Congress of CUNY helped fund my research project—revising the database, verifying and correcting all the old entries, collecting new ones, and editing the essays for this edition. Special thanks go to Professor Ngozi Agbim, Chief Librarian at LaGuardia Community College, for her support and encouragement which helped to see the project through.

Many libraries and their staffs made helpful contributions, such as the Dance Collection at Lincoln Center and the Donnell Media Center of The New York Public Library, New York University's Bobst Library, and the Program for Art on Film at Pratt Institute. Numerous distributors and independent producers filled out data sheets and provided detailed information. Eric Monder, a specialist on the director George Sidney, submitted invaluable data for the listings of Sidney's musical dance films.

Thanks also to Barbara Abrash and Catherine Egan, editors of *Mediating History: The MAP Guide to Independent Video by and about African American, Asian American, Latino, and Native American People*, whose format served as an inspiration for this work; and to my husband, Mel, and children, Jessica and Matthew Spain, who provided solid moral support and cheerful endurance.

Introduction
LOUISE SPAIN

"THE MECHANISM BY WHICH the style of dance is passed from generation to generation is fragile, even haphazard. The ballets of the past have no literal script; the only clues to form and content are vague descriptive notations and an equally unreliable oral tradition. The choreographic imprint, like a magnificent sand castle, is washed away by time, leaving behind only the footprints of the architect and the musical score."

Gelsey Kirkland with Greg Lawrence, *Dancing on My Grave: An Autobiography*, New York: Doubleday & Company, Inc., 1986.

It is just this transitory nature of the genre as noted by ballerina Gelsey Kirkland which recorded dance retains, and then a new hybrid is formed—dance on camera.

At a meeting of the Board of Directors of Dance Films Association held on January 7, 1969, the minutes indicate that Ms. Emily Jones, then the Executive Director of the Educational Film Library Association (EFLA), "suggested that one important function of DFA should be that of providing a Union Catalog of all available films on dance, including pertinent technical, descriptive and distribution data. The primary service function of the organization, she stated, must NOT be that of a film library."

Thereafter, Ms. Susan Braun, the first Executive Director and Founding President, guided the organization in producing catalogs of dance films and videos. Several different versions were self-published in the '70s and '80s, until Princeton Book Company issued the first *Dance Film and Video Guide* compiled by Deirdre Towers for DFA in 1991, upon which this new edition is based.

Form and Content

Dance on Camera: A Guide to Dance Films and Videos is a resource tool for members of the dance profession, educators, librarians, curators, programmers, producers, directors, and those interested in dance on film and video. There are over 1,400 entries—about two thirds from the 1991 edition which were retained, verified and revised, more than 400 new titles, and 100 new entries for musical dance feature films. To be listed, films and videotapes simply had to be in current distribution in the United States. No sale or rental prices have been given, since these differ from source to source and change without notice. No attempt has been made to disclaim or endorse the quality of the material.

Indexes

The Guide is indexed according to the screen credits (Choreographer, Composer, Director, Dancer, Dance Company) as listed in the Title Indes (except for producer), and under categories such as style of dance (Ballet, Ballroom, Folk, Modern, Jazz, Tap, etc.); type (Anthropological, Documentary Portraits, Experimental, Cinedance, Instructional); geographical location, and other subject areas such as Dance History, Dance Therapy, Children, Pantomime, Choreography, Circus Arts, and Collaboration. Many titles are indexed under multiple categories.

There are also separate indexes for Awards, Excerpts, and Series. Users may access films and videos by any of these elements simply by turning to the relevant index.

References Used

Distributors' catalogs, flyers, and data entry forms.

Green, Stanley. *Encyclopedia of the Musical Film.* New York: Oxford University Press, 1981.

Halliwell, Leslie. *Halliwell's Film Guide*, Fifth Edition. New York: Charles Scribner's Sons, 1986.

Taylor, John Russell and Arthur Jackson. *The Hollywood Musical.* New York: McGraw-Hill Book Company, 1971.

Thomas, Tony. *That's Dancing.* New York: Harry N. Abrams Inc., 1984.

Dance Films Association (DFA)

DFA publishes a bimonthly newsletter for members, *Dance on Camera News*, announcing new releases, interviews, resources, competitions, festivals, and funding sources. Members also have telephone access to the continually updated database, and may view a number of films available solely through DFA.

DFA sponsors the oldest competitive dance film and video festival, Dance on Camera, held annually in New York City. In December, 1996, the New York Film Society at Lincoln Center co-sponsored the Dance on Camera Festival at the Walter Reade Theater. Additional activities and services include members' use of a tri-standard monitor, research on titles, curatorial assistance, and marketing/distribution suggestions.

Legal Obligations

When arrangements are made for film or video rentals or purchase, the borrower accepts the following obligations: to use them for nontheatrical, nonprofit, nonbroadcast purposes only, and not to duplicate them in whole or in part.

Disclaimer

To the best of our knowledge and ability, the information contained in *Dance on Camera* was true at the time of publication. Although distributors frequently change their addresses and their holdings, the list of distributors and resources at the end of the indexes was correct at the time of publication. The editor and Dance Films Association do not assume and hereby disclaim any liability for any errors or omissions, whether resulting from inaccurate information, negligence, or any other cause. In order to submit information about omitted or new titles, or to correct old data for future editions, please contact the editor in care of the publisher or Dance Films Association, 31 West 21st Street, 3rd floor, New York, NY 10010, (212) 727-0764.

Choreography for Camera:
A Historical Perspective
Evann Siebens

Evann Siebens trained at the Royal Ballet School and was a dancer with the National Ballet of Canada and the Bonn Ballet in Germany. She is presently studying film production and philosophy at New York University.

"In most dance films the dancer, knowing little of the possibilities of camera and cutting, works in terms of theatrical composition; the filmmaker, knowing little about theatrical choreographic integrity, refuses to sit still and concerns himself with photographic pictorial effects which usually have nothing to do with the intentions of the dancer. The usual unsatisfactory result is neither fish nor fowl—it is neither good film nor good dance." [1]

Written in 1945 by Maya Deren, this passage aptly describes the core problem that affects many dance films. To simply transfer a piece of dance from proscenium stage to film is to ignore the spatial freedom of film, whereas to overemphasize the movement of the camera as opposed to that of the dancers takes away from the kinesthetic qualities of the dance. Space is not the only variable element, however. Film time varies greatly due to editing choices, whereas live dance movement creates a smooth linear continuity. The energy of live performance is also inherently different from that of film. The challenge is to find a true synthesis between the two mediums, and effectively translate a three-dimensional, kinetic art form into a two-dimensional one.

Dance films have existed since the invention of the motion picture. Edward Muybridge's photographic inventions and use of multiple cameras—an early forerunner of film—were used to study both animal and human movement that could not be seen through direct observation. Dance films were recorded by Thomas Edison as early as 1895, including *Annabelle's Serpentine Dance* and *Annabelle's Butterfly Dance*, and the Pathé Brothers and Georges Méliès started creating movement films soon after. Archival footage of legendary dance figures Ruth St. Denis in 1906, Doris Humphrey in 1924, Katherine Dunham in 1941 and Martha Graham in 1943, are rare visible artifacts of some of the pioneers of American modern dance, while film snippets of Russian ballerina Anna Pavlova give the balletomane a glimpse of her performing genius.

Aside from being archival and historical documents, dance films exist in a large variety of forms and genres, including: films incorporating dance into a narrative story or into its form (as in the musical), documentaries, performance records, instructional videos, music videos, etc. Yet in spite of the magnitude of the output, very few films have been successful in combining the two mediums in a true synthesis. The problems of stage to screen transference were first encountered when plays written for the theatre were filmed. Most people believed in the superiority of live theatre and its visceral connection between the audience and the performer, and renounced the new medium as mere visual distraction. This same argument is used in relation to dance film today; namely, that dance loses its force and immediacy when it is transferred from the live performance arena.

Still, there have been filmmakers and/or choreographers who have achieved this symbiosis of dance and film, among whom Maya Deren, Busby Berkeley, Martha Graham, Doris Humphrey, Norman McLaren, and Merce Cunningham in collaboration with Charles Atlas and Elliot Caplan are among the most successful. What have these filmmakers and/or dance-makers done to achieve this union? Is there a particular way of filming dancers, or of choreographing for the camera? Have they solved the essential problems of space, time and energy and, if so, how? Essentially, what is the language of dance film? A good dance film director should not only move actors and/or dancers but also be able to "choreograph" the camera's movement. Similarly, a choreographer and director are both working creatively towards a vision, as well as orchestrating elements of design, music, performance, and the technical aspects of dance and film in order to create a final project.

Not surprisingly, filmmaker Maya Deren, innovator and pioneer not only of dance film but of experimental film in general, was a dancer who worked for choreographer Katherine Dunham. All of Deren's films, most noticeably *Meshes of the Afternoon*, express a deep understanding of movement; they not only explore the range of the dancer's movements, but also the *space* within which the dancer moves. An appreciation of how dance and space interrelate is crucial in film, for the perspective of a film camera is an inversion of the proscenium stage. On stage, the space across the front is widest, becoming smaller as it recedes back. Conversely, a

[1] Maya Deren. "Choreography for the Camera." *Dance Magazine.* October, 1945. pp 20–12.

film frame is at its narrowest closest to the camera's eye, becoming larger as it recedes back. Not only does filmed dance have the ability to focus attention on *exactly* what it wants its audience to notice, it also has the freedom of omnidirectional space within the frame.

Deren's film *A Study in Choreography for Camera* deals with this exploration of space and uses cinematic techniques to enhance the choreographic movement. The opening sequence, a long, circular pan, shows the dancer appearing in three different places in the same glade of trees. This illusion is achieved through careful in-camera editing combined with the continuous movement of the camera, creating a world where space and time are distorted. Deren later uses the dancer's movement to motivate a change of location: a développé which, in a match-on-action cut, continues its course, but in a different location. The thrust of the movement and familiarity of the single leg are used to orient the viewer in spite of the abrupt jump cut. It also illustrates Deren's innovative use of space by using a disturbing change to emphasize the fluidity and constant presence of the dancer. Film time is explored by showing the dancer spotting (a head technique used by dancers to avoid dizziness), and gradually speeding the camera up to give the illusion of extraordinarily fast pirouettes. Later, time is slowed down as the dancer moves into slow motion jêtés over and around the camera. This particularly emphasizes the freedom of the camera's perspective as compared to that of a stage audience, and gives an exquisite sense of flight and weightlessness—the goal of many dancers and choreographers. The movement and thrust of Deren's short film is achieved by her exploration of both cinematographic and choreographic dance techniques.

Busby Berkeley, another innovative dance filmmaker, is renowned for his large-scale, extravagantly patterned dance numbers created for numerous musical films in the 1930s and '40s (see also Eric Monder's essay, "The Velvet Light Trip Fantastic: A 'History' of the Hollywood Dance Musical"). Berkeley strove to emancipate the camera from its static, frontal position, and choreographed its movements even more than those of the dancers. He reacted against the stationary, full-bodied style employed by dance cinematographers of the time, influenced by Fred Astaire, who believed that dance should be filmed in full figure long shots. Astaire is quoted as having said, "Either the camera will dance or I will." This is still often the paradigm as to how dance *should* be filmed, yet much of Astaire's success lies in his own performing genius.

Berkeley's abstraction of the single dancer to part of a larger picure is seen most particularly in his famous overhead or kaleidoscopic shots. Taken immediately from overhead (and so losing any sense of depth or perspective that a lower shot would provide), the dancers become part of a whole, moving, abstract picture or pattern. These patterns often serve a symbolic purpose, as seen in the early film *Gold Diggers of 1933*. In the penultimate dance number "The Shadow Waltz," the images move from individual shots of women playing violins to a macrocosm of dancers playing violins. With violins lit in the darkened, abstract space, the groups of women become one large, glittering violin being played with a lit bow. Berkeley continually creates larger patterns or shapes out of groups of women whether they be violins, pianos or flowers, indicating a universal vision. Most importantly, these images could only be seen with the aid of a moving film camera; one could never see Berkeley's choreographic shapes on a proscenium stage.

Martha Graham's film *Night Journey* exemplifies how stage choreography can be transposed to camera with an innate understanding of camera, dance space, and movement. Directed by Alexander Hammid, husband of Maya Deren, its beautiful images are derived from the superb use of the foreground and background planes, giving depth and dimension to the dancing. The choreography moving on a diagonal towards and away from the camera has a strong kinetic sense, as the dancers move into close-up, and then rapidly disappear into the distance. The camera work is static, with many long shots and few edits; the movement comes essentially from the performers as they move in and out of the frame, giving a deep impression of off-screen space. This is especially effective with the "Greek chorus" of women as they "comment", through movement, on the actions of Jocasta and Oedipus the King, who are both in frame most of the time. Shot in black and white with low-key lighting, the stylized minimalist set, costumes, and clear, white, neutral space dramatize and enhance the tonality and beauty of the entire film. Extremely sensitive to the choreographer's work, the filmmaker has not only effectively transposed the performance piece to film, but has also made a new work of art.

One of the pioneers of modern dance in America, choreographer Doris Humphrey, filmed much of her work for archival purposes. Yet *Air for the G String*, originally choreographed in 1928 and made into a film in 1934, is an early example of a beautiful, integrated dance film. The central figure was danced by Humphrey herself, yet it is essentially an ensemble piece for five women, with the imbalance between the group and soloist explored in the choreography and reflected in the shooting style of the film. Nearing the climax, the five dancers move from a straight line into a gradual circular pattern, their weight back as they shift from slow, languorous walking to accented triplets. As they proceed into a tighter circle, the film cuts from a full frontal shot to an oblique, overhead shot which emphasizes the circularity of the choreographic shape. This choice of shot preserves the choreographic integrity of the movement pattern, and enhances the abstractly beautiful circular shape created by the dancers. The film includes footage of all the choreography, yet near the end focuses on Humphrey as she slowly, deliberately lifts her arms and face in a moment of spiritual revelation. The ecstasy and beauty of this climatic moment is incredibly moving as we look upon a rare and living portrait of Humphrey's passion for her art. The film ends as it begins, with all five dancers in a single line, lyrically and sonorously moving through the music and the dance.

Another successful dance film orchestrator is the animator Norman McLaren. His film *Pas de Deux* (1968) is a ballet choreographed for a man and a woman by Ludmilla Chirlaeff. The film is shot in simple long shot, yet the slow motion images are completely altered through the use of an optical printer; the superimposition of frames results in multiple, overlapping images. The choreographic progression of the dance becomes larger and more expansive, and is matched with a similar optical effect; the single images of the dancers double and triple until multiple images proliferate. This tasteful and artistic film takes a simple pas de deux and, through technical means, expands it into an abstract and pure dance experience.

More recently, important explorations in dance film have been undertaken by Merce Cunningham in collaboration with directors Charles Atlas and Elliot Caplan. Cunningham, a major choreographer of American modern dance, is an innovator of dance space and its omnidirectional capabilities. Rather than relying on the conventions of a proscenium stage, or frontal space, he considered any open space to be equal to, and just as important, as any other place. This lack of directional orientation, and the nature of Cunningham's movement, translates particularly well to film, and the way the camera sees movement.

Charles Atlas's film *Channels/Inserts* is a study in space and dual events occurring concurrently with dancers moving in and out of the frame, oblivious to the camera's own movement or presence. As the camera follows one dancer, the film frame is opened or expanded to show the other dancers still in the background of the previous space, thus evolving into an interaction between the two locations. The constant movement of the dancers and camera, as well as the use of depth, is important for this illusion to work, with the foreground and background emphasis resulting in a three-dimensional image. The energy and kinesis that this film emits proves that any energy lost from a lack of physical presence can be regained through the kinetic movement of the camera. Cunningham's work with Atlas and presently with Caplan (especially the beautifully luminescent film *Beach Birds for Camera* discussed in Virginia Brooks' essay "Some Thoughts on Filming Dance: A Conversation with Elliot Caplan"), are important in that they actively explore the uniqueness of dance created for the camera.

The above films and filmmakers cover only a fraction of dance film history. Many choreographers and filmmakers are presently collaborating and experimenting in this exciting, and not yet fully explored art form. Still, audiences accustomed to live dance performances sometimes find dance film unsatisfying and miss the energy of a live, visceral performance. Yet in many ways, dance film comes closer to a pure, true conception of dance that evolved in a social context, only later becoming conventionalized into performance form. Most dances originate in a studio, with a proscenium or "front" created for standardized performance spaces. Yet to choreograph for and with a camera is to explore space, time and energy from a different, and perhaps more basic aspect of dance. The difficulty of effectively synthesizing or marrying the two art forms is overwhelming to many filmmakers and/or choreographers, yet as the above examples illustrate, wonderful films have been made, inspiring hope for the future. As Maya Deren wrote in her essay "Choreography for the Camera:"

"It is my earnest hope that film-dance will be rapidly developed and that, in the interest of such a development, a new era of collaboration between dancers and filmmakers will open up—one in which both would pool their creative energies and talents towards an integrated art expression." (Ibid p. 11).

Some Thoughts on Filming Dance:
A Conversation with Elliot Caplan
Virginia Brooks

Virginia Brooks is Professor of Film and Head of Production at Brooklyn College of the City University of New York. She has made documentary and record films of dance for more than twenty years, produced archival video for the School of American Ballet since 1980, and written on the art and craft of filming dance for Ballet Review, Dance Magazine, *and* Dance Research Journal.

Note: This is an edited transcript of a discussion with filmmaker Elliot Caplan on some of the factors involved in bringing dance to the screen. Caplan came to the Cunningham Dance Foundation in 1977, starting out as a cameraman and assistant to Charles Atlas. Since 1984, as co-director and editor with Merce Cunningham, Caplan has been responsible for all of the company's work in film and television. Most recently he created two award-winning programs—the documentary *Cage/Cunningham*, and the extraordinary film *Beach Birds for Camera*.

VB—When you begin a project to film something that already exists as a stage production, what is the first thing you do?

EC—The first thing I do is to look at [the choreography]. I get or make a tape of the whole choreography—a worktape, a single shot, wide angle, from the front center.

VB—Not from the side? What about the aspect ratio, can you get back far enough to get it all in?

EC—In fact, when I have to do a taping for that purpose I set the lines and the dancers stay inside. And I study it.

VB—What do you look for?

EC—I look for the choreography to guide me in what's to happen with the camera. It is not as though I bring in a separate structure. I watch what happens, and usually the choreography suggests direction, placement, focal length of the lens, distance, and some way to continue from that point. It might not necessarily be the beginning of the dance; I might see a particular shot in the middle of the dance and then I'll work backwards. When we begin to work, Merce and I sit at a table with a monitor. I place the camera somewhere, and we just start. It either works or it doesn't. I make changes. We work very much on the spot and then we notate all of these things. We go through section by section that way. And I try to adapt my notation to his choreographic

delineation, so if he calls it section 1, part A, I do the same, so we have a way to relate to each other. Also, the technique tape that we made around the time of *Deli Commedia* [the first piece for which Caplan was solely responsible] gave me a great insight into breaking down the dance, how the technique looked on camera, because then I saw the technique expanded into movement . . . I believe my way of understanding the dance came from painting because, to me, I was dealing with a frame. I had enough of an understanding of film at that time to approach it very pragmatically so I looked at the frame like a blank canvas, and I dealt with weight, and shape, and color, and balance; my way into the dance was in fact through weight. I didn't have a memory for movement, Merce's dancers didn't perform to any music, there was no story, so it was very hard for me to look at this and remember these bits of choreography.

VB—So while it would be crazy to come to a dance you have never seen and expect to film it, by the same token, even if you see it, you can't learn the dance; you have to learn what happens in *dances*. If somebody has their weight on their right foot, they can't readily move in that direction.

EC—Exactly.

VB—So, even though you might be seeing the dance for the first time you know what the structure of the thing can be, even if you don't know exactly what is going to happen.

EC—Once I established that way of looking at the dance through the weight, I had a new confidence and I could really place my frame where I needed it to be, and I knew that the body wasn't going to do something unpredictable.

VB—We agree there's no one way to film dance, but there are decisions you need to make for any project. When you look at the design of a piece, and decide where you are going to place the camera, you have said there shouldn't be any dance happening off the screen . . . but that is not possible always. Sometimes you want to show some detail. How do you choose the detail? Or is detail too disrupting?

EC—No . . . there's a section at the end of *Beach Birds* where there's a single male dancer, David Kulik, and he's doing a solo and he's looking up, his arms are up. Then he looks down and he looks [like this] across the stage and I chose to cut away and show what he was looking at.

VB—Standard narrative technique.

EC—Right. It was three dancers doing something; those things are happening in the space at the same time but the way I dealt with it in the film is that it's what he's looking at. In fact those dancers were there all the time and he's not really looking at them. Merce doesn't even have them doing that on stage I don't think, but I made this little narrative thing that helped me in the film. Most of the time the only important thing is that the dancing is on the screen, it's not happening someplace else. In *Changing Steps*, however, we broke the frame, and we let dancers go out and in, framed parts of the body; we cut into things already in progress, cut away to something else. Anything went in *Changing Steps* because of the nature of that choreography. It can be all mixed up; it can be done in different orders.

VB—People will look at different places when they are looking at it on the stage anyway.

EC—Yes, and Merce uses it as event material, all mixed up.

VB—But how do you choose which detail to focus on?

EC—I think probably I film a lot of [detail] and I later figure it out in the editing room.

VB—How would you start training someone else to do this job?

EC—I'd send them to the Metropolitan Museum of Art to look at paintings. I really would. I know myself, I can't tell you how much I get from paintings. Sometimes I get ideas from film. I go to a film and it gives me an idea into a film. In *Points in Space* I had gone to see Kurosawa's *Ran*, and that idea of space collapsed one on top of the next.

VB—The planes . . .

EC—That's what I used in *Points in Space*. But that's rare, because I don't think there are that many good films out there, commercial films, to take from that way . . . To train someone, you know it's so hard; I was photographing Merce's work for two years before I began to understand it. I've told him that. I've said it publicly and it's like anything else, you just need to dedicate yourself to something, you need to just keep doing it.

VB—So you think that working with one choreographer as you have, and analysing what his movement looks like and being able to capture it in a way that's meaningful on the screen is the ideal way to proceed. I mean, as opposed to the situations where someone goes in and does one thing after another in a particular space but there are a lot of different styles.

EC—I think it is an ideal way, but it's a rare way that doesn't happen.

VB—It's too expensive to have somebody on board.

EC—I'm the only filmmaker working for a dance company anywhere. There isn't another. There are other filmmakers who work with dance. Those people should be employed to make the films of dance rather than the people who do music videos who think they know about dance but don't. It's just like any other field, it needs its own discipline. You have to deal with the issues of movement.

VB—Well, that's one of the exciting things about it; the *subject* of dance is movement, and for me, in any film the most interesting part is the movement, whether it is the subject movement or the camera movement. But when the subject is dance, and the subject of dance is movement, then you have a big responsibilty for presenting that movement. It is very different from dialogue, where you can just do over-the-shoulder cuts back and forth and so on.

EC—Well, in fact that's true. What you're really suggesting is a language of movement which filmmakers, depending on their level of craft, exploit or not. Good filmmakers exploit it. They do things that are exciting in terms of movement that relate to story.

VB—What else can we say about training?

EC—It is so hard to say; there are no two dances that are alike. I approach my work in a very practical way and I don't try to step out in front of what I think is the purpose of the film, which is to show the dancing. One needs to start from that purpose. It seems in all of the film that I see the filmmaker has too much of an ego, and wants to express him or herself. That's what kills the dance.

VB—It *can* kill the dance if you don't know what you are doing.

EC—The only way to do this is to start at a school level; we have to have schools and programs that are dedicated to teaching students how to photograph dance, give them the tools and allow them to explore this so it is something they become interested in.

VB—What it looks like on the screen . . .

EC—. . . a chance to figure it out.

VB—Well, I think that's true. It shouldn't become just one of the things you do without as much freedom, because if you're filming dance somebody else has a creative stake in the project. If you are really an imaginative filmmaker you will do something else where you can have all of the control. If filming dance is a valid enterprise in its own right, then film and dance people are more likely to choose doing it together.

EC—They have to be able to see it and break it down in some way visually. If it is going to be a straight documentation there most likely is a place in the sequence to cut to a different angle. If you can cut from one side to another, you look for those places, and they either dance the piece three or four times and you shoot it completely from each side, or they do it to that point and you know where to cut, and they stop, and you change position, and then they continue.

VB—. . . after you've made your new setup.

EC—Most of the time, something made for the stage doesn't work as well on camera and it has to be changed to allow the camera to be closer, be more intimate with the thing that it's photographing . . . so there needs to be someone in the making of the stage piece that would be sympathetic to that idea of changing the work. Assuming there's time, you take that person and sit him down in front of a monitor and you put a video camera on the piece and you look at it and say, for instance, 'Look, this person is blocking that one. Can we move this person over here?' You begin to deal with the issues that are necessary to make something clear for the camera. Otherwise, you are just setting it up and shooting it and doing just what came before.

VB—And some parts will work because the camera happens to be in the right place and other parts won't, so you will actually be doing a disservice to the total piece.

EC—I just went to the Presenters' Conference . . . I was curious; I went to everyone's booth and everyone has video, even if it is a music person. And ninety percent of the stuff suffered from this lack, from not making something that took the camera into account. 'We have our thing, it's set, now you just set up a camera and you are going to shoot this.'

VB—With no thought for the light . . .

EC—With no thought for anything. And if film was approached that way no one would want to go to the movies.

VB—It would be the same as just setting a camera up in front of a theater piece.

EC—A wonderful thing would be some sort of national institute, a group of people that would travel to places documenting for companies, the way things should be done, capturing these pieces properly. Or people would come to New York and there would be a studio . . .

VB—Set up and ready with the all the lights and a proper floor . . .

EC—It needs to be done right, otherwise dance on film will always stay where it has been. That's why music video is so exciting, and has taken off so much because they made it specifically for television.

VB—Right, but you know something else about music video? The music is inviolate. It's being used for presenting the songs; they are not really interested in the dance or the visuals for their own sake. The music is what they are selling and the music is not compromised in any way; it is recorded in the most beautiful manner, with all the tracks and studio time and all the rest of it. The dance is just something to put on the screen to keep people's eyes engaged while they're listening to the songs.

EC—You know there was an article recently in a magazine called *International Arts Manager*, and I'm tired of people writing about dance on camera as though it's new. It's not new any more. Some of us have been doing it for twenty years.

VB—And thinking about it, . . . and others were doing it before us.

EC—You and I know it's not new any more. There is a body of work out there. The AMEX [International Music Center, Vienna] festival we went to, there were how many programs?

VB—There were more than 150 . . .

EC—In that year alone! So let's get on with it, we're not talking about this new art form anymore. Maybe it's new to you if you're nineteen years old.

VB—It's true; it's time for people to study what has been done and move on.

Dance Literacy:
Programming and Teaching with Film
Deirdre Towers

Deirdre Towers, President of Alegrias Productions and Vice President of the Board of Dance Films Association, is a dancer who has edited Dance on Camera News *for DFA since 1982, and has written about dance for many other publications. Parts of this essay first appeared in* Dance Teacher Now *(Raleigh, North Carolina).*

IMAGINE AN ENGLISH TEACHER making a course plan without a reading list, a piano teacher giving his students only his own compositions to practice, or an aspiring writer who had only read essays by his teachers. Preposterous! Teaching without source materials is unusual in most disciplines. However, many dance teachers overlook the opportunity to introduce the inspiration and example available in dance films and videos.

Unlike writers, musicians or visual artists who have vast libraries, scores, and museums to explore, dancers generally have to rely upon the resources of their local teachers and performers. Many teachers have gathered a repertoire from their own professional experience, or gained a sophisticated approach to improvisation, and/or could recreate choreography through dance notation. However, even in these cases, the students have a limited perspective.

The video revolution has swept in the option of dance literacy. Over 3,000 dance films and videos are now distributed in the United States, with an equivalent number on music and the visual arts. Dancers can spin the globe and study the dance of wherever their finger lands. They can push back the clock and slip into another era. Anna Pavlova, Sergei Diaghilev, Irene Castle, or Hermes Pan become household friends. Whatever their fancy might be, students can now sample a smorgasbord of choices. Presenters, teachers, and curators can design series and curricula with far more freedom and imagination than ever before.

To whet the appetite, start with a jaunty mix of graphics and tap called *Visual Shuffle*, a sweet look at loneliness with *Le Bal*, a poetic treatment of revenge (*Blood Wedding*), and the urge to fly (*Airdance*). Lost in America? Try *Forbidden City, USA*, the documentary on Chinese Americans barred from Hollywood. For the ballerina in the making, have her experience the 1957 *A Dancer's World*.

For the main course, how about a series? A dance film or video series can help sustain community interest in the arts, especially when funding for live performances is in serious

jeopardy. Consider developing a series around the process, the craft of dance, opening with Natalia Makarova's *A Class of Her Own*, or *Sylvie Guillem at Work*, and then closing with the *Dance in America*'s specials on George Balanchine. Video biographies are proliferating, so a portrait series could be easily assembled. As a starting point, sample *Genius On the Wrong Coast*, the documentary on the choreographer/innovator Lester Horton, or *Hanya, Portrait of a Pioneer* on Hanya Holm. Another series could be constructed around ideas and issues. The award-winning documentary *Positive Motion* shows Anna Halprin coaxing a group of men with AIDS to express their fears and anger. *Partners, Brothers, Pas de Deux, Milt and Honi*, either literally or figuratively explore relationships.

For the presenter intent on audience development, film series with guest speakers can be a wonderful magnet. Entice music and dance lovers with a program split with two interpretations of the same music or the same story: Ravel's "Bolero" choreographed for an ensemble by Maurice Béjart (*Bolero*) and the sensuous duet by Lar Lubovitch (*Fandango*); or three versions of *Romeo and Juliet* with choreography by Yuri Grigorovich, Rudolf Nureyev and Kenneth MacMillan. Invite musicians, dancers, and directors to debate the variances in musicality, technical polish, and dramatic credibility. Make a bow to cross-culturalism with films on social dancing around the world and offer classes simultaneously.

To return to the nitty gritty of the classroom, a holistic approach to dance training feeds the mind, body and spirits of students through a guided use of the video library. Whether the assignment is to decipher why a certain piece is moving, or how a ballet or musical is structured, the students will discover the multiple options to express any emotion, circumstance or abstract idea. They will perceive how different cultures relate to the audience, to space and to stillness.

A dance teacher can jump into the role of historian by simply suggesting videos that support his/her vision and training. A teacher schooled in the technique of Jose Limon, for example, can take the dancers beyond and behind the technique by placing Limon in the context of his peers. Viewing the documentaries *Trailblazers of Modern Dance*, *The Men Who Danced* on Ted Shawn, and/or the performance works of Alwin Nikolais or Martha Graham will grant the students a multidimensional understanding of their art.

As a guide or counselor, the teacher can gently direct the

energy of student productions by suggesting specific videos. For example, for a dancer drawn to dance theatre, show *What Do Pina Bausch and Her Dancers Do in Wuppertal?* and *Anna Sokolow, Choreographer*. For a minimalist dancer, introduce her/him to Eiko and Koma's *Lament* beautifully shot by James Byrne or Laura Dean's *Tympani*. These videos will speed their development and build a sophistication and subtlety into their approach.

For students whose hearts are set on making the BIG TIME, put them in the producer's chair. Have them dissect commercial films such as *Dirty Dancing* or *The Nutcracker*. Discuss the moments of anticipation, shadings, and even missed opportunities on the part of either the performers or the choreographer. Gage the depth of what is or is not being communicated, the illusions, allusions, energies, and patterns. Watch *Singin' in the Rain* to see how each dance sequence either helps advance the plot or give us new insight into the characters. Compare two interpretations of *Sleeping Beauty* to examine the variances in musicality, technical polish, and the use of classic literature.

By examining the production value of videos, students learn to recognize the approach of the director and the editors. Was the dance well adapted for the camera? Does the cameraman support or hinder the dance? Studying dance in the media makes the students keenly aware of communication through body movements, the psychological implications behind everyday gestures, postures, and rhythms. This intelligence prepares the young dancers for a variety of careers as directors, social workers, psychologists, and managers.

Especially for students who doubt their commitment to a performance career, steer them towards an intellectual approach to dance. Have them research the source materials behind a production, such as studying the score along with a video, or reading the stories that inspired the classic ballets. Take a theme, such as adolescence, and assemble a program that demonstrates how different cultures acknowledge life's passages with Gianfranco Norelli's *Sunrise Dance* about the Apache native American ritual, *Shaman's Journey* or *Serama's Mask*.

Alternatively, perhaps the dancer has more of an inclination to join the world of cinematographers. Support his/her enthusiasms with a series on dance-film experiments including *Early Dance Films*, *Maya Deren: Experimental Films*, director/composer Meredith Monk's *Ellis Island*, Emile Ardolino's *He Makes Me Feel Like Dancin'* and Canadian animator Norman McLaren's *Narcissus*. Consider the investment of bringing in the marvelous film exhibition *Before Hollywood: Turn of the Century Film from American Archives* which includes the first efforts of Thomas Edison's *Annabelle's Serpentine Dance* and *Annabelle's Butterfly Dance*.

Finally, videos can also answer questions or solve dilemmas. Perhaps a parent is anxious to know more about the background of a local teacher. Look for a video of the company the teacher performed with or of the creator of the technique she/he follows. Oftentimes, videos can be borrowed or studied on the premises of a company, even though they may not be released for commercial distribution. A dancer desperately seeking direction can shop for her identity by looking at videos. Collaborating artists can quickly educate themselves through the use of videos. A composer commissioned to do a piece may find solace and amusement by watching Wynton Marsalis try to communicate with Peter Martins in *Accent On The Offbeat*.

Enjoy the wealth of opportunities! For help in finding a film or for suggestions on developing a curriculum or a series, please contact Dance Films Association.

The Velvet Light Trip Fantastic:
A "History" of the Hollywood Dance Musical

ERIC MONDER

Eric Monder is the author of George Sidney *(Greenwood Press, 1994,) and has contributed articles to* The New York Times, Film Comment, *and* The Motion Picture Guide.

THE HISTORY OF THE Hollywood musical has usually been told in unenlightening terms, from its "primitive" beginnings (in the late 1920s and early '30s) to its "refined" peak years (in the 1940s and '50s) to its "decline" (in the 1960s and beyond). Likewise, musicals that have emphasized dance have mostly been judged in terms of their stylistic components (performance, staging, design), rather than by the degree to which they divorce themselves from their inherent theatricality. Yet, throughout Hollywood musical history, "dance musicals," whether based on stage properties or not, were routinely filmed like stage shows. Only occasionally would a director challenge the genre technologically as well as artistically. Thus, a linear history of the musical does not reveal a true progression of cinematic development, but a constant tension between old, theatrical and new, filmic components.

Dance in Hollywood film begins in earnest during the 1930s with the aesthetic debate between Busby Berkeley and Fred Astaire. Both choreographers came from the stage, but Astaire was also the star of his films. He preserved the theatrical element of his material with his long-take, wide-shot dances opposite Ginger Rogers in their famous RKO musicals—*Flying Down to Rio* (1933), *Top Hat* (1935), *Shall We Dance* (1937), et al. In these films, Astaire worked closely with directors and screenwriters in order to "integrate" the dances naturally into the narratives. Meanwhile, Berkeley's numbers in Warner Bros.' "backstage" musicals, including *42nd Street* (1933), *The Gold Diggers of 1933* (1933), and *Dames* (1934), were casually inserted spectaculars in storylines that Berkeley usually did not direct. Berkeley, however, increased the dimensions of the stage by using trick shots and odd camera angles (including his trademark overhead shot), and by editing each film cel to music (Astaire edited as little as possible). While Astaire's intimate, canned ballroom style was more immediately influential on movie musicals, Berkeley was the first director to create movement through editing and camerawork, rather than traditional staging.

Although many musicals continued to feature big production numbers throughout the Depression and World War II, the economic frugality of the period forced a scaled-down approach that dovetailed nicely with Astaire's simpler style.

The Metro-Goldwyn-Mayer producer, Arthur Freed, became well-known for making the best musicals in the 1940s—e.g. *Meet Me in St. Louis* (1944), *On the Town* (1949). These featured streamlined production numbers, usually with few performers, and were based on the Astaire "integrated" model (Astaire worked for Freed several times in the 1940s and '50s). When Busby Berkeley joined the famous Freed "unit" in 1939, even he altered his style, and in 1942's *For Me and My Gal*, starring Gene Kelly and Judy Garland, Berkeley relinquished the choreographer's job altogether, directing only the dramatic scenes. Ironically, by the time Berkeley started work on Freed's production of *Annie Get Your Gun* in 1949, he was fired because his direction was considered too stagebound.

During Hollywood's "Golden Age", from the 1930s through the '50s, other studios (Warner Bros., 20th Century-Fox, etc.) either made pale imitations of the MGM/Astaire-style integrated dance film, or updated the old backstage musical formula (minus the innovations of Busby Berkeley). Typically, in these films, such choreographers as Hermes Pan, Robert Alton, LeRoy Prinz, Jack Cole, Nick Castle, and Michael Kidd, took over musical numbers from directors who were either too busy with other chores or too untrained in musical staging.

In the meantime, critics hailed the MGM approach of advancing plots and developing characters through dance. As a consequence, several young choreographers became directors under Arthur Freed's watch, including: Charles Walters (*Good News* [1947], *Easter Parade* [1948]); Stanley Donen (*Royal Wedding* [1951], *Seven Brides for Seven Brothers* [1954]), and Donen in tandem with Gene Kelly (*On the Town* [1949], *Singin' in the Rain* [1952]). Kelly's quasi-balletic variation on the Astaire paradigm was praised for injecting the modern dance styles of Martha Graham and others. Perhaps the most acclaimed director working for Freed, Vincente Minnelli, also came from a theater background (as an art director), yet Minnelli, too, integrated dance numbers in a theatrical, albeit fluid, sophisticated style—e.g. in *The Pirate* (1948), *An American in Paris* (1951), and *Brigadoon* (1954).

Another director, George Sidney, also worked occasionally at the Freed unit at MGM—*The Harvey Girls* (1946), *Annie Get Your Gun* (1950), *Show Boat* (1951) and, likewise, worked on the musical portions of his films. But Sidney used a more cinematic approach than his contemporaries. Unlike most of the other directors and choreographers, Sidney did not come from either a theatrical or a pure dance background but, rather, learned all aspects of filmmaking through his experience as an assistant director at the studio. Like Berkeley, Sidney commented on the theatrical nature of his material by using more cutting, camerawork and trick effects than Minnelli-Walters-Donen-Kelly; but, unlike Berkeley, Sidney undercut the divertissement of the spectacle with ironic, self-reflexive touches. In "Life Upon the Wicked Stage" (in *Show Boat*), for example, the performers of a stage act (Marge and Gower Champion) had to duck under and run around the camera—out of camera range—in order to appear in different parts of the space, as different characters, during the lengthy takes. Thus, Sidney exposed the limitations of a famous theater piece by exploring the endless possibilities of the cinema.

In the 1950s and '60s, most musicals were either literal adaptations of stage shows like *Oklahoma!* (1955), *West Side Story* (1961), and *My Fair Lady* (1964), or were influenced by the musical strains of rock n' roll. During this era, only George Sidney continued to expand the vocabulary of the form by deconstructing the theatrical elements in such adap-

tations as *Kiss Me Kate* (1953, in 3-D), *Pal Joey* (1957), *Bye Bye Birdie* (1963) and *Half a Sixpence* (1968). The "rock" musicals, which reflected changing musical tastes, incorporated the latest teenage dance crazes, but it took Sidney, again, to make the quintessential rock 'n roll musical, *Viva Las Vegas* (1964, starring Elvis Presley and Ann-Margret), which was also the first of its kind to cut shots to fast, hard-edged rock rhythms. Sidney's popular film immediately influenced the British director, Richard Lester, who introduced the rock group, the Beatles, in *A Hard Day's Night* (1964) and *Help!* (1965), and choreographer-turned-director, Bob Fosse, who edited his own dances in *Sweet Charity* (1969), *Cabaret* (1972), and *All that Jazz* (1979). By the 1980s, in fact, Sidney's revolutionary montage techniques were regularly employed by rock video directors.

And yet, despite the influence of Sidney's formal dynamism on new musical forms, Hollywood since the 1970s has continued to produce and market standard film adaptations of Broadway shows like *The Wiz* (1978), *Annie* (1982), and *A Chorus Line* (1985). Evidently, there will always be a dialectic between traditional and aesthetically progressive approaches to dance on film—no matter what advances have been made.

Dance on Film and Video at the Library of Congress
DAVID PARKER

David Parker is the Acting Head of the Curatorial Section, Motion Pictures, Broadcasting and Recorded Sound Division, The Library of Congress. He has compiled/co-authored Guide to Dance in Films *and is the maker of the film* Anna Sokolow Directs "Odes."

THE MOST IMPORTANT EVENT influencing dance resources at The Library of Congress was the invention of the motion picture. For the first time, it was possible to capture a dancer's image fully. Movies profoundly changed the nature of dance documentation. Because dance is a camera subject that moves, filmmakers—later followed by producers of television and videotape—have been drawn to dancing images since movies began. Researchers at the Library can see films made before the turn of the century, such as *Imperial Japanese Dance* (1894), *Annabelle's Fire Dance* (1897) or *National Geisha Dance of Japan* (1902).

From the first, dance films were exhibited as part of the program, from instructional films on how to do contemporary social dances to *Classical Dances by Countess Thamara De Swirsky* (1912). During the silent era, choreography was pioneered for dramatic feature films such as *Intolerance* and *The Ten Commandments*. Sporadic filming was also done that was not intended for public exhibition: e.g., Anna Pavlova filmed half a dozen works in 1924.

Almost immediately dance scholars, seeing the tremendous potential of capturing dance, began to exploit film as a medium for enriching resources for research. Many hours of films of dance rehearsals, oral history and interviews—such as those with Martha Graham and Ruth Page—are held by the Library.

By the early 1930s, the advent of sound had boosted film production of many dance performances which are represented in the Library by hundreds of shorts featuring dancers such as Agnes de Mille dancing in 1930, "Snakehips" Tucker in 1933, and a series of tabloid musicals built around eccentric dancer Hal LeRoy.

By the mid-thirties, the popularity of the series of Busby Berkeley and Astaire and Rogers musical films prompted Hollywood to produce a large number of musicals, often in bi-annual "Broadway Melody", "Gold Diggers" and "Follies" series. These document dance works of such talents as Eleanor Powell, Paul Draper, and George Balanchine.

The Library's original commission of Aaron Copland and Martha Graham for the work which became *Appalachian Spring* (1959) offers the scholar extensive paper documentation to consult, along with the video and film recordings of productions of the work made decades later.

Virtually half of the films made in Hollywood during the peak wartime years were some form of musical, many including dance. The Library's holdings document work of such contributors as Kathryn Dunham and The Nicholas Brothers. America's wartime allies were featured in shorts and feature films such as *Bayaderka* and the Red Army Dancers' *A Nation Dances*; less theatricalized ethnic dance documentation, also reflected in the field recordings of vernacular dance, are available in the Library's Archive of Folk Culture in the Jefferson Building in Washington, DC. Apart from musicals, the genre of biographical dramas has included the work of dancers from Lilian Harvey as *Fanny Ellsler* (1937), to Tamara Toumanova in *Deep in My Heart* (1954) and *Tonight We Sing*. "Backstage" stories and historical dramas have provided settings for choreography by such artists as Lester Horton, Valerie Bettis and Jack Cole.

Throughout the era of sound films, theatricalized versions of popular social dances have been choreographed for inclusion in topical film dramas, from "The Grizzly Bear" of the ragtime era through the rock and roll dances to Latin dance permutations of the recent past.

As a result of this technological breakthrough, the Library's motion picture collection holds more than one hundred thousand films and videos, in which dance is prominent in many hundreds of films and in hundreds more videotapes. Dancing also became a major component of feature film compilations of musicals, such as *That's Dancing* (1985) and the three anthologies of *That's Entertainment* (1974, 1976, 1993).

The Library's collections of dance in films expanded greatly in number from the early 1940s until the present. Many of these productions are documentaries of famous dance companies such as the Paris Opera Ballet, Ballet Russe, the Royal Ballet, the Bolshoi, the Kirov, the La Scala Opera Ballet, and the San Francisco Ballet.

Holdings produced for television range from Ray Bolger dancing in a commercial to many network variety series regularly featuring dance. They include *Ballets de France, The Bell Telephone Hour, Omnibus*, and *Dance in America*.

The development of videotaping as a means to record dance has produced major changes in dance research. Creators of dance can now produce records of dance quickly and relatively inexpensively; this is as true for practitioners of all kinds of vernacular dance as it is for theatrical dance. As a result, a rich treasure of dance literature awaits analysis and study.

The Library's acquisition of such materials has been enormously enhanced by the 1976 revision of the copyright law. This provides for the copyright registration of choreographic works. As a result of this provision, the Library has received thousands of such dance videotapes, including numerous deposits from George Balanchine (*Square Dance, Chaconne, Stars and Stripes,*) and Agnes de Mille (*The Bitter Weird, Bloomer Girl* and *Conversations About the Dance*).

The relative permanence of film/video has prompted a dramatic change in expectations of creators of dance. Choreographers know that their work can become a part of artistic history long after they cease choreographing or dancing. This realization has spurred increased interest at the Library in attempting to preserve all aspects of dancers' and choreographers' creative work. Such new awareness of historical perspective has become an important tool for the acquisition of dance collections at the Library.

Especially during the past half century, choreographers and dancers have developed and maintained personal collections of extraordinary value. Among the most significant such collections in The Library of Congress are those of Bob Fosse/Gwen Verdon, Martha Graham and Franziska Boas. The Library's collections of materials of Franziska Boas documents many dimensions of her career as dancer, educator and social activist. All share a dependence on the moving image as a prime document of the creative artist.

The Fosse/Verdon Collection in particular is such an example: a comprehensive assemblage of the high achievements of Bob Fosse and Gwen Verdon. Through documentation of the period of their professional lives, one can construct a rich picture of the dancer's world on Broadway, in movies and on television. It contains a videotaped performance of Fosse's stage musical *Pippin* and a six-page analysis of the direction of the production by Fosse.

As with other such Library collections, the photographs, manuscripts and other papers of this collection are available in the Library's Music Division; video, film and audio materials are available in the reading rooms of the Motion Picture, Broadcasting and Recorded Sound Division, in the Madison Building, in Washington, DC.

The Library doesn't loan films or videotapes. All moving image works must be viewed on the premises. Access is available to those who are doing scholarly research and are above high school age. Appointments to view films or videos must be made several days in advance. Viewing is done on film or video viewing machines from 8:30 AM to 5:00 PM on weekdays. In the vast majority of cases, there is no subject index for dance films and videos, which must be accessed alphabetically by titles, located by first consulting other reference sources.

EDITOR'S NOTE: The titles mentioned in these essays are listed in the Guide only if they have been found to be in United States distribution.

Dance on Camera Title Index

¡A BAILAR! THE JOURNEY OF A LATIN DANCE COMPANY
1988, 37 and 29 min. color film, video
Distributor: The Cinema Guild
Producer: Catherine Calderón
Director: Catherine Calderón
Choreographer: Eddie Torres
Principal Dancer: Eddie Torres
Composer: Tito Puente
Category: SOCIAL, HISPANIC
Dance on Camera Festival 1991 Honorable Mention
New York City's *salseros*—Hispanic club and street dancers—prepare for their first public performance at the Apollo Theatre in Harlem.

ACCENT ON THE OFFBEAT
1993, 90 min. color video
Distributors: Laserdisc Fan Club
Producers: Peter Gelb, Susan Froemke
Directors: Peter Gelb, Susan Froemke
Choreographer: Peter Martins
Principal Dancers: Heather Watts, Jock Soto, Albert Evans, Wendy Whelan, Nikolaj Hübbe, Melinda Roy, Nilas Martins
Dance Company: New York City Ballet
Composer: Wynton Marsalis
Category: COMPOSITION, COLLABORATION
Dance on Camera Festival 1994 Bronze Award
A commissioned score by Wynton Marsalis and choreography by Peter Martins provides the backdrop for a documentary on the collaborative artistic process of these two artists, culminating with the performance of the ballet at the New York State Theatre.

ACCUMULATION WITH TALKING PLUS WATER MOTOR
1986, 10 min. color video
Series: Alive From Off Center
Distributor: KTCA-TV
Producer: KTCA-TV
Director: Jonathan Demme
Choreographer: Trisha Brown
Principal Dancer: Trisha Brown
Category: MODERN, EXPERIMENTAL
Modern dancer Trisha Brown simultaneously tells three stories and performs two solos.

THE ACHIEVERS: KATHERINE DUNHAM
1988, 15 min. color video
Distributor: PennState
Principal Dancer: Katherine Dunham
Category: DOCUMENTARY PORTRAITS, AFRICAN-AMERICANS
Katherine Dunham—dancer, choreographer, teacher and anthropologist—is interviewed and presented as instrumental in changing the status of the African-American dancer from entertainer to artist.

ACROBATIC DANCE OF THE SNAKE MAIDENS
1968, 33 min. color film
Distributor: PennState
Producer: Wissen
Director: H. Himmelheber
Category: ANTHROPOLOGICAL, AFRICA
Three small girls from the villages of Dan and Guere along the western Ivory Coast in Africa perform acrobatic feats to the accompaniment of drums and an iron clinking instrument. Then, they are whirled into the air by their trainer and wound around his body like snakes.

ACROBATS OF GOD
1968, 22 min. color film, video
Series: Three By Martha Graham
Distributors: Pyramid, Kent State, University of Minnesota, Viewfinders
Producers: John Houseman, H. Poindexter for Martha Graham Center
Director: David Wilson
Choreographer: Martha Graham
Principal Dancers: Martha Graham, Bertram Ross, Robert Cohan, Mary Hinkson, Helen McGehee, Takako Asakawa, Clive Thompson
Dance Company: Martha Graham Dance Company
Composer: Carlos Surinach
Category: MODERN, DANCE HISTORY
Set Designer: Isamu Noguchi
Graham's dance celebrating the trials, denials, glories and delights of being a dancer adapted for television by John Butler.

ADOLESCENCE
1966, 22 min. b&w film
Distributor: Indiana University
Director: Vladimir Forgency
Principal Dancers: Sonia Petrovna, Madame Egorova
Composers: Frédéric Chopin, Niccolo Paganini
Category: BALLET, CHILDREN
Sonia Petrovna, a young French girl, studies ballet with eighty-four-year-old Madame Egorova, a former star of Serge Diaghilev's Ballets Russes. Despite her diligence, she fails her first audition. French dialogue with English subtitles.

ADOLESCENCE OF BALLET
1993, 20:10 min. color video
Distributor: Hal Bergsohn Associates
Producers: Isa and Hal Bergsohn
Director: Hal Bergsohn
Choreographer: Isa Bergsohn
Principal Dancers: Adair Landborn, Thom Carlyle
Category: DANCE HISTORY
As part of a dance history series intended for use in the classroom, the video traces the historical development of dance from early Greek theatre to the Elizabethan court. Live dance sequences demonstrate a pavane and a gaillard.

ADRIENNE CHERIE INTERPRETS DANCES OF INDIA
1988, 35 min. color video
Distributor: ACA Enterprises
Producer: Adrienne Cherie
Director: Louis Zweier
Choreographers: Adrienne Cherie, Sujata
Principal Dancer: Adrienne Cherie
Composer: Jay Scott Hacklemann
Category: INDIA, INSTRUCTIONAL
Performances of *Alarippu* (invocational dance), *Devadasi* (temple dance), *Parvathi* (dance of a goddess), *Water Maiden* (Kathak dance), *Fish Story*, and *Tara* (hand ballet), plus exercises for the hands.

ADVENTURES IN ASSIMILATION
1992, 8 min. color video
Distributors: Third World Newsreel, The Kitchen
Director: Richard Dean Moss
Choreographer: Richard Dean Moss
Principal Dancer: Richard Dean Moss
Category: MODERN
Using movement within a fixed frame, Moss expresses self-discovery and identity through his choreography and dance.

ADZO
1994, 3 min. b&w video
Distributor: Duster Films
Producer: Matthew M. Hauser
Director: Matthew M. Hauser
Choreographer: Matthew M. Hauser
Composer: Matthew M. Hauser
Category: ANIMATION, AFRICA
Dance on Camera Festival 1994 Honorable Mention
An animation of African dance, in which energetic drumming accompanies two dancers in an original composition in the traditional style of the Ewe-speaking people of Ghana. Shouts of *Adzo*, which translates as "Monday," could refer to a dancer born on a Monday.

AEROS
1990, 33 min. color video
Distributors: Electronic Arts Intermix, Museum of Modern Art
Producer: Susan A. Fait
Director: Burt Barr
Choreographer: Trisha Brown
Dance Company: Trisha Brown Company
Composer: Richard Landry
Category: MODERN COMPANIES
Impressions of the company in Russia, and the collaboration between choreographer-performer Trisha Brown and designer-painter-photographer Robert Rauschenberg. The dancers, clad in silver unitards, move by the blinding lights of the set.

AFGHANISTAN DANCES (3 films)
1963, 10–14 min. color, b&w film (silent)
Distributor: PennState
Producer: Wissen
Category: FOLK, ASIA
Three silent films of folk dances performed by

men in Pashtun and Tadzhik in Badakhshan, and Pashtun in Wardak, Afghanistan.

AFGHANISTAN: MEN'S DANCE WITH PANTOMIMIC INTERLUDE
1963, 10 min. color film
Distributor: PennState
Producer: Wissen
Director: Herman Schlenker
Category: FOLK, ASIA
In a valley surrounded by mountains, seven men dance to a drum and wood instrument, with horses and a herd of cows in the distance. The film closes in on the men's bodies draped in robes. The wind whistles as the men clap and move their line dance around an open circle.

AFRICA DANCES
1967, 27 min. color film, video
Series: International Zone Series
Distributor: United Nations Visual Materials Library
Producer: United Nations Television
Director: Ramakantha Saarma
Choreographers: Italo Zambo, Hamidou Bangoura
Principal Dancers: Italo Zambo, Hamidou Bangoura
Dance Company: Les Ballets Africains of the Republic of Guinea
Category: AFRICA, FOLK
Narrator: Alistair Cooke
Les Ballets Africains, founded shortly after Guinea achieved its independence, performs at the United Nations General Assembly for the anniversary of the Universal Declaration of Human Rights. Introduction by Ambassador Ashkar Marof of Guinea.

AFRICAN CARVING: A DOGON KANAGA MASK
1974, 19 min. color film
Distributor: Phoenix
Producer: Film Study Center of Harvard University
Director: Eliot Elisofon
Category: RELIGIOUS/RITUAL, AFRICA
The Dogons of Mali, West Africa perform a masked dance to release a dead man's spirit. Prior to the ritual, a man carves a mask from the wood of a Tagoda tree in a secluded cave. His carving gestures are repeated later by the masked dancers.

AFRICAN MUSICIANS
1957, 15 min. b&w film
Distributor: PennState
Producer: Gérard de Boe
Director: Gérard de Boe
Category: FOLK, AFRICA
African musicians play traditional Congolese music on indigenous instruments including tom-toms, plucked harps, horns, xylophones, and flutes, ending with a dance performance.

AFRICAN RELIGIOUS AND RITUAL DANCES
1971, 19 min. color film, video
Series: Tell It Like It Was
Distributors: Carousel Films, PennState
Producer: WCAU-TV/Philadelphia
Director: Dick Danjotell
Category: AFRICA, RELIGIOUS/RITUAL
Michael Babatunde Olatunji and his company re-enact the cult dances of the Yorubas, *Invocation to Igunnu,* and the *Ritual Fire Dance* to Shango, the God of Thunder.

AFTERNOON OF A FAUN
1973, 11 min. color film
Distributor: Dance Film Archive
Producer: John Mueller
Director: John Mueller
Choreographer: Vaslav Nijinsky
Principal Dancer: Vaslav Nijinsky
Composer: Claude Debussy
Category: BALLET, DANCE HISTORY
An approximate reconstruction of the ballet choreographed and performed by Vaslav Nijinsky in 1912 using still photographs and drawings set to the music of Claude Debussy.

AILEY DANCES
1982, 85 min. color video
Distributors: Dance Horizons, Viewfinders, Media Basics
Producers: James Lipton for ABC Video Enterprises and National Video Corporation
Director: Tim Kiley
Choreographer: Alvin Ailey
Principal Dancers: Judith Jamison, Donna Wood, Maxine Sherman, Roman Brooks, Deborah Manning, Ronald Brown
Composers: Duke Ellington, Ralph Vaughan Williams, Alice Coltrane, Laura Nyro
Category: MODERN, AFRICAN-AMERICANS
The African-American modern dance company recorded live at New York's City Center performs *Night Creatures, Cry the Lark Ascending,* and the famous spiritual *Revelations.*

AIR FOR THE G STRING
1934, 7 min. b&w film
Distributors: Dance Films Association, Dance Film Archive
Choreographer: Doris Humphrey
Principal Dancers: Doris Humphrey, Ernestine H. Stodell, Cleo Athenoes, Dorothy Lathrop, Hyla Rubin
Composer: Johann Sebastian Bach
Category: MODERN, DANCE HISTORY
The work of modern dance pioneer Doris Humphrey (1895–1958), which shows five women in floor-length robes, framed by two pillars, performing the adagio from Bach's *Air For the G String.* This dance, which premiered in 1928, plays an important role in the history of American modern dance.

AIRDANCE and LANDINGS
1987, 30 min. color video
Series: Alive From Off Center
Distributor: KTCA-TV
Producer: KTCA-TV
Director: Michael Schwartz
Choreographer: Elizabeth Streb
Principal Dancer: Elizabeth Streb
Category: MODERN, CINEDANCE
A collaboration by the director and choreographer-performer on two short pieces using risk-oriented situations: *Airdance,* during which Streb never touches the ground, and *Landings,* a series of touchdowns on specially designed pads. Both exemplify how an editor can shape the environment and rhythm of movement in a video dance.

AIRWAVES
1974, 5 min. color film
Distributor: Film-makers' Cooperative
Director: Dave Gearey
Choreographer: Dana Reitz
Category: MODERN
The tall, lithe minimalist in collaboration with a poet-director who hopes that "the dancer, like clouds, makes visible the winds."

AL GILBERT PRESENTS (60 videos)
1955–90, 60–90 min. color video
Distributor: Stepping Tones
Producer: Stepping Tones
Principal Dancer: Al Gilbert
Category: INSTRUCTIONAL, CHILDREN
One of the first to produce a series of teaching tapes, California-based tap teacher Al Gilbert has a line of graded technique and routine tapes, with voice-over instructions in tap, jazz, ballet, Hawaiian, and pointe, geared for children and adults.

ALBANIAN COUNTRY FOLKDANCES (3 films)
1971, 7–12 min. color, b&w film
Distributor: PennState
Producer: Wissen
Category: FOLK, EUROPE
From the country bordered by the former Yugoslavia and Greece, folkdances from Metohija (7 min.), men's dances from Zur (12 min.), women's dances from Zur (7 min.).

ALICE IN WONDERLAND: A DANCE FANTASY
1993, 27 min. color video
Distributors: V.I.E.W., Corinth, Facets
Dance Company: Prague Chamber Ballet
Category: BALLET, CHILDREN
Alice, the Mad Hatter, Cheshire Cat and Queen are brought to life in this dance fantasy as original as the story it tells. Ballet, mime, acrobatics and theatre combine with magnificent sets and costumes to dramatize the classic Lewis Carroll tale.

ALICIA ALONSO: ALICIA
1976, 75 min. color film, video
Distributors: Video Artists International, Music Video Distributors, Corinth, Viewfinders, New Yorker
Producer: Cuban Film Institute
Director: Victor Casaus
Choreographers: Marius Petipa, Alberto Alonso
Principal Dancers: Alicia Alonso, Azari Plisetski
Dance Company: Ballet National de Cuba
Composers: Léon Minkus, Cesare Pugni, Peter Ilyich Tchaikovsky, Georges Bizet, Adolphe Adam
Category: BALLET, DOCUMENTARY PORTRAITS
This portrait of Cuban ballerina Alicia Alonso includes interviews and excerpts from *Gisèlle* (Act I), *Don Quixote, Grand Pas de Quatre, The Black Swan* from *Swan Lake,* and Alberto Alonso's *Carmen.* Both Spanish and English narration available.

ALICIA WAS FAINTING
1994, 37 min. color film
Distributor: Forefront Films
Producer: Núria Olivé-Bellés
Director: Núria Olivé-Bellés
Choreographer: Núria Olivé-Bellés

Principal Dancers: Maggie Thom, Ruthanne Gereghty, Curtis Robertson, Núria Olivé-Bellés
Composer: Nana Simopoulos
Category: CHILDREN
School of Visual Arts 1994 Dusty Award for Best Picture, Best Director, Best Editor, National Educational Film and Video Festival Silver Apple Award, Bravo Independent Channel 1994 Award
A drama about a fourteen-year-old girl who faces adolescence alone after her mother dies, expressing her awakening to womanhood through flashbacks and daydreams.

ALL THAT JAZZ
1979, 120 min. color film, video, laser
Distributors: Films Inc., CBS/Fox, Facets
Producer: Columbia
Director: Bob Fosse
Choreographer: Bob Fosse
Principal Dancers: Ann Reinking, Leland Palmer, Erzsebet Foldi, Ben Vereen, Roy Schneider
Composers: Barry Mann, Peter Allen, Cynthia Weil, Jerry Leiber, Mike Stoller, Henry Creamer
Category: FEATURES, JAZZ
Feature film based on the life of Bob Fosse, who reveals his obsessions, his creative drive, his loves and phobias, as he struggles with his weakening heart. Dancers appear in rehearsal, in his dreams, and in his home, when his daughter and his latest girlfriend treat him to a specially choreographed gift. Dance numbers include *Everything Old Is New Again*.

ALL THE BEST FROM RUSSIA
1977, 60 min. color video
Distributor: Mastervision
Producers: Nielsen Aerns and Canadian Broadcasting Company
Director: Don Haldane
Dance Company: Bolshoi Ballet, Don Cossack Dancers, Armenian Folk Ensemble
Category: FOLK, EUROPE
Snatches of Russian cultural entertainment, from the robust and rough to the polished, interspersed with informal interviews, landscape scenes, and shots of the treasures at the Hermitage Museum. The documentary conveys the feeling of the culture, the energy of the artists, yet with no specific dance excerpts to be noted.

ALMIRA 38
1978, 19:30 min. b&w film
Distributor: Film-makers' Cooperative
Director: Nancy LaRue Kendall
Choreographer: Gay Delanghe
Principal Dancer: Gay Delanghe
Category: MODERN, EXPERIMENTAL
A dance poem in tribute to a woman in search of freedom.

ALVIN AILEY: MEMORIES AND VISIONS
1974, 54 min. color film, video
Distributors: Phoenix, University of California Extension Center, Kent State, University of Minnesota
Producers: Ellis Haizlip and Alonzo Brown for WNET/13
Director: Stan Lathan
Choreographer: Alvin Ailey
Principal Dancers: Judith Jamison, Sara Yarborough, Dudley Williams, Tina Yuan

Dance Company: Alvin Ailey American Dance Theatre
Composers: Ralph Vaughan Williams, Patricia Sciortini, Howard Roberts, Leon Russell
Category: MODERN, AFRICAN-AMERICANS
A performance documentary introduced by the late choreographer with excerpts from *Blues Suite*, *Cry the Lark Ascending*, *Mary Lou's Mass*, *Hidden Rites*, *Cry*, *A Song for You*, *Revelations*, *House of the Rising Sun*, *The Lord Saves*, *Act of Contrition*.

ALWAYS FOR PLEASURE
1978, 58 min. color film, video
Distributors: Flower Films, Museum of Modern Art, Music Video Distributors, University of California Extension Center, Facets, Film-makers' Cooperative, Buffalo State
Producer: Les Blank
Director: Les Blank
Category: NATIVE AMERICANS, UNITED STATES
American Film Festival 1978 Blue Ribbon, CINE Golden Eagle
Documentary on the Black Indian dances and parades as part of the celebrations in Mardi Gras in New Orleans, with stops at a jazz funeral and St. Patrick's Day festivities.

AMERICAN BALLET THEATRE: A CLOSE-UP IN TIME
1973, 90 min. color film
Distributor: Arthur Cantor, Inc.
Director: Jerome Schur
Choreographers: Antony Tudor, Agnes de Mille, Alvin Ailey, Michel Fokine, Marius Petipa, Harold Lander, Lev Ivanov, David Blair
Principal Dancers: Cynthia Gregory, Ivan Nagy, Sallie Wilson, Christine Sarry, Eleanor D'Arturo, Ted Kivitt, Marcos Paredes
Dance Company: American Ballet Theatre
Composers: Arnold Schoenberg, Peter Ilyich Tchaikovsky, Aaron Copland, Frédéric Chopin, Karl Czerny, Duke Ellington
Category: BALLET COMPANIES
The choreographers and company founder Lucia Chase discuss the American Ballet Theatre's history and repertoire. Selections from *Pillar of Fire* (Tudor-Schoenberg), Black Swan Pas de Deux from *Swan Lake* (Ivanov-Petipa/Tchaikovsky), *Les Sylphides* (Fokine/Chopin), *Rodeo* (de Mille/Copland), *Études* (Lander-Czerny), and *The River* (Ailey/Ellington).

AMERICAN BALLET THEATRE AT THE MET
1984, 100 min. color video, laser
Distributors: Home Vision, Laserdisc Fan Club, Music Video Distributors, Corinth, Media Basics
Producer: Robin Scott for National Video Corporation
Director: Brian Large
Choreographers: Marius Petipa, Michel Fokine, George Balanchine, Kenneth MacMillan, Natalia Makarova
Principal Dancers: Mikhail Baryshnikov, Cynthia Gregory, Cynthia Harvey, Fernando Bujones, Amanda McKerrow, Patrick Bissell, Martine Van Hamel
Dance Company: American Ballet Theatre
Composers: Sergei Prokofiev, Léon Minkus, Léo Delibes, Frédéric Chopin
Category: BALLET COMPANIES

Four ballets filmed at the Metropolitan Opera House: the *Pas de Deux* from *Paquita* (Makarova after Petipa/Minkus), *Les Sylphides* (Fokine/Chopin), *Pas de Deux* from *Sylvia* (Balanchine/Delibes), and *Triad* (MacMillan/Prokofiev).

AMERICAN BALLET THEATRE IN SAN FRANCISCO
1985, 105 min. color video, laser
Distributors: Dance Horizons, Corinth
Producer: National Video Corporation
Director: Brian Large
Choreographers: Paul Taylor, Antony Tudor, Kenneth MacMillan, Marius Petipa, Lynn Taylor-Corbett
Principal Dancers: Natalia Makarova, Fernando Bujones, Cynthia Gregory, Kevin McKenzie
Dance Company: American Ballet Theatre
Composers: George Frederick Handel, Ernest Chausson, Peter Ilyich Tchaikovsky, Sergei Prokofiev, Louis Gottschalk
Category: BALLET COMPANIES
Dance on Camera Festival 1987 Silver Award
Among the selections are: *Jardin aux Lilas* (Tudor-Chausson), the *Black Swan Pas de Deux* from *Swan Lake* (Petipa/Tchaikovsky), *Romeo and Juliet* (MacMillan/Prokofiev), *Airs* (Taylor-Handel), and *Great Galloping Gottschalk*.

AMERICAN BALLROOM DANCING (6 videos)
1979–87, 60–102 min. color video
Distributor: Jim Forest Videotapes
Producer: Jim Forest
Choreographer: Bobbi McDonald
Principal Dancers: Jim Forest, Bobbi McDonald
Category: BALLROOM, INSTRUCTIONAL
A comprehensive training course in American ballroom (fox-trot, waltz, swing, hustle, polka, peabody, soft-shoe) and Latin (cha-cha, tango, rumba, mambo, samba, merengue, bossa nova, bolero, and paso doble). Demonstrated by the late Jim Forest, an itinerant teacher-performer, and Bobbi McDonald, 1974 Grand Nationals Professional American Latin Champion and compiler of the American Standard of Ballroom Dancing.

AN AMERICAN IN PARIS
1951, 113 min. color film, video, laser
Distributors: Swank, MGM/UA
Producer: MGM
Director: Vincente Minelli
Choreographer: Gene Kelly
Principal Dancers: Gene Kelly, Leslie Caron
Composer: George Gershwin
Category: FEATURES, MUSICALS
Academy Award
An American artist living in Paris falls in love with a Parisian dancer. Along with dance numbers *I Got Rhythm*, *'S Wonderful*, *Embraceable You*, and *Love is Here to Stay*, is the *American in Paris* dream ballet (seventeen minutes long), wherein Kelly explores the city, depicted in the styles of such artists as Dufy, Renoir, Van Gogh, etc.

AMERICAN INDIAN SOCIAL DANCING
1980, 28 min. color film
Distributor: Green Mountain Cine
Producer: Nick Manning
Director: Nick Manning
Category: NATIVE AMERICANS
Social dances performed and described by Iro-

quois Indians living in the northeast United States.

AMERICAN MUSICALS: FAMOUS PRODUCTION NUMBERS
1929–35, 38 min. b&w film
Distributor: Museum of Modern Art
Directors: David Butler, Lloyd Bacon, Mervyn LeRoy, Busby Berkeley, Thornton Freeland
Choreographers: Seymour Felix, Busby Berkeley, Dave Gould, Hermes Pan
Principal Dancers: Ruby Keeler, Ginger Rogers, Dick Powell, Fred Astaire
Composers: Harry Warren, Vincent Youmans, Buddy DeSylva
Category: MUSICALS
A sampling from the early musical films showing how the challenge of combining sound and dance performance was met.

AMICI DANCE
9 min. color video
Distributor: Franciscan Communications
Producer: CTVCA
Category: DANCE THERAPY, DISABILITIES
Group improvisation by mentally handicapped people filmed in California.

AMIR: AN AFGHAN REFUGEE MUSICIAN'S LIFE IN PESHAWAR, PAKISTAN
1985, 52 min. color PAL video
Distributor: Documentary Educational Resources
Producer: Royal Anthropological Institute
Director: John Baily
Category: ANTHROPOLOGICAL, DOCUMENTARY PORTRAITS
Bilan Ethnographique, Musée de l'Homme 1986 Prix Spécial de Jury, Society for Visual Anthropology 1989 Award of Excellence
A documentary on the life of Afghan refugee Amir Mohammad, a professional musician—his living conditions in Peshawar and his longing to return to Herat. Music and dance performances include resistance songs at a Pakistani wedding.

EL AMOR BRUJO
1986, 100 min. color film, video
Distributors: Swank, Facets
Director: Carlos Saura
Choreographer: Antonio Gades
Principal Dancers: Antonio Gades, Cristina Hoyos
Composer: Manuel de Falla
Category: FEATURES, FLAMENCO
The last of a trilogy by one of Spain's most perceptive directors (see *Blood Wedding, Carmen*), involving a famous flamenco troupe and a young Spanish widow obsessed with visions of her husband, who dances nightly with his ghost.

AMPHIBIAN
1985, 9 min. color video (silent)
Distributor: Electronic Arts Intermix
Producer: Mary Lucier
Director: Mary Lucier
Choreographer: Elizabeth Streb
Principal Dancer: Elizabeth Streb
Category: EXPERIMENTAL, MODERN
Abstraction of a body in natural environments of water, land and air, in a collaboration between modern dancer Elizabeth Streb and a videographer known for her installations and poetic approach to landscapes.

ANASTENARIA
1969, 17 min. b&w film
Distributor: University of California Extension Center
Producer: Peter Haramis
Director: Peter Haramis
Category: RELIGIOUS/RITUAL, EUROPE
Documentary of the fire-dancing and sacrificial ceremony held in Serres in Northern Greece. The villagers sacrifice an animal and divide it among themselves. The initiates dance in a trance on embers, unmarked by the flames.

ANATOMY AS A MASTER IMAGE IN TRAINING DANCERS
1989, 59 min. color video
Distributors: Dance Horizons, AAHPERD
Producer: Ruth Solomon
Director: Gus Solomons
Category: INSTRUCTIONAL
Dance on Camera Festival 1989 Gold Award
Fundamental movement principles basic to any dance style or technique presented in a warmup class geared for dancers at the University of Santa Cruz.

THE ANATOMY LESSON
1968, 25 min. color film, video
Distributor: Consulate General of the Netherlands
Producers: Stewart Lippe, Margaret Dale
Director: Stewart Lippe
Choreographer: Glen Tetley
Principal Dancers: Jaap Flier, Willy de la Bye, Alexandre Radius, Ger Thoma
Dance Company: Nederlands Dans Theatre
Composer: Marcel Landowski
Category: BALLET, ART
A ballet inspired by Rembrandt's 1632 group portrait entitled *The Anatomy Lesson of Dr. Tulp*. In a series of flashbacks, one sees the tormented past of the man on the dissecting table.

ANCHORS AWEIGH
1945, 145 min. color film, video, laser
Distributors: Facets, Swank, MGM/UA
Producer: MGM
Director: George Sidney
Choreographers: Gene Kelly, Stanley Donen
Principal Dancers: Gene Kelly, Frank Sinatra
Composers: Jule Styne, Sammy Cahn
Category: FEATURES, MUSICALS
Two sailors on leave in Hollywood attempt to further a singer's career in this popular World War II musical. Kelly's dance numbers, with Sinatra in his first dancing role, include the *Mexican Hat Dance, We Hate to Leave*, and *Sinbad the Sailor*, one of the first combinations of animation and live action with the animated cartoon character Jerry the Mouse, telling the story of *The King Who Couldn't Dance*.

THE ANCIENT ART OF BELLY DANCING
1977, 30 min. color film, video
Distributor: Phoenix
Producer: Stewart Lippe
Director: Stewart Lippe
Principal Dancers: Little Egypt, Janis Lippe, Theodora Leavens
Dance Company: Juliana and Bal Anat Dancers, Babaganous Dancers
Category: DANCE HISTORY, BELLY DANCE, MIDDLE EAST

History of this five thousand-year-old art supported by stills of sculpture, paintings, and locations inspired by and associated with the dance, along with performances by today's dancers in clubs, studios, and outdoor events. Includes rare footage of Little Egypt at the 1893 Chicago World's Fair.

AND STILL WE DANCE
1989, 60 min. color film, video
Distributor: Searchlight
Director: Ashley James
Category: FOLK, FESTIVALS
Dance on Camera Festival 1989 Gold Award
San Francisco's tenth annual Ethnic Folk Festival, featuring dances of the Philippines, Eastern Europe, Asia, Africa, Spain and the Americas, performed by dancers living in the Bay area.

THE ANGEL OF TIME
1991, 10 min. color video
Distributors: Canyon Cinema, Film-makers' Cooperative
Producer: Silvianna Goldsmith
Director: Silvianna Goldsmith
Choreographer: Jenny Burrill
Principal Dancer: Jenny Burrill
Category: EXPERIMENTAL
Using experimental effects, the dance is dedicated to the human spirit that can fly or not, as seen by a pair of artificial wings worn by the dancer.

ANIMA
1988, 15 min. color video
Distributor: Locketz, Jan Marce
Producer: Jan Marce Locketz
Director: Jan Marce Locketz
Choreographer: Jan Marce Locketz
Principal Dancers: Earne Stevenson, Barbara Ziegler, Zonni Bauer, Barbara Canner, Nina d'Abbracci, Rob O'Neil
Composer: Uakti
Category: EXPERIMENTAL
Abstract study in slow-motion, with sensual closeups of dancers jumping, turning, and colliding.

ANIMAL DANCES: PHYE-MA-LEB AND SAN-GE
1968, 4 min. color film
Distributor: PennState
Producer: Wissen
Category: FOLK, CHINA
A folk dance from Tibet inspired by the flight of a butterfly, accompanied by flute and solo voice, and another folk dance in honor of snow lions, accompanied by drums, cymbals, and flute.

ANIMALS IN MOTION
1968, 7 min. color film (silent)
Distributor: Biograph Entertainment
Producer: John Straiton
Director: John Straiton
Category: DANCE HISTORY
Experimental documentary on the components of movements, with stills by Edward Muybridge (1830–1904) of women, men and children dancing, boxing and exercising.

ANITA: DANCES OF VICE
1987, 85 min. color film, video
Distributors: First Run/Icarus, Facets
Producer: Rosa von Praunheim
Director: Rosa von Praunheim

Category: FEATURES

The scandalous Anita Berber, an open bisexual and drug user who danced nude in public in 1920s Berlin, is the subject of this film. She choreographed such pieces as *Vice*, *Horror*, and *Ecstasy*.

ANNA KARENINA

1974, 120 and 81 min. color film, video, laser

Distributors: Kultur, Home Vision, Corinth, Dance Horizons, Viewfinders, Media Basics

Producer: Mosfilm Studios

Choreographer: Maya Plisetskaya

Principal Dancers: Maya Plisetskaya, Alexander Godunov, Vladimir Tihonov, Yuri Vladimirov

Dance Company: Bolshoi Ballet

Composer: Rodion Shchedrin

Category: BALLET, FEATURES

The first work by Russian prima ballerina Maya Plisetskaya based on Leo Tolstoy's tragic novel of a woman who abandons her husband and child for a man who subsequently abandons her. Set to music composed by Plisetskaya's husband.

ANNA SOKOLOW, CHOREOGRAPHER

1978, 20 min. color, b&w film, video

Distributors: Dance Horizons, Museum of Modern Art

Producers: Lucille Rhodes and Margaret Murphy

Directors: Lucille Rhodes, Margaret Murphy

Choreographer: Anna Sokolow

Principal Dancer: Anna Sokolow

Composers: Kenyon Hopkins, Johann Sebastian Bach, Carl Maria von Weber

Category: DANCE HISTORY, DOCUMENTARY PORTRAITS, CHOREOGRAPHY

Chicago International Film Festival 1978 Gold Plaque

Portrait of modern choreographer Anna Sokolow, who began her career in the 1930s studying with Martha Graham and Louis Horst. Illustrated with moments of her teaching class and directing excerpts from *Rooms* (a series of solos and ensemble pieces suggesting urban alienation) and *Dreams* (a memorial to victims of the Holocaust).

ANNIE

1982, 128 min. color film, video

Distributor: Films Inc.

Producer: Columbia

Director: John Huston

Choreographer: Arlene Phillips

Principal Dancer: Ann Reinking

Composer: Charles Strouse

Category: FEATURES, MUSICALS

The comic book depression-era orphan Annie, Daddy Warbucks, Grace Farsell and Miss Hannigan, come to life in a musical extravaganza. Numbers include *It's a Hard Knock Life*, *Easy Street*, and *Tomorrow*.

ANNUNCIATION

1977, 16 min. color film, video

Distributor: Phoenix

Director: Marcelo Epstein

Choreographer: Sandra Adominas

Principal Dancer: Sandra Adominas

Composer: Joellen Lapidus

Category: EXPERIMENTAL

Dance on Camera Festival 1977

Moments from a woman's past, present and future life to reveal her many levels of consciousness.

ANTIGONE/RITES OF PASSION

1990, 85 min. color film, video

Distributors: Mystic Fire Video, Film-makers' Cooperative

Producer: Amy Greenfield

Director: Amy Greenfield

Choreographer: Amy Greenfield

Principal Dancers: Amy Greenfield, Bertram Ross, Janet Eilber

Composers: Glenn Branca, David Van Tiegham, Elliott Sharp, Paul Lemos, Diamanda Galas

Category: MODERN, EXPERIMENTAL

This is a dance film of the 400 B.C. Greek drama of the woman who defied the state to bury her brother. Filmed in woods, caves, and deserts, and in Albany, New York.

ANTONY TUDOR

1992, 60 min. color, b&w film, video

Distributor: Dance Horizons

Producer: Swedish Television

Directors: Viola Aberle, Gerd Anderson

Choreographer: Antony Tudor

Principal Dancers: Nora Kaye, Hugh Laing, Sallie Wilson

Category: BALLET, DOCUMENTARY PORTRAITS, CHOREOGRAPHY

A documentary with rare interviews of Tudor (1908–1987) as well as of Agnes de Mille, Nora Kaye, Sallie Wilson, Margaret Craske and Martha Hill. Old footage and newer interpretations of Tudor classics are juxtaposed with the interviews. Excerpts include: *Dark Elegies*, *Pillar of Fire*, *Jardin aux Lilas*, *Romeo and Juliet*, *Judgment of Paris*, *Undertow*, and *The Leaves are Fading*.

ANYUTA

1982, 68 min. color video

Distributors: Kultur, Home Vision, Corinth, Viewfinders, Media Basics

Director: Alexander Belinsky

Choreographer: Vladimir Vassiliev

Principal Dancers: Vladimir Vassiliev, Ekaterina Maximova

Dance Company: Bolshoi Ballet, Kirov Ballet, Maly

Composer: Valery Gavrilin

Category: FULL-LENGTH BALLETS, DANCE DRAMA

A narrative ballet inspired by Anton Chekhov's *Anna Round the Neck,* a novel depicting a young woman forced to marry a rich but indifferent husband. Eventually, she finds admirers crowding at her feet.

APPALACHIAN JOURNEY

1991, 60 min. color video

Series: American Patchwork

Distributor: PBS Video

Category: FOLK, UNITED STATES

A journey with host Alan Lomax into the mountain valleys where country music was born, exploring the historical mix of cultures which resulted in the region's unique blend of ballads, legends, fiddling, banjo picking, and square dancing.

APPALACHIAN SPRING

1959, 31 min. color, b&w film

Distributors: Phoenix, Dance Film Archive, Kultur, Indiana University, PennState, Lane Education

Producer: Nathan Kroll for WQED-TV/Pittsburgh

Director: Peter Glushanok

Choreographer: Martha Graham

Principal Dancers: Martha Graham, Linda Hodes, Stuart Hodes, Bertram Ross, Helen McGehee, Ethel Winter, Miriam Cole, Matt Turney

Dance Company: Martha Graham Dance Company

Composer: Aaron Copland

Category: MODERN, DANCE HISTORY

Set Designer: Isamu Noguchi

Venice International Film Festival, Edinburgh Film Festival

Martha Graham performs in the 1958 filming of her stark classic, which premiered in 1944, of a pioneer wedding in the Appalachian Mountain wilderness. Dance Film Archive also carries the 1976 version from the PBS series *Dance in America* (33 min.), performed by Yuriko Kimura, Tim Wengard, David Hatch Walker, Janet Eilber and the Graham Company.

ARAB DANCES FROM CENTRAL SUDAN (11 films)

1965–65, 4–10 min. color film

Distributor: PennState

Producer: Wissen

Category: FOLK, MIDDLE EAST

A couple dance *Djersiss*, as performed by the Omar and Haddad Arabs in Chad, Africa, with clapping and leaping to the rhythms of women singing songs in praise of the rich and famous. An excerpt of the *Al Beher* dance performed by couples; the *Am Haraba*, originally a war dance; the *Kifet* dance, in which women and girls sing, clap and sway in a semicircle until the men advance, choose partners, dance in couples, and then withdraw to pick new partners. Finally, the *Zinugi*, a circle dance and *Nugarafolk*, a line dance.

ARABIAN DANCES

1960, 3 min. b&w film

Distributor: PennState

Producer: Wissen

Category: FOLK, MIDDLE EAST

A social dance common among the camel herdsmen of southern Arabia, performed by both men and women after they have led their animals to drink at a nearby spring.

ARGENTINE TANGO (2 videos)

1991, 1992, 60 and 40 min. color video

Distributor: Tanguero Productions

Producer: Tanguero Productions

Choreographers: Alberto Toledano, Loreen Arbus

Principal Dancers: Alberto Toledano, Loreen Arbus

Category: SOCIAL, INSTRUCTIONAL

Teachers: Alberto Toledano and Loreen Arbus

The basics of "salon style" tango are presented, along with a brief history of the dance and short demonstration sections.

L'ARMARI

1991, 12 min. color video

Distributor: Olivé-Bellés, Núria

Producer: Núria Olivé-Bellés

Director: Núria Olivé-Bellés

Choreographer: Javier De Frutos

Principal Dancers: Javier De Frutos, Michael Fine

Composer: Richard Wagner
Category: MODERN
A man stays in his closet and remembers his lover, his sadness, and his lover's departure.

ART AND DANCE
1993, 15 min. color video
Distributor: Films for the Humanities and Sciences
Principal Dancer: Rick Benedict
Category: DOCUMENTARY PORTRAITS
A young dancer speaks of his commitment and passion for dance, along with an art student and computer student.

ART AND MOTION
1952, 16 min. color film
Distributor: Encyclopedia Britannica
Producer: University of California Extension Center
Category: ART, INSTRUCTIONAL
This teachers' guide explains motion as an integral element in the visual arts, demonstrated by a dancer and a skater. Reviews contemporary trends and ways in which artists use motion in painting, mobiles, and camera techniques.

ART AND TECHNIQUE OF THE BALLET
1967, 11 min. b&w film
Distributor: The Cinema Guild
Producer: Richard Scheinflug for Lehrfilm-Institut
Choreographers: Lev Ivanov, Marius Petipa
Principal Dancers: Helmut Ketels, Christa Kempf, Uta Graf
Composer: Peter Ilyich Tchaikovsky
Category: INSTRUCTIONAL, BALLET
Depicts the formal vocabulary of ballet, and examines the Pas de Quatre from Swan Lake, in rehearsal and performance.

THE ART OF BODY MOVEMENT (11 programs)
1970, 12–63 min. b&w film, video
Distributor: Mettler Studios
Producer: Will Carbo
Director: Barbara Mettler
Category: INSTRUCTIONAL, IMPROVISATION
Teacher: Barbara Mettler
Improvisations by amateurs of all ages before an audience at the Tucson Creative Dance Center. Created by Barbara Mettler, whose films and videos on improvisation include: Movimiento Creativo en Costa Rica (1989, in Spanish, 31 min.); Baby Dance (1989, 12 min., four young mothers dancing with their babies); The Language of Movement (1985, 24 min.); Pure Dance (1980, 58 min.); Creative Dance for Children (four films, 1966–1977, 63 min.); Group Dance Improvisation (1979, 34 min.); A New Direction in Dance (1978, 58 min., group improvisation).

THE ART OF DANCING: AN INTRODUCTION TO BAROQUE DANCE
1979, 21 min. b&w video
Distributor: ARC Videodance
Producers: Jeff Bush and Celia Ipiotis
Directors: Jeff Bush, Celia Ipiotis
Choreographers: Catherine Turocy, Kellom Tomlinson, Louis Pecour
Principal Dancers: Catherine Turocy, Ann Jacoby, Roger Tolle
Category: DANCE HISTORY
A lesson on the minuet based on Kellom Tomlin-

son's dance manual The Art of Dancing, published in London in 1720, with a demonstration of notation symbols, comments on execution and style, followed by a short sequence of Minuet d'Omphalle by Louis Pecour, 1704, a state version of the ballroom minuet.

ART OF MEMORY
1987, 36 min. color video
Distributors: Electronic Arts Intermix, Facets
Director: Woody Vasulka
Principal Dancer: Daniel Nagrin
Category: MODERN, EXPERIMENTAL
Modern dancer Daniel Nagrin appears briefly in this multidimensional, antiwar protest structured in seven acts. Black and white footage of Nagrin's Watergate Sketches, shot in the early 1970s by the Vasulkas, is inset as a symbol of civic opposition.

ART OF SILENCE: PANTOMIMES WITH MARCEL MARCEAU (13 films)
1975, 7–11 min. color film
Distributor: Encyclopedia Britannica
Producer: John Barnes
Director: John Barnes
Principal Dancers: Marcel Marceau, Pierre Verry
Category: PANTOMIME
Thirteen short sketches, available individually, by the French master of pantomime: Pantomime: The Language of the Heart (10 min.) discusses the technique and philosophy of the art with illustrative clips; Cage (9 min.) is a rendering of a man struggling to escape the invisible walls around him; Creation of the World (11 min.) recounts the story of Adam and Eve; Dream (9 min.); Hands (7 min.) is a struggle between good and evil; Maskmaker (9 min.) shows the vulnerable craftsman; Painter (8 min.) demonstrates how one can make others see the invisible; Sideshow (9 min.) shows the tightrope walker; Youth, Maturity, Old Age, Death (8 min.) illustrates the cycle of life, and the Bip series recreates Marceau's famous character.

THE ART OF THE TWENTIETH CENTURY BALLET
1985, 75 min. color video, laser
Distributors: Viewfinders, Home Vision
Choreographer: Maurice Béjart
Principal Dancers: Jorge Donn, Shonach Mirk
Dance Company: Ballet of the 20th Century
Composers: Maurice Ravel, Gustav Mahler
Category: BALLET
Three of Béjart's works performed to Ravel's Bolero and Mahler's Symphony No. 5 (4th movement) and Symphony No. 3 (4th–6th movements).

ARTISTS OF THE DANCE
1977, 56 min. color video
Distributor: Louise Tiranoff Productions
Producer: Louise Tiranoff
Director: Louise Tiranoff
Choreographers: Doris Jones, Claire Haywood
Principal Dancer: Sandra Fortune
Category: CHOREOGRAPHY, AFRICAN-AMERICANS
Two African-American choreographers and teachers direct and choreograph a production in their school in Washington, D.C. One of their students, Sandra Fortune, the first African-American dancer to win the international ballet

competition in Varna, performs a solo, The Black Swan.

ARUANA MASKED DANCES
1959, 20 min. color film (silent)
Distributor: PennState
Producer: Wissen
Director: H. Schultz
Category: ANTHROPOLOGICAL, LATIN AMERICA
The ritual in the village of Jatoba in the Araguaia region of Brazil, during which men in masks run to the village, dance with the women, and return home.

AS SEEN ON TV
1987, 30 min. color video
Series: Alive From Off Center
Distributor: Electronic Arts Intermix
Producer: Susan Dowling
Director: Charles Atlas
Principal Dancers: Bill Irwin, Beatríz Rodriguez
Category: EXPERIMENTAL, COMEDY
Irwin plays a job-hunting hoofer who goes to a television audition only to be drawn inside the monitor. Trapped in the world of television, he stumbles through electronic adventures, cavorts with the soap opera stars and attempts to dance with a ballerina.

ASHANTI DANCE ADJEMLE AT KOUADJIKRO
1968, 12 min. color film
Distributor: PennState
Producer: Wissen
Director: H. Himmelheber
Category: ANTHROPOLOGICAL, AFRICA
In Baule, Ivory Coast, young men perform an acrobatic dance to the accompaniment of three drums, an iron bell, rattle calabash, and rub-rattle. In 1967, a three-minute record was also made of the Gbagba dance of Baule, for which the performers wear masks parodying sheep, women, and a cowherd.

ASHES, MIST AND WIND BLOWN DUST
1987, 30 min. color video
Distributor: Dance On Video
Producer: Norwegian Broadcasting Corporation
Director: Jannike Falk
Choreographer: Kjersti Alveberg
Principal Dancer: Claude Paul Henry
Composer: Antonio Bibalo
Category: EXPERIMENTAL
Grand Prix International Vidéo-Danse Festival 1988 Experimental Category
A surreal dance video from Norway divided into sections introduced by quotes from Henrik Ibsen's Peer Gynt.

ASIA SOCIETY COLLECTION (b&w videos)
1960–90, 30 min. each b&w video
Distributor: Asia Society
Producer: Asia Society
Principal Dancers: Teh-cheng P'Ansori, Djimat Chang, Saeko Ichinohe
Category: ASIA, FOLK
Performance record of artists invited to the New York Center: P'Ansori (Korea's leading singer and mime Kim So-Hee with three musicians who play the kayageum, kuhmoongo and the p'iri); The Topeng Dance Theatre of Bali (Djimat performs a scene from The End of King Bungkut

with gamelan accompaniment); *Traditional Japanese Dance* (Koisaburo Nishikawa and Company perform *Fuji Musume*, *Kotkobuki Sambaso*, and *Sagi Musume*); *Chinese Shadow Plays* (lecture-demonstration by Chang Tehcheng); *Saeko Ichinohe and Company* (modern dance inspired by Japanese tradition with poems recited by Joan Baez).

ASIA SOCIETY COLLECTION (color videos)
1960–90, 30 min. each color video
Distributor: Asia Society
Producer: Beate Gordon for Asia Society
Principal Dancers: Surasena, Yamini Krishnamurti, Hung-Yen Hu, Ock Lee Sun, Sitara, Birju Maharaj, Bando Yaenosuke, Osaka Garyokai
Category: ASIA, FOLK
Established in 1960, the Asia Society of New York City produced and recorded over twelve hundred performances by Asian companies and artists invited to the Asia Society by impresario Beate Gordon: *Heen Baba and his Dance and Drum* (Surasena dances *Vannamas*, in praise of the butterfly and the elephant, and part of the *Ves*, the sacred ritual of Sri Lanka); *Yamini Krishnamurti: South Indian Dance*, *The Nine Classical Sentiments* (in the Bharata Natyam style); *The Frog who Became a Queen* (Kuchipudi); *Aak: Korean Court Music and Dance* (one-thousand-year-old tradition performed in long silk gowns); *Pongsam Masked Dance Drama from Korea* (three of seven episodes of a festive comedy); *Masked Dance Drama of Bhutan* (pantomime from a small Himalayan Kingdom called Pholay Molay); *The Fuijan Hand Puppets from the People's Republic of China* (five-hundred-year-old tradition with acrobatics, song and dance); *Kathakali: South Indian Dance Drama from the Kerala Kalamandalam* (sixteenth-century technique stemming from martial arts combined with music, sung text, mime and dance); *Chhau: The Masked Dance of Bengal* (ancient Indian war dances which incorporate stories from the *Ramayana*); *Hu Hung-Yen: Aspects of Peking Opera* (demonstrates makeup and a scene from *The Butterfly Dream* and *The Scarf Dance*); *Sun Ock Lee: Korean Dancer*, *Sal Poo Ri I* (a dance originating from shamanistic rituals); *Shinjang Nori and Seung Moo* (originally performed by monks as part of a meditation); *Dancers and Musicians of the Burmese National Theatre* (exercises which form the basis of Burmese dances); *Nat Votaress* (an appeal to the spirits, and from the *Ramayana*, a contest between kings for the hand of Sita); *Martial Arts of Kabuki from the National Theater Institute of Japan* (demonstrates stage fighting and two excerpts from *Hama Matsukaze* and *Kujira No Danmari*); *Thovil: Ritual Chanting, Dance and Drumming of Exorcism* (demon-masked dancers eat fire, twirl torches and perform four other dances from Sri Lanka); *Bugaku: The Traditional Court, Temple and Shrine Dances from Japan* (the ceremonial dance of the Japanese Imperial Household); *Yakshagana: Ritual Dance Theater from South Kanara, India* (rituals and Hindu tales enacted through dance and drama); *Sitara* (an invocation to the elephant god *Ganesha*, the *Toru Tukra*, *Mayur Nritya* [peacock], and *Tatkar*, all in the Indian Kathak style); *Penca and Topeng Babakan from Sunda, Indonesia* (dances based on martial arts and animal movements with masks from an-

cient Javanese stories); *Kathak: North Indian Dance* (*Vandana*, a prayer dance, and *Geetopadesh*, the gambling scene from the *Mahabharata*); *Bunraku Puppet Theatre of Japan* (the Japanese art of handling large dolls on stage and the craft of making them); *The Awaji Puppet Theatre of Japan* (scenes from classic Japanese tales and demonstration of how to manipulate the puppets); *Nido Tichiuchi: Revenge of the Two Sons* (a dance drama from Okinawa of two sons who disguise themselves to deceive and kill their father's murderer); *Saiko Ichinohe Dance: East and West* (Japanese and Western dance patterns compared and demonstrated by New York-based Saeko Ichinohe); *Forgotten Dances* (three Japanese folk dances and a drum demonstration performed by the Japanese Folk Dance Group); *Music and Dance of the Siberian Asians* (native Siberians of the Nanai Ulchi and Koryak tribes performing music, shaman dances, storytelling, and songs with pantomime); *Encounter with the Gods: Orissi Dance with Sanjuka Panigrahi* (Indian *orissi* dance performed by an internationally recognized master).

ASLI ABADI SERIES
1977, 10 min. color film
Distributor: Embassy of Malaysia
Dance Company: Badan Budaya, Kememterian
Category: FOLK, ASIA
A series of traditional Malaysian dances.

ASPECTS OF SYMMETRY
1970, 18 min. color film
Distributor: International Film Bureau
Producer: Polytechnic Institute of Brooklyn
Category: INSTRUCTIONAL
Mathematicians, scientists, artists and dancers explore the presence and application of symmetry in their respective fields.

ATTITUDES IN DANCE
1964, 28 min. b&w film
Distributor: Dance Film Archive
Director: Merrill Brockway
Choreographers: Norman Walker, Gerald Arpino
Principal Dancers: Lisa Bradley, Lawrence Rhodes, Paul Sutherland, Cora Cahan, Norman Walker
Composers: Maurice Ravel, Alan Hovhannes, Antonio Vivaldi, Vittorio Rieti
Category: MODERN
Four works by Gerald Arpino, the director of the Robert Joffrey Ballet, and Norman Walker, the head of the dance department at Adelphi University: *Ballet for Four* (Arpino/Ravel); *Sea Shadow* (Arpino/Ravel); *Courtly Duet* (Walker-Vivaldi); and *Dance Finale* (Walker-Hovhannes).

AUDITION POWER: PART I, KNOWING WHAT IT TAKES TO BE CHOSEN and PART II, WORKING THE HOLLYWOOD SYSTEM
1992, 45 and 51 min. color video
Distributors: Dance Horizons, Instructional Video
Producer: Choreographer's Resource Center
Director: Del Jack
Principal Dancers: David Kloss, Carrie Kloss
Category: INSTRUCTIONAL
Prepares dance students for the audition experience, with dancers explaining the process: how it works, and how to gain a competitive edge.

AWA ODORI
1971, 15 min. color film
Distributors: Iowa State, The Japan Foundation
Producer: Broadcast Programming Center of Japan
Category: FOLK, JAPAN
A documentary of a four-hundred-year-old tradition honoring All Souls Day of Buddhism observed by the Japanese every August 15th in Tokushima City, Japan. Forty groups of dancers rehearse and perform from dawn to midnight.

¡AY, CARMELA!
1990, 100 min. color film, video
Distributor: Films Inc.
Producer: Miramax
Director: Carlos Saura
Choreographer: Alberto Portillo
Principal Dancers: Carmen Maura, Andrés Pájares
Category: FLAMENCO, FEATURES
The story of a pro-Republican cabaret trio of flamenco dancers and musicians captured by Franco's Fascist soldiers who were forced to sing and dance for their enemies, and for their lives. In Spanish, with English subtitles.

BABES IN ARMS
1939, 91 min. b&w video, laser
Distributors: Facets, Swank, MGM/UA
Producer: MGM
Director: Busby Berkeley
Choreographer: Busby Berkeley
Principal Dancers: Judy Garland, Mickey Rooney
Composer: Richard Rodgers
Category: FEATURES, MUSICALS
Based upon the Rodgers and Hart Broadway musical, the story depicts the children of old-time vaudevillians, who avoid being sent to a work farm by staging their own show.

BABES ON BROADWAY
1941, 118 min. b&w video, laser
Distributors: Facets, MGM/UA
Producer: MGM
Director: Busby Berkeley
Choreographer: Busby Berkeley
Principal Dancers: Judy Garland, Mickey Rooney, Ray McDonald
Composer: Burton Lane
Category: FEATURES, MUSICALS
Sequel to *Babes in Arms*, with the kids performing on Broadway.

BACKSTAGE AT THE KIROV
1984, 78 min. color film, video
Distributors: New Yorker, Corinth, Facets, Media Basics
Producers: Kenneth Locker and Gregory Saunders
Director: Derek Hart
Choreographer: Marius Petipa
Principal Dancers: Altynai Asylmuratova, Oleg Vinogradov, Olga Moiseyeva, Konstantin Zaklinsky, Galina Mezentseva
Dance Company: Kirov Ballet
Composer: Peter Ilyich Tchaikovsky
Category: BALLET COMPANIES
This inside look at the Kirov Ballet of Leningrad focuses on a young girl about to make her debut as the Swan Queen, followed by excerpts from *Swan Lake*.

BAHIA: AFRICA IN THE AMERICAS
1988, 58 min. color video
Distributors: University of California Extension Center

Directors: Giovanni Brewer, Michael Brewer
Category: LATIN AMERICA, AFRICA
The Brazilian state of Bahia is known as the "capital of African culture in the Americas" because of the importation of large numbers of slaves from Nigeria, Angola and the Congo, where the Yoruba religion is practiced. Limited numbers of dance sequences, along with music, art and food, show how African cultural traditions have been preserved by the people of Bahia, especially in their *Candomblé* religion.

LE BAL
1980, 112 min. color film, video
Distributor: Direct Cinema
Producer: Almi/Warner Brothers
Director: Ettore Scola
Principal Dancers: Etienne Guichard, Francesca de Rosa
Category: FEATURES, SOCIAL
Best Foreign Film of 1983
Set in a Paris dance hall from the 1930s to the 1980s, the film suggests a political and historical perspective of France by using a silent cast of individuals who come alone and leave alone, yet communicate to each other through body language and the social dance typical of each decade.

BAL-ANAT
1975, 20 min. color film
Distributor: Canyon Cinema
Producer: John Carney
Director: John Carney
Category: BELLY DANCE
Traces the development of a belly dancing troupe in the San Francisco Bay area, from studio training to a live performance at The Renaissance Pleasure Fair.

BALANCES
1980, 9:30 min. color film, video
Distributor: Coe Film Associates
Producer: Cine Light Productions
Director: Whitney Green
Choreographer: Tomm Ruud
Principal Dancers: Allyson Deane, Nancy Dickson
Dance Company: San Francisco Ballet
Composer: Aram Khachaturian
Category: BALLET
Three San Francisco Ballet members rehearse with the choreographer and then perform *Mobile*, a trio set to the adagio from Khachaturian's *Gayne*.

THE BALANCHINE ESSAYS: ARABESQUE
1995, 45 min. color video
Series: The Balanchine Library
Distributors: Dance Horizons, WarnerVision Entertainment, Viewfinders, Facets
Choreographer: George Balanchine
Principal Dancers: Merrill Ashley, Suki Schorer
Dance Company: New York City Ballet
Category: CHOREOGRAPHY
The first program in the Balanchine technique series demonstrating his innovative style and technique. Others released in 1996 are: *Passé* and *Attitude* (43 min.), and *Port de Bras* and *Épaulement* (45 min.).

BALI BEYOND THE POSTCARD
1992, 60 min. color, b&w video
Distributors: Filmakers Library, Coe Film Associates, PennState, University of Minnesota

Producer: Nancy Dine
Director: Peggy Stern
Category: BALI
Dance on Camera Festival 1992 Gold Award, National Educational Film and Video Festival 1992 Gold Apple, American Film and Video Festival 1992 Honorable Mention
A story about a Balinese family whose gamelan music and *Legong* dance tradition spans four generations, as the mature dancer passes down the legacy by training the youngest nine-year-old member, Ni Luh Kade.

BALI: ISLE OF TEMPLES
1978, 27 min. color film
Distributor: Coronet/MTI
Producer: Bay Street Pictures Corporation
Category: BALI, RELIGIOUS/RITUAL
Barong and *Ketjack* dances are seen amidst the bustle of the marketplace: weaving, painting, rice harvesting, a Hindu play shadow play, festivals, and religious ceremonies.

BALI MECHANIQUE
1992, 17 min. color film
Distributors: Film-makers' Cooperative, Canyon Cinema
Producer: Henry Hills
Director: Henry Hills
Dance Company: Tirta Sari, Gunung Sari, Samara Jati
Composers: Wayan Lotring, Richard Rodgers
Category: BALI, COMEDY
A two-part self-reflective study of the dance and rhythms of life in Bali. The first section presents a complete *Legong* dance, performed by three young girls, representing King Lasem, Princess Rankesari (whom he has abducted and is attempting to seduce), and a servant. The second section, in ironic contrast, weaves together footage of lush rice terraces and the "erotic bumblebee" of *Oleg Tambulilingan* dance to give a humorous literalization of another vision of Bali(the Westerners' paradise on Earth(to the accompaniment of *Bali Hai*, from the Broadway musical *South Pacific*.

BALI: THE MASK OF RANGDA
1974, 30 min. color film, video
Distributor: Hartley Film Foundation
Producer: Elda Hartley
Director: Elda Hartley
Category: RELIGIOUS/RITUAL, BALI
The Balinese seek the link between man and God, conscious and unconscious, by dancing in village squares: *Barong-Rangda* and *Ketjak*, both trance dances to ward off evil spirits.

BALI TODAY
1967, 18 min. color film
Distributor: Hartley Film Foundation
Producer: Elda Hartley
Director: Elda Hartley
Category: BALI, ANTHROPOLOGICAL
Narrator: Dr. Margaret Mead
Anthropologist Dr. Margaret Mead talks about modern life relative to the slow-to-change island of Bali, its people, culture, and religion. Balinese painting, music and native dances are shown as part of two ceremonies, a wedding and cremation of the dead.

BALLADE
1978, 28 min. color video
Distributor: FACSEA
Producer: Espace et Mouvement
Director: Pierre Marie Goulet
Category: FOLK, EUROPE
A collection of folk songs and dances from France.

IL BALLARINO: THE ART OF RENAISSANCE DANCE
1990, 33 min. color video
Distributor: Dance Horizons
Producer: Julia Sutton
Directors: Julia Sutton, Johannes Holub
Choreographer: Negri Caroso, reconstructed by Julia Sutton
Principal Dancers: Patricia Rader, Charles Perrier
Category: DANCE HISTORY, INSTRUCTIONAL
Dance on Camera Festival 1993 Honorable Mention
The Dancing Master is a demonstration and description of sixteenth-century renaissance court dances for couples and groups, which are also analyzed and taught. Accompanied by period musical instruments, dancers perform finished pieces in full costume.

BALLERINA
1963, 28 min. b&w film
Distributor: National Film Board of Canada
Producers: Nicholas Balla and National Film Board of Canada
Director: George Kaczender
Choreographers: George Kaczender, Ludmilla Chiriaeff
Principal Dancer: Margaret Mercier
Dance Company: Les Grands Ballets Canadiens
Composer: Sergei Prokofiev
Category: BALLET, DOCUMENTARY PORTRAITS
Prima ballerina Margaret Mercier, graduate of Sadler's Wells (now Royal Ballet) School, rehearses a scene from *Cinderella*.

BALLERINA: LYNN SEYMOUR
1979, 60 min. color video
Distributor: Mastervision
Producer: Pat Ferns for Nielsen-Ferns
Director: Karin Altmann
Choreographers: Frederick Ashton, Lar Lubovich, Kenneth MacMillan, Lynn Seymour
Principal Dancers: Lynn Seymour, Rudolf Nureyev, Galina Samsova, Stephen Jefferies, Christopher Gable, Werner Dittrich, David Wall
Composers: Alexander Scriabin, Kurt Weill, André Messager, Leo Janácek, Sergei Prokofiev
Category: BALLET, DOCUMENTARY PORTRAITS
Portrait of the English ballerina and character actress with rehearsals, interviews, and performance excerpts of *The Two Pigeons*, *Romeo and Juliet*, and *Intimate Letters*.

THE BALLERINAS
1987, 108 min. color film, video
Distributors: Kultur, Dance Horizons, Viewfinders, Home Vision
Producer: Polivideo-TVE
Choreographers: Michel Fokine, Marius Petipa, Anna Pavlova, Jean Coralli, Lev Ivanov, Jules Perrot, Léonide Massine

Principal Dancers: Vladimir Vassiliev, Carla Fracci, Peter Shaufuss, Richard Cragun
Composers: Adolphe Adam, Peter Ilyich Tchaikovsky, Frédéric Chopin, Léo Delibes, Cesare Pugni
Category: BALLET, FEATURES
Italian prima ballerina Carla Fracci portrays the romantic ballerinas of the nineteenth-century: Maria Taglioni, Carlotta Grisi, Anna Pavlova, Fanny Elssler, Tamara Karsavina, and others, while Peter Ustinov plays the role of Théophile Gautier, the ballet critic-poet, and then Sergei Diaghilev, the impresario. Excerpts from *La Sylphide*, *Le Papillon*, *Gisèlle*, *La Cachucha*, *Coppélia*, *Sleeping Beauty*, *Esmeralda*, *Les Sylphides*, and *La Farrucha*.

BALLET
1995, 170 min. color film
Distributor: Zipporah Films
Producer: Frederick Wiseman
Director: Frederick Wiseman
Choreographer: Frederick Ashton
Principal Dancers: Alessandra Ferri, Cynthia Harvey, Susan Jaffe, Christine Dunham, Julio Bocca, Wes Chapman
Dance Company: American Ballet Theatre
Composers: Peter Ilyich Tchaikovsky, César Franck, Igor Stravinsky
Category: BALLET COMPANIES
A backstage glimpse of the American Ballet Theatre as seen in cinema-verité style over seven weeks of rehearsal and three weeks on tour. With choreographers-ballet masters Agnes de Mille, Irina Kolpakova, David Richardson, and Michael Somes.

BALLET: A CAREER FOR BOYS
1979, 11 min. color film, video
Distributor: Carousel Films
Producer: Judy Reemtsma for CBS News
Choreographer: Lev Ivanov
Principal Dancer: Peter Bole
Dance Company: New York City Ballet
Composer: Peter Ilyich Tchaikovsky
Category: BALLET, CHILDREN
A profile of a twelve-year-old dance student, Peter Bole, talking candidly to CBS News correspondent Sharron Lovejoy about the difficulties of pursuing a ballet career. Scenes from a dress rehearsal of *The Nutcracker* with Peter in the role of the Prince are shown.

BALLET ADAGIO
1971, 10 min. color film, video
Distributors: Dance Film Archive, Pyramid, Indiana University, Kent State, Biograph Entertainment, Buffalo State University of Minnesota
Producer: National Film Board of Canada
Director: Norman McLaren
Choreographers: David Holmes, Asaf Messerer
Principal Dancers: Anna Marie Holmes, David Holmes
Composer: Tomaso Albinoni
Category: BALLET, CINEDANCE
A slow-motion take of the classic ballet duet *Spring Waters*, using slow-motion and enhanced lighting.

BALLET CLASS (3 videos)
1981, 40–60 min. color video
Distributors: Kultur, Dance Horizons, Viewfinders, Karol, Home Vision, Instructional Video

Producers: Seymour Klempner, Marc Chase Weinstein, and Gary Jacinto for AVHL
Directors: Lee Kraft, Gary Donatelli
Principal Dancers: Cynthia Harvey, Peter Fonseca, Allison Potter
Composers: Whit Kellog, Doug Corbin, Lynn Stanford
Category: INSTRUCTIONAL, BALLET
Ballet Class For Beginners (40 min), *Ballet Class For Intermediate-Advanced* (56 min.) and *Shape-Up* (58 min.), an exercise program designed for dancers and non-dancers. Taught by David Howard, the New York-based teacher and coach, former soloist with the Royal Ballet and National Ballet of Canada.

BALLET COMES TO BRITAIN
1972, 26 min. b&w video
Series: Ballet For All
Distributor: The Media Guild
Director: Nicholas Ferguson
Choreographers: Vaslav Nijinsky, Léonide Massine, Bronislava Nijinska, Ninette de Valois
Principal Dancers: Christopher Bruce, David Wall, Marilyn Williams, Brenda Last, Johaar Mosaval
Dance Company: Royal Ballet, Ballet Rambert
Composers: Claude Debussy, Gioacchino Rossini, François Poulenc, Gavin Gordon
Category: BALLET, EUROPE
Most of these excerpts are from English versions of Diaghilev ballets: the Ballet Rambert version of Nijinsky's *L'Après-midi d'un Faun*, the can-can duet from Massine's *Boutique Fantasque* (1919), the hostess' solo from Nijinska's *Les Biches* (1924). Also excerpts from Ninette de Valois' *The Rake's Progress*.

BALLET ENTERS THE WORLD STAGE
1972, 26 min. b&w video
Series: Ballet For All
Distributor: The Media Guild
Director: Nicholas Ferguson
Choreographers: August Bournonville, Jean Coralli
Principal Dancers: Margaret Barbieri, Nicholas Johnson, Marion Tate, Bridget Taylor
Dance Company: Ballet For All
Composers: Adolphe Adam, Herman Severin Lovenskjöld
Category: PANTOMIME, BALLET
A version of *Gisèlle* for four dancers, piano and viola. Narrator David Blair touches on the innovations of dancing on toe, dancing with less cumbersome costumes, and communicating through mime, all of which were introduced at the time of *Gisèlle's* premiere. The sylph's opening dance in Bournonville's *La Sylphide* is also shown.

BALLET ETOILES
1989, 20 min. color video
Distributor: FACSEA
Principal Dancers: Sylvie Guillem, Patrick Dupond
Category: BALLET
Rehearsal and discussion between two megastars of the French ballet. In French or English versions.

BALLET FAVORITES
1988, 59 min. color video
Distributors: Home Box Office, Laserdisc Fan Club, Viewfinders

Producer: National Video Corporation
Directors: John Vernon, Peter Wright, Preben Montell, Colin Nears, Brian Large, Elena Macharet
Choreographers: Marius Petipa, Lev Ivanov, Jean Coralli, Kenneth MacMillan, Mikhail Baryshnikov, Frederick Ashton, Konstantin Sergeyev, Aleksandr Gorsky
Principal Dancers: Cynthia Harvey, Natalia Makarova, Lesley Collier, Mikhail Baryshnikov, Anthony Dowell, Alessandra Ferri, Wayne Eagling, Galina Mezentseva, Konstantin Zaklinsky
Dance Company: American Ballet Theatre, Kirov Ballet, Royal Ballet
Composers: Adolphe Adam, Peter Ilyich Tchaikovsky, Sergei Prokofiev, Léon Minkus
Category: BALLET COMPANIES
Excerpts of films of three ballet companies, with a compilation of solos, pas de deux and ensembles from *Don Quixote*, *Swan Lake*, *The Nutcracker*, *Romeo and Juliet*, *Sleeping Beauty*, and *Gisèlle*.

BALLET FOLKLÓRICO NACIONAL DE MÉXICO
1988, 110 and 45 min. color video
Distributors: Gessler, Media Basics
Producer: Gessler
Choreographer: Silvia Lozano
Dance Company: Ballet Folklórico Nacional de México
Category: FOLK, LATIN AMERICA
Performance by Mexico City's globe-trotting troupe of eighty dancers, presenting the traditional music and dance of Mexico. The selections include *Boda Tarasca*, *Jarabe Mixteco*, *El Norte*, *Los Quetzales*, *Alegría Jaliscience*, and *La Huasteca*. Worksheets created by Thomas Alsop are also provided.

BALLET IN JAZZ
1962, 11 min. b&w film
Distributor: The Cinema Guild
Producer: Roto-Film GmbH/Hamburg
Director: Hans Reinhard
Choreographer: Heinz Schmieder
Principal Dancers: Heinz Schmieder, Maria Litto, F. Friedman, R. Owens
Composer: Siegfried Franz
Category: JAZZ, BALLET
A German ballet influenced by American jazz dance.

BALLET LEGENDS: THE KIROV'S NINEL KURGAPKINA
1993, 40 min. color video
Distributors: V.I.E.W., Corinth
Producer: Göstelradio
Director: V. Butoman
Principal Dancer: Ninel Kurgapkina
Dance Company: Kirov Opera Ballet
Composers: Léon Minkus, Johann Strauss, Riccardo Drigo, Adolphe Adam, Dmitri Shostakovich, Peter Ilyich Tchaikovsky
Category: BALLET, DOCUMENTARY PORTRAITS
Ninel Alexandrovna Kurgapkina was a leading prima ballerina with Russia's Kirov Ballet for twenty-five years. She was renowned for her distinctive style, impeccable technique, and passionate acting. She is seen in excerpts from *Don Quixote*, *Waltz*, *Harlequinade*, *Le Corsaire*, and *Sleeping Beauty*.

BALLET MECHANIQUE
1924, 15 min. b&w film
Distributors: Museum of Modern Art, Biograph
    Entertainment
Director: Fernand Léger
Category: EXPERIMENTAL, TECHNOLOGY
Images of wire whisks and funnels, copper pots
    and lids, tinned and fluted baking pans, com-
    bined with shots of a woman climbing again
    and again a steep flight of stairs with a heavy
    sack on her back. The only film made by the
    French painter Fernand Léger, an artist of the
    Cubist School. The film plays with the theme of
    the mechanization of humans and the human-
    ization of objects.

BALLET ROBOTIQUE
1983, 8 min. color film, video
Distributors: Pyramid, Kent State
Producer: Bob Rogers
Director: Bob Rogers
Composers: Georges Bizet, Peter Ilyich Tchai-
    kovsky
Category: EXPERIMENTAL, TECHNOLOGY
In this winner of eighteen awards, pirouetting ro-
    bots at the General Motors assembly line drill
    holes in auto shells, spray paint on chassis, and
    shoot welding sparks in time to the cannon fire
    of the *1812 Overture.*

BALLET RUSE
1989, 35 min. color video
Series: State of the Art
Distributor: Music Video Distributors
Producer: Eirc S. Luskin for New Jersey Network
Director: Eric Vuolle
Choreographer: Peter Anastos
Dance Company: Garden State Ballet
Composers: Frédéric Chopin, Peter Ilyich Tchai-
    kovsky
Category: BALLET, COMEDY
Emmy Award
This farce by the choreographer known for his
    work with Ballet Trockadero and American Bal-
    let Theatre includes two ballets: *Yes Virginia,
    Another Piano Ballet* in which Anastos pokes
    fun at the genre of ballets set to Chopin's piano
    music; and *Forgotten Memories,* which mocks
    adulterous triangles.

BALLET STUDY FILMS (6 films)
1950s, 5–16 min. b&w film
Distributor: Dance Film Archive
Choreographers: Michel Fokine, Marius Petipa,
    Lev Ivanov, Enrico Cecchetti
Principal Dancers: Lois Smith, David Adams, Nina
    Novak, Michael Maule, Melissa Hayden
Composers: Peter Ilyich Tchaikovsky, Frédéric
    Chopin, Léo Delibes
Category: BALLET, INSTRUCTIONAL
Classical pas de deux and excerpts including: *Blue
    Bird* (*Pas de Deux*); *Coppélia* (*Wedding Pas de
    Deux*); *Sleeping Beauty* (*Pas de Deux* and varia-
    tions); *Swan Lake* (Act II excerpts); and *Les Syl-
    phides* (excerpts).

BALLET WITH EDWARD VILLELLA
1970, 27 min. color film, video
Distributors: Coronet/MTI, Learning Corporation
    of America, Modern Talking Picture Service, In-
    sight Media, Indiana University, Kent State,
    PennState, University of Minnesota
Producer: Robert Saudek for I.Q. Films
Choreographers: George Balanchine, Marius Pet-
    ipa, Jean Coralli
Principal Dancers: Patricia McBride, Edward Vil-
    lella
Dance Company: New York City Ballet
Composers: Igor Stravinsky, Adolphe Adam
Category: BALLET, DOCUMENTARY POR-
    TRAITS
Narrator: Edward Villella
American Film Festival
Edward Villella illustrates the muscular power and
    control necessary to partner a ballerina. Ex-
    cerpts from *Giselle* (Coralli/Adam 1841) dem-
    onstrate the qualities of classical ballet. A
    segment of *Apollo* (Balanchine/Stravinsky 1967)
    and *Rubies,* from the three-act ballet *Jewels* (Ba-
    lanchine/Stravinsky 1967), represent the neo-
    classical style.

THE BALLET WORKOUT
1987, 83 min. color video
Distributors: Kultur, Dance Horizons, Home Vi-
    sion
Producer: Instructional Video Systems
Choreographer: Melissa Lowe
Principal Dancer: Melissa Lowe
Category: INSTRUCTIONAL, BALLET
This is a way to achieve a lithe, supple body, im-
    prove your carriage, and attain the look and
    grace of a professional dancer.

THE BALLET WORKOUT II
1993, 70 min. color video
Distributors: Kultur, Dance Horizons, Home Vi-
    sion, Facets
Producer: Rob Sabal
Choreographer: Melissa Lowe
Principal Dancer: Melissa Lowe
Category: INSTRUCTIONAL, BALLET
Two new workouts which address the goal of
    achieving and maintaining the look of a profes-
    sional dancer.

BALLET'S GOLDEN AGE (1830–1846)
1966, 10 min. color, b&w film
Distributors: Kent State, UCLA Instructional
    Media Library
Producer: Walter P. Lewishon
Category: BALLET, DANCE HISTORY
Prints of the romantic ballerinas Marie Taglioni
    (1804–1884), Fanny Essler (1810–1884), Car-
    lotta Grisi (1821–1899), and Lucile Grahn
    (1821–1907), with quotations from letters and
    reviews to convey a sense of the period.

BALLROOM DANCING (3 videos)
1987, 1991, 1993, 57, 48 and 60 min. color video
Distributors: Kultur, Karol, Instructional Video,
    Home Vision, Facets (Advanced)
Director: Rick Allen Lippert
Principal Dancers: Terese Mason, Susan Major,
    Randolph Scott
Category: BALLROOM, INSTRUCTIONAL
Ballroom Dancing for Beginners, Intermediate and
    Advanced, offer lessons in the fox-trot, tango,
    waltz, rumba, cha-cha and swing.

**BALLROOM DANCING: THE
INTERNATIONAL CHAMPIONSHIPS**
1993, 60 min. color video
Distributor: V.I.E.W.
Producer: Vaclav Klecka
Director: Jaroslav Gajda
Principal Dancers: Donnie Burns, Gaynor Fair-
    weather, Karen Hilton, Marcus Hilton
Category: BALLROOM
The world's top-ranked couples compete in the
    international Latin and Modern ballroom dance
    competition. Features special performances of
    cha-cha, samba, quickstep, paso doble, jive and
    more, as well as solos by the reigning world
    champions of ballroom.

THE BAND WAGON
1953, 111 min. color film, video, laser
Distributors: Facets, Swank, MGM/UA
Producer: MGM
Director: Vincente Minelli
Choreographers: Fred Astaire, Michael Kidd
Principal Dancers: Fred Astaire, Cyd Charisse
Composer: Arthur Schwartz
Category: FEATURES, MUSICALS
An aging legendary performer, who is washed-up
    in Hollywood, makes a comeback in a Broad-
    way musical. Based upon the original Broadway
    revue, musical dance numbers include *That's
    Entertainment, A Shine on Your Shoes, Dancing
    in the Dark,* and the ballets *The Beggar Waltz*
    and *The Girl Hunt* for corps de ballet.

BANGUZA TIMBILA
1982, 30 min. color video
Distributor: PennState
Producer: Ron Hallis
Director: Ron Hallis
Category: AFRICA, FOLK
Ten players of hand-made *timbilas,* which are sim-
    ilar to marimbas, accompany fifteen dancers
    performing in Banguza, Mozambique.

BARBARA IS A VISION OF LOVELINESS
1978, 6 min. b&w film
Distributor: Phoenix
Producer: Lightworks
Director: Bruce Elder
Category: EXPERIMENTAL
An experimental film of a dancing figure creating
    abstract forms in black and white.

**BARBARA MORGAN: EVERYTHING IS
DANCING**
1983, 18 min. color video
Distributor: Museum of Modern Art
Producer: Edgar B. Howard for Checkerboard
    Foundation
Principal Dancer: Martha Graham
Category: DOCUMENTARY PORTRAITS, NA-
    TIVE AMERICANS
Photographer Barbara Morgan, known to the
    dance world for the photos she took of Martha
    Graham in the 1930s and '40s, recounts her first
    encounters with Native American rituals in the
    Southwest, and explains how movement and
    dance became important subjects for her.

THE BARKLEYS OF BROADWAY
1949, 109 min. color film, video, laser
Distributors: Facets, Swank, MGM/UA
Producer: MGM
Director: Charles Walters
Choreographers: Fred Astaire, Robert Alton,
    Hermes Pan
Principal Dancers: Fred Astaire, Ginger Rogers
Composer: Harry Warren
Category: FEATURES, BALLROOM

A successful musical team is split when the female half seeks fulfillment in meaningful drama—only to find that she's happier in musical comedy. Dance routines include: *The Swing Trot, You'd Be Hard to Replace, Bouncin' the Blues,* and *They Can't Take That Away From Me.*

BAROQUE DANCE 1675–1725

1979, 23 min. color film, video
Distributors: University of California Extension Center, Dance Film Archive
Producer: Allegra Fuller Snyder
Director: Allegra Fuller Snyder
Principal Dancers: Sue Wanven, Ron Taylor
Category: DANCE HISTORY
Dance on Camera Festival Certificate of Merit
Introduces the social and theatrical dancing of the baroque period in context with the architecture landscape gardening, music, design and costume of that time. Includes a *Suite for Theatre* (rondeau, minuet, hornpipe and slow air) and *Suite for Diana and Mars.* Demonstrates the minuet's hand and finger movements and ways to interprete baroque notation. Accompanied by a 104-page book.

BART COOK: CHOREOGRAPHER

1987, 30 min. color video
Distributor: Museum of Modern Art
Producer: Patsy and Jeff Tarr for the Checkerboard Foundation
Director: Fitzgerald, Kit
Choreographer: Bart Cook
Composer: Gioacchino Rossini
Category: DOCUMENTARY PORTRAITS, CHOREOGRAPHY
Shows Bart Cook of the New York City Ballet working with students from the School of the American Ballet, closing with a performance of his choreography.

BARYSHNIKOV AT WOLF TRAP

1976, 50 min. color video
Distributors: Kultur, Dance Horizons, Viewfinders, Home Vision
Producer: WETA Inc.
Choreographers: Arthur Saint-Léon, Michel Fokine, Leonid Jacobson, Marius Petipa
Principal Dancers: Mikhail Baryshnikov, Gelsey Kirkland, Marianna Tcherkassky
Category: BALLET
Host: Beverly Sills
Baryshnikov's American television debut, at the peak of his artistic talents, recorded at the Wolf Trap Farm Park for the Performing Arts in Virginia, featuring him in pas de deux from both *Coppélia* and *Don Quixote* with his first American partner, Gelsey Kirkland. Also excerpts from *Le Spectre de la Rose,* and a solo performance of *Vestris,* in which he had enormous success in his native Russia.

BARYSHNIKOV DANCES SINATRA

1988, 60 min. color video
Distributors: Dance Horizons, Viewfinders, Karol, Home Vision, Media Basics
Producer: Don Mischer
Choreographer: Twyla Tharp
Principal Dancers: Mikhail Baryshnikov, Deirdre Carberry, Elaine Kudo, Susan Jaffe, Robert La Fosse, Cheryl Yeager
Dance Company: American Ballet Theatre

Composers: Alexander Glazunov, Franz Joseph Haydn, Joseph Lamb
Category: BALLET
Baryshnikov plays an impossible, irresistible lover in *Sinatra Suite;* a virtuoso clown in *Push Comes to Shove,* the pun-filled satire set to rags by Joseph Lamb and symphonies of Joseph Haydn; and a sweet-tempered partner in *The Little Ballet.* Also called *Baryshnikov by Tharp* and *Baryshnikov, Tharp and Sinatra.*

BARYSHNIKOV: THE DANCER AND THE DANCE

1983, 82 min. color video
Distributors: Kultur, Home Vision, Dance Horizons, Viewfinders
Producers: Harriet and Victor Millrose with Melvyn Bragg and London Weekend Television
Director: Tony Cash
Choreographers: Choo San Goh, Marius Petipa
Principal Dancers: Mikhail Baryshnikov, Marianna Tcherkassky
Dance Company: American Ballet Theatre
Composer: Samuel Barber
Category: BALLET, DOCUMENTARY PORTRAITS
Narrator: Shirley MacLaine
Mikhail Baryshnikov rehearses, coaches and performs his commissioned ballet *Configurations,* choreographed by the late Choo San Goh. In the course of his reflection on his career and early training in Russia, Baryshnikov, in footage as a young man, performs the role of the pirate in *Le Corsaire.*

BASIC PRINCIPLES OF POINTE/PARTNERING

(2 videos)
1994, 45 min. each color video
Distributor: Dance Horizons
Category: INSTRUCTIONAL
Exercises for all levels of ballet students with Patricia Dickinson. Also available: *Pointe To Pointe* (40 min.), ballet barre exercises for beginning/intermediate pointe students.

BASIC SWORD

1987, 100 min. color video
Distributor: Chandra of Damascus
Producer: Chandra of Damascus
Choreographer: Chandra of Damascus
Principal Dancer: Chandra of Damascus
Category: MIDDLE EAST
Balancing, twirling, turning techniques of using the sword in Middle Eastern dance.

BATHING BEAUTY

1944, 101 min. color video, laser
Distributor: MGM/UA
Producer: MGM
Director: George Sidney
Choreographers: Jack Donahue, Robert Alton, John Murray Anderson
Principal Dancers: Esther Williams, Red Skelton
Composer: Johnny Green
Category: FEATURES, MUSICALS
The first and best Esther Williams swim showcase disrupts its marital mix-up plot with colorful set pieces, including an exciting Latin *Joropa* dance, a eurythmics comedy sketch with Skelton which spoofs the ballet classics, and a water ballet finale which includes a tribute to Busby Berkeley.

THE BAUHAUS DANCES OF OSKAR SCHLEMMER: A RECONSTRUCTION

1986, 31:15 min. color video
Distributor: The Kitchen
Producers: Mary Salter and Debra McCall
Directors: Robert Leacock, Debra McCall
Composer: Craig Gordon
Category: MODERN, DANCE HISTORY
A reconstruction of the abstract dances made in Germany as a spin off of the energy and philosophy emanating from the Bauhaus, the influential German school of art and architecture founded in 1919.

LA BAYADÈRE (Kirov Ballet)

1977, 126 min. color video
Distributors: Kultur, Home Vision, Viewfinders, Corinth
Producer: Göstelradio
Director: Elena Macharet
Choreographers: Vakhtang Chabukiani, Vladimir Ponomaryov, Marius Petipa
Principal Dancers: Gabriela Komleva, Tatiana Terekova, Rejen Abdyev
Dance Company: Kirov Ballet
Composer: Léon Minkus
Category: FULL-LENGTH BALLETS
The 1877 three-act ballet based on the Indian classic *Kalisdasa: Sakuntala* and *The Cart of Clay,* filmed live at the Kirov Theatre. Murdered by a jealous lover, Nikia the Bayadère continues to haunt a young warrior, Solor, who remains the object of her affection even as she dances in the Kingdom of the Shades.

LA BAYADÈRE (Royal Ballet)

1991, 120 min. color video, laser
Distributors: Kultur 1326, Home Vision BAY020, Viewfinders, Dance Horizons, Corinth, Laserdisc Fan Club
Producer: Cameras Continales/Amaya
Director: Derek Bailey
Choreographer: Natalia Makarova, after Marius Petipa
Principal Dancers: Altynai Asylmuratova, Irek Mukhamedov, Darcey Russell
Dance Company: Royal Ballet
Composer: Léon Minkus
Category: FULL-LENGTH BALLETS
La Bayadère (The Temple Dancer) is based on an ancient Indian poem. The ballet concerns the love between Nikiya and Solor. Solor is obliged to wed Ganeatti, who murders her rival, Nikya. Overcome with grief, Solor envisions the slain maiden inviting him to join her in the Kingdom of the Shades. In their final dance together, they manage to find a measure of happiness among the phantoms of other maidens who have died of unrequited love. This Covent Garden performance has been hailed as the definitive production.

BEACH BIRDS FOR CAMERA

1992, 28 min. color, b&w 35mm film, video
Distributors: Cunningham Dance Foundation, VPI
Producer: Cunningham Dance Foundation
Director: Elliot Caplan
Choreographer: Merce Cunningham
Dance Company: Merce Cunningham Dance Company
Composer: John Cage

Category: CINEDANCE, MODERN
IMZ Dance Screen Festival 1993 Award, Dance on Camera Festival 1993 Best of Show
The first Cunningham filmdance shot on 35mm wide-screen begins in black and white at the Industria Superstudio, New York, and then cuts to color footage shot in the main soundstage at the historic Kaufman Astoria Studios, New York. The third segment is an exclusive interview with Merce Cunningham.

BEAR DANCE
1988, 13 min. color film, video
Distributors: PennState, Encyclopedia Britannica
Producer: James Ciletti in cooperation with Southern Utes and Ute Mountain Utes of Colorado
Director: James Ciletti
Category: NATIVE AMERICANS
The Ute Indians' joyful rite of spring which pays tribute to the tribe's legendary protector.

BEAUTY AND THE BEAST
1966, 50 min. color film, video
Distributor: Home Vision
Producer: Gordon Waldear for ABC Film Release
Choreographer: Lew Christensen
Principal Dancers: Robert Gladstein, Lynda Meyer, David Anderson
Dance Company: San Francisco Ballet
Composer: Peter Ilyich Tchaikovsky
Category: FULL-LENGTH BALLETS
Narrator: Hayley Mills
A fairy tale about a beautiful girl who saves her father's life by agreeing to live with a beast who magically transforms himself into a prince.

BECAUSE WE MUST
1989, 50 min. color video
Distributors: Electronic Arts Intermix, The Kitchen
Producer: Jolyon Wimhurst for Channel 4
Director: Charles Atlas
Choreographer: Michael Clark
Principal Dancer: Michael Clark
Dance Company: Michael Clark Company
Composers: Frédéric Chopin, T. Rex, Graham Lewis, Velvet Underground, Dome
Category: COMEDY, BALLET
A satiric romp in which trained male ballet dancers from London prance about in drag and sing around the grand piano. Punctuated by repeated regurgitations from the lead and a nude woman dancing by with a roaring chain saw.

BEDHAYA: THE SACRED DANCE
1994, 20 min. color video
Distributor: Stanford University
Producer: Shanty Harmayn
Director: Shanty Harmayn
Dance Company: Surakarta Court Dancers
Category: ASIA, RELIGIOUS/RITUAL
Dance on Camera Festival 1995 Honorable Mention
This documentary, shot in Indonesia, portrays three generations of court dancers from the palace of Surakarta through interviews with former and current dancers.

BEEHIVE
1985, 15 min. color film, video
Distributors: Facets, Moore, Frank
Producer: Frank Moore
Director: Frank Moore
Choreographer: Jim Self
Principal Dancers: Jim Self, Teri Weksler
Composer: Man Parrish
Category: MODERN, NATURE
Bessie Award 1985, Dance on Camera Festival 1987 Honorable Mention
A bumbling drone unwittingly causes a worker bee to be transformed into a queen. A related ballet by the same title was commissioned by the Boston Ballet and premiered in 1987. The cast included thirty-six bees and eight flowers.

BEFORE HOLLYWOOD: TURN OF THE CENTURY FILM FROM AMERICAN ARCHIVES (6 programs)
1895–1915, 68–108 min. b&w film
Distributor: American Federation of Arts
Producer: American Federation of Arts
Directors: W.K.L. Dickson, William Heise
Principal Dancer: Annabelle Moore
Category: DANCE HISTORY
Program I of the series includes dance shorts made in 1895–96: *Annabelle Butterfly Dance*, *Annabelle Serpentine Dance*, and *Serpentine Dance*, produced by the Edison Manufacturing Company in the period when film cameras and projectors were just being developed. Selected by the late Jay Leyda, renowned historian of early cinema and American literature, and Charles Musser, film scholar and filmmaker. Also organized as a touring film series from American Federation of Arts is *A History of the American Avant-Garde Cinema*, with seven programs showing thirty-six films produced by twenty-eight artists between 1943 and 1972, including the works of Maya Deren.

BEGINNINGS
1976, 30 min. color film
Distributor: Arthur Cantor, Inc.
Producers: Maren and Reed Erskine
Directors: Maren and Reed Erskine
Choreographer: Arthur Saint-Léon
Dance Company: New York City Ballet
Composer: Léo Delibes
Category: BALLET, INSTRUCTIONAL
Dance Teachers: Suki Shorer, Alexandra Danilova
Dance on Camera Festival 1977 Honorable Mention
This study of the School of American Ballet, founded in 1934 by Lincoln Kirstein and George Balanchine, shows the aims and attitudes of the students and faculty, who demonstrate the ballet vocabulary, and conclude with scenes from a performance of *Coppélia*, choreographed by Balanchine/Danilova after Saint-Léon.

THE BEGINNINGS OF TODAY
1972, 26 min. b&w video
Series: Ballet For All
Distributor: The Media Guild
Director: Nicholas Ferguson
Choreographers: Michel Fokine, Marius Petipa
Principal Dancers: Anna Pavlova, Shirley Grahame, Graham Usher
Composers: Frédéric Chopin, Peter Ilyich Tchaikovsky, Igor Stravinsky
Category: BALLET, DANCE HISTORY
Celebrates the poetic expression of the romantic period with excerpts from *Les Sylphides*, *Swan Lake*, *Sleeping Beauty*, and *Petroushka*. Rare footage shows Anna Pavlova performing two solos, *La Nuit* and *The Dying Swan*.

BEHIND THE MASK
1975, 52 min. color film
Series: Tribal Eye
Distributors: University of California Extension Center, UCLA Instructional Media Library, University of Minnesota
Producer: BBC-TV
Category: ANTHROPOLOGICAL, RELIGIOUS/RITUAL, AFRICA
Narrator: David Attenborough
The masks of the Dogon people of Mali, Africa, are used in ritual ceremonies that include singing and dancing.

BELL DANCE FOR THE CONJURATION OF THE SACRED BUSH COW
1954, 3:30 min. b&w film (silent)
Distributor: PennState
Producer: Wissen
Director: E. Leuzinger
Category: ANTHROPOLOGICAL, AFRICA, RELIGIOUS/RITUAL
Dancers of Afo, Nigeria swing large iron bells and civet cat pelts as symbols of the sacred bush cow, their protective power, to drive evil spirits away.

THE BELLE OF NEW YORK
1952, 82 min. color video
Distributors: Facets, Swank, MGM/UA
Producer: MGM
Director: Walters, Charles
Choreographer: Robert Alton
Principal Dancers: Fred Astaire, Vera-Ellen
Composer: Harry Warren
Category: FEATURES, TAP
A playboy seeks the love of a woman in the Salvation Army. Dance numbers include a figure dance on an ice pond on skates and a tap dance atop the Washington Square arch. Also, *Baby Doll*, *Oops*, *Naughty But Nice*, and *I Wanna Be a Dancin' Man*.

BELLY DANCE! MAGICAL MOTION
1985, 57 min. color video
Distributors: Magical Motion Enterprises, Instructional Video
Producer: Cheryl Simon known as Atea
Director: Mitch Merback
Choreographer: Cheryl Simon
Principal Dancer: Cheryl Simon
Composer: Ramal LaMarr
Category: BELLY DANCE, INSTRUCTIONAL
Introduction to belly dance technique with historical background, exercises for finger cymbals and veil work, with a chapter on costuming and examples of the *baladi* and Saudi-style garments, as well as cabaret costumes.

BELLY DANCE! SLOW MOVES; BELLY DANCE! FAST MOVES (2 videos)
1996, 40 min. each color video
Distributor Magical Motion Enterprises
Instructor: Atea
Category: BELLY DANCE, INSTRUCTIONAL
Sequels to *Belly Dance: Magical Motion*, presenting beginner and intermediate instruction in the fast and slow movements of classical belly dance.

BERIMBAU
1974, 12 min. color film
Distributor: New Yorker
Producer: Tony Talbot
Director: Tony Talbot
Category: LATIN AMERICA, MARTIAL ARTS
In this ethnomusicology film, Nana, a black musician, uses a *berimbau*, a one-stringed musical bow, to play traditional melodies to accompany the *capoeira*, a dance based on the Brazilian martial art form. Presents the history and harmonies of the *berimbau*, one of the oldest musical instruments.

BESIDE HERSELF
1987, 7:45 min. b&w film
Distributor: Film-makers' Cooperative
Directors: Power Boothe, Caitlin Cobb
Choreographer: Caitlin Cobb
Composer: A. Leroy
Category: EXPERIMENTAL
A nonverbal dialogue between a woman in black on one side of the screen and the same woman in white on the other.

BEST OF ALL A DANCER
1983, 11 min. color film, video
Distributor: Direct Cinema
Producers: Richard Heus and Robert Marinaccio
Director: Richard Heus
Choreographers: David Morgan, Rusty Hartman
Principal Dancer: Rusty Hartman
Composer: Warren R. McCommons
Category: DANCE THERAPY, DISABILITIES
Rusty Hartman, a thirty-two-year-old man with Down's Syndrome, performs dances he choreographed over the last eight years with the help of a supportive teacher. An inspiring example of how dance and music can ease communication and self-esteem.

BEYOND ROUTINE
1995, 35 min. color video
Series: Tools For Choreography
Distributor: ClearWater Productions
Producer: Don Gosselin
Director: Neil Colligan
Choreographer: Daryl Gray
Composers: Yellen and Ager
Category: INSTRUCTIONAL, CHOREOGRAPHY
Puts choreographic method to work in a vaudevillian production number *Happy Feet*, deconstructing and explaining how it is put together. Available with instructional workbook and audiotape.

BEYOND THE MAINSTREAM: POSTMODERN DANCERS
1980, 60 min. color video
Series: Dance in America
Distributor: Films Inc.
Producers: Merrill Brockway, Carl Carlson
Director: Merrill Brockway
Choreographers: Trisha Brown, Laura Dean, David Gordon, Yvonne Rainer, Steve Paxton, Kei Takei
Principal Dancers: Yvonne Rainer, David Gordon, Steve Paxton, Trisha Brown
Dance Company: Grand Union
Category: CHOREOGRAPHY, DOCUMENTARY PORTRAITS

A representation of the lives and art of the dancers-choreographers as seen through interviews and excerpts of their dance pieces: *Contact Improvisation, Line Up, Glacial Decoy, A Trio, Chair, The Matter, Light, Dance.*

BILL T. JONES: DANCING TO THE PROMISED LAND
1994, 60 min. color video
Distributors: V.I.E.W., Facets, Dance Horizons
Producer: Antelope West/BBC-TV
Director: Mischa Scorer
Choreographer: Bill T. Jones
Principal Dancer: Bill T. Jones
Dance Company: Bill T. Jones/Arnie Zane Dance Company
Category: CHOREOGRAPHY, DOCUMENTARY PORTRAITS
Dance on Camera Festival 1994 Gold Award
Modern dancer-choreographer Bill T. Jones explains his approach to his work based on *Uncle Tom's Cabin,* with rehearsal and performance excerpts.

BILL T. JONES: STILL/HERE WITH BILL MOYERS
1995, 60min. color video
Distributor: WNET
Producers: David Grubin & Alice Markowitz
Directors: David Grubin & Alice Markowitz
Choreographer: Bill T. Jones
Principal Dancer: Bill T. Jones
Dance Company: Bill T. JonesArnie Zane Dance Company
Category: DANCE THERAPY
A record compiled by Bill Moyers and David Grubin of the making of Bill T. Jones' *StillHere*, a controversial dance which explores the feelings of one hundred non-dancers who were facing life-threatening illnesses such as AIDS.

BILLBOARDS
1993, 75 min. color video, laser
Series: Dance in America
Distributor: Dance Horizons
Producer: Gerald Arpino
Director: Bailey, Derek
Choreographers: Dean, Laura, Charles Moulton, Margo Sappington, Peter Pucci
Dance Company: Robert Joffrey Ballet
Composer: Prince
Category: FULL-LENGTH BALLETS, COLLABORATION
A rock ballet set to the music of Prince, an acclaimed pop artist, and performed by the Robert Joffrey Ballet, a well-known dance company.

BINO-DANCE
1963, 2 min. b&w film (silent)
Distributor: PennState
Producer: Wissen
Category: FOLK, ASIA
Filmed in the Pacific, men and women from Tabiteuea, Gilbert Islands perform *Bino*, a traditional folk dance performed from a sitting position. *Kawawa,* the introductory song and dance of the Gilbert Island, *Kamei, Wa N'Tarawa* and the *Kabuakaka* were other brief dance films produced by Wissen.

BIRDS OF A FEATHER
1990, 28 min. color video
Distributor: University of California Extension Center

Producers: Birds of a Feather and Show Place Video Productions
Category: DANCE THERAPY
A dance therapy film in which five members of a troupe dance, sing, and act despite their individual disabilities. Signed for the hearing impaired.

BITTER MELONS
1971, 30 min. color film
Distributors: Documentary Educational Resources, University of California Extension Center
Producer: Center for Documentary Anthropology
Director: John Marshall
Category: ANTHROPOLOGICAL, AFRICA
CINE Golden Eagle, American Film Festival Blue Ribbon
Igwikhwe bushmen of the Kalahari Desert area in southwest Africa, perform animal songs about the tribe's dependence upon the land for their livelihood, and their continual search for water. Shot in the mid-1950s as part of a Peabody Museum expedition.

BLACK AND WHITE
1985, 7 min. color film
Distributor: Gross, Sally
Director: Joan Kurahara
Choreographer: Sally Gross
Composer: Gary Haase
Category: EXPERIMENTAL, ART
Dance on Camera Festival 1986 Honorable Mention
An experimental effort to superimpose the movements of dancers with slides painted by Joan Kurahara.

THE BLACK BOOTS
1995, 10 min. 35mm film
Distributor: BAM Productions
Producer: Bridget A. Murnane
Director: Bridget A. Murnane
Choreographer: Marcus Schulkind
Dancer: Jeanine Durning
Dance Company: Marcus Schulkind Dance Company
Composer: Louis Gottschalk, Igon Tkachenko
Category: EXPERIMENTAL
This film revolves around the loss and retrieval of one woman's love of and devotion to dance. The film cuts from dance class to street, to beach, to ballroom, to park, to classroom with the ever mobile boots as the transitional focus.

BLACK GIRL
1982, 30 min. color film, video
Series: Planning Ahead
Distributor: University of California Extension Center
Producer: Berkeley Productions
Directors: Hal and Marilyn Weiner
Category: AFRICAN-AMERICANS, CHILDREN
American Film Festival, National Council on Family Relations, National Educational Film and Video Festival
A young African-American teenager drops out of school and secretly takes a job as a dancer and waitress at a local bar. She dreams of becoming a ballet dancer but doesn't know how to pursue her goal in the face of violent opposition from her family.

BLACK TIGHTS
1962, 120 min. color film, video
Distributors: Dance Film Archive, Viewfinders,
    Video Artists International
Producer: Joseph Kaufman
Director: Terence Young
Choreographer: Roland Petit
Principal Dancers: Roland Petit, Zizi Jeanmaire,
    Moira Shearer, Cyd Charisse, Hans Van Manen,
    Henning Kronstram
Composers: Georges Bizet, Marius Constant, Jean-
    Michel Damase
Category: BALLET, FEATURES
Narrator: Maurice Chevalier, Costumes: Yves
    Saint Laurent
A feature film set in Paris consisting of four bal-
    lets: *Carmen*, in which a cigarette girl seduces a
    young soldier and leaves him for a matador; *Cy-
    rano de Bergerac*, based on the play by Edmond
    Rostand about a man's attempt to woo his love
    by proxy through a young soldier; *Diamond
    Cruncher*, about a beautiful pickpocket who has
    a passion for eating stolen diamonds; and *A
    Merry Mourning* (originally known as *Devil in
    Twenty-Four Hours*), in which a woman pur-
    chases a black dress to dance with a suitor who
    murdered her husband.

BLOOD WEDDING
1981, 71 min. color film, video
Distributors: Alegrías, Xenon
Producer: Emiliano Piedra
Director: Carlos Saura
Choreographer: Antonio Gades
Principal Dancers: Antonio Gades, Cristina Hoyos
Category: FLAMENCO, FEATURES
The first of a trilogy of flamenco dance-theatre
    works by Saura (see *Carmen, El Amor Brujo*),
    based on Federico García Lorca's tragic play of
    a young bride who runs off with a previous
    lover. Subsequently, her lover and new husband
    kill each other.

THE BLUE ANGEL
1988, 78 min. color video
Distributors: Kultur, Home Vision, Dance Hori-
    zons, Viewfinders, Corinth, Media Basics
Producers: Telemondis, La Sept, FR3, and WK
    Productions
Director: Dirk Sanders
Choreographer: Roland Petit
Principal Dancers: Dominique Khalfouni, Roland
    Petit, Pierre Aviotte
Dance Company: Ballet National de Marseille
Composer: Lou Bruder
Category: FULL-LENGTH BALLETS
Based on the story by Heinrich Mann of Rosa
    Frohlich, the cabaret dancer Josef von Sternberg
    made so famous with his 1930 classic starring
    Marlene Dietrich. The ballet flirts with the joys
    of toying with a man's obsessive lust.

BLUE SNAKE
1986, 58 min. color video
Distributors: Bullfrog Films, Rhombus Interna-
    tional
Producers: TV Ontario and Canada Council, Niv
    Fichman, and Louise Clark for Rhombus Inter-
    national
Director: Niv Fichman
Choreographer: Robert Desrosiers
Dance Company: National Ballet of Canada

Composers: John Lang, Ahmed Hassan
Category: BALLET, DOCUMENTARY POR-
    TRAITS
Dance on Camera Festival Gold Award, American
    Film and Video Red Ribbon, San Francisco In-
    ternational Film Festival Golden Gate Award
Cannibalism, revenge and transcendence, the un-
    usual sequence for this surreal ballet commis-
    sioned by the National Ballet of Canada,
    unfolds through rehearsals, costume fittings,
    and performance. This collaborative effort
    equally involves all the participating artists and
    producers.

BLUE STUDIO: FIVE SEGMENTS
1976, 15 min. color film, video (silent)
Distributor: Cunningham Dance Foundation
Producer: Cunningham Dance Foundation
Director: Charles Atlas
Choreographer: Merce Cunningham
Principal Dancer: Merce Cunningham
Category: CINEDANCE, EXPERIMENTAL
A solo performed in a fifteen-by-fifteen-foot stu-
    dio seemingly transformed through chromakey,
    a method whereby imagery can be superim-
    posed on a blue backdrop, giving the choreog-
    rapher the freedom to transport the dancers to
    any environment, real or surreal, or to dance
    with multiple clones of himself. See also the
    variation on this film by Nam June Paik in
    Merce By Merce By Paik.

BOB RIZZO'S BALLET CLASS FOR KIDS
1993, 50 min. color video
Distributor: Dance Horizons
Dance Company: Riz-Biz Kidz
Category: INSTRUCTIONAL, CHILDREN,
    BALLET
The class focuses on developing vocabulary, tech-
    nique and correcting errors of the one-to-two-
    year student, including ballet barre, center com-
    binations and Grand Waltz.
BOB RIZZO'S 50 TURNS AND JUMPS
1994, 60 min. color video
Distributor: Dance Horizons
Category: INSTRUCTIONAL
Turn and jump variations for beginning through
    advanced dancers.

BOB RIZZO'S JAZZ CLASS FOR KIDS
1993, 55 min. color video
Distributor: Dance Horizons
Dance Company: Riz-Biz Kidz
Category: INSTRUCTIONAL, CHILDREN, JAZZ
The class for beginner to advanced nine-to-six-
    teen-year-old student includes jazz barre, floor
    stretches and progressions.

THE BODY AS AN INSTRUMENT
1972, 27 min. color video
Series: Dance as an Art Form
Distributors: Pro Arts, UCLA Instructional Media
    Library
Producer: Chimerafilm
Director: Warren Leib
Choreographer: Murray Louis
Dance Company: Murray Louis Dance Company
Composer: Alwin Nikolais
Category: MODERN, INSTRUCTIONAL
Narrator: Murray Louis
After examining a variety of the sizes, shapes and
    temperaments represented by a group of actors,
    athletes, children, animals and university dance

students, Murray Louis assures us that anyone
    can dance. Louis performs excerpts of his reper-
    toire with his company.

BODY ROCK
1984, 94 min. color film, video
Distributor: Films Inc.
Producer: Trans Atlantic
Director: Marcelo Epstein
Choreographer: Susan Scanlan
Principal Dancer: Lorenzo Lamas
Dance Company: The Body Rock Crew
Category: FEATURES, BREAK DANCE
A music video-style story of a group of young am-
    bitious rap singers, break-dancers and graffiti
    artists.

BODY TALK: EIGHT MOVEMENT THERAPIES
1975, 58 min. b&w video
Distributor: Meyer, Sybil
Producer: American Dance Therapy Association
    (Northern California Chapter)
Director: Sybil Meyer
Category: DANCE THERAPY
Eight sessions at a dance therapy conference with
    an explanation of the therapy goals and a vari-
    ety of approaches for self-expression and non-
    verbal communication.

BODY TJAK
1992, 7 min. color video
Distributor: In Motion Productions
Producer: Skip Blumberg
Director: Skip Blumberg
Choreographers: Keith Terry, I Wayan Dibia
Category: COLLABORATION
Lively collaboration between a rhythmic American
    and a Balinese *Ketchak* choreographer involves
    a mixed cultural company of twenty-four danc-
    ers-musicians-puppeteers.

BOLD STEPS
1984, 81 min. color video
Distributors: Corinth, Viewfinders
Producer: Canadian Broadcasting Corporation
Director: Cyril Frankel
Choreographers: Marius Petipa, Harold Lander,
    Erik Bruhn, Constantin Patsalas, Glen Tetley
Principal Dancers: Karen Kain, Erik Bruhn, Ru-
    dolf Nureyev, Celia Franca, Lorna Geddes, Mik-
    hail Baryshnikov
Dance Company: National Ballet of Canada
Composers: Peter Ilyich Tchaikovsky, Karl Czerny,
    Morton Gould, Léon Minkus, Harry Freedman,
    Bohuslav Martinu
Category: BALLET COMPANIES
Traces the development of the Toronto-based Na-
    tional Ballet of Canada with statements by the
    founder-former artistic director Celia Franca,
    and former dancer Lorna Geddes, supported by
    stills and footage. Rehearsals under Erik
    Bruhn's direction of *Études* (Lander-Czerny),
    Here We Come (Bruhn/Gould), *La Bayadère*
    (Petipa/Minkus), *Don Quixote* (Petipa/Min-
    kus), *Oiseaux Exotiques* (Patsalas/Freedman),
    Sphinx (Tetley/Martinu), *Swan Lake* (Petipa/
    Tchaikovsky), and performances at the com-
    pany's gala.

BOLERO
1961, 15 min. b&w film, video, laser
Distributors: Dance Film Archive, Corinth
Producer: Jean-Luc Landier

Director: Jean-Luc Landier
Choreographer: Maurice Béjart
Principal Dancer: Duska Sifinos
Dance Company: Ballet of the 20th Century
Composer: Maurice Ravel
Category: BALLET, COMEDY

A comically erotic ballet in which a soloist pulses above a circle of men sitting in chairs who gradually join forces with ritualistic ardor. One of the few works currently available by Maurice Béjart. For information on his films transferred to video, contact the Belgian Consulate.

BOLERO and PICTURES AT AN EXHIBITION
1994, 66 min. color video
Distributor: Dance Horizons
Choreographers: Lar Lubovitch, Moses Pendleton
Dance Company: Momix
Composers: Maurice Ravel, Modest Petrovich Mussorgsky
Category: MODERN, EXPERIMENTAL, ART

Contemporary interpretations of familiar music— one a love duet juxtaposed against a giant clockwork, and the other, the actual paintings coming to life.

THE BOLSHOI BALLET
1967, 90 min. color video
Distributors: Kultur, Viewfinders, Home Vision
Producer: Mosfilm Studios
Directors: Leonid Lavrovsky, Alexander Shelenkov
Choreographer: Leonid Lavrovsky
Principal Dancers: Raisa Struckhova, Nina Timofeyeva, Alla Osipenko, Natalya Bessmertnova, Ekaterina Maximova
Dance Company: Bolshoi Ballet
Composers: Sergei Prokofiev, Sergei Rachmaninov, Maurice Ravel
Category: BALLET COMPANIES
Dance on Camera Festival 1986

Rehearsal and performance of *Paganini* (Lavrovsky/Rachmaninov 1960) depicting the violin virtuoso inspired by his muse, *The Stone Flower* (Lavrovsky/Prokofiev 1954) about a sculptor's obsession with perfection, *Bolero* and *Waltz*.

THE BOLSHOI BALLET: GALINA ULANOVA
1991, 95 min. color video
Distributors: Video Artists International, Viewfinders, Dance Horizons, Media Basics
Producer: Paul Czinner
Director: Paul Czinner
Principal Dancers: Galina Ulanova, Nikolai Fadeyechev, Raisa Struchkova,
Dance Company: Bolshoi Ballet
Composers: Boris Asafiev, Peter Ilyich Tchaikovsky, Mikhail Ivanovich Glinka, Charles Gounod, Sergei Rachmaninov, Camille Saint-Saëns, Adolphe Adam
Category: BALLET COMPANIES

Paul Czinner's film of the Bolshoi on the first-ever tour of Great Britain in 1956, with Ulanova in a complete *Gisèlle* and six shorter works: *Dance of the Tartars* from the *Fountain of Bakhchisarai*; *Spanish Dance* from *Swan Lake*; *Polonaise* and *Cracovienne* from *Ivan Susanin*; *Walpurgisnacht* from *Faust*; *Spring Waters*; *The Dying Swan*.

BOLSHOI: DIVERTISSEMENTS
1986, 120 min. color video, laser
Distributor: Laserdisc Fan Club
Producers: Colin Nears and BBC-TV
Director: John Vernon
Choreographers: Marius Petipa, Yuri Grigorovich, Michel Fokine
Principal Dancers: Irek Mukhamedov, Natalya Bessmertnova, Nina Ananiashvili
Dance Company: Bolshoi Ballet
Composers: Peter Ilyich Tchaikovsky, Aram Khachaturian, Léon Minkus, Frédéric Chopin
Category: BALLET COMPANIES

Flamboyant divertissements filmed at the Battersea Pavilion in London with the following selections: *Les Sylphides*, *Spartacus* (Act II), *Sleeping Beauty*, *La Bayadère*, *Swan Lake*, *The Golden Age*, *Spring Waters*, *Don Quixote*.

BOLSHOI PROKOFIEV GALA
1991, 170 min. color video
Distributors: Kultur, Viewfinders, Corinth, Home Vision
Producer: Mikhail Litvinov
Directors: Dimitri Sarantopoulos, Nikita Tikhonov, George Zarafonitis
Choreographer: Yuri Grigorovich
Principal Dancers: Natalia Arkhipova, Maria Bilova, Ludmila Semenyaka, Nina Semizorova, Yuri Vasyuchenko, Aleksandr Vetrov
Dance Company: Bolshoi Ballet
Composer: Sergei Prokofiev
Category: BALLET

This centennial gala features the Bolshoi Ballet's brightest stars performing in excerpts from three great ballets, including *Romeo and Juliet*, *Ivan The Terrible*, and *The Stone Flower*, to celebrate the one hundredth birthday of Prokofiev.

BOLSHOI SOLOISTS CLASSIQUE
1987, 42 min. color video, laser
Distributors: V.I.E.W., Corinth
Producer: Soviet Film and TV
Choreographers: Mikhail Lavrosky, Michel Fokine, Nina Timofeyeva
Principal Dancers: Nina Timofeyeva, Mikhail Lavrovsky
Dance Company: Bolshoi Ballet
Composers: Peter Ilyich Tchaikovsky, Adolphe Adam, George Gershwin, Tomaso Albinoni, Camille Saint-Saëns
Category: BALLET

Program of solos and duets performed by dancers who both became members of the Bolshoi in 1961, including: *The Dying Swan* (Fokine/Saint-Saëns); *Porgy and Bess* (Lavrovsky/Gershwin); *Adagio* (Timofeyeva/Albinoni); and *Pas de Deux Classique* (Timofeyeva/Adam).

BONE DREAM
1977, 7:30 min. b&w video
Distributor: ARC Videodance
Producers: Jeff Bush and Celia Ipiotis
Directors: Jeff Bush, Celia Ipiotis
Choreographers: Eiko and Koma
Principal Dancers: Eiko and Koma
Category: EXPERIMENTAL, BUTOH
Dance on Camera Festival 1979

A meditation in the nude made in collaboration with the New York-based Japanese couple Eiko and Koma, trained in the *Butoh* school.

BONNIE BIRD DEMONSTRATES GRAHAM TECHNIQUE
1938–39, 12 min. b&w film (silent)
Distributor: Dance Film Archive
Principal Dancers: Bonnie Bird
Category: MODERN, INSTRUCTIONAL

A member of Martha Graham's company filmed at the Greek Theatre at Mills College, doing the floor exercises developed by the modern dance pioneer.

BOOK OF DAYS
1988, 75 min. color, b&w 35mm film, video
Distributor: The Stutz Company
Producer: Tatge/Lasseur Productions
Director: Meredith Monk
Choreographer: Meredith Monk
Category: MODERN

Connects thematic material about the meaning of time from the Middle Ages days of war, plague and fear of the Apocalypse to the modern world racial and religious conflict, AIDS and the fear of nuclear annihilation.

BOOK OF SHADOWS
1992, 24:30 min. color video
Distributors: Canyon Cinema, Facets
Producer: Janis Mattox
Director: Don Ferguson
Choreographer: Marci Javril
Principal Dancers: Marci Javril, Riccardo Morrison
Composer: Janis Mattox
Category: MODERN, EXPERIMENTAL

Dance on Camera Festival 1993 Honorable Mention, Worldfest Houston 1993, Philadelphia International Film Festival 1993, Baltimore Independent Film and Video Festival 1993, East Bay Video Festival 1992, American Film and Video Festival

Ritually invokes the transmission of feminine powers through a book of shadows, the secret record of rituals, healings and special knowledge handed down by a wise woman-shaman-witch to her apprentices.

BORN FOR HARD LUCK: PEG LEG SAM JACKSON
197?, 29 min. color film
Distributor: Tom Davenport Films
Director: Tom Davenport
Principal Dancer: Arthur (Peg Leg Sam) Jackson
Category: UNITED STATES, DOCUMENTARY PORTRAITS

Portrait of one of the last of the medicine show entertainers who played his blues harmonica, sang and danced to attract a crowd in the rural south for men pitching snake oil and other dubious cures.

BORN TO DANCE
1936, 108 min. b&w film, video, laser
Distributors: Facets, Films Inc., Swank, MGM/UA
Producer: MGM
Director: Roy del Ruth
Choreographer: Dave Gould
Principal Dancers: Eleanor Powell, Buddy Ebsen, Vilma Ebsen
Composer: Cole Porter
Category: FEATURES, MUSICALS

Three sailors on leave meet the hostess of a lonely hearts club in New York. The dance numbers include: *Hey, Babe, Hey, Easy to Love, I've Got You Under My Skin, Rap Tap on Wood*, and *Swingin' the Jinx Away*, set on a battleship.

BOURNONVILLE BALLET TECHNIQUE
1992, 45 min. color video
Distributor: Dance Horizons

Choreographer: August Bournonville
Dance Company: Royal Danish Ballet
Category: INSTRUCTIONAL, BALLET

Fifty *enchainements* (exercises) selected and reconstructed by Vivi Flindt and Knud Arne Jurgenson, demonstrate one of the world's major techniques developed by the nineteenth-century Danish choreographer.

BOYCEBALL
1991, 14 min. color video
Distributor: Filmakers Library
Producer: Robert H. Lieberman
Director: Robert H. Lieberman
Choreographer: Larry Bradley
Dance Company: The Ithaca Ballet
Composer: Willaim Boyce
Category: CHILDREN
Dance on Camera Festival 1992 Honorable Mention

A community-based ballet company creates a short ballet that will appeal to school-age audiences. Using baseball as a theme and music by the eighteenth-century composer, William Boyce, we see it from conception to performance.

BRANCHES
1975, 6:30 min. color film
Distributor: Film-makers' Cooperative
Director: Dave Gearey
Principal Dancers: Carol Marcy, Dana Reitz, Nannette Sievert
Composer: Malcolm Goldstein
Category: EXPERIMENTAL

An ode to the sensuality and mystery of light filtering through bodies climbing among branches.

BREAK
1983, 27:48 min. color video
Distributor: KTCA-TV
Producers: Mark Lowry and Kathryn Escher for Twin Cities Public TV
Director: Kathryn Escher
Choreographer: Bill T. Jones
Principal Dancers: Bill T. Jones, Maria Cheng, Eric Barsness, Stephen Rueff
Composer: Graham Lewis
Category: MODERN, EXPERIMENTAL

Feelings of social unrest pushed this African-American choreographer-performer to create a group dance set in a striking landscape of dunes, cliffs, and gullies.

BREAKIN'
1984, 87 min. color video
Distributors: MGM/UA, Swank
Producer: MGM
Director: Joel Silberg
Principal Dancers: Michael Chambers, Lucinda Dickey, Adolfo Quiñones
Category: FEATURES, JAZZ, BREAK DANCE

Feature filmed in Los Angeles about a struggling jazz dancer who teams up with two break-dancers to win a competition.

BREAKING: STREET DANCING
1981, 23 min. color video
Distributor: Gotham City Filmworks
Director: Ramsey Najm
Category: BREAK DANCE, AFRICAN-AMERICANS, HISPANIC

Dance on Camera Festival 1982 Gold Award
Displays the competitive street dance of African-Americans and Hispanics living in New York City's South Bronx(a blend of martial arts, acrobatics and disco, done to rap music.

BRIGADOON
1954, 108 min. color film, video, laser
Distributors: Facets, Films Inc., Swank, MGM/UA, Laserdisc Fan Club
Producer: MGM
Director: Vincente Minelli
Choreographer: Gene Kelly
Principal Dancers: Gene Kelly, Cyd Charisse
Composer: Frederick Loewe
Category: FEATURES, MUSICALS

The charms of Brigadoon, a village in the Scottish highlands, are discovered by two lost Americans. Dance numbers include *The Chase* and *The Heather on the Hill.*

BRINGING TO LIGHT
1992, 10 min. color film
Distributor: Beeman, Andrea
Producers: Andrea Beeman and Susan Kraft
Directors: Andrea Beeman, Susan Kraft
Choreographers: Andrea Anwar, Susan Kraft, La Yoanna
Principal Dancers: Andrea Anwar, Susan Kraft, La Yoanna
Composer: Miki Navazio
Category: MODERN
Dance on Camera Festival 1992

Explores how a woman is affected emotionally, intellectually and physically by pregnancy, using imagery from Middle Eastern, American modern and flamenco dance. Dancer-choreographer Susan Kraft was seven months pregnant at the time she performed the modern dance solo in the film.

BRITISH BALLET TODAY
1972, 26 min. b&w video
Series: Ballet For All
Distributor: The Media Guild
Director: Nicholas Ferguson
Choreographers: Kenneth MacMillan, Frederick Ashton
Principal Dancers: David Blair, Kerrison Cooke, Ronald Emblem, Brenda Lest, Patricia Ruenne
Dance Company: Ballet For All
Composers: Dmitri Shostakovich, Ferdinand Hérold
Category: BALLET, EUROPE

Duet from MacMillan's *Concerto,* followed by parts of Ashton's 1960 character ballet *La Fille Mal Gardée.*

BROADWAY MELODY OF 1936
1935, 101 min. b&w video
Distributors: Facets, Swank, MGM/UA
Producer: MGM
Director: Roy del Ruth
Choreographer: Dave Gould
Principal Dancers: Eleanor Powell, Buddy Ebsen, Vilma Ebsen
Composer: Nacio Herb Brown
Category: FEATURES, TAP

A Broadway producer and a columnist clash.
Dance numbers include: *Broadway Rhythm* and *You Are My Lucky Star.*

BROADWAY MELODY OF 1938
1937, 113 min. b&w video
Distributors: Facets, Swank, MGM/UA
Producer: MGM
Director: Roy del Ruth
Choreographer: Dave Gould
Principal Dancers: Eleanor Powell, George Murphy, Buddy Ebsen, Judy Garland
Composer: Nacio Herb Brown
Category: FEATURES, TAP

Problems backstage threaten the opening of a Broadway show. Dance numbers include *Your Broadway and My Broadway.*

BROADWAY MELODY OF 1940
1939, 102 min. b&w film, video, laser
Distributors: Films Inc., Facets, Swank, MGM/UA
Producer: MGM
Director: Norman Taurog
Choreographers: Fred Astaire, Bobby Connolly
Principal Dancers: Fred Astaire, Eleanor Powell, George Murphy
Composer: Cole Porter
Category: FEATURES, TAP

Two male dancers compete for the lead in a Broadway show, as well as for the star. Musical dance numbers include *Between You and Me, I Concentrate on You, I Am the Captain,* and the dance finale *Begin the Beguine* on a mirrored floor.

BROADWAY TAP (2 videos)
1988–89, 45 min. each color video
Distributor: Hoctor Products
Producer: Studio Music Corporation
Choreographer: Sonya Kerwin
Principal Dancer: Sonya Kerwin
Category: INSTRUCTIONAL, TAP

Routines by one of the Rockettes, the dance team in residence at Radio City Music Hall in New York City.

BRUSH AND BARRE: THE LIFE AND WORK OF TOULOUSE-LAUTREC IN DANCE AND MUSIC
1979, 59 min. color film, video
Distributor: University of California Extension Center, UCLA Instructional Media Library
Choreographer: Linda Fowler
Category: ART, EXPERIMENTAL

Documents the development and performance of *Treclau,* a multimedia dance theatre piece and master's thesis performed by university students. The performance is intercut with stills of Henri de Toulouse-Lautrec's paintings and graphics, with characters performing in costumes patterned after Lautrec.

BRYONY BRIND'S BALLET: THE FIRST STEPS
1988, 45 min. color video
Distributors: Kultur, Dance Horizons, Instructional Video
Producer: John Watkinson
Director: John Watkinson
Choreographer: Joan Lawson
Principal Dancer: Bryony Brind
Composer: Paul Stobart
Category: BALLET, INSTRUCTIONAL

A principal with the Royal Ballet explains the basic principals and movements of ballet.

BUCKDANCER
1966, 6 min. b&w film, video
Distributor: University of California Extension Center

Producer: Bess Lomax Hawes
Principal Dancer: Ed Young
Category: AFRICAN-AMERICANS, FOLK
Recorded on the Sea Islands of Georgia, African-American musicians dance on a front porch accompanied by voices, clapping, and broomsticks. A craftsman shows how he made his fife and how it is played.

BUFFALO SOLDIER
1981, 11 min. color film, video
Distributors: Museum of Modern Art, Coe Film Associates
Producer: Urban Communications Group
Director: Robert Handley
Choreographer: Carole Morisseau
Principal Dancers: Carl Bailey, Warren Spears
Dance Company: Detroit City Dance Company
Composer: Quincy Jones
Category: AFRICAN-AMERICANS
CINE Golden Eagle, Emmy Award
Forerunner of the feature film *Glory,* this dance heralds the heroic deeds of the U.S. African-American cavalry soldiers of the Ninth and Tenth regiments who fought in the Civil War.

BUILDING CHILDREN'S PERSONALITIES WITH CREATIVE DANCE
1953, 30 min. color film
Distributor: UCLA Instructional Media Library
Producers: Lawrence P. Frank, Jr., Gary Goldsmith
Category: INSTRUCTIONAL, CHILDREN
Dance Teacher: Gertrude Copley Knight
Guiding children, age five to ten, to gain confidence through the training and discipline of dance. The teacher suggests word pictures and praises the children's efforts to translate them into movement.

BUJONES IN CLASS
1986: 31 min. color video
Distributors: Kultur, Corinth, Viewfinders, Home Vision, Instructional Video, Dance Horizons
Producer: Mary Aixa Calleiro
Director: Zeida Cecilia-Méndez
Principal Dancer: Fernando Bujones
Category: BALLET, INSTRUCTIONAL
The ballet star executes his ballet barre and center combinations, with emphasis on posture, placement and the classical ballet movements. Also includes Bujones in 1974 Varna competition.

BUJONES: IN HIS IMAGE
1986, 57 min. color video, laser
Distributors: Kultur, Viewfinders, Corinth, Home Vision
Producer: Mary Aixa Calleiro
Director: Zeida Cecilia-Méndez
Choreographer: Maurice Béjart
Principal Dancer: Fernando Bujones
Dance Company: American Ballet Theatre
Category: BALLET
Excerpts of Bujones' greatest performances, with excerpts form *Le Corsaire, Swan Lake, Don Quixote, Seven Greek Dances,* and *La Bayadère.*

BULLFIGHT
1975, 9 min. color film
Distributor: Museum of Modern Art
Producer: Halcyon Films
Director: Shirley Clarke
Choreographer: Anna Sokolow
Principal Dancer: Anna Sokolow

Composer: Norman Lloyd
Category: EXPERIMENTAL, MODERN
Modern solo suggesting the perspectives of both the bull and the matador, intercut with scenes of a bullfight. Anna Sokolow's arms curve with the grace and power of a Spanish dancer.

BUSTER COOPER WORKSHOP VIDEOS (28 videos)
1981–1987, 30 min. each color video
Distributor: Buster Cooper Dance Videos
Producer: Buster Cooper
Category: INSTRUCTIONAL, CHILDREN
Teachers: Buster Cooper, Terry Wolter, David Storey, W.M. Martin, Nathalie Krassovska, Eileen McKee
Popular tunes ranging from *Boogie Woogie Bugle Boy, Material Girl, The Way You Make Me Feel* to *Little Shop of Horrors.* Graded ballet, jazz and tap classes with routines and notes.

BUSTER COOPER'S HOW TO TAP (6 videos)
1986, 60 min. each color video
Distributor: Buster Cooper Dance Videos
Producer: Buster Cooper
Category: INSTRUCTIONAL, TAP, CHILDREN
Teacher: Buster Cooper
Barre, center and travelling steps with a routine and notes for grades one through six. Also available, *Buster Cooper's Tap Routines* with two routines: *Darkness* and *Golden Slippers.*

BUTOH: BODY ON THE EDGE OF CRISIS
1990, 89 min. color film, video
Distributor: Michael Blackwood Productions
Producer: Michael Blackwood Productions
Director: Christian Blackwood
Choreographers: Tatsumi Hijikata, Kazuo Ohno, Min Tanaka, Yoko Ashikawa, Akaji Maro, Isamu Ohsuka, Natsu Nakajima, Ushio Amagatsu, Yukio Waquari
Dance Company: Sankai Juku, Dai Rakuda Kan, Maijuku, Byakko-sha, Hakutoboh, Muteki-sha
Category: BUTOH, JAPAN
Examines *Butoh,* the Japanese dance movement that attempts to reestablish the traditional links between dance, music, myth and mask, while making links between inner life and everyday existence. The documentary covers the history of this revolutionary movement with interviews, rehearsals, archival footage, including that of the master Tatsumi Hijikata in his 1960 work *Revolt of the Flesh.*

BYE BYE BIRDIE
1963, 112 min. color film, video, laser
Distributors: Films Inc., Facets, Laserdisc Fan Club
Producer: Columbia
Director: George Sidney
Choreographer: Onna White
Principal Dancers: Ann-Margret, Janet Leigh, Bobby Rydell, Dick Van Dyke
Composers: Charles Strouse, Lee Adams
Category: FEATURES, MUSICALS
An adaptation of the Broadway hit about a rock star who invades a small midwestern town. When he is drafted, a girl is chosen to send him off on live television with a kiss. Dance numbers include *Put On a Happy Face* which mixes live action with animation, *The Shriners' Ballet, Kids,* and the split screen *Telephone Hour.* The bigger production numbers, including *A Lot of*

Livin' To Do and a *Sleeping Beauty* parody, are both lavish and amusing.

CABARET
1972, 124 min. color film, video
Distributors: Swank, CBS/Fox
Producer: Warner Brothers
Director: Bob Fosse
Choreographer: Bob Fosse
Principal Dancers: Liza Minnelli, Joel Grey
Composer: John Kander
Category: FEATURES, NIGHTCLUB
Academy Award
This musical became almost as notorious as its subject, the Kit Kat Klub, Berlin's hotbed of vice and anti-Semitism, in pre-World War II Germany. The choreography shows the power of movement to manipulate emotions and the eye of the camera to clarify that intention. Dance numbers include *Money, Money* and *Cabaret.*

THE CACHUCHA
1980, 14 min. color film
Distributor: Dance Film Archive
Choreographer: Jean Coralli
Principal Dancer: Margaret Barbieri
Category: DANCE HISTORY, HISPANIC
The Spanish dance accompanied by castanets made popular in the middle of the nineteenth-century by Fanny Elssler. Reconstructed in England from Zorn notation by Dr. Ann Hutchinson Guest.

CAGE/CUNNINGHAM
1991, 95 min. color, b&w video
Distributors: VPI, Kultur, Dance Horizons
Producer: Cunningham Dance Foundation
Director: Elliot Caplan
Choreographer: Merce Cunningham
Dance Company: Merce Cunningham Dance Company
Composer: John Cage
Category: COLLABORATION, DOCUMENTARY PORTRAITS
IMZ Dance Screen Festival 1992 Best Documentary
Documentary of composer John Cage and choreographer Merce Cunningham, two American artists who have collaborated for more than forty-five years, tracing the history of their association and the influence they have had in the art, literary, dance and music worlds.

CALL OF THE DRUM: NAPOLEONIC DANCES
1972, 28 min. color video
Distributor: Orion Enterprises
Producer: WTTW-TV/Chicago
Director: Richard Carter
Choreographer: Gus Giordano
Dance Company: Gus Giordano Dance Company
Category: JAZZ
Set to French marches, the dance plays around the theme of Napoleon's conflicting drives for love and glory.

THE CALL OF THE JITTERBUG
1989, 30 min. color video
Distributors: Filmakers Library, PennState, Buffalo State, University of Minnesota
Producers: Tana Ross, Jesper Sørensen, Vibeke Winding
Directors: Tana Ross, Jesper Sørensen, Vibeke Winding

Category: SOCIAL, DANCE HISTORY
American Film and Video Festival 1989 Blue Ribbon, CINE Golden Eagle 1989
Interviews with musicians and dancers, plus vintage footage in this tribute to the dance craze that swept the nation in the 1930s and crossed the color barrier.

CAN-CAN
1960, 130 min. color film, video, laser
Distributors: Films Inc., Facets, Laserdisc Fan Club
Producer: Twentieth Century Fox
Director: Walter Lang
Choreographer: Hermes Pan
Principal Dancers: Juliet Prowse, Shirley McLaine, Frank Sinatra
Composer: Cole Porter
Category: FEATURES, NIGHTCLUB
A lawyer and a cabaret owner battle frequent raids because it is illegal to perform the can-can in Parisian nightclubs of the 1890s. Dance numbers include *Can-Can* and *Adam and Eve Ballet.*

CAN YOU SEE ME FLYING? A PORTRAIT OF TERRY SENDGRAFF
1991, 28 min. color video
Distributors: Filmakers Library, Indiana University
Producer: Fawn Yacker
Director: Fawn Yacker
Choreographer: Terry Sendgraff
Principal Dancer: Terry Sendgraff
Category: DOCUMENTARY PORTRAITS, DISABILITIES
Dance on Camera Festival 1992 Honorable Mention
A dancer, who started dancing at age forty-one, created her own dance form, "Motivity," utilizing low-flying, multilevel trapezes. Despite a mastectomy in her fifties, she continues to perform and teach. Features several performances, including *Hovering.*

CANADIANS CAN DANCE
1966, 22 min. color film, video
Distributor: National Film Board of Canada
Producer: National Film Board of Canada
Director: John Howe
Dance Company: Butler Irish Dancers, Danube Swabian Youth, Estonian Folk Group, Hawaiian Dancers, Kalya Ukrainian Dancers, Macedonian Folklorists, Moravian and Slovak Dancers, Netherlands Folklore Circle, Polish St. Stanislaus Youth
Category: FOLK, CANADA
Gathering of fifteen hundred amateur folk dancers at the annual Canadian National Exhibition in Toronto.

CANON IN D
1977, 8 min. color film
Distributor: Brooks, Virginia
Director: Virginia Brooks
Choreographer: Nolan T'sani
Dance Company: School of American Ballet
Composer: Johann Pachelbel
Category: BALLET
A single camera record of a work for four dancers filmed at the school.

CAN'T RUN BUT
1992, 3:40 min. color video
Distributor: St. Ann's School

Producer: St. Ann's School
Director: Moving Image II, under faculty advisor Deborah Dobski
Composer: Paul Simon
Category: CHILDREN, CINEDANCE
This dance video was created by the Moving Image II class and the high school dance class at St. Ann's School in Brooklyn Heights. The initial idea was to create a dance which could only exist on film or video. Paul Simon gave permission to use his song, *Can't Run But,* for the project.

CAPRICCIO ESPAGNOL (Spanish Fiesta)
1941, 20 min. color film
Distributor: Dance Films Association
Producer: Warner Brothers
Director: Jean Negulesco
Choreographers: Léonide Massine, Argentinita
Principal Dancers: Tamara Toumanova, Alexandra Danilova, Frederic Franklin, André Eglevsky, Léonide Massine
Dance Company: Ballet Russe de Monte Carlo
Composer: Nikolai Rimsky Korsakov
Category: BALLET, HISPANIC
The 1939 ballet of five divertissements, inspired by the regional rhythms and folk dance of Spain: *Alborado,* a dance of Galicia; *Variation,* a *Seguidillas* from New Castile played with castanets; *Alborado,* a comic interlude; *Gypsy Scene and Dance;* and *Fandango Asturiana.*

CAREFREE
1938, 83 min. b&w film
Distributors: Films Inc., Media Basics
Producer: RKO
Director: Mark Sandrich
Choreographer: Hermes Pan
Principal Dancers: Fred Astaire, Ginger Rogers
Composer: Irving Berlin
Category: FEATURES, MUSICALS
A patient under psychoanalysis because of so frequently postponing her wedding day, falls in love with her analyst. Dance numbers include *The Yam.*

CARMEN
1984, 99 min. color film, video
Distributors: Swank
Producer: Orion
Director: Carlos Saura
Choreographer: Antonio Gades
Principal Dancers: Cristina Hoyos, Laura del Sol, Antonio Gades
Composers: Paco da Lucia, Georges Bizet
Category: FLAMENCO, FEATURES
This second in the flamenco trilogy made by the Spanish director with Antonio Gades, (see *Blood Wedding, El Amor Brujo*), toys with the structure of a play-within-a-play. Carmen, the original femme fatale, exercises her erotic skill both on and offstage. Hollywood's 1948 version of the story is called *The Loves of Carmen,* starring Rita Hayworth and Glenn Ford.

CARMEN (Ballet National de Marseille)
1980, 44 min. color video
Distributors: Kultur, Home Vision CAR060, Corinth
Producer: Telmondis, FR3
Director: Dirk Sanders
Choreographer: Roland Petit

Principal Dancers: Mikhail Baryshnikov, Zizi Jeanmaire, Denys Ganio
Dance Company: Ballet National de Marseille
Composer: Georges Bizet
Category: FULL-LENGTH BALLETS
A sensual dance version of the Bizet classic, whose highlight is an erotic duet in which the characters express their fatal attraction to one another. Recorded not long after Baryshnikov's defection.

CARMEN (Bolshoi Ballet)
1973, 73 min. color film, video, laser
Distributors: Kultur, Home Vision, Corinth, Karol, Viewfinders
Producer: Corinth Films
Director: Vadim Derbenev
Choreographers: Alberto Alonso, Vladimir Vassiliev, Marius Petipa, Michel Fokine
Principal Dancers: Maya Plisetskaya, Nikolai Fadeyechev
Dance Company: Bolshoi Ballet
Composers: Georges Bizet, Alexander Glazunov, Johann Sebastian Bach, Rodion Shchedrin, Camille Saint-Saëns
Category: BALLET, DOCUMENTARY PORTRAITS
The Russian ballerina Maya Plisetskaya stars in excerpts from her most famous roles, with *Carmen Suite,* choreographed by a Cuban and a Russian, as the centerpiece. Also included are scenes from *Raymonda, Prelude* and *The Dying Swan.*

CARNIVAL OF RHYTHM
1989, 20 min. b&w film
Distributor: Dance Films Association
Producer: Warner Brothers
Director: Jean Negulesco
Choreographer: Katherine Dunham
Principal Dancers: Katherine Dunham, Talley Beatty, Archie Savage, Lavinia Williams, Syvilla Fort
Category: FOLK, LATIN AMERICA, AFRICA
Features songs and dances from Brazil, a South American Indian courtship dance, and a dance from Africa, presented by the influential African-American dancer-researcher. Among the dances are *Ciudade Maravillosa, Los Indios, Batucada,* and *Adeus Terras.*

CARNIVAL OF SHADOWS
1989, 58 min. color film, video
Distributor: Bullfrog Films
Producers: Niv Fichman, Barbara Willis Sweete for Rhombus International
Director: Barbara Willis Sweete
Composer: R. Murray Schaefer
Category: MODERN, CIRCUS ARTS
Combining opera, dance, rock video, fairy tale and horror movie, based on the Greek myth of the Minotaur. Set within the grounds of an old-time outdoor carnival, over one hundred performers are presented, including singers, dancers, actors, musicians, acrobats, magicians, jugglers and fire-eaters.

CAROLE MORISSEAU AND THE DETROIT CITY DANCE COMPANY
1979, 14 min. color film
Distributors: Museum of Modern Art, PennState
Producer: Sue Marx
Director: Sue Marx

Choreographer: Carole Morisseau
Dance Company: Detroit City Dance Company
Category: MODERN COMPANIES
Emmy Award 1980, CINE Golden Eagle Award 1980
Young company in rehearsal and in an opening night performance with the choreographer expressing her views about dance and her dreams for her company.

THE CAROLINA SHAG
1987, 90 min. color video
Distributor: Jim Forest Videotapes
Producer: Jim Forest
Category: INSTRUCTIONAL, SOCIAL
Teacher: Jackie McGee
National Professional champions of the shag, a popular social dance in the southeastern United States, break down all its steps with a final demonstration.

CAROUSEL
1956, 128 min. color film, video
Distributors: Facets, Films Inc.
Producer: 20th Century Fox
Director: Henry King
Choreographers: Rod Alexander, Agnes de Mille
Principal Dancer: Jacques d'Amboise
Composer: Richard Rodgers
Category: FEATURES, MUSICALS
The film alternates between the afterworld and the story of a handsome but shiftless carnival barker who marries a mill girl. The news that they are to have a child causes him to commit a robbery in which he is killed. Sixteen years after his death, he posthumously visits his daughter to resolve any conflict. Jacques d'Amboise appears in the *Carousel Ballet*; other dance numbers are *June is Bustin' Out All Over* and *A Real Nice Clambake.*

THE CATHERINE WHEEL
1982, 90 min. color video, laser
Distributors: Home Vision, Viewfinders, Corinth, Media Basics
Producer: National Video Corporation
Director: Twyla Tharp
Choreographer: Twyla Tharp
Dance Company: Twyla Tharp Dance Company
Composer: David Byrne
Category: MODERN, EXPERIMENTAL
Originally designed for Broadway, refashioned for television, using animation, computer-generated figures, shadow play and reverse action. The production grew out of Twyla Tharp's fascination for Saint Catherine, the fourth-century martyr condemned to die on a spiked wheel.

CAUGHT
1987, 8 min. b&w video
Distributor: Romano, Roberto
Producer: Roberto Romano
Director: Roberto Romano
Choreographer: David Parsons
Principal Dancer: David Parsons
Composer: Robert Fripp
Category: MODERN, EXPERIMENTAL
Solo shot in an urban ruin with the strobe-lit images of the former Paul Taylor dancer in leaping, hurtling flight.

CAVALCADE OF DANCE
1941, 10 min. b&w film
Distributor: Dance Films Association
Producer: Warner Brothers
Director: Jean Negulesco
Principal Dancer: Yolanda Veloz
Category: BALLROOM, HISPANIC
Ballroom dances presented by a famous ballroom team of the 1940s: *Maxixe* from Brazil, one step, tango from Argentina, Charleston, black bottom, jitterbug, rumba, *chiapenecas* (Mexican waltz). With narration.

CAVE
1990, 11 min. color video
Distributor: Olivé-Bellés, Núria
Producer: Dennis O'Connor
Director: Núria Olivé-Bellés
Choreographer: Dennis O'Connor
Principal Dancer: Dennis O'Connor
Category: MODERN
A centaur, painted blue, sneaks into a small blue room and plays with a television and a telephone.

CELEBRATION: A HISTORY OF THE SADLER'S WELLS ROYAL BALLET
1989, 50 min. color video
Distributors: Home Vision, Dance Horizons, Viewfinders
Producer: Jaras Entertainment/IFPA Ltd.
Director: Jolyon Winhurst
Choreographers: Frederick Ashton, Kenneth MacMillan, Robert Helpmann, Lynn Taylor Corbett
Dance Company: Royal Ballet
Composers: Ferdinand Hérold, Adolphe Adam, Edward Deldevez, Léon Minkus
Category: BALLET COMPANIES
Narrator: James Mason
Dance on Camera Festival 1990 Silver Award
Documentary on Sadler's Wells Ballet and its brilliant, strong-willed founder, Dame Ninette de Valois, combines performances, rehearsals, interviews, and archival footage from company performances. Excerpts from *Polonia, Gisèlle, La Fille Mal Gardée, Paquita, Three Pictures,* and *Elite Syncopations.*

A CELEBRATION OF LIFE: DANCES OF THE AFRICAN-GUYANESE
1993, 43 min. color video
Distributor: The Cinema Guild
Producer: Kean Gibson
Director: Kean Gibson
Category: ANTHROPOLOGICAL, AFRICA
Traditional dance in Guyana has been affected by many cultures, mainly Spanish, Dutch, French, British, African, East Indian, Portuguese and Chinese, which have been blended into this multicultural society. The African-Guyanese dances featured celebrate freedom from slavery, upcoming weddings, dance ceremonies at an African-style wake, and religious ceremonies incorporating African drumming and dancing.

A CELEBRATION OF ORIGINS
1992, 45 min. color film, video, PAL
Distributor: Documentary Educational Resources
Producer: Doug Lewis
Directors: Patsy and Timothy Asch
Category: ANTHROPOLOGICAL
Society for Visual Anthropology Award of Excellence, Festival Dei Popoli Award
Depicts the ritual life of the people of the domain of Wai Brama in eastern Flores, Indonesia. The film focuses on a small group of ritual leaders who struggle to hold the celebration in the absence of the source of the domain, the ritual leader of the community, who died after initiating the rituals. Many of the important principles of order in the domain are manifested in the Celebration of Origins including those governing relations between men and women, human beings and the deity and spirits, and the clans and houses which constitute the domain.

A CELEBRATION OF ROCK
1971, 28 min. b&w video
Distributor: Orion Enterprises
Producer: Richard Carter for WTTW-TV/Chicago
Director: Richard Carter
Choreographer: Gus Giordano
Dance Company: Gus Giordano Dance Company
Composer: Gus Giordano
Category: JAZZ, BALLET
Features *The Matriarch,* a jazz ballet about a blind girl, her lover and her overprotective mother, set to the music *In a Gada da Vida* performed by Chicago's Onstage Majority, and two short jazz pieces, *Scorpio,* and *The Getaway.*

CERBERUS
1978, 30 min. color video
Distributor: Solaris
Producer: Henry Smith
Director: Skip Sweeney
Choreographer: Henry Smith
Principal Dancers: Henry Smith, Sebastian Ellison, Kris Varjan, Harvey Konigsberg, Miguel Rivera
Composer: Teiji Ito
Category: MARTIAL ARTS, EXPERIMENTAL
In this fantasy shot near San Francisco, Henry Smith populates the woods and beaches of northern California with shamans, warriors and spirits, a sword-wielding Angel of Death, and the hero, Cerberus, the clown warrior. Combining elements of Japanese theatre, dance and martial arts, Cerberus exposes his relationships to himself, his enemies, and his gods.

A CERTAIN AGE
1991, 60 min. color video
Series: Smithsonian World
Distributor: PBS Video
Producers: WETA and The Smithsonian Institution
Category: DOCUMENTARY PORTRAITS
This program features portraits of remarkable senior citizens, including an interview with the late choreographer and dancer, Agnes de Mille.

A CHAIRY TALE
1957, 10 min. b&w film, video
Distributors: International Film Bureau, University of California Extension Center, UCLA Instructional Media Library, Buffalo State, University of Minnesota
Producer: National Film Board of Canada
Director: Norman McLaren
Composers: Ravi Shankar, Chatur Lal, Modu Mullick
Category: EXPERIMENTAL, ANIMATION
A young man performs a sort of pas de deux with a chair (animated by Evelyn Lambart) that refuses to be sat upon.

CHAMPIONS
1992, 2:30 min. color video
Distributor: In Motion Productions

Producer: Skip Blumberg
Director: Skip Blumberg
Choreographer: The Champions
Dance Company: The Champions
Category: CHILDREN
Preteen girls perform cheers in a ghetto style that crosses cheerleader movements and rap. This is a performance by a super energetic Brooklyn cheers crew.

CHANCE DANCE

1976, 16 min. b&w film, video
Distributor: University of California Extension Center
Producer: Trudi Ferguson
Director: Jim Stodell
Category: EXPERIMENTAL
Dance on Camera Festival 1978 Honorable Mention
Three pairs of dancers demonstrate the notion of chance or randomness in dance.

CHANCE ENCOUNTERS

1992, 7 min. b&w film, video
Distributor: Overfoot
Producer: Jody Oberfelder-Riehm
Director: Jody Oberfelder-Riehm
Choreographer: Jody Oberfelder-Riehm
Principal Dancer: Jody Oberfelder-Riehm
Dance Company: Overfoot Dance Company
Composer: A. Leroy
Category: COLLABORATION
Dance on Camera Festival 1992 Honorable Mention
An experimental film exploring the collaboration among choreographer, cinematographer, editor and composer.

CHANGING STEPS

1989, 35 min. color, b&w video
Distributors: Cunningham Dance Foundation, Museum of Modern Art
Producers: Cunningham Dance Foundation and La Sept
Directors: Elliot Caplan, Merce Cunningham
Choreographer: Merce Cunningham
Dance Company: Merce Cunningham Dance Company
Composer: John Cage
Category: MODERN COMPANIES
Dance on Camera Festival 1990 Gold Award
Choreographed in 1973, adapted for television in 1988, these ten solos are intercut with footage of a West German tour, and flashbacks of the original cast in rehearsal.

CHANNELS/INSERTS

1982, 32 min. color film, video
Distributor: Cunningham Dance Foundation
Producer: Cunningham Dance Foundation
Director: Charles Atlas
Choreographer: Merce Cunningham
Dance Company: Merce Cunningham Dance Company
Composer: David Tudor
Category: CINEDANCE, EXPERIMENTAL
The directors place the cast and scenes in such a way as to give the sense of dual events happening concurrently. They divided the studio into sixteen possible areas for dancing. Cunningham then applied the *I Ching* to determine the order in which the divisions were used. Atlas employed cross-cutting to indicate the simultane-ity of events, as well as travelling mattes or wipes to allow for diversity in the continuity of the image.

CHARLES WEIDMAN: ON HIS OWN

1990, 59 min. color, b&w video
Distributor: Dance Horizons
Producer: Charles Weidman Dance Foundation
Directors: Virginia Brooks, Janet Mendelsohn
Choreographer: Charles Weidman
Principal Dancers: Doris Humphrey, Charles Weidman
Composers: Johannes Brahms, Johann Sebastian Bach, Roy Harris, Lionel Nowak
Category: MODERN, DOCUMENTARY POR-TRAITS
Narrator: Alwin Nikolais
Dance on Camera Festival 1991 Silver Award, Dance Screen Festival 1990 Special Prize of the Jury
The career of modern dance pioneer Charles Weidman is traced from his roots in Lincoln, Nebraska, to the last work he choreographed in 1974. Describes his years as performer with Denishawn, his renowned association with Doris Humphrey, and the last thirty years on his own.

CHARLESTON

1927, 20 min. b&w film (silent)
Distributors: Biograph Entertainment, Facets
Director: Jean Renoir
Principal Dancers: Catherine Hessling, A. Cerf
Category: DANCE HISTORY, COMEDY
One of the first efforts by the French director Jean Renoir. A silent, comic fantasy with gyrating seminude dancers.

CHARMAINE'S HAWAIIAN/TAHITIAN VIDEO PEARLS (2 videos)

1989, 80 min. each color video
Distributor: Charmaine
Producer: Charmaine
Principal Dancer: Charmaine
Category: HULA, INSTRUCTIONAL
Forty routines showing Tahitian *aprimas* and *oteas*, Hawaiian ancient, modern and religious sit-down hulas, with emcee notes on history and costuming. Available individually or together on one tape.

CHE CHE KULE: EXERCISES FOR KIDS

1990, 59 min. color video
Distributor: Ile Ife Films
Producer: Bayne Williams Film Company
Choreographer: Arthur Hall
Principal Dancer: Arthur Hall
Category: INSTRUCTIONAL, CHILDREN
Children's class designed by African-American dancer Arthur Hall, filmed in two Vermont elementary schools. Title refers to the Ghanaian dance evocative of the movements of rowing and boating.

CHECKMATE

1990, 45 min. color video
Distributors: Video Artists International, Viewfinders, Corinth
Choreographer: Ninette de Valois
Dance Company: Sadler's Wells Royal Ballet
Composer: Arthur Bliss
Category: FULL-LENGTH BALLETS
Portrays a game of love and death, played accord-ing to the rules of the game of chess. The Black Queen first captures the Red Queen, then defeats the Red Knight, and finally delivers the Red King to her warriors. This ballet is rooted in English traditions.

CHIANG CHING: A DANCE JOURNEY

1982, 30 min. color film, video
Distributor: University of California Extension Center
Producer: Lana Pih Jokel
Director: Lana Pih Jokel
Choreographer: Chaing Ching
Principal Dancer: Chaing Ching
Category: CHINA, DOCUMENTARY POR-TRAITS
Dance on Camera Festival, Asian-American International Film Festival Honoree, Hong Kong Film Festival Honoree
A portrait of a talented Chinese American dancer-choreographer, Chiang Ching. Traces her childhood in China, where she trained at the Peking Dance Academy and became a teenage movie star in Hong Kong. Several performances filmed in New York City and during a triumphant return visit to China reveal her style, which combines the rigor of the traditional Chinese dance with the free expression of the West.

CHILDREN DANCE

1970, 14 min. b&w film
Distributor: University of California Extension Center
Producers: Geraldine Diamondstein and Naima Prevots
Directors: Geraldine Diamondstein, Naima Prevots
Category: CHILDREN, INSTRUCTIONAL
Teachers: Geraldine Diamondstein, Naima Prevots
Children, ages five to nine, express their feelings, moods and ideas through rhythmic patterns and improvisations. Suggests ways that nonspecialists can awaken children's creativity in movement.

THE CHILDREN OF THEATRE STREET

1978, 92 min. color film, video
Distributors: Kino, Kultur, Dance Horizons, Corinth, Viewfinders, Home Vision, Media Basics
Producers: Earl Mack and Jean Dalyrmple for Mack-Vaganova
Directors: Earl Mack, Jean Dalyrmple, Robert Dornhelm
Principal Dancers: Galina Messenzeva, Konstantin Zaklinsky
Category: BALLET COMPANIES, CHILDREN
Narrator: Princess Grace of Monaco
This documentary on one of the world's finest ballet schools, the Vaganova Choreographic Institute (the Kirov School) in Leningrad, focuses on three students at different stages of development, examining the intense competition for admission and the eight years of subsequent training.

CHILDREN ON THE HILL

1982, 20 min. color video
Series: The Educational Performance Collection
Distributor: Dance Notation Bureau
Producer: Dance Notation Bureau
Choreographer: Moses Pendleton
Category: CHILDREN, NOTATION

Musicians: King Sunny Ade and the African Beats, Air Beleu, Budd Palmer, Mighty Diamonds

Taped performance at City College of dance featuring two male roles: The Grub, a thick lumpy being in a green padded costume and Mojo, a composite character choreographed by one of the founders of Pilobolus. Comes with an introductory article on labanotation, intermediate/ advanced level notated score by Terri Richards, critical text, and study/performance rights to the dance.

CHILDREN WITH A DREAM

1992, 27 min. color film
Distributor: Carousel Films
Producer: Barbara Shelly
Director: Karen Grossman
Dance Company: Central Pennsylvania Youth Ballet
Category: INSTRUCTIONAL, CHILDREN
Dance on Camera Festival 1992 Honorable Mention, NEFVF Festival 1992 Silver Apple
At the Central Pennsylvania Youth Ballet, founded by Marcia Dale, young children make an extraordinary commitment to the study of classical ballet. Classes, rehearsals and performances reveal the grueling schedule which produces technically proficient dancers at the cost of a normal childhood.

CHILDREN'S DANCES

1965, 9 min. color film
Distributor: PennState
Producer: Wissen
Category: FOLK, AFRICA, CHILDREN
Ten Dangaleat girls in Chad present seven dances of their own tribe and those of neighboring Arabs and Dadjo.

CHINESE FOLK ARTS

1976, 24 min. color video
Distributor: Iowa State
Producer: Free China Film Syndicate
Category: FOLK, CHINA
Introduces dragon and lion dances along with the traditional folk arts of shadow puppetry, embroidery, paper cutting, kite flying, lanterns, and puppet shows.

CHINESE, KOREAN AND JAPANESE DANCE

1964, 30 min. color film
Distributors: Asia Society, PennState, UCLA Instructional Media Library
Producer: Bureau of Audio-Visual Instruction, New York
Director: Clifford Ettinger
Principal Dancers: Cho Wan-kyung, Hu Hung-yen, Hu Yung-fang, Suzushi Hanayagi
Category: ASIA, FOLK
Traditional steps and patterns explained by impresario Beate Gordon with performances of *Sorceress Dance* and the *Old Man's Dance* (Korea), *Word Dance* and the *Scarf Dance* (China), and *Kabuki* (Japan).

CHOICE CHANCE WOMAN DANCE

1971, 44 min. color film
Distributors: Film-makers' Cooperative, Canyon Cinema
Director: Ed Emshwiller
Principal Dancers: Carolyn Carlson, Becky Arnold, Susan Lazarus

Composers: Joan Friedman, David Borden, Steve Drews
Category: EXPERIMENTAL, WOMEN
A meditation, typical of its time, considering women in their various states of awareness: while alone, with a child or adult, or as professionals. A group improvisation inspired by the paradoxes and dilemmas confronting women today.

THE CHOPI TIMBILA DANCE

1980, 40 min. color film, video
Distributor: PennState
Producer: Wissen
Director: Andrew Tracey
Composer: Venancio Mbande
Category: ANTHROPOLOGICAL, AFRICA
African music specialist Andrew Tracey and Mozambiquan composer Venancio Mbande explain the elements of Chopi xylophone orchestral music and its relationship to *mgodo*, a suite of movements.

A CHOREOGRAPHER AT WORK: JOHN BUTLER

1960, 29 min. b&w film, video
Series: A Time To Dance
Distributor: Indiana University
Producer: Jac Venza for WNET/13
Choreographer: John Butler
Principal Dancers: Glen Tetley, Carmen de Lavallade, James Moore, Bambi Linn
Category: MODERN, CHOREOGRAPHY
Teacher-commentator Martha Myers and John Butler discuss how a choreographer works, and demonstate with members of his company the elements of rhythm, space, and theme with excerpts from Butler's *Three Promenades With the Lord.*

CHOREOGRAPHY

1964, 11 min. b&w film
Distributor: The Cinema Guild
Producer: Lehrfilm-Institut
Director: Richard Scheinflug
Choreographers: Heinz Claus, Christa Kempf
Principal Dancers: Heinz Claus, Christa Kempf
Composer: Johann Sebastian Bach
Category: BALLET, CHOREOGRAPHY
A documentary on a ballet choreographer's creative process and vision, concluding with a performance.

CHOREOGRAPHY BY BALANCHINE (3 videos)

1977, 1980, 1995, 60 min. each color video
Series: Dance in America, The Balanchine Library
Distributors: WarnerVision Entertainment, Viewfinders, Dance Horizons
Producer: Emile Ardolino
Director: Merrill Brockway
Choreographer: George Balanchine
Principal Dancers: Suzanne Farrell, Peter Martins, Merrill Ashley, Robert Weiss, Patricia McBride
Dance Company: New York City Ballet
Composers: Maurice Ravel, Wolfgang Amadeus Mozart, Paul Hindemith, Gabriel Fauré, Igor Stravinsky
Category: BALLET
Narrator: Edward Villella
Performances by the New York City Ballet of such Balanchine works as *Tzigane, Andante, The Four Temperaments, Chaconne, Prodigal Son, Stravinsky Violin Concerto* and selections from *Jewels.*

A CHORUS LINE

1985, 113 min. color video
Distributor: Facets
Producer: Columbia
Director: Richard Attenborough
Choreographer: Jeffrey Hornaday
Principal Dancers: Alyson Reed, Audrey Landers, Gregg Burge, Charles McGowan
Composer: Marvin Hamlisch
Category: FEATURES, MUSICALS
An adaptation of the Broadway musical in which dancers auditioning for a new production reveal their insecurities and aspirations. Musical numbers include *Dance 10, Looks 3, I Can Do That,* and *Surprise, Surprise.*

CHRISTY LANE'S LINE DANCING

1992, 40 min. color video
Distributor: Dance Horizons
Category: INSTRUCTIONAL, UNITED STATES
Teacher: Christy Lane
Instruction in a dance popular in country bars and dance nightclubs. The dances include: *Achy Breaky Cowboy Boogie, Cowboy Cha-Cha, Elvira Dance* and *Walkin' Wazie.*

CHRYSALIS

1973, 21:30 min. color film
Distributors: Canyon Cinema, Museum at Large
Director: Ed Emshwiller
Choreographer: Alwin Nikolais
Dance Company: Alwin Nikolais Dance Company
Category: EXPERIMENTAL, IMPROVISATION
Improvised choreography and cinema techniques from slow-motion to pixillation altered in post-production by the late Ed Emshwiller, backed by a sound track made with the voices of the dancers.

CHUCK DAVIS, DANCING THROUGH WEST AFRICA

1987, 28 min. color film, video
Distributors: Filmakers Library, Buffalo State
Directors: Gorham Kindem, Jane Desmond
Choreographer: Chuck Davis
Dance Company: African-American Dance Ensemble
Category: AFRICA, AFRICAN-AMERICANS
Dance on Camera Festival 1987 Honorable Mention, CINE Golden Eagle
Tour of Chuck Davis' African-American Dance Ensemble through Senegal and Gambia, focusing on three tribes: Wolof, Mandinka, and Diola. Reveals their warmth and respect for dance, and concludes with a community performance celebrating peace and love.

CINDERELLA (Berlin Comic Opera Ballet)

1987, 75 min. color video
Distributors: V.I.E.W., Karol, Corinth
Producers: Deutsche Fersefunk and Defa Studio Film
Choreographer: Tom Schilling
Principal Dancers: Hannelore Bey, Roland Gawlick
Dance Company: Berlin Comic Opera Ballet
Composer: Sergei Prokofiev
Category: FULL-LENGTH BALLETS, CHILDREN
Performance documentary of this three-act classic ballet based on the fairy tale by the seventeenth-century poet Charles Perrault about an unloved

young women who is pursued by a prince she happens to meet at the one ball she ever attends.

CINDERELLA (Bolshoi Ballet)
1961, 81 min. color film, video, laser
Distributors: Kultur, Home Vision CIN040, Corinth, Laserdisc Fan Club
Producer: International Historic Films
Directors: Alexander Rowe, Rostislav Zakharov
Choreographer: Rostislav Zakharov
Principal Dancers: Raisa Struchkova, Gennadi Lediakh, Ekaterina Maximova
Dance Company: Bolshoi Ballet
Composer: Sergei Prokofiev
Category: FULL-LENGTH BALLETS, CHILDREN
A 1945 version of the fairy tale described above, filmed with multiple cameras with the orchestra of the State Academic Bolshoi Theatre.

CINDERELLA (Bolshoi Ballet)
1984, 81 min. color film
Distributor: Kultur, Corinth
Producer: International Historic Films
Directors: Alexander Rowe, Rostislav Zakharov
Principal Dancers: Raisa Struchkova, Gennadi Lediakh, Ekaterina Maximova
Dance Company: Bolshoi Ballet
Composer: Sergei Prokofiev
Category: FULL-LENGTH BALLETS, CHILDREN
The 1961 Russian color motion picture version of the timeless fairytale. Using multiple cameras to create a variety of shots and special effects, the film results in an unusual performance.

CINDERELLA (Lyon Opera Ballet)
1990, 87 min. color video, laser
Distributors: Home Vision CIN020, Corinth, Viewfinders, Media Basics
Producer: Reiner Moritz
Director: Mans Reutersward
Choreographer: Maguy Marin
Dance Company: Lyon Opera Ballet
Composer: Sergei Prokofiev
Category: FULL-LENGTH BALLETS, CHILDREN
This modern rendition of the classic fairy tale (described above) sets the ballet in a doll's house with all the masked characters only as mobile as their wooden bodies will allow. The Swedish director heightens the vulnerability of this approach by the use of close-ups.

CINDERELLA (Paris Opera Ballet)
1989, 125 min. color laser
Distributors: Corinth, Dance Horizons, Viewfinders
Producers: La Sept and SFP of Paris and National Video Corporation of London
Directors: Colin Nears, Rudolf Nureyev
Choreographer: Rudolf Nureyev
Principal Dancers: Sylvie Guillem, Charles Jude, Isabelle Guérin, Monique Loudières, Rudolf Nureyev
Dance Company: Paris Opera Ballet
Composer: Sergei Prokofiev
Category: FULL-LENGTH BALLETS, CHILDREN
Nureyev transports Charles Perrault's classic fairy tale into the art deco world of Hollywood in the 1930s, where Cinderella escapes her miserable existence at home. With outlandish set designs, costumes, and giant pinup girls, the ballet frolics around the dream of immediate and complete salvation from mediocrity. Other versions of Perrault's tale: the 1964 feature film starring

Ginger Rogers, and Walt Disney's animated film of 1950.

CINDERELLA: A DANCE FANTASY
1993, 31 min. color video
Distributor: V.I.E.W.
Producer: Frantz Film Production
Choreographer: Tom Schilling
Principal Dancers: Hannelore Bey, Roland Gawlick
Dance Company: Berlin Comic Opera Ballet
Composer: Sergei Prokofiev
Category: BALLET, CHILDREN
Prokofiev's timeless score is the musical backdrop for the elegant and expressive dancing, which will delight children and adults alike. Colorful costumes and sets complete the magical mood of one of the most romantic stories ever told.

CIRCLE OF THE SUN
1960, 30 min. color film
Distributors: National Film Board of Canada, University of California Extension Center, University of Minnesota
Producer: Tom Daly for National Film Board of Canada
Director: Colin Low
Category: NATIVE AMERICANS
The tribal councils, pow wows and dances of the Blood Indians of Alberta, Canada, testify to the power of circles. The *Sundance* is captured on film for the first time.

CIRCLES I
1971, 7 min. color film
Distributor: Film-makers' Cooperative
Producer: Doris Chase
Director: Doris Chase
Composer: Morton Subotnik
Category: EXPERIMENTAL, ANIMATION
Circles revolve in, around, and through each other with a sensitivity to their musical accompaniment.

CIRCLES II
1972, 12 min. color film, video
Distributors: Doris Chase Productions, Coronet/MTI, Indiana University, Film-makers' Cooperative
Producers: Frank Olney and Robert Brown
Director: Doris Chase
Choreographer: Mary Staton
Dance Company: Mary Staton Dance Ensemble
Composer: William O. Smith
Category: ANIMATION, EXPERIMENTAL
Avant Garde Festival 1972, CINE Golden Eagle 1973, American Film Festival 1973
Explores the dimensions of color and spatial relations as dancers move through themes and variations around giant fiberglass circles.

CIRCLES: CYCLES KATHAK DANCE
1988, 28 min. color film, video
Distributors: University of California Extension Center, Indiana University
Producer: Robert Gottlieb
Director: Robert Gottlieb
Principal Dancers: Shawati Sen, Daksha Sheith, Jai Kishan
Category: INDIA, GESTURES
Dance on Camera Festival 1989 Honorable Mention, American Film Festival Red Ribbon, Na-

tional Educational Film and Video Festival Silver Apple
Explores the traditions of *Kathak*, the one-thousand-year-old classical dance of northern India, which reflects influences of both Hindu and Islamic cultures. Includes excerpts of its vast repertoire and stills of paintings reflective of the dance.

CIRCUMCISION
1965, 16 min. color film
Distributor: PennState
Producer: Wissen
Category: RELIGIOUS/RITUAL, AFRICA
As part of the public circumcision ceremony, women and girls of the Haddad tribe perform the *goshele* dance in front of the house where the boys are secluded for seven days. Filmed in Southern Wadai in Central Sudan, Africa.

CLASSIC KIROV PERFORMANCES
1992, 110 min. color, b&w video
Distributors: Kultur, Viewfinders, Corinth, Home Vision, Facets
Producer: Castle Communications
Principal Dancers: Anna Pavlova, Galina Ulanova, Tatiana Terekova, Natalia Dudinskaya, Vakhtang Chabukiani
Dance Company: Kirov Ballet
Category: BALLET COMPANIES
Rare archival films of the greatest ballet performances at the Kirov Theatre, St. Petersburg, from 1930 to the present. Contains Anna Pavlova in her legendary role of the Dying Swan. Includes excerpts from *Sleeping Beauty, La Bayadère, Don Quixote, Gayane, Chopiniana, Ruslan and Ludmila, The Nutcracker, Cinderella, Prince Igor, The Dying Swan, Raymonda, Fountain of Bakhchisarai, Romeo and Juliet, Taras Bulba,* and *Esmeralda.*

CLASSICAL BALLET
1960, 29 min. b&w film, video
Series: A Time To Dance
Distributors: Indiana University, UCLA Instructional Media Library
Producer: Jac Venza for WNET/13
Choreographers: Marius Petipa, Lev Ivanov, Louis Merante
Principal Dancers: Maria Tallchief, André Eglevsky, Linda Yourth, George Li
Composers: Peter Ilyich Tchaikovsky, Léo Delibes
Category: BALLET, INSTRUCTIONAL
Teacher-commentator Martha Myers discusses the rules of classical ballet. Students of the Eglevsky school demonstrate the essential ballet steps and positions. Maria Tallchief and André Eglevsky perform a pas de deux from *Swan Lake* and Louis Merante's *Sylvia* (1876). Another pas de deux from Marius Petipa's *Sleeping Beauty* is performed by Linda Yourth and George Li, who also performs the *Blue Bird* male variation.

CLINIC OF STUMBLE
1948, 13 min. color film
Distributors: Film-makers' Cooperative, Museum of Modern Art
Producers: Sidney Peterson and Hy Hirsh
Directors: Sidney Peterson, Hy Hirsh
Choreographer: Marian Van Tuyl
Principal Dancers: Beth Osgood, Barbara Bennion, Edith Wiener
Composer: Gregory Tucker

Category: EXPERIMENTAL, COMEDY
Dance on Camera Festival 1978 Honorable Mention
An experiment in superimposition of ballet images, with three women in long dresses and bonnets riding scooters, sitting, reading, dancing alone and together in a space adorned with exotic lamps.

CLOUD DANCE
1980, 13 min. color film
Distributor: Film-makers' Cooperative
Directors: Robyn Brentano, Andrew Horn
Choreographer: Andrew de Groat
Composer: Michael Galasso
Category: EXPERIMENTAL, ART
Poet: Christopher Knowles
Sculptor: Lenore Tawney
Improvised solo in *Four Armed Cloud*, a translucent maze of over thirteen thousand threads installed at the New Jersey State Museum. Edited with blackouts to create a rhythmic unity between the dance, poetry, music and sculpture.

CLYTEMNESTRA
1982, 90 min. color video
Series: Dance in America
Distributor: Films Inc.
Producers: Emile Ardolino, Judy Kinberg
Directors: Emile Ardolino, Judy Kinberg
Choreographer: Martha Graham
Principal Dancers: Martha Graham, Yuriko Kimura
Dance Company: Martha Graham Dance Company
Composer: Halim El-Dabh
Category: FULL-LENGTH BALLETS
A reconstruction of Martha Graham's 1958 work based upon Aeschylus' trilogy *The Oresteia*.

COAST ZONE
1983, 27 min. color film, video
Distributor: Cunningham Dance Foundation
Producer: Cunningham Dance Foundation
Director: Charles Atlas
Choreographer: Merce Cunningham
Dance Company: Merce Cunningham Dance Company
Composers: Larry Austin, The Beachcombers
Category: MODERN, CINEDANCE
American Film Festival
Merce Cunningham and Charles Atlas explore the layering possibilities of video by contrasting back and foreground figures dancing in the vaulted Synod House of the Cathedral of St. John the Divine in New York City. The camera moves around the thirteen dancers, at one point circling the action in a single trajectory.

THE COLLABORATORS: CAGE, CUNNINGHAM, RAUSCHENBERG
1987, 55 min. color video
Distributor: Cunningham Dance Foundation
Producer: KETC-TV
Choreographer: Merce Cunningham
Dance Company: Merce Cunningham Dance Company
Composer: John Cage
Category: MODERN, COLLABORATION
A discussion among the choreographer and his longtime collaborators, painter Robert Rauchenberg and composer John Cage, is moderated by dance critic David Vaughan, with archival

footage of *Travelogue, Minutiae,* and *Antic Meet* intercut throughout. *Coast Zone,* a piece choreographed in 1983, completes the program.

COLLECTED WORKS OF ELIZABETH STREB
1987, 34 min. color video
Distributor: The Kitchen
Producer: Elizabeth Streb
Director: Carol Steinberg
Choreographer: Elizabeth Streb
Principal Dancer: Elizabeth Streb
Category: MODERN
A compilation which displays Streb's daring and adventurous choreographic work.

COLOR IN DANCE
1973, 5 min. color film
Distributor: Iowa State
Category: EXPERIMENTAL
A still camera catches the movements of dancers behind a screen, their shadows and effects emanating from three colored spotlights.

COME DANCE WITH ME
1992, 66 min. color video
Distributor: University of California Extension Center
Director: Claudia Wilke
Category: DANCE THERAPY
Movement therapist Trudi Schoop is profiled in this documentary at the age of eighty-eight, working with a group of long-term patients at a psychiatric clinic in Switzerland. By sharing their world for three weeks and encouraging them to express their emotions and visions through movement, the patients begin to respond under her guidance. In German with English subtitles.

THE COMPANY
1984, 9:30 min. color video
Distributor: Ririe-Woodbury Dance Company
Producer: KUTV-TV/Salt Lake City
Principal Dancers: Shirley Ririe, Joan Woodbury
Dance Company: Ririe-Woodbury Dance Company
Category: MODERN COMPANIES, INSTRUCTIONAL
Dance on Camera Festival 1985 Honorable Mention
Cofounders of a modern company based at the University of Utah work with their students.

COMPLETE FLAMENCO DANCE TECHNIQUE (8 videos)
1986, 90 min. each color video
Distributor: Morca Foundation
Producer: Téo Morca
Director: Téo Morca
Choreographer: Téo Morca
Category: FLAMENCO, INSTRUCTIONAL
Emmy Award
Videos describing a balanced approach to learning Spanish flamenco dance, its rhythmic structure and style, from an American teacher known for his vast repertoire. Also available from the Morca Foundation: *Téo Morca in Solo Concert,* and *Antología Flamenca*.

THE CONCERT
1987, 12 min. color video
Distributors: Coe Film Associates, Pyramid
Producers: Claude and Julian Chagrin
Principal Dancer: Julian Chagrin

Category: COMEDY, EXPERIMENTAL
Cavorting on the black and white pavement behind London's Royal Albert Hall, a pianist dances on his "keyboard" with a charm and whimsy reminiscent of Charlie Chaplin.

THE CONQUEST OF EMPTINESS
1993, 45 min. color video
Distributor: University of California Extension Center
Producer: Claudia Wilke
Frankfurt (Germany) International Dance Screen Festival Honoree; Munich (Germany) International Film Festival Honoree
Therapist: Trudi Schoop
Category: DANCE THERAPY
At ninety, dance therapist Trudi Schoop talks about herself, her work, her dance career, and her experiences with the normal and the insane. The film includes archival footage of her dancing and her pioneering work in dance therapy.

CONTEMPORARY DANCE TRAINING (2 videos)
1989, 25 and 65 min. color video
Distributor: Dance Horizons
Category: MODERN, INSTRUCTIONAL
Part 1 *Off-Center—A Step Into Modern Dance,* an introduction to modern dance vocabulary, and Part 2 *The Class, Do It!,* a supplement to classwork, taught by Phyllis Gutelius

COPLAND PORTRAIT
1975, 29 min. color film
Distributor: National Technical Information Service
Producer: United States Information Agency
Choreographer: Eugene Loring
Dance Company: American Ballet Theatre
Category: BALLET, COMPOSITION
American Film Festival Blue Ribbon
A documentary about composer Aaron Copland, born in Brooklyn in 1900, with musical excerpts from his *Appalachian Spring, Rodeo,* and a dance sequence from *Billy the Kid*.

COPPÉLIA (Ballets de San Juan)
1980, 110 min. color video
Distributors: Kultur, Home Vision, Corinth, Viewfinders, Media Basics
Choreographer: Arthur Saint-Léon
Principal Dancers: Fernando Bujones, Ana María Castañón
Dance Company: Ballets de San Juan
Composer: Léo Delibes
Category: FULL-LENGTH BALLETS
The 1870 ballet classic about a mechanical doll that comes to life, her quiet beauty in contrast to that of the lively real-life heroine.

COPPÉLIA (Kirov Ballet)
1993, 92 min. color video
Distributors: Viewfinders, Dance Horizons
Choreographer: Oleg Vinogradev
Principal Dancers: Elvira Tarasova, Peter Rusanov, Irina Shapchits, Mikhail Zavialov
Dance Company: Kirov Ballet
Composer: Léo Delibes
Category: FULL-LENGTH BALLETS
Delibes' ballet performed by the Kirov.

COPPÉLIA: ACT II
1967, 26 min. b&w video
Distributor: Orion Enterprises

Producer: WTTW-TV/Chicago
Director: Richard Carter
Choreographers: Lev Ivanov, Enrico Cecchetti
Dance Company: Illinois Ballet
Composer: Léo Delibes
Category: BALLET
The second act of the 1870 ballet, based on E.T.A.
Hoffmann's fairy tale *Der Sandman*, about a
mechanical doll in the mysterious workshop of
Dr. Coppelius. Adapted by Richard Ellis and
Christine Duboulay.

CORROBOREE: THE AUSTRALIAN BALLET
1951, 10 min. b&w film
Distributor: PennState
Choreographer: Rex Reid
Dance Company: Australian Ballet
Composer: John Antill
Category: BALLET, AUSTRALIA
The *Corroboree*, an aboriginal dance festival, is
recreated by Australia's national ballet com-
pany.

LE CORSAIRE
1988, 86 min. color, b&w video, laser
Distributors: Dance Horizons, Kultur, Corinth
Choreographer: Marius Petipa
Principal Dancers: Yevgeny Neff, Altynai Asylmur-
atova, Faroukh Ruzimatov, Yelena Pankova
Dance Company: Kirov Ballet
Composer: Léo Delibes
Category: FULL-LENGTH BALLETS
The colorful nineteenth-century spectacle per-
formed in its entirety in a 1987 revival.

CORTÈGE OF EAGLES
1969, 38 min. color film, video
Series: Three By Martha Graham
Distributors: Pyramid, Kent State, PennState, Uni-
versity of Minnesota, Viewfinders
Producers: John Houseman and H.R. Poindexter
Director: David Wilson
Choreographer: Martha Graham
Principal Dancers: Martha Graham, Bertram Ross,
Robert Cohan, Clive Thompson, Mary Hink-
son, Takako Asakawa
Dance Company: Martha Graham Dance Com-
pany
Composer: Eugene Lester
Category: MODERN, DANCE HISTORY
Set in Troy at the time of its fall, choreographer
Martha Graham portrays the bereaved Queen
Hecuba, wife of King Priam, who wrestles with
the inevitable collapse of her kingdom and is
driven to violence.

COSTUMING: SKIRT AND ACCESSORIES
1988, 120 min. color video
Distributor: Chandra of Damascus
Producer: Chandra of Damascus
Category: INSTRUCTIONAL, BELLY DANCE
Lecture/demonstration covering costume construction techniques and ideas for Middle Eastern dance. The same distributor-producer
carries other two-hour lectures/demonstrations
such as *Beading and Design* and *Bra and Belt
Construction Class II*.

THE COTTON CLUB
1984, 127 min. color film, video
Distributors: Swank, New Line
Producer: Orion
Director: Francis Coppola
Choreographers: Gregory Hines, Maurice Hines,
Charles "Honi" Coles, Michael Smuin, Henry
LeTang
Principal Dancers: Gregory Hines, Maurice Hines,
Charles "Honi" Coles
Composers: Duke Ellington, Harry Akst-Grant
Clarke, Joseph Meyer, Roger Wolfe Kahan
Category: FEATURES, TAP
This feature, starring Richard Gere, Diane Lane
and Nicolas Cage, offers top-notch dancing and
loving, amidst dubious business associations
carried on in one of Harlem's most popular
nightclubs of the late 1920s. Talent triumphs
despite the climate of racism and crime.

COUNTRY CORNERS
1976, 27 min. color film, video
Distributor: Phoenix
Producers: Robert Fiore and Richard Nevell, with
White Mountain Films
Principal Dancer: Ed Larkin
Category: DANCE HISTORY, UNITED STATES
Dance on Camera Festival 1978
Traces the history of contra dance back to the ar-
rival of the first settlers in New England, with
Ed Larkin and his dancers of East Bethel, Ver-
mont presenting the traditional and less ortho-
dox forms.

COURT DANCE: TAIHEIRAKU and
ETENRAKU (2 films)
1972, 44 and 30 min. color film
Distributor: The Japan Foundation
Producer: EC Japan Archives
Category: JAPAN
Taiheiraku, a dance of eternal peace, is performed
by the music department of the Imperial
Household. Four dancers, armed with Chinese-
style helmets, swords, and spears, represent
warriors ushering in the age of peace. The second film features the court music of *Etenraku*
in which the winds and percussion gradually
drop out, leaving the strings (*Koto* and *Biwa*) in
a solo role.

COVER GIRL
1944, 107 min. color video, laser
Distributors: Facets, Laserdisc Fan Club
Producer: Columbia
Director: Charles Vidor
Choreographers: Stanley Donen, Gene Kelly, Sey-
mour Felix, Jack Cole
Principal Dancers: Gene Kelly, Rita Hayworth,
Phil Silvers
Composer: Jerome Kern
Category: FEATURES, NIGHTCLUB
A nightclub dancer gets a chance at Broadway
stardom after winning a magazine covergirl
contest, but eventually returns to her club in
Brooklyn. The dance numbers include *Make
Way for Tomorrow* and *Alter Ego* in which Kelly
appears to be dancing with himself.

CRWDSPCR
1996, 55 min. color film
Distributor: Cunningham Dance Foundation
Producer: Cunningham Dance Foundation
Director: Elliot Caplan
Choreographer: Merce Cunningham
Dance Company: Merce Cunningham Dance
Company
Composer: John King
Category: MODERN, TECHNOLOGY

Dance on Camera Festival 1996 Gold Award
Features the choreographic process of Merce Cunningham's experiments with the computer program *Life Forms* as directed by Elliot Caplan.
John King composed the music by transforming
sounds from a steel Dobro slide guitar. Mark
Lancaster designed the multicolored costumes
to reflect the same vertical and horizontal divisions that the computer program makes of the
body.

CREATION OF THE WORLD: A SAMBA
OPERA
1978, 56 min. color film, video
Distributor: The Cinema Guild
Director: Vera de Figueiredo
Category: SOCIAL, LATIN AMERICA
Venice International Film Festival Venice People's
Award
Photographed during the carnival in Rio de Ja-
neiro, the Beija Flor Samba School sets a story
of genesis, according to Yoruba mythology, to
dance, song, and drum.

CREATIVE MOVEMENT: A STEP TOWARDS
INTELLIGENCE FOR CHILDREN AGES 2–8
1993, 80 min. color video
Distributors: Kultur, Dance Horizons, Home Vi-
sion
Producer: Melissa Lowe
Choreographer: Melissa Lowe
Category: INSTRUCTIONAL, CHILDREN
Encourages children to have fun as they clap, sing
and move to music. Children develop balance,
coordination, self-awareness and self-expres-
sion through games and improvisation.

CREOLE GISÈLLE
1988, 88 min. color video
Distributors: Kultur, Home Vision, Facets, Dance
Horizons, Viewfinders
Producers: Danmarks Radio, WNET-TV/13
Director: Thomas Grimm
Choreographers: Jean Coralli, Jules Perrot, Fred-
eric Franklin
Principal Dancers: Virginia Johnson, Eddie Shell-
man, Lowell Smith
Dance Company: Dance Theatre of Harlem
Composer: Adolphe Adam
Category: FULL-LENGTH BALLETS, AFRICAN-
AMERICANS
Transplants the classic story ballet, originally set
in Europe, to New Orleans and layers it with a
suggestion of the class war between African-
Americans in the 1800s.

CRIME PAYS
1984, 5 min. color video
Distributor: Murphey, Claudia
Director: Michael Moser
Choreographer: Claudia Murphey
Composers: Daryl Hall, John Oates
Category: MODERN
Dance on Camera Festival 1985
A modern dance inspired by the body language of
prisoners.

CROOKED BEAK OF HEAVEN
1975, 52 min. color film
Series: Tribal Eye
Distributors: University of California Extension
Center, University of Minnesota, UCLA In-
structional Media Library

Producer: BBC-TV
Category: NATIVE AMERICANS
Narrator: David Attenborough
The Kwakiutl and other Indian tribes of the Pacific Northwest are known for their potlatch ceremonies—theatrical dances in which an individual's most valued possessions are distributed to his guests and kinsmen.

THE CROW/SHOSHONE SUNDANCE

1992, 56 min. color film
Distributor: Thunderous Productions
Category: NATIVE AMERICANS
The sacred act of preparing for and participating in a sundance ceremony are depicted in the film, shot in Montana and authorized by the Crow Nation.

CULTIC DANCES IN A BUDDHIST PAGODA NEAR HUE

1963, 20 min. color film
Distributor: PennState
Producer: Wissen
Director: John Barnes
Category: RELIGIOUS/RITUAL, ASIA
Initiated by a Buddhist priest, this ceremony in Vietnam is dominated by women dancing before an altar, who claim to have been ordered to do so by ghosts.

CUNNINGHAM DANCE TECHNIQUE: ELEMENTARY LEVEL

1985, 35 min. color video
Distributor: Cunningham Dance Foundation
Producer: Cunningham Dance Foundation
Director: Elliot Caplan
Choreographer: Merce Cunningham
Principal Dancers: Alison Cutri, Jill Diamond, Nancy Langsner, Kate Troughton
Category: INSTRUCTIONAL, MODERN
Teachers: Susan Alexander, Ruth Barnes, Merce Cunningham, June Finch, Susana Hayman-Chaffey, Chris Komar
Dance on Camera Festival 1985
Cunningham dancers, students and teachers demonstrate sequential exercises and simple combinations of movements, intercut with footage of classes. Merce Cunningham, whose no-nonsense technique has been evolving since 1959, offers a running commentary.

CUNNINGHAM DANCE TECHNIQUE: INTERMEDIATE LEVEL

1987, 55 min. color video
Distributor: Cunningham Dance Foundation
Producer: Cunningham Dance Foundation
Directors: Elliot Caplan, Merce Cunningham
Choreographer: Merce Cunningham
Principal Dancers: Heidi Kreusch, David Kulick, Larissa McGoldrick, Dennis O'Connor, Yukie Okuyama, Carol Teitelbaum
Category: INSTRUCTIONAL, MODERN
Teachers: Merce Cunningham, Diane Frank, Catherine Kerr, Chris Komar, Robert Kovich, Rob Remley
The second in the educational series, this video offers a narrated technique class set in the Westbeth studio in New York, with narration and commentary by Merce Cunningham.

CUP/SAUCER/TWO DANCERS/RADIO

1965/1983, 23 min. color film
Distributor: Film-makers' Cooperative
Director: Jonas Mekas
Choreographers: Kenneth King, Phoebe Neville
Category: COMEDY, EXPERIMENTAL
An essay in pop art style in a performance recorded in 1965, and later translated into a film on alienation which gives equal emphasis to all the elements listed in the title. Neville, dressed in bra, girdle, curlers and toe shoes, marches across the floor on pointe with a radio clasped to her ear. King, dressed in an undershirt, shorts, and black tie, does calisthenics.

CURTAIN UP

1982, 27 min. color film
Distributors: International Film Bureau, Coe Film Associates, University of Minnesota
Producers: Royal Opera House, Charles Thompson
Director: Jolyon Winhurst
Choreographers: Frederick Ashton, Kenneth MacMillan, Marius Petipa, Enrico Cecchetti
Principal Dancers: David Ashmole, Desmond Kelly, Margaret Barbieri, Marion Tate, Susan Crow, David Bintley
Dance Company: Sadler's Wells Royal Ballet
Composers: Léo Delibes, Scott Joplin, André Messager, Ferdinand Hérold
Category: BALLET COMPANIES
Discussions about touring, training, and the importance of professionalism. Excerpts from *Coppélia* (Petipa and Cecchetti/Delibes), *Elite Syncopations* (MacMillan/Joplin), *The Two Pigeons* (Ashton/Messager), *La Fille Mal Gardée* (Ashton/Hérold). Guide available with ballet synopses and short history of the Sadler's Wells and of ballet.

DADDY LONGLEGS

1955, 126 min. color film, video
Distributors: Films Inc., Facets
Producer: Twentieth Century Fox
Director: Jean Negulesco
Choreographers: Roland Petit, David Robel, Fred Astaire
Principal Dancers: Fred Astaire, Leslie Caron
Composer: Alex North
Category: FEATURES, BALLET
A romance blooms between a French orphan girl and her anonymous American benefactor. Ballet sequences include *Daddy Long Legs, Guardian Angel, Dream,* and *Sluefoot.*

DAISY AND HER GARDEN: A DANCE FANTASY

1994, 38 min. color video
Distributor: V.I.E.W.
Producer: Czech Television
Director: Pavel Smok
Choreographer: Pavel Smok
Principal Dancer: Marta Balzarova
Dance Company: Czech Television Arts Company
Category: BALLET, CHILDREN
A magical tale told through dance, music and poetic narration.

DAMBIO FESTIVAL DANCE FROM CENTRAL SUDAN

1965, 9 min. color film
Distributor: PennState
Producer: Wissen
Category: FESTIVALS, AFRICA
Women performing at the annual feast of the *margai* for the Diongor clan in Chad, evidently tipsy from too much millet beer, attempt to keep the beat in this festival dance. Quarrels break out and the dance dissolves.

DAMES

1934, 90 min. b&w film, video, laser
Distributors: Swank, Facets
Producer: Warner Brothers
Director: Ray Enright
Choreographer: Busby Berkeley
Principal Dancers: Ruby Keeler, Joan Blondell
Composer: Harry Warren
Category: FEATURES, MUSICALS
This typical "backstage musical" film tells the story of a songwriter-singer trying to raise money for a new show, the aspiring actress he loves and a wisecracking, gold digging actress during the production of a Broadway musical. Dance numbers include *Dames* and *I Only Have Eyes For You.*

A DAMSEL IN DISTRESS

1937, 103 min. b&w film
Distributor: Films Inc.
Producer: RKO
Director: George Stevens
Choreographers: Hermes Pan, Fred Astaire
Principal Dancers: Fred Astaire, George Burns, Gracie Allen
Composer: George Gershwin
Category: FEATURES, TAP
Original Story: P.G. Wodehouse
Astaire plays a popular American dancer who, while appearing in London, falls in love at first sight. Dance numbers include: *Put Me To the Test, Stiff Upper Lip,* and *Nice Work If You Can Get It,* reprised as a drum solo and dance by Astaire.

DANCE

1980, 4 min. color film
Distributor: PennState
Category: ANIMATION
This animated film uses one red and one blue character who dance together beautifully, each to a different tune. An allegory of relationships among friends, neighbors, races, and countries.

THE DANCE

1960, 74 min. b&w film, video
Distributor: The Cinema Guild
Producer: Deutsche Wochenschau
Director: Heinrich Weidman
Choreographers: Katherine Dunham, Mary Wigman, Harald Kreutzberg, Alan Carter, Kurt Jooss, Dore Hoyer
Principal Dancers: Katherine Dunham, Ludmilla Tcherina, John Kriza, Melissa Hayden, Harald Kreutzberg, Dore Hoyer
Dance Company: Kurt Jooss Dance Company
Composer: Frederick Cohen
Category: DANCE HISTORY, DOCUMENTARY PORTRAITS
Mime: Marcel Marceau
Teacher: Lola Roget
This historical documentary includes the work of Katherine Dunham based on native dances of Africa, continues with folk dances from fifteen nations, today's social dances (waltz, fox-trot and mambo), and culminates with ballet and modern performances. Mary Wigman, the German choreographer, appears in a brief sequence

teaching her students. Kurt Jooss' company performs the classic antiwar ballet *The Green Table.*

DANCE: A REFLECTION OF OUR TIMES

1960, 29 min. b&w film, video
Series: A Time To Dance
Distributor: Indiana University
Producer: Jac Venza for WNET/13
Choreographer: Herbert Ross
Principal Dancers: John Kriza, Ruth Ann Koesun, Lupe Serrano, Sallie Wilson, Scott Douglas, Enrique Martínez
Dance Company: American Ballet Theatre
Category: DANCE ANALYSIS, ART, BALLET
Herbert Ross, dancer, choreographer and producer of such features as *The Turning Point* and *Dancers,* evaluates dance as a means of social commentary in light of artists' efforts in other disciplines. Members of the company perform excerpts from Ross' *Paeon* (1957) and *Caprichos* (1949), based on Goya's etchings on man's weaknesses.

DANCE AND GROW: DEVELOPMENTAL DANCE ACTIVITIES FOR THREE THROUGH EIGHT-YEAR-OLDS

1994, 50 min. color video
Distributor: Dance Horizons
Director: Betty Rowen
Category: INSTRUCTIONAL, CHILDREN
Developmental activities for three through eight-year-olds based on Betty Rowen's book *Dance and Grow.*

DANCE AND HUMAN HISTORY

1974, 40 min. color film, video
Series: Movement Style and Culture
Distributors: University of California Extension Center, UCLA Instructional Media Library, Indiana University, PennState, Buffalo State
Producer: Alan Lomax
Directors: Alan Lomax, Forrestine Paulay
Category: ANTHROPOLOGICAL, DANCE ANALYSIS
Analyzing dance from a geometric perspective, Alan Lomax explains his theory, developed from a ten-year cross-cultural study. He grouped types of dance in terms of linear, curvilinear or spiral tendencies, and whether the dancer's torso is moved as a block or divided into units. Three variables(climate, method of food production, and sexual division of labor(-appear to determine the shape of dance, as exemplified by footage taken around the world.

DANCE AND MYTH: THE WORLD OF JEAN ERDMAN (3 videos)

1993, 53, 59, and 67 min. color video
Distributor: Uroboros, Dance Horizons
Producers: Jeff Bush and Celia Ipiotis for ARC Videodance, Dan Berkowitz
Directors: Celia Ipiotis, Nancy Allison, Dan Berkowitz
Choreographer: Jean Erdman,
Principal Dancers: Nancy Allison, Leslie Dillingham, Dianne Howarth, Muna Tseng, Stephen Nunley, David Rousseve
Composers: John Cage, Claude Debussy, Louis Harrison, Louis Horst, Otto Janowitz, Béla Bartók, Henry Cowell, Ezra Laderman
Category: MODERN, DOCUMENTARY PORTRAITS, DANCE HISTORY
Narrator: Jean Erdman

Part 1, *The Early Dances,* recreates the choreographer's work from 1942–48. Part 2, *The Group Dances,* recreates the choreographer's major group dances from 1949–50. Part 3, *The Later Solos,* recreates the choreographer's solo works from 1951–57. All are intercut with archival and contemporary footage, and are narrated by Erdman, a leading dancer-choreographer of the post-pioneer period of American modern dance. Excerpts include *The Transformations of Medusa, Hamadryad, Passage, Ophelia, Creature on a Journey, Daughters of the Lonesome Isle, The Perilous Chapel, Solstice, Pierrot, The Moon, Changingwoman,* and *Fearful Symmetry.*

DANCE AND TRANCE OF BALINESE CHILDREN

1995, 43 min. video
Distributor: Filmakers Library
Producer: Jay Haley, Madeleine Richeport-Haley
Category: BALI, CHILDREN
Combining footage taken by Margaret Mead and Gregory Bateson in the 1930s with new footage, this documentary affirms the living tradition of Balinese dance by showing the ongoing training of children through repetition, imitation and forceful manipulation into correct positions.

DANCE: ANNA SOKOLOW'S *ROOMS*

1967, 30 min. b&w film
Series: USA Dance Series
Distributors: Indiana University, PennState, UCLA Instructional Media Library, University of Minnesota
Producer: Jac Venza for WNET/13
Director: Dave Geisel
Choreographer: Anna Sokolow
Principal Dancers: Anna Sokolow, Ze'eva Cohen, Jack Moore, Jeff Duncan
Composer: Kenyon Hopkins
Category: MODERN, DOCUMENTARY PORTRAITS
A brief introduction to and performance of *Rooms,* the four-part classic (*Escape, Going, Desire* and *Panic*) choreographed in 1954. As she sets one or more in a room, Sokolow expresses the sense of isolation, alienation, loneliness and hunger of the soul.

DANCE BABY DANCE (2 videos)

1985, 30 min. each color video
Distributor: Hoctor Products
Producer: Hoctor Products
Category: INSTRUCTIONAL, JAZZ
Teacher: Jimmie Ruth White
Jazz routines for teachers and students.

DANCE BLACK AMERICA

1984, 90 min. color film
Distributors: Dance Horizons, Facets
Producers: State University of New York, Brooklyn Academy of Music, Pennebaker Associates
Directors: Chris Hegedus, D.A. Pennebaker
Choreographers: Alvin Ailey, Charles Moore
Principal Dancers: Alvin Ailey, Charles Moore
Dance Company: Mama Lu Parks' Jazz Dancers, Alvin Ailey American Dance Theatre, Chuck Davis Dance Company, Jazzy Double Dutch Jumpers, Charles Moore Dance Theatre, Garth Fagan's Bucket Dance Theatre, Magnificent Force
Category: AFRICAN-AMERICANS, DOCUMENTARY PORTRAITS

Narrator: Geoffrey Holder
Dance on Camera Festival 1985
An onstage/offstage documentary showing a cross section of the personalities and styles within the African-American dance world, from a festival held at the Brooklyn Academy of Music. Dances performed included *Fontessa and Friends, Lindy Hop, From Before, Ostrich, Lenjen-Go Man-Diani, Junkie, Juba* and *Cakewalk.*

DANCE CHROMATIC

1959, 7 min. color film
Distributor: Film-makers' Cooperative
Director: Ed Emshwiller
Principal Dancer: Nancy Fenster
Composer: Louis Harrison
Category: EXPERIMENTAL, ART
Creative Film Foundation Award of Exceptional Merit
"A fusion of dance, abstract painting, and a percussive score achieving a hypnotic and strongly rhythmic synthesis," said the late Ed Emshwiller, recognized for his experiment with video effects and his collaborations with artists of many media.

DANCE CLASS

1970s, 9 min. color film
Distributor: National Film Board of Canada
Producer: National Film Board of Canada
Director: Joan Henson
Choreographer: Peter Randazzo
Dance Company: Toronto Dance Theatre
Category: MODERN COMPANIES
Company members of the Toronto Dance Theatre rehearse *A Thread of Sand,* choreographed by a Martha Graham disciple.

DANCE CLASS WITH SERENA

1989, 97 min. color video
Distributor: Serena
Producer: Serena
Director: Alan Wilson
Principal Dancer: Serena
Category: BELLY DANCE, INSTRUCTIONAL
Comprehensive course on Middle Eastern dance, with tips on posture, isolations, hip articulations, hand and arm routines, by the New York-based Serena, author of *The Belly Dance Book,* published by McGraw Hill. Also available from Serena is her *Visions of Salome,* a 1986 concert taped at Riverside Church.

DANCE CONTEST IN ESIRA

1936, 11 min. b&w film
Distributor: Museum of Modern Art
Producer: Nordisk, Denmark
Director: Paul Fejos
Category: ANTHROPOLOGICAL, AFRICA
An early anthropological film study of a dance contest held by several tribes in the village of Esira in Madagascar, with the meaning of the dances explained and modern cinematic techniques used.

DANCE DELILAH, DANCE!

1988, 30 min. color video
Distributor: Visionary Dance Productions
Producer: Visionary Dance Productions
Choreographer: Delilah
Principal Dancer: Delilah
Composer: Steven Flynn
Category: BELLY DANCE

Seven belly dance solos with Middle Eastern rhythms and modalities, excerpted from her three volume *Delilah's Belly Dance Workshop*. A short narrative introduces the artistry and discipline of this Seattle-based performer.

DANCE DESIGN: MOTION

1975, 19 min. color film
Distributor: AAHPERD
Producer: The Athletic Institute
Director: Robert Cooley
Choreographer: Lynda Davis
Principal Dancers: Lynda Davis, Susan Kennedy, Mary Ann Kellogg, Clay Taliaferro
Composer: Larry Attaway
Category: INSTRUCTIONAL
A teacher's guide with advice on how to build a kinetic vocabulary, develop a continuity of movement, and create design concepts.

DANCE DESIGN: SHAPING

1975, 16 min. color film
Distributor: AAHPERD
Producer: The Athletic Institute
Director: Robert Cooley
Principal Dancers: Clay Taliaferro, Mary Ann Kellogg, Susan Kennedy, Lynda Davis
Composer: Larry Attaway
Category: INSTRUCTIONAL
With the camera placed below a transparent floor, the viewer sees how dancers use the values of shape and time for accent, punctuation, and clarification.

DANCE DESIGN: SPACE

1975, 19 min. color film
Distributor: AAHPERD
Producer: The Athletic Institute
Director: Robert Cooley
Principal Dancers: Lynda Davis, Susan Kennedy, Mary Ann Kellogg, Clay Taliaferro
Category: INSTRUCTIONAL
This teacher's aid shows how dancers relate to and move through space.

DANCE ELEVEN

1976, 8 min. color film, video
Series: Doris Chase Dance Series—Four Solos
Distributors: Film-makers' Cooperative, Doris Chase Productions, Museum of Modern Art
Producer: Doris Chase
Director: Doris Chase
Principal Dancer: Cynthia Anderson
Composer: Laurie Spiegel
Category: MODERN, EXPERIMENTAL
A woman dances a duet with her own image, multiplied, blurred, and dissolved through feedback techniques. The surrounding space is transformed into a viscous atmosphere of colored light, which responds and bends to the dance.

DANCE EX MACHINA

1986, 2:00 min. color video
Distributor: The Kitchen
Director: John Sanborn, Mary Perillo
Choreographer: Cyndi Lee
Principal Dancer: Mary Ellen Strom
Category: ANIMATION
A solo dance piece in which the directors first explored the potential of rotoscoping using the HARRY Animation System.

THE DANCE EXPERIENCE (9 videos)

1985–1990, 60–90 min. color video
Distributor: Tremaine Dance Conventions
Producer: Tremaine Dance Convention
Category: JAZZ, TAP, INSTRUCTIONAL
Teachers: Joe Tremaine and others from his faculty
American Video Conference Award
Ten to twelve routines per tape, created by Californian teachers who tour the country with competitive conventions. Also available from Tremaine: *Jazz Technique, Progressions and Turns* and *Tap Technique.*

A DANCE FANTASY

1980s, 7:30 min. color film
Distributor: Coe Film Associates
Producer: Sue Gilbert
Director: Sue Gilbert
Category: CHILDREN
A little girl meets a life-size puppet in a costume warehouse. Sparks fly as they waltz, tango, soft-shoe, and clown around until her mother appears, breaking the spell.

DANCE FESTIVAL: MAKIRITARE (2 films)

1955, 1969, 8 and 7 min. color film
Distributor: PennState
Producer: Wissen
Category: FESTIVALS, LATIN AMERICA
The earlier film shows a dance festival held by the Makiritare of the Orinoco Head Water Region in Venezuela. Festival participants in the later film sport patterns painted on their bodies with red vegetable dye, and move in a line to suggest a herd of grunting wild boars.

DANCE FIVE

1976, 5 min. color film
Distributors: Film-makers' Cooperative, Doris Chase Productions
Producer: Doris Chase
Director: Doris Chase
Choreographer: Kei Takei
Principal Dancer: Kei Takei
Composer: Timothy Thompson
Category: MODERN, EXPERIMENTAL
Sculptor: Doris Chase
A dancer's movements around a kinetic sculpture are intertwined with optical patterns, creating a dynamic kaleidoscope.

A DANCE FOR 15 PREGNANT WOMEN

1992, 12 min. color video
Distributor: Pentacle
Producer: Myrna Packer
Director: Harmony Vanover-Feldman
Choreographers: Myrna Packer, Art Bridgman
Dance Company: Art Bridgman/Myrna Packer
Composer: Naaz Hosseini
Category: MODERN, WOMEN
Dance on Camera Festival 1993 Honorable Mention
A documentary based on the performance of *Water's Edge*, a dance for fifteen pregnant women.

DANCE FOUR

1977, 6:30 min. color film
Series: Doris Chase Dance Series—Three Solos
Distributors: Museum of Modern Art, Doris Chase Productions
Producer: Doris Chase
Director: Doris Chase

Choreographer: Kei Takei
Composers: George Kleinsinger, Eric Eigen, Mike Mahaffey
Category: MODERN, EXPERIMENTAL
Another collaboration between the Asian choreographer Kei Takei and the filmmaker-sculptor Doris Chase.

DANCE: FOUR PIONEERS

1966, 30 min. b&w film
Series: USA Dance Series
Distributors: PennState, Dance Film Archive, Indiana University, Lane Education, University of Minnesota
Producer: Jac Venza for WNET/13
Director: Charles S. Dubin
Choreographers: Martha Graham, Doris Humphrey, Charles Weidman, Hanya Holm
Principal Dancers: Chester Wolenski, Lola Huth
Dance Company: American Dance Theatre
Composer: Johann Sebastian Bach
Category: DANCE HISTORY, CHOREOGRAPHY, MODERN
Introduces four of the most influential American choreographers. Film clips from 1934 show the four working at Bennington College, Vermont. The American Dance Theatre perform Doris Humphrey's *Passacaglia*, shot at Lincoln Center.

DANCE FRAME

1978, 7 min. color film, video
Distributors: Film-makers' Cooperative, Doris Chase Productions
Producer: Doris Chase
Director: Doris Chase
Choreographer: Sara Rudner
Principal Dancer: Sara Rudner
Composer: Joan LaBarbara
Category: MODERN, EXPERIMENTAL
An effort to create the third dimension in which the lines of a dancer are juxtaposed with a colored, geometric form.

DANCE IMAGING

1994, 30 min. color video
Distributor: Cernik, Eva
Producers: Eva Cernik, Fritz Penning
Director: Eva Cernik
Choreographer: Eva Cernik
Principal Dancer: Eva Cernik
Category: MIDDLE EAST, INSTRUCTIONAL
A teaching video created out of an extensive collection of images used in twenty years of teaching. Steps are likened to things in motion in everyday life, shown in comparison to the step, and then shown in a dance both with the image and then without. It is intended to train the eye of both the dancer and general onlooker to see images created by the dancer. All dancing is done in Middle Eastern style.

DANCE IN AMERICA (over 75 titles)

1976-present, 60 min. each color video
Distributors: Dance Collection, Lincoln Center (on-site viewing only)
Producers: Merrill Brockway, Jac Venza, Emile Ardolino, Judy Kinberg for WNET/13 in association with a variety of European broadcasters
Directors: Merrill Brockway, Thomas Grimm, Judy Kinberg, Emile Ardolino
Dance Company: The foremost dance companies in America

Category: DOCUMENTARY PORTRAITS,
UNITED STATES
Four programs a year broadcast on national public
television produced with the aim of preserving
and sharing the best of American dance.

DANCE: IN SEARCH OF *LOVERS*
1966, 30 min. b&w film
Series: USA Dance Series
Distributor: Indiana University
Producers: Jac Venza and Virginia Kassel for
WNET/13
Choreographer: Glen Tetley
Principal Dancers: Carmen de Lavallade, Mary
Hinkson, Scott Douglas
Category: MODERN, CHOREOGRAPHY
With Tetley's ballet *Lovers* as the centerpiece, the
choreographer reveals how he integrates his
story line, choreography, costumes, sets, and
music.

DANCE IN THE SUN
1953, 7 min. b&w film
Distributor: Museum of Modern Art
Producer: Shirley Clarke
Director: Shirley Clarke
Choreographer: Daniel Nagrin
Principal Dancer: Daniel Nagrin
Category: EXPERIMENTAL, MODERN
A solo by the modern dance pioneer, who begins
in a studio and makes his final statement on a
beach.

THE DANCE INSTRUMENT
1975, 27 min. color film
Series: The Dance Experience
Distributor: AAHPERD
Producer: The Athletic Institute
Director: Robert Cooley
Principal Dancers: Lynda Davis, Susan Kennedy,
Mary Ann Kellogg, Clay Taliaferro
Composer: Larry Attaway
Category: INSTRUCTIONAL
This teachers' guide explores the range of creative
possibilities within movement.

DANCE LIKE A RIVER: ODADAA!
DRUMMING AND DANCING IN THE U.S.
1985, 45 min. color film, video
Distributor: Indiana University
Producers: Barry Dornfeld and Tom Rankin for
Oboade Institute of African Culture
Director: Yacub Addy
Choreographer: Yacub Addy
Dance Company: Odadaa
Category: AFRICA, FOLK COMPANIES
Dance on Camera Festival 1989 Silver Award
Documents the dance styles, purpose and per-
formances of a nine-member Ga dance com-
pany from Ghana West Africa, based in
Washington, D.C.

DANCE MASKS: THE WORLD OF MARGARET
SEVERN
1983, 33 min. color film, video
Distributor: University of California Extension
Center
Producer: Peter Lipskis
Director: Peter Lipskis
Choreographer: Margaret Severn
Principal Dancer: Margaret Severn
Category: MODERN, DOCUMENTARY POR-
TRAITS

Dance on Camera Festival, American Film Festival, Choice Outstanding Nonprint Media
Award
In the 1920s and '30s, Margaret Severn was acclaimed for her short mask dances, each of
which portrayed a character or emotion. At age
eighty, Severn performs briefly and comments
on the stills and film clips of her prime.

DANCE: NEW DIRECTIONS
1980, 20 min. color film, video
Distributor: FACSEA
Producer: French Ministry of Foreign Affairs
Choreographer: Douglas Dunn
Principal Dancer: Michel Dénard
Category: MODERN, CHOREOGRAPHY
Teacher: Alwin Nikolais
A performance at Alwin Nikolais' school for cho-
reographers on the banks of the Loire River, in
which Dénard, a principal with the Paris Opera
Ballet, performs a composition by American
modern dance choreographer Douglas Dunn.

DANCE: NEW YORK CITY BALLET
1966, 30 min. b&w film
Series: USA Dance Series
Distributors: PennState, University of California
Extension Center, Indiana University, Univer-
sity of Minnesota
Producer: Jac Venza for WNET/13
Director: Charles S. Dubin
Choreographer: George Balanchine
Principal Dancers: Jacques d'Amboise, Suzanne
Farrell, Arthur Mitchell, Melissa Hayden, Patri-
cia McBride, Edward Villella
Dance Company: New York City Ballet
Composers: Igor Stravinsky, Louis Gottschalk,
Peter Ilyich Tchaikovsky
Category: BALLET COMPANIES, CHOREOG-
RAPHY
Choreographer George Balanchine discusses his
philosophy of classical ballet, along with ex-
cerpts from *Agon* (Farrell and Mitchell), *Pas de
Deux* (Hayden and d'Amboise), *Tarantella* (Mc-
Bride and Villella), and *Meditation* (Farrell and
d'Amboise).

DANCE NINE
1983, 4 min. color film, video
Series: Doris Chase Dance Series—Four Solos
Distributors: Film-makers' Cooperative, Doris
Chase Productions, Museum of Modern Art
Producer: Doris Chase
Director: Doris Chase
Principal Dancer: Gus Solomons
Composer: George Kleinsinger
Category: MODERN, EXPERIMENTAL
A modern dancer seemingly partners kinetic pat-
terns generated by a Rutt/Etra video synthe-
sizer. His image is multiplied and colored into
an abstract collage.

DANCE OF DARKNESS
1989, 56 min. color video, laser
Distributor: Electronic Arts Intermix
Producer: La Sept in association with WGBH/
WNET New Television
Director: Edin Veléz
Principal Dancers: Tatsumi Hijikata, Kazuo Ohno
Dance Company: Dai Rakuda Kan, Byakko Sha,
Hakutoboh
Category: BUTOH, EXPERIMENTAL
A personal statement as well as a historical per-

spective of the Japanese dance *Butoh*, born in
the 1960s in the middle of the worldwide ques-
tioning of values. Edin Velez eliminated the
confines of the frame by alternately using footage of rehearsals and performances shot outdoors and in studios and then combining
several kinetic images. Tatsumi Hijikata and
Kazuo Ohno, *Butoh's* cocreators, express their
search to "break through the normal to individ-
ualism, away from Japanese good manners to
personal freedom."

DANCE OF THE AGES/ON THE SHORE
1913, 6 min. b&w film (silent)
Distributor: Dance Film Archive
Director: Ted Shawn
Principal Dancer: Ruth St. Denis
Category: MODERN, DANCE HISTORY
A "trick" film made by modern dance pioneer Ted
Shawn with theatrical posings by his partner,
Ruth St. Denis, in 1906.

DANCE OF THE BUSHCLEARING SOCIETY
GUA
1968, 11 min. b&w film
Distributor: PennState
Producer: Wissen
Director: H. Himmelheber
Category: ANTHROPOLOGICAL, AFRICA
Men in Dan, Ivory Coast, dance for their employ-
ers, both before and after clearing woodland for
plantations. Every employee must be equally
gifted as a dancer and a laborer in order to hold
his job.

DANCE ON THE WIND
1994, 30 min. color video
Distributor: The Cinema Guild
Producers: Marty Frame, Ivor Miller, Jeremy
Brecher, Jill Cutler
Principal Dancer: Eno Washington
Category: AFRICAN-AMERICANS
Documents the life and work of Eno Washington,
an African-American dancer and cultural activ-
ist, portraying his early experience of African-
American religious and secular movement tra-
ditions, his study of African dance, and his dis-
covery of unrecognized connections between
African and African-American dance.

DANCE ON VIDEO: AN INTRODUCTION TO
VIDEOTAPING DANCE
1979, 30 min. b&w video
Distributor: ARC Videodance
Producers: Jeff Bush and Celia Ipiotis
Directors: Jeff Bush, Celia Ipiotis
Choreographer: Celia Ipiotis
Principal Dancer: Celia Ipiotis
Category: INSTRUCTIONAL, CINEDANCE
Ideas and experiences about the problems, bene-
fits, and techniques of videotaping dance. Best
suited for closed-circuit viewing in a workshop,
discussion or research context. Includes three
versions of *Motherless Child* choreographed by
Celia Ipiotis, the producer-host for the televi-
sion series *Eye on Dance*.

DANCE ON: WITH BILLIE MAHONEY
1980-present, 29 min. each color video
Distributor: Dance On Video
Producers: Billie Mahoney and Dance Films Asso-
ciation
Category: DANCE HISTORY

Host: Billie Mahoney

A one-on-one cable talk show hosted by a dancer, dance notator, and teacher, with guests representing the spectrum of the dance world. Often includes archival and historical information on American dance. In relaxed conversations, dancers talk freely about themselves and their experiences. With close to 250 taped in New York until 1989, *Dance On* is now produced in Kansas City and has been taped with internationally known guests at sites worldwide.

A DANCE ORIENTAL EXTRAVAGANZA (2 videos)

1992, 1993, 120 and 90 min. color video
Distributor: Kahreen and Kira
Producers: Kahreen and Kira
Directors: Kahreen and Kira
Principal Dancers: Olgui Jajouka, Suzanna Del Vecchio, Kahreen and Kira
Dance Company: Kismet Dancers of Miami, Step Sisters
Category: BELLY DANCE

Features all styles of Middle Eastern dance.

DANCE OUTLINE

1978, 4 min. color film
Distributor: Doris Chase Productions
Producer: Doris Chase
Director: Doris Chase
Choreographer: Sara Rudner
Principal Dancer: Sara Rudner
Composer: Joan LaBarbara
Category: CINEDANCE, MODERN

A dance conceived for the camera by a modern dancer in collaboration with video pioneer Doris Chase.

DANCE PRELUDES (4 videos)

1987, 60 min. each color video
Distributor: Video D
Producer: Philadelphia Dance Alliance
Director: Dennis Diamond
Choreographers: Senta Driver, José Limón, Richard Weiss
Principal Dancers: Senta Driver, José Limón, Richard Weiss, Finis Jhung, Daniel Lewis, William Soleau, Christine Redpath
Dance Company: Pennsylvania Ballet, Harry
Category: BALLET, COMPOSITION, MODERN
Teachers: Finis Jhung, Daniel Lewis

Four documentaries on the creative process: *Pennsylvania Ballet In Rehearsal*; *Harry*, Senta Driver talking about her modern company which performs segments of *Video 5000*, *Missing Persons* and *Reaches*; *Finis Jhung's Ballet For Adult Beginners* by the popular New York-based teacher; and *José Limón Technique*, an hour class with Daniel Lewis on the basics of the modern style devised by the late José Limón.

DANCE: ROBERT JOFFREY BALLET

1966, 30 min. b&w film
Series: USA Dance Series
Distributor: Indiana University
Producer: Jac Venza for WNET/13
Director: Charles S. Dubin
Choreographers: Robert Joffrey, Anna Sokolow, Gerald Arpino
Principal Dancers: Lisa Bradley, Robert Blankshine, Luís Fuente
Dance Company: Robert Joffrey Ballet

Composers: Louis Harrison, T. Marcer, Antonio Vivaldi
Category: BALLET COMPANIES

Early film of Jac Venza's with rehearsal session and excerpts from *Pas de Deeses*, based on a nineteenth-century French lithograph, and *Gamelan* (Joffrey), *Opus 65* (Sokolow), *Incubus* and *Viva Vivaldi* (Arpino).

DANCE SEVEN

1976, 8 min. color film, video
Series: Doris Chase Dance Series—Four Solos
Distributors: Film-makers' Cooperative, Doris Chase Productions, Museum of Modern Art
Producer: Doris Chase
Director: Doris Chase
Principal Dancer: Marnee Morris
Composer: Teiji Ito
Category: MODERN, EXPERIMENTAL

Through postproduction effects of feedback, de-beaming, and superimposition, a former New York City Ballet dancer appears as a moving painting, fragmented by color separations, her figure juxtaposed with close-ups of her face.

DANCE SPACE

1980, 14 min. color film
Distributor: Coe Film Associates
Producer: National Dance Institute
Director: John Avildsen
Principal Dancers: Jacques d'Amboise, Mikhail Baryshnikov
Category: CHILDREN

Features Jacques d'Amboise, former principal with the New York City Ballet who founded the National Dance Institute. He supervises rehearsals of his students drawn from the public schools of the five boroughs of New York City and their annual performances with guest artists at Lincoln Center and Madison Square Garden. (See also *He Makes Me Feel Like Dancin'*).

DANCE SQUARED

1963, 4 min. color film
Distributor: International Film Bureau
Producer: National Film Board of Canada
Director: Norman McLaren
Category: ANIMATION

The distinguished animator awakens a sense of how geometry underlines every movement by dividing, subdividing, and gyrating squares.

DANCE TEN

1977, 8 min. color film, video
Series: Doris Chase Dance Series—Three Solos
Distributors: Film-makers' Cooperative, Doris Chase Productions, Museum of Modern Art
Producer: Doris Chase
Director: Doris Chase
Choreographer: Jonathan Hollander
Composer: William Bolcomb
Category: MODERN, EXPERIMENTAL

Modern dance solo with a video-synthesized image of a kinetic sculpture, a "rocker" by sculptor Doris Chase.

DANCE THEATRE OF HARLEM

1976, 60 min. color film, video
Series: Dance in America
Distributor: Indiana University
Producers: PBS, RM Arts, GmbH and BBC-TV
Director: Merrill Brockway

Choreographers: Geoffrey Holder, Arthur Mitchell, George Balanchine, Lester Horton
Principal Dancers: Stephanie Dabney, Ronald Perry, Stanley Perryman, Eddie Shellman, Yvonne Hall
Dance Company: Dance Theatre of Harlem
Composers: Judith Hamilton, Edvard Grieg
Category: BALLET COMPANIES, AFRICAN-AMERICANS

Dance on Camera Festival 1980 Gold Award

Members of the African-American dance company appear informally and in rehearsal, and perform two movements from *Forces of Rhythm*, set to *Do the Breakdown* and *He Ain't Heavy, He's My Brother*; *Bugaku*, George Balanchine's dance which premiered in 1963; *The Beloved* (Horton/Hamilton); restaged by James Truitte; *The Holberg Suite* (Mitchell/Grieg); and *Dougla*, Hindu and African ritual choreographed by Holder.

DANCE THEATRE OF HARLEM

1988, 117 min. color video
Distributors: Home Vision, Dance Horizons, Viewfinders, Corinth, Voyager, Films Inc., Karol, Media Basics, Facets
Producer: WNET-TV/New York with RM Arts and Danmarks Radio
Director: Thomas Grimm
Choreographers: Agnes de Mille, Robert North, Lester Horton, Arthur Mitchell
Dance Company: Dance Theatre of Harlem
Composers: Morton Gould, Franz Schubert, Bob Downes, Judith Hamilton, Milton Rosenstock
Category: BALLET COMPANIES, AFRICAN-AMERICANS

American Film and Video Festival 1991

Four ballets by the New York-based company: de Mille's *Fall River Legend*, inspired by Lizzie Borden's 1892 murder of her father and stepmother; North's *Troy Game*, an acrobatic satire of the macho man; Horton's *The Beloved*, a duet in which a jealous man strangles his wife whom he suspects of being unfaithful; Mitchell's *John Henry*, a tale of the "steel drivin' man" who challenged the steam drill, but died with a hammer in his hand.

THE DANCE THEATRE OF HARLEM

198?, 14 min. color video
Distributor: Films for the Humanities and Sciences
Category: BALLET COMPANIES, AFRICAN-AMERICANS

A segment from *60 Minutes* which shows how the establishment of a dance company which would provide Harlem youngsters with opportunities in professional ballet has resulted in the growth of a world-class troupe.

DANCE THERAPY: THE POWER OF MOVEMENT

1983, 30 min. color film, video
Distributors: University of California Extension Center, Kent State, University of Minnesota
Producer: American Dance Therapy Association
Director: Norris Brock
Category: DANCE THERAPY
Dance Therapists: Joan Chodorow, Jane Downes, Susan Sandel, Barbara Estrin, Sharon Chaiklin
Dance on Camera Festival, National Coalition of Arts Therapy Association Honoree

Five dance therapists work with their patients, ranging from an emotionally disturbed child in a psychiatric hospital to geriatric patients in a nursing home, demonstrating that movement can communicate, even when words fail.

DANCE THREE
1977, 8:30 min. color film
Distributors: Film-makers' Cooperative, Doris Chase Productions
Producer: Doris Chase for WNYC-TV
Director: Doris Chase
Choreographer: Kei Takei
Principal Dancer: Kei Takei
Composer: George Kleinsinger
Category: MODERN, EXPERIMENTAL
A dance based on a theme from Takei's series called *Light Part Nine*.

DANCE TO THE GREAT MOTHER
199?, 45 min. color video
Distributor: Visionary Dance Productions
Producer: Visionary Dance Productions
Director: Steven Flynn
Choreographer: Delilah
Principal Dancer: Delilah
Composer: Sirocco
Category: BELLY DANCE, WOMEN
Delilah portrays Isis, the Great Mother, using belly dance to celebrate the feminine creative principle. Performed during the last trimester of her pregnancy, Delilah's dance portrays the joy and mystery of the arrival of new life through the female body. An in-depth interview, discussing both the creation of this dance and the meaning of belly dancing for women, follows the performance.

DANCE TO THE MUSIC
1980, 30 min. color video
Series: Jumpstreet
Distributor: Iowa State
Principal Dancer: Charles "Honi" Coles
Dance Company: Rod Rodgers Dance Troupe
Category: JAZZ, TAP, AFRICAN-AMERICANS
Explores the African-American musical heritage from its African roots to its influence on modern American music.

DANCE TO THE MUSIC (4 videos)
1980s, 30 min. each color video
Distributor: Hoctor Products
Producer: Studio Music Corporation
Category: INSTRUCTIONAL, JAZZ
Teachers: Kit Andree, Scott Benson, Dawn Carfton, Daryl Retter, Valene Tueller, Jimmi Ruth White
Jazz routine demonstrations accompanied by drum and rhythm tracks.

A DANCE TRIBUTE TO MICHAEL JORDAN
1989, 30 min. color video
Distributor: Orion Enterprises
Producer: Gus Giordano
Choreographer: Gus Giordano
Dance Company: Gus Giordano Dance Company
Category: JAZZ, AFRICAN-AMERICANS
A dance biography of the agile basketball player from his dribbling youth to his superstar status today. Substantiated with news clips of the athlete and interviews with the dancers.

THE DANCE WORKS OF DORIS HUMPHREY: *WITH MY RED FIRES* AND *NEW DANCE*
1972, 60 min. color video
Distributor: Dance Horizons
Choreographer: Doris Humphrey
Principal Dancer: Doris Humphrey
Dance Company: American Dance Festival Company
Composer: Wallingford Riegger
Category: MODERN, DANCE HISTORY
Features three dances created in the 1930s by the modern dance pioneer (*New Dance, Variations and Conclusion, With My Red Fires*) which dramatize the conflicts between men and women, the individual and the group, and the power of love—maternal, romantic, and fraternal—and its capacity for passionate and destructive excesses.

THE DANCER
1994, 100 min. color video
Distributor: First Run/Icarus
Director: Donya Seuer
Choreographer: Donya Seuer
Dancers: Anneli Alhanko, Katja Bjorner, Natalia Makarova
Category: FEATURES, DOCUMENTARY PORTRAITS
This film depicts the world which envelops a young dancer of the Swedish Ballet School.

DANCER FOR THE CORONATION
1988, 8 min. color film
Distributor: Film-makers' Cooperative
Director: Caroline Avery
Category: MODERN, EXPERIMENTAL
Caroline Avery, a painter who switched to film as her canvas in the early 1980s, plays with light and shadow to give the illusion of a dancer folding back on herself.

A DANCER MUST DANCE
5 min. color video
Distributor: Coe Film Associates
Producer: New Zealand National Film Unit
Principal Dancer: Peter Gannett
Dance Company: Royal New Zealand National Ballet
Category: BALLET COMPANIES
Shows the Royal New Zealand National Ballet in class and performance.

DANCER REHEARSING
1994, 3:17 min. color video
Distributor: Backalley Productions
Producer: Mark Wilcken
Director: Mark Wilcken
Choreographer: Julie Goncalves
Principal Dancer: Julie Goncalves
Composer: Grant McKee
Category: MODERN
A brief look into the life of a dancer and her pianist as they struggle with artistic expression and scheduling conflicts.

DANCERS
1987, 97 min. color film, video
Distributors: Warner Home Video, Corinth, Facets, Swank
Producer: Cannon Films
Director: Herbert Ross
Choreographers: Marius Petipa, Mikhail Baryshnikov

Principal Dancers: Mikhail Baryshnikov, Alessandra Ferri, Julie Kent
Dance Company: American Ballet Theatre
Composer: Adolphe Adam
Category: FEATURES, BALLET
While on tour in Italy, an innocent corps member falls for the company playboy. During a performance of *Gisèlle*, she recognizes that she is living the part of Gisèlle and flees from the theatre. Stronger of heart than the onstage Gisèlle, she gets a tattoo and returns to her apologetic boyfriend.

A DANCER'S GRAMMAR
1977, 18 min. color film, video
Distributors: Phoenix, University of California Extension Center, University of Minnesota
Producer: Nina Feinberg
Director: Nina Feinberg
Principal Dancers: Lawrence Rhodes, Lois Bewley
Category: BALLET, INSTRUCTIONAL
Dance on Camera Festival 1977
Barre and center work of two dancers showing the differences for the male and female bodies. Portrays dancers perfecting their craft through sweat and discipline.

DANCERS IN SCHOOL
1971, 45 min. color film, video
Distributors: Pennebaker Associates, PennState
Producer: D.A. Pennebaker
Director: D.A. Pennebaker
Principal Dancers: Bella Lewitsky, Virginia Tanner, Murray Louis
Category: INSTRUCTIONAL, CHILDREN
Three methods of teaching children demonstrated in the Improving Public Awareness of Concepts of Telecommunications (IMPACT) program sponsored by the National Endowment's Artists in the Schools program and the Office of Education.

A DANCER'S WORLD
1957, 30 min. b&w film, video
Distributors: Phoenix, Kultur, Museum of Modern Art, Indiana University, University of California Extension Center, Kent State, Iowa State, Lane Education, University of Minnesota
Producer: Nathan Kroll for WGED-TV/Pittsburgh
Director: Peter Glushanok
Choreographer: Martha Graham
Principal Dancers: Martha Graham, Mary Hinkson, Bertram Ross, Yuriko Kimura, Helen McGehee, Gene McDonald, Ellen Siegel, David Wood, Miriam Cole, Lillian Biersteker, Robert Cohan, Ethel Winter
Dance Company: Martha Graham Dance Company
Composer: Cameron McCosh
Category: DANCE HISTORY, MODERN COMPANIES
Venice International Film Festival, American Film Festival
Choreographer-dancer Martha Graham shares her philosophy of life as a dancer. In her dressing room, she talks about the dancer's world as she prepares for the role of Jocasta in her choreographic work *Night Journey*. Her company demonstrates their own technical and psychological preparation and then rehearses the dance.

DANCES AND RITES AFTER THE DEATH OF A TRIBAL CHIEF
1962, 12 min. b&w film
Distributor: PennState
Producer: Wissen
Category: AFRICA, ANTHROPOLOGICAL, RELIGIOUS/RITUAL
From the Angas tribe in Nigeria, West Africa, a glimpse into the sacrificial ceremonies following the death of a chief in Pankshin.

DANCES FROM DJAYA (5 films)
1964–65, 4–10 min. color film
Distributor: PennState
Producer: Wissen
Category: FOLK, AFRICA
Three circle dances from Central Sudan, Africa: the *Parama;* the *Napa* with twenty boys dancing while girls sing songs of praise; the *Bardjat,* and three *djele* dances with the boys' long turban scarves waving in the air.

DANCES FROM THE CASBAH
1990s, 48 min. color video
Distributor: Bastet Productions
Producer: Bastet Productions
Choreographer: Kathryn Ferguson
Principal Dancer: Kathryn Ferguson
Dance Company: Xanadu Dancers
Category: BELLY DANCE
Collage of four solos (*Amethyst, The Copper Flute, Dreams of Matahara,* and *Shaqawa*) blending traditional Oriental dance with Western elements. Also includes *Just Beyond Subliminal,* a short experimental work which combines Oriental dance with abstract video art. The dancer's edition also includes a *Directory of Oriental Dance Resources* and *Rick's Café,* an early Kathryn Ferguson video performance.

DANCES OF BUDDHIST PILGRIMS
1957, 4 min. color film (silent)
Distributor: PennState
Producer: Wissen
Category: ANTHROPOLOGICAL, CHINA
A man and a woman on a pilgrimage to a Buddhist monastery earn food for their Tibetan journey by chanting and dancing.

DANCES OF INDIA: KATHAKALI
1945, 10 min. b&w film
Distributors: Kent State, Lane Education
Producer: Films of the Nations
Category: GESTURES, INDIA, DANCE DRAMA
Explains the gesture language of India's dance drama and shows three episodes from the *Mahabarata* which was filmed in its entirety in 1990 during the run of Peter Brooks' production at the Brooklyn Academy of Music in New York.

DANCES OF MEXICO: ANIMAL ORIGINS
1981, 12 min. color film
Distributor: Tempo Films
Directors: Mary Joyce, Annette MacDonald
Category: FOLK, NATURE
The continuing importance of the deer, bird, snake and horse is demonstrated in the dances of Mexico.

DANCES OF SOUTHERN AFRICA
1973, 55 min. color film, video
Distributor: PennState

Producer: Gei Zantziger
Director: Gei Zantziger
Category: FOLK, AFRICA
Recreational dances performed by men working in the mines of South Africa and in the Tribal Trust lands: the *Xhosa* shaking dance; high-kicking *Ndlamu* dance of the Zingili Zulo; and the tumbling dance of the Ndau tribes.

DANCES OF THE SILK ROAD: AN INTRODUCTION TO UZBEK AND GEORGIAN DANCE (2 videos)
1988–90, 60 min. each color video
Distributor: Uzbek Dance Society
Dance Company: Bakhor Ensemble
Category: FOLK, ASIA
Solo and ensemble performances of the Turkic-speaking Sunni Muslim people with historical photos and stills of the art and elaborate costumes in the first video. The second focuses on the traditional dance of the Republic of Georgia (the ancient dances from the Caucasus Mountains between the Black and Caspian Seas. Poetry, folklore and architecture are interwoven with the dance sequences to demonstrate how the cultural legacy of the Georgian peoples is expressed through dance. Also available: *The Bakhor Ensemble In Concert,* filmed in Tashkent.

DANCES OF THE WORLD (16 videos)
1987, 30–60 min. color video
Distributors: AAHPERD, Dance Horizons, Facets
Principal Dancer: John Ramsey
Dance Company: Kentucky College Country Dancers, Folklórico Gauteque Ballet, Compania Folklórica Las Mesas de Cayey, Ballet Folklórico de Colima, Grupo Folklórico del Departamento de Bellas Artes, Guadalajara, Clan Na Gael, Rinnceoiri Idirnaisiunta, An Oige Na H'Eireann Dance Groups, Monkseaton Dancers of Newcastle-upon-Tyne
Category: FOLK, INTERNATIONAL
Filmed at Folkmoot, Asheville, North Carolina, this series shows the colorful dances of Ireland, England, Korea, Mexico, Puerto Rico, Poland, Russia, and the Appalachian region.

DANCING (8 videos)
1993, 60 min. each color video
Distributors: Dance Horizons, Viewfinders, Home Vision, Insight Media, Buffalo State, Facets, Media
Basics
Producer: PBS
Principal Dancers: Jacques d'Amboise, Twyla Tharp, 1980,
Category: INTERNATIONAL
Narrator: Raul Trujillo
This eight part series, filmed in eighteen countries from India to the former USSR, and from Brazilian to African-American forms, explores dance as a form of communication and expression in a variety of cultural contexts. Examples span the spectrum from staged ballet to urban street dance to traditional myth and ritual. Individual titles are: *The Power of Dance, The Lord of the Dance, Sex and Social Dance, Dance at Court, New Works New Forms, Dance Centerstage, The Individual and Tradition,* and *Dancing in One World.*

DANCING BOURNONVILLE
1980, 48 min. color film
Distributor: Audience Planners

Producers: Royal Danish Ministry for Foreign Affairs and the Danish Government Film Office
Choreographers: August Bournonville, Hans Beck
Principal Dancers: Erik Bruhn, Kirsten Ralov, Hans Brenaa, Ib Anderson, Mette Honningen, Mette-Ida Kirk
Dance Company: Royal Danish Ballet
Category: BALLET, DANCE HISTORY, CHOREOGRAPHY
The traditions and training methods of the prolific Danish dancer-choreographer August Bournonville (1805–1879), as developed and codified by Hans Beck with excerpts from his ballets at different stages of preparation, from rehearsal to performance.

DANCING FOR MR. B.: SIX BALANCHINE BALLERINAS
1989, 90 and 43 min. color film, video
Series: The Balanchine Library
Distributors: Direct Cinema, WarnerVision Entertainment, Viewfinders, Dance Horizons, Facets
Producer: Anne Belle
Director: Anne Belle
Principal Dancers: Mary Ellen Moylan, Maria Tallchief, Melissa Hayden, Allegra Kent, Merrill Ashley, Darci Kistler
Dance Company: New York City Ballet
Category: BALLET, DOCUMENTARY PORTRAITS
Dance on Camera Festival 1991
A documentary in homage to choreographer George Balanchine with six ballerinas (each representing a different era in Balanchine's career with the New York City Ballet (recounting how the artist influenced their lives and how they keep his ballets and inspiration alive.

DANCING FREE
1992, 7 min. color film, video
Distributor: Cadigan, Katie
Producer: Katie Cadigan
Director: Katie Cadigan
Choreographer: Bonnie Bernstein
Category: DANCE THERAPY
After years of feeling disassociated and alienated from their bodies, a group of incest survivors at a YWCA in Palo Alto, CA seek out a dance therapy group which ultimately liberates them from the destructive legacy of their abusive childhoods.

DANCING FROM THE INSIDE OUT
1994, 28 min. color video
Distributor: Dancing Video
Producers: Thaïs Mazur, Sarah Shockley
Director: Sarah Shockley
Choreographers: Thaïs Mazur, Nina Haft
Principal Dancers: Judith Smith, Bonnie Lewkowicz, Uli Schmitz
Dance Company: AXIS Dance Troupe
Composer: Mark Gray
Category: DISABILITIES
Dance on Camera Festival 1994 Silver Award
Tells the story of three extraordinary professional dancers with disabilities and their paths to acceptance: Uli, who was afflicted with polio at age three; Bonnie, a dancer for ten years prior to a major car accident; and Judy, a championship horsewoman before a severe spinal cord injury. Their stories are highlighted by scenes of their daily lives, and working out a wheelchair dance in rehearsal.

DANCING GIRLS OF LAHORE
1993, 40 min. color video
Distributor: Filmakers Library
Producer: Ahmad Jamal
Category: DOCUMENTARY PORTRAITS, WOMEN
An ancient tradition of dancing girls who were courtesans to the nobility still exists in the Islamic state of Pakistan. Saira and Taira hope to become film stars, but entertain in the traditional forms of song, dance and poetry to support their brothers and father.

DANCING HANDS
1988, 30 min. color video
Series: Alive From Off Center
Distributors: Electronic Arts Intermix, In Motion Productions
Producer: John Schott for KTCA-TV
Director: Skip Blumberg
Choreographers: Keith Terry, Ellen Fisher, Blondell Cummings, Sally Hess, Wendy Perron, Robert La Fosse
Composer: Frank Maya
Category: MODERN, EXPERIMENTAL
Dance on Camera Festival 1989 Honorable Mention
A series of nine short dances performed exclusively with hand and arm gestures, conceived for the camera by an assortment of modern ballet and funk dancers.

THE DANCING MAN: PEG LEG BATES
1992, 60 min. color, b&w video
Distributor: PBS Video
Producers: Dave Davidson and Amer Edwards in association with Hudson West Productions and South
Carolina ETV
Category: AFRICAN-AMERICANS, TAP, DISABILITIES
Traces the extraordinary life of Clayton "Peg Leg" Bates who, despite a debilitating injury at age twelve, went on to become a tap dance legend. The eighty-four-year old Bates recounts some of the triumphs he experienced and obstacles he encountered.

DANCING ON THE EDGE
1989, 28 min. color video
Series: Alive From Off Center
Distributor: KQED-TV
Producer: Linda Schaller
Directors: Tim Boxell, Gino Tanasescu
Choreographers: Rinde Eckert, Margaret Jenkins, Joe Goode, Ellen Bromberg
Principal Dancers: Rinde Eckert, Margaret Jenkins, Joe Goode, Ellen Bromberg
Category: MODERN
Dance on Camera Festival 1990 Honorable Mention
Features three avant-garde dance works by Bay Area dancers-choreographers.

DANCING OUTLAW
1991, 30 min. plus 30 min. selected outtakes, color video
Distributor: Flower Films
Producer: Jacob Young
Principal Dancer: Jesco White
Category: UNITED STATES, FOLK
Emmy Award
Jesco White, a backwoods mountain dancer from Boone County, West Virginia, reveals how dancing saved him from a life of substance abuse, violence and alcoholism.

THE DANCING PROPHET
15 min. color film, video
Distributor: Franciscan Communications
Director: Bruce Baker
Choreographer: Doug Crutchfield
Category: DOCUMENTARY PORTRAITS
CINE Golden Eagle
Pressured by his father to become a minister, Doug Crutchfield rebelled and found his own ministry in dance, as demonstrated by his interpretation of Christ's healing of the sick.

THE DANCING PROPHET
1970, 25 min. color film, video
Distributor: Pyramid
Director: Edmund Penney
Choreographer: Ruth St. Denis
Principal Dancer: Ruth St. Denis
Category: DANCE HISTORY, MODERN, DOCUMENTARY PORTRAITS
This documentary on the modern dance pioneer Ruth St. Denis traces her development and thought with still photographs, historical footage, graphics, recreated dance sequences and solo dances by St. Denis. Dame Alicia Markova, Jack Cole and Sir Anton Dolin discuss her influence.

DANCING SCHOOL
1980, 6 min. color film, video
Distributor: Phoenix
Producers: Hungarofilm, Panzonia Film Studios
Director: Peter Szoboszlay
Category: CHILDREN, ANIMATION
This imaginative animated film features a most unusual dancing class, where the young dancers' minds, as well as their feet, soar through space and time. Led by a most unusual dance instructress (who persists in turning herself into a piano), the children of the class are encouraged to exercise their imaginations freely, admitting them to a world of fantasy and adventure far removed from the mundane dance exercises they must perform.

DANCING THROUGH THE MAGIC EYE: A PORTRAIT OF VIRGINIA TANNER
1979–84, 35 min. color video
Distributor: Virginia Tanner Creative Dance Center
Producer: Virginia Tanner Creative Dance Center
Director: Claudia Sisemore
Principal Dancers: Mary Ann Lee, Linda Smith, Virginia Tanner
Category: INSTRUCTIONAL, CHILDREN
Interviews with the Salt Lake City-based pioneer who developed a method of teaching children which awakens their creativity and belief in themselves.

DANCING THRU
1940s, 33 min. b&w film
Distributor: Dance Film Archive
Choreographers: Marius Petipa, Jack Billings, Chris Gil
Principal Dancers: Galina Ulanova, Jack Billings, Diane Chase, Chris Gil
Category: BALLET, TAP
Whimsical views of international dance styles, with an excerpt of *Swan Lake* performed by Russian prima ballerina Galina Ulanova, as well as two styles of tap: ballroom tappers Jack Billins and Diane Chase and acrobatic tapper Chris Gil.

DANCING'S ALL OF YOU
1982, 23:30 min. color film, video
Distributors: Coe Film Associates, De Nonno Pix
Director: Tony De Nonno
Principal Dancers: Alfredo Gustar, Carol Hess
Category: TAP, DOCUMENTARY PORTRAITS
Tales from a sixty-two-year-old hoofer who performed with Billie Holiday, Ella Fitzgerald, Dizzy Gillespie and Duke Ellington, as he coaches his students and performs *The Tune of the Hickory Stick* and swirls around a young lady on a rooftop. Romance and reality merge as the two perform tap, soft-shoe, and ballroom duets.

DANZANTE
1992, 28 min. color video
Distributor: PBS Video
Producer: Miguel Grunstein
Director: Miguel Grunstein
Dance Company: Danza Azteca de Anahuac
Category: NATIVE AMERICANS, RELIGIOUS/RITUAL
A striking depiction of the ritual dances and beliefs of Ancient Aztec and Toltec Mayan cultures described and enacted by the five-member dance troupe

DANZAS REGIONALES ESPAÑOLAS
1966, 14 min. color film
Series: El Español por el Mundo
Distributors: Indiana University, University of California Extension Center, Kent State, PennState
University of Minnesota
Producer: Encyclopedia Britannica
Category: FOLK, HISPANIC
Dances of Spain performed on stage, in patios and courtyards with historical references and scenes of the different regions where the dances originated. Narrated in Spanish.

DAPHNIS AND CHLÖE
1988, 61 min. color video
Distributors: Home Vision, Viewfinders, Corinth, Media Basics
Producer: BBC-TV
Director: Derek Bailey
Choreographer: Graeme Murphy
Principal Dancers: Carl Morrow, Victoria Taylor, Paul Saliba, Kim Walter
Dance Company: Sydney Dance Company
Composer: Maurice Ravel
Category: FULL-LENGTH BALLETS
Dance on Camera Festival 1989 Gold Award
Not to be confused with the versions by Michel Fokine, John Cranko, or George Skibine, this story of love lost and regained is choreographed here by Australian Graeme Murphy in a pop vein(dancing nymphs swirling about on roller skates, Pan descending on a cloud, and Cupid swooping by on a skateboard.

DARE TO DANCE
1995, 40 min. color video
Distributor: Grey Dawn Productions
Producer: Justin Harris

Director: Justin Harris
Dance Company: Pacific Northwest Ballet
Category: CHILDREN, INSTRUCTIONAL
This documentary, designed to inspire and motivate young dancers, follows three dancers aged 10, 14 and 17 as they take class, rehearse and perform. Also featured are interviews with teachers, parents and professional dancers.

DAVID GORDON: PANEL
1986, 20 min. color video
Series: Alive From Off Center
Distributor: KTCA-TV
Producer: KTCA-TV
Director: David Gordon
Choreographer: David Gordon
Principal Dancers: David Gordon, Valda Setterfield
Category: MODERN, CHOREOGRAPHY
Highlights the work of the choreographer in two autobiographical duets. In *Dorothy and Eileen*, two women dance while confiding stories about their mothers. In *Close-Up*, Gordon and his wife, Valda Setterfield, suggest the dynamics of relationships.

DAVIDSBÜNDLERTANZE
1981, 43 and 86 min. color video, laser
Series: The Balanchine Library
Distributors: Corinth, WarnerVision Entertainment, Media Basics, Viewfinders, Dance Horizons, Facets, Laserdisc Fan Club
Producer: Catherine Tatge for National Video Corporation
Director: Merrill Brockway
Choreographer: George Balanchine
Principal Dancers: Suzanne Farrell, Jacques d'Amboise, Peter Martins, Ib Anderson, Karin von Aroldingen, Adam Luders, Sara Leland, Heather Watts
Dance Company: New York City Ballet
Composer: Robert Schumann
Category: FULL-LENGTH BALLETS
A ballet set to Schumann's cycle of eighteen piano pieces, for four couples who suggest Schumann's inner turmoil

DAY ON EARTH
1972, 20 min. color film
Distributors: Dance Film Archive, UCLA Instructional Media Library
Director: Dwight Godwin
Choreographer: Doris Humphrey
Principal Dancers: Peter Sparling, Janet Eilber
Dance Company: Juilliard Dance Company
Composer: Aaron Copland
Category: MODERN, DANCE HISTORY
Choreographed in 1947 by Doris Humphrey, this work for a man, wife, child, and girl suggests the cycles of life and love. Reconstructed for two Juilliard students who became members of Martha Graham's company and then developed solo careers.

DEAF LIKE ME
1981, 23:30 min. color video
Distributor: Franciscan Communications
Producer: Barr Films
Director: Jim Callner
Category: PANTOMIME, CHILDREN, DISABILITIES
The story of Yollie, a shy, deaf ten-year-old, who

responds to a mime who she later discovers is also deaf.

DEBBIE DEE TAP TECHNIQUE (4 videos)
1985–86, 90–105 min. color video
Distributor: Taffy's By Mail
Principal Dancer: Debbie Dee
Category: TAP, INSTRUCTIONAL
Teacher: Debbie Dee
Technique classes for different levels with turns, combinations, exercises and progressions.

DEBONAIR DANCERS
1986, 27 min. color film
Distributor: Filmakers Library
Producer: Alison Nigh-Strelich
Category: INSTRUCTIONAL, DANCE THERAPY, DISABILITIES
Narrator: Jack Lemmon
Dance on Camera Festival 1987 Honorable Mention, CINE Golden Eagle 1986
Mentally disabled young men and women improve through dancing under the supervision of John Soiu, a California ballroom dance instructor active among the disabled for over forty years.

DECLARATION OF INDEPENDENCE
1993, 15 min. color video
Distributor: Harnett, Daniel
Producer: Edith Stephen
Director: Daniel Harnett
Choreographer: Edith Stephen
Dance Company: Electric Current Dance Company
Category: MODERN
Created from a series of three dances, *Second Hand Rose*, *The Peacock,* and *Declaration of Independence,* the film creates an imaginative interpretation by taking the inherent qualities in the dance and exaggerating its rhythm.

DEEP HEARTS
1980, 53 min. color film, video
Distributors: Phoenix, PennState, University of California Extension Center, UCLA Instructional Media Library
Producer: Harvard University Film Study Center
Director: Robert Gardner
Category: AFRICA, ANTHROPOLOGICAL
Ritual dances called *berewol*, in which the younger men, wearing elaborate costumes and makeup, compete in a contest of beauty. Performed by nomads of the Bororo Fulani tribe of the Niger Republic in Africa.

DEEP IN MY HEART
1954, 132 min. color video, laser
Distributors: Facets, MGM/UA
Producer: MGM
Director: Stanley Donen
Choreographer: Eugene Loring
Principal Dancers: Gene Kelly, Cyd Charisse, Fred Kelly, Ann Miller
Composer: Sigmund Romberg
Category: FEATURES, MUSICALS
Musical biography of the composer, Sigmund Romberg. Dance numbers include *One Alone, I Love To Go Swimmin' With Wimmin,* and *It.*

THE DELHI WAY
1960, 45 min. color film
Distributor: New Yorker

Producer: Asia Society
Director: James Ivory
Category: INDIA
Documentary recording of classical Indian dancers by the maker of *Room With A View.*

DELI COMMEDIA
1985, 18 min. color film, video
Distributor: Cunningham Dance Foundation
Producer: Cunningham Dance Foundation
Directors: Elliot Caplan, Merce Cunningham
Choreographer: Merce Cunningham
Dance Company: Merce Cunningham Dance Company
Composer: Pat Richter
Category: MODERN, SOCIAL
American Film Festival
Merce Cunningham's bow to vaudeville with hints of cakewalk, tango, and lindy woven into his modern mode.

DELILAH & SIROCCO . . . LIVE & WILD!
1992–93, 82 min. color video
Distributor: Visionary Dance Productions
Producers: Delilah, Steven Flynn
Directors: Delilah, Steven Flynn
Choreographer: Delilah
Principal Dancer: Delilah
Composer: Sirocco
Category: IMPROVISATION, MIDDLE EAST
Seven dance performances that display the improvisational interaction between dancer and musician. Shot on Maui, with some dances by the sea and in the jungle.

DELILAH'S BELLY DANCE WORKSHOP (3 videos)
1988, 90 min. each color video
Distributor: Visionary Dance Productions
Producers: Delilah, Steven Flynn
Choreographer: Delilah
Principal Dancer: Delilah
Composer: Steven Flynn
Category: BELLY DANCE, INSTRUCTIONAL
Instructor: Delilah
Nafisa Magazine 1990, 1991, 1992 Best Instructional Video
Exercises by the Seattle-based teacher-performer for the hips, torso, arms, hands, zills and rhythms on Volume I; fast hips, *Baladi, Masmoudi* and *Karshilama* veil technique on Volume II; undulations, belly rolls, coin tricks, floor work and the Turkish drop with four demonstration pieces on Volume III.

DELILAH'S COSTUME WORKSHOP (2 videos)
199?, 180 min. color video
Distributor: Visionary Dance Productions
Producer: Visionary Dance Productions
Director: Steven Flynn
Choreographer: Delilah
Principal Dancer: Delilah
Composer: Steven Flynn
Category: BELLY DANCE, INSTRUCTIONAL
Instructor: Delilah
Includes belly dance costuming, construction techniques, design ideas, materials, practical tips and secrets, and costuming history, including a "dancing" belly dance fashion show.

DENISHAWN: THE BIRTH OF MODERN DANCE
1988, 40 min. color, b&w video
Distributors: Kultur, Dance Horizons, Viewfinders, Corinth, Home Vision

Producer: New Jersey Center Dance Collective
Directors: Clark Santee, Delia Gravel Santee
Choreographer: Ruth St. Denis
Dance Company: New Jersey Center Dance Collective
Category: MODERN, DOCUMENTARY PORTRAITS, DANCE HISTORY
A documentary history of one of America's most influential dance companies. Founded by Ruth St. Denis and Ted Shawn at the beginning of the century, the troupe known as Denishawn has become legendary for its unique approach to modern dance. Archival footage and reconstructions of *Schubert Waltzes, Floor Plastique, Chœur Danse, Incense* and *Bakawali Nautch* are juxtaposed with dramatizations of the elderly St. Denis and Shawn.

DERVISH
1972, 18 min. color video (silent)
Distributor: Eclipse
Producer: Amy Greenfield
Director: Amy Greenfield
Choreographer: Amy Greenfield
Principal Dancer: Amy Greenfield
Category: EXPERIMENTAL
Superimpositions of a spinning figure wrapped in a white sheet.

THE DESPERATE HEART
1974, 21 min. color film, video
Distributor: Beals, Margaret
Choreographer: Valerie Bettis
Principal Dancer: Margaret Beals
Category: MODERN
Valerie Bettis' famous dance solo performed by Margaret Beals under Bettis' direction. The two artists and dance critic Walter Terry discuss the challenges of passing on a role.

DHANDYO
1961, 3 min. b&w film
Distributor: PennState
Producer: Wissen
Category: FOLK, ASIA
Stick dance of the Fakirani, a nomadic group of the Jat in the Indus delta of West Pakistan, performed at a celebration in honor of the ancestor Sanwelo.

DIALOGUE FOR CAMERAMAN AND DANCER
1972–74, 25 min. color video
Distributor: Film-makers' Cooperative
Producer: Amy Greenfield
Director: Amy Greenfield
Choreographer: Amy Greenfield
Principal Dancer: Amy Greenfield
Category: EXPERIMENTAL, CINEDANCE
As the camera circles and follows a nude woman, we hear the cameraman and the dancer share their feelings on the experience.

DIDO AND AENEAS
1995, 55 min. color video
Distributor: Rhombus International, Bullfrog
Producer: Daniel Iron
Director: Barbara Willis Sweete
Dancer: Mark Morris
Dance Company: Mark Morris Dance Group
Composer: Henry Purcell
Category: FULL-LENGTH BALLETS
Dance on Camera Festival 1996 Silver Award

This adaptation of the provocative dance production by Mark Morris takes a fresh and controversial approach to the baroque operatic masterwork by Henry Purcell. Dido, the noble queen of Carthage, has fallen in love with the Trojan prince, Aeneas. While the court celebrates the imminent union of the two monarchs, the evil sorceress with her coven of witches plots their downfall. Romance leads to heartbreak and tragedy.

DIGITAL DANCE
1984, 5 min. color video
Distributor: Murphey, Claudia
Producer: Claudia Murphey
Director: Michael Moser
Choreographer: Claudia Murphey
Category: EXPERIMENTAL
Dance on Camera Festival 1985
Experiment in digital effects used to clarify the themes of equality, trust, and interdependence.

DINIZULU AND HIS AFRICAN DRUMMERS, DANCERS AND SINGERS
1991, 13:30 min. color video
Series: Alive From Off Center
Distributor: In Motion Productions
Producer: Skip Blumberg
Director: Skip Blumberg
Choreographer: Nina Dinizulu
Dance Company: Dinizulu and his African Drummers, Dancers and Singers
Category: AFRICA
One of the first African-American cultural performance companies founded in 1947 and the oldest still in existence performs the *Gum Boot Rhythm Dance,* a South African Zulu miner's dance; *goma,* a Ghanaian square drum played with hands and bare feet; *Limwe Weche,* an emotional Congolese song of mourning; and *Adjobo,* an acrobatic dance of the vitality of the Ghanaian Ewe people.

DIONYSUS
1963, 26 min. color film
Distributor: Film-makers' Cooperative
Producer: Charles Boultenhouse
Director: Charles Boultenhouse
Principal Dancers: Louis Falco, Anna Duncan, Nicholas Magallanes, Flower Hujer
Composer: Teiji Ito
Category: CINEDANCE, EXPERIMENTAL
The film medium is used to convey the psychological states of the Greek myth of Pentheus: circling handheld cameras for intoxication; slow-motion pans for hypnosis; single frame cutting for dismemberment; multiple exposures for metamorphosis. A young Louis Falco opens the film with his leaps superimposed on double images of fists and flowers.

DIRTY DANCING
1987, 100 min. color film, video
Distributor: Swank, Vestron
Producer: Vestron
Director: Emile Ardolino
Choreographer: Kenny Ortega
Principal Dancers: Patrick Swayze, Jennifer Grey
Composers: Franke Previte, John DeNicola, Donald Markowitz, Patrick Swayze, Merry Clayton
Category: FEATURES, SOCIAL
A young woman learns under pressure to dance as

an emergency substitute for a professional club dancer while vacationing with her family.

DISCOVERING AMERICAN INDIAN MUSIC
1971, 24 min. color video
Series: Discovering Music
Distributors: Insight Media, Indiana University, University of Minnesota
Producer: Bernard Wilets
Composer: Louis Ballard
Category: NATIVE AMERICANS
American Indian tribes from around the country gather to perform their songs and dances, and share ritual ceremonies.

DISCOVERING RUSSIAN FOLK MUSIC
1975, 23 min. color film, video
Series: Discovering Music
Distributor: Kent State
Producer: Bernard Wilets
Category: FOLK, EUROPE
Plaintive songs, swirling dances, and explanations of the traditional and contemporary uses of music in villages, cities, and churches in Russia.

DISCOVERING THE MUSIC OF AFRICA
1967, 22 min. color film
Series: Discovering Music
Distributors: Insight Media, PennState, University of California Extension Center
Producer: Bernard Wilets
Category: AFRICA, FOLK
Social and ceremonial dances of Africa performed with featured drummer Robert Ayittee of Ghana.

DISCOVERING THE MUSIC OF INDIA
1969, 22 min. color video
Series: Discovering Music
Distributor: Indiana University
Producer: Bernard Wilets
Category: FOLK, INDIA, GESTURES
Introduces the Carnatic music and instruments used in the South, and the Hindustani music and instruments of the North of India. Concludes with a dance in which the artist implies the lyrics of a song through hand gestures and facial expressions.

DISCOVERING THE MUSIC OF LATIN AMERICA
1969, 20 min. color film, video
Series: Discovering Music
Distributors: Insight Media, Kent State, Iowa State, Indiana University
Producer: Bernard Wilets
Category: FOLK, LATIN AMERICA
Explores the evolution of the Latin American dance and music from Indian and Spanish traditions. Demonstrates the pre-Columbian instruments and the Latin American dance rhythms.

DISCOVERING THE MUSIC OF THE MIDDLE AGES
1968, 20 min. color video
Series: Discovering Music
Distributors: Kent State, Iowa State, Indiana University
Producer: Bernard Wilets
Category: FOLK, EUROPE
Performances of a peasant's dance, *caccia,* madrigal and court dance, troubadour's song, and ex-

planations of the development of polyphony and medieval instruments.

DISCOVERING THE MUSIC OF THE MIDDLE EAST

1968, 20 min. color film
Series: Discovering Music
Distributor: Lane Education
Producer: Bernard Wilets
Category: FOLK, MIDDLE EAST

Explores the music dating back to the seventh century of the conquering Mohammedan peoples' movement through the Middle East, the Balkans, Africa and Spain, illustrated by dancers and musicians. Points out the ornamented melodies and the asymmetrical rhythms played by the oud, santir, *qanun, cimbalum* and *dumbek,* along with the dancers of several countries. Shows their influence on classical composers such as Rimsky-Korsakov, Khatchaturian, Mozart and Beethoven.

DISCOVERING YOUR EXPRESSIVE BODY WITH PEGGY HACKNEY

1981, 60 min. color video
Distributor: Dance Horizons
Principal Dancer: Peggy Hackney
Category: INSTRUCTIONAL, MODERN

A University of Washington dance professor, who is also a certified Laban movement analyst, presents ways to become aware of vertical and diagonal connections, moving with three spatial pulls, propelling and spiraling. The demonstration is based on the fundamentals of Irmgard Bartenieff.

DOLLY, LOTTE, AND MARIA

1988, 60 min. color film, video
Distributor: First Run/Icarus
Producer: Rosa von Praunheim
Principal Dancers: Lotte Göslar, Maria Piscator
Category: DOCUMENTARY PORTRAITS, PANTOMIME

A tribute to avant-garde, aristocracy, revolution and enduring careers through interviews with dancer and clown Lotte Göslar, singer Dolly Haas, and dancer Maria Piscator.

DON QUIXOTE (American Ballet Theatre)

1983, 90 min. color video, laser
Distributors: Corinth, Home Vision, Media Basics
Producer: National Video Corporation
Director: Brian Large
Choreographer: Mikhail Baryshnikov after Marius Petipa and Alexander Gorsky
Principal Dancers: Cynthia Harvey, Victor Barbee, Mikhail Baryshnikov
Dance Company: American Ballet Theatre
Composer: Léon Minkus
Category: FULL-LENGTH BALLETS

Baryshnikov's production based on an episode from the Spanish classic by Miguel de Cervantes in which Don Quixote believes he has found his Dulcinea, his vision of perfection, when he meets Kitri. She, however, is already trying to avoid her father's chosen suitor so that she can run off with Basil (Baryshnikov). Filmed at New York's Metropolitan Opera House.

DON QUIXOTE (Australian Ballet)

1972, 109 min. color film, video, laser
Distributors: Kultur, Home Vision DON060, Viewfinders, Karol, Corinth, Laserdisc Fan Club, Dance Film Archive (*Pas De Deux* and *Finale,* 20 min.)
Producer: John Hargreaves
Director: Rudolf Nureyev
Choreographers: Rudolf Nureyev with Robert Helpmann, Marius Petipa
Principal Dancers: Rudolf Nureyev, Lucette Aldous, Colin Peasley
Dance Company: Australian Ballet
Composer: Léon Minkus
Category: FULL-LENGTH BALLETS

This version of the 1869 Gorsky/Petipa ballet was restaged by Nureyev for the 1970 Adelaide Festival of the Arts.

DON QUIXOTE (Kirov Ballet)

1988, 120 min. color video
Distributors: Kultur, Home Vision DON070, Dance Horizons, Viewfinders, Corinth
Producer: Göstelradio
Choreographers: Marius Petipa, Aleksandr Gorsky
Principal Dancers: Tatiana Terekova, Faroukh Ruzimatov, Vladimir Ponomaryov
Dance Company: Kirov Ballet
Composer: Léon Minkus
Category: FULL-LENGTH BALLETS

The four-act ballet filmed live at the Leningrad State Kirov Theatre.

DON QUIXOTE (Russian State Perm Ballet)

1992, 120 min. color video
Distributors: Kultur, Dance Horizons, Viewfinders, Home Vision DON170, Facets
Producer: Arts Core
Director: Vladimir Salimbaev
Choreographers: Aleksandr Gorsky, Marius Petipa
Principal Dancers: Nina Ananiashvili, Aleksei Fadeyechev, Aleksandr Astafiev, Evgeny Katusov
Dance Company: Russian State Perm Ballet
Composer: Léon Minkus
Category: FULL-LENGTH BALLETS

A joyous new production of the ballet which tells the tale of an old knight who dreams of chivalry and tilts at windmills.

DORIS CHASE DANCE SERIES: FOUR SOLOS

1976–80, 24 min. color film, video
Series: Four By Doris Chase
Distributors: Museum of Modern Art, Film-makers' Cooperative
Producer: Doris Chase
Director: Doris Chase
Principal Dancers: Marnee Morris, Gus Solomons, Cynthia Anderson, Gay Delanghe
Composers: Teiji Ito, George Kleinsinger, Spiegel, Laurie, Jelly Roll Morton
Category: MODERN, EXPERIMENTAL

Dance Seven with Marnee Morris (8 min.); *Dance Nine* with Gus Solomons (4 min.); *Dance Eleven* with Cynthia Anderson (8 min.); and *Jazz Dance* with Gay Delanghe (4 min.). Solo performances filmed with many special effects of feedback, de-beaming, superimposition, colored lights, and abstract patterns. See entries under individual titles.

DORIS CHASE DANCE SERIES: THREE SOLOS

1975–80, 27 min. color film, video
Distributor: Museum of Modern Art
Producer: Doris Chase
Director: Doris Chase
Choreographers: Sara Rudner, Jonathan Hollander, Kei Takei
Principal Dancers: Sara Rudner, Jonathan Hollander, Kei Takei
Composers: Joan LaBarbara, George Kleinsinger, William Bolcomb
Category: MODERN, EXPERIMENTAL
Sculptor: Doris Chase
Avignon Film Festival, Melbourne Filmex, Chicago International Film Festival, Berlin Film Festival

Dance Four with Kei Takei (6:30 min.); *Dance Ten* with Jonathan Hollander (9:30 min.); and *Variation II* with Sara Rudner (11 min.). See entries under individual titles.

DORIS HUMPHREY TECHNIQUE: THE CREATIVE POTENTIAL

1992, 45 min. color, b&w video
Distributor: Dance Horizons
Director: Ernestine Stodelle
Principal Dancer: Doris Humphrey
Category: DANCE HISTORY, MODERN

Features the 1934 *Air for the G String,* excerpts from the 1936 film on the Humphrey technique, and performances of three early Humphrey dances, *Quasi-Valse, Two Ecstatic Themes,* and *Etude Patetico.*

LE DORTOIR (The Dormitory)

1990, 53 min. color video
Distributors: Bullfrog Films, Rhombus International
Producer: Niv Fichman for Rhombus International
Director: François Girard
Choreographers: Danielle Tardif, Gilles Maheu
Principal Dancer: Gilles Maheu
Dance Company: Carbone 14
Composers: Bill Vorn, Gaëtan Gravel
Category: MODERN, DANCE DRAMA
National Educational Film and Video Festival 1992 Gold Apple, International Emmy Awards 1991 Best Performing Arts, Prix Gémeaux 1992 Best Arts Special, Golden Gate Awards 1992 First Prize

An adaptation of Gilles Maheu's internationally acclaimed stage production which features Maheu and his company, Carbone 14. The program tells the story of a man's journey back into memory and imagination to escape, and finally overcome, a personal crisis. Set in a convent dormitory, it is a disturbing, nostalgic chronicle of fleeting impressions told through dance, music and images that range from the erotic to the violent.

DREAM DANCES OF THE KASHIA POMO: THE BOLE-MARU RELIGIOUS WOMEN'S DANCES

1964, 30 min. color film, video
Distributors: University of California Extension Center, PennState
Category: NATIVE AMERICANS, RELIGIOUS/ RITUAL

Pomo women demonstrate the dances of the Bole-Maru dream religion nearly a century after it evolved, reflecting recent influences of Christianity and World War II. The five dances are: *The Hand Power Dance, Star Hoop Dance, Feast Dance, Marriage Dance* and *War Flag Dance.*

THE DRUMMAKER

1978, 37 min. b&w film, video
Distributor: PennState

Producer: Smithsonian Institution Office of Folklife Programs
Category: NATIVE AMERICANS
William Bineshi Baker Sr., an Ojibwa Indian on the Lac Court Orielles Reservation in northern Wisconsin, demonstrates the art of drummaking and expresses his belief in tradition.

THE DRUMS OF WINTER (Uksuum Cauyai)
1988, 90 min. color film, video, PAL
Distributor: Documentary Educational Resources
Producers: Sara Elder and Len Kamerling
Directors: Sara Elder, Len Kamerling
Category: ANTHROPOLOGICAL
National Educational Film and Video Festival Silver Apple, International Arctic Festival Grand Prize, Society for Visual Anthropology Award of Excellence, American Film Festival Blue Ribbon
An exploration of the traditional dance, music and spiritual world of the Yup'ik Eskimo people in the village of Emmonak on the Bering Sea coast. The film follows the villagers as they prepare for a ceremonial gathering, practicing their songs and dances. Interviews and contemporary images are juxtaposed with archival footage of early Christian missionaries.

DU BARRY WAS A LADY
1943, 101 min. color video
Distributors: Facets, Swank, MGM/UA
Producer: MGM
Director: Roy del Ruth
Choreographer: Charles Walters
Principal Dancer: Gene Kelly
Composer: Cole Porter
Category: FEATURES, MUSICALS
New Yorker Red Skelton imagines himself back in the court of King Louis XIV. Dance numbers include *Do I Love You?*

DUET
199?, 10:30 min. b&w film
Distributor: Overfoot
Producer: Jody Oberfelder-Riehm
Director: Jody Oberfelder-Riehm
Choreographer: Jody Oberfelder-Riehm
Principal Dancer: Jody Oberfelder-Riehm
Composer: Michel Florian
Category: MODERN, WOMEN
Dance on Camera Festival 1991
In her eighth month of pregnancy, the dancer-choreographer and her unborn child are partners, moving to the sound of fetal heartbeats and conveying a sense of wonder.

DUNE DANCE
1980, 40 min. color film
Distributor: Dance Film Archive
Producer: Carolyn Brown
Director: Carolyn Brown
Principal Dancers: Sara Rudner, Wendy Rogers, Bruce de St. Croix, Jean Churchill, Robert Seder, Jumay Chu, Meg Harper, Charles Atlas, Robert Clifford
Category: MODERN, EXPERIMENTAL, IMPROVISATION
Photographed on the dunes of Cape Cod in Massachusetts, the movement was not staged but rather improvised, and directly affected by the sand or the camera.

THE DUTCH NATIONAL BALLET
1983, 50 min. color video
Distributor: Coe Film Associates

Producer: Radio Nederlands TV
Choreographers: Rudi van Dantzig, Hans van Manen, Toer van Schayk
Dance Company: Dutch National Ballet
Composers: Franz Liszt, Charles Ives
Category: BALLET COMPANIES, CINEDANCE
Two ballets seen from inception to performance: *Live* (van Manen/Liszt), a video-ballet for two dancers, a cameraman and screen, and *Life* (van Dantzig and van Schayk/Ives), a theatre spectacular with a message of concern about today's world.

DYING SWAN
1973, 3 min. b&w film
Distributor: Dance Film Archive
Choreographer: Michel Fokine
Principal Dancer: Vera Fokine
Composer: Camille Saint-Saëns
Category: BALLET, DANCE HISTORY
Over fifty still photographs of Vera Fokine performing the solo choreographed by her husband were taken from Fokine's 1925 book. These stills were then synchronized with the music according to the published requirements of the choreographer.

EARLY DANCE (2 videos)
1995, 24 and 30 min. color video
Distributor: Dance Horizons
Producer: Isa Partsch Bergsohn
Director: Hal Bergsohn
Principal Dancers: Angine Fèves, Charles Perrier
Category: DANCE HISTORY
Part 1, *From the Greeks to the Renaissance*, covers dance history from the Greek theatre to the Elizabethan court. Part 2, *The Baroque Era*, shows the development of music, dance and theatre in the French court style.

EARLY DANCE FILMS 1894–1912
1965, 12 min. b&w film (silent)
Distributors: Dance Film Archive, UCLA Instructional Media Library, Iowa State
Producers: Pathé Brothers, American Mutoscope, Biograph, Georges Melies and Thomas Edison
Principal Dancers: Cathrina Bartho, Loie Fuller, Annabelle Moore, Ella Lola Karina
Category: MODERN, DANCE HISTORY
The first dancers ever filmed! Among the eleven shorts are *Annabelle*, *Nymph and the Waves*, *Flag Dance*, *Animated Picture Studio*, and *Chrissie Sheridan*. Also called *Dance On Film, 1894–1912: Part 1*.

EARTHMATTERS
1992, 7 min. color video
Distributor: WHYY-TV 12
Director: Glen Holsten
Choreographer: Birgitta Herrman
Principal Dancers: Birgitta Herrman, Tonio Guerra
Dance Company: Ausdrückstanz Dance Theatre
Composer: Mark Baechtle
Category: MODERN
Images of the earth are combined with layers of dance, exploring the relationship between humans and the planet they live on.

EASTER PARADE
1948, 103 min. color film, video, laser
Distributors: Swank, Facets, MGM/UA
Producer: MGM

Director: Charles Walters
Choreographers: Fred Astaire, Robert Alton
Principal Dancers: Fred Astaire, Judy Garland, Ann Miller
Composer: Irving Berlin
Category: FEATURES, MUSICALS
Covering the time period from the day before Easter 1912, to Easter Sunday 1913, a dancing star (Astaire) and an unknown (Garland) form a new partnership, after his regular partner (Miller) leaves to join the Ziegfeld Follies. Dance numbers include *It Only Happens When I Dance With You, Beautiful Faces Need Beautiful Clothes, I Have a Piano, Ragtime Violin, A Couple of Swells,* and *Drum Crazy.*

THE EBB AND FLOW
1979, 52 min. color film
Series: The Magic of Dance
Distributors: Dance Film Archive, University of Minnesota
Producer: Patricia Foy for BBC-TV
Director: Patricia Foy
Choreographers: George Balanchine, Marius Petipa, Jules Perrot, John Durang, Mary Skeaping
Principal Dancers: Mikhail Baryshnikov, Rudolf Nureyev, Margot Fonteyn, Yoko Morishita, Shimizu Tetsutaro, Wayne Sleep, Desmond Kelly, Vyvyan Lorrayne, Esbart Dansire de Rubi
Composers: Igor Stravinsky, Léon Minkus, Adolphe Adam
Category: BALLET, DANCE HISTORY
Narrator: Margot Fonteyn
As part of a historical series, this episode includes a discussion of Anna Pavlova and a visit to Peter Ilyich Tchaikovsky's home. Among the excerpts are: Skeaping's reconstruction of *Flore and Sephry;* John Durang's hornpipe; *Gisèlle* performed by Fonteyn and Nureyev in 1962; the adagio from *Don Quixote* performed by Morishita and Tetsutaro; the cell scene from *Petroushka* with Fonteyn and Baryshnikov; a duet from Balanchine's *Apollo* performed by Lorrayne and Kelly; and a Spanish *jota* performed by de Rubi.

ECHOES OF JAZZ
1966, 30 min. color film
Series: USA Dance Series
Distributors: Lane Education, University of Minnesota
Producer: Jac Venza for WNET/13
Director: Charles S. Dubin
Choreographers: John Butler, Donald McKayle, Grover Dale
Principal Dancers: Grover Dale, Charles "Honi" Coles, Dudley Williams, Paula Kelly, William Luther, Buzz Miller, Mary Hinkson, John Butler
Composers: Jelly Roll Morton, Duke Ellington, Gunther Schuller
Category: JAZZ, TAP, INSTRUCTIONAL
Traces the development of American jazz dance from tap dance in the vaudeville form of the 1900s, to the orchestrated jazz of the '30s, to the abstract music of the '60s. Honi Coles explains and demonstrates tap steps such as sand shuffle, waltz clog, time step, buck-and-wing. McKayle's *Storyville,* Dale's *New Orleans 1900,* and a piece by John Butler are also performed.

EDDIE BROWN'S *SCIENTIFIC RHYTHM*
1991, 30 min. color video
Distributor: Images

Producer: Sharon Arslanian
Director: Sharon Arslanian
Principal Dancer: Eddie Brown
Composer: Sharon Arslanian
Category: TAP, INSTRUCTIONAL
Dance on Camera Festival 1991 Silver Award
A veteran hoofer who appeared with Bill Robinson's revue in the '30s and the Art Tatus Show in the '40s, explains his own unique style of tap dance: fast, crisp shuffles, solid flat-footed stamps, staccato heel drops, and graceful crossovers, all executed with a seemingly effortless lightness. He demonstrates how he applied "Scientific Rhythm" to a variety of music/dance forms: Highland fling, soft-shoe, swing, and waltz clog. Also included are improvised dances to three jazz standards: *Just Friends, Indiana,* and *Mellow Tone.*

EDO: DANCE AND PANTOMIME

1972, 50 min. color film, video
Distributors: Asia Society, Museum at Large
Producers: Asia Society and Museum at Large
Directors: Hans Namuth, Paul Valkenberg
Dance Company: Taneo Wakayama and Company
Category: ASIA, PANTOMIME
This three-part film recreates the Lincoln Center performance of three dance pantomimes of the Tokugama period (1600–1867): *Orochi Taiji* (Destroying the Eight-Headed Serpent); *Keishin Aikoku* (Homage to the Gods and Love for the Homeland); and *Kotobuki Jishi* (The Felicitous Lion).

EIGHT GREAT STEPS TO CHOREOGRAPHY

1995, 40 min. color video
Series: Tools For Choreography
Distributor: ClearWater Productions
Producer: Don Gosselin
Director: Neil Colligan
Choreographer: Daryl Gray
Composers: Felix Mendelssohn, Georges Bizet, Richard Strauss
Category: INSTRUCTIONAL, CHOREOGRAPHY
Presents eight fundamental choreographic concepts utilized with eight ballet steps, demonstrating how to construct dances for small and large groups. Available with instructional workbook and audiotape.

ELECTRIC BOOGIE

1983, 30 min. color film, video
Distributor: Filmakers Library
Producers: Tana Ross and Freke Vuijst
Category: SOCIAL, DOCUMENTARY PORTRAITS
American Film Festival 1984 Blue Ribbon
Four boys from the Bronx live, eat and sleep "electric boogie".

ELEGY

1982, 9 min. color film
Distributor: Debra Zalkind Talking Dance Foundation
Producer: Debra Zalkind
Director: Jay Schlossberg Cohen
Choreographer: Debra Zalkind
Principal Dancer: Debra Zalkind
Composer: Gabriel Fauré
Category: MODERN
A young girl tries to come to an understanding of death, as choreographed by a former member

of the modern dance companies of Lar Lubovitch and Twyla Tharp.

ELEMENT

1973, 12 min. b&w film, video
Distributor: Film-makers' Cooperative
Director: Amy Greenfield
Choreographer: Amy Greenfield
Principal Dancer: Amy Greenfield
Category: EXPERIMENTAL
A woman falls, rolls, and rises out of mud, as a metaphor of primordial ooze. Exploring weight, tension and texture in repetitive patterns, the collaborators probe for the essence of female sensuality. *Tides,* also available from Film-makers' Cooperative, is a similar exercise film set in water rather than mud and set in slow-motion.

ELEMENT

1989, 8 min. color video
Distributor: Deborah Gladstein and Sam Kanter
Producers: Deborah Gladstein, Sam Kanter
Director: Sam Kanter
Principal Dancers: Deborah Gladstein, Jennifer Lane, Robbyn Scott
Category: EXPERIMENTAL
Explores the expressive force of simple gestures and stillness in the context of the body's relationship to water. The moving water of a sunlit stream creates a dynamic textural background for ever changing configurations of abstracted images of the nude form.

THE ELEMENTS OF DANCE

1989, 15 min. color video
Series: Arts Alive
Distributor: Ririe-Woodbury Dance Company
Producer: Agency for Instructional Television/Bloomington, Indiana
Director: Shirley Ririe
Category: INSTRUCTIONAL, CHILDREN
Dance on Camera Festival 1989 Gold Award
Scripted for teenagers to show how dance training can help develop athletic skills.

ELIOT FELD: ARTISTIC DIRECTOR

1971, 58 min. color video
Distributor: Michael Blackwood Productions
Producer: Michael Blackwood Productions
Directors: Christian Blackwood, Michael Blackwood
Choreographer: Eliot Feld
Principal Dancers: Eliot Feld, Christine Sarry
Dance Company: American Ballet Theatre
Composers: Gustav Mahler, Johannes Brahms
Category: BALLET, DOCUMENTARY PORTRAITS
Commentator: Clive Barnes
Saga of Eliot Feld's initial struggles to form a company for an appearance at the Spoleto Festival, and his American debut at the Brooklyn Academy of Music. Among the excerpts are: *At Midnight, Meadowlark,* and *Intermezzo.*

ELLIS ISLAND

1982, 30 min. color, b&w film, video
Distributor: The Stutz Company
Producer: Bob Rosen for WGBH-TV/Boston
Directors: Meredith Monk, Bob Rosen
Choreographer: Meredith Monk
Composer: Meredith Monk
Category: EXPERIMENTAL

Atlanta Film Festival, San Francisco International Film Festival, CINE Golden Eagle
In this chilling portrait of New York City's chief entry station for immigrants to the U.S., the camera sweeps past the debris of decaying buildings to rest on a group of turn-of-the-century immigrants, whose predicament is relayed through dance and simple, telling gestures.

EMPEROR JONES

1972, 26 min. color film
Distributor: Dance Film Archive
Producer: Steeg Productions
Choreographer: José Limón
Principal Dancers: Clay Taliaferro, Edward DeSoto
Dance Company: American Dance Festival Professional Repertory Company
Category: MODERN, DANCE DRAMA
1920 play about an ex-convict Pullman porter who ruled a West Indian island through fear and exploitation.

ENCOUNTER

1970, 10 min. color film
Distributor: Film-makers' Cooperative
Producer: Amy Greenfield for Dance Circle of Boston
Director: Amy Greenfield
Choreographer: Amy Greenfield
Principal Dancers: Rima Wolff, Amy Greenfield
Category: MODERN, EXPERIMENTAL, WOMEN
Struggle within one woman and between two women.

ENDANCE

1988, 30 min. color video
Series: Alive From Off Center
Distributors: Electronic Arts Intermix, KTCA-TV
Producer: KTCA-TV
Directors: John Sanborn, Mary Perillo
Principal Dancer: Timothy Buckley
Composer: "Blue" Gene Tyranny
Category: MODERN, EXPERIMENTAL
One man's bittersweet farewell to the dance world, with a synthesis of performance, interviews, personal commentary and comic interludes.

THE ENDURING ESSENCE: THE TECHNIQUE AND CHOREOGRAPHY OF ISADORA DUNCAN, REMEMBERED AND RECONSTRUCTED BY GEMZE DE LAPPE

1990, 60 min. color video
Distributor: Images
Producer: Sharon Arslanian
Director: Sharon Arslanian
Choreographer: Isadora Duncan
Principal Dancers: Sharon Arslanian, Gemze de Lappe
Category: INSTRUCTIONAL, MODERN
Reconstructor: Gemze de Lappe
A professional dancer-director-teacher recalls her early Duncan training and describes how she has applied that technique in her approach to dance. Includes a class at Smith College and six dances originally choreographed by Duncan and reconstructed by de Lappe: *Ballspiel, Classical Duet, Water Study, Blessed Spirits, Three Graces,* and *The Mother.*

L'ENFANT ET LES SORTILEGES

1987, 51 min. color video, laser
Distributors: Home Vision, Dance Horizons, Corinth

Producer: National Video Corporation
Director: Hans Hulscher
Choreographer: Jiri Kylian
Dance Company: Nederlands Dans Theatre
Composer: Maurice Ravel
Category: BALLET, DANCE DRAMA
Dance on Camera Festival 1987 Gold Award
Based on a poem by Colette, in which a boy refuses to do his homework and destroys his surroundings after he's punished. The ballet begins as the objects in his room come to life seeking revenge.

ENIGMA VARIATIONS
1970, 33 min. color film
Distributor: Dance Film Archive
Producer: James Archibald
Director: James Archibald
Choreographer: Frederick Ashton
Principal Dancers: Svetlana Beriosova, Anthony Dowell, Stanley Holden, Derek Rencher
Dance Company: Royal Ballet
Composer: Edward Elgar
Category: BALLET, DANCE DRAMA
This English story-ballet is a grand bow to the Edwardian composer, Edward Elgar, created with colorful characters by the director of the Royal Ballet, Sir Frederick Ashton.

ENTR'ACTE
1924, 18 min. b&w film (silent)
Distributor: Dance Film Archive
Director: Rene Clair
Choreographer: Jean Borlin
Dance Company: Ballets Suédois
Composer: Erik Satie
Category: BALLET, DANCE HISTORY
Rene Clair's second film, a zany, Dada-inspired, silent masterpiece, formed part of Jean Borlin's *Relache* performed by the Ballets Suédois. The music by Erik Satie was performed live at screenings of the silent film.

ENTROPY: REVERSE TO OMEGA
1993, 15 min. color video
Distributor: Valk, Achmed
Producer: Achmed Valk
Director: Achmed Valk
Choreographer: Achmed Valk
Dance Company: Kansas State Repertory Dance Company
Composer: Glenn Grayson
Category: CINEDANCE
A multicamera, high-tech dance made for video that explores the cyclical and metaphysical nature of beginnings and endings, as represented by the Omega point.

ERICK HAWKINS
1964, 15 min. b&w film
Distributor: UCLA Instructional Media Library
Producer: UCLA
Dance Company: Erick Hawkins Dance Company
Category: MODERN COMPANIES
Hawkins, a former Martha Graham dancer, performs dances from his repertory with his company, followed by a discussion of possible interpretations of the pieces, their significance in the modern dance movement, and the relationship of modern dance to the other performing arts.

ERICK HAWKINS' AMERICA
1992, 57 min. color video
Distributor: Dance Horizons
Choreographer: Erick Hawkins
Dance Company: Erick Hawkins Dance Company
Composers: Alan Hovhannes, Virgil Thomson, David Diamond
Category: MODERN, DOCUMENTARY PORTRAITS
Features Hawkins' work on American themes: *Plains Daybreak, Hurrah!, Ahab, God's Angry Man, Classic Kite Tails,* and *Black Lake.*

ERIK BRUHN: ARTIST OF THE BALLET
1973, 21 min. color film
Distributor: Audience Planners
Producer: Danish Government Film Office
Principal Dancers: Erik Bruhn, Carla Fracci
Category: BALLET, DOCUMENTARY PORTRAITS
Commentator: Clive Barnes
An interview with world-renowned Danish ballet dancer, the late Erik Bruhn, onstage, in a television studio, as ballet master, and in rehearsal with the Italian prima ballerina Carla Fracci.

THE ERIK BRUHN GALA: WORLD BALLET COMPETITION
1983, 90 min. color video
Distributors: Home Vision, Corinth, Viewfinders
Producers: RM Arts and Canadian Broadcasting Corporation
Director: Norman Campbell
Principal Dancers: Karen Kain, Glen Tetley, Natalia Makarova, Kevin McKenzie, Owen Montague, Bonnie Moore, Martine Lamy
Dance Company: National Ballet of Canada, Royal Ballet, Royal Danish Ballet, American Ballet Theatre
Category: BALLET, FESTIVALS
Gala for the first Erik Bruhn prize competition held in Toronto, Canada, with dancers from four of the companies with which he is most closely associated, in honor of the great dancer and choreographer. Includes an excerpt from *Swan Lake.*

ESSENTIAL BALLET: RUSSIAN BALLET
1994, 90 min. color video, laser
Distributors: Laserdisc Fan Club, Home Vision, Facets
Principal Dancers: Yulia Makhalina, Andris Liepa, Larissa Lezhina, Faroukh Ruzimatov, Maya Plisetskaya, Nina Ananiashvili
Dance Company: Kirov Ballet
Composer: Peter Ilyich Tchaikovsky
Category: BALLET
Stars of the Russian ballet in performance in London and Moscow. Part 1 presents the Kirov at the Royal Opera House and part 2 is a special outdoor performance in Moscow's Red Square. Excerpts include: *Swan Lake, The Nutcracker, Diana and Actaeon, Sleeping Beauty, Don Quixote, Le Corsaire, Gisèlle,* and *The Firebird.*

ESSENTIALS OF TAP TECHNIQUE
1990, 6:30 min. color video
Distributors: Electronic Arts Intermix, Circuit Theatre, In Motion Productions
Producer: Susan Goldbetter
Director: Skip Blumberg
Choreographers: Charles Charles Cook;

Principal Dancers: Charles Cook, Brenda Bufalino, Kevin Ramsey
Category: INSTRUCTIONAL, TAP
Dance on Camera Festival 1991 Silver Award
A graphic analysis of tap dance essentials. Red tap shoes open this artful short with slow-motion and amplified sound for the actual flaps, stamps, and tempos to get the rhythms. Each expert demonstrates his or her trademark steps with inserts of the full body.

ETERNAL CIRCLE
1952, 12 min. b&w film
Distributor: Dance Film Archive
Director: Herbert Seggelke
Choreographer: Harald Kreutzberg
Principal Dancer: Harald Kreutzberg
Composer: Freiderich Wilckens
Category: MODERN, DANCE HISTORY
A masked solo, choreographed in the 1930s by a German dancer born in Czechoslovakia in 1902, depicting a drunk, a prostitute, a king, and finally, death.

ETHNIC DANCE AROUND THE WORLD
1983, 24 min. color film, video
Distributor: Phoenix
Producer: Wayne Mitchell
Category: FOLK, INTERNATIONAL
Examples of dances from the Americas, Asia, Africa, Europe and Australia explain why dances and music vary from one culture to the next. Depicts the religious basis of many dances, as well as dances for planting and harvesting, courtship, and entertaining royalty.

ETHNIC DANCE: ROUNDTRIP TO TRINIDAD
1960, 29 min. b&w film, video
Series: A Time To Dance
Distributor: Indiana University
Producer: WGBH-TV/Boston
Choreographer: Geoffrey Holder
Principal Dancers: Geoffrey Holder, Carmen de Lavallade
Category: CARIBBEAN
Explores the significance of Caribbean dance in the context of concert dance, with performances of *Bele,* adapted from the European minuet, *Yanvallou,* part of the voodoo ritual, and *Banda,* a Haitian dance of death.

ÉTUDE IN FREE
1982, 8 min. color video
Distributor: ARC Videodance
Producers: Jeff Bush and Celia Ipiotis
Directors: Jeff Bush, Celia Ipiotis
Choreographer: Dianne McIntyre
Principal Dancer: Dianne McIntyre
Composer: Bobby McFerrin
Category: EXPERIMENTAL, MODERN
Coordinating body, mind, and voice, in a style akin to singer Bobby McFerrin's, the dancer builds a quiet, lyric solo to an explosive high and then lets it fade to black.

EVA AS DANCER (2 videos)
199?, 120 min. each color video
Distributor: Cernik, Eva
Principal Dancer: Eva Cernik
Category: MIDDLE EAST
Excerpts chosen from the dance career of Eva Cernik from 1980–91. Includes veil, nightclub, sword, and whirling dervish dances (Volume I)

and many others such as classical Oriental, East European gypsy and Kuwaiti traditional dances (Volume II), taped indoors and outdoors with live music.

AN EVENING WITH ALVIN AILEY AMERICAN DANCE THEATRE

1987, 110 min. color video
Distributors: Home Vision, Viewfinders, Corinth, Voyager, Facets
Producer: RM Associates
Director: Thomas Grimm
Choreographers: Alvin Ailey, Judith Jamison, Talley Beatty
Dance Company: Alvin Ailey American Dance Theatre
Composers: Alice Coltrane, Laura Nyro, Gospel and Blues
Category: MODERN COMPANIES, AFRICAN-AMERICANS
Dance On Camera Festival 1987 Honorable Mention
Performance tape of *Divining,* choreographed by Judith Jamison, former company member and current director of the Ailey company, *Stack-Up* by Talley Beatty, and two by the founder Alvin Ailey, *Revelations,* and the solo *Cry.*

AN EVENING WITH KYLIAN AND THE NEDERLANDS DANS THEATRE

1987, 87 min. color video, laser
Distributors: Home Vision, Dance Horizons, Viewfinders, Corinth
Producer: RM Associates
Directors: Hans Hulscher, Torbjörn Ehrnvall
Choreographer: Jiri Kylian
Dance Company: Nederlands Dans Theatre
Composers: Igor Stravinsky, Toru Takemitsu, Claude Debussy, Leo Janácek
Category: BALLET COMPANIES
Dance on Camera Festival 1987 Silver Award
Four ballets by the acclaimed Dutch choreographer: *Svadebka* (*Les Noces*) set to music of Igor Stravinsky, *La Cathédrale Engloutie* (Debussy), *Sinfonietta* (Janácek), and *Torso* (Takemitsu).

AN EVENING WITH THE BALLET RAMBERT

1986, 103 min. color video
Distributors: Home Vision, Dance Horizons, Viewfinders, Corinth
Producer: RM Arts
Director: Thomas Grimm
Choreographers: Robert North, Christopher Bruce
Dance Company: Ballet Rambert
Composers: Bill Withers, Leo Janácek
Category: BALLET COMPANIES
Dance on Camera Festival 1987 Honorable Mention
Three pieces by the British-based ballet company founded by Marie Rambert in 1926. Performances of *Lonely Town, Lonely Street* (North/Withers), *Intimate Pages* (Bruce/Janácek), *Sergeant Early's Dream,* with choreography by Christopher Bruce set to folk songs.

AN EVENING WITH THE ROYAL BALLET

1963, 85 min. color video, laser
Distributors: Kultur, Dance Horizons, Viewfinders, Corinth, Home Vision, Media Basics
Producer: British Home Entertainment
Directors: Anthony Asquith, Havelock Allan
Choreographers: Michel Fokine, Rudolf Nureyev, Marius Petipa, Frederick Ashton
Principal Dancers: Margot Fonteyn, Rudolf Nureyev, Antoinette Sibley, David Blair
Composers: Peter Ilyich Tchaikovsky, Frédéric Chopin, Adolphe Adam
Category: BALLET COMPANIES
Performances of *La Valse,* and excerpt from *Les Sylphides, Pas de Deux* from *Le Corsaire,* and *Aurora's Wedding* from *Sleeping Beauty* filmed live at the Royal Opera House, Covent Garden, London.

EVENT FOR TELEVISION

1977, 56 min. color film, video
Series: Dance in America
Distributor: Cunningham Dance Foundation
Producer: Emile Ardolino
Director: Merrill Brockway
Choreographer: Merce Cunningham
Principal Dancer: Merce Cunningham
Composers: John Cage, David Tudor
Category: MODERN
Cunningham performs excerpts from *Minutiae* (1954), *Septet* (1953), *Antic Meet* (1958), *Scramble* (1967), *Rainforest* (1968), *Sounddance* (1974), and *Video Triangle* (1976)

EVERYBODY DANCE NOW

1992, 60 min. color video
Series: Dance in America
Distributor: VPI
Producer: Margaret Selby
Choreographers: Cholly Atkins, Jamale Graves, Michael Kidd
Principal Dancers: James Brown, Madonna, Michael Jackson, Janet Jackson, Paula Abdul, M.C. Hammer
Category: MUSIC VIDEOS
Peabody Award 1992, Montreux Golden Rose Festival Bronze Prize
A spectrum of dance in music videos, from street performers to superstars. Dancers, choreographers and film directors share their insight along with footage from the videos.

EVERYTHING YOU SHOULD KNOW ABOUT HAWAIIAN/TAHITIAN HULA (2 videos)

1990, 60 min. (Tahitian), 80 min. (Hawaiian), color video
Distributor: Charmaine
Principal Dancer: Charmaine
Category: HULA, INSTRUCTIONAL
Variations with step and arm movements, background history, and an explanation of language and costumes.

EXCERPTS FROM *WITHOUT A PLACE*

1992, 7 min. color video
Distributor: Julie Miller Productions
Producer: Julie Miller
Director: Julie Miller
Choreographer: Joe Goode
Principal Dancers: Elizabeth Burnitt, Suellen Einairsen
Dance Company: Joe Goode Performance Group
Composers: Erik Walker, Joe Goode
Category: MODERN, EXPERIMENTAL
Dance on Camera Festival 1992
Interviews and performance footage of the Joe Goode Performance Group showcase an innovative blend of postmodern dance and experimental theatre.

EXOTIC AND ACROBATIC DANCES

1900, 10 min. b&w film (silent)
Distributor: Dance Film Archive
Category: DANCE HISTORY
Silent film from the turn-of-the-century featuring Spanish exhibition dancing and contortionists.

THE EYE HEARS, THE EAR SEES

1970, 59 min. color film
Distributors: National Film Board of Canada, Karol
Producers: National Film Board of Canada and BBC-TV
Choreographer: Ludmilla Chiriaeff
Principal Dancers: Margaret Mercier, Vincent Warren
Category: DOCUMENTARY PORTRAITS, CINEDANCE
Narrators: Gavin Millar, Grant Munro
Norman McLaren explains his attraction to film and his discontent with conventional techniques. Includes excerpts from his films *Hen Hop* and *Pas de Deux.*

THE EYE ON DANCE COLLECTION (over 325 programs)

1981–present, 30 min. each color video
Distributor: ARC Videodance
Producers: Jeff Bush and Celia Ipiotis for ARC Videodance
Category: DANCE HISTORY
The oldest weekly issue-based television series on dance and dance history hosted by Celia Ipiotis, now running prime time in the New York Metropolitan area on WNYC/TV, offers a standard format of one to three guests with short performance clips or stills. With a collection of over 325 programs, the series includes intensive coverage of the issues affecting the world of dance and an introduction to the broad spectrum of artists, producers, technicians, and specialists in support services. The topics range from collaborations, health, partnering, reconstructions, to tricks of surviving as an artist. The complete collection is available for viewing at the Dance Collection of The New York Public Library at Lincoln Center.

FALL RIVER LEGEND

1971, 10 min. color film
Distributors: AIMS Media, University of Minnesota
Producer: Bob Shanks
Director: Bob Shanks
Choreographer: Agnes de Mille
Principal Dancers: Sallie Wilson, Lucia Chase, Tom Adair
Dance Company: American Ballet Theatre
Composer: Morton Gould
Category: DANCE DRAMA, BALLET
Excerpts from the 1948 ballet based on the true story of Lizzie Borden, accused of murdering her father and stepmother with an axe in 1892. Filmed at Sturbridge, Massachusetts.

FALLING DOWN STAIRS

1995, 56 min. color video
Series: Inspired by Bach
Distributor: Rhombus International
Producer: Niv Fichman
Director: Barbara Willis Sweete
Dancer: Mark Morris

Dance Company: Mark Morris Dance Group
Composer: Johann Sebastian Bach
Category: COLLABORATION, DOCUMENTARY PORTRAITS
Dance on Camera Festival 1996 Gold Award
In this episode we see renowned cello virtuoso Yo-Yo Ma embark on an intense year-long collaboration with Mark Morris, the "enfant terrible" of the American dance world. The film follows Morris and Ma to New York, Boston, Toronto, and Jacob's Pillow, documenting their collaboration with remarkable intimacy, humor and candor. The finale is a spectacular performance of J.S. Bach's *3rd Cello Suite* especially for the screen with stunning costumes by designer Isaac Mizrahi.

FALLING OFF THE BACK PORCH
1983, 15 min. color video
Series: The Educational Performance Collection
Distributor: Dance Notation Bureau
Producer: Dance Notation Bureau
Choreographer: Clay Taliaferro
Composer: Claude Debussy
Category: MODERN, NOTATION
Taped performance at Arizona State University of a dance that acknowledges the challenge of living with inconsistencies. Multimedia kit provides advanced level labanotated score by Mary Corey, critical text, and study/performance rights.

FAME
1980, 127 min. color film, video
Distributors: Swank, MGM/UA
Producer: United Artists
Director: Alan Parker
Choreographer: Louis Falco
Principal Dancers: Gene Ray, Carol Massenberg
Composer: Michael Gore
Category: FEATURES, MUSICALS
Set in Manhattan's celebrated High School of the Performing Arts, the story concerns the hopes and dreams of eight young would-be stars. Musical numbers include the audition sequence and *Hot Lunch*.

FAN AND BUBBLE DANCES
1942, 9 min. b&w film
Distributor: Dance Film Archive
Principal Dancers: Sally Rand, Faith Bacon
Category: DANCE HISTORY
Sally Rand set the reputation of strippers in America on a new track by artfully disguising her nude body with a giant fan.

FAN TECHNIQUES FOR ORIENTAL DANCE (2 videos)
1988–89, 63 and 85 min. color video
Distributor: Chandra of Damascus
Choreographer: Chandra of Damascus
Principal Dancer: Chandra of Damascus
Category: MIDDLE EAST
A discussion of various types of fans with demonstrations of ways to use each type in Middle Eastern dance. In the second video, the demonstration shows how to use a fan with a veil, along with tips on dancing with two and three veils together.

FANDANGO
1991, 15 min. color video
Distributor: Rhombus International
Producers: Barbara Willis Sweete and Niv Fichman
Director: Barbara Willis Sweete
Choreographer: Lar Lubovich
Principal Dancers: Sylvain Lafortune, Mia Babalis
Composer: Maurice Ravel
Category: CINEDANCE, MODERN
International Emmy Awards 1992 Best Performing Arts, Chicago International Film Festival 1992 First Prize
Uses a moving camera to capture two dancers performing in a timeless, indefinable setting dominated by a gigantic clockwork wheel ceaselessly turning. Part 2 of *Pictures on the Edge*.

FANTASIA
1940, 120 min. color film, video
Distributors: Buena Vista, Facets
Producer: Walt Disney
Director: Ben Sharpsteen
Composers: Johann Sebastian Bach, Peter Ilyich Tchaikovsky, Paul Dukas, Igor Stravinsky, Ludwig van Beethoven, Modest Petrovich Mussorgsky, Franz Schubert
Category: ANIMATION, FEATURES
Eight concert pieces choreographed through animation. The Sorcerer's Apprentice, among other animated characters, moves with a grace and musicality few ballerinas would dare to challenge. Also to be noted for its brilliant choreographic invention within animated form: Disney's *Lady and the Tramp* (1955), *Sleeping Beauty* (1959), *Dumbo* (1941), available through Buena Vista.

A FANTASY GARDEN BALLET CLASS: BALLET INSTRUCTION WITH GARDEN CREATURES FOR PRE-SCHOOLERS and CLASS II (2 videos)
1992, 1996, 40 min. each color video
Distributors: Kultur, Dance Horizons
Producer: New Sounds for Dance
Category: CHILDREN, INSTRUCTIONAL, BALLET
These unique ballet classes, created especially for preschoolers, associates each of the five basic ballet steps with flowers and garden animals. Help children remember ballet terminology easily and enjoy warm-up, stretching and strengthening exercises, rhythmics, elementary ballet steps and floor exercises.

FANTASY OF FEET
1970, 8 min. color film, video
Series: Magic Movements Unit 3 Let's See Series
Distributor: Encyclopedia Britannica
Category: CHILDREN, INSTRUCTIONAL
Little feet walk, dance, run and jump in sandals, flippers, slippers, boots, and barefoot. Encourages children to realize how shoes and the surfaces they're designed for affect our movements.

FASHIONS OF 1934
1934, 78 min. b&w video
Distributor: Facets
Producer: Warner Brothers
Director: William Dieterle
Choreographer: Busby Berkeley
Category: FEATURES, MUSICALS
A con man and his girlfriend steal the latest Paris creations.

FEATHERS
3 min. color film
Distributor: Dance Film Archive

Choreographer: William Dunas
Category: WOMEN, DANCE HISTORY
Classically oriented solos for women.

FESTIVAL IN COMMEMORATION OF THE DEAD
1965, 14 min. color film
Distributor: PennState
Producer: Wissen
Category: AFRICA, RELIGIOUS/RITUAL, FESTIVALS
In a village in Mali, sacrificial goats and millet beer are brought to a festival in which dancers wearing *kanaga* masks appear. A similar ceremony is filmed in *Festival in Commemoration of the Dead at Ningari*, also from PennState.

FESTIVAL OF THE DANCE
1973, 60 min. color film
Distributor: Dance Film Archive
Producer: Ted Steeg
Director: Ted Steeg
Choreographers: Doris Humphrey, Martha Graham, Charles Weidman, José Limón
Composers: Heitor Villa-Lobos, Lionel Nowak, Wallingford Riegger
Category: MODERN, FESTIVALS
A company performs modern dance classics at the American Dance Festival at Connecticut College in 1972, with shots of auditions, rehearsals and performance excerpts from *Emperor Jones*, *Flickers*, *New Dance*, and *With My Red Fires*.

FIDDLER ON THE ROOF
1971, 169 min. color film, video, laser
Distributors: Facets, Swank, MGM/UA
Producer: United Artists
Director: Norman Jewison
Choreographers: Tom Abbott, Jerome Robbins
Principal Dancers: Neva Small, Rosalind Harris, Michele Marsh
Composer: Jerry Bock
Category: FEATURES, MUSICALS
Adapted from the stories of Sholom Aleichem about the efforts of Tevye, a milkman in a Russian shtetl of 1905, to find traditional marriages for his four daughters. Dance numbers include *Wedding Celebration* and *Chava Ballet*.

FIELDS
1987, 11 min. color video
Distributor: Electronic Arts Intermix
Director: James Byrne
Choreographer: Susan Hadley
Composer: Bradley Sowash
Category: MODERN, EXPERIMENTAL
Filmed in plowed fields and in an urban plaza where dancers clad in suits suggest the gestures of farmers.

THE FIGHT
1992, 8 min. b&w film
Distributor: Frameline
Producer: Núria Olivé-Bellés
Director: Núria Olivé-Bellés
Choreographer: Núria Olivé-Bellés
Principal Dancers: Javier De Frutos, Ramón Baeza, Larry Goldhuber
Composer: Núria Olivé-Bellés
Category: MODERN
Krakow Film Festival 1994 Golden Dinosaur Egg, Cinevue International Film Festival (Florida) 1994 Second Place

Body-to-body in a boxing ring, two men measure themselves by their physical strength, power, and an unexpected challenge.

LA FILLE MAL GARDÉE (Basler Ballett)
1987, 78 min. color laser
Distributor: Viewfinders
Producers: WDR and UNITEL Film
Director: Josie Montes-Baquer
Choreographer: Heinz Spoerli
Dance Company: Basler Ballett
Composers: Louis Joseph, Ferdinand Hérold, Peter Ludwig Hertel
Category: FULL-LENGTH BALLETS
Tells the story of a farmer's daughter who manages to win the man she loves despite her mother's effort to marry her off to a dim-witted wealthy suitor.

LA FILLE MAL GARDÉE (Royal Ballet)
1981, 98 min. color video, laser
Distributors: Home Box Office, Home Vision, Music Video Distributors, Corinth, Media Basics
Producer: National Video Corporation
Director: John Vernon
Choreographer: Frederick Ashton
Principal Dancers: Lesley Collier, Michael Coleman, Leslie Edwards
Dance Company: Royal Ballet
Composer: Ferdinand Hérold
Category: FULL-LENGTH BALLETS
Instilling obedience in willful children has never been easy, whether in 1879, the premiere of this ballet by Jean Dauberval, or in 1960, the debut for Frederick Ashton's version. Ashton adds various English folk dances (maypole, morris, sword and Lancashire clog) to give a rustic feeling to the story of a young girl evading a planned marriage.

FILM WITH THREE DANCERS
1970, 20 min. color film
Distributors: Canyon Cinema, Film-makers' Cooperative
Director: Ed Emshwiller
Principal Dancers: Carolyn Carlson, Emery Hermans, Bob Beswick
Category: MODERN, EXPERIMENTAL
Sorrento Film Festival, Whitney Art Museum Series
A trio of dancers, first in leotards, then blue jeans, then nude, are shown in stylized and abstract images accompanied by naturalistic and abstract sounds.

THE FIREBIRD
1980s, 55 min. color video
Distributors: Home Vision, Viewfinders, Corinth, Media Basics
Producer: RM Arts
Director: Thomas Grimm
Choreographer: Glen Tetley
Dance Company: Royal Danish Ballet
Composer: Igor Stravinsky
Category: FULL-LENGTH BALLETS
RAI Prize, Prix Italia
A firebird, kept in an enchanted garden, is guarded by a severe Victorian family. With the help of her lover, the firebird liberates herself from the family's bonds. Not to be confused with the original *Firebird* choreographed by Michel Fokine and premiered by Diaghilev's Ballets Russes in 1910, Adolph Bolm's version of 1945, or George Balanchine's of 1949.

FIRST SOLO
1982, 10 min. color video
Distributor: Rush Dance Company
Director: Davidson Gigliotti
Choreographer: Patrice Regnier
Principal Dancer: Sallie Wilson
Category: MODERN
Solo created for the ballerina known for her interpretation of Antony Tudor's ballets.

FIRST STEPS
1984, 26 min. color film, video
Distributor: Phoenix
Producers: Ted Haimes and Pamela Emil
Director: Ted Haimes
Category: CHILDREN, INSTRUCTIONAL, CIRCUS ARTS
Each fall, representatives of the Alvin Ailey Dance Center and the New York School for Circus Arts/Big Apple Circus audition public school students in search of gifted dancers and acrobats. The film follows the students through the year as they study the arts of the trampoline, trapeze, tightrope, and dance.

FLAMENCO
1986, 70 min. color video
Distributors: Alegrías, Films For the Humanities and Sciences, PennState
Producer: Spanish Television
Directors: Reni Mertens, Walter Marti
Principal Dancers: Pepa Guerna, Antonio el Divino
Category: FLAMENCO, HISPANIC
Teacher: Ciro
Jota, bulerías, soleares, malagueña, and *cante jondo,* intercut with sweeps of the landscape, performed by young and old for friends in the four corners of Spain.

FLAMENCO
1994, 100 min. color film
Distributor: New Yorker
Producer: Juan Lebrón
Director: Carlos Saura
Principal Dancer: Joaquín Cortés
Category: FLAMENCO, FEATURES
A performance film featuring three hundred of the greatest musicians, singers and dancers in the art of flamenco.

FLAMENCO AT 5:15
1969, 30 min. color film, video
Distributor: Direct Cinema
Producers: Cynthia Scott and Adam Symansky for National Film Board of Canada
Director: Cynthia Scott
Category: FLAMENCO, INSTRUCTIONAL
Academy Award 1983 Best Documentary Short
Advanced students at the National Ballet School of Canada demonstrate their Spanish dance expertise under the guidance of their teachers, Susana and Antonio Robledo.

FLAMENCO GITANO
1969, 21 min. b&w film
Distributor: PennState
Producer: Wissen
Category: FLAMENCO, HISPANIC
Spanish gypsies demonstrate five types of Andalusian dance: *soleares, alegrías, tanguillos, tientos* and *bulerías,* accompanied by guitars and *palmas.*

FLAMENCOS DE LA LUZ (8 videos)
1984–94, 32–60 min. color video
Distributors: Alegrías, Dance Horizons
Producer: Pilar Pérez de Guzmán
Director: Antonio G. Olea
Principal Dancers: Pilar Pérez de Guzmán, Manuel Badillo
Composer: Miguel Rivera
Category: FLAMENCO, INSTRUCTIONAL
Guitarist: Miguel Rivera
Singer: Rafael Fajardo
Comprehensive course on flamenco with concentrated lessons in: *sevillanas,* the popular social dance for couples once the pastime of the Andalusians but now in discos all over Europe (*Course in Sevillanas,* 60 min.); the basics of heelwork, arms, rhythms and the dancer's relationship with the guitarist (*The Basics of Flamenco Dance,* 45 min.); the sensuality of the flamenco-rumba (*Course in Rumba,* 50 min.); the speed and precision of castanets (*Course in Castanets,* 54 min.); the *cante* or accompanying song of flamenco (*Danza Flamenco de Hoy,* 60 min.); a flamenco performance taped in a *tablao* (nightclub) in Madrid (*Show Flamenco,* 40 min.); modern, classical and gypsy styles of guitar (*The Spanish Guitar,* 45 min.); and a performance by Angelita Vargas dancing with her eight-year-old niece and other young dancers, featuring *bulerías* and tangos (*¡Fiesta Gitana!,* 32 min.). Available in either Spanish or English.

THE FLAPPER STORY
1985, 29 min. color film, video
Distributor: The Cinema Guild
Director: Lauren Lazin
Category: SOCIAL, WOMEN
Academy of Picture Arts and Science Documentary Merit Award, Chicago International Film Festival Silver Plaque, Philadelphia International Film Festival, CINE Golden Eagle Award
A mix of contemporary interviews and archival film footage examining the provocative "new woman" of America's Roaring Twenties.

FLASHDANCE
1983, 95 min. color film, video
Distributors: Films Inc., Paramount
Producer: Paramount
Director: Adrian Lyne
Choreographer: Jeffrey Hornaday
Principal Dancers: Marine Jahan, Jennifer Beals, Michael Nouri
Category: FEATURES, JAZZ
Blue-collar worker by day, erotic dancer by night, and lover whenever feasible, the heroine shocks and delights the stodgy jury when she auditions for the Pittsburgh Ballet.

FLICKERS
1972, 19 min. color film
Distributor: Dance Film Archive
Producer: Ted Steeg
Director: Ted Steeg
Choreographer: Charles Weidman
Principal Dancer: Linda Tarnay
Dance Company: Professional Repertory Company at Connecticut College
Category: MODERN, DANCE HISTORY

A zany spoof of silent movies in four parts: *Hearts Aflame, Wages of Sin, Flowers of the Desert* and *Hearts Courageous*. Originally choreographed in 1941, with Doris Humphrey and Charles Weidman in the leading roles.

FLUTE OF KRISHNA
1926, 10 min. color film (silent)
Distributor: Dance Film Archive
Producer: Eastman Kodak Company
Choreographer: Martha Graham
Principal Dancers: Robert Ross, Evelyn Sabin, Betty MacDonald, Suzanne Vacanti
Category: MODERN, DANCE HISTORY
Choreographed by Martha Graham while in residence at the Eastman School of Music, which produced this silent film as part of an experiment with a two-color process.

FLYING DOWN TO RIO
1933, 89 min. b&w film, video, laser
Distributors: Films Inc., Facets
Producer: RKO
Director: Thornton Freeland
Choreographers: Dave Gould, Fred Astaire, Hermes Pan
Principal Dancers: Fred Astaire, Ginger Rogers, Dolores del Rio
Composer: Vincent Youmans
Category: FEATURES, TAP
A musical combining the elements of dance, song, and aviation with a South American background. Best known for its "floorshow" finale, which consists of a large-scale dance on a fleet of airplanes. It is also known for Astaire and Roger's first dance on screen together, *The Carioca*. Other dance numbers include *Orchids in the Moonlight* and *Music Makes Me*.

FLYING LOTUS: CHAMPION ACROBATS OF CHINA
1992, 43 min. color video
Distributor: V.I.E.W.
Producers: The Beijing Scientific and Educational Film Studio
Category: CIRCUS ARTS
Female champion acrobats perform innovative routines based on the twenty-five hundred-year-old tradition. Routines include: *Ten Levels to the Heavens* (pyramid of benches), *High Above . . . the Flower Opens* (bicycle balancing), and *The Peacock Spreads Its Tail* (stunt cycling).

FOLKLÓRICO
1989, 29 min. color video
Distributor: Barr Films
Producer: Center Communications
Category: FOLK, LATIN AMERICA
Rehearsals, performances and interviews with experts on the folk music and dance of Mexico and southwestern United States.

FOLKMOOT USA (30 videos)
1984, color video
Producer: Folkmoot USA
Distributor: Folkmoot USA
Category: FOLK, FESTIVALS
Launched in 1984 by Dr. Clinton Border, a retired surgeon, Folkmoot is the largest international folk festival in the United States. On the average, three hundred and fifty folk dancers perform in schools and street fairs for eleven days. Twelve videos cover the annual event while others highlight the following countries: England, France, Germany, Ireland, Italy, Korea, Mexico, Poland, Puerto Rico, Russia, Spain. In addition there are videos focusing on Appalachia, clogging, folk games, a compilation video titled *The Best of Folkmoot USA*, *The North Carolina International Folk Festival*, and *1984 A Documentary*.

FOLLOW THE FLEET
1936, 110 min. b&w film, video, laser
Distributors: Films Inc., Facets, Laserdisc Fan Club, Media Basics
Producer: RKO
Director: Mark Sandrich
Choreographers: Fred Astaire, Hermes Pan
Principal Dancers: Fred Astaire, Ginger Rogers, Randolph Scott
Composer: Irving Berlin
Category: FEATURES, TAP
A former vaudeville team—a sailor and a dance hall singer—meet again in a ballroom in San Francisco. Dance numbers include *Let Yourself Go, I'd Rather Head a Band*, and *Let's Face the Music and Dance*.

FONTEYN AND NUREYEV: THE PERFECT PARTNERSHIP
1985, 90 min. color video, laser
Distributors: Kultur, Dance Horizons, Viewfinders, Corinth, Home Vision
Producer: Peter Batty
Choreographers: Frederick Ashton, Marius Petipa
Principal Dancers: Margot Fonteyn, Rudolf Nureyev, Ninette de Valois
Composers: Sergei Prokofiev, Peter Ilyich Tchaikovsky
Category: BALLET, DOCUMENTARY PORTRAITS
Narrator: Robert Powell
This retrospective traces the Fonteyn-Nureyev partnership from its inception in 1962 to conclusion in 1978, with commentary, behind-the-scenes footage, and excerpts from *Marguerite and Armand, Romeo and Juliet, Le Corsaire, Lucifer, Sleeping Beauty*, and *Les Sylphides*.

FOOTAGE
1976, 9:30 min. color film
Distributor: Film-makers' Cooperative
Director: Dave Gearey
Principal Dancers: Dana Reitz
Category: EXPERIMENTAL
Anthology Film Archives 1980
Feet running, digging into mud and sand, playing with the air, and casting shadows.

FOOTLIGHT PARADE
1933, 104 min. b&w film, video, laser
Distributors: Swank, Facets
Producer: Warner Brothers
Director: Lloyd Bacon
Choreographer: Busby Berkeley
Principal Dancers: James Cagney, Ruby Keeler
Composers: Harry Warren, Sammy Fain
Category: FEATURES, MUSICALS
One of the legendary "backstage musicals" of 1933 about the personal and professional problems encountered by a kinetic imaginative director who is creating a series of mini-musicals known as prologues. Musical numbers include *Shanghai Lil* and *By a Waterfall*.

FOOTLOOSE
1984, 106 min. color film, video
Distributors: Films Inc., Paramount
Producer: Paramount
Director: Herbert Ross
Choreographer: Lynn Taylor-Corbett
Principal Dancers: Kevin Bacon, Lori Singer
Category: FEATURES, JAZZ
A city boy visits an uptight, small town in the Midwest and gets everyone to dance, forbidden among the majority of people in this Bible Belt town, who have been following the dictates of local religious authorities.

FOR DANCERS
1989, 17 min. color film
Distributor: Picture Start, BAM Productions
Producer: Bridget Murnane
Director: Bridget Murnane
Principal Dancers: Fred Strickler, Iris Pell, Louise Burns, Susan Rose
Composers: Megan Roberts, Benjamin Britten
Category: TAP, MODERN
Dance on Camera Festival 1990 Honorable Mention
Fred Strickler, a tap dancer, Louise Burns, a former Merce Cunningham dancer, and Susan Rose, a Boston-based modern dancer-choreographer, perform their own choreography and a work by Bella Lewitzky.

FOR ME AND MY GAL
1942, 100 min. b&w video
Distributors: Facets, Swank, MGM/UA
Producer: MGM
Director: Busby Berkeley
Choreographer: Bobby Connolly
Principal Dancers: Gene Kelly, Judy Garland, George Murphy
Composer: George W. Meyer
Category: FEATURES, MUSICALS
A female vaudevillian has to choose between two partners.

FOR THE LOVE OF DANCE
1981, 57:46 min. color film, video
Distributor: National Film Board of Canada
Producer: National Film Board of Canada
Directors: Michael McKennirey, Cynthia Scott, David Wilson, John D. Smith
Dance Company: Les Grands Ballets Canadiens, National Ballet of Canada, Toronto Dance Theatre, Le Groupe de la Place Royale, Winnipeg Ballet, Winnipeg Contemporary Dance Company, Anna Wyman Dance Theater
Category: BALLET COMPANIES
Dance on Camera Festival 1982 Award
A panorama of dance in Canada featuring seven of the country's leading dance companies.

FOR THE SPIDER WOMAN
1970s, 16 min. color film (silent)
Distributor: Dance Film Archive
Choreographer: Jane Comfort
Principal Dancer: Jane Comfort
Category: MODERN, EXPERIMENTAL, WOMEN
The dancer is seen in a solo repeated at various stages of her pregnancy.

FORBIDDEN CITY, U.S.A.
1989, 56 min. color film, video
Distributors: CrossCurrent Media

Producer: Arthur Dong
Director: Arthur Dong
Principal Dancers: Tony and Wing, Mary Mammon, Dottie Sun, Jack Mei Ling
Composer: Gary Stockdale
Category: NIGHTCLUB, DOCUMENTARY PORTRAITS
Dance on Camera Festival 1991
This documentary takes us back to San Francisco's Forbidden City nightclub, the Chinese Cotton Club of the 1930s and '40s. Chinese American performers who appeared regularly at the club discuss how their careers were thwarted by racism. Clips of their performances are included.

42ND STREET

1933, 89 min. b&w film, video, laser
Distributors: Facets, Swank
Producer: Warner Brothers
Director: Lloyd Bacon
Choreographer: Busby Berkeley
Principal Dancers: Ruby Keeler, Dick Powell
Composer: Harry Warren
Category: FEATURES, MUSICALS
One of the legendary "backstage musicals" of 1933, the story traces the many pitfalls along the line to the final production of a Broadway-bound musical comedy. Known for its large-scale musical numbers choreographed by Berkeley, *42nd Street* was one of the first musicals to take full advantage of the medium of film. Musical numbers include: *42nd Street* and *Shuffle Off to Buffalo*.

FOUR DANCE CLASSES IN EGYPT

1980s, 120 min. color video
Distributor: Cernik, Eva
Producer: Eva Cernik
Category: MIDDLE EAST, INSTRUCTIONAL
Teachers: Raqia Hassan, Hana Hassan, Khairiya Maazin
Instructional video on Middle Eastern dance, with the first two classes in the Cairo cabaret style, the third in the *Reda* style with a *Saiidi* routine, the final, a *Ghawazi* cane dance accompanied by *rababa* and *darabukas*.

FOUR JOURNEYS INTO MYSTIC TIME

1978, 109 min. color film
Distributor: Museum of Modern Art
Producers: Shirley Clarke, Marian Scott, Spiral Productions
Director: Shirley Clarke
Choreographer: Marian Scott
Dance Company: University of California at Los Angeles Dance Company
Category: EXPERIMENTAL
Dance on Camera Festival 1979 Honors Award
Of the four journeys, *Mysterium* explores the dynamic union of masculine and feminine, *Initiation* examines the mystery of ancient rites, *Trance* shows a dancer, through video electronics, creating the aura surrounding a soul in transition, and *One-Two-Three* is a comic waltz.

FOUR MOVES IN SPACE: A VIDEODANCE SUITE

1980, 29 min. color video
Distributor: ARC Videodance
Director: Jeff Bush
Choreographer: Celia Ipiotis
Principal Dancer: Celia Ipiotis
Category: EXPERIMENTAL, CINEDANCE

Solos ranging from the stark *A Pity* to the multi-layered and chromafaceted *Galaxy Ebb Tide*, to *Chappaquiddick Evening Song*, shot on the beach after the Kennedy incident, and *Crimson Blue*.

FOUR SOLOS FOR FOUR WOMEN

1980, 28 min. color video
Distributor: Film-makers' Cooperative
Producer: Amy Greenfield
Director: Amy Greenfield
Choreographer: Amy Greenfield
Principal Dancers: Amy Greenfield, Suzanne Gregoire, Susan Hendrickson, Sudabeh Keshmirian
Category: MODERN, WOMEN
Camera: Richard Leacock
Dramatic, personal movement designed for close-ups of four women who arch, stretch, and bend with their hair unbound, their bodies wrapped in satin.

THE FOUR TEMPERAMENTS

1980, 30 min. color film
Series: Dance in America
Distributors: Dance Film Archive, Dance Horizons, Facets
Producer: Emile Ardolino for WNET/13
Director: Merrill Brockway
Choreographer: George Balanchine
Principal Dancers: Bart Cook, Merrill Ashley, Daniel Duell, Peter Martins, Suzanne Farrell, Robert Weiss
Dance Company: New York City Ballet
Composer: Paul Hindemith
Category: FULL-LENGTH BALLETS
Dance on Camera Festival 1981
The 1946 ballet by the late Russian-born choreographer.

FOUR WOMEN

1979, 4 min. color video
Distributor: Third World Newsreel
Producer: Ilanga Witt
Director: Julie Dash
Dance Company: Harlem Preparatory School students
Composer: Nina Simone
Category: WOMEN, AFRICAN-AMERICANS
A dance interpretation of the ballad of Nina Simone on four common stereotypes of African-American women.

FRACTIONS I

1978, 33 min. color, b&w film, video
Distributor: Cunningham Dance Foundation
Producer: Cunningham Dance Foundation
Director: Charles Atlas
Choreographer: Merce Cunningham
Principal Dancers: Karole Armitage, Louise Burns, Graham Conley, Ellen Cornfield, Meg Eginton, Lisa Fox, Chris Komar, Robert Kovich
Dance Company: Merce Cunningham Dance Company
Composer: John Gibson
Category: MODERN, CINEDANCE
A dance choreographed for the camera with the objective of discovering the flexibility of perspective. Dancers appear both outside and within four monitors, all contained within the frame of a fifth monitor.

FRACTURED VARIATIONS and VISUAL SHUFFLE

1986, 14 min. color video
Series: Alive From Off Center

Distributors: The Kitchen, Electronic Arts Intermix
Producer: KTCA-TV
Directors: John Sanborn, Mary Perillo
Choreographer: Charles Moulton
Principal Dancers: Charles Moulton, Beatrice Bogorad, Jackie Goodrich, Christopher Pilafian, Guillermo Resto
Composers: Bill Buchen, Scott Johnson
Category: EXPERIMENTAL, CINEDANCE
Dance on Camera Festival 1986
Two experimental dance collaborations in which the choreography is as much fixed in post as preproduction, as dancers pass through environments created with the HARRY Animation System, ADO, and other special effects devices.

FRAGMENTS: MAT/GLASS

1975, 18 min. b&w video
Distributor: Film-makers' Cooperative
Producer: Amy Greenfield
Director: Amy Greenfield
Choreographer: Amy Greenfield
Principal Dancer: Ben Dolphin
Category: MODERN, CINEDANCE
Two-channel videotape edited by Amy Greenfield from a live video dance performance at New York City's Kitchen Center, during which two cameras shot a solo with live monitors surrounding the performance area to register close-ups, pullbacks, and image inversions.

FRAGMENTS OF VOYAGES IN AFRICA

1984, 30 min. color video
Distributor: Solaris
Producer: Henry Smith
Director: Henry Smith
Principal Dancer: Henry Smith
Dance Company: Solaris Dance Theatre
Category: AFRICA, MODERN
Combines on-location African footage shot along the Congo River, in tribal villages, in the rain forest, and along the rapids of the Congo River, with studio-shot dance impressions of three trips to Senegal, Ghana, and the Congo made by Solaris Dance Theatre in 1980–83.

FRANK HATCHETT: INSPIRATION

1984, 60 min. color video
Distributor: Taffy's By Mail
Producers: Ted and Diane Sorensen for Danzing
Category: INSTRUCTIONAL, JAZZ
Teacher: Frank Hatchett
This documentary catches the excitement of a typical New York jazz class with its intense energy and blend of talent, shapes, ages and personalities. Led by a popular teacher on the dance teachers' convention circuit. Workbook also available.

FRANK HATCHETT PRESENTS SIZZLIN' HOT JAZZ

1989, 30 min. color video
Distributor: Taffy's By Mail
Producer: Frank Hatchett
Category: JAZZ, INSTRUCTIONAL
Warm-up exercises, isolations, progressions and routines by the New York-based jazz teacher.

FRANKIE MANNING'S BIRTHDAY VIDEO

1994, 5.20 min. color video
Distributor: Beam Productions
Producer: Kathy Lacommare and Stuart Math

Director: Stuart Math
Category: SOCIAL
Dance on Camera Festival 1995 Honorable Mention
Legendary lindy-hopper and choreographer Frankie Manning celebrated his eightieth birthday in May 1994, in a four-day celebration in New York City's streets, ballrooms, studios and homes. This video tribute to Manning and the lindy was shown as part of his birthday celebration. In it, lindy-hoppers from all over the globe dance to Manning's favorite song, *Shiny Stockings*.

FRED ASTAIRE LEARN TO DANCE (5 videos)
1989, 30 min. each color video
Distributor: Best Film and Video
Principal Dancers: Lee Santos, Peggy Santos
Category: INSTRUCTIONAL, SOCIAL
Lessons for beginners with two dances taught in each video in the styles of Latin (cha-cha and salsa), ballroom (fox-trot and waltz), swing (lindy and jitterbug), and country western (cotton-eyed joe and polka).

FRENCH CAN-CAN
1954, 105 min. color video
Distributor: Interama
Producer: Franco London
Director: Jean Renoir
Category: FEATURES, NIGHTCLUB
Recreates the excitement and sensuality of the Moulin Rouge dance style, as a Parisian impresario unsuccessfully tries to mount a production. The high-kicking dance with its splits and garter belt tossings provides the centerpiece for the show.

FRENCH FOLK DANCING (20 videos)
1987, 45 and 55 min. color video
Distributor: Gessler
Producer: Cindy López
Director: Greg Markle
Category: FOLK, INSTRUCTIONAL
A teaching kit with audiotape, manual, and performance tape featuring high school students from Colorado. Volume I: *Le Branle à Six* from Brittany, accompanied by a *biniou*, or bagpipe, and a *bombarde*, an oboe-like instrument; *La Boulangère* from Alsace-Lorraine, which resembles the United States' western square dance; *La Contre-Danse* from Haiti. Volume II: *Le Branle du Quércy*, *Saint Ferreul* from Catalonia, and *La Bastrinque* from Québec.

FROM AN ISLAND SUMMER
1984, 15 min. color video
Distributor: The Kitchen
Producer: WGBH-TV/Boston
Director: Charles Atlas
Choreographer: Karole Armitage
Principal Dancer: Karole Armitage
Category: EXPERIMENTAL, CINEDANCE
Atlas juxtaposes Armitage's choreography, featuring two dancers, against contrasting New York backdrops.

FROM SAN FRANCISCO: DANCING ON THE EDGE
1989, 30 min. color video
Series: Alive From Off Center
Distributor: KTCA-TV

Producer: Linda Schaller for KQED-TV and KTCA-TV
Directors: Gino Tanasescu, Tim Boxell
Choreographers: Margaret Jenkins, Rinde Eckert, Ellen Bromberg, Joe Goode
Principal Dancers: Margaret Jenkins, Rinde Eckert, Ellen Bromberg, Joe Goode
Category: MODERN
Dance on Camera Festival 1990 Honorable Mention
Shoebirds/Atlantic, a new music theatre piece developed and performed by choreographers Margaret Jenkins and Rinde Eckert; Ellen Bromberg's adaptation of her work *The Black Dress*, which examines gender roles; and *29 Effeminate Gestures*, choreographer Joe Goode's examination of sexual stereotypes.

FULL CIRCLE: THE WORK OF DORIS CHASE
1974, 10:30 min. color film, video
Distributors: PennState
Producer: Elizabeth Wood
Director: Doris Chase
Choreographer: Mary Staton
Dance Company: Mary Staton Dance Ensemble
Composer: George Kleinsinger
Category: MODERN, DOCUMENTARY PORTRAITS
This documentary of Doris Chase, painter-sculptor-filmmaker, explains how she became interested in creating sets for choreographers and being involved in media.

FULL OF LIFE A-DANCIN'
1978, 29 min. color film
Distributors: Phoenix, University of California Extension Center
Producers: Robert Fiore and Richard Nevell
Director: Robert Fiore
Principal Dancer: Floyd King
Dance Company: Southern Appalachian Cloggers
Category: FOLK, UNITED STATES
American Film Festival
Features a champion clog dancing team from the southern Appalachian mountains, accompanied by fiddles and banjoes.

FUNDAMENTAL DANCE SIGNS
1991, 21 min. color video
Distributor: AAHPERD
Producers: Sue Gill and Diane V. Hottendorf
Category: DISABILITIES, INSTRUCTIONAL
For teachers of dance whose students use sign language, covering creative movement, ballroom dance, choreography, ballet and tap dance.

FUNNY FACE
1957, 103 min. color film, video
Distributors: Films Inc., Facets
Producer: Paramount
Director: Stanley Donen
Choreographers: Fred Astaire, Eugene Loring
Principal Dancers: Fred Astaire, Audrey Hepburn
Composer: George Gershwin
Category: FEATURES, MUSICALS
The love story of a fashion photographer (Astaire) and a Greenwich Village intellectual (Hepburn) who has gone to Paris to model. Dance numbers include *Let's Kiss and Make Up*, *He Loves and She Loves*, and *Funny Face*.

FUNNY GIRL
1968, 151 min. color film, video
Distributors: Facets, Films Inc.

Producer: Columbia
Director: William Wyler
Choreographer: Herbert Ross
Principal Dancers: Barbra Streisand, Tommy Rall
Composer: Jule Styne
Category: FEATURES, MUSICALS
Academy Award: Barbra Streisand
Based upon the life of Fanny Brice and her stormy romance with her husband, Nick Arnstein, who was involved in shady financial dealings. Dance numbers include *Roller Skate Rag*, *The Swan*, and *Don't Rain on My Parade*.

FUNNY HOUSE
1988, 11 min. color video
Distributor: Eccentric Motions
Producer: Trinity Square Video
Director: Pooh Kaye
Choreographer: Funny House
Dance Company: Funny House Co-op
Category: ANIMATION, CHILDREN
Canada Council Best of 1988
A comical story about two girl gangs fighting for the same space. The video utilizes blue box effects and frozen frame animation, and was the product of a four-week workshop in Toronto at Trinity Square Video. Pooh Kaye directed the workshop of dancers, costume designers and media artists.

GAGAKU *BAIRO* IN TWO STYLES
1972, 17 min. color film
Distributor: PennState
Producer: Wissen
Category: JAPAN
Two variations of a Japanese dance set to music of the Imperial Court and Shinto shrines, with instrumental composition in 6/4 meter and a dance in 5/4 meter.

GAITÉ PARISIENNE
1941, 20 min. color film
Distributor: Dance Films Association
Producer: Warner Brothers
Director: Jean Negulesco
Choreographer: Léonide Massine
Principal Dancers: Léonide Massine, Frederic Franklin, Milada Miladova, Nathalie Krassovksa, Igor Youskevitch, Casimir Kokitch, James Starbuch, André Eglevsky, Lubov Roudenko
Dance Company: Ballet Russe de Monte Carlo
Composer: Jacques Offenbach
Category: FULL-LENGTH BALLETS, NIGHTCLUB
The festive, one-act ballet revolves around the exploits of a wealthy Peruvian in a Paris nightclub in the 1890s.

GAITÉ PARISIENNE
1954, 38 min. b&w film, video
Distributors: Dance Film Archive, Dance Horizons, Viewfinders, Corinth, Video Artists International
Director: Victor Jessen
Choreographer: Léonide Massine
Principal Dancers: Alexandra Danilova, Frederic Franklin, Leon Danielian
Dance Company: Ballet Russe de Monte Carlo
Composer: Jacques Offenbach
Category: NIGHTCLUB, DANCE HISTORY
A balletomane's surreptitious attempts to capture the spirited ballet on film between 1948 and 1954 despite the obstacle of having his camera

confiscated by dutiful ushers in the middle of performances.

GALA
1982, 90 min. color film, video
Distributor: Karol
Producer: National Film Board of Canada
Directors: John D. Smith, Cynthia Scott, Michael McKennirey
Dance Company: Winnipeg Contemporary Dance Company, National Ballet of Canada
Category: BALLET, MODERN
A performance record.

GALINA ULANOVA
1964. 37 min. b&w film
Distributor: Corinth
Producer: Central Documentary Film Studio, Moscow
Directors: Leonid Kristi, Maria Slavinskaya
Choreographers: Michel Fokine, Leonid Lavrovsky, Jean Coralli, Rostislav Zakharov
Principal Dancer: Galina Ulanova
Dance Company: Kirov Ballet, Bolshoi Ballet
Composers: Sergei Prokofiev, Adolphe Adam, Frédéric Chopin, Boris Asafiev
Category: BALLET, DOCUMENTARY POR-TRAITS
The life and art of the Russian ballerina Galina Ulanova, from her early days with the Kirov Ballet to her later role as a teacher at the Bolshoi Ballet School. Includes excerpts of her performances of *Gisèlle* (Coralli/Adam), *Romeo and Juliet* (Lavrovsky/Prokofiev), *Les Sylphides* (Fokine/Chopin), and *The Fountain of Bakhchisarai* (Zakharov/Asafiev).

GAMEEL GAMAL (Oh! Beautiful Dancer)
1976, 24 min. color film, video
Distributors: Phoenix, Kent State, Iowa State
Producer: Gordon Inkeles
Principal Dancers: Taia Amina, Katarina
Category: BELLY DANCE, INSTRUCTIONAL
Four belly dances with two beginning dancers helping each other through their first nightclub performance. Features a class in Middle Eastern dance by Roman Ballardine.

THE GANG'S ALL HERE
1943, 103 min. color film
Distributors: Films Inc., Swank
Producer: 20th Century Fox
Director: Busby Berkeley
Choreographer: Busby Berkeley
Principal Dancer: Carmen Miranda
Composer: Harry Warren
Category: FEATURES, MUSICALS
Wartime musical story of a serviceman, a chorus girl, and a Park Avenue socialite. Berkeley's way-out choreography includes *The Lady in the Tutti Frutti Hat*, and *The Polka Dot Polka*.

GATERE-DANCE
1964, 3 min. color film
Distributor: PennState
Producer: Wissen
Director: G. Koch
Category: ANTHROPOLOGICAL, WOMEN
A woman's dance in Onotoa, Gilbert Islands, accompanied by a chorus.

THE GAY DIVORCEE
1934, 105 min. b&w film, video, laser
Distributors: Facets, Films Inc., Laserdisc Fan Club
Producer: RKO
Director: Mark Sandrich
Choreographers: Fred Astaire, Dave Gould, Hermes Pan
Principal Dancers: Fred Astaire, Ginger Rogers, Betty Grable
Composer: Cole Porter
Category: FEATURES, TAP
Astaire is a dancer mistakenly thought by Rogers to be a professional correspondent with whom she must spend the night at an English resort to win a divorce. Complications arise when the real correspondent shows up at the hotel. Dance numbers include *Don't Let It Bother You*, *Night and Day*, *The Continental*, and *Let's K-nock K-neez*.

GBAGBA MASK DANCE AT ASOUAKRO (2 films)
1968, 21 and 28 min. color film
Distributor: PennState
Producer: Wissen
Category: FOLK, FESTIVALS, AFRICA
Filmed during a festival in Baule, Ivory Coast, the *Gbagba* is performed by a boy wearing a bird mask.

GEE, OFFICER KRUPKE
1975, 25 min. color film, video
Distributor: PennState
Producer: Edward A. Mason
Director: Edward A. Mason
Choreographer: Robert Berger, after Jerome Robbins
Principal Dancers: Harvard College students
Composer: Leonard Bernstein
Category: MUSICALS
American Film Festival Blue Ribbon, Chicago International Film Festival Silver Plaque
A documentary on the process of building a college production of the musical *West Side Story*, from the first read-through to the opening night.

GENIUS ON THE WRONG COAST
1993, 90 min. color video
Distributor: Green River Road
Producer: Lelia Goldoni
Director: Lelia Goldoni
Choreographer: Lester Horton
Principal Dancers: Alvin Ailey, Carmen de Lavallade, Bella Lewitsky, Eleanor Brooks, Jimmy Truitte, Lelia Goldoni
Dance Company: Lester Horton Dancers
Category: DOCUMENTARY PORTRAITS, MODERN COMPANIES
Dance on Camera Festival 1994 Silver Award
A biography of legendary West Coast choreographer, Lester Horton (1909–1953), including interviews with his dancers, critics and friends, and glimpses of the environment and social milieu in which he created. The documentary chronicles the development of his aesthetic from his humble beginnings in Indiana through the political and social ferment of the 1930s, and includes rare archival footage of his work.

GEOGRAPHY AND METABOLISM
1987, 23:30 min. color video
Series: Alive From Off Center
Distributor: Electronic Arts Intermix
Producer: KTCA-TV/St. Paul
Directors: John Sanborn, Mary Perillo
Choreographer: Molissa Fenley
Category: MODERN, EXPERIMENTAL
Three barefoot girls dance in the wide-open spaces of a southwestern desert for the airborne cameraman, who swoops about like a drunken hawk. In the second half, the camera again dances with two women in a draped studio.

GERD BOHNER
0 min. color film
Distributor: Modern Talking Picture Service
Producer: German Government
Choreographer: Oskar Schlemmer
Principal Dancer: Gerd Bohner
Category: MODERN, DOCUMENTARY POR-TRAITS
This portrait of Gerd Bohner, a dancer-choreographer who was considered an outsider in the German dance scene, includes scenes from Oskar Schlemmer's *Das Triadisches Ballett*.

GERMAN FOLK DANCES
1988, 42 min. color video
Distributor: Gessler
Producer: Gessler
Director: Cindy López
Category: FOLK, EUROPE, INSTRUCTIONAL
Students perform *Siebenschritt* from Bavaria, *Strommt em Babeli* from Switzerland and *Das Fenster* from Germany. Teaching kit includes dance instructions and a costume guide.

GHOST DANCES
1989, 41 min. color video
Distributors: Home Vision, Viewfinders
Producer: Independent Films Producers Association
Choreographer: Christopher Bruce
Dance Company: Ballet Rambert
Composer: Victor Jara
Category: BALLET, LATIN AMERICA
A performance video inspired by a letter from the widow of Chilean folksinger and writer Victor Jara, a victim of the Chilean military coup that brought Augusto Pinochet to power. The ballet evokes the gaiety and courage the South American people maintain despite oppression and murder.

GISÈLLE (American Ballet Theatre)
1969, 90 min. color video, laser
Distributors: Corinth, Viewfinders, Home Vision GIS060
Producer: Unitel
Director: Ugo Niebling
Choreographer: David Blair after Jean Coralli and Jules Perrot
Principal Dancers: Carla Fracci, Erik Bruhn
Dance Company: American Ballet Theatre
Composer: Adolphe Adam
Category: FULL-LENGTH BALLETS
The romantic ballet in two acts is based on the story by Théophile Gautier on a theme by Heinrich Heine, in which a country girl with a weak heart dies when she realizes her lover is not only an aristocrat, but is betrothed. She joins the Wilis, a bevy of ladies who have suffered a similar fate, and receives her guilt-ridden, grave-visiting lover. Filmed in Berlin, Germany.

GISÈLLE (American Ballet Theatre)
1976, 95 min. color video, laser
Series: Live From Lincoln Center

Distributors: Paramount, Media Basics, Facets
Producer: Lincoln Center
Directors: John Goberman, Robert Schwarz
Choreographers: Jean Coralli, Jules Perrot
Principal Dancers: Natalia Makarova, Mikhail Baryshnikov, Martine van Hamel
Dance Company: American Ballet Theatre
Composer: Adolphe Adam
Category: FULL-LENGTH BALLETS
Emmy Award
The full-length production filmed at the Metropolitan Opera House.

GISÈLLE (Ballet Nacional de Cuba)

1964, 90 min. b&w film, video
Distributors: Video Artists International, Music Video Distributors, Viewfinders, Corinth
Producer: Cuban Film Institute
Director: Enrique Piñeda Barnet
Choreographers: Alicia Alonso, Jean Coralli, Jules Perrot
Principal Dancers: Alicia Alonso, Azari Plisetski, Fernando Alonso
Dance Company: Ballet Nacional de Cuba
Composer: Adolphe Adam
Category: FULL-LENGTH BALLETS
Dance on Camera Festival 1979
Full-length ballet performed and choreographed by the Cuban ballerina Alicia Alonso in her prime, after the original by Jean Coralli and Jules Perrot.

GISÈLLE (Ballet Teatro Municipal of Rio de Janeiro)

1984, 104 min. color video
Distributors: Kultur, Viewfinders, Corinth, Home Vision GIS050
Producer: Fernando Bujones
Choreographers: Marius Petipa, Jean Coralli, Jules Perrot
Principal Dancers: Fernando Bujones, Ana Botafogo
Dance Company: Ballet Teatro Municipal of Rio de Janeiro
Composer: Adolphe Adam
Category: FULL-LENGTH BALLETS
Bujones stars as Count Albrecht at the peak of his career with the Ballet Teatro Municipal of Rio de Janeiro, in Brazil.

GISÈLLE (Bavarian State Ballet)

1979, 78 min. color video
Distributors: Kultur, Viewfinders, Home Vision GIS070, Facets
Producer: ATV Network Ltd.
Choreographers: Jules Perrot, Jean Coralli
Principal Dancers: Rudolf Nureyev, Lynn Seymour, Monica Mason, Gerd Larson
Dance Company: Bavarian State Ballet
Composer: Adolphe Adam
Category: FULL-LENGTH BALLETS
Nureyev stars as Albrecht in this version. Gisèlle is danced by Canadian prima ballerina, Lynn Seymour and the Queen of the Wilis is portrayed by Monica Mason of the Royal Ballet.

GISÈLLE (Bolshoi Ballet)

1974, 85 min. color video
Distributors: Kultur, Corinth, Music Video Distributors, Viewfinders, Facets
Producer: Lothar Bock Associates, GmbH
Choreographer: Yuri Grigorovich
Principal Dancers: Natalya Bessmertnova, Mikhail Lavrovsky, Galina Kozlova
Dance Company: Bolshoi Ballet
Composer: Adolphe Adam
Category: FULL-LENGTH BALLETS
The full-length classic filmed live at the Bolshoi Theatre in Moscow.

GISÈLLE (Bolshoi Ballet)

1990, 90 min. color video
Distributors: Viewfinders, Corinth, Home Vision GIS020, Media Basics
Producers: NHK and Japan Arts Corporation
Director: Shuji Fujii
Choreographers: Jean Coralli, Jules Perrot, Marius Petipa, Yuri Grigorovich
Principal Dancers: Natalya Bessmertnova, Yuri Vasyuchenko, Maria Bilova
Dance Company: Bolshoi Ballet
Composer: Adolphe Adam
Category: FULL-LENGTH BALLETS
Recorded live at the Bolshoi Theatre in Moscow.

GISÈLLE (Kirov Ballet)

1983, 115 min. color video, laser
Distributors: Home Box Office, Corinth
Producer: National Video Corporation
Director: Preben Montell
Choreographers: Jean Coralli, Jules Perrot
Principal Dancers: Galina Mezentseva, Konstantin Zaklinsky
Dance Company: Kirov Ballet
Composer: Adolphe Adam
Category: FULL-LENGTH BALLETS
Filmed in Leningrad.

GISÈLLE . . . THE MAKING OF

1996, 29 min. color video
Distributor: V.I.E.W.
Producer: EuroArts/Brilliant Media Productions
Director: Dietrich Lehmstedt
Choreographer: Marcia Haydee
Dancers: Jean-Christopher Blavier, Richard Cragun, Tamas Detrich, Birgit Kell, Melinda Witham
Dance Company: Stuttgart Ballet Company
Composer: Adolphe Adams
Category: BALLET
Ballerina-choreographer Marcia Haydee discusses and demonstrates her version of *Gisèlle*, created for the Wütembergisches Staatstheater in Stuttgart, Germany.

GLEN TETLEY: PORTRAIT OF THE CHOREOGRAPHER

1994, 58 min. color video
Distributor: Michael Blackwood Productions
Producer: Michael Blackwood Productions
Director: Michael Blackwood
Choreographer: Glen Tetley
Dance Company: Het Nationale Ballet of Amsterdam
Category: CHOREOGRAPHY, DOCUMENTARY PORTRAITS
A portrait of the choreographer and his work, filmed both in Amsterdam during rehearsals of the Het Nationale Ballet and in New York. Includes interviews with Tetley.

GODUNOV: THE WORLD TO DANCE IN

1983, 60 min. color video
Distributors: Kultur, Viewfinders, Corinth, Home Vision
Producer: Peter Rosen with Metromedia
Director: Peter Rosen
Choreographer: Marius Petipa
Principal Dancers: Alexander Godunov, Cynthia Gregory, Maya Plisetskaya
Composer: Adolphe Adam
Category: BALLET, DOCUMENTARY PORTRAITS
Alexander Godunov, a former Bolshoi dancer whose rugged face became familiar to America's movie-going public through his spot appearances in such films as *Witness*, discusses his career on a performance tour across America soon after his defection. Includes rehearsal and performance excerpts of his solo in *Le Corsaire*.

GOLD DIGGERS OF 1933

1933, 98 min. b&w video, laser
Distributors: Facets, Swank
Producer: Warner Brothers
Director: Mervyn Le Roy
Choreographer: Busby Berkeley
Principal Dancers: Ruby Keeler, Ginger Rogers
Composer: Harry Warren
Category: FEATURES, MUSICALS
One of the "backstage musicals" of 1933 in which chorus girls seeking husbands are suspected of being gold diggers. Dance numbers include *We're in the Money*, *Remember My Forgotten Man*, and *The Shadow Waltz*.

GOLD DIGGERS OF 1935

1935, 95 min. b&w video
Distributors: Facets, Swank
Producer: Warner Brothers
Director: Busby Berkeley
Choreographer: Busby Berkeley
Category: FEATURES, MUSICALS
A charity show is to be presented at a New Hampshire summer resort. Dance numbers include *The Words Are In My Heart*, and *The Lullaby of Broadway*.

GOLDBERG VARIATIONS

1992, 30 min. color video
Distributor: The Kitchen
Producer: KAAT Theater in association with The Kitchen
Director: Walter Verdin
Choreographer: Steve Paxton
Principal Dancer: Steve Paxton
Category: IMPROVISATION, MODERN
Features Steve Paxton in an improvisational mode.

THE GOLDEN AGE

1987, 113 min. color laser
Distributors: Laserdisc Fan Club, Corinth
Producer: Robin Scott for National Video Corporation with Göstelradio-Soviet TV and BBC-TV
Director: Colin Nears
Choreographer: Yuri Grigorovich
Principal Dancers: Irek Mukhamedov, Natalya Bessmertnova
Dance Company: Bolshoi Ballet
Composer: Dmitri Shostakovich
Category: FULL-LENGTH BALLETS, NIGHTCLUB
Stereo Review 1987 Video of the Year Award
This three-act ballet, set in a nightclub popular among the bourgeoisie in the 1920s, revolves around the rivalry between a fisherman and a gang leader and their love for the same woman.

THE GOLDWYN FOLLIES
1938, 120 min. color video
Distributors: Home Box Office, Facets
Producer: Samuel Goldwyn
Director: George Marshall
Choreographer: George Balanchine
Principal Dancer: Vera Zorina
Dance Company: Metropolitan Opera Ballet
Composer: George Gershwin
Category: FEATURES, MUSICALS
Hollywood musical choreographed by the cofounder of the New York City Ballet, George Balanchine.

GOLI MASK DANCE
1968, 31 min. color film
Distributor: PennState
Producer: Wissen
Director: H. Himmelheber
Category: AFRICA, ANTHROPOLOGICAL
Three or four pairs of masked men of Baule, Ivory Coast, try to surpass each other by dancing to the hot rhythms of rattle calabashes played by a men's chorus.

GRAND CONCERT
1951, 102 min. color film
Distributor: Corinth
Producer: Mosfilm Studios
Director: Vera Stroyeva
Choreographers: Marius Petipa, Mikhail Lavrovsky
Principal Dancers: Galina Ulanova, Olga Lepeshinskaya, Maya Plisetskaya, Marina Semyonova, Mikhail Lavrovsky
Composers: Peter Ilyich Tchaikovsky, Sergei Prokofiev
Category: BALLET
Opera and ballet scenes with Galina Ulanova, Olga Lepeshinskaya and others. Included are excerpts from *Swan Lake*, *Prince Igor*, and Lavrovsky's *Romeo and Juliet*.

LE GRATIE D'AMORE (The Graces of Love)
1992, 32 min. color video
Distributor: Historical Dance Foundation
Choreographers: Caroso, Arbeau, Negri
Category: DANCE HISTORY
A complete collection of renaissance court dances from the late 1500s: galliards, pavanes, Canaries, Branles, figure dances, couple and group dances. In Spanish with English subtitles.

GREASE
1978, 110 min. color video
Distributor: Facets
Producer: Paramount
Director: Randal Kleiser
Choreographer: Patricia Birch
Principal Dancers: John Travolta, Olivia Newton-John
Composer: Jim Jacobs
Category: FEATURES, MUSICALS
A satirical view of the teenaged greasers of the '50s at Rydell High School. Dance numbers include *You're the One That I Want*.

GREAT BALLERINA
1950, 7 min. b&w film
Distributor: Lane Education
Producer: Lenfilm Studios, U.S.S.R.
Choreographer: Marius Petipa

Principal Dancers: Galina Ulanova, Vladimir Preobrajensky
Composer: Peter Ilyich Tchaikovsky:
Category: BALLET
The *Pas de Deux* from the second act of *Swan Lake* shot in the Bolshoi Theatre and performed by Galina Ulanova and Vladimir Preobrajensky. An excerpt from the feature *Russian Ballerina*.

GREAT PERFORMANCE IN DANCE
1960, 29 min. b&w film, video
Series: A Time To Dance
Distributor: Indiana University
Producer: Jac Venza for WGBH-TV/Boston
Choreographers: Léonide Massine, Marius Petipa, Arthur Saint-Léon, Valerie Bettis
Principal Dancers: Anna Pavlova, Alexandra Danilova, Frederic Franklin, Edith Jerell, Thomas Andrew, Argentinita, Vernon and Irene Castle
Composers: Peter Ilyich Tchaikovsky, Johann Strauss, Léo Delibes
Category: DANCE HISTORY, CHOREOGRAPHY, BALLET
Shows how one dancer may interpret choreography quite differently from another. Danilova and Franklin perform a duet from Massine's *Le Beau Danube* and Jerell and Andrew demonstrate an alternate version. Danilova and Franklin also perform excerpts from Bettis' *A Streetcar Named Desire*, as well as the classics *Swan Lake* and *Coppélia*. Martha Myers and dance critic Walter Terry discuss the interplay of dancer and choreographer and the process of creating a role. Film clips of ballerina Anna Pavlova, flamenco dancer Argentinita and ballroom team Vernon and Irene Castle are also shown.

GRIOT NEW YORK
1995, 87 min. color video
Series: Dance in America
Distributors: Dance Horizons, WNET
Choreographer: Garth Fagan
Dance Company: Garth Fagan's Bucket Dance Theatre
Composer: Wynton Marsalis
Category: MODERN
Griot, meaning storyteller or keeper of the collective memory, is a West African term applied to a work about New York City.

HAA SHAGOON
1983, 29 min. color film, video
Distributor: University of California Extension Center
Producer: Joseph Kawaky
Director: Joseph Kawaky
Category: NATIVE AMERICANS
Documents a day of Tlingit Indian ceremonies held along the Chilkoot River in Alaska. Prayers, songs and dances are interpreted by a tribal elder.

HAIL THE NEW PURITAN
1986, 84 min. color video
Distributor: The Kitchen
Producer: Channel 4/London
Director: Charles Atlas
Choreographer: Michael Clark
Principal Dancer: Michael Clark
Category: MODERN: EXPERIMENTAL
Fantasy day-in-the-life of Michael Clark, a dancer trained at the Royal Ballet School who then pursued his own choreography with a punk sensi-

bility. Filmed in the streets of London, at clubs, parties, and in his home.

HAIR
1979, 121 min. color film, video
Distributors: Swank, MGM/UA
Producer: United Artists
Director: Milos Forman
Choreographer: Twyla Tharp
Principal Dancer: Twyla Tharp
Dance Company: Twyla Tharp Dance Company
Composer: Galt MacDermot
Category: FEATURES, MUSICALS, MODERN
An Oklahoma farm boy travels to New York before going into the army. In Central Park, he meets a group of long haired free spirits who subsequently help him escape from his basic training camp. Notable for the dance audience because of the choreography by modern dancer Twyla Tharp.

HALF A SIXPENCE
1968, 148 min. color video
Distributor: Paramount
Producer: Paramount
Director: George Sidney
Choreographers: Gillian Lynn, Virginia Mason
Principal Dancers: Tommy Steele, Julia Foster
Composer: David Heneker
Category: FEATURES, MUSICALS
A wistful, engaging adaptation of the West End and Broadway hit based on H.G. Wells' *Kipps*. The dances include the elaborate *Money to Burn*, *Flash*, *Bang*, *Wallop*, and the simple, charming title tune.

HANYA: PORTRAIT OF A DANCE PIONEER
1984, 55 min. color film, video
Distributors: Dance Horizons, AAHPERD
Producers: Marilyn Cristofori and Nancy Mason Hauser
Directors: John Ittleson, Marilyn Cristofori, Nancy Mason Hauser
Choreographer: Hanya Holm
Principal Dancer: Hanya Holm
Dance Company: Don Redlich Dance Company
Composer: Kenny Davis
Category: MODERN, DOCUMENTARY PORTRAITS, CHOREOGRAPHY
Narrators: Julie Andrews, Alfred Drake
Commentators: Alwin Nikolais, Glen Tetley
Dance on Camera Festival 1985 Grand Prize
Portrait of Hanya Holm, a German American choreographer who helped shape modern dance in the United States. There are clips from her early and late performances, conversations which reveal her belief in hard work and improvisation, and interviews with Alwin Nikolais and Glen Tetley who worked with her. Valerie Bettis dances in the Holm style outdoors in Colorado, where Holm taught for forty years.

THE HARD NUT
1992, 87 min. color video
Distributors: Dance Horizons, Home Vision, Viewfinders
Choreographer: Mark Morris
Dance Company: Mark Morris Dance Group
Composer: Peter Ilyich Tchaikovsky
Category: FULL-LENGTH BALLETS
An outrageous spoof of *The Nutcracker*, featuring the antics of a dysfunctional family at Christmastime.

HARMONICA BREAKDOWN

1995, 15 min. video
Distributor: Filmakers Library
Producer: A Singh Productions
Directors: Darshan Singh-Bhuller, Tom Hurwitz
Choreographer: Jane Dudley
Dancer: Sheron Wray
Composer: Sonny Terry
Category: AFRICAN-AMERICANS

Part performance, part documentary, the solo choreographed by Jane Dudley in 1938 depicts the hardship and courage of ordinary people in the context of Dorothea Lange's black and white photos of sharecroppers in the deep South during the Depression.

HARVEST DANCES (2 films)

1957, 20 and 15 min. color film
Distributor: PennState
Producer: Wissen
Category: ANTHROPOLOGICAL, LATIN AMERICA

Filmed in Venezuela during the *Tamunangue* festivities in honor of San Antonio, the feast starts with a fighting game, followed by seven different dances and a song to venerate the saint. In the shorter film made the same year at the time of the maize harvest, the Ayaman celebrate the great *Tura* together with the mestizo population around a frame of maize and sugar cane stalks.

THE HARVEY GIRLS

1946, 104 min. color video, laser
Distributor: MGM/UA
Producer: MGM
Director: George Sidney
Choreographer: Robert Alton
Principal Dancers: Ray Bolger, Cyd Charisse, Judy Garland, Angela Lansbury
Composers: Harry Warren, Johnny Mercer
Category: FEATURES, MUSICALS

An original musical comedy about the pioneering Harvey House waitresses of the 1890s which includes a Ray Bolger tap dance, an Angela Lansbury can-can, a Cyd Charisse ballet, a waltz ensemble, and the famous production number *On the Atchison, Topeka and the Santa Fe*.

HAVE A FLING WITH DANCE (2 videos)

1988, 30 and 45 min. color video
Distributor: Hoctor Products
Producer: Studio Music Corporation
Category: INSTRUCTIONAL, JAZZ
Teachers: Valene Tueller, Darryl Retter

Tap and jazz routines are broken down so that the viewer can follow and then perform.

HE MAKES ME FEEL LIKE DANCIN'

1983, 51 min. color film, video
Distributors: Direct Cinema, University of Minnesota
Producers: Emile Ardolino, Judy Kinberg, and Edgar J. Scherick Associates
Director: Emile Ardolino
Choreographer: George Balanchine
Composers: Lee Norris, Martin Charnin
Category: INSTRUCTIONAL, CHILDREN

Academy Award 1983 Best Documentary Feature, Emmy Award 1984, Christopher Award, American Film Festival 1985 Emily Award

Jacques d'Amboise, former New York City Ballet principal dancer, auditions children to participate in his National Dance Institute. Representing a cross section of New York City's multiethnic population, one thousand children learn to dance and perform in the *Event of the Year* at Madison Square Garden with guest artists Judy Collins, Kevin Kline, and other celebrities.

HELEN: QUEEN OF THE NAUTCH GIRLS

1972, 30 min. color, b&w film
Distributor: New Yorker
Producer: Merchant/Ivory
Director: Anthony Korner
Category: INDIA, NIGHTCLUB

This musical profile of India's answer to Busby Berkeley provides insight into modern India and the Westernization of its dance through its best-known nightclub performer. Helen is also seen in excerpts from her Bombay and Madras films.

HELEN TAMIRIS IN NEGRO SPIRITUALS

1958, 17 min. b&w film
Distributor: Dance Films Association
Director: Marcus Blechman
Choreographer: Helen Tamiris
Principal Dancer: Helen Tamiris
Category: AFRICAN-AMERICANS
Singers: Eugene Brice, Muriel Rahn

Dance critic John Martin introduces Helen Tamiris, choreographer of many musicals (including *Showboat*, *Tough and Go*, and *Annie Get Your Gun*), revues and films. Tamiris then performs her solos: *Go Down Moses*, *Swing Low, Sweet Chariot*, *Git on Board*, *Crucifixion*, and *Joshua Fit the Battle of Jerico*.

HELICAL WIND

1983, 10 min. color video
Distributor: Deborah Gladstein and Sam Kanter
Producers: Deborah Gladstein, Sam Kanter
Director: Sam Kanter
Choreographer: Deborah Gladstein
Principal Dancer: Deborah Gladstein
Category: EXPERIMENTAL

The dancer twists, turns and leaps through black space as slow-motion takes reveal the subtleties of her gestures.

HELLO DOLLY

1969, 118 min. color film, video, laser
Distributors: Facets, Films Inc.
Producer: Twentieth Century Fox
Director: Gene Kelly
Choreographer: Michael Kidd
Principal Dancers: Barbra Streisand, Tommy Tune
Composer: Jerry Herman
Category: FEATURES, MUSICALS

A widowed matchmaker pursues a wealthy grain merchant in 1890s New York. Dance numbers include *Put on Your Sunday Clothes*.

HELP ME TO DREAM

1992, 5 min. b&w film, video
Distributor: WHYY-TV 12
Director: Glen Holsten
Choreographer: Michael A. Carson
Principal Dancers: Sheila Zagar, Michael A. Carson
Dance Company: Ausdrückstanz Dance Theater
Category: MODERN

Dance on Camera Festival 1993 Silver Award

Provides the viewer with thirty-five pieces of a fifty-piece puzzle about relationships, sexual identification and the sexual conflicts in human nature. The writer-choreographer's work is influenced by the German Expressionist films of the 1930s.

HERALD'S ROUND

1982, 8 min. color video
Distributor: ARC Videodance
Director: Celia Ipiotis
Choreographer: Peter Sparling
Principal Dancer: Peter Sparling
Composer: Johann Sebastian Bach
Category: MODERN, EXPERIMENTAL

A canon made in postproduction, in which a former Martha Graham soloist marks out his soul's domain and confronts his own image in a dialogue with himself.

HERE AND NOW WITH WATCHERS

1983, 5:45 min. b&w film
Distributor: Film-makers' Cooperative
Director: Jonas Mekas
Principal Dancer: Erick Hawkins
Category: EXPERIMENTAL, MODERN

Former Martha Graham dancer Eric Hawkins, who formed and toured internationally with his own modern dance company, and longtime collaborator-composer-musician Lucia Dlugoszewski, share a concert under the wandering eye of the camera. Commissioned originally by a magazine called *Show* and salvaged by the filmmaker twenty years later.

HERITAGE OF CHINESE OPERA

1978, 31 min. color video
Distributor: Iowa State
Category: CHINA, OPERA

Illustrates the falsetto singing, symbolism in gait and gesture, acrobatics, costumes, and face painting in Chinese opera, which has a history of more than thirteen centuries.

HIGH NOON

1992, 4 min. b&w film
Distributor: Wagman, Vera
Producer: Vera Wagman
Director: Vera Wagman
Choreographer: Vera Wagman
Principal Dancers: Donatella Accardi, Diane Mateo
Composers: Frédéric Chopin, Enzio Morricone
Category: DANCE DRAMA

Depicts the psychodrama that occurs between two rival ballerinas.

THE HIGHWAYMAN

1958, 13 min. b&w film
Distributor: Kent State
Producer: Kurt Simon for McGraw Hill
Principal Dancers: Jerry Jackson, María Elena Aza
Composer: John Sentes
Category: MODERN
Narrator: John Carradine

Duet set to a recitation of Alfred Noye's poem *The Highwayman*.

HIP HOP SP

1990, 11 min. color video
Distributor: Third World Newsreel
Director: Francisco César
Category: LATIN AMERICA, CHILDREN

Sao Paulo's hip hop movement as depicted by

young blacks through dance, music and graffiti, reveals their view of black Brazilian history.

HIROSHIMA
1989, 10 min. color film
Distributor: Coe Film Associates
Producer: Maciek Albrecht
Director: Maciek Albrecht
Choreographer: Claire Iwatsu
Principal Dancer: Claire Iwatsu
Composer: Saniem Bennett
Category: EXPERIMENTAL
Dance On Camera Festival 1989 Gold Award
An experimental work made in reaction to the bombing of Hiroshima.

HOLIDAY INN
1942, 101 min. b&w video, laser
Distributors: Facets, Laserdisc Fan Club, Swank
Producer: Paramount
Director: Mark Sandrich
Choreographers: Fred Astaire, Danny Dare
Principal Dancers: Fred Astaire, Marjorie Reynolds
Composer: Irving Berlin
Category: FEATURES, MUSICALS
A Connecticut farm is the setting for a nightclub celebrating such holidays as Christmas. Musical numbers include *You're Easy to Dance With* and *White Christmas.*.

HOLIDAY OF BALLET
1982, 49 min. color film
Distributors: Kultur, Corinth, Home Vision
Principal Dancers: Amanda McKerrow, Andris Liepa
Category: BALLET, FESTIVALS
A record of the International Competition of Ballet Artists in Moscow in 1981, where Washington D.C.-native Amanda McKerrow became the first American dancer to win a gold medal.

HOLLYWOOD CLOWNS
1979, 120 min. b&w video
Distributor: MGM/UA
Producer: MGM
Principal Dancers: Charlie Chaplin, Laurel and Hardy, Buster Keaton, Martin and Lewis
Category: PANTOMIME, COMEDY, FEATURES
Compilation of the best from the funniest funnymen, all of whom held their audience by their choreography as much as by their scripts.

HONI COLES: THE CLASS ACT OF TAP
1993, 58 min. color video
Distributor: VPI
Producer: Susan Pollard
Director: James Swenson
Choreographer: Charles "Honi" Coles
Principal Dancer: Charles "Honi" Coles
Category: TAP
Features scenes of the vaudeville era in which Honi grew up, including clips with the masters, John Bubbles and Bill Robinson, historical footage of early Honi Coles dance numbers, and interviews with Honi, his students and colleagues.

HOPI KACHINAS
1962, 10 min. color film
Distributor: Lane Education
Producer: Jack Breed for ACI Films
Director: Jack Breed
Category: NATIVE AMERICANS

Documentary on the religion of the Hopi Indian tribe with particular focus on the kachina dolls, little wooden images of dancers, made to represent supernatural spirits.

HOUSE OF TRES
1990, 16 min. color video
Series: Alive From Off Center
Distributor: KTCA-TV
Producer: Mindy Golberg for Epoch Films
Directors: Jeff Preiss, Diane Martel
Choreographer: Diane Martel
Principal Dancer: Willi Ninja
Dance Company: House of Chanel, House of Afrika
Composer: Dmitri
Category: BREAK DANCE, CHILDREN
House, hip hop and voguing street styles fabricated and polished by the boys of New York, who grew up break dancing, throwing karate kicks, and mocking the cool strut of fashion runways.

HOW BALLET BEGAN
1975, 26 min. b&w video
Series: Ballet For All
Distributor: The Media Guild
Director: Nicholas Ferguson
Choreographers: August Bournonville, Kenneth MacMillan, Marius Petipa, Jean Coralli, Georges Noverre, John Weaver, Mary Skeaping
Dance Company: Ballet For All
Composers: Léo Delibes, Peter Ilyich Tchaikovsky, Jean Lully
Category: BALLET, DANCE HISTORY
First in the British series of seven films presented on Thames Television. Traces ballet from the mid-seventeenth-century royal European courts through the early nineteenth-century. Excerpts from *Ballet de la Nuit* (1653), Weaver's *Loves of Mars and Venus* (1716), Noverre's *Petits Riens* (1778), Bournonville's *Konservatoriet* (1849), Petipa's *Sleeping Beauty*, and MacMillan's *Concerto*.

HOW BALLET WAS SAVED
1975, 26 min. color video
Series: Ballet For All
Distributors: The Media Guild, PennState
Director: Nicholas Ferguson
Choreographer: Arthur Saint-Léon
Principal Dancers: Janet Francis, Margaret Barbieri, Alison Howard, Spencer Parker, Oliver Symons
Composer: Léo Delibes
Category: BALLET, DANCE HISTORY
Originally, ballet was performed only by men. When women started to assume roles in the 1800s the male dancers, with the exception of the Russians, rebelled. Includes excerpts from the 1870 version of *Coppélia*, based on the memories of Paulette Dynalix, in which a woman plays Franz.

HOW DO YOU FEEL, EMPEROR'S NEW CLOTHES, ROCKER
1977, 29 min. color film, video
Distributors: Doris Chase Productions, Film-makers' Cooperative
Producer: Doris Chase
Director: Doris Chase
Principal Dancers: Kei Takei, Lloyd Ritter, Jonathan Hollander, Nancy Cohen

Composer: George Kleinsinger
Category: EXPERIMENTAL, MODERN, ANIMATION
The first of these three experimental pieces by the sculptor-painter-videographer who explored video in the '60s and '70s is an animated film on body movement and self-awareness geared to children. The second presents a duet in a fable, while the third, a solo performed by Jonathan Hollander, demonstrates how the Rutt-Etra video synthesizer alters the image of one of Chase's sculptures made for the dance.

HOW TO IMPROVE YOUR BALLET TECHNIQUE/PIROUETTES/POINTE TECHNIQUE WITH RONI MAHLER (3 videos)
1991, 1993, 1994, 60 min. each color video
Distributor: Dance Horizons
Category: INSTRUCTIONAL
Exercises for pre-pointe and beginning students in *Pointe Technique,* intermediate/advanced students in *Pirouettes,* and for the pre-professional in *Ballet Technique.*

HOW TO MOVE BETTER
1975, 20 min. color film, video
Series: The Dance Experience
Distributor: AAHPERD
Producer: The Athletic Institute
Choreographer: Lynda Davis
Principal Dancer: Lynda Davis
Category: INSTRUCTIONAL
Tips on how to correct alignment errors and build a positive self-image.

HUMPHREY TECHNIQUE
1936, 10 min. b&w film (silent)
Distributor: Dance Film Archive
Choreographer: Doris Humphrey
Principal Dancers: Letitia Ide, Beatrice Seckler, Edith Orcutt, Katherine Manning
Category: MODERN, DANCE HISTORY, INSTRUCTIONAL
Demonstrations of the modern technique devised by Doris Humphrey.

HUPA INDIAN WHITE DEERSKIN DANCE
1958, 11 min. color film
Distributors: Barr Films, UCLA Instructional Media Library
Producer: Arthur Barr Productions
Category: NATIVE AMERICANS
A glimpse into the ten-day deerskin dance ceremony of the Hupa Indians of Northwestern California, the most advanced and best-known tribe of the Athabascan family. Wearing elaborate costumes, the dancers recite long narratives studded with magical formulas for success and well-being.

I AM A DANCER
1973, 90 min. color film, video
Distributors: Home Box Office, Media Basics, Viewfinders
Producer: Evdoros Demetriou for EMI Film Productions
Director: Pierre Jourdan
Choreographers: August Bournonville, Glen Tetley, Frederick Ashton, Marius Petipa
Principal Dancers: Rudolf Nureyev, Margot Fonteyn, Carla Fracci, Lynn Seymour, Michael Somes, Leslie Edwards
Composers: Franz Liszt, Herman Severin Loven-

skjöld, Peter Ilyich Tchaikovsky, Karlheinz Stockhausen

Category: BALLET, DOCUMENTARY POR-
TRAITS

Rudolf Nureyev, born in Ufa, USSR in 1938, prepares and then performs sequences from the
classics: *Marguerite and Armand, Les Sylphides,*
Sleeping Beauty and *Field Figures.*

I CAN DANCE: INTRODUCTION TO BALLET
FOR CHILDREN

1989, 30 min. color video

Distributors: Kultur, Dance Horizons, Instructional Video, Home Vision

Producer: Surefoot Partners/Debra Maxwell

Director: Ron Kantor

Category: BALLET, INSTRUCTIONAL, CHIL-
DREN

Introduces children to the wonderful world of ballet and dance. Designed specifically for children,
this program follows a child's first ballet lesson,
emphasizing both the technique and the fun of
ballet.

I HATE TO EXERCISE, I LOVE TO TAP

1984, 86 min. color video

Distributors: Kultur, Dance Horizons

Producer: Marilyn Shapiro

Director: Dave Hilmer

Choreographer: Gene Castle

Principal Dancer: Bonnie Franklin

Composer: Shelly Markham

Category: TAP, INSTRUCTIONAL

Bonnie Franklin teaches the basic steps, how to
build combinations and dance popular tap routines such as the soft-shoe, the waltz clog and
the time step, and how to dance into shape
while learning tap at the same time.

I WILL NOT BE SAD IN THIS WORLD

1992, 20 min. color video

Distributor: Ping Chong and Company

Producer: Ping Chong and Company

Director: Ping Chong

Choreographer: Ping Chong

Principal Dancers: Nancy Alfaro, Jürgen Bamberger, Ching Gonzalez, Jeannie Hutchins, Paul
Langland

Dance Company: Ping Chong and Company

Composer: Djivan Gasparian

Category: MODERN, EXPERIMENTAL

Dance on Camera Festival 1993 Silver Award

A metaphorical work which juxtaposes the ele-
mental nature of existence against the abilities
of an individual to remain human. The work
focuses on the body, at once beautiful and
threatened by our persistent denial and forget-
fulness.

IBRAHIM FARRAH PRESENTS RARE
GLIMPSES: DANCES FROM THE MIDDLE
EAST, VOLUME I

1993–94, 55 min. color, b&w video

Distributor: Farrah, Ibrahim

Producer: Andrea Beeman

Choreographers: Ibrahim Farrah, Nadia Gamal

Principal Dancers: Fatima, Nadia Gamal

Category: BELLY DANCE, DANCE HISTORY,
MIDDLE EAST

Ibrahim Farrah, the Middle Eastern dance choreographer, teacher, performer and publisher of
Arabesque magazine, presents five rare glimpses
of North African and Middle Eastern dance film

from the last century. Farrah introduces and
comments on each clip, beginning with Fatima
filmed in 1897 by Thomas Edison, probably the
first belly dancer ever recorded on film.

ICE SKATING SHOWCASE: GREAT ROUTINES
OF THE 1980S

1990, 60 min. color video

Distributor: V.I.E.W.

Principal Dancers: Scott Hamilton, Torvill and
Dean, Dorothy Hamill, Robin Cousins, The
Protopopovs, Linda Fratianne

Category: ICE DANCE

A compilation of the very best of world professional figure skaters of the 1980s, performing
fourteen of their finest routines.

ILONA VERA'S BALLET CLASS

1988, 73 min. color video

Distributors: Kultur, Viewfinders, Home Vision,
Instructional Video

Producer: Levine/Trowbridge

Category: BALLET, INSTRUCTIONAL

Teacher: Ilona Vera

Explains the Vaganova method of training, which
shaped such Russian greats as Mikhail Baryshnikov, Natalia Makarova, and Anna Pavlova.
The instructor was born in Hungary and received her training at the Ballet Institute in Bu-
dapest.

IMAGE: A DANCER

1974, 37 min. color film

Distributor: Arthur Cantor, Inc.

Principal Dancer: Christopher Aponte

Category: DOCUMENTARY PORTRAITS,
BALLET

This portrait of the motivations and ambitions of
a young dancer in New York is a visual, intro-
spective study of his world—class, rehearsal,
home and performance. It reveals the frustration and celebration of this arduous profession.

IMAGE: FLESH AND VOICE

1969, 77 min. b&w film

Distributors: Film-makers' Cooperative, Canyon
Cinema

Director: Ed Emshwiller

Principal Dancers: Carolyn Carlson, Emery Hermans

Category: MODERN, EXPERIMENTAL

Von Sternberg Prize for Most Original Feature
Film, Mannheim Festival 1970

"A structural interplay of sound, image and sensual tensions"(a plotless feature as explained by
the filmmaker.

IMAGE OF A DANCER

1989, 32 min. color film, video

Distributor: The Cinema Guild

Director: Bruce Nicholson

Dance Company: Marin Ballet

Category: BALLET, CHILDREN

International Film and TV Festival of New York
Silver Medal, Houston International Film Festival Bronze Award

Three young dancers studying with the Marin Ballet in California are shown in class sessions, rehearsals, and public performance, interspersed
with interviews with the dancers and their in-
structors that reveal the intense competition of
the world of professional dance.

IMAGES IN DISTRACTED TIME

1980, 20 min. color, b&w video

Distributor: ARC Videodance

Producer: Jeff Bush

Director: Jeff Bush

Choreographer: Celia Ipiotis

Principal Dancer: Celia Ipiotis

Category: CINEDANCE, MODERN

Solos made specifically for the camera: *Good Thing*
Gone, Finisterre, Motherless Child IV, A Pity,
Take One, and *Solo.*

IMMORTAL SWAN

1935, 38 min. b&w film

Distributor: Museum of Modern Art

Producer: Victor Dandre

Director: Nakhimoff, Edward

Choreographers: Michel Fokine, Laurent Novikov,
Anna Pavlova, Marius Petipa

Principal Dancers: Anna Pavlova, Pierre Vladimiroff

Composers: Camille Saint-Saëns, Frédéric Chopin,
Léon Minkus

Category: BALLET, DANCE HISTORY

In 1935, four years after the death of the great
Russian ballerina Anna Pavlova, her husband
and manager Victor Dandre assembled this collection of performance excerpts from *Invitation*
to the Dance, La Nuit, California Poppy, Don
Quixote, Coqueteries de Columbine, Danse Grec-
que, and *Dragonfly.* Lost for some time, it is one
of the few authentic documents of Pavlova with
scenes of her relaxing, strolling in the garden
and talking to her pet swans. Synchronized by
Vladimir Launitz and Aubrey Hutchins.

IMPROVISATION

1977, 5 min. color video

Distributors: Film-makers' Cooperative, Doris
Chase Productions

Producer: Doris Chase

Director: Doris Chase

Choreographer: Kei Takei

Principal Dancer: Kei Takei

Category: CINEDANCE, MODERN

Modern solos choreographed for television and altered in postproduction to create a kinetic
painting.

IMPROVISATION TO BANSURI FLUTE AND
SEASCAPES

1990, 30 min. color video

Distributor: Beals, Margaret

Producer: Margaret Beals

Director: Roberto Romano

Composers: Judith Pearce, G.S. Sachdev

Category: MODERN, IMPROVISATION

A record of two solos: *Improvisation* (Beals/Sach-
dev) and *Seascapes* (Beals/Pearce), which uses
text from Virginia Woolfe's novel *The Waves,*
performed in St. Mark's Church in New York.

IMPROVISATIONS TO CHOPIN

1985, 30 min. color video

Distributor: Beals, Margaret

Producer: Margaret Beals

Composer: Frédéric Chopin

Category: MODERN, IMPROVISATION

Improvisations of selected *Nocturnes, Preludes* and
Ballades, played by pianist Thomas Hrynkiv.

IMPULSES

1974, 40 min. color film

Distributor: Beals, Margaret

Producer: Impulses Foundation
Director: Peter Powell
Principal Dancer: Margaret Beals
Category: MODERN, IMPROVISATION
Introduced by Walter Terry, the Impulses Company interact spontaneously and demonstrate the art of improvisation. The company consists of three musicians, a singer, a monologist and a dancer.

IN A JAZZ WAY: A PORTRAIT OF MURA DEHN
1986, 30 min. color film, video
Distributor: Filmakers Library
Producers: Louise Ghertler and Pamela Katz
Directors: Louise Ghertler, Pamela Katz
Principal Dancer: Mura Dehn
Category: JAZZ, DOCUMENTARY PORTRAITS
American Film Festival 1986 Blue Ribbon
The late Mura Dehn, a young RussianAmerican who frequented Harlem's Savoy Ballroom in the 1930s, caught the manic inspiration of the lindy and bebop dancers on film, when she wasn't dancing herself. Dehn, eighty-two years old at the time of this film, recounts those halcyon days.

IN A REHEARSAL ROOM
1975, 11 min. color film, video
Distributors: Films Inc., Dance Film Archive, Coe Film Associates
Director: David Hahn
Choreographer: William Carter
Principal Dancers: Cynthia Gregory, Ivan Nagy
Composer: Johann Pachelbel
Category: BALLET
A love-at-first-sight duet danced by two principals with the American Ballet Theatre.

IN CONCERT: PROFILE OF GUS GIORDANO JAZZ DANCE CHICAGO
1987, 37 min. color video
Distributor: Orion Enterprises
Director: Marcia Standiford
Choreographer: Gus Giordano
Dance Company: Gus Giordano Jazz Dance Chicago
Category: JAZZ, DOCUMENTARY PORTRAITS
Features *The Rehearsal Continues, Hot Tamales,* and *On the Corner,* as well as discussions with the Chicago-based jazz choreographer.

IN HEAVEN THERE IS NO BEER?
1984, 51 min. color film
Distributors: Flower Films, Museum of Modern Art, University of California Extension Center, Facets Buffalo State, Film-makers' Cooperative
Producer: Les Blank
Director: Les Blank
Principal Dancers: Walt Solek, Jimmy Sturr, Marion Lush
Category: FOLK, SOCIAL, UNITED STATES
Dance on Camera Festival 1985, Sundance Special Jury Award, Melbourne International Film Festival Grand Award
A celebration of the dance, food, music, friendship and religion of the polka subculture. Poles, Czechs, Germans, young and old, romp away in the eleven-day Polkabration in New London, Connecticut, a polka mass at the International Polka Association convention in Milwaukee, a Polish wedding in Wisconsin and a church lawn party in Buffalo.

IN MOTION WITH MICHAEL MOSCHEN
1991, 57:30 min. color video
Distributor: PBS Video, In Motion Productions
Producer: Skip Blumberg
Director: Skip Blumberg
Choreographer: Michael Moschen
Principal Dancer: Michael Moschen
Composer: David Van Tieghem
Category: CIRCUS ARTS
Michael Moschen(a movement artist, manipulator of geometric forms, and sculptor in motion(combines elements of dance, circus skills, percussion, performance art, and principles of physics into a unique art form.

IN PARIS PARKS
1954, 15 min. color film
Distributor: Museum of Modern Art
Director: Shirley Clarke
Composer: Lanoue Davenport
Category: CHILDREN, CINEDANCE
Children's rhythms as they play in the parks of Paris, cinematically choreographed.

IN PRAISE OF FOLLY
1975, 52 min. color film
Distributor: Films Inc.
Producer: Comacico
Director: Roland Petit
Choreographer: Roland Petit
Principal Dancer: Jean Cau
Composer: Marius Constant
Category: BALLET
Brief ballets on the follies of violence, publicity, machinery, power, love and drugs. Based on a 1966 stage work.

IN THE BLINK OF AN EYE . . . (AMPHIBIAN DREAMS) IF I COULD FLY I WOULD FLY
1987, 25 min. color video
Distributor: Electronic Arts Intermix
Producer: Mary Lucier with WNET/WGBH New Television
Director: Mary Lucier
Principal Dancer: Elizabeth Streb
Composer: Earl Howard
Category: EXPERIMENTAL, MODERN
Evolution from black void to a natural world to a white void. A unique collaboration, one of three with modern dancer Elizabeth Streb, with provocative juxtapositions, close-ups and timing.

IN THE LAND OF THE WAR CANOES
1973, 47 min. b&w video
Distributor: University of California Extension Center
Director: Edward S. Curtis
Category: NATIVE AMERICANS, ANTHROPOLOGICAL
The dance-dramas of the traditional potlatch ceremony of the Kwakiutl Indians of the Pacific Northwest were filmed in the summer of 1914 at villages on Vancouver Island by photographer Edward S. Curtis. The present version added a sound track with authentic Kwakiutl music and narrative.

INDEX
1972, 5 min. b&w film
Distributor: Friedman, Gene
Producer: Gene Friedman
Director: Gene Friedman
Choreographers: Judith Dunn, Gene Friedman

Principal Dancers: Tony Holder, Judith Dunn
Composer: Bill Dixon
Category: EXPERIMENTAL, MODERN
In this experimental film, a duet becomes a sextet through multiple exposures.

INDIA CABARET
1986, 60 min. color film, video
Distributor: Filmakers Library
Director: Mira Nair
Category: INDIA, NIGHTCLUB
American Film Festival 1986 Blue Ribbon, Athens International Film Festival 1986 Golden Athena
Focuses on a group of female strippers who work in a Bombay nightclub, showing the ordinary life the dancers lead during the day, and their transformation in the dressing room into "queens of the night."

INDIA: HAUNTING PASSAGE
1965, 60 min. color film
Series: World Theatre Series
Distributor: PennState
Producer: Newmark Films
Director: Robin Hardy
Dance Company: Little Ballet Troupe of Bombay
Composer: Ravi Shankar
Category: INDIA: DANCE DRAMA
Rajashtan puppets perform *Ramayana,* the classic Sanskrit epic of Rama dethroned and exiled with his wife Sita, who is abducted by a demon king. With the help of a monkey king and general, Rama frees Sita and regains his kingdom. Following this performance is a puppet-ballet fable by Satyajit Ray with music by Ravi Shankar and a performance by The Children's Little Theatre Unit of Calcutta, intercut with a montage of twentieth-century India.

INDIANS OF THE PLAINS, SUNDANCE CEREMONY
1954, 11 min color film
Distributors: Lane Education, University of Minnesota
Producer: James Larsen for Academy Films
Director: James Larsen
Category: NATIVE AMERICANS
The annual *Sundance* includes selecting the site, establishing the camp, preparing the tepees, and the dance ceremonies in the several lodges. The concluding *Grass Dance* involves everyone present.

INDICATIONS OF DISTANCE AND DIRECTION IN THE HONEYBEE: ROUND AND WAGGLE DANCE
1979, 19 min. color film
Distributor: PennState
Producer: Wissen
Category: NATURE
Analyzes the rhythm, energy expenditure, and buzzing of bees doing the round and tail-wagging dance as part of their foraging routine.

INNER RHYTHM
1986, 29 min. color film, video
Distributor: Bullfrog Films
Producers: Niv Fichman and Louise Clark
Director: Niv Fichman
Choreographer: Robert Desrosiers
Composers: John Lang, Ahmed Hassan
Category: COMPOSITION, BALLET, COLLABORATION, CHOREOGRAPHY

American Film Festival Blue Ribbon

Insight into the collaboration between two composers as they create the score for *Blue Snake,* based on videotapes of Desrosiers' silent dance commissioned by the National Ballet of Canada. The choreographer then incorporates their tapes into his rehearsals, gradually developing and refining the score and choreography.

INSIDE EYES
1987, 10 min. color video
Distributor: Electronic Arts Intermix
Director: James Byrne
Choreographer: Victoria Marks
Principal Dancer: Victoria Marks
Category: MODERN, CINEDANCE
Modern dancers shove, hold, lift and crash into the lens as the cameraman swoops among the bodies.

INSIDE THE HOUSE OF FLOATING PAPER
1984, 4:50 min. color film
Distributor: Eccentric Motions
Producer: Pooh Kaye
Director: Pooh Kaye
Composer: John Kilgore
Category: EXPERIMENTAL, ANIMATION
Black Maria Film Festival 1984 Award
Set in the ruins of a New York City shipping wharf, a man and woman struggle to communicate within a world animated by unseen forces.

INSTRUCTIONAL BALLET TAPES DIRECTED BY DOROTHY LISTER (4 videos)
1985, 30 min. each color video
Distributor: Hoctor Products
Category: BALLET, INSTRUCTIONAL, CHILDREN
Teacher: Dorothy Lister
Four tapes, graded pre-ballet and levels 1–3, designed by a performer-choreographer who ran the children's department of the Joffrey School of Ballet. Notes and two record albums also available.

INTENSIVE COURSE IN ELEMENTARY LABANOTATION (5 videos)
1988, 20 min. each color video
Distributor: Dance Horizons
Producer: Laban Institute
Category: INSTRUCTIONAL, NOTATION
Teacher: Jill Beck
Ten basic lessons in labanotation, the system of recording dance on paper, set in a classroom with students learning symbols, asking questions and performing dance exercises. Comes with a thirty-page workbook.

INTERNATIONAL STYLE LATIN DANCING (3 videos)
1988, 60–120 min. color video
Distributor: Jim Forest Videotapes
Producer: Jim Forest
Category: BALLROOM, INSTRUCTIONAL, HISPANIC
Teachers: Keith Todd, Keren Alexis
Southeastern and Florida champions present the cha-cha, samba, rumba, paso doble and jive in the bronze, silver, and gold levels set by the international ballroom competitions.

INTERNATIONAL STYLE MODERN DANCING (7 videos)
1980s, 60 min. each color video
Distributor: Jim Forest Videotapes

Producer: Jim Forest
Principal Dancer: Jim Forest
Category: BALLROOM, INSTRUCTIONAL
Teachers: Maxwell Bishop and Gwynneth Bishop
Demonstration and detailed instructions by British champions currently in Port Charlotte, Florida. Covers the bronze, silver, and gold levels of the modern syllabus for the waltz, tango, foxtrot and quickstep. Performance in tails and gown conclude each tape.

INTRODUCTION TO BALLROOM DANCING
1988, 60 min. color video
Distributors: Taffy's By Mail, Home Vision
Category: INSTRUCTIONAL, BALLROOM
Teacher: Margot Schotz
Swing, rumba, cha-cha, waltz, fox-trot for beginners, as taught by a member of the Imperial Society of Teachers.

AN INTRODUCTION TO BELLY DANCE
1986, 122 min. color video
Distributor: Bastet Productions
Producer: Bastet Productions
Principal Dancer: Kathryn Ferguson
Category: BELLY DANCE, INSTRUCTIONAL
Houston International Film Festival Silver Award
Shimmy variations, steps, and isolation techniques to *beledy* rhythm, a basic in Arabic-Turkish dance. Also body waves, circles, hip sways and muscle-stretching movements for *taxim* and *chiftitelli* rhythms.

INTRODUCTION TO DANCE MEDICINE: KEEPING DANCERS DANCING
1992, 50 min. color video
Distributor: Dance Medicine Education Fund
Producer: Susan Macaluso
Director: Susan Macaluso
Category: DANCE THERAPY, DISABILITIES
Dance on Camera Festival 1992 Honorable Mention
Shows the dancer as an artist, but also an athlete prone to injuries. Orthopedist Dr. William Hamilton, and physical therapists Marika Molnar and Katy Keller, describe causes of these injuries and the specialized care needed. Dancers from *A Chorus Line*, Dance Theatre of Harlem, ABT and others, demonstrate the dance steps and tell their stories.

AN INTRODUCTION TO UZBEK DANCE
1992, 60 min. color video
Distributor: Uzbek Dance Society
Producer: Steven Flynn
Director: Laurel Gray
Choreographers: Isakar Akilov, Mukarram Turganbaeva
Dance Company: Bakhor Ensemble
Category: FOLK
After providing a brief historical and cultural overview of Uzbekistan, this video introduces the three major regional schools of Uzbek dance with examples performed by leading soloists and ensembles.

INTROSPECTION
1941–46, 6:15 min. color film
Distributor: Film-makers' Cooperative
Director: Sara Kathryn Arledge
Principal Dancers: James Mitchell, John R. Baxter
Category: EXPERIMENTAL

Disembodied dancers float through a black space, forming a rhythmic, abstract design.

INVENTION IN DANCE
1960, 29 min. b&w film, video
Series: A Time To Dance.
Distributors: Indiana University, Buffalo State, Lane Education, UCLA Instructional Media Library
Producer: Jac Venza for WNET/13
Choreographers: Alwin Nikolais, Isadora Duncan
Principal Dancer: Ruth St. Denis
Dance Company: Henry Street Playhouse Dance Company
Category: MODERN, DANCE HISTORY
Dancer-composer-designer Alwin Nikolais and Martha Meyers discuss modern dance pioneers Isadora Duncan and Ruth St. Denis, the Denishawn school, and its students Martha Graham, Charles Weidman and Doris Humphrey. Slides and film clips of St. Denis in *Radha*, and a demonstration of the Duncan technique by Sima Boriosivana, are included along with excerpts from Nikolais' *Web, Discs, Noumenon and Fixation* which illustrate his innovations in electronic music, lighting, and costumes.

INVISIBLE DANCE
1981, 12 min. color film
Distributor: Dance Film Archive
Choreographer: David Woodberry
Principal Dancer: David Woodberry
Dance Company: David Woodberry Dance Company
Composer: Laurie Spiegel
Category: MODERN
Dancing in the streets of New York City, oblivious to the crowds.

INVITATION TO KABUKI
3 min. color film
Distributor: The Japan Foundation
Producer: Sakura Motion Picture
Category: JAPAN, DANCE DRAMA
An introduction to the Japanese dramatic form dating from the sixteenth-century, with makeup and costume sessions, the techniques behind the stylized acting and dancing, and the role of musicians in narration and accompaniment. With excerpts from several of the most popular Japanese plays: *Terakoya, Yoshitsuna, Senbonzakura,* and *Kochiyama.*

INVITATION TO THE DANCE
1956, 93 min. color film, video
Distributors: Swank, Films Inc.
Producer: MGM
Director: Gene Kelly
Choreographer: Gene Kelly
Principal Dancers: Gene Kelly, Carol Haney, Igor Youskevitch, Tamara Toumanova, Diana Adams
Composers: Jacques Ibert, André Previn, Nikolai Rimsky-Korsakov
Category: FEATURES, ANIMATION
Academy Award, Berlin Film Festival Grand Prize
Gene Kelly's first effort as a solo director-choreographer with three ballets: *Circus, Ring Around the Rosy* and *Sinbad the Sailor,* partially animated by the Hanna-Barbera studios.

INVOCATION: MAYA DEREN
1987, 53 min. color, b&w film, video
Distributor: Women Make Movies

Director: Jo Ann Kaplin
Category: DOCUMENTARY PORTRAITS
Narrator: Helen Mirren
Biography of the charismatic avant-garde film-maker, poet and anthropologist.

IOWA BLIZZARD '73

1973, 11 min. b&w film
Distributor: Summers, Elaine
Producer: Elaine Summers
Director: Bill Rowley
Category: CINEDANCE, MODERN
A dance in a snow-covered field, with images of the dancers multiplied through film laboratory superimpositions of identical footage in forward, reverse, and slow-motion.

IROQUOIS SOCIAL DANCE I AND II

1980, 18 min. each color film, video
Distributor: Green Mountain Cine
Producer: Nick Manning
Director: Nick Manning
Principal Dancer: Mike Mitchell
Category: INSTRUCTIONAL, NATIVE AMERICANS
An overview of the Iroquois social dances in the first film, and how to do them in the second.

ISADORA

1968, 138 min. color video
Distributor: MCA/Universal
Producer: Universal
Director: Karol Reisz
Category: FEATURES, DANCE HISTORY
Cannes Film Festival 1969 Best Actress, 10 Best Films of the Year
A dramatization of the life of the celebrated modern dancer with Vanessa Redgrave and Jason Robards Jr.

ISADORA DUNCAN: MOVEMENT FROM THE SOUL

1988, 60 min. color film, video
Distributor: Direct Cinema
Producer: Geller-Goldfine Productions
Directors: Dayna Goldfine, Daniel Geller
Choreographer: Isadora Duncan
Principal Dancers: Madeleine Lytton, Lori Belilove, Julie Harris
Dance Company: Oakland Ballet
Composers: Frédéric Chopin, Franz Schubert, Christoph Gluck, Johann Strauss, Alexander Scriabin
Category: MODERN, DANCE HISTORY
Dance on Camera Festival 1990 Gold Award, San Francisco International Film Festival 1989 Golden Gate Award
A documentary based on the writings and letters of Isadora Duncan (1877–1927), the San Francisco-born dancer. A revolutionary artist and rebel who dared to defy the turn-of-the-century Victorian and Puritan mores, Duncan's artistic and social milieu is depicted through archival footage, stills, and news clippings. The solo dances and duet performed include: *Dance of the Furies, Dance of the Blessed Spirits, Narcissus, Gypsy Mazurka, Water Study, Classical Duet, Military March, The Mother, The Revolutionary,* and *The Blue Danube.*

ISADORA DUNCAN: TECHNIQUE AND CHOREOGRAPHY

1978, 29 min. color film
Distributor: Brooks, Virginia
Producer: Virginia Brooks
Director: Virginia Brooks
Choreographer: Isadora Duncan
Principal Dancers: Gemze de Lappe, Hortense Kooluris, Julia Levien
Dance Company: Isadora Duncan Dance Ensemble
Composers: Frédéric Chopin, Franz Schubert, Alexander Scriabin
Category: MODERN, INSTRUCTIONAL
Technique class and perfomances of Schubert's *Three Graces* and *Water Study* waltzes, Chopin's *Mazurka for Two* and *Polonaise Militaire*, and Scriabin's *The Mother* and *The Revolutionary* études.

ISADORA DUNCAN: TECHNIQUE AND REPERTORY

1994, 60 min. color video
Distributor: Dance Horizons
Producer: Dance Arts Foundation
Directors: Julia Levien, Andrea Mantell-Seidel
Choreographer: Isadora Duncan
Dance Company: Isadora Duncan Dance Ensemble
Composers: Frédéric Chopin, Franz Schubert, Johann Strauss
Category: DANCE HISTORY, INSTRUCTIONAL
Dance material includes class work used for teaching Duncan dance—basic technique and patterns—correlating to the text *Duncan Dance—A Guide for Young People Ages Six to Sixteen* by Julia Levien, with performances of original Duncan repertory from 1905 to 1923 such as *Southern Roses Waltz, Dubinushka, Under the Scarf,* and *Slow Mazurka.*

ISADORA DUNCAN: THE BIGGEST DANCER IN THE WORLD

1966, 67 min. b&w film
Distributor: Biograph Entertainment
Producer: BBC-TV
Director: Ken Russell
Principal Dancer: Vivien Pickles
Category: MODERN, FEATURES, DANCE HISTORY
In this feature based on the life of modern dance pioneer Isadora Duncan, the dancer is portrayed as an eccentric genius languishing over her lack of fulfillment as an artist and as a lover.

ISLAND OF THE RED PRAWNS

1978, 52 min. color film, video
Distributor: University of California Extension Center
Category: ANTHROPOLOGICAL, ASIA
In preparations for a wedding between the children of two chieftains in the Fiji Islands, people dance ecstatically on burning coals. During the feast, dancers and singers tell the legend of sacrosanct red prawns.

IT DOESN'T WAIT

1990, 8 min. color video
Series: Alive From Off Center
Distributor: KTCA-TV
Producers: KTCA-TV and Openhaus
Director: Mark Openhaus
Choreographer: Doug Elkins
Principal Dancer: Doug Elkins
Composers: Bob Clarida, Ken Walicki
Category: EXPERIMENTAL, MODERN
Dancers emerge and disappear in street settings, as

choreographed by a former break-dancer who studied ballet, modern dance, aikido and Peking Opera traditions.

ITAM HAKIM ITOPIIT (We Someone, the Hopi)

1984, 58 min. color video
Distributors: Phoenix, Facets
Producers: ZDF TV and IS Productions
Director: Victor Masayesva Jr.
Category: NATIVE AMERICANS
Storyteller: Ross Macaya
In recognition of the Hopi Centennial, this program integrates images of native and Hopi Indian life, history, mythology, ritual music and performances with the life and stories of Hopi. In the Hopi language with English subtitles.

IT'S ALWAYS FAIR WEATHER

1955, 101 min. color film, video, laser
Distributors: Facets, Swank, MGM/UA, Laserdisc Fan Club
Producer: MGM
Directors: Gene Kelly, Stanley Donen
Choreographers: Gene Kelly, Stanley Donen
Principal Dancers: Gene Kelly, Cyd Charisse, Dan Dailey, Michael Kidd
Composer: André Previn
Category: FEATURES, MUSICALS
Intended as a sequel to *On the Town* in which three ex-soldiers meet for their tenth reunion, only to find they have little in common until brought together through a television show. Notable for two street dances, one with garbage cans and the other by Kelly on roller skates (*I Like Myself*) and also for Cyd Charisse's routine with boxers at Shillman's gym (*Baby You Knock Me Out*).

IVAN THE TERRIBLE (Bolshoi Ballet)

1977, 91 and 120 min. color film, video, laser
Distributors: Kultur, Home Vision, Corinth, Viewfinders
Producer: Mosfilm Studios
Director: L. Ohrimenko
Choreographer: Yuri Grigorovich
Principal Dancers: Yuri Vladimirov, Natalya Bessmertnova, Boris Akimov
Dance Company: Bolshoi Ballet
Composer: Sergei Prokofiev
Category: FULL-LENGTH BALLETS
The classic ballet depicting key episodes in the life of Ivan IV, the cruel sixteenth-century Russian Czar, in this story of murder and intrigue.

IVAN THE TERRIBLE (Bolshoi Ballet)

1990, 120 min. color video, laser
Distributors: Viewfinders, Kultur, Corinth, Home Vision, Media Basics
Producers: Primetime Entertainment, NHK, Japan Arts Corporation, and Video/Film Bolshoi
Choreographer: Yuri Grigorovich
Principal Dancers: Irek Mukhamedov, Natalya Bessmertnova, Gedeminas Taranda
Dance Company: Bolshoi Ballet
Composer: Sergei Prokofiev
Category: FULL-LENGTH BALLETS
Recorded live at the Bolshoi Theatre in Moscow.

JAPAN: THE FROZEN MOMENT

1965, 60 min. b&w film
Series: World Theatre Series
Distributor: PennState
Category: JAPAN, DANCE DRAMA

The dance, music and poetry of Japan's *Noh*, *Ka-buki*, and *Bunraku* theatre traditions, with scenes from the *Noh* play *Matsukaze*.

JAZZ (2 videos)
1985, 30 min. each color video
Distributor: Hoctor Products
Producer: Studio Music Corporation
Category: INSTRUCTIONAL, JAZZ
Teacher: Scott Benson
Technique class and six complete jazz routines.

JAZZ DANCE
1980, 4 min. color film, video
Series: Doris Chase Dance Series—Four Solos
Distributors: Film-makers' Cooperative, Museum of Modern Art
Producer: Doris Chase
Director: Doris Chase
Principal Dancer: Gay Delanghe
Composers: Jelly Roll Morton, Scott Joplin
Category: MODERN, EXPERIMENTAL
Transformed through synthesized images, the dancer interprets the bouncing rhythms of Jelly Roll Morton. Director Doris Chase explains, "I used an outline generator and controlled the time sequence with a slow-motion disc to choreograph with the dancer."

JAZZ DANCE CLASS 1989
1989, 60 min. color video
Distributor: Orion Enterprises
Producer: James F. Robinson
Dance Company: Gus Giordano Dance Company
Category: JAZZ, INSTRUCTIONAL
Teacher: Gus Giordano
Jazz dance instruction with Chicago-based teacher Gus Giordano, covering the warm-up, walks, center barre, and basic technique. With interview and performance.

JAZZ DANCE CLASS WITH GUS GIORDANO
1984, 63 min. color video
Distributors: Kultur, Dance Horizons, Orion Enterprises, Home Vision
Producers: Wendell and Marge Moody for All Night Moving Pictures
Director: James F. Robinson
Choreographer: Gus Giordano
Composer: Michael Morales
Category: INSTRUCTIONAL, JAZZ
Teacher: Gus Giordano
Interview, performance footage and class with the Chicago-based teacher, Gus Giordano.

THE JAZZ DANCE JIGSAW
1990, 115 min. color video
Distributor: Orion Enterprises
Producer: Jazz Dance World Congress
Director: Meg Amato
Category: JAZZ
Combines the history and growth of jazz dance with highlights of the First Jazz Dance World Congress, held in Evanston, Illinois in 1990. Includes excerpts of concert footage from jazz dance companies from around the world, plus interviews and panel discussions.

JAZZ DANCE WITH CHRISTY LANE (4 videos)
199?, 50 min. each color video
Distributors: Dance Horizons, Instructional Video
Category: INSTRUCTIONAL, JAZZ
Teacher: Christy Lane

Four programs—beginning, low intermediate, high intermediate, and advanced—teach jazz technique and combinations in an easy-to-follow way.

JAZZ FOR KIDZ: PROGRESSIONS AND COMBINATIONS WITH BOB RIZZO (3 videos)
1993, 42, 35, and 35 min. color video
Distributor: Dance Horizons
Category: CHILDREN, INSTRUCTIONAL, JAZZ
Three programs—*Beginner, Intermediate,* and *Advanced*—teach techniques and short routines using children of different ages performing battements, pirouettes, kicks and jumps.

JAZZ HOOFER: BABY LAURENCE
1981, 28 min. color film, video
Distributor: Rhapsody Films
Producer: Bill Hancock
Director: Bill Hancock
Principal Dancers: Baby Laurence, Bill "Bojangles" Robinson, John Bubbles, King Rastus Brown
Composers: Charlie Parker, Art Tatum
Category: TAP, DOCUMENTARY PORTRAITS
Records the bebop dance style and life of one of the great old tap dancers, Baby Laurence. Includes performances of King Rastus Brown, Bill Robinson and John Bubbles, with unusual film clips of musicians Charlie Parker and Art Tatum, whose music inspired Baby Laurence.

JAZZ JAZZ JAZZ
1988, 30 min. color video
Distributor: Hoctor Products
Producer: Studio Music Corporation
Category: INSTRUCTIONAL, JAZZ
Teacher: Richard Pierlon
Jazz routines and technique for turns and jumps.

JAZZ PARADES: FEET DON'T FAIL ME NOW
1990, 60 min. color, b&w video
Series: American Patchwork
Distributors: Pacific Arts, PBS Video
Producer: Alan Lomax
Category: JAZZ
New Orleans, birthplace of American jazz, is the setting for an exploration by Alan Lomax of neighborhood dances, social clubs, a rooftop dancer named Spiderman, and Mardi Gras.

JEAN ERDMAN: OUT OF CHAOS, *AMOR*
1967, 14 min. b&w film
Distributor: Lane Education
Producer: Jean V. Cutler
Director: Jean V. Cutler
Choreographer: Jean Erdman
Principal Dancer: Jean Erdman
Category: MODERN, DOCUMENTARY PORTRAITS
Jean Erdman, a former Martha Graham soloist, teaches a class at the University of California in Los Angeles, and performs a solo, *Amor.*

JEAN-LOUIS BARRAULT: A MAN OF THE THEATRE
1984, 58 min. color film
Distributor: Arthur Cantor, Inc.
Producer: Helen Gary Bishop
Director: Muriel Balash
Category: PANTOMIME, DOCUMENTARY PORTRAITS
A portrait of the mime-actor-director-entrepre-

neur Jean-Louis Barrault with scenes of his performances and interviews with colleagues, including stage director Peter Brook and actress Jeanne Moreau.

JEAN-LOUIS BARRAULT: THE BODY SPEAKS
1984, 28 min. color film
Distributor: Arthur Cantor, Inc.
Producer: Helen Gary Bishop
Director: Muriel Balash
Category: PANTOMIME
Excerpts from the one-man show of the French mime filmed live in Lincoln Center's Alice Tully Hall in June, 1981.

JESUS, SON OF MAN
1988, 70 min. color video
Distributor: Coe Film Associates
Producer: Hungarian MTV
Choreographer: Ivan Marko
Principal Dancer: Ivan Marko
Dance Company: Hungarian State Opera Ballet Company
Composer: Franz Liszt
Category: FULL-LENGTH BALLETS, RELIGIOUS/RITUAL
A dance oratorio.

LE JEUNE HOMME ET LA MORT
1965, 15 min. color film, video
Distributor: FACSEA
Director: Roland Petit
Choreographer: Roland Petit
Principal Dancers: Rudolf Nureyev, Zizi Jeanmaire
Composer: Johann Sebastian Bach
Category: BALLET, DANCE DRAMA
Inspired by playwright Jean Cocteau, this dramatic ballet is a landmark film for its sensitive camera work and acrobatic choreography. Rudolf Nureyev plays the tormented young man, originally played by Jean Babilee. Zizi Jeanmaire provides the noose.

JITTERBUG: BEGINNERS! and JITTERBUG 2: INTERMEDIATE (2 videos)
1992, 60 min. each color video
Distributor: Dance Horizons
Producer: West Coast Dance Productions
Principal Dancers: Kyle Webb, Susan Parisi
Category: SOCIAL, INSTRUCTIONAL
Instruction in dancing the jitterbug at two levels.

JITTERING JITTERBUGS
1940s, 11 min. b&w film
Distributor: Dance Film Archive
Category: SOCIAL, DANCE HISTORY
Social dances, big apple and jitterbug performed in a Harlem ballroom.

JOHN CRANKO
1970, 7 min. color film, video
Distributor: Modern Talking Picture Service
Choreographer: John Cranko
Principal Dancers: Marcia Haydee, Richard Cragun
Dance Company: Stuttgart Ballet
Category: BALLET, DOCUMENTARY PORTRAITS, CHOREOGRAPHY
Interviews and practice sessions with Marcia Haydee and Richard Cragun about the late choreographer who developed the Stuttgart Ballet Company of Germany into a company of international significance.

JOHN LINDQUIST: PHOTOGRAPHER OF DANCE
1980, 28 min. color film
Distributor: Brodsky & Treadway
Producer: Brodsky & Treadway
Director: Robert P. Brodsky
Choreographer: Norman Walker
Principal Dancers: Christian Holder, Joyce Cuoco, Youri Vamos
Category: MODERN, DOCUMENTARY POR-TRAITS
Portrait of the staff photographer at Jacob's Pillow Dance Festival and his working style and philosophy. Shows him at age eighty-nine photographing dancers at Jacob's Pillow and shows numerous photographs of Ted Shawn, Ruth St. Denis, Alicia Alonso, and Christian Holder.

JONATHAN AND THE ROCKER
1977, 26 min. color video
Distributor: Doris Chase Productions
Producer: Doris Chase
Director: Doris Chase
Choreographer: Jonathan Hollander
Principal Dancer: Jonathan Hollander
Composers: William Bolcomb, Timothy Thompson, George Kleinsinger
Category: MODERN, EXPERIMENTAL
A modern dancer performs a duet with a sculptural form which is animated by the Rutt-Etra video synthesizer.

JOSÉ GRECO: IN PERFORMANCE
1959, 26 min. b&w video
Distributors: Dance Horizons, Corinth
Producers: Video Artists International, New England Conservatory
Principal Dancer: José Greco
Category: FOLK, HISPANIC
José Greco appeared live on the *Voice of Firestone* telecast on January 5, 1959. This video of that performance shows the dancer at the peak of his career, surrounded by his troupe of dancers, singers and instrumentalists. Selections include: *Pastoral Romance* (traditional folk dance of Galicia); *Castellana* (traditional folk dance of Castille); *Córdoba* (Andalusian Serenade); *Granada* (traditional folk dance of the *gitanos* of Andalusia); and *Wedding Dance* (traditional folk dance of Valencia).

JOSEPH'S LEGENDE
1991, 66 min. color video
Distributors: Home Vision, Viewfinders, Corinth
Choreographer: John Neumeier
Principal Dancers: Judith Jamison, Kevin Haigen, Karl Musil, Franz Wilhelm
Dance Company: Vienna State Opera Ballet
Composer: Richard Strauss
Category: FULL-LENGTH BALLETS
A performance of the ballet in one act based on the Biblical story.

THE JOY OF BACH
1979, 60 min. color video
Distributor: Vision Video
Producer: Lutheran Film Associates
Director: Paul Lammers
Choreographer: Manfred Schnelle
Principal Dancers: Téo Morca, Nellie Cotto, Floyd Chisholm, Marina Otto

Dance Company: Jacobs Pillow Dancers, Jeff Duncan Dancers
Composer: Johann Sebastian Bach
Category: MODERN
A salute to the composer with five dances set to the Allegro from *Concerto for Two Harpsichords in C Minor*, *Fugue in D Minor*, the Presto from *Concerto No. 5 for Harpsichord*, the Allegro from the *Violin Concerto in A Minor*, and *Air from Orchestral Suite No. 3 in D Major*.

THE JUDSON PROJECT TAPES (13 videos)
1980–1982, 2–83 min. b&w video
Distributor: The Kitchen
Producer: Bennington College
Principal Dancers: Elaine Summers, Yvonne Rainer, Phoebe Neville, Steve Paxton, Arleen Passloff, Jackson Maclow, John Herbert McDowell, David Gordon, Simone Forti, Al Carmines, Philip Corner, Lucinda Childs, Trisha Brown, Alex Hay, Robert Rauchenberg
Category: MODERN COMPANIES
The founding members of the experimental modern dance group active in New York City's Judson Church in the 1960s discuss their work, which is illustrated with archival footage.

JUMP
1984, 15 min. color video
Distributor: The Kitchen
Producer: Le Ministère de la Culture Octet et Network
Director: Charles Atlas
Choreographer: Philippe Decoufle
Musicians: Joseph Biscuit and The Residents
Category: EXPERIMENTAL, COMEDY
The cheerful, fragmented style of the director matches the nonchalant angularity of the French choreographer whose dancers sport whimsical costumes and headdresses by Lulu and Bill Tornado.

JUNCTION
1965, 12 min. color film
Distributors: Dance Film Archive, Burckhardt, Rudolph
Producer: Rudolph Burckhardt
Director: Rudolph Burckhardt
Choreographer: Paul Taylor
Principal Dancers: Bettie de Jong, Carolyn Adams, Dan Wagoner, Daniel Grossman, Paul Taylor, Elizabeth Walton
Dance Company: Paul Taylor Dance Company
Composer: Johann Sebastian Bach
Category: MODERN
A quick paced work for the *First* and *Fourth Suites for Unaccompanied Cello*.

JUPITER'S DARLING
1955, 96 min. color video, laser
Distributor: MGM/UA
Producer: MGM
Director: George Sidney
Choreographers: Hermes Pan, Gower Champion
Principal Dancers: Marge and Gower Champion, Esther Williams
Composers: Burton Lane, Harold Adamson
Category: FEATURES, MUSICALS
A lavish spoof of both wide-screen spectacles and the Hannibal legend which includes an Esther Williams underwater ballet in which marble statues come to life. The Champions dance in a slave market and around trained elephants.

JUST FOR FUN
1980s. 30 min. color video
Distributor: Hoctor Products
Producer: Studio Music Corporation
Category: INSTRUCTIONAL, JAZZ
Teacher: Mallory Graham
Jazz routines.

JUST FOR ME
1984, 27 min. color film, video
Distributor: Phoenix
Producer: Lauren Productions, Ltd. for the National Film Board of Canada
Director: Louis Tupper
Category: DANCE THERAPY, WOMEN
Three women take time from their families and businesses to dance and have fun.

THE JVC VIDEO ANTHOLOGY OF WORLD MUSIC AND DANCE (30 videos)
1988, 37–60 min. color video
Distributor: Multicultural Media
Producer: Victor Company of Japan, Ltd.
Category: FOLK, DANCE HISTORY
Contains five hundred folk music and dance performances from more than one hundred countries in Europe, Asia, Oceania, Africa and the Americas, in both excerpted and original film footage format. Accompanied by nine companion volumes with descriptive information.

THE JVC/SMITHSONIAN FOLKWAYS VIDEO ANTHOLOGY OF MUSIC AND DANCE OF AFRICA (3 videos)
1996 47–56 min. color video
Distributor: Multicultural Media
Producer: Victor Company of Japan, Ltd.
Category AFRICA, FOLK
A three-video/three-booklet collection containing seventy-five performances from Egypt, Uganda, Senegal, the Gambia, Liberia, Ghana, Nigeria, Kenya, Malawi, Botswana and South Africa.

THE JVC/SMITHSONIAN FOLKWAYS VIDEO ANTHOLOGY OF MUSIC AND DANCE OF EUROPE (2 videos)
1996 58 min. each color video
Distributor: Multicultural Media
Director: Kunihiko Nakagawa
Producer: Victor Company of Japan, Ltd.
Category: EUROPE, FOLK
A two-video/two-booklet collection of fifty-eight performances from Iceland, the Faroe Islands, Denmark, Ireland, Scotland, Wales, England, France, Italy, the Czech Republic, Hungary, Romania and Serbia.

THE JVC/SMITHSONIAN FOLKWAYS VIDEO ANTHOLOGY OF MUSIC AND DANCE OF THE AMERICAS (6 videos)
1996 43–59 min. color video
Distributor: Multicultural Media
Producer: Victor Company of Japan, Ltd.
Category UNITED STATES, CARIBBEAN, LATIN AMERICA, FOLK
A collection of one hundred fifty eight performances from Canada, the United States, the Caribbean and Central and South America, each video accompanied by a book.

KA
1986, 16:40 min. color video
Distributor: Freedman, Laurie

Producer: Laurie Freedman
Director: David Kedem
Choreographer: Laurie Freedman
Principal Dancer: Sally-Anne Friedland
Composer: David Geyra
Category: EXPERIMENTAL, MODERN
Dance on Camera Festival Silver Award for Experimental Video
A woman meets a desert spirit, which she takes to be her *Ka*, the Egyptian term for one's double who shadows us in life in preparation for life after death. Shot in the Judean Desert and the Dead Sea, Israel.

KABUKI: CLASSIC THEATRE OF JAPAN
1964, 30 min. color film
Distributor: The Japan Foundation
Producer: Kaga Productions
Category: DANCE DRAMA, JAPAN
Excerpts from four plays of Kabuki, which three hundred years ago developed the stylized gesture and speech of the classical Japanese theatrical tradition, with the dance sequences from *Musume Dojoji* and *Kagami Jishi*.

KALAHARI
1984, 7:30 min. color video
Distributors: Deborah Gladstein and Sam Kanter
Producers: Deborah Gladstein and Sam Kanter
Director: Sam Kanter
Choreographer: Deborah Gladstein
Category: MODERN, EXPERIMENTAL
Portions of dancers' bodies sweep across a black screen and freeze. Slow-motion images appear and disappear, driven by a rhythmic, pulsating sound track.

KALAKSHETRA: DEVOTION TO DANCE
1985, 50 min. color video
Distributor: Centre Communications
Producer: Griffin Productions
Director: Anthony Mayer
Choreographer: Rukmini Devi
Dance Company: Kalakshetra
Category: DANCE DRAMA, INSTRUCTIONAL, INDIA
American Film Festival Blue Ribbon, Dance on Camera Festival 1986 Silver Award
Kalakshetra, India's center for the performing arts, was headed by Rukmini Devi, who devoted her life to the cultural enrichment of children's education and the performance of the epic dance dramas which are the life blood of India's artistic heritage. This video portrays the daily life of the center, showing the teaching and learning process, culminating in a spectacular exposition of dance drama performed at Kalakshetra's Festival of the Performing Arts.

KALYIAN
1986, 10 min. color, b&w video
Distributor: Electronic Arts Intermix
Producer: Barbara Sykes-Dietze
Director: Barbara Sykes-Dietze
Choreographers: Barbara Sykes-Dietze, Jan Heyn-Cubacub
Principal Dancers: Barbara Sykes-Dietze, Jan Heyn-Cubacub
Composer: Richard Woodbury
Category: MARTIAL ARTS, ASIA
Dance on Camera Festival 1986 Honorable Mention
Kalyian is derived from *Kali*, a Philippine warrior martial art founded by the blind princess from the island of Sumar. This tape is a modern day personification of the female warrior spirit, combining elements of technology with dance.

KARATE RAP
1989, 4:30 min. color video
Distributor: Samurai Studios
Producer: David Seeger
Choreographer: Michael Scott Gregory
Principal Dancers: Charlotte d'Amboise, Jay Poindexter
Category: MARTIAL ARTS, MUSIC VIDEOS
Dance on Camera Festival 1989 Gold Award
A tongue-in-cheek promotion of martial arts presented as a music video.

KAREN KAIN: BALLERINA
1977, 54 min. color video
Distributor: Mastervision
Producers: Richard Nielsen and Pat Ferns
Director: Philip McPhedran
Choreographers: John Cranko, Roland Petit
Principal Dancers: Karen Kain, Frank Augustyn, Rudy Bryans, Roland Petit
Dance Company: Ballet National de Marseille
Composers: Georges Bizet, Sergei Prokofiev
Category: BALLET, DOCUMENTARY PORTRAITS
Follows a National Ballet of Canada ballerina on tour in *Carmen* with a French company, the Ballet de Marseille, directed by Roland Petit, and performing a duet from John Cranko's *Romeo and Juliet*. Karen Kain speaks openly about her fears and aspirations with British dance critic Clement Crisp.

KASHIA MEN'S DANCES: SOUTHWESTERN POMO INDIANS
1963, 40 min. color film, video
Series: American Indian Series
Distributors: University of California Extension Center, UCLA Instructional Media Library
Producer: C.C. Macaulay
Director: Clyde B. Smith
Category: NATIVE AMERICANS
Four Pomo dances performed in elaborate headdresses and costumes on the Kashia Reservation on the northern Californian coast in a specially made brush enclosure. The dances, a blend of the ancient and more recently developed religion Bole Maru, celebrate spring, the coming of the salmon, harvest initiation into a secret society or adulthood, and healing the sick. Dances shown are: *Toto*, *Lehuye*, *Bighead*, and *The Ball Dance*.

KATHAK
1949, 10 min. b&w film
Distributor: Lane Education
Producer: Indian Government Information Services
Category: INDIA, GESTURES
North India's favorite classical dance performed with an explanation of hand and finger gestures and facial and body expressions.

KATHERINE DUNHAM
1988, 15 min. color video
Distributor: Encyclopedia Britannica
Producer: Turner Broadcasting
Principal Dancer: Katherine Dunham
Category: MODERN, DOCUMENTARY PORTRAITS, AFRICAN-AMERICANS
A profile of Katherine Dunham, an African-American matriarch of dance, with Hollywood film clips, historical materials, and footage of Dunham's school in East St. Louis. Explores Haitian culture, a subject of much fascination for Dunham, and a complete performance of *Rites de Passage*.

KATHY'S DANCE
1978, 28 min. color film, video
Distributor: Direct Cinema
Producer: Anne Drew
Choreographer: Kathy Posin
Principal Dancer: Kathy Posin
Category: MODERN, INSTRUCTIONAL
American Film Festival 1978 Blue Ribbon
Captures a modern dancer's joyful exuberance and sense of purpose as she teaches, choreographs and performs.

KAZE-NO-KO
1984, 13 min. color video
Distributor: Asia Society
Director: Richard Brevar
Choreographer: Yukio Sekiva
Dance Company: Kaza-no-ko Troupe
Category: PANTOMIME, JAPAN
Dance on Camera Festival 1985
A Japanese troupe of dance-mime performers tells the story of *The Ugly Duckling*, using origami and Japanese *Noh* figures.

KEI TAKEI
1976, 29 min. color video
Distributor: Doris Chase Productions
Producer: Doris Chase
Dance Company: Moving Earth Company
Category: MODERN, CINEDANCE
Using the dance movements of Kei Takei and the Moving Earth Company as themes, avant-garde effects are employed to create video art.

KEMOKO SANO TEACHES AFRICAN DANCE FROM THE REPUBLIC OF GUINEA
1991, 54 min. color video
Distributor: Sano Videos
Producer: Kemoko Sano
Director: Kemoko Sano
Choreographer: Kemoko Sano
Dance Company: Merveilles d'Afrique, Ballets Africains of the Republic of Guinea
Composer: Kemoko Sano
Category: AFRICA, INSTRUCTIONAL
Part I (44 min.) is a lesson in seven traditional rhythm patterns from the Republic of Guinea, demonstrated by dancers in a seaside setting in Guinea, West Africa. Part II (10 min.) is the opening night of Les Ballets Africains' engagement at the Sadler's Wells Theatre in London, September 1990, from the arrival of troupe members at the theatre to a postperformance party.

KHMER COURT DANCE
1992, 75 min. color video
Distributor: Documentary Educational Resources
Producer: Sam-Ang Sam/Naomi Hawes Bishop
Director: John Bishop
Choreographer: Chan Moly Sam
Dance Company: Khmer Studies Institute
Category: ASIA

Studio production of two tapes about Cambodian classical dance.

KICKER DANCIN' TEXAS STYLE: HOW TO DO THE TOP TEN COUNTRY AND WESTERN DANCES LIKE A TEXAS COWBOY
0 min. color video
Distributor: AAHPERD
Category: FOLK, INSTRUCTIONAL, UNITED STATES
Teachers: Shirley Fushing, Patrick McMillan
The basics of the ten popular Texan dances.

KINETIC COLOR IN DANCE
1976, 7 min. color film
Distributor: Iowa State
Producer: R.B. Lindenmeyer
Category: EXPERIMENTAL, MODERN
The shadow of three modern dancers behind a translucent screen is lit from the side and back.

THE KING AND I
1956, 133 min. color video
Distributor: Facets
Producer: 20th Century Fox
Director: Walter Lang
Choreographer: Jerome Robbins
Principal Dancers: Gemze de Lappe, Yuriko Michiko, Dusty Worrall
Composer: Richard Rodgers
Category: FEATURES, MUSICALS
A movie version of the Broadway musical about the Victorian teacher of the Crown Prince of Siam, whose position against slavery influenced her pupil. Dances include *The Small House of Uncle Thomas.*

KING KAMEHAMEHA HULA COMPETITION: 14th AND 15th ANNUAL (3 videos)
1987, 1989, 110, 90, and 70 min. color video
Distributor: Kalama Productions
Producer: David Kalama
Director: Roland Yamamoto
Principal Dancer: Tangaroa Teamaru
Category: HULA, FESTIVALS
Highlights of the hula competitions in honor of the first king of Hawaii with *kahiko* (ancient hula) *auana* (modern hula), and the *oli* (Hawaiian chanting), shot in Hawaii.

KING KONG IN A BLANKET
1978, 9 min. color film, video
Distributor: Ile Ife Films
Producer: Bayne Williams Film Company
Director: Nan Ross
Principal Dancer: John Carrafa
Composer: Brad Terry
Category: DANCE THERAPY
Dance on Camera Festival 1979
Portrait of Spindleworks, a workshop for mentally retarded adults in Brunswick, Maine, selected as one of ten model sites by the National Committee of the Arts for the Handicapped. Dancer John Carrafa, a longtime member of Twyla Tharp's company, shares his joy of moving with the workshop members who also spin yarn and hook rugs.

THE KIROV BALLET: CLASSIC BALLET NIGHT
1988, 95 min. color video
Distributors: V.I.E.W., Corinth
Producer: Soviet Film and TV
Choreographers: Agrippina Vaganova, Marius Petipa, August Bournonville, Arthur Saint-Léon, Anton Dolin
Principal Dancers: Irina Kolpakova, Gabriela Komleva, Tatiana Terekova, Alla Sizova, Galina Mezentseva, Sergei Berezhnoi, Vitali Afanaskov, Natalia Bolshkova, Vadim Gouliaev, Boris Blankov, Svetlana Efrenova, Valeri Emets, Elena Evteeva
Dance Company: Kirov Ballet
Composers: Cesare Pugni, Riccardo Drigo, Edvard Helsted
Category: BALLET COMPANIES
Program from Russia includes: *Diana and Actaeon* (Vaganova/Pugni) performed by Terekova and Berezhnoi; *Esmeralda* (Petipa/Drigo) performed by Komleva and Afanaskov; *Flower Festival at Genzano* (Bournonville/Helsted) performed by Bolshkova and Gouliaev; *The Canteen Keeper* (Saint-Léon/Pugni) performed by Sizova, Blankov and Kirov soloists; *The Venice Carnival* (Petipa/Pugni) performed by Efrenova and Emets; *Pas de Quatre* (Dolin/Pugni) performed by Kolpakova, Komleva, Evteeva, and Mezentseva.

THE KIROV BALLET IN LONDON
1988, 126 min. color video
Distributors: Kultur, Corinth, Dance Horizons, Home Vision
Producer: BBC-TV
Choreographer: Oleg Vinogradov
Principal Dancers: Faroukh Ruzimatov, Altynai Asylmuratova, Natalia Makarova
Dance Company: Kirov Ballet
Category: BALLET
Contains excerpts from many of the world's greatest ballets: *La Bayadère* (*Kingdom of the Shades*); *Esmeralda* (*Pas de Six*); *La Vivandière* (*Pas de Deux*); *Le Papillon* (*Pas de Deux*); *Swan Lake* (*Pas de Deux*); *Don Quixote* (*Pas de Deux*); *Le Corsaire* (*Le Jardin Animé*). A highlight is a special guest appearance by Natalia Makarova, reunited with her former company after an absence of seventeen years.

KIROV SOLOISTS: INVITATION TO THE DANCE
1989, 54 min. color video
Distributors: V.I.E.W., Corinth
Producer: Soviet Film and TV
Choreographers: Nikolai Kovmir, Roland Petit, V. Timofeev, Marius Petipa, L. Lebedev, Paul Taglioni, Agrippina Vaganova
Principal Dancers: Irina Kolpakova, Tatiana Terekova, Sergei Berezhnoi, Olga Tchenchikova
Dance Company: Kirov Ballet
Composers: Cesare Pugni, J.M. Jarre, Norbert Burgmuller, Heitor Villa-Lobos, Jacques Offenbach
Category: BALLET COMPANIES
Performance and rehearsals of six ballets by the great Russian troupe: *Diana and Actaeon* (Vaganova/Pugni); *Nôtre Dame de Paris* (Petit/Jarre); *Pas de Deux* (Timofeev/Burgmuller); *Carnival de Venise* (Petipa/Pugni); *Bachiana* (Lebedev/Villa-Lobos); and *Le Papillon* (Taglioni/Offenbach). Between each, ballerina Kolpakova takes the viewer backstage.

KISS ME KATE
1953, 109 min. color film, video
Distributors: Swank, MGM/UA
Producer: MGM
Director: George Sidney
Choreographers: Hermes Pan, Bob Fosse
Principal Dancers: Ann Miller, Tommy Rall, Bobby Van, Bob Fosse
Composer: Cole Porter
Category: FEATURES, MUSICALS
A film version of the Broadway show about a theatrical troupe putting on a musical version of Shakespeare's *Taming of the Shrew*, with the offstage sparring of the two stars in tandem with their onstage performance. Dance numbers include: *From This Moment On, Too Darn Hot, Always True To You in My Fashion, Why Can't You Behave?* and *Tom, Dick and Harry.*

KIT'S KIDS
1980s, 30 min. color video
Distributor: Hoctor Products
Producer: Studio Music Corporation
Category: INSTRUCTIONAL, JAZZ, CHILDREN
Teacher: Kit Andree
Jazz routines for kids.

KONTAKION: A SONG OF PRAISE
1972, 26 min. color video
Distributor: The Media Guild
Producer: Thames Television
Choreographer: Barry Moreland
Principal Dancer: William Louther
Dance Company: London Contemporary Dance Theatre
Composer: Peter Maxwell Davis
Category: BALLET, RELIGIOUS/RITUAL
A contemporary ballet depicting Christ's birth, baptism, ministry, healing, crucifixion and resurrection. *Kontakion* is the Greek word for "a song of praise."

KOREA: PERFORMING ARTS: THE WONDERFUL WORLD OF KIM SUNG HEE
1979, 21 min. color film
Series: Korea
Distributors: Indiana University, Coe Film Associates, Lane Education, Coronet/MTI
Producer: Centron
Director: Harold Harvey
Principal Dancer: Kim Sung Hee
Category: DANCE DRAMA, ASIA
American Film Festival
Traditional dances performed by Kim Sung Hee of the National Theatre of Seoul, who explains that the central theme in all Korean performing arts is unity with nature.

KUMU HULA: KEEPERS OF A CULTURE
1989, 85 min. color film, video
Distributors: Rhapsody Films, Facets, Kino, Music Video Distributors
Producers: Robert Mugge and Vicky Holt Takamine
Directors: Lawrence McConkey, Eric Roland, Robert Mugge
Principal Dancers: Iris Nalei Napaepae-Kunewa
Dance Company: Halau O Kaleiho Ohie
Category: HULA
Chanting to the Goddess Pele on the Island of Kilauea and performing animal-inspired pieces, a group of Hawaiians share the history and traditions of the hula, the dance imported from Polynesia. The documentary is one of three on Hawaii that honors the advice *Au'a'la e tama e tona motu*, which in translation means "Hold fast, o child, to your heritage."

KYLIAN COLLECTION
1991, 91 min. color laser
Distributor: Corinth
Choreographer: Jiri Kilian
Dance Company: Nederlands Dans Theatre
Composers: Franz Joseph Haydn, Claude Debussy, Arnold Schoenberg, Carlos Chavez
Category: BALLET
Performances include Haydn's symphonies *The Clock* and *La Chasse,* Debussy's *Silent Cries,* Schoenberg's *Transfigured Night* and Chavez' *Stamping Ground.*

LACHO DROM
1994, 103 min. color film, video
Distributor: New Yorker Films
Producer: Michele Ray Gavras
Director: Tony Gatlif
Category: INTERNATIONAL
Shot in eight countries from Afghanistan to Spain, a gypsy leads a tour into the hearts of his own people solely through amazing photography, music and dance.

THE LADY OF THE CAMELLIAS
1987, 125 min. color video
Distributors: Kultur, Viewfinders, Corinth, Home Vision, Media Basics
Producer: Polyphon with Fernseh, Hamburg
Director: John Neumeier
Choreographer: John Neumeier
Principal Dancers: Marcia Haydee, Ivan Liska
Dance Company: Hamburg Ballet
Composer: Frédéric Chopin
Category: FULL-LENGTH BALLETS, DANCE DRAMA
Dance on Camera Festival 1988 Gold Award
Inspired by the nineteenth-century French novel by Alexander Dumas, John Neumeier choreographed this beautifully shot and designed film of a courtesan's love for a younger man, forbidden by his father and further complicated by her tuberculosis.

LAMBACHEN and STEINHAUSER LANDLER
(2 films)
1970, 1973, 8 and 10 min. b&w film
Distributor: PennState
Producer: Wissen
Category: FOLK, EUROPE
The dance from Lambach im Traunviertel, Austria accompanied by accordion, two violins and double bass, followed by Bavarian polka.

LAMBETH WALK: NAZI STYLE
1942, 2 min. b&w film
Distributor: Biograph Entertainment
Category: EXPERIMENTAL
Satirical World War II propaganda and a takeoff on the popular ballroom dance of the 1940s.

LAMENT
1951, 16 min. b&w film
Distributors: Dance Films Association, PennState, Lane Education
Producer: Walter V. Strate
Director: Walter V. Strate
Choreographer: Doris Humphrey
Principal Dancers: José Limón, Letitia Ide, Ellen Love
Composer: Norman Lloyd
Category: MODERN, DANCE HISTORY
Re-staged for film, this dark trio honors the death of a bullfighter as Federico García Lorca's poem *Lament for Ignacio Sánchez Mejías* is recited.

LAMENT
1985, 9 min. b&w video
Distributor: Electronic Arts Intermix
Producer: Walker Art Center, Minneapolis
Director: James Byrne
Choreographers: Eiko and Koma
Principal Dancers: Eiko and Koma
Composer: Karma Moffett
Category: EXPERIMENTAL, MODERN
A duet performed in two adjacent puddles of water with low lighting that catches the pool reflections and sculpts the slowly twisting naked bodies.

LAMENTATION
1943, 10 min. color film
Distributors: Dance Films Association, National Archives
Producer: Harmon Film Foundation
Directors: Mr. and Mrs. Simon Moselsio
Choreographer: Martha Graham
Principal Dancer: Martha Graham
Composer: Zoltán Kodály
Category: MODERN, DANCE HISTORY
John Martin, former dance critic of the *New York Times,* gives a brief history of modern dance and discusses dance as a medium of expression. Martha Graham performs excerpts from her 1930 solo, accompanied by Louis Horst on the piano. Twisting in her costume which covers her from head to toe, Graham becomes a sculptural study of agony.

THE LANGUAGE OF DANCE
1960, 29 min. b&w film
Series: A Time To Dance
Distributor: Indiana University
Producer: Jac Venza for WNET/13
Principal Dancers: José Limón, Pauline Koner, Lucas Hoving, Betty Jones, Robert Powell, Lola Huth
Dance Company: José Limón Company
Composer: Norman Dello Joio
Category: MODERN, DANCE HISTORY
Choreographer-dancer José Limón and teacher Martha Meyers talk about the language of dance and movement. The film features Limón's *There is a Time,* a classic choreographed in 1956, inspired by the line in the book of *Ecclesiastes,* "To everything there is a season, and a time to every purpose under the heaven."

THE LAST DANCING ISADORABLE
1988, 30 min. color video
Distributor: Bardsley, Kay
Producer: Kay Bardsley
Choreographer: Maria-Theresa Duncan
Principal Dancers: Maria-Theresa Duncan, Clive Thompson
Category: MODERN, DANCE HISTORY, DOCUMENTARY PORTRAITS
Focus on the life and career of the late Maria-Theresa Duncan, an adopted daughter of Isadora Duncan, portrayed through stills, paintings and clips of her performances, including *March Slav,* in the 1920s and in 1976.

LAURETTA: MADONNA OF THE SENIOR CITIZEN SET
1989, 20 min. color video
Distributor: Motion Pixels
Producer: Jean de Boysson
Director: Jean de Boysson
Category: DOCUMENTARY PORTRAITS, BELLY DANCE
Dance on Camera Festival 1990 Honorable Mention
An uninhibited sixty-three-year-old retired factory worker talks about her second career, belly dancing, and performs in community events.

LEARN HOW TO DANCE (82 videos)
1986–91, 60 min. each color video
Distributor: Butterfly Video
Producer: Sherry Greene for Butterfly Video
Director: Sherry Greene
Category: BALLROOM, INSTRUCTIONAL
Teacher: Kathy Blake
Series includes lessons in the fox trot, jitterbug, waltz, tango, samba, cha-cha, rumba, merengue, mambo, disco hustle, Charleston, polka, salsa, line dances, west coast swing, peabody, children, lambada. Also available through Butterfly, eleven titles with David Nicholas, Boston makeup artist, and a two-and-a-half hour preview tape.

LEARNING TO DANCE IN BALI
1930s, 13 min. b&w film, video
Distributors: University of California Extension Center, PennState
Producers: Margaret Mead and Gregory Bateson
Director: Gregory Bateson
Principal Dancer: I. Mario
Category: ANTHROPOLOGICAL, BALI
Narrator: Margaret Mead
This landmark film by anthropologists Margaret Mead and Gregory Bateson, demonstrates the extraordinary means of passing on a traditional Balinese dance through manipulation and imitation. Mead advocated recording all her observations whether by words or camera, and thereby transformed the method of social anthropological research. The footage was taken by Bateson in the 1930s and narrated by Mead just before her death in 1978.

LEE'S FERRY
1982, 8 min. color film
Distributor: Gross, Sally
Director: Susan Brockman
Choreographer: Sally Gross
Principal Dancer: Sally Gross
Composer: Keith Jarrett
Category: EXPERIMENTAL, ART
Painter: Joan Kurahara
Dance on Camera Festival 1982 Honorable Mention
A moving landscape is formed by the dancer's images combined with a series of projected light from painted slides.

THE LEGACY OF THE CHOREOGRAPHY OF ISADORA DUNCAN
1988, 45 min. color video
Distributor: Dance Films Association
Producers: Julia Levien with Dance Films Association
Director: Penny Ward
Choreographer: Isadora Duncan
Principal Dancers: Julia Levien, Hortense Kooluris
Dance Company: Isadora Duncan Dance Ensemble

This remake of a remake had its stage debut in 1864 with choreography by the Frenchman Arthur Saint-Léon. Based on a Russian fairytale by Yershov Ivanushka, a young man befriends a horse with magical powers, which helps him to win the love of a woman, trick a half-witted Czar, and live happily ever after as a prince.

LITTLE LIEUTENANT
1993, 6 min. color film, video
Distributors: Canyon Cinema, Film-makers' Cooperative
Producer: Sally Silvers
Directors: Sally Silvers, Henry Hills
Choreographer: Sally Silvers
Dance Company: Sally Silvers and Dancers
Composer: Kurt Weill
Category: MODERN
Dance on Camera Festival 1993 Silver Award
A look back at the late Weimar era with its struggles and celebrations leading up to world war as seen through current day eyes. Scored to John Zorn's arrangement of the Kurt Weill song, *Little Lieutenant of the Loving God,* and drawing its imagery both from the original song and its defiantly idiosyncratic rearrangement, the film presents a prismatic reading of what was originally a solo dance.

THE LITTLEST REBEL
1935, 70 min. b&w video
Distributors: CBS/Fox, Films Inc., Facets
Producer: Twentieth Century Fox
Director: David Butler
Principal Dancers: Shirley Temple, Bill "Bojangles" Robinson
Category: FEATURES, TAP, CHILDREN
Of the nineteen movies the child star made in the thirties, this one is notable for her duet on the stairs with one of the all-time great hoofers, Bill Robinson. The story line follows Shirley's determination to save her father, a confederate soldier, even if it requires a visit to President Lincoln.

LIVE AND REMEMBER (Wo Kiksuye)
1987, 29 min. color video
Distributor: Solaris
Producer: Solaris in association with South Dakota Public TV
Principal Dancers: Sir Ben Black Bear, Marty Good Bear, Lloyd One Star
Composer: Ironwood Singers
Category: NATIVE AMERICANS
San Francisco International Film Festival 1988 Best of Show
Opening with footage of a Sweat Lodge Ceremony, a source of spiritual strength, this documentary shows Lakota Indian elders, medicine men, and dancers discussing the challenge of keeping their native culture alive. Shot on the Rosebud Reservation in South Dakota, the dance footage includes performances of the *Eagle, Sneak-Up,* and *Hoop-Dance,* with examples of fancy dancing.

LIVE VIDEO DANCE
1987, 6:20 min. color video
Distributor: Electronic Arts Intermix
Producer: Kit Fitzgerald
Director: Kit Fitzgerald
Choreographer: Stephanie Woodard
Principal Dancer: Stephanie Woodard

Composer: Peter Zummo
Category: MODERN, EXPERIMENTAL
Electronic cloning allows a colorfully clad solo dancer to create her own responsive environment and a mobile backdrop which races off to the left, sinks and disappears. The dancer pulses in place with gentle curves of the torso and arms, seemingly unimpressed by her visual echo.

LIVING AMERICAN THEATER DANCE
1982, 11 min. color film, video
Distributors: Phoenix, University of Minnesota
Producer: John Alper for Mayqueen Productions
Director: John Alper
Choreographer: Lee Theodore
Principal Dancers: Lee Theodore, Ann Reinking
Dance Company: American Dance Machine
Category: MUSICALS
The American Dance Machine, a living archive of over forty-five Broadway routines, rehearse musical classics under the tutelage of the late Lee Theodore, founder of the company.

LOCALE
1980, 30 min. color film, video
Distributor: Cunningham Dance Foundation
Producer: Cunningham Dance Foundation
Director: Charles Atlas
Choreographer: Merce Cunningham
Composer: Takehisa Kosugi
Category: MODERN, CINEDANCE
The camera moves with, around, and among the dancers at different speeds, its movements choreographed as precisely as those of the performers. Three kinds of cameras were used: Steadicam, Movieola crab dolly and an Elemac dolly with a crane arm, to provide a wide range of perspective and intensity.

LODELA
1996 27 min, b&w 35mm film
Distributor: National Film Board of Canada
Producer: John Sirabella, National Film Board of Canada
Director: Philippe Baylaucq
Choreographer: José Navas
Dancers: Chi Long, José Navas
Composer: Eric Longsworth
Category: EXPERIMENTAL
Dance on Camera Festival 1996 Bronze Award
An arresting study in nude photography as an abstraction, featuring the choreography of Venezuela-born, Montréal-based José Navas. The camera switches from two perspectives, that of the audience and that of the performer, balancing negative and positive spaces.

LONGEST TRAIL
1986, 58 min. color film, video
Series: Movement Style and Culture
Distributors: University of California Extension Center, University of Minnesota
Category: NATIVE AMERICANS
Explores the dance traditions of Native Americans and shows over fifty of their dances. Also recounts the settlement of the New World by peoples who crossed the Bering Straight land bridge eons ago.

LOOK! WE HAVE COME THROUGH
1978, 11 min. b&w film
Distributor: Phoenix

Producer: Lightworks
Director: Bruce Elder
Category: EXPERIMENTAL, CINEDANCE
Various devices of shooting and editing are used to parallel the intent of the choreography.

LOOKING FOR ME
1970, 29 min. b&w film, video
Distributors: University of California Extension Center, PennState, Iowa State, Buffalo State
Producers: Virginia Bartlett and Norris Brock for the Shady Lane School, Pittsburgh, PA
Category: DANCE THERAPY
CINE Golden Eagle, American Psychological Association Honoree
Reveals the delights of experiencing one's body and documents the success of therapist Janet Adler in bringing two autistic girls out of their shells. For later film on Adler, see *Still Looking* under title entry.

LORD OF THE DANCE/DESTROYER OF ILLUSION
1986, 108 min. color film, video
Distributor: Mystic Fire Video
Producer: Richard Kohn
Principal Dancer: Trulshig Rinpoche
Category: ASIA, RELIGIOUS/RITUAL
American Film Festival 1987 Red Ribbon
A metaphysical travelogue to Nepal and the Mani-Rimdu festival of "awakening." The Buddhist monks perform a series of thirteen dances to depict gods in battle with malevolent supernatural forces, as part of a Tibetan Tantric ritual.

LOVELY TO LOOK AT
1952, 102 min. color film, video
Distributors: Facets, Swank, MGM/UA
Producer: MGM
Director: Mervyn Le Roy
Choreographer: Hermes Pan
Principal Dancers: Ann Miller, Marge and Gower Champion
Composer: Jerome Kern
Category: FEATURES, MUSICALS
Remake of the 1934 film *Roberta,* about six Americans' business and romantic complications in their elegant dress salon in Paris. Dance numbers include *I Won't Dance, Smoke Gets In Your Eyes,* and *I'll Be Hard To Handle.*

LOVERS FRAGMENTS
1995, 19 min. color video
Distributor: AlienNation Company
Producer: Johannes Birringer
Director: Johannes Birringer
Choreographer: Johannes Birringer, Imma Sarries-Zgonc
Dancer: Imma Sarries-Zgonc
Dance Company: AlienNation Company
Composer: André Marquetti
Category: EXPERIMENTAL
Five bisexual lovers trapped in an abandoned building explore their erotic and spiritual fantasies.

THE LOVERS OF TERUEL
1962, 90 min. color film, video
Distributors: Kultur, Viewfinders, Home Vision, Corinth
Producer: Janus
Director: Raymond Rouleau
Choreographer: Milko Sparemblek

Principal Dancer: Ludmilla Tcherina
Composer: Mikis Theodorakis
Category: FULL-LENGTH BALLETS, FLA-MENCO
In a play-within-a-play, the star of a gypsy troupe identifies with her role as Duchess Isabelle of Teruel, who dances nightly in public squares waiting for the return of her lover, who is killed by her betrothed. The parallel in her own life becomes unbearable and she destroys herself. Cinematographers are Claude and Pierre Renoir.

LOWER EXTREMITY DANCE MEDICINE: ORTHOPEDIC EXAMINATION WITH DR. WILLIAM HAMILTON
1995, 50 min. color video
Distributors: Dance Medicine Education Fund, Dance Horizons
Producer: Susan Macaluso
Director: Susan Macaluso
Dance Company: New York City Ballet, Dance Theatre of Harlem, Hartford Ballet
Category: DANCE THERAPY, DISABILITIES
Detailed evaluation of specific dance injuries, with physical examinations of the foot, ankle, and lower leg. Class and performance footage accentuate explanations of dance movement, technique and alignment.

LUDMILA SEMENYAKA: BOLSHOI BALLERINA
1989, 60 min. color video
Distributors: Kultur, Viewfinders, Corinth, Home Vision
Producer: Gosteleradio
Choreographer: Marius Petipa
Principal Dancers: Ludmila Semenyaka, Andris Liepa, Mikhail Lavrovsky, Alexander Bogatyrev
Dance Company: Bolshoi Ballet
Composers: Peter Ilyich Tchaikovsky, Arno Babadjanyan, Adolphe Adam, Riccardo Drigo, Arif Melikov
Category: BALLET, DOCUMENTARY PORTRAITS
Leningrad-born Semenyaka made her first impression internationally at the 1969 Moscow Competition. Three years later, she was invited to join the Bolshoi Ballet in Moscow. Here she performs in *Sleeping Beauty, A Solar Duet, Gisèlle, Legend of Love, The Talisman, The Nutcracker, Spartacus,* and *Swan Lake.*

LUIGI (3 videos)
1988, 60 min. each color video
Distributor: Hoctor Products, Dance Horizons
Producer: Studio Music Corporation
Choreographer: Luigi
Principal Dancers: Luigi, Francis Roach, Ande Handler
Category: INSTRUCTIONAL, JAZZ
Teacher: Luigi
Complete technical breakdown of the New York-based teacher's fluid jazz style, for beginning through advanced level students. Known for his exacting warm-up and his line of instructional records, Luigi has trained countless performers in his jazz technique identifiable by its grace, nuance, and lyricism.

LUMIA I and II: THE DESIGN OF DANCE (2 films)
1974, 7 min. each color film
Distributor: Iowa State

Producer: R.B. Lindenmeyer
Category: EXPERIMENTAL
Interplay of red, green and blue lights and shadows with a dancer seen behind a translucent screen.

LUMINAIRE
1985, 6 min. color video
Distributor: The Kitchen
Directors: John Sanborn, Dean Winkler
Choreographer: Charles Moulton
Principal Dancer: Charles Moulton
Category: EXPERIMENTAL, CINEDANCE
Patterns choreographed through postproduction with the dancer caught in an electronic web.

THE LURE AND THE LORE
1988, 15 min. color video
Distributor: Third World Newsreel
Director: Ayoka Chenzira
Choreographer: Thomas Pinnock
Principal Dancer: Thomas Pinnock
Category: FOLK
Pinnock's "immigrant folktales" are performed, using traditional Jamaican folklore to depict his migration to New York and illustrate the influence of both worlds on his choreography.

MA'BUGI: TRANCE OF THE TORAJA
1971, 21 min. color film
Distributor: University of California Extension Center
Category: ANTHROPOLOGICAL, ASIA, RELIGIOUS/RITUAL
Depicts a ritual that restores the balance of well-being for a village in the highlands of Sulawesi (Celebes), Indonesia. Filmed in the Rantekasimpo village of the Makale district, known for its spectacular elaborations of this rite of renewal and invigoration.

MACBETH
1980, 105 min. color video
Distributors: Kultur, Home Vision, Viewfinders, Corinth, Media Basics
Producer: Göstelradio
Director: Vladimir Vassiliev
Choreographer: Vladimir Vassiliev
Principal Dancers: Aleksei Fadeyechev, Nina Timofeyeva
Dance Company: Bolshoi Ballet
Composer: Kirill Molchanov
Category: FULL-LENGTH BALLETS
William Shakespeare's tale of murder and intrigue filmed live at the Bolshoi Theatre in Moscow. The choreographer focuses on the meeting of the three witches, the ambition of Lady Macbeth, the murders of King Duncan and Banquo and the torment suffered by Macbeth and his wife after they claimed the throne.

MACHITO: A LATIN JAZZ LEGACY
1987, 58 min. color, b&w film, video
Distributor: First Run/Icarus
Producer: Carlos Ortíz
Director: Carlos Ortíz
Category: HISPANIC, JAZZ
Frank "Machito" Grillo, Cuban maracas player and band leader, popularized the Latin jazz music of his homeland and introduced it at Harlem nightspots such as the Cotton Club. Historic footage of 1920s Cuba and Hollywood

production numbers are included in this documentary.

MADE IN THE BRONX
1981, 30 min. color, b&w video
Distributor: Museum of Modern Art
Producer: Susan Fanshel
Director: Susan Fanshel
Choreographer: Lanny Lasky
Principal Dancers: Ron Love, Chuck Davis, Jim Gross, Paul Pines
Composers: Basha Alperin, Ron Love
Category: CHILDREN, ART
American Film Festival Red Ribbon, Sinking Creek Film Festival James Blue Documentary Award
Documents a workshop in creativity which was organized in the Bronx for adults with children in neighborhood community centers. The members enthusiastically explore art, poetry, music and dance.

MADEMOISELLE FIFI
1993, 18 min. b&w video
Distributors: Video Artists International, Facets
Choreographer: Zachary Zolov
Principal Dancers: Alexandra Danilova, Roman Jasinsky, Michael Maule
Composer: Theodore Lajarte
Category: BALLET
In 1955, Danilova was brought to the Canadian Broadcasting Corporation studios in Montréal to dance the lead part in a new work written especially for the occasion. The live telecast which resulted is here presented, the only existing record of the artist in a complete performance.

THE MAGANA BAPTISTE SIXTH ANNUAL BELLY DANCE FESTIVAL
1989, 90 min. color video
Distributor: Magana Baptiste Royal Academy
Producer: Magana Baptiste Royal Academy
Principal Dancers: Devi Ananda Baptiste, Horacio Cifuentes
Composer: Nabil El Ansari
Category: BELLY DANCE, FESTIVALS
Californian school recital for teachers and dancers. Also available on Middle Eastern dance: *Mr. and Miss Belly Dance Contest, San Francisco* (1988 and 1987), *Dr. Mo Geddawi's August 1988 Workshop,* and *Hoacio Cifuentes' Instructional Volumes I and II.*

MAGDALENE
1992, 12 min. color video
Distributor: Echo Productions
Producer: Cinzia Fascino
Director: Cinzia Fascino
Choreographer: Cinzia Fascino
Principal Dancers: Mabel Ferragut, Beth Spicer
Composer: Dead Can Dance
Category: MODERN, RELIGIOUS/RITUAL
Dance on Camera Festival 1993 Honorable Mention
A fictional exploration of the character from the Gospels. The words spoken by the Master from Nazareth released the soul of Mary Magdalene the Courtesan, and transformed her life into a quest for eternity.

MAGIC MEMORIES ON ICE (2 videos)
199?, 97 and 78 min. color video
Distributor: ABC Sports

Category: ICE DANCE
Features three decades of figure skating performances. Ice dance tapes are also available from NBC Sports (800) 999–0988 (*Nutcracker on Ice*); CBS Video (800) 747–7999 (*Winter Olympics*); and A & E (800) 423–1212 (*Planets on Ice*).

THE MAGIC OF THE BOLSHOI BALLET

1987, 60 min. color video
Distributors: Kultur, Home Vision, Dance Horizons, Corinth
Producer: Göstelradio
Choreographer: Marius Petipa
Principal Dancers: Maya Plisetskaya, Galina Ulanova, Vladimir Vassiliev, Natalya Bessmertnova, Ekaterina Maximova
Dance Company: Bolshoi Ballet
Category: BALLET COMPANIES
A comprehensive retrospective of the past fifty years of the two hundred-year-old Bolshoi Ballet, with rare footage of performances and classes including scenes from *Sleeping Beauty, Romeo and Juliet, Don Quixote, Gisèlle,* and *Swan Lake.*

THE MAGIC OF THE KIROV BALLET

1988, 60 min. color video, laser
Distributors: Kultur, Home Vision, Viewfinders, Dance Horizons, Corinth
Producers: Göstelradio and the Entertainment Video Company
Choreographer: Marius Petipa
Principal Dancers: Faroukh Ruzimatov, Tatiana Terekova, Olga Chenchikova
Dance Company: Kirov Ballet
Composers: Léon Minkus, Riccardo Drigo, Peter Ilyich Tchaikovsky, Alexander Glazunov
Category: BALLET COMPANIES
Pas de deux selections from the Kirov's classical repertoire include: *Entry of the Shades* and *Indian Dance* from Act II of *La Bayadère, Le Corsaire, Sleeping Beauty,* the *Spanish Dance* from Act II of *Raymonda, Swan Lake, Paquita,* and *Don Quixote.*

THE MAGNIFICENT BEGINNING

1979, 52 min. color film, video
Series: The Magic of Dance
Distributors: Dance Film Archive, University of Minnesota
Producer: Patricia Foy for BBC-TV
Choreographers: Mary Skeaping, Frederick Ashton, Maximillien Gardel, Roland Petit
Principal Dancers: Roland Petit, Zizi Jeanmaire, David Wall, Wendy Ellis, Ronald Emblem
Dance Company: Royal Swedish Ballet, Royal Ballet, Dance Academy of Peking
Composers: Rebel, Henry Purcell, Etienne-Nicolas Méhul, Ferdinand Hérold, Huang AnLun
Category: BALLET
Narrator: Margot Fonteyn
The fifth program in the series presents Louis XIV as the champion of ballet, with a tour of the Paris Opera and the Drottningholm Theatre in Sweden. The Royal Swedish Ballet performs three ballets of Mary Skeaping: *Le Camargo, Cupid Out of His Humor,* and *La Dansomania.* The Royal Ballet performs extracts from Ashton's *La Fille Mal Gardée* and the bedroom scene from Roland Petit's *Carmen.* The Dance Academy of Peking performs *The Little Match Girl.*

MAKAHIKI FESTIVAL

1987, 53 min. color video
Distributor: Kalama Productions
Producer: Kalama Productions
Director: Roland Yamamoto
Principal Dancer: Waimea Falls Park
Category: HULA, FESTIVALS
Tenth annual festival in Haleiwa, Hawaii, with games and activities reminiscent of the original *makahiki* held by Hawaiians before contact with western civilization. Solo dances in *kahiko* (ancient) and *auana* (modern) hula. This is the only solo competition in which men and women compete equally in Hawaii.

MAKAROVA: IN A CLASS OF HER OWN

1985, 60 min color video
Distributors: Video Artists International, Dance Horizons, Viewfinders, Media Basics, Corinth
Producer: National Video Corporation
Director: Derek Bailey
Choreographer: Roland Petit
Principal Dancers: Natalia Makarova, Roland Petit, Irina Yakobsen
Category: BALLET, DOCUMENTARY PORTRAITS
Natalia Makarova takes a private class with her Russian coach Irina Yakobsen. Makarova's voice offers information on her development of roles, her insight into the differences between the romantic and classical techniques and the Russian and Western approach to dance.

MAKAROVA RETURNS

1989, 60 min. color video
Distributors: Kultur, Viewfinders, Dance Horizons, Corinth, Home Vision
Producer: BBC-TV
Director: Derek Bailey
Principal Dancer: Natalia Makarova
Composer: Peter Ilyich Tchaikovsky
Category: BALLET, DOCUMENTARY PORTRAITS
In this emotionally charged program, ballerina Natalia Makarova returns to the Kirov nearly twenty years after her defection from the USSR. "Natasha" is reunited with her family, gives a tour of the theatre, and dances again with the Kirov Ballet in a performance of *Eugen Onegin.*

MAKING BALLET: KAREN KAIN AND THE NATIONAL BALLET OF CANADA

1995, 86 min. color video
Distributor: V.I.E.W.
Director: Anthony Assopardi
Choreographer: James Kudelka
Principal Dancer: Karen Kain
Dance Company: National Ballet of Canada
Composer: Frédéric Chopin
Category: BALLET COMPANIES
Behind-the-scenes glimpse into the National Ballet of Canada's making of *The Actress* with Canada's prima ballerina Karen Kain.

MAKING DANCES: SEVEN POSTMODERN CHOREOGRAPHERS

1980, 89 min. color video
Distributor: Michael Blackwood Productions
Producer: Michael Blackwood Productions
Director: Michael Blackwood
Choreographers: Trisha Brown, Lucinda Childs,

Douglas Dunn, David Gordon, Kenneth King, Meredith Monk, Sara Rudner
Principal Dancers: Trisha Brown, Lucinda Childs, Douglas Dunn, David Gordon, Kenneth King, Meredith Monk, Sara Rudner
Category: MODERN, CHOREOGRAPHY
Performances and interviews with seven modern dancer-choreographers active in the 1970s, who were inspired by the Martha Graham-Merce Cunningham tradition. Performances include: *Accumulation With Talking Plus Water Motor* by Brown; *Dance* by Childs; *Foot Rules* by Dunn; *An Audience With the Pope, One Part of the Matter* by Gordon; *World Raid* by King, *Education of the Girlhild, Dolman Music* by Monk; and *Modern Dances* by Rudner.

THE MAKING OF A BALLET

1973, 38 min. color film, video
Distributors: Consulate General of the Netherlands, Coe Film Associates
Producer: Jan Vrijman
Choreographer: Rudi van Dantzig
Dance Company: Dutch National Ballet
Category: BALLET, COMPOSITION
This documentary on the making of a ballet shows the obsessiveness of the creative process. The ballet, an adaptation of Jerzy Kosinski's *The Painted Bird,* centers around a man who remains indifferent to violent attacks and is subsequently destroyed.

MALAMBO DEL SOL

1990, 6 min. color video
Distributor: Alegrías
Producer: Taller Latinoamericano
Director: Bernardo Palombo, Donna Light
Choreographers: Deirdre Towers, Brenda Chambers
Dance Company: Ballet Las Pampas
Category: EXPERIMENTAL, FOLK
This urban folktale uses the road as a symbol of the link between traditional culture and modern society, with parade footage taken in New York City and Peru. Las Pampas performs the Argentinian *malambo* in traditional gaucho dress in the city streets and parks.

MALAYSIAN DANCES (7 films)

1974–78, 10 min. each color film
Distributor: Embassy of Malaysia
Dance Company: National Cultural Troupe
Category: FOLK, ASIA
Folk dances, including the Farmers' Dance which depicts work in the rice fields and the self-reliance of the villagers, are shown in two films. A five-part film of the Asian variety show in Kuala Lumpur features artists from Indonesia, Malaysia, Philippines, Singapore, and Thailand.

MAN BLONG CUSTOM

1976, 52 min. color film
Series: Tribal Eye
Distributors: Iowa State, University of Minnesota, University of California Extension Center
Producer: BBC-TV
Category: RELIGIOUS/RITUAL, ASIA
Narrator: David Attenborough
Sacred ceremonies performed in the cult house in the jungle-covered mountains of the New Hebrides and on the Solomon Islands, where the sea spirit dances are shown.

MAN WHO DANCES: EDWARD VILLELLA
1968–80, 54 min. color film, video
Distributor: Direct Cinema
Producer: Robert Drew
Choreographer: George Balanchine
Principal Dancers: Edward Villella, Patricia Mc-
Bride
Category: BALLET, DOCUMENTARY POR-
TRAITS
Emmy Award
Edward Villella, artistic director of the Miami Bal-
let, partners Patricia McBride in rehearsals with
choreographer George Balanchine, founder of
the New York City Ballet. They perform *Rubies*
from Balanchine's *Jewels* and the *Pas de Deux*
from *Tarantella*.

MANON
1982, 126 min. color video, laser
Distributors: Home Box Office, Home Vision,
Music Video Distributors, Corinth, Media Ba-
sics
Producer: National Video Corporation
Director: Colin Nears
Choreographer: Kenneth MacMillan
Principal Dancers: Jennifer Penney, Anthony
Dowell
Dance Company: Royal Ballet
Composer: Jules Massenet
Category: FULL-LENGTH BALLETS
The story of a love so obsessive and self-destruc-
tive that a young man of good social standing
sacrifices everything to satisfy a woman of dubi-
ous morality. Based on the 1731 novel by Abbé
Prévost, set to the music written for the opera
composed in 1884.

MARCEAU ON MIME
1974, 22 min. color film, video
Distributor: AIMS Media
Producer: Gesture Productions
Director: John Gould
Category: PANTOMIME
Mime: Marcel Marceau
The French mime artist discusses his art.

MARCEL MARCEAU OU L'ART DU MIME
1961, 17 min. b&w film, video
Distributor: FACSEA
Director: P. Paviot
Category: PANTOMIME
Mime: Marcel Marceau
The French mime at home, surrounded by memo-
rabilia of pantomime through the ages, and on
stage as Bip and Don Juan. In French or English
versions.

MARGOT FONTEYN IN LES SYLPHIDES
1947, 8 min. b&w film
Distributor: Dance Film Archive
Choreographer: Michel Fokine
Principal Dancers: Margot Fonteyn, Michael
Somes
Dance Company: Royal Ballet
Composer: Frédéric Chopin
Category: BALLET
An excerpt from *Little Ballerina*, a British feature,
with a movement of *Les Sylphides*. The perform-
ance is intercut with backstage scenes.

THE MARGOT FONTEYN STORY
1989, 90 min. color video, laser
Distributors: Home Vision, Dance Horizons,
Viewfinders, Corinth

Producer: RM Arts
Director: Patricia Foy
Principal Dancers: Frederick Ashton, Robert Helpmann, Rudolf Nureyev, Anton Dolin, Ninette
de Valois, Margot Fonteyn
Composers: Adolphe Adam, Peter Ilyich Tchaikovsky
Category: BALLET, DOCUMENTARY POR-
TRAITS
Dance on Camera Festival 1990 Gold Award,
American Film Festival Blue Ribbon
Prima Ballerina Assoluta Dame Margot Fonteyn
speaks from her home in Panama to tell her life
story on the eve of her seventieth birthday. Her
memories are intercut with interviews with
mentors, partners and protegés, such as Ninette
de Valois, Frederick Ashton, Robert Helpmann,
and Rudolf Nureyev, plus archival footage of
Fonteyn in *Ondine*, *Swan Lake*, and *Gisèlle*.

THE MARRAKESH FOLK FESTIVAL AND MORE!
1984, 60 min. color video
Distributor: Morocco
Producer: Morocco
Category: FOLK, FESTIVALS
A record of the entire Marrakesh Folk Festival,
plus city and country *Schikhatt*, male *Schikhatt*
and tray dances, all narrated by Morocco.
Filmed on-site during live performances.

MARTHA CLARKE: LIGHT AND DARK
1980, 54 min. color film
Distributors: Phoenix, University of California Ex-
tension Center, University of Minnesota
Producer: Joyce Chopra
Director: Joyce Chopra
Choreographer: Martha Clarke
Principal Dancers: Martha Clarke, Felix Blaska
Category: MODERN, DOCUMENTARY POR-
TRAITS
Dance on Camera Festival
Reveals the imaginative sources, creative process
and working habits of Martha Clarke, former
Pilobolus member internationally celebrated for
her daring approach to theatre. Four dances,
about loneliness, being a woman, and the
strangeness of performance, are developed over
the course of a year in her rural studio in Con-
necticut, from the hard work of refining and
rehearsing to learning from the audience.

MARTHA GRAHAM, AN AMERICAN ORIGINAL IN PERFORMANCE
1958, 93 min. b&w video, laser
Distributors: Kultur, Dance Horizons, Viewfind-
ers, Corinth, Home Vision, Facets
Producer: Nathan Kroll for WQED-TV/Pittsburgh
Directors: Peter Glushanok, Aexander Hammid
Principal Dancers: Martha Graham, Miriam Cole
Composers: Aaron Copland, William Schuman
Category: MODERN, DANCE HISTORY
A trilogy of films made in Martha Graham's mid-
dle years: *A Dancer's World*, *Night Journey*, and
Appalachian Spring (see individual entries).

THE MARTHA GRAHAM DANCE COMPANY
1976, 90 min. color film
Series: Dance in America
Distributors: Indiana University, University of
California Extension Center, WarnerVision En-
tertainment
Producer: WNET/New York

Director: Merrill Brockway
Choreographer: Martha Graham
Principal Dancers: Peter Sparling, Elisa Monte,
Peggy Lyman, Takako Asakawa, Janet Eilber
Dance Company: Martha Graham Dance Com-
pany
Composers: Zoltán Kodály, Louis Horst, Aaron
Copland, Samuel Barber
Category: MODERN COMPANIES
Narrator: Gregory Peck
Dance on Camera Festival 1977, American Film
Festival 1977 Red Ribbon
Choreographer Martha Graham introduces her
dances: *Diversion of Angels* (1948), *Lamentation*
(1930), *Frontier*, *Adorations*, *Appalachian Spring*
(1944) and Medea's solo danced by Takako Asa-
kawa from *Cave of the Heart*.

MARTHA GRAHAM: THE DANCER REVEALED
1994, 60 min. color video
Series: Dance in America
Distributors: Dance Horizons, Viewfinders, Facets
Producer: Dominique Lasseur
Director: Catherine Tatge
Choreographer: Martha Graham
Principal Dancer: Martha Graham
Category: MODERN, DOCUMENTARY POR-
TRAITS
Narrator: Claire Bloom
The modern dance pioneer who died in 1991 at
age ninety-seven is seen in historical film clips
speaking about her art as well as in performance
of such works as *Heretic*, *Lamentation*, *Frontier*,
Appalachian Spring, *Every Soul is a Circus*,
American Document, *Primitive Mysteries*, and
Night Journey. Her former partner and husband
Erick Hawkins, biographer Agnes de Mille, Gra-
ham dancers Jane Dudley, Pearl Lang and Rob-
ert Cohan, are interviewed.

MARTHA GRAHAM: THREE CONTEMPORARY CLASSICS
1984, 85 min. color video
Distributors: Corinth, Music Video Distributors,
Media Basics
Producers: Judy Kinberg and Jac Venza for
WNET-TV/13
Director: Thomas Grimm
Choreographer: Martha Graham
Principal Dancers: Takako Asakawa, Teresa Ca-
pucilli
Dance Company: Martha Graham Dance Com-
pany
Composers: Gian Carlo Menotti, Samuel Barber,
Carl Nielsen
Category: MODERN, DANCE HISTORY
Performances of three works, *Errand into the
Maze*, *Acts of Light*, and *Cave of the Heart*. The
first was choreographed in 1947 on the myth of
Theseus and a woman's struggle with fear; the
second premiered in 1947, set to a commis-
sioned score by Samuel Barber; and the third
was choreographed by Graham in her eighties
on the subject of Medea, the jilted, vengeful
Goddess.

MARY WIGMAN: FOUR SOLOS
1929, 10 min. b&w film (silent)
Distributors: Dance Film Archive, Museum of
Modern Art
Choreographer: Mary Wigman
Principal Dancer: Mary Wigman

Category: MODERN, DANCE HISTORY

The influential German dancer performs four solos: *Seraphic Song, Pastorale, Dance of Summer,* and *Witch Dance.* At the time of filming she had completed her studies in Switzerland with Rudolph von Laban, the father of labanotation, and opened her own school in Dresden.

MARY WIGMAN: MY LIFE IS DANCE

1986, 29 min. color video
Distributor: Modern Talking Picture Service
Director: Ulrich Tegeder
Choreographer: Mary Wigman
Principal Dancers: Mary Wigman, Hanya Holm, Yvonne Georgi, Harald Kreutzberg, Dore Hoyer, Susanna Linke
Category: MODERN, DOCUMENTARY PORTRAITS

This documentary of the German modern dancer and choreographer, made in honor of her one hundredth birthday shows clips of *Wanderings* filmed in 1926, *Witch Dance* (1926), *Swinging Landscape* (1929) and *Deathmark* (1930).

MARY WIGMAN: 1886–1973: *WHEN THE FIRE DANCES BETWEEN THE TWO POLES*

1982, 45 min. color film, video
Distributors: Dance Horizons, University of California Extension Center, UCLA Instructional Media Library
Producers: Allegra Fuller Snyder and Annette MacDonald
Directors: Allegra Fuller Snyder, Annette MacDonald
Principal Dancer: Mary Wigman
Category: MODERN, DOCUMENTARY PORTRAITS

Dance on Camera Festival Honorable Mention, Grand Prix International Vidéo-Danse Festival

Study of the life and work of Mary Wigman, Germany's foremost innovator in modern dance. Historical footage shows her working with students, and highlights Wigman's performances from 1923–1942 in *Seraphic Song, Dance of Summer, Witch Dance,* and her last performance in 1942, *Farewell and Thanksgiving.*

THE MARYINSKY BALLET

1993, 147 min. color video
Distributors: Home Vision, Facets, Corinth
Producer: Danmarks Radio Aarhus Dance Studio
Director: Thomas Grimm
Choreographers: Michel Fokine, Oleg Vinogradov, Marius Petipa, N. and S. Legat, Arthur Saint-Léon
Principal Dancers: Altynai Asylmuratova, Larissa Lezhina, Konstantin Zaklinsky, Faroukh Ruzimatov
Dance Company: Maryinsky Ballet (formerly the Kirov)
Composers: Frédéric Chopin, Igor Stravinsky, Samuel Barber, Riccardo Drigo, Adolph Adam, Joseph Bayer, Cesare Pugni, Léon Minkus
Category: BALLET COMPANIES

The Maryinsky Ballet, formerly the Kirov Ballet, performs a program of classical and contemporary works: *Barber's Adagio, Chopiniana, Petroushka, Le Corsaire, Pas de Deux, The Fairy Doll, Markitenka Pas de Six,* and *Paquita.*

MASS

1990, 11:40 min. color video
Series: Alive From Off Center

Distributor: Electronic Arts Intermix
Producer: Mary Lucier
Director: Mary Lucier
Choreographer: Elizabeth Streb
Principal Dancers: Elizabeth Streb, Paula Gifford, Henry Beer, Jorge Collazo, Peter Larose, Christopher Batenhorst
Category: EXPERIMENTAL, MODERN

Examining force and resistance in the case of a group acting as a unified body, this third collaboration between Mary Lucier and Elizabeth Streb is a metaphor for the survival of an artist's vision in an urban environment. In a succession of brightly colored interludes shot from distorted perspectives, Streb's dancers seem to be floating, flying, pushing or being pushed by large buildings. Available both as a three channel installation and single video.

MASTERS OF TAP

1988, 61 and 40 min. color video
Distributors: Home Vision, Viewfinders
Producer: IFPA Ltd.
Director: Nierenberg, George
Choreographers: Charles "Honi" Coles, Chuck Green, Will Gaines
Principal Dancers: Charles "Honi" Coles, Chuck Green, Will Gaines
Category: TAP, DANCE HISTORY

A sentimental journey through the history of tap with three masters.

MAYA DEREN: EXPERIMENTAL FILMS

1943–59, 76 min. b&w film, video
Distributors: Mystic Fire Video, Women Make Movies
Producer: Alexander Hackenschmied
Director: Maya Deren
Principal Dancer: Talley Beatty
Category: EXPERIMENTAL, CINEDANCE

Enchanted by the power of movement and the challenges of space and time, Maya Deren was America's first dance filmmaker. She said, "Each film was built as a chamber and became a corridor, like a chain reaction." The collection includes *Meshes of the Afternoon, At Land, A Study in Choreography for Camera, Ritual in Transfigured Time, Meditation on Violence* and *The Very Eye of Night.* See individual titles for descriptions.

MAYERLING

1994, 135 min. color video, laser
Distributors: Viewfinders, Laserdisc Fan Club, Corinth, Facets, Home Vision
Producer: BBC-TV
Choreographer: Kenneth MacMillan
Principal Dancers: Lesley Collier, Irek Mukhamedov, Viviana Durante, Darcey Bussell
Dance Company: Royal Ballet
Composer: Franz Liszt
Category: FULL-LENGTH BALLETS

A ballet enacting the story of Austrian Crown Prince Rudolph, and the culmination of his love affair with the seventeen-year-old Mary Vetsera in their double suicide.

MEDEA

1979, 110 min. color video
Distributors: Kultur, Home Vision, Viewfinders, Media Basics
Producer: Göstelradio
Director: Elgudja Zhgenti

Choreographer: Georgiy Aleksidze
Principal Dancers: Marina Goderdzishvili, Vladimir Lulukhadze
Composer: Revaz Gabichvadze
Category: FULL-LENGTH BALLETS

The one-act ballet filmed in the Soviet Union is based on Euripides's drama of lost love, adultery, revenge, and murder.

MEDIATION ON VIOLENCE

1948, 13 min. b&w film
Distributors: Mystic Fire Video, Museum of Modern Art, Film-makers' Cooperative
Producer: Maya Deren
Director: Maya Deren
Choreographer: Maya Deren
Category: EXPERIMENTAL, CINEDANCE

The movements and rhythms of the Wu-tang and Shao-Lin schools of Chinese boxing filmed as patterns with flute and drum accompaniment by Maya Deren, a prime mover of the avante-garde in the late 1930s and '40s.

MEDICINE FIDDLE

1992, 81 min. color video
Distributor: University of California Extension Center
Producer: Michael Loukinen for Up North Films
Category: NATIVE AMERICANS

National Educational Film and Video Festival Gold Apple, American Indian Film Festival Special Merit Award, CINE Golden Eagle, American Folklore Society honoree, American Film Festival honoree

The fiddling and dancing traditions of Native and Métis families both in the U.S. and Canada are featured. The fiddle entered Native American tradition in the seventeenth-century when introduced by French fur traders and the Scots, and by Irish immigrants a century later. Today's fiddling and step-dancing of these cultures, together with their spiritual ideals, reflect this early influence. Dancers and fiddlers are from the Ojibwa, Menominee, Métis and Ottawa groups.

MEET ME IN ST. LOUIS

1944, 113 min. color, film, video, laser
Distributors: Facets, Swank, MGM/UA
Producer: MGM
Director: Vincente Minelli
Choreographer: Charles Walters
Principal Dancers: Judy Garland, Margaret O'Brien
Composer: Hugh Martin
Category: FEATURES, MUSICALS

Story of a year in the life of an American family in turn-of-the-century St. Louis. Musical numbers include: *Under the Bamboo Tree, The Trolley Song,* and *Meet Me In St. Louis.*

MEHANG SUSAH

1984, 11 min. color video
Distributor: Penny Ward Video
Producer: Penny Ward
Director: Penny Ward
Choreographer: Mia Borgatta
Principal Dancer: Mia Borgatta
Category: EXPERIMENTAL

Dance on Camera Festival 1985 Honorable Mention

Taped outdoors among bamboo grasses, a woman blends with the environment in this gestural dance. The title may be translated as "Indeed it is difficult."

THE MEN WHO DANCED: THE STORY OF TED SHAWN'S MALE DANCERS 1933–1940

1986, 30 min. color, b&w video
Distributor: Dance Horizons
Producer: Ron Honsa
Choreographer: Ted Shawn
Dance Company: Ted Shawn and the members of his original troupe
Category: MODERN, DANCE HISTORY
Dance on Camera Festival 1986 Grand Prize
A reunion of the members of Ted Shawn's all-male troupe includes interviews, flashback stills, and performance footage. Founded in 1933 at Jacob's Pillow, the company had a daily routine of working in the fields, dancing, and building their performance center in the Berkshires.

MERCE BY MERCE BY PAIK

1978, 30 min. color video
Distributors: Cunningham Dance Foundation, Electronic Arts Intermix
Producer: Cunningham Dance Foundation
Directors: Nam June Paik, Shigeko Kubota, Charles Atlas
Choreographer: Merce Cunningham
Principal Dancer: Merce Cunningham
Composers: David Held, Earl Howard, John Cage
Category: EXPERIMENTAL, MODERN, CINEDANCE
This experimental video with dance choreographed for the camera illustrates that time and movement are reversible. Includes Cunningham's *Blue Studio* (1976) directed by Charles Atlas, later altered by Nam June Paik who also added a sound track, and *Merce and Marcel* with excerpts from a 1964 performance of Cunningham's *Septet* in Helsinki, and Russell Connor's interview with Marcel Duchamp.

MERCE CUNNINGHAM

1980, 60 min. color film, video
Distributor: Cunningham Dance Foundation
Producer: London Weekend Television
Director: Geoff Dunlop
Choreographer: Merce Cunningham
Principal Dancers: Karole Armitage, Louise Burns, Ellen Cornfield, Meg Eginton, Chris Komar
Composers: John Cage, Takehisa Kosugi
Category: MODERN
Rehearsals and commentaries by Merce Cunningham, Carolyn Brown, Karole Armitage, and Chris Komar, plus excerpts from Cunningham's *Travelogue*, *Squaregame*, and *Exchange*.

MERCE CUNNINGHAM AND COMPANY

1982, 45 min. color film, video
Distributor: Cunningham Dance Foundation
Producer: L'Institut National de L'Audiovisual with Cunningham Dance Foundation
Director: Benoît Jacquot
Choreographer: Merce Cunningham
Dance Company: Merce Cunningham Dance Company
Category: MODERN COMPANIES, DOCUMENTARY PORTRAITS
Presented in English and French with English subtitles, this documentary explores Cunningham's method of choreography, his employment of random methods to determine the order of dance sequences through use of the *I Ching*, his

collaboration with John Cage, and his relationship with the dancers. Cunningham candidly reveals his ideas through interviews and rehearsal and performance excerpts of *Trails*, *Scramble*, *Aeon*, *Quartet*, *Suite for Five*, *Roadrunners*, and *Fractions*.

MEREDITH MONK

1985, 56 min. color video
Series: Four American Composers
Distributor: Mystic Fire Video
Producer: Revel Guest
Director: Peter Greenaway
Choreographer: Meredith Monk
Principal Dancer: Meredith Monk
Category: CHOREOGRAPHY
The choreography of this multimedia artist is featured as she performs excerpts from several of her works: *Dolman Music*, *Traveling*, *Quarry*, *Ellis Island*, and *Turtle Dreams*.

THE MERRY WIDOW

1983, 60 min. color video
Distributors: Kultur, Dance Horizons, Home Vision, Viewfinders, Media Basics, Corinth
Producer: Chicago Educational Television
Director: Dick Carter
Choreographer: Ruth Page
Principal Dancers: Peter Martins, Patricia McBride, Rebecca Wright, George de la Peña
Dance Company: New York City Ballet
Composer: Franz Lehár
Category: FULL-LENGTH BALLETS
Premiered at Chicago's Lyric Opera in 1955, this romantic ballet is set to the music of the three-act operetta written in 1905 by the Hungarian composer Franz Lehár. The plot revolves around a ball and the intricacies of various love affairs among turn-of-the-century Paris bourgeoisie.

MESHES OF THE AFTERNOON

1943, 14 min. b&w film
Distributors: Museum of Modern Art, Mystic Fire Video, Biograph Entertainment
Director: Maya Deren
Choreographer: Maya Deren
Principal Dancers: Maya Deren, Alexander Hammid
Composer: Teiji Ito
Category: EXPERIMENTAL, MODERN
An experimental film using movement to create a surrealist nightmare. Components include a woman, a mysterious reappearing figure, a key dropping, a knife and a man.

MESQUAKIE

1976, 10 min. color film
Distributor: Iowa State
Category: NATIVE AMERICANS
Shows the philosophy, ritual dances, and art of the Mesquakie tribe of American Indians.

MEXICAN DANCES (2 films)

1971, 17 and 18 min. color film, video
Distributor: AIMS Media
Producer: Association Film Services
Choreographer: Raul Macías
Dance Company: Ballet Folklórico Estudiantíl
Category: FOLK, LATIN AMERICA
Student production of Mexican folk dances at Lincoln High School in Los Angeles. The first film shows excerpts of the *Tilingo Lingo Iguana*, *La*

Bamba, *La Negra*; the second shows *El Carretero*, *Amor de Madre*, *Las Adelitas*, *Los Machetes*, *Alazanas*, and *Járabe Tapático*.

MGODO WA MBANGUZI

1973, 53 min. color film, video
Distributor: PennState
Producers: Gei Zantziger and Andrew Tracey
Directors: Gei Zantziger, Andrew Tracey
Category: AFRICA, ANTHROPOLOGICAL
Performances in a Chopi village in southern Mozambique accompanied by xylophone orchestras. Study guide available.

MICHAEL MOSCHEN

1986, 20 min. color video
Series: Alive From Off Center
Distributor: Electronic Arts Intermix, In Motion Productions
Producer: KTCA-TV in association with the Brooklyn Academy of Music
Director: Skip Blumberg
Principal Dancer: Michael Moschen
Category: CIRCUS ARTS
In three solo pieces, the juggler-illusionist demonstrates his prowess with crystal balls, glowing rods and shooting flames.

MIDEASTERN DANCE: AN INTRODUCTION TO BELLY DANCE

1986, 122 min. color video
Distributor: Bastet Productions
Producers: Gerald Harwood, Sarajean Allen Harwood, Kathryn Ferguson
Director: Gerald Harwood
Choreographer: Kathryn Ferguson
Principal Dancer: Kathryn Ferguson
Category: BELLY DANCE, INSTRUCTIONAL
Houston International Film Festival Silver Award
A complete course, beginning through advanced, including an explanation of Middle Eastern music.

MILDRED: THE FIRST 90 YEARS

1989, 29 min. color video
Distributor: Terra Nova
Producer: Melinda Productions
Category: DOCUMENTARY PORTRAITS
A portrait of a woman ninety years old and still dancing with vibrancy and power.

MILT AND HONI

1996, 90 min. color film
Distributor: Louise Tiranoff Productions
Producer: Louise Tiranoff Productions
Director: Louise Tiranoff
Choreographer: Charles "Honi" Coles
Principal Dancers: Charles "Honi" Coles, Brenda Buffalino
Composers: Duke Ellington, Milt Hinton
Musicians: Cab Calloway, Dizzy Gillespie, Milt Hinton
Category: TAP, AFRICAN-AMERICANS, JAZZ
Dance on Camera Festival 1996 Silver Award
This documentary is about the friendship and long working relationship of two legends of American jazz, bass player Milt Hinton, and the late tap dancer Honi Coles. Using the original and archival footage that spans the last century, it shows couples doing the Charleston, Honi Coles and his brother at the Cotton Club, jazz greats Cab Calloway and Dizzy Gillespie and tap dancer, Brenda Buffalino. The two artists re-

hearse alone and perform together, and reminisce about their sixty years' friendship over lunch at a Chinese restaurant.

THE MIME
1966, 29 min. b&w film
Distributor: PennState
Producers: Robert Rosen and Arthur Miller for Center for Mass Communication
Category: PANTOMIME
Mime: Tony Montararo
The training, discipline and ingenuity of a mime based in Maine, who performs and presents his personal views on mime and its effects on his private life.

THE MIME OF MARCEL MARCEAU
1972, 23 min. color video
Distributor: Coronet/MTI
Producer: Paris Match
Director: David Camus
Category: PANTOMIME
Mime: Marcel Marceau
The French master plays Bip, the director of a theatre company, along with other characters, and shows the study behind each gesture, and the nuance of expression demanded before it is perfected.

MIME TECHNIQUE: PART I
1977, 27 min. color film, video
Distributor: Phoenix
Producer: Stewart Lippe
Director: Stewart Lippe
Category: PANTOMIME, INSTRUCTIONAL
Mime: Paul Gaulin
An ape, transformed into a man, takes a walk in the park where he finds a book on mime instruction. He acts out the instructions and attempts variations.

MIMI GARRARD DANCE THEATRE
1989, 30 min. color video
Distributor: Mimi Garrard Dance Theatre
Producer: Mimi Garrard
Choreographer: Mimi Garrard
Dance Company: Mimi Garrard Dance Theatre
Category: MODERN COMPANIES
Composite of short excerpts from several repertory works by this modern dancer known for her dramatic character studies.

MINING DANCES (4 films)
1968, 21–25 min. color film
Distributor: PennState
Producer: Wissen
Category: AFRICA, ANTHROPOLOGICAL
Sotho-Ndebele, Mpondo, Setapo and Chopi dancers around the mines of the Vlakfontein near Johannesburg-Roodepoort, South Africa.

MIRACLE OF BALI: A RECITAL OF MUSIC AND DANCING
1972, 39 min. color film
Distributor: Buffalo State
Producers: John Coast and David Attenborough for BBC/Xerox
Category: BALI
Presents classical Balinese dance and gamelan music with the narrator describing the four types of musical ensembles. A chorus of 150 men chant for the legendary monkey dance which dates back to the third century.

MIRROR OF GESTURE
1974, 21 min. color film, video
Distributor: University of California Extension Center
Producer: Los Angeles County Museum of Art
Category: GESTURES, INDIA, ART
Shots of Indian sculpture are intercut with sequences of classical Indian dance to suggest the correspondence between the two arts.

MISS JULIE
1964, 37 min. b&w film
Distributor: Dance Film Archive
Producer: Mans Reutersward for Sveriges TV 2
Director: Mans Reutersward
Choreographer: Birgit Cullberg
Dance Company: Royal Swedish Ballet
Composer: Ture Rangström
Category: BALLET, DANCE DRAMA
The 1950 classic by the Swedish choreographer who was a pioneer in creating dances for the camera. Based on August Strindberg's play of 1888, it depicts a love-hate relationship between the sexes and social classes.

MIXED DOUBLE
1973, 5 min. color film
Distributor: Audience Planners
Producer: Danish Government Film Office
Choreographer: Eske Holm
Principal Dancers: Eske Holm, Sorella Englund
Composer: Stig Kreutzfeldt
Category: EXPERIMENTAL, BALLET
An experimental ballet film featuring a pas de deux.

MODERN BALLET
1960, 29 min. b&w film
Series: A Time To Dance
Distributors: Indiana University, UCLA Instructional Media Library
Producer: Jac Venza for WNET/13
Choreographers: Antony Tudor, Marius Petipa, Lev Ivanov
Principal Dancers: Antony Tudor, Nora Kaye, Hugh Laing, Yekaterina Geltzer, Vasily Tichomiroff
Composers: Peter Ilyich Tchaikovsky, Arnold Schoenberg, Frederick Delius, William Schuman
Category: BALLET, DANCE HISTORY
British choreographer Anthony Tudor and Martha Myers discuss the developments in the ballet world of the 1940s, the change of subject and mood and reasons for retaining the classical vocabulary. *Swan Lake* excerpt included, along with Tudor's *Pillar of Fire, Undertow, Romeo and Juliet, Dim Luster, Jardin aux Lilas,* and *Gala Performance* performed by his original cast.

MODERN DANCE: CHOREOGRAPHY AND THE SOURCE
1966, 20 min. color film
Distributor: Kent State
Producers: Hildegard L. Spreen and Margaretta Fristoe for Bailey Films
Category: MODERN, CHOREOGRAPHY
Affirms that the source of creativity is within us and the inspiration to dance is all around us. *Sumer Is Icumen In, Farandole, Greensleeves*

Duet and *Boxes* are performed by the students of San Jose State College.

MODERN DANCE: COMPOSITION
1959, 12 min. b&w film
Distributor: Kent State
Producer: Thorne Films
Category: MODERN, DANCE ANALYSIS
Teacher: Patricia Eckert
Students at the University of Colorado analyze the elements of dance composition and develop dances of their own entitled *Celebration* and *Lament.*

MODERN DANCE: CREATIVE IMAGINATION AND CHOREOGRAPHY
1965, 17 min. color film
Distributor: Kent State
Producers: Hildegard L. Spreen and Margaretta Fristoe for Bailey Films
Category: MODERN, CHOREOGRAPHY
Students of San Jose State College illustrate how an imaginative choreographer discovers new relationships and concepts in common subject matter by performing a children's dance, a whimsy, pantomime, and period piece.

MODERN DANCE: THE ABC OF COMPOSITION
1964, 13 min. color film
Distributor: Kent State
Producers: Hildegard L. Spreen and Margaretta Fristoe for Bailey Films
Category: MODERN, COMPOSITION
Presents the compositional problems of using rhythmic patterns, architectural shapes, and complementary movements.

MOIMO FESTIVAL DANCE FROM CENTRAL SUDAN
1964, 5 min. color film
Distributor: PennState
Producer: Wissen
Category: FESTIVALS, AFRICA
Circle dance for men and women, accompanied by flutes and drums, performed at the *motyoro* feast of the Dangaleat in Chad, Africa.

MOISEYEV DANCE COMPANY: A GALA EVENING
1980, 70 min. color video
Distributors: V.I.E.W., Viewfinders, Media Basics
Producer: Soviet Film and TV
Choreographer: Igor Moiseyev
Dance Company: Moiseyev Dance Company
Category: FOLK COMPANIES
This virtuoso folk dance troupe founded in 1937 in the Soviet Union presents: *Suite of Russian Folk Dances, Moldavian Suite, Old City Quadrille, The Soccer Match, Tajik's Dance of Happiness, Azerbaijan Shepherd Dance Suite,* and *Ukrainian Gopak Dance.* This gala evening was held at the Congress Hall in Moscow as part of the 1980 Olympic Cultural Program.

MOKO JUMBIE: TRADITIONAL STILT WALKERS
1991, 15 min. color video
Distributor: Filmakers Library
Producer: Karen Kramer
Director: Karen Kramer
Principal Dancers: Kenneth Nakeem Williams, Olukose Wiles

Dance Company: William "Bungo" Hinton Ensemble

Category: AFRICA, FOLK

Moko Jumbie, or "dancing spirit," is illustrated by the ten-foot high stilt walkers who perform at street festivals, Caribbean celebrations, and religious ceremonies in West Africa.

A MOMENT IN LOVE

1957, 8 min. color film

Distributor: Museum of Modern Art

Director: Shirley Clarke

Choreographer: Anna Sokolow

Principal Dancers: Carmela Gutierrez, Paul Sanasardo

Composer: Norman Lloyd

Category: CINEDANCE, EXPERIMENTAL

An example of "cinedance," a dance designed for the camera, merging movements and images in a cinematic choreography of the relationship of two lovers.

MOMENT OF LIGHT: THE DANCE OF EVELYN HART

1991, 48 min. color film, video

Distributors: Bullfrog Films, Rhombus International

Producer: Blue Morpho Films with the National Film Board of Canada

Director: Gordon M. Reeve

Choreographers: Uwe Scholz, Rudi van Dantzig, Agrippina Vaganova

Principal Dancers: Evelyn Hart, Kader Belarbi, Rex Harrington, Manuel Legris, Robert Maccherndl

Dance Company: Royal Winnipeg Ballet, Paris Opera Ballet

Composers: Wolfgang Amadeus Mozart, Sergei Prokofiev, Cesare Pugni

Category: BALLET, DOCUMENTARY PORTRAITS

National Educational Film and Video Festival, Oakland, 1993 Bronze Apple, Columbus International Film and Video Festival 1993 Bronze Plaque

The film follows Evelyn Hart, one of the great interpreters of classical ballet, from a premiere in Munich to the Paris Opera House for her debut as Juliet with Kader Belarbi as Romeo. The film concludes in Winnipeg with a riveting performance on the very stage where her dance career began. Through candid interviews she reveals the physical and emotional strain which accompanies her brief moments of ecstasy as she reaches for perfection. Other works performed include *Sleeping Beauty, Klavierkoncert Es-Dür,* and *Esmeralda.*

MONEY

1985, 15 min. color film

Distributors: Film-makers' Cooperative, Canyon Cinema

Producer: Henry Hills

Director: Henry Hills

Principal Dancers: Sally Silvers, Pooh Kaye, Yoshiko Chuma

Category: ART, EXPERIMENTAL

Black Maria Festival Director's Award

Presents the resistance of the Downtown New York art community to the first Reagan term. Features poets and musicians as well as dancers, exploring common tendencies, themes, modes, and tropes among experimental art and artists

of that era, while itself participating in these radical explorations.

MOON

1988, 6 min. b&w film

Distributor: Film-makers' Cooperative

Directors: Power Boothe, Caitlin Cobb

Principal Dancers: Margaret Albertson, Tina Dudek, Valerie Gutwirth, Nancy Sakamoto

Composer: Brooks Williams

Category: EXPERIMENTAL

A dance mediation on the nature of the moon, eggs, circular saws and love, this abstract film, according to the director, is a surrealist wheel of fortune.

MOON GATES: THREE VERSIONS

1974, 15:30 min. color film

Distributors: Film-makers' Cooperative, Doris Chase Productions

Producer: Doris Chase

Director: Doris Chase

Choreographer: Mary Staton

Dance Company: Mary Staton Dance Ensemble

Composer: George Kleinsinger

Category: MODERN, EXPERIMENTAL

Sculptor: Doris Chase

A compilation of *Moongates I, II, III* in which the Mary Staton company dances with a commissioned sculpture, seen in its purity and then transformed through a video synthesizer and transferred back to film and optically printed.

MOOR'S PAVANE (VARIATIONS ON THE THEME OF OTHELLO)

1950, 15 min. color film

Distributor: PennState

Director: Walter V. Strate

Choreographer: José Limón

Principal Dancers: José Limón, Lucas Hoving, Betty Jones, Ruth Currier

Dance Company: José Limón Company

Composer: Henry Purcell

Category: MODERN, DANCE DRAMA

Inspired by William Shakespeare's *Othello,* this modern dance suggests the jealousy and passion of the tragedy within the framework of a court dance.

MORNING STAR (CHOLPON)

1961, 75 min. color film

Distributor: Corinth

Producer: Lenfilm Studios

Director: Roman Tikhomirov

Choreographer: Nurden Turgelev

Principal Dancers: Nurden Turgelev, Reinia Chokeyeva, Uram Sarbagishev, Bibisara Beishenaliyeva, S. Abdusilov

Dance Company: Kirghizian State Opera and Ballet Theatre

Composer: Mikhail Rauchwergher

Category: FULL-LENGTH BALLETS

A ballet based on a legend from the Tien-Shan Mountains of Kirghizia in Central Asia. Cholpon is in love with Nurdin, but their happiness is threatened by an old sorceress who turns herself into a beautiful young woman. Cholpon's love proves stronger than the sorceress' magic.

MOROCCO AND THE CASBAH DANCE EXPERIENCE

1986, 120 min. color video

Distributor: Morocco

Producer: Morocco

Director: Morocco

Choreographer: Morocco

Principal Dancer: Morocco

Dance Company: Morocco and the Casbah Dance Experience

Composer: Mark Kyrkostas

Category: MIDDLE EAST, FOLK

Full concert of Middle Eastern and North African folk dance and music, based on Morocco's extensive field research and Middle Eastern and North African dance experience. Taped on site during performance.

MOROCCO, BODY AND SOUL (3 films)

1987, 26 min. each color film, video

Distributor: First Run/Icarus

Director: Izza Genini

Category: FOLK, MIDDLE EAST

Three documentary films shot in Morocco: *Hymns of Praise* in which participants in a pilgrimage to the sanctuary of Moulay Idriss I dance themselves into a trance; *Lutes and Delights* about Abdelsadek Chekara and his orchestra, interpreters of Arab-Andalusian music; and *Aita,* symbolizing the climactic cry of a female troubadour performing with dancers and musicians at religious ceremonies, marriages, and circumcisions.

MOTHER AND CHILD /50

1996, 19 min. color video

Distributor: ARC Videodance

Producer: Jeff Bush

Choreographer: Maureen Fleming

Dancer: Maureen Fleming

Composer: David Lawson

Category: BUTOH, EXPERIMENTAL

A choreographic meditation of the psychic female from the stage work *Eros,* performed in a *Butoh* style and recorded at fifty percent of the original speed.

MOTION

1972, 32 min. color video

Series: Dance as an Art Form

Distributor: Pro Arts

Producer: Chimerafilm

Director: Warren Leib

Choreographer: Murray Louis

Composer: Alwin Nikolais

Category: MODERN, IMPROVISATION

Narrator: Murray Louis

Advocates the joy of movement: professional and amateur dancers roll down hills, fall into snow banks and run along beaches. Choreographer-dancer-narrator Murray Louis improvises and performs excerpts from his dances *Facits* and *Personnae.*

MOURNING CELEBRATIONS FROM ETHIOPIA (2 films)

1951, 5–8 min. b&w film (silent)

Distributor: PennState

Producer: Wissen

Category: RELIGIOUS/RITUAL, AFRICA

Excerpts from the hour-long dances in Shangama in southern Ethiopia in honor of the deceased, with a pantomime to drive away the demons. The burial concludes with the burning of the deceased's hut. In the second film, the Sala tribe express their sympathy with choral processions and dances before the burial.

MOURNING DANCES FROM CHAD (5 films)
1964–65, 4–9 min. color, b&w film
Distributor: PennState
Producer: Wissen
Category: RELIGIOUS/RITUAL, AFRICA
Shows a mourning dance performed by three women and a man from the Mukulu tribe armed with a spear. Other films show the *Darangaba,* a circle dance, and the *Mutu Dodi,* stamping dances from the Kenga village of Barama, Chad.

MOVEMENT EXPLORATION: WHAT AM I
1968, 11 min. color film
Distributor: Kent State
Producer: Film Associates
Category: INSTRUCTIONAL, CHILDREN
Children mimic birds, animals and machines, in their exploration of movement.

MOVEMENT IN CLASSIC DANCE: THE PELVIC AREA
1980, 11 min. color film, video
Distributor: Indiana University
Director: Phil Stockton
Choreographer: Anna Paskevska
Principal Dancers: Jeanine Murrell, Leslie Horn, Scotty Martin
Category: BALLET, INSTRUCTIONAL
Dancers demonstrate correct alignment of the pelvic area, with slow-motion scenes and anatomical illustrations to detail the functions of the hip, leg, and abdominal muscles in controlling the pelvis.

MOVING PASTURES
1988, 20 min. color video
Distributor: Beals, Margaret
Choreographer: Margaret Beals
Principal Dancer: Margaret Beals
Composer: G.S. Sachdev
Category: MODERN, IMPROVISATION
Two solos improvised to Bansuri flute and pre-scored piano with pianist André Gribou.

A MOVING PICTURE
1989, 54 min. color film, video
Distributors: Bullfrog Films, Rhombus International
Producer: Rhombus International
Director: Jurgen Lutz
Choreographer: Ann Ditchburn
Principal Dancers: Ann Ditchburn, Robert Desrosiers
Dance Company: National Ballet of Canada
Composers: Kate Bush, Leonard Cohen, Laurie Anderson, Buffy Sainte Marie, André Gagnon, Jennifer Warnes
Category: CINEDANCE, ANIMATION
International Film and TV Festival of New York Gold Award, Gemini Awards (Toronto) Best Performing Arts Special, Rose d'Or (Switzerland)
Laced with animation and optical wizardry, the film presents a group of talented dancers in and out of rehearsals in a spacious, sunny loft in Toronto.

MOVING TOWARD HEALTH
1992, 28 min. color video
Distributor: University of California Extension Center
Producer: Sandy Dibbell-Hope

Category: DANCE THERAPY
Authentic Movement, a form of dance and movement therapy, is used in a support group of survivors of breast cancer. The documentary shows that this therapy can be a powerful tool for women, using movement to help them cope with cancer and its aftermath.

MOVING TRUE
1973, 19 min. b&w film, video
Distributor: Creative Arts Rehabilitation Center
Director: Barry Shapiro
Principal Dancer: Chryssa
Category: DANCE THERAPY
Dance Therapist: Anne Olin
Dance therapy session with a female patient suffering from deep withdrawal and insecurity.

MUNICH COOPERS' DANCE
1963, 17 min. color film
Distributor: PennState
Producer: Wissen
Category: FOLK, EUROPE
Male members of the Coopers of Munich, Germany, perform a historic guild dance in traditional costume with a brass band followed by two hoop swingers.

MURRAY LOUIS IN CONCERT: VOLUME I, DANCE SOLOS
1989, 52 min. color video
Distributor: Dance Horizons
Choreographer: Murray Louis
Principal Dancer: Murray Louis
Composers: Alwin Nikolais, and others
Category: MODERN, CHOREOGRAPHY
Filmed from 1972–1988, this tape spans the career of the modern dancer who collaborated with composer Alwin Nikolais. Solos performed from 1953 to the present are intercut with posters, stills, and comments by the artist about the evolution of his work and his choreographic technique. *Déja-vu, Chimera, Junk Dances,* and ten other solos are included.

MUSIC BOX
1980, 30 min. color video
Distributor: Orion Enterprises
Producers: Wendell and Marge Moody
Director: James F. Robinson
Choreographer: Gus Giordano
Musicians: Sensational Nightingales
Category: JAZZ, EXPERIMENTAL
CINE Golden Eagle, Silver Cindy-IFPA, Angel Award
A man trudging home from work through a dreary, icy city is surprised by gospel singing and dancing angels dressed in tuxedos.

MUSIC, DANCE AND FESTIVAL AMONG THE WAIAPI INDIANS OF BRAZIL
1987, 39 min. color video
Distributor: University of California Extension Center
Producer: Victor Fuks
Category: FESTIVALS, LATIN AMERICA
Festival of Indians from the Amazon rain forest, with importance placed on *caxiri* (beer) and the reinforcement of their identity and social order through participation in festivals.

MUSIC MAKERS OF THE BLUE RIDGE
1965, 48 min. color film
Distributors: PennState, Indiana University

Producer: WNET-TV/New York
Category: FOLK, UNITED STATES
Singing and dancing with the hillbillies of the Blue Ridge Mountains of western North Carolina, with fiddle, banjo, cittern and guitar accompaniment. Flashes on groundhogs, moonshine stills, and mules pulling plows to set the scene.

THE MUSIC MAN
1962, 151 min. color video
Distributor: Facets
Producer: Warner Brothers
Director: Morton da Costa
Choreographers: Onna White, Tom Panko
Principal Dancers: Timmy Everett, Susan Luckey
Composer: Meredith Willson
Category: FEATURES, MUSICALS
The screen version of the stage musical of 1957, in which a fast-talking music man tricks the citizens of River City, Iowa into believing that he can turn the town's youth into a marching band. Musical numbers include *Seventy-Six Trombones,* and *Trouble.*

THE MUSIC OF THE DEVIL, THE BEAR AND THE CONDOR
1989, 52 min. color video
Distributor: The Cinema Guild
Director: Mike Akester
Category: ANTHROPOLOGICAL, LATIN AMERICA
In annual music festivals at carnival time in the Andes, the sacred, magical ceremonies of the Aymara Indians bring devils, bears and sacred spirits to life in the form of dancers in elaborate costumes.

MY FAIR LADY
1964, 170 min. color film, laser
Distributors: Swank, Laserdisc Fan Club
Producer: Warner Brothers
Director: George Cukor
Choreographer: Hermes Pan
Principal Dancer: Audrey Hepburn
Composer: Frederick Loewe
Category: FEATURES, MUSICALS
Academy Award
Musical inspired by George Bernard Shaw's *Pygmalion,* of the remaking of a cockney flower girl into an upper-class British lady. Musical numbers include *Wouldn't It Be Lovely, With A Little Bit of Luck, Get Me To The Church On Time,* and *I Could Have Danced All Night.*

NAGRIN VIDEOTAPE LIBRARY OF DANCE (16 films and videos)
1948–90, 30–120 min. color, b&w film, video
Distributor: Nagrin, Daniel
Choreographer: Daniel Nagrin
Principal Dancer: Daniel Nagrin
Category: MODERN, JAZZ
Performances by the modern dance soloist entitled *Solos* (1948–67), *Four Films* (1948–65), *The Peloponnesian War* (1968), *Two Works by the Workgroup* (1972–73), *Spring* (1965), *Changes* (1948–74), *Jazz Changes* (1958–74), *Ruminations* (1976), *The Getting Well Concept* (1965–78), *The Fall* (1977), *Jacaranda* (1979), *Poems off the Wall* (1981), *Dance as Art, Dance as Entertainment* (1975), *The Art of Memory* (1985), *Jazz and Me* (1990), plus the *Nagrin Videotape Library Sampler* with four selections from each of the tapes (100 min.).

NAPOLI

1986, 98 min. color video, laser
Distributors: Laserdisc Fan Club, Corinth, Media Basics
Producer: Robin Scott for National Video Corporation in association with Danmarks Radio
Director: Kirsten Ralov
Choreographer: August Bournonville
Principal Dancers: Linda Hindberg, Arne Vilumsen
Dance Company: Royal Danish Ballet
Composers: Edvard Helsted, Gioacchino Rossini, Niels Gade, Holger Simon Pauli, Lumbye
Category: FULL-LENGTH BALLETS
In this three-act classic ballet first performed in 1842, Teresina, the beloved of an Italian fisherman, is swept overboard on a romantic cruise. Despite the protests of a water spirit who falls in love with her, Gennaro wins her back, providing ample cause for celebration when the couple returns to land.

NARCISSUS

1983, 22 min. color film, video
Distributors: International Film Bureau, National Film Board of Canada
Producer: National Film Board of Canada
Director: Norman McLaren
Choreographer: Fernand Nault
Principal Dancers: Jean-Louis Morin, Sylvain LaFortune
Category: MODERN, EXPERIMENTAL
Dance on Camera Festival Gold Award, American Film and Video Festival Honorable Mention
Modern dance duet depicting the theme of self-obsession and the isolation of self-infatuation. In his fifty-ninth and last film, animator-experimental director Norman McLaren fed the images through an optical printer so that the two bodies merge, multiply, flicker and fade.

NATASHA

1985, 70 min. color video, laser
Distributors: Kultur, Dance Horizons, Viewfinders, Corinth, Home Vision
Producers: Julia Matheson and Robin Scott for National Video Corporation
Director: Derek Bailey
Choreographers: Roland Petit, Michel Fokine, Kenneth MacMillan, Frederick Ashton, Maurice Béjart, George Balanchine, Gennaro
Principal Dancers: Natalia Makarova, Tim Flavin, Anthony Dowell, Gary Chryst
Dance Company: Norman Maen Dancers
Composers: Georges Bizet, Camille Saint-Saëns, Jules Massenet, Frédéric Chopin, Johann Sebastian Bach, Sergei Prokofiev
Category: BALLET, DOCUMENTARY PORTRAITS
Best Arts Program of the Year by British Television
The Russian-born ballerina Natalia Makarova (Natasha) demonstrates her versatility and rich repertory by performing excerpts from Balanchine's *On Your Toes,* the ballets *Romeo and Juliet* (MacMillan/Prokofiev), *Manon* (MacMillan/Massenet), *A Month in the Country* (Ashton/Chopin), *Carmen* (Petit/Bizet), *Proust Remembered* (Petit), *Bach Sonata* (Béjart/Bach), *Begin the Beguine* (Gennaro/Porter), and solos *Dying Swan* (Fokine/Saint-Saëns) and *Les Sylphides* (Fokine/Chopin).

NATIONAL FOLK FESTIVAL (3 films)

1950, 30 min. each color film
Distributor: National Technical Information Service
Category: FOLK, INTERNATIONAL, FESTIVALS
The three short films include folk dances from West Germany, Philippines, New England, and Scotland (Part 1); Poland, England, Croatia, Native America, Lithuania, Ukraine, Texas and Tennessee (Part 2); Israel, Russia, Czechoslovakia, and square dances from America (Part 3).

THE NATIONAL FOLK TROUPE OF EGYPT (FIRQUA KAWMIYYA)

1984, 80 min. color video
Distributor: Morocco
Producer: Morocco
Category: FOLK, MIDDLE EAST
This film illustrates the influence of Soviet and ballet elements in Egyptian folk-inspired theatre dance, narrated and explained by Morocco from concerts in 1980 and 1982 in Mansoura and Cairo, Egypt.

NAVAJO NIGHT DANCES

1957, 11 min. color film
Distributors: Kent State, Lane Education
Producer: Walter P. Lewisohn for Coronet Films
Category: NATIVE AMERICANS
Produced in cooperation with the National Congress of American Indians, the film presents three dances performed during a nine-day healing chant: *Dance of the Plumed Arrow, Feather,* and *Fire Dance.*

NEMETON

1992, 10 min. color video
Distributor: Lieff, Judith
Producer: Judith Lieff
Director: Judith Lieff
Choreographer: Judith Lieff
Principal Dancers: Barbara Koch Zerhoven, Nicole Carter, Alison Newell
Composer: Mark Duggan
Category: MODERN
Dance on Camera Festival 1992 Honorable Mention
A mythical story drawing upon elements of Celtic mythology. Three women conveying sexual potency, maternal instincts and frustration merge into one.

NEW DANCE

1986, 24:30 min. color video
Distributor: Electronic Arts Intermix, In Motion Productions
Director: Skip Blumberg
Choreographer: Charles Moulton
Principal Dancers: Charles Moulton, Michael Moschen
Dance Company: Moulton Ensemble
Category: MODERN, CIRCUS ARTS
Three pieces, two modern and one circus arts, shot by a filmmaker known for his spare style and attention to the essential beauty within each subject: *Toward a Minimal Choreographer* (1 min), Charles Moulton's *Nine Person Precision Ball Passing* (8 min.), *Michael Moschen: Solos* (15.30 min.).

THE NEW DANCE GROUP GALA CONCERT

1994, 160 min. color video
Distributor: American Dance Guild
Producer: American Dance Guild
Director: Holub, Johannes
Principal Dancers: Talley Beatty, Valerie Bettis, Charles Weidman, Pearl Primus, Donald McKayle, Jean Erdman, Anna Sokolow, Daniel Nagrin, Sophie Maslow
Category: DANCE HISTORY
A performance of eighteen dances and excerpts from the 1930s to 1970s, recreated to honor and celebrate the achievements of the New Dance Group, which developed or influenced several generations of important modern dances and choreographers through its school, dance company, and artists. Dances include *Mourner's Bench, The Desperate Heart, Lynchtown, The Negro Speaks of Rivers, Rainbow 'Round my Shoulder, The Transformations of Medusa, Lyric Suite,* and many others.

NEW DANCE: RECORD FILM

1972, 30 min. color film
Distributor: Dance Film Archive
Choreographers: Doris Humphrey, Charles Weidman
Principal Dancers: Linda Tarnay, Peter Woodin
Dance Company: Connecticut College Repertory Company
Composer: Wallingford Riegger
Category: MODERN, DANCE HISTORY
A single, fixed-camera view of a reconstruction of the 1935 modern dance classic of affirmation, performed at The American Dance Festival at Connecticut College.

NEW ENGLAND DANCES

1990, 30 min. color video
Distributor: Documentary Educational Resources
Producer: John Bishop
Director: John Bishop
Category: FOLK, UNITED STATES
A view of some of the old dances in New England and their callers and musicians. In Maine, Phil Johnson calls squares in Lebanon with the Maple Sugar Band and and Charlie Mitchell does contra dances in Northport. Massachussets venues include John Campbell and Norman MacEarchern in Watertown, William Chaisson and Joe Cormier in Waltham, and Arcade Richard and Victor Albert in Leominster.

NEW YORK POST WAVE

1995, 19 min. color video
Distributor: High Frequency Wavelengths
Producer: High Frequency Wavelengths
Director: Marilynn Danitz
Choreographer: Marilynn Danitz
Dancer: Anne Walsemann
Dance Company: High Frequency Wavelengths
Composer: Ingram Marshall
Poet: Allen Ginsberg
Category: EXPERIMENTAL
An experimental work integrating dance, poetry and video art and expressing the impact on the human psyche by our daily news barrage. Created in collaboration with the poet Allen Ginsberg.

THE NEXT STEP

1994, 97 min. color 35mm film, video
Distributor: FIlmopolis
Director: Christian Faber
Writer-Producer: Aaron Reed
Producer: Hank Blumenthal

Choreographer: Donald Byrd
Dancers: Denise Faye, Gerry McIntyre, Rick Negron
Composers: Mio Morales, Brian Otto, Roni Skies
Category: FEATURES, THEATRE, JAZZ
A bold, sexy Broadway dance film whose protagonist is a male dancer suffering from retirement denial. He confuses his emotional and professional life with brief liaisons that ruin his longterm relationship. One show closes, another begins, but this time he's not one of the chosen.

NIGHT JOURNEY
1961, 29 min. b&w film, video
Distributors: Phoenix, Kultur, University of California Extension Center, Kent State, PennState, University of Minnesota
Producer: Nathan Kroll
Director: Alexander Hammid
Choreographer: Martha Graham
Principal Dancers: Martha Graham, Bertram Ross, Paul Taylor
Dance Company: Martha Graham Dance Company
Composer: William Schuman
Category: MODERN, DANCE HISTORY
Set Designer: Isamu Noguchi
Berlin Film Festival Special Award
Martha Graham's masterpiece of a woman trying to reconcile herself to the fact that she has unknowingly engaged in an incestuous relationship. The work, which premiered in 1947, drew inspiration from the surrealist novel by André Coffrant, about a bride, a poet, a black magician, and the Greek legend of Oedipus.

NIGHT ON THE SEA OF GALILEE: ISRAEL FOLK DANCE FESTIVAL
1981, 60 min. color video
Distributors: Kultur, Viewfinders, Karol
Producer: Iroex
Category: FOLK, MIDDLE EAST, FESTIVALS
The top Hebrew folkloric and Chassidic dance groups, in colorful native costumes, perform in a festival at Zemach on the shores of the Sea of Galilee.

NIJINSKA: A LEGEND IN DANCE
1988, 58 min. color, b&w video
Distributor: KQED-TV
Producer: Linda Schaller
Director: Linda Schaller
Choreographer: Bronislava Nijinska
Dance Company: Royal Ballet, Het Nationale Ballet of Amsterdam, Oakland Ballet, Robert Joffrey Ballet, Ballet Russe de Monte Carlo, Ballet Rambert, American Ballet Theatre
Category: DANCE HISTORY, CHOREOGRAPHY, BALLET
Narrator: Mikhail Baryshnikov
Dance on Camera Festival 1990 Silver Award
A portrait of the first female choreographer in the history of ballet. Rare historical clips of various ballet companies are highlighted along with her masterpieces *Les Noces* and *Les Biches*.

NIJINSKY
1980, 125 min. color video
Distributors: Paramount, Viewfinders
Producer: Paramount
Director: Herbert Ross
Choreographers: Michel Fokine, Kenneth MacMillan, Vaslav Nijinsky

Principal Dancers: Leslie Browne, George de la Peña, Carla Fracci
Composers: Claude Debussy, Nikolai Rimsky-Korsakov, Robert Schumann, Igor Stravinsky, Carl Maria von Weber
Category: FEATURES, BALLET
Alan Bates stars in a feature film on the life and times of Vaslav Nijinsky, the ill-fated Russian choreographer-dancer, with a focus on his relationship with his possessive boss-lover, Sergei Diaghilev. Includes excerpts from *Le Spectre de la Rose*, *L'Après-midi d'un Faun*, and *Games*.

NIK AND MURRAY
1986, 56 min. color film, video
Distributor: Museum of Modern Art
Producer: Christian Blackwood
Director: Christian Blackwood
Choreographer: Murray Louis
Composer: Alwin Nikolais
Category: MODERN, DOCUMENTARY PORTRAITS, COLLABORATION
Chicago International Film Festival Gold Plaque Award, Houston International Film Festival Gold Award
Follows Alwin Nikolais and Murray Louis, his collaborator of more than twenty years, catching the two artists on stage, in dressing rooms, and at "happenings" around the world. Includes clips of *School for Bird People* performed in the streets of Aix-en-Provence, France.

NINA ANANIASHVILI AND INTERNATIONAL STARS (4 videos)
1994, 57 min. each color video
Distributors: Video Artists International, Facets
Choreographers: Michel Fokine, Marius Petipa, August Bournonville, Lev Ivanov, V. Elizariev, Rostislav Zakharov, Jean Coralli, Jules Perrot, Aleksandr Gorsky, Victor Giovsky
Principal Dancers: Nina Ananiashvili, Faroukh Ruzimtov, Irma Noradze, Yuri Posokhov, Irina Dorofeeva, Vadim Pisarev, Rose Gad, Alexander Kolpin, Aleksei Fadeyechev, Darci Kistler, Tatiana Terekova, Andris Liepa, Elisabeth Platel, Nicholas Le Riche, Zhanna Ayupova, Igor Selensky
Dance Company: Bolshoi Ballet, Royal Danish Ballet, Kirov Ballet, Philadelphia Russian Ballet, New York City Ballet, Düsseldorf Ballet, Paris Opera Ballet
Category: BALLET, DOCUMENTARY PORTRAITS
These videos were recorded when Nina Ananiashvili visited Japan in 1991 (Volumes 1 and 2) and 1993 (Volumes 3 and 4). In Volume 1 she is seen as the young girl in *Le Spectre de la Rose*, and in the *Grand Pas de Deux* from *Sleeping Beauty*. In Volume 2 she performs *The Dying Swan, Moods,* and the *Grand Pas* from *Don Quixote*. In Volume 3 she performs *Pas de Quatre* and the *Pas de Deux* from *Raymonda*. In Volume 4 she performs an extended episode from *Don Quixote*—the *Grand Pas*.

NINE VARIATIONS ON A DANCE THEME
1967, 13 min. b&w film, video
Distributors: University of California Extension Center, Kent State, UCLA Instructional Media Library
Producer: Hilary Harris
Director: Hilary Harris
Choreographer: Bettie de Jong

Principal Dancer: Bettie de Jong
Dance Company: Paul Taylor Dance Company
Composer: McNeil Robinson
Category: EXPERIMENTAL, MODERN, CINEDANCE
Edinburgh Film Festival 1966, San Francisco International Film Festival 1966, Cork 1966, Mannheim Festival 1966
A dance phrase choreographed and performed by a former member of Paul Taylor's company for the camera as a means of exploring the possibilities of filming dance. The director developed nine variations in the camera viewpoint and its transformations in the editing process.

NO MAPS ON MY TAPS
1979, 58 min. color film, video
Distributor: Direct Cinema
Producer: George T. Nierenberg
Director: George Nierenberg
Choreographers: Sandman Sims, Chuck Green, Bunny Briggs
Principal Dancers: Sandman Sims, Chuck Green, Bunny Briggs
Category: TAP, DOCUMENTARY PORTRAITS, DANCE HISTORY
American Film Festival 1979 Blue Ribbon
Insight into tap dancing with historical footage from the 1930s and portraits of three master hoofers, with a finale at Harlem's Small's Paradise, hosted by Lionel Hampton and his big band.

NOCTURNAE
1996, 8 min. b&w/color film, video
Distributor: Echo Productions
Producer: Cinzia Fasino
Director: Cinzia Fasino
Choreographer: Muriel Melançon
Dancer: Lacy James
Composers: Maurizio Lanzalaco, Cinzia Fasino
Category: EXPERIMENTAL
Inspired by the theme of the Annunciation, a celestial messenger appears to a young woman absorbed in the solitude of the night and reveals to her that she carries within her the seeds of immortality.

NOH DRAMA
1965, 30 min. color film, video
Distributor: The Japan Foundation
Producer: Sakura Motion Picture
Category: JAPAN, DANCE DRAMA
An explanation of Japan's six-hundred-year-old dramatic tradition with a formal procession of musicians and chorus onto the stage. Selections from plays include the dance performances of *Shojo* and *Takasago*. Also available from The Japan Foundation, three videos: *Introduction to Noh: Noh Play; Funabenke;* and *Introduction to Noh: Noh and Shimai*.

NOT FOR LOVE ALONE
1983, 24 min. color video
Series: The Educational Performance Collection
Distributor: Dance Notation Bureau
Producer: Dance Notation Bureau
Choreographer: Buzz Miller
Composers: Alexander Scriabin, John Cage
Category: JAZZ, NOTATION
Taped performance at Ohio State University of this modern/jazz dance in eight sections. Comes with advanced labanotated score by Jane Mar-

riett, introductory article on labanotation, critical text for students and reconstructors, and study/performance rights to the dance.

NSAMBO DANCE FESTIVAL AT ISANGI (2 films)
1976, 11 and 17 min. b&w film (silent)
Distributor: PennState
Producer: Wissen
Category: FOLK, AFRICA, FESTIVALS
A dance festival with folk and acrobatic dancers filmed in Ekonda, Zaire, and Central Africa.

N/UM TCHAI: THE CEREMONIAL DANCE OF THE !KUNG BUSHMEN
1969, 20 min. b&w film, video
Distributors: Documentary Educational Resources, University of California Extension Center, PennState
Producer: Peabody Museum
Director: John Marshall
Category: ANTHROPOLOGICAL, AFRICA
A documentary of an all-night medicine dance in the Kalahari Desert of southwest Africa during which several !Kung Bushmen go into a trance and exercise special healing powers. *N/um* can be translated as medicine or supernatural potency. Divided into two parts, the first offers an analysis of the dances, and the second shows the ceremony without narration.

THE NUTCRACKER (American Ballet Theatre)
1976, 79 min. color video, laser
Distributors: MGM/UA, Home Vision NUT050, Viewfinders, Corinth, Media Basics
Producer: CBS
Director: Heinz Liesendahl
Choreographers: Mikhail Baryshnikov, Tony Charmoli, Lev Ivanov
Principal Dancers: Gelsey Kirkland, Mikhail Baryshnikov
Dance Company: American Ballet Theatre
Composer: Peter Ilyich Tchaikovsky
Category: FULL-LENGTH BALLETS, CHILDREN
Emmy Award
The best-selling dance tape in the United States and longest-running dance program on television is this version of the full-length ballet based on the E.T.A. Hoffman fairy tale which premiered in St. Petersburg, Russia, in 1892. The Christmas special focuses on the little girl who dreams her new nutcracker doll becomes an adoring prince who fights off the invasion led by the Mouse King, and brings her a sampling of the dances from around the world.

THE NUTCRACKER (Bolshoi Ballet)
1978, 100 min. color video
Distributors: Corinth, Kultur 0062, Home Vision NUT030, Viewfinders (120 min.), Karol
Producer: Göstelradio
Director: Yuri Grigorovich
Choreographer: Yuri Grigorovich
Principal Dancers: Ekaterina Maximova, Vladimir Vassiliev
Dance Company: Bolshoi Ballet
Composer: Peter Ilyich Tchaikovsky
Category: FULL-LENGTH BALLETS, CHILDREN
Live from the Bolshoi Theatre, the Christmas favorite known as *Mezhdunarodnaya Kniga*. Set in a small Russian town in the mid-nineteenth-century, a child overcomes the tragedy of her

brother breaking her new doll by falling asleep and fabricating fate as she'd like it to be.

THE NUTCRACKER (Bolshoi Ballet)
1978, 87 min. color video
Distributors: Corinth, Kultur 1201, Home Vision NUT040
Producer: Lothar Beck Associates, GmbH
Principal Dancers: Vladimir Vassiliev, Ekaterina Maximova, Gordeyev Vyacheslav, Nadia Pavlova
Dance Company: Bolshoi Ballet
Category: FULL-LENGTH BALLETS, CHILDREN
A double casting for the lead roles for the ballet filmed live at the Bolshoi Theatre in Moscow.

THE NUTCRACKER (Bolshoi Ballet)
1989, 145 min. color video
Distributors: Viewfinders, Corinth, Music Video Distributors, Media Basics
Producers: NHK, Primetime Entertainment, Video/Film Bolshoi and Japan Arts Corporation
Director: Yuri Grigorovich
Choreographer: Yuri Grigorovich
Principal Dancers: Natalia Arkhipova, Irek Mukhamedov, Yuri Vetrov
Dance Company: Bolshoi Ballet
Composer: Peter Ilyich Tchaikovsky
Category: FULL-LENGTH BALLETS, CHILDREN
Recorded live at the Bolshoi Theatre in Moscow.

THE NUTCRACKER (New York City Ballet)
1992, 90 min. color film, video, laser
Distributors: Warner Home Video, Media Basics, Laserdisc Fan Club
Producers: Robert Krasnow, Arnon Milchan and Robert Hurwitz
Director: Emile Ardolino
Choreographer: George Balanchine
Principal Dancers: Darci Kistler, Damian Woetzel, Kyra Nichols, Wendy Whelan, McCauley Culkin
Dance Company: New York City Ballet
Composer: Peter Ilyich Tchaikovsky
Category: FULL-LENGTH BALLETS, CHILDREN
Narrator: Kevin Kline
New York City Ballet's classic production of George Balanchine's *The Nutcracker*.

THE NUTCRACKER (Paris Opera Ballet)
1992, 90 min. color video, laser
Distributors: Dance Horizons, Home Vision NUT060, Corinth, Viewfinders
Producer: Rudolf Nureyev
Choreographer: Rudolf Nureyev after Lev Ivanov
Principal Dancers: Elisabeth Maurin, Laurent Hilaire
Dance Company: Paris Opera Ballet
Composer: Peter Ilyich Tchaikovsky
Category: FULL-LENGTH BALLETS, CHILDREN
Tchaikovsky's ballet choreographed by Nureyev.

THE NUTCRACKER (Royal Ballet)
1985, 120 min. color video
Distributors: Viewfinders, Music Video Distributors
Producer: National Video Corporation with BBC-TV
Choreographers: Lev Ivanov, Peter Wright
Principal Dancers: Lesley Collier, Anthony Dowell, Julia Rose
Dance Company: Royal Ballet
Composer: Peter Ilyich Tchaikovsky

Category: FULL-LENGTH BALLETS, CHILDREN
Production devised by Peter Wright, director of the Sadler's Wells Royal Ballet, with Tchaikovsky ballet expert Roland John Wiley, to combine the original staging with modern effects.

OBATALA
1993, 17 min. b&w video
Distributor: Ile Ife Films
Producer: Bruce Williams
Director: Bruce Williams
Choreographer: Arthur Hall
Principal Dancer: Arthur Hall
Dance Company: Arthur Hall Afro-American Dance Ensemble
Category: AFRICAN-AMERICANS
Dance on Camera Festival 1993 Honorable Mention
For many years the Arthur Hall Afro-American Dance Ensemble, active from 1958 to 1988, performed *Obatala,* about the Yoruba Orisha responsible for all created forms, as its signature piece. In 1993, a tribute to Arthur Hall was staged in Philadelphia, bringing him back for the first time in five years, as seen in this film.

OBSEQUIES FOR DECEASED REGIONAL CHIEFTAINS (5 films)
1954–56, 4–9 min. color, b&w film (silent)
Distributor: PennState
Producer: Wissen
Category: RELIGIOUS/RITUAL, ANTHROPOLOGICAL, AFRICA
Films made in Upper Volta, West Africa (now known as Burkina Faso) of the mask dances from Nuna and the war and harvest dances and mock combat from Kasena, with much pomp and solemnity.

THE OFFICIAL DOCTRINE
1967, 3 min. b&w film
Distributor: Friedman, Gene
Producer: Gene Friedman
Director: Gene Friedman
Choreographers: Judith Dunn, Gene Friedman
Principal Dancer: Judith Dunn
Category: EXPERIMENTAL, CINEDANCE
Solo by Judith Dunn is photographed with special film to create an avant-garde style in which the film techniques are part of the creative approach to the dance.

OKLAHOMA!
1955, 148 min. color video, laser
Distributors: CBS/Fox, Facets
Producer: Twentieth Century Fox
Director: Fred Zinnemann
Choreographer: Agnes de Mille
Principal Dancers: Bambi Lynn, Gene Nelson, James Mitchell, Marc Platt
Composer: Richard Rodgers
Category: FEATURES, MUSICALS
Agnes de Mille choreographed this famous Broadway musical of the Southwest, advancing the plot based on Lynn Riggs' *Green Grow the Lilacs.* The 1943 musical, adapted for cinema, honored de Mille's stage choreography, which set a new standard for musical theatre. Dance numbers include *Everything's Up to Date in Kansas City.*

OLD TIME DANCES
1980s, 95 min. color video
Distributor: Jim Forest Videotapes

Category: INSTRUCTIONAL, SOCIAL
Teachers: George and Betty Montgomery
The Montgomerys of Palm Beach, known for their regular appearances at the Breakers Hotel, perform and teach the bunny hug, turkey trot, maxixe, castle walk, black bottom, Charleston, shag, peabody, polka, waltz, and two-step.

OLIVER!
1968, 153 min. color film, video, laser
Distributors: Facets, Films Inc, Laserdisc Fan Club
Producer: Columbia
Director: Carol Reed
Choreographer: Onna White
Principal Dancers: Mark Lester, Jack Wild
Composer: Lionel Bart
Category: FEATURES, MUSICALS
Academy Award
A musical based on Charles Dickens' novel *Oliver Twist*, about the adventures of orphans who are members of Fagan's band of pickpockets in nineteenth-century London. Musical numbers include *Food Glorious Food*, *I'd Do Anything*, and *Consider Yourself At Home*.

ON THE MOVE: THE CENTRAL BALLET OF CHINA
1986, 60 min. color film, video
Distributor: Direct Cinema
Producer: Catherine Tatge
Director: Merrill Brockway
Dance Company: Central Ballet of China
Category: BALLET COMPANIES, CHINA
Dance on Camera Festival 1987 Gold Award, Directors Guild of America 1988 Best Documentary Award
Making their American debut, the company performs at the Brooklyn Academy of Music and takes classes with Paul Taylor, Alvin Ailey, and at the School for American Ballet. The documentary registers their mixed reactions to American culture.

ON THE TOWN
1949, 98 min. color film, video, laser
Distributors: Swank, Laserdisc Fan Club, MGM/UA
Producer: MGM
Directors: Gene Kelly, Stanley Donen
Choreographers: Gene Kelly, Stanley Donen
Principal Dancers: Gene Kelly, Frank Sinatra, Vera-Ellen, Ann Miller, Jules Munshin, Betty Garrett
Composer: Leonard Bernstein
Category: FEATURES, MUSICALS
A screen version of the 1944 Broadway musical, shot on location in New York, in which three sailors on shore leave meet and fall in love with three girls. Dance numbers include *Miss Turnstile's Ballet*, *Prehistoric Man*, *New York, New York, Main Street*, and *A Day in New York Ballet*.

ON YOUR TOES
1939, 94 min. b&w film, video
Distributor: Swank
Producer: MGM
Director: Ray Enright
Choreographer: George Balanchine
Principal Dancers: Vera Zorina, Eddie Albert
Composer: Richard Rodgers
Category: FEATURES, MUSICALS
Broadway musical of backstage jealousies at the ballet. Includes a performance of *Slaughter on Tenth Avenue* and *Princess Zenobia Ballet*.

ON YOUR TOES . . . THE MAKING OF
1996, 30 min. color video
Distributor: V.I.E.W.
Producer: EuroArts/Brilliant Media Productions
Director: Gabriele Henke
Choreographer: Larry Fuller
Dancers: Jean-Christophe Blavier, Richard Cragun, Randy Diamond, Stephen Greenston, Marcia Haydee, Birgit Keil, Vladimir Klos
Dance Company: Stuttgart Ballet Company
Composer: Richard Rodgers
Category: MUSICALS
A behind-the-scenes look at the recreation of the 1936 Broadway musical choreographed by George Balanchine.

ONCE AGAIN
1974, 3:45 min. color film
Distributor: Film-makers' Cooperative
Director: Dave Gearey
Choreographer: Dana Reitz
Category: COMEDY, EXPERIMENTAL
Art Gallery of Ontario Dance and Film Festival 1977
A comical, stop-action scene of a woman expecting a telephone call, looking out the window of a stark angular room.

THE ONDEKO-ZA IN SADO
1973, 60 min. color film
Distributor: The Japan Foundation
Producer: Tagayasu Den
Category: JAPAN
Japanese young people, who have rejected established society, search for meaning through running and studying traditional Japanese music and dance.

THE ONE I SEE
1984, 27 min. color video
Distributor: Dance Rep
Director: Peter Reed
Principal Dancers: Principals from American Ballet Theatre, Robert Joffrey Ballet, and Eliot Feld Company
Category: EXPERIMENTAL
A triptych: *The One I See* (filmed in a deserted warehouse), *Abandoned*, and *Searching* (filmed in Silvercup Studios). Shaped with pedestrian movements and fall and recovery rhythms, the three films are joined through an "us and them" theme, a defensive attempt to be alone with an inner strength despite an environment devoid of comforts.

ONEGIN
1987, 96 min. color video, laser
Distributors: Home Vision, Viewfinders, Corinth
Producer: National Video Corporation
Directors: Norman Campbell, Reid Anderson
Choreographer: John Cranko
Principal Dancers: Sabine Allemann, Frank Augustyn
Dance Company: National Ballet of Canada
Composer: Peter Ilyich Tchaikovsky
Category: FULL-LENGTH BALLETS
Dance On Camera Festival 1987 Gold Award
Choreographed in 1965 for the Stuttgart Ballet, the dramatic ballet stems from Alexander Pushkin's 1831 tragic poem of unrequited love.

ONEIRO: IN THE SHADOW OF ISADORA
1987, 14 min. color video
Distributor: Film-makers' Cooperative
Director: Silvianna Goldsmith
Choreographer: Lori Belilove, based on Isadora Duncan dances and techniques;
Principal Dancer: Lori Belilove
Composer: Maurice Ravel
Category: EXPERIMENTAL, MODERN
Five dances in the Isadora Duncan style superimposed on images of Greek temples, paintings, sculptures and the Aegean Isles depict a dream (*oneiro* in Greek) in which the self surrenders to its shadow. Shot using a Grass Valley switcher and computer-generated effects.

OP ODYSSEY
1978, 17 min. color video
Distributor: Doris Chase Productions
Producer: Doris Chase
Director: Doris Chase
Choreographer: Valerie Hammer
Principal Dancers: Jonathan Hollander, Esther Chaves
Composer: Mike Mahaffey
Category: MODERN, EXPERIMENTAL
Paris Festival d'Automne Grand Prize
An excerpt from a multimedia piece with dance, music, kinetic sculpture and film, based on Diane Wakowski's poetry.

ORFEUS AND JULIE
1970, 7 min. color film
Distributor: Audience Planners
Choreographers: Sorella Englund, Eske Holm
Principal Dancers: Sorella Englund, Eske Holm
Category: ANIMATION, BALLET
Abstraction of a pas de deux performed by two members of the Royal Danish Ballet.

AN ORIGINAL BILL ROBINSON VIDEO
1985, 60 min. color video
Distributor: Mayer, Julia
Producer: Julia Mayer
Choreographer: Bill "Bojangles" Robinson
Principal Dancer: Julia Mayer
Category: TAP, INSTRUCTIONAL
Tap routines taught to Julia Mayer by Bill Robinson, followed by exercises.

AN ORIGINAL JULIA MAYER VIDEO
1990, 120 min. color video
Distributor: Mayer, Julia
Producer: Julia Mayer
Principal Dancer: Julia Mayer
Category: INSTRUCTIONAL, TAP
An instructional video on the Charleston, followed by a chair routine, two intermediate, one beginner and three advanced tap routines for study.

ORISUN OMI (THE WELL): PROLOGUE TO THE YORUBA CYCLE
1978–82, 28 min. color, b&w film, video
Distributor: Ile Ife Films
Producer: Bayne Williams Film Company
Director: Arthur Hall
Choreographer: Arthur Hall
Principal Dancer: Ron Tayton
Dance Company: Bahia State Ballet
Composer: Ogun Kotoko
Category: FOLK, LATIN AMERICA
Filmed on location in Salvador da Bahia, Brazil,

choreographer Arthur Hall directs a modern company of the Federal University in a cultural exchange sponsored by the Partners of the Americas. Layered images suggest the depth of myth contained in the dances and the African influence in South America.

OTHER VOICES, OTHER SONGS: THE ARMENIANS
1989, 30 min. color video
Distributor: Filmakers Library
Producer: Sapphire Productions
Dance Company: Sayat Nova Armenian Folk Dance Company
Category: FOLK, EUROPE
Dance on Camera Festival 1990 Honorable Mention
Archival photos recall life in the old country, while Armenian Americans strive to keep their culture alive by teaching the traditional dances and performing them at community events.

OTHER VOICES, OTHER SONGS: THE GREEKS
1989, 30 min. color video
Distributor: Filmakers Library
Producer: Sapphire Productions
Dance Company: Mandala Folk Dance Company
Category: FOLK, EUROPE
Shot in both Europe and America, the documentary examines the roots of Hellenic music and the pivotal role of traditions in Greek life. Shows songs and dances by several Greek American companies.

OUR TOWN: THE MAKING OF A BALLET
1993, 52 min. color video
Distributor: Leben Productions
Producer: John Leben
Director: John Leben
Choreographer: Philip Jerry
Principal Dancers: Shayne Dutkiewicz, Kevin Carpenter
Dance Company: Grand Rapids Ballet
Composer: Aaron Copland
Category: BALLET, COLLABORATION
This moving story of life and death in a small town in New England is based on Thornton Wilder's play *Our Town*, and is set to the music of American composer, Aaron Copland. The candid interviews with dancers, artistic directors and the rehearsal sequences give viewers a unique behind-the-scenes look into the creative process of staging a ballet. The program then presents a performance at the Grand Rapids Civic Theatre.

OUT OF THE LIMELIGHT, HOME IN THE RAIN
1979, 52 min. color film, video
Series: The Magic of Dance
Distributors: Dance Film Archive, University of Minnesota
Producers: BBC-TV and Time-Life Films
Director: Patricia Foy
Choreographer: Frederick Ashton
Principal Dancers: Margot Fonteyn, Rudolf Nureyev, Michael Somes
Dance Company: Royal Ballet
Composers: Edward Elgar, Franz Liszt
Category: BALLET, DOCUMENTARY PORTRAITS
Narrator: Margot Fonteyn

Tour of the Royal Opera House at Covent Garden, the setting for a gala honoring Margot Fonteyn on her sixtieth birthday. Fonteyn performs *Salut d'Amour* with its choreographer Frederick Ashton, followed by Ashton's *Marguerite and Armand*.

P FUNK
1996, 12:25 min. color video
Distributor: WHYY-TV
Producer: Glen Holsten
Director: Glen Holsten
Choreographer: Rennie Harris
Dancer: Rennie Harris
Dance Company: Rennie Harris Pure Movement
Category: MUSIC VIDEOS
This video combines the aesthetics of rap, music videos, and documentary talk shows to make a positive statement.

THE PAINTED PRINCESS
1994, 15 min. color film, video
Distributor: Eccentric Motions
Producer: Eccentric Motions
Director: Pooh Kaye
Choreographer: Pooh Kaye
Principal Dancers: Kendall Alway, David Roe
Dance Company: Eccentric Motions
Composers: John Kilgore, Pooh Kaye
Category: ANIMATION, CHILDREN, ART
Dance on Camera Festival 1994 Silver Award
This live action/animation film was inspired by Diego Velázquez' portraits of the sixteenth-century Spanish court. On the day of the portrait sitting of a Spanish princess, we go off on a raucous, romantic journey through a deserted palace, swirling forests, and an enchanted circus, as she discovers that art can change her life.

PALENQUE: UN CANTO
199?, 48 min. color video
Distributor: New Day Films
Director: María Raquel Bozze
Category: LATIN AMERICA
Latin American descendants of African slaves preserve their ancestors' culture in music, dance and social relationships.

PALM PLAY
1980, 30 min. color film, video
Series: Movement Style and Culture
Distributor: University of California Extension Center
Producers: Alan Lomax, Irmgard Bartenieff, Forrestine Paulay
Directors: Alan Lomax, Irmgard Bartenieff, Forrestine Paulay
Category: ANTHROPOLOGICAL, GESTURES
Illustrates six types of palm gestures prevalent in the dances of the Far East, Indonesia, and Europe, as an attempt to understand the nature of their respective societies.

PANTOMIMES
1954, 20 min. color film, video
Distributor: FACSEA
Category: PANTOMIME
Mime: Marcel Marceau
The French mime Marcel Marceau plays dice with life, chases butterflies, tames wild beasts, and portrays life's passages: adolescence, maturity, old age.

PARADES AND CHANGES
1965, 40 min. b&w film
Distributor: Canyon Cinema
Director: Anna Halprin
Dance Company: San Francisco Dancers Workshop
Category: EXPERIMENTAL
A product of the sixties, dancers relate to space, trap doors, scaffolding, and a weather balloon. In Act II, nude dancers tear rolls of paper.

PARAFANGO
1983–84, 29 min. color, b&w video
Distributor: The Kitchen
Producer: Institut National de la Communication Audiovisuelle
Director: Charles Atlas
Choreographer: Karole Armitage
Principal Dancers: Michael Clark, Philippe Decoufle, Nathalie Richard, Jean Guizeroix, Karole Armitage
Category: EXPERIMENTAL, MODERN
A montage of studio rehearsals with plots and subplots revolving around the choreographer and four male partners with dramatic narrative. Includes scenes of war, collapsing buildings, falling trees, and a bored cashier watching television.

PARCELLE DE CIEL
1987, 18 min. color video
Distributor: Electronic Arts Intermix
Producer: MCR Productions, La Sept, INA, AR-CANAL
Director: Robert Cahen
Choreographer: Susan Buirge
Composers: Charles Ives, Henry Purcell, Anton Webern, Johann Sebastian Bach
Category: MODERN, EXPERIMENTAL
Slow-motion, stop-action abstraction of a barefoot group dance choreographed by an American-based in southern France.

PARIS
1982, 26 min. color video
Distributor: KTCA-TV
Producers: Mark Lowry and Kathryn Escher
Director: Mark Lowry, Kathryn Escher
Choreographers: Meredith Monk, Ping Chong
Principal Dancers: Meredith Monk, Ping Chong
Category: MODERN, EXPERIMENTAL
First performed in 1972 as part of a travelogue series, this dance theatre piece on journeys, both imaginary and real, was shot in an abandoned grain mill in Minneapolis, fusing avant-garde dance, music, and theatre to evoke a vision of turn-of-the century Left Bank bohemian life.

PARIS DANCES DIAGHILEV
1991, 84 min. color video, laser
Distributors: Dance Horizons, Home Vision, Corinth, Viewfinders, Facets
Choreographers: Michel Fokine, Vaslav Nijinsky, Bronislava Nijinska
Dance Company: Paris Opera Ballet
Composers: Igor Stravinsky, Carl Maria von Weber, Claude Debussy
Category: BALLET
Performances of *Petroushka*, *Le Spectre de la Rose*, *L'Après-midi d'un Faun*, and *Les Noces*.

THE PARIS OPERA BALLET: SEVEN BALLETS
1989, 66 min. color video, laser
Distributors: V.I.E.W., Corinth
Producer: 8 Productions
Choreographers: Norbert Schmucki, Marius Petipa
Principal Dancers: Patrick Dupond, Sylvie Guillem, Noëlla Pontois, Manuel Legris
Dance Company: Paris Opera Ballet
Composers: Peter Ilyich Tchaikovsky, Edvard Grieg, Daniel Auber, Camille Saint-Saëns, Jean Sibelius
Category: BALLET COMPANIES
American Video Conference Award
Features five ballets by Schmucki: *Escamillo, Le Petit Pan, Bambou* (extract), *Rixe,* and *Une Femme,* as well as Petipa's *Grand Pas Classique,* and the *White Swan Pas de Deux* from *Swan Lake.*

THE PARIS OPERA BALLET: SIX BALLETS
1987, 58 min. color video, laser
Distributors: V.I.E.W., Corinth
Producer: 8 Productions
Choreographers: Norbert Schmucki, Marius Petipa
Principal Dancers: Patrick Dupond, Noëlla Pontois, Claude De Vulpian
Dance Company: Paris Opera Ballet
Composers: Peter Ilyich Tchaikovsky, Manuel Valera, Dmitri Shostakovich, Giacomo Meyerbeer
Category: BALLET COMPANIES
Five ballets by Schmucki: *Tchaikovsky Ballet, Deltat, Elphemera, Paillettes,* and *The Ice Skaters,* also Petipa's *Black Swan Pas de Deux* from *Swan Lake.*

PARISIAN FOLLIES
1920s, 8 min. b&w film
Distributor: Dance Film Archive
Principal Dancer: Josephine Baker
Category: NIGHTCLUB, AFRICAN-AMERICANS
Cabaret and nightclub acts from Paris, including the African-American comedienne-dancer-singer who stunned Europe, Josephine Baker.

PARTNERING FOR THE THEATRE ARTS (2 videos)
0 min. each color video
Distributor: Jim Forest Videotapes
Category: INSTRUCTIONAL, BALLROOM
Teachers: François Szony, Toni Ann Gardella
A world famous adagio team performs and teaches a waltz and paso doble, and demonstrates many of their lifts in real time and slow-motion.

PARTNERS
1980, 22:30 min. color film, video
Distributor: Schulz, Larry
Producer: Larry Schulz
Principal Dancers: Bill Davies, Sandra Cameron
Category: BALLROOM
Two ballroom dance champions practice and perform five classic dances—fox-trot, slow waltz, tango, quickstep, Viennese waltz—and discuss their partnership and the future of ballroom dance.

PAS DE DEUX
1968, 14 min. b&w film, video
Distributors: Museum of Modern Art, National Film Board of Canada, University of Minnesota, University of California Extension Center, Dance Film Archive, Biograph Entertainment, Coe Film Associates Indiana University, PennState, Iowa State
Producer: National Film Board of Canada
Director: Norman McLaren
Choreographer: Ludmilla Chiriaeff
Principal Dancers: Margaret Mercier, Vincent Warren
Category: BALLET, EXPERIMENTAL, CINEDANCE
American Film Festival Blue Ribbon, Canadian and British Film Awards
Two white-clad principals of Les Grands Ballets Canadiens, silhouetted by rear lighting and multiplied through the exposure of individual frames up to eleven times, perform a simple pas de deux dance movement. A landmark film in the development of collaborations between dancers and filmmakers.

PAS DE DEUX
1984, 81 min. color video
Distributors: Dance Horizons, Viewfinders, Music Video Distributors, Media Basics
Producer: Mark I. Rosenthal
Director: Ted Lin
Choreographers: Marius Petipa, Filippo Taglioni
Principal Dancers: Patricia McBride, Wayne Eagling, Ravena Tucker, Michel Dénard, Ghislaine Thesmar, Yoko Morishita
Category: BALLET
Selections from *Sleeping Beauty, La Sylphide, Le Corsaire,* and *Don Quixote.*

PAS DE QUATRE and THE CHARIOTEER
1968, 29 min. b&w video
Distributor: Orion Enterprises
Producer: WTTW-TV/Chicago
Director: Richard Carter
Choreographers: Jules Perrot, Anton Dolin, Dom Orejudos
Dance Company: Illinois Ballet
Composers: Cesare Pugni, Samuel Barber
Category: BALLET
Pas de Quatre, created by Jules Perrot in 1845 to display the talents of the four greatest ballerinas of the day, was reconstructed here by British dancer Anton Dolin. Also included is *The Charioteer,* a modern ballet depicting the horses and drivers of the Gods, choreographed by Dom Orejudos to the music of Samuel Barber.

PASSAGE
1993, 10 min. color film, video
Distributor: Shimin, Tania
Producer: Tania Shimin
Director: Tania Shimin
Choreographer: Tania Shimin
Principal Dancer: Annette Pu
Composer: Daniel Barry
Category: MODERN
Dance on Camera Festival 1993 Honorable Mention
A poetic meditative homage to the land and to ancient peoples worldwide, expressive of our brief passage through time, filmed at the ancient cave dwellings of Tsankawi, New Mexico.

PAUL TAYLOR AND COMPANY: AN ARTIST AND HIS WORK
1968, 32 min. color film, video
Distributors: Pyramid, Lane Education, PennState, UCLA Instructional Media Library, University of Minnesota
Producers: Paul Steeg and Harris Communications
Director: Ted Steeg
Choreographer: Paul Taylor
Principal Dancer: Paul Taylor
Dance Company: Paul Taylor Dance Company
Composers: Ludwig van Beethoven, Carlos Surinach, Franz Joseph Haydn
Category: MODERN COMPANIES, DOCUMENTARY PORTRAITS
Narrator: Clive Barnes
One of the few films on the internationally acclaimed modern dancer, who began his career with Martha Graham and is seen rehearsing excerpts from *Lento, Agathe's Tale, Orbs, Three Epitaphs, Aureole,* and *Piece Period.*

THE PAUL TAYLOR DANCE COMPANY
1978, 60 min. color video
Series: Dance in America
Distributor: WarnerVision Entertainment
Producers: Emile Ardolino and Judy Kinberg
Director: Emile Ardolino, Judy Kinberg
Choreographer: Paul Taylor
Dance Company: Paul Taylor Dance Company
Composer: Johann Sebastian Bach
Category: BALLET
Two works are performed: *Esplanade,* set to the music of Bach's E-major and D-minor violin concertos and *Runes,* a Druid-inspired dance of mystery and imagination.

PAUL'S PIECE OF SKY
1993, 56 min. color video
Distributor: Moving Visions Productions
Producer: Nikila Cole
Director: Nikila Cole
Choreographer: Paul Hall
Dance Company: Paul Hall Contemporary Dance Company
Composer: Pat Metheny
Category: MODERN COMPANIES, AFRICAN-AMERICANS
A young, struggling, multicultural dance company in the '90s is documented performing at the Sixth International Conference for Blacks in Dance, with an intimate look at the preparations, travels, and ups and downs of this vibrant young company.

PAVLOVA: A TRIBUTE TO A LEGENDARY BALLERINA
1983, 81 min. color video
Distributors: Kultur, Dance Horizons, Home Vision
Producers: Pierre Morin, Micheline Charest, Ronald A. Winberg for Société Radio Canada/Premiere Performance Corporation
Director: Pierre Morin
Choreographers: Marius Petipa, Anna Pavlova, Ann Marie de Angelo, Hilary Cartwright, Michel Fokine
Principal Dancers: Amanda McKerrow, Ann Marie de Angelo, Marianna Tcherkassky, Patrick Bissell, Valentina Kozlova, Frank Augustyn
Composers: Léon Minkus, Riccardo Drigo, Peter Ilyich Tchaikovsky, Léo Delibes, Fritz Kreisler, Camille Saint-Saëns
Category: BALLET, DOCUMENTARY PORTRAITS
Narrator: Leslie Caron

A tribute to the globetrotting Russian ballerina Anna Pavlova with film clips, photography, and memorabilia drawn from her thirty-year career, and choreography by the former Joffrey dancer Ann Marie de Angelo. Scenes from *Don Quixote*, *Sleeping Beauty*, *Gisèlle*, and *The Dying Swan*.

THE PENNSYLVANIA BALLET: DA MUMMY, NYET MUMMY
1993, 10 min. color video
Distributor: WHYY-TV 12
Choreographer: Christopher d'Amboise
Principal Dancers: Anne White, Giorgio Madia
Dance Company: Pennsylvania Ballet
Composer: Dmitri Shostakovich
Category: BALLET, CHOREOGRAPHY
Dance on Camera Festival 1993 Honorable Mention
Offers a behind-the-scenes look at the making of a new ballet by choreographer Christopher d'Amboise. Gives a rare glimpse into rehearsals, costume and set designs, as the company prepares for the dance's world premiere.

PERIL OF ANGELS
1993, 6:30 min. color, b&w video
Distributor: Dusty Nelson Pictures
Producer: Bill Egle
Director: Dusty Nelson
Choreographer: Nita Little Nelson
Principal Dancers: Michele de la Reza, Peter Kope, Lorn MacDougal
Category: MODERN, EXPERIMENTAL
Dance on Camera Festival 1994 Honorable Mention
Divine intervention in the ebb and flow of passionate romance, with the dance sequences shot in color and intercut with black and white narratives.

THE PERSISTENT IMAGE and VALSE
1969, 24 min. b&w video
Distributor: Orion Enterprises
Producer: WTTW-TV/Chicago
Director: Richard Ellis, Christine DuBoulay, Richard Carter
Choreographers: Dom Orejudos, Hy Somers
Dance Company: Illinois Ballet
Composers: Sergei Prokofiev, Mikhail Ivanovich Glinka
Category: BALLET
Orejudos' *The Persistent Image,* set in the Victorian era, revolves around an adulterous theme, a lodger copulating with the matron of the household. *Valse* is choreographed in the classical style by Hy Somers.

PETER MARTINS: A DANCER
1979, 54 min. color video
Distributors: Kultur, Viewfinders, Corinth, Home Vision, Buffalo State
Producer: Danmarks Radio and Film Company
Director: Jorgen Leth
Choreographers: George Balanchine, Peter Martins, Jerome Robbins
Principal Dancers: Peter Martins, Suzanne Farrell, Heather Watts, Daniel Duell
Composers: Igor Stravinsky, Peter Ilyich Tchaikovsky
Category: BALLET, DOCUMENTARY PORTRAITS
The Danish-born artistic director of New York

City Ballet trains, rehearses with choreographer Jerome Robbins, fusses over his costumes, and performs duets from George Balanchine's *Chaconne*, *Agon* and *Tchaikovsky Pas de Deux*, while he expresses his feelings about himself, his work and his company. Heather Watts and Daniel Duell perform Martin's *Calcium Light Night*.

A PHANTASY
1952, 7:30 min. color film
Distributor: International Film Bureau
Producer: National Film Board of Canada
Director: Norman McLaren
Composer: Maurice Blackburn
Category: ANIMATION
Canadian animator Norman McLaren used pastel drawings and cutouts for a dance accompanied by saxophone and synthesizer.

PICTURES AT AN EXHIBITION
1991, 34 min. color 1 inch video
Distributor: Rhombus International
Producer: Niv Fichman
Director: Bernar Hébert
Choreographer: Moses Pendleton
Principal Dancers: Karl Baumann, Jim Cappeletti, Kelly Holcombe, Cynthia Quinn, Rebecca Stern
Dance Company: Momix
Composer: Modest Petrovich Mussorgsky
Category: MODERN
Emmy Award Best Performing Arts, Chicago International Film Festival 1992 Gold Hugo Award
A journey into the creative genius of Mussorgsky and his arranger Ravel, traveling into the world beyond the pictures with the dancers of Momix.

PILOBOLUS AND JOAN
1973, 58 min. color video
Distributor: Electronic Arts Intermix
Producer: WNET-TV/New York
Director: Ed Emshwiller
Principal Dancer: Joan McDermott
Dance Company: Pilobolus Dance Theatre
Category: MODERN, COMEDY, EXPERIMENTAL
Reversing Kafka's *Metamorphosis*, a cockroach becomes a man, or rather four men, clumsily but artfully attached, and falls in love with Joan. Responding to her in urban streets, her modest apartment and a pastoral lake, the beast manages as best it can despite occasional dismemberings and momentary aerial flights. With narration and special effects.

PILOBOLUS DANCE THEATRE
1977, 60 min. color video
Series: Dance in America
Distributor: WarnerVision Entertainment
Producers: Emile Ardolino, Judy Kinberg, Merrill Brockway
Director: Emile Ardolino, Judy Kinberg
Principal Dancers: Martha Clarke, Moses Pendleton
Dance Company: Pilobolus Dance Theatre
Category: MODERN
This program features four dances which span the dance company's history: *Walkyndon*, *Momix*, *Aliane*, and *Molly's Not Dead*.

THE PIRATE
1948, 102 min. color film, video, laser
Distributors: Facets, Laserdisc Fan Club, Swank, MGM/UA

Producer: MGM
Director: Vincente Minelli
Choreographers: Robert Alton, Gene Kelly
Principal Dancers: Judy Garland, Gene Kelly, Nicholas Brothers
Composer: Cole Porter
Category: FEATURES, MUSICALS
A carnival performer on a Caribbean tour takes on the identity of a swashbuckling pirate in order to make a romantic overture. Dance numbers include *The Pirate Ballet*, *Mack the Black*, and *Be a Clown*.

PLANES, TRAINS, AUTOMOBILES
199?, 10:45 min. color video
Distributor: DeVivo, Kerry
Director: Kerry DeVivo
Choreographer: Kerry DeVivo
Principal Dancers: Chris Harris, Kaile Larson, Elizabeth Haselwood
Composer: Randall S. McIntosh
Category: MODERN, EXPERIMENTAL
Reflects on the difficulties and rewards of long distance relationships in a variety of locations—an airport, on an airplane, and at an intersection—juxtaposing dancers, images, and a variety of environments.

THE PLANETS
1994, 60 min. color film, 1 inch video
Producers: Niv Fichman and Barbara Willis Sweete
Director: Barbara Willis Sweete
Choreographer: Lar Lubovitch
Principal Dancers: Paul Duchesnay, Isabelle Duchesnay, Brian Orser, Sonia Rodriguez
Composer: Gustav Holst
Category: ICE DANCE
A television special incorporating solo and ensemble ice dance, precision group skating, conventional dance, and synchronized swimming.

PLASMASIS
1974, 14 min. color film
Distributor: The Cinema Guild
Director: Melchor Casals
Principal Dancers: Caridad Martínez, Lázaro Carreno
Dance Company: Ballet Nacional de Cuba
Composer: Sergio Fernandez Barroso
Category: BALLET
A modern Cuban ballet on the evolution of man.

PLISETSKAYA DANCES
1964, 70 min. b&w film, video
Distributors: Corinth, Kultur, Dance Horizons, Viewfinders, Home Vision, Insight Media
Producer: Central Documentary Film Studio
Director: Vasili Katanyan
Choreographers: Marius Petipa, Lev Ivanov, Agrippina Vaganova;Vakhtang Chabukiani, Aleksandr Gorsky, Arthur Saint-Léon, Leonid Yacobson
Principal Dancers: Maya Plisetskaya, Yuri Zhdanov, Vladimir Vassiliev
Dance Company: Bolshoi Ballet
Composers: Peter Ilyich Tchaikovsky, Alexander Glazunov, Sergei Prokofiev, Léon Minkus
Category: BALLET, DOCUMENTARY PORTRAITS
Presents rare footage of Maya Plisetskaya, Bolshoi Ballet's prima ballerina, as a child, during her career and in performance of *Swan Lake*, *Laure-*

ncia, Spartacus, The Little Humpedback Horse, Khovanschina, Raymonda, The Stone Flower, Romeo and Juliet, Walpurgisnacht and *Don Quixote.*

A POEM OF DANCES ALSO KNOWN AS PLISETSKAYA: CARMEN
1973, 73 min. color video
Distributors: Corinth, Home Vision
Producer: Mosfilms Studios
Director: Vadim Derbenev
Choreographers: Alberto Alonso, Vladimir Vassiliev
Principal Dancers: Maya Plisetskaya, Nikolai Fadeyechev
Dance Company: Bolshoi Ballet
Composers: Peter Ilyich Tchaikovsky, Georges Bizet, Alexander Glazunov, Johann Sebastian Bach
Category: BALLET, DOCUMENTARY PORTRAITS
The Russian ballerina Maya Plisetskaya in some of her most famous roles from *Carmen Suite, Raymonda, Prelude,* and *The Dying Swan.*

THE POINT IS
1986, 7:10 min. color video
Distributor: Coe Film Associates, Kineped Films
Producer: Sheila Kogan
Director: Yudi Bennett
Dance Company: American Ballet Theatre
Category: BALLET
A documentary about toe shoes.

POINTE BY POINT
1988, 45 min. color video
Distributors: Kultur, Dance Horizons, Home Vision
Producer: Ross Alley
Director: Greg Lofton
Principal Dancer: Deborah Noakes
Category: BALLET, INSTRUCTIONAL
Teacher: Barbara Fewster
Guidelines to develop safe habits and muscular strength on pointe are presented in four sections: types of feet, preparations of the ballet shoe, study in pointe for beginners and, finally, placement.

POINTS IN SPACE
1986, 55 min. color film, video
Distributors: Cunningham Dance Foundation, Kultur, Dance Horizons, Viewfinders, Home Vision, Corinth, Viewfinders
Producers: Bob Lockyer of BBC-TV and Cunningham Dance Foundation
Director: Elliot Caplan, Merce Cunningham
Choreographer: Merce Cunningham
Dance Company: Merce Cunningham Dance Company
Composer: John Cage
Category: MODERN, COMPOSITION
Prague Plaque D'Or, American Film Festival, International Film and Television Festival
Rehearsals and interviews with the artists take the viewer through the complexities of bringing new dance to television.

POLYNESIAN DANCES FROM THE ELLICE ISLANDS (4 films)
1960, 2–8 min. b&w film
Distributor: PennState
Producer: Wissen

Category: FOLK, ASIA, IMPROVISATION
An improvisational solo performed to two *Fakanau* narrative songs accompanied by a drum; a *Fatele,* a woman's dance accompanied by a large men's chorus; two minutes of a *Siva* song from the Samoan Islands with a couple improvising; and a group of girls singing *Viki,* a song of praise, illustrated with arm and hand movements.

PORTRAIT OF AN ARTIST
1984, 28 min. color film, video
Distributors: Coe Film Associates, Women Make Movies
Producer: Robin Schanzenbach
Director: Robin Schanzenbach
Category: DOCUMENTARY PORTRAITS, ART
American Film Festival, Berlin Film Festival, Lyon Documentary Film Festival
Traces the career of Doris Chase as a painter, sculptor, film/video artist, and designer and builder of kinetic sculpture for dancers. Follows her personal and artistic evolution over thirty years.

A PORTRAIT OF GISÈLLE
1987, 98 min. color film, video
Distributors: Wombat, Kultur, Dance Horizons, Viewfinders, Corinth, Home Vision, University of Minnesota
Producer: Joseph Wishy for ABC Video Enterprises
Director: Muriel Balash
Choreographers: Jean Coralli, Jules Perrot
Principal Dancers: Alicia Alonso, Yvette Chauvire, Carla Fracci, Alicia Markova, Olga Spessivtzeva, Galina Ulanova, Natalia Makarova, Patricia McBride
Composer: Adolphe Adam
Category: BALLET, DANCE HISTORY
Dance on Camera Festival 1982 Gold Award, Academy Award
Sir Anton Dolin explains the plot of *Gisèlle* and its performance history, lending insights into its technical and dramatic demands. Eight of the greatest Gisèlles illustrate the points with rare films of their performances dating from as early as 1932. Dolin prepares New York City Ballet's Patricia McBride for the title role.

POSITIVE MOTION
1992, 37 min. color video
Distributor: University of California Extension Center
Producer: Andy A. Wilson
Director: Andy A. Wilson
Choreographer: Anna Halprin
Dance Company: Positive Motion Dance Company
Composers: Jules Beckman, Norman Rutherford
Category: DANCE THERAPY
Dance on Camera Festival 1992 Best in Festival, Grand Prix International Vidéo-Danse Festival Award (France), Film Arts Foundation Festival Honoree, Dance Screen Festival Honoree (Berlin)
The men of an HIV/AIDS group in San Francisco are helped to use the dance to express their feelings, find support in each other, and combat the fears and isolation of their condition.

POW WOW!
1980, 16 min. color film, video
Distributors: Coronet/MTI, University of Minnesota

Producer: Centron
Category: NATIVE AMERICANS
Insight into Indian culture, ceremonies, and traditional dances, including the *Fire Dance* of the Chiricahua Apaches and the *Gourd Dance* of the Comanches, at a pow wow or *wacipi.*

PRAISE HOUSE
1992, 30 min. color video
Distributor: Third World Newsreel
Director: Julie Dash
Choreographer: Willa Jo Zawole Zollar
Dance Company: Urban Bush Women
Category: AFRICAN-AMERICANS, RELIGIOUS/RITUAL
Set in the South, the spirit of her ancestors moves a young woman to dance, based on rhythms and rituals passed down from African slaves.

PREPARING TO DANCE
1984, 15 min. color film, video
Series: The Dance Experience
Distributors: Kent State, Iowa State, University of Minnesota
Producer: The Athletic Institute
Choreographer: Lynda Davis
Category: INSTRUCTIONAL
Demonstrates the components of proper training for a dancer.

PRIMITIVE MOVERS
1983, 30 min. color film
Distributor: Rose, Kathy
Director: Kathy Rose
Principal Dancer: Kathy Rose
Category: ANIMATION
The creator dances in front of and with her animated films, which range from the figurative to the cubistic and abstract.

THE PRINCE OF BROADWAY
1980s 30 min. color video
Distributor: Hoctor Products
Producer: Studio Music Corporation
Category: INSTRUCTIONAL, TAP
Teacher: Thommie Walsh
Jazz routines by Thommie Walsh, a Broadway gypsy.

THE PRINCE OF THE PAGODAS
1992, 194 min. color video
Distributors: Viewfinders, Corinth, Home Vision
Producers: Derek Bailey for BBC-TV and National Video Corporation
Director: Derek Bailey
Choreographer: Kenneth MacMillan
Principal Dancers: Darcey Bussell, Jonathan Cope
Dance Company: Royal Ballet
Composer: Benjamin Britten
Category: FULL-LENGTH BALLETS
A ballet set in a magical kingdom of the east about a young girl in search of her identity.

PRINCESS TAM TAM
1992, 77 min. b&w film, video
Distributors: Kino, Music Video Distributors, Facets
Director: Edmond Greville
Principal Dancer: Josephine Baker
Category: FEATURES, JAZZ
Singer-dancer-comedienne Josephine Baker stars as a wild young Tunisian who a rich author tries to civilize, but then succumbs to her charms.

PRIVATE PERFORMANCE
1992, 5 min. b&w video
Distributor: WIMM Productions
Producer: Morgan V. Spurlock
Director: Morgan V. Spurlock
Choreographer: Marcus Galante
Principal Dancers: Dani Raese, Michelle Jacobi, Marcus Galante
Composer: Bohuslav Martinu
Category: MODERN, EXPERIMENTAL
Dance on Camera Festival 1994 Honorable Mention
This short made as a student project asks the question, "Who are we to judge who is and isn't sane?" Looking for food in the park, a homeless man joins two women dancing. For a moment he is transported into a different world by the beauty of the dance.

PROCESSION: CONTEMPORARY DIRECTIONS IN AMERICAN DANCE
1967, 19 min. b&w film, video
Distributor: University of California Extension Center
Producer: Mark McCarty
Director: Mark McCarty
Principal Dancer: Anna Halprin
Dance Company: Dancer's Workshop Company
Category: MODERN, DOCUMENTARY PORTRAITS
Anna Halprin explains her approach to "total theatre" as a journey through space, adapting and responding to the light and sounds of outdoor environments. The dancers manipulate objects, costumes and forms, performing selections from *Procession*.

LA PROMENADE
1993, 11:30 min. color video
Distributor: Motion Pixels
Producer: Jean de Boysson
Director: Jean de Boysson
Choreographer: Yves Musard
Principal Dancers: Yves Musard, Dennis O'Connor, Sarah Perron
Dance Company: Yves Musard and VaDancers
Composer: Eve-Marie Breglia
Category: CINEDANCE, MODERN
Dance on Camera Festival 1993 Honorable Mention
Based on images from a dance installation by Yves Musard, conceived for Dan Graham's rooftop Urban Park Project, the video explores the idea of "screen choreography" by setting an interrelated series of shots to motion, making the screen a stage for a galaxy of orbiting perspectives.

PULCINELLA/SOLDAT
1988–89, 66 min. color video
Distributors: Home Vision, Viewfinders, Corinth
Producer: Bob Lockyer
Director: Bob Lockyer
Choreographers: Ashley Page, Richard Alston
Principal Dancers: Christopher Carney, Amanda Britton, Gary Lambert, Glenn Wilkinson
Dance Company: Ballet Rambert
Composer: Igor Stravinsky
Category: FULL-LENGTH BALLETS
Uproarious adventures of *Pulcinella* (Page/Stravinsky), the Tuscan version of the puppet, Punch. *Soldat* (Alston/Stravinsky) tells the tra-

ditional folk tale of the soldier and the devil in a battle of wits for the soldier's soul.

PULL YOUR HEAD TO THE MOON
1992, 12 min. color video
Distributor: KTCA-TV
Producer: Alive-TV
Director: Ayoka Chenzira
Choreographer: David Rousseve
Principal Dancers: Aziza, Sondra Loring, Renée Redding-Jones, David Rousseve, Genevieve Rousseve, Julie Tolentino, Charmaine Warren
Composer: Public Enemy
Category: COLLABORATION, MODERN
Dance Screen Festival 1992 Best Original Choreography
A collaboration between choreographer and filmmaker which centers on text and movement. The artists trace the experience of choreographer Rousseve's current New York life and that of his Creole grandmother growing up in Louisiana during the 1920s.

PURE REMAINS
199?, 3:15 min. color video
Distributor: DeVivo, Kerry
Director: Kerry DeVivo
Choreographer: Kerry DeVivo
Principal Dancers: Chris Harris, Peg Volpe Posnick
Composer: Jesse Manno
Category: MODERN, EXPERIMENTAL
A journey through water and on land, filmed in Colorado mountains, lakes and creeks.

PUSS IN BOOTS
1986, 98 min. color video
Distributors: Home Vision, Viewfinders, Media Basics
Producer: Interama
Choreographer: Roland Petit
Principal Dancer: Patrick Dupond
Dance Company: Ballet National de Marseille
Composer: Peter Ilyich Tchaikovsky
Category: FULL-LENGTH BALLETS
Based on Charles Perrault's 1697 fairytale of a ingenious cat who secures a fortune and a wife for his master, a penniless young miller.

PUTTIN' ON THE RITZ
1974, 4 min. color film
Distributor: Kent State
Producer: Contemporary Films
Director: Antoinette Starkiewicz
Composer: Irving Berlin
Category: TAP, ANIMATION
In this animated tribute to Fred Astaire, a tap-dancing silhouette leads a chorus line through the song sung by Astaire.

QUARRY
1978, 80 min. color film
Distributor: Dance Film Archive
Producer: Amram Nowak Associates
Director: Amram Nowak
Choreographer: Meredith Monk
Principal Dancer: Meredith Monk
Composer: Meredith Monk
Category: MODERN, CHILDREN
Dance on Camera Festival 1978 Certificate of Honor, OBIE Award
This theatre piece is made up of a lullaby, march

and requiem depicting a child's half-comprehending vision of war and holocaust.

RABL
1985, 7:40 min. color video
Distributor: Coe Film Associates
Producer: Rush Dance Company
Director: Ed Lachman
Choreographer: Patrice Regnier
Principal Dancers: Anthony Stafford, Annette White
Dance Company: Rush Dance Company
Composer: Carter Burwell
Category: ANIMATION, TECHNOLOGY
The love-hate relationship between man and computer enacted through duet and computer graphics, with disembodied floating arms and legs. Created by the animator responsible for the effects in *The Catherine Wheel*.

RADHA
1941, 19 min. color film
Distributor: Dance Film Archive
Director: Dwight Godwin, Dwight
Choreographer: Ruth St. Denis
Principal Dancers: Ruth St. Denis, Donald Saddler
Composer: Edouard Lalo
Category: MODERN, DANCE HISTORY
Narrator: Walter Terry
The modern dance pioneer Ruth St. Denis, framed by a corps of men, was filmed outside Jacob's Pillow in 1941. The cinematographer edited the footage in 1972 and inserted still photographs from other performances in between sections of the dance. Dance critic Walter Terry provides a six-minute introduction.

RADL AND HATSCHO FROM JIHLAVA (2 films)
1963, 14 min. color film
Distributor: PennState
Producer: Wissen
Category: FOLK, EUROPE
The fanfare songs and dances of Moravian farmers performed in a studio, along with the *Hatscho*, a dance that begins in three-quarter time, transforms into a polka rhythm, and ends in a gallop.

RAG TO ROCK TO DISCO
1980, 47 min. color video
Distributor: Orion Enterprises
Director: Victor Summa
Category: JAZZ, DANCE HISTORY
Narrator: Gus Giordano
A history of jazz dance from the 1920s through the 1970s, with segments of jazz classics culminating with the disco craze.

RAGAS FOR SWAMI SATCHIDANANDA
1974, 15 min. color film
Distributor: Beals, Margaret
Choreographer: Margaret Beals
Principal Dancer: Margaret Beals
Composers: Ravi Shankar, Collin Walcott
Category: MODERN
Two dances based on yoga postures and forms, introduced by the choreographer.

RAINFOREST
1972, 30 min. color film
Distributor: Pennebaker Associates
Producer: D.A. Pennebaker, Public Broadcasting Laboratory

Director: D.A. Pennebaker
Choreographer: Merce Cunningham
Principal Dancers: Merce Cunningham, Carolyn Brown
Dance Company: Merce Cunningham Dance Company
Composer: David Tudor
Category: MODERN, COMPOSITION
Set Designer: Andy Warhol
Performance and interview with composer John Cage and a segment of a rehearsal.

THE RAKE'S PROGRESS

1990, 45 min. color video
Distributors: Video Artists International, Corinth, Viewfinders
Choreographer: Ninette de Valois
Principal Dancers: David Morse, Nicola Katrak, Kim Reeder
Dance Company: Sadler's Wells Royal Ballet
Composer: Gavin Gordon
Category: BALLET, ART
One of the first classics of the native English school of ballet, which premiered in 1935. The choreographer calls the ballet her *Homage to Hogarth,* a reference to the brilliant British caricaturist whose paintings inspired her work.

RAVEL

1989, 105 min. color film, video
Distributors: Rhombus International, Bullfrog Films
Producer: Rhombus International
Director: Larry Weinstein
Choreographers: Robert Desrosiers, David Earle
Principal Dancers: Rosemarie Arroyave, Eric Tessier-Lavigne
Dance Company: Toronto Dance Theatre
Composer: Maurice Ravel
Category: COMPOSITION
Pianist Alicia de Larocha plays with the Montréal Symphony Orchestra in this documentary homage to the French composer Maurice Ravel (1875–1937), with two dance sequences, home movies, stills, interviews, and the composer's unpublished letters.

RAYMONDA (Bolshoi Ballet)

1984, 146 min. color video
Distributors: Kultur, Home Vision, Dance Horizons, Viewfinders, Corinth, Media Basics
Choreographers: Marius Petipa, Gedeminas Taranda
Principal Dancers: Ludmila Semenyaka, Irek Mukhamedov, Gedeminas Taranda
Dance Company: Bolshoi Ballet
Composer: Alexander Glazunov
Category: FULL-LENGTH BALLETS
This ballet, which premiered in 1898 in St. Petersburg, centers around a medieval tale of the kidnapping of Raymonda, a noble lady betrothed to the white knight Jean de Brienne.

RAYMONDA (Bolshoi Ballet)

1989, 136 min. color video
Distributors: Viewfinders, Corinth, Facets, Media Basics
Producers: NHK Enterprises, Video/Film Bolshoi, and Japan Arts Corporation
Choreographers: Marius Petipa, Aleksandr Gorsky, Yuri Grigorovich
Principal Dancers: Natalya Bessmertnova, Yuri Vasyuchenko, Gedeminas Taranda

Dance Company: Bolshoi Ballet
Composer: Alexander Glazunov
Category: FULL-LENGTH BALLETS
Recorded live at the Bolshoi Theatre in Moscow, Russia.

REAL EGYPTIAN FOLK

1986, 60 min. color video
Distributor: Morocco
Producer: Morocco
Dance Company: Mahmoud Reda Troupe
Category: FOLK, MIDDLE EAST
Ghawazee, Dervish, Candelabrum, Tahtiyb, Nubian, Sudanese dances shot on location, narrated and explained by Morocco.

REALITY OF A DREAMER: RIVER NORTH DANCE COMPANY

1993, 27 min. color video
Distributor: HMS Media
Producers: Scott Silberstein and Matt Hoffman
Director: Matt Hoffman
Choreographers: Sherry Zunker Dow, Frank Chaves, Ginger Farley, Derrick Evans
Dance Company: River North Dance Company
Musicians: Eurythmics, Judy Garland, K.D. Lang, The Neville Brothers, Red Hot Chili Peppers, Luther Vandross
Category: MODERN COMPANIES, JAZZ
River North Dance Company blends contemporary jazz dance styles with popular music from the '40s through the '90s. This documentary offers a close look at six pieces from their diverse repertoire.

RECKIN' SHOP *LIVE FROM BROOKLYN*

1992, 25 min. color video
Distributor: KTCA-TV
Producer: Alive-TV
Director: Diane Martel
Category: DOCUMENTARY PORTRAITS
Hong Kong Lesbian and Gay Film Festival
An intimate portrait of the mecca of hip hop, and the original dance crew from a thriving subculture.

RECREATIONAL DANCES FROM CENTRAL SUDAN (4 films)

1964, 6–10 min. color film
Distributor: PennState
Producer: Wissen
Category: FOLK, AFRICA
From the Dangaleat people of Chad in central Africa a couple dance, the *Gisess,* is accompanied by two drummers and a chorus of girls. Two circle dances, the *Patie* and *Bidjerua,* are accompanied by flutes, drums, rattle, *parna,* and cultic wind instruments, all of which carry the *Kaltumandasa,* an energetic dance for the young.

RED DETACHMENT OF WOMEN

1968, 105 min. color film
Distributor: Third World Newsreel
Producer: People's Republic of China
Category: CHINA, BALLET, WOMEN
The famous ballet from China depicts a women's military unit during the Chinese Revolution, blending traditional Western theatre, Peking opera, folk dance, calisthenics and acrobatics.

THE RED SHOES

1948, 135 min. color film, video, laser
Distributors: Films Inc., Paramount, Home Vision, Corinth, Biograph Entertainment

Producer: J. Arthur Rank Organization
Directors: Michael Powell, Emeric Pressburger
Choreographers: Robert Helpmann, Léonide Massine
Principal Dancers: Moira Shearer, Ludmilla Tcherina, Robert Helpmann, Léonide Massine, Allan Carter
Dance Company: Royal Ballet
Composer: Brian Easdale
Category: FEATURES, BALLET
The classic feature film is based on the Hans Christian Andersen fairy tale. A young ballerina, obsessed with her art, marries a young composer equally absorbed in his. Torn between loyalties to her director and her love, the ballerina meets a tragic ending.

THE REFINER'S FIRE

1977, 6 min. color film
Distributor: Phoenix
Producers: Keith Beasley, Richard Grossman and Carl Hemenway
Category: ANIMATION
Squares attempt to dance with circles, suggesting our dilemma as to whether or not to conform to society.

REFLECTIONS OF A DANCER: ALEXANDRA DANILOVA, PRIMA BALLERINA ASSOLUTA

1981, 52 min. color film, video
Distributor: Direct Cinema
Producer: Anne Belle
Director: Anne Belle
Choreographers: Marius Petipa, Michel Fokine
Principal Dancers: Alexandra Danilova, Frederic Franklin
Composers: Léon Minkus, Nicholas Tcherepnine
Category: BALLET, DOCUMENTARY PORTRAITS
Alexandra Danilova, the renowned dancer who left Russia with George Balanchine and later joined Serge Diaghliev's Ballets Russes, coaches her students at the School of American Ballet for a performance of *Le Pavillon d'Armide* (Fokine/Tcherepnine.) While setting *Paquita* (Petipa/Minkus) for the Cincinnati Ballet Company, she demonstrates with her former partner Frederic Franklin.

THE REHEARSAL

1980, 28 min. color video
Distributor: Orion Enterprises
Director: Richard Carter
Choreographer: Gus Giordano
Category: BALLET
Emmy Award, PBS Award, Ohio State Award
During a class, two dancers who dislike one another rehearse a pas de deux that is a celebration of love.

THE REHEARSAL: A ROCK BALLET

1985, 82 min. color video
Distributor: Coe Film Associates
Producer: Hungarian MTV
Dance Company: Hungarian State Opera Ballet Company
Composer: Johann Sebastian Bach
Category: BALLET, FEATURES
Hungarian ballet dancers prepare for a performance of Bach's *St. John's Passion.* They are interrupted by refugees seeking asylum, and subsequently disrupted by their persecutors.

REINCATNATED
1984, 6 min. color film, video
Distributor: Coe Film Associates
Producer: Patricia Jaffe
Director: Patricia Jaffe
Principal Dancer: Rita Nachtmann
Category: COMEDY, PANTOMIME
A cat tries to nap, but is continually awakened by the sounds of the household around her.

REMEMBERING THELMA
1981, 15 min. color film, video
Distributor: Women Make Movies
Producer: Kathe Sandler
Director: Kathe Sandler
Principal Dancer: Thelma Hill
Dance Company: Alvin Ailey American Dance Theatre, New York Negro Ballet
Category: MODERN, DOCUMENTARY PORTRAITS, AFRICAN-AMERICANS
Dance on Camera Festival 1982
Thelma Hill was one of the most sought after modern dance teachers in the country when she died in a tragic accident in 1977. A pillar in the development of African-American dance, Hill and her engaging spirit is captured through footage and stills of her days as a performer with the original Alvin Ailey Dance Theater and the New York Negro Ballet of the 1950s.

REPETITIONS
1984, 45 min. color, b&w video
Distributor: Electronic Arts Intermix
Producer: Image Video
Director: Marie André
Choreographer: Anne Teresa de Keersmaeker
Principal Dancer: Anne Teresa de Keersmaeker
Category: MODERN, CHOREOGRAPHY, DOCUMENTARY PORTRAITS
During rehearsals in Brussels for *Elena's Aria* (presented in the United States at the Brooklyn Academy of Music), the choreographer talks with her dancers. The close-ups, candids, and momentary shots of the world outside the studio help to convey the fragmented feeling of the creative process.

REQUIEM FOR A SLAVE
1966, 27 min. b&w video
Distributor: Orion Enterprises
Producer: WTTW-TV/Chicago
Director: Karen Prindel
Principal Dancers: Earnest Morgan, Rita Roles
Composer: J. Mark Quinn
Category: JAZZ, DANCE DRAMA
Emmy Award
An operatic dance-drama set in a burial ground, where the wife and friends of a dead slave have gathered for graveside services. As mourners sing eulogies, the action flashes back to happier times.

RETRACING STEPS: AMERICAN DANCE SINCE POSTMODERNISM
1988, 89 min. color film, video
Distributor: Michael Blackwood Productions
Producer: Michael Blackwood Productions
Director: Michael Blackwood
Choreographers: Blondell Cummings, Jim Self, Johanna Boyce, Bill T. Jones, Arnie Zane, Stephen Petronio, Molissa Fenley, Diane Martel, Wendy Perron

Principal Dancers: Blondell Cummings, Jim Self, Johanna Boyce, Bill T. Jones, Arnie Zane, Stephen Petronio, Molissa Fenley, Diane Martel, Wendy Perron
Composers: Peter Gordon, Ryuichi Sakamoto, David Cunningham, Giuseppe Verdi, Diane Martel, David Linton, David Munson, A. Leroy, Lenny Picket
Category: MODERN, DANCE HISTORY
Dance on Camera Festival 1989
The eclecticism found in American dance in the 1980s. Performances include: *Second Sight, Esperanto, Separate Voices* (Fenley); *Fever Swamp, Freedom of Information Part 3, Holzer Duett . . . Truisms, The Gift/No God Logic* (Jones/Zane); *Untitled '87* and *Brother Jackass* (Martel); *#3, Walk-In, Simulacrum Reels* (Petronio); *The Tree Isn't Far From Where The Acorn Falls* and *Women, Water and a Waltz* (Boyce); *Arena* (Perron); *Alabama Trilogy* (Self); *Moving Pictures, Aerobics,* and *Basic Strategies* (Cummings).

RHYTHM 'N RED SHOES
1980s, 30 min. color video
Distributor: Hoctor Products
Producer: Studio Music Corporation
Choreographer: Mallory Graham
Principal Dancer: Mallory Graham
Category: INSTRUCTIONAL, JAZZ
Jazz routines by teacher Mallory Graham.

RHYTHMETRON: THE DANCE THEATRE OF HARLEM WITH ARTHUR MITCHELL
1973, 52 min. color film
Distributors: PennState, University of Minnesota
Producer: Milton A. Fruchtman
Director: Milton A. Fruchtman
Choreographer: Arthur Mitchell
Principal Dancer: Arthur Mitchell
Dance Company: Dance Theatre of Harlem
Category: BALLET, AFRICAN-AMERICANS, DOCUMENTARY PORTRAITS
Narrator: Brock Peters
American Film Festival (Blue Ribbon)
A documentary on Arthur Mitchell, the former New York City Ballet dancer who developed the first African-American classical ballet company in the United States. Mitchell teaches his students in the basement of a Harlem church. Dance Theatre of Harlem company members demonstrate a ballet barre to Philadelphia school children and then perform excerpts from Mitchell's *Fête Noire, Biosfera,* and *Rhythemetron.*

RITES OF PASSING
1981, 15 min. b&w film, video
Distributor: High Tide Dance
Producer: Risa Jaroslow for High Tide Dance
Director: Nancy Schreiber
Choreographer: Risa Jaroslow
Principal Dancer: Risa Jaroslow
Category: MODERN
Dance on Camera Festival 1982
A dance for twelve women on the sand of the Battery landfill in lower Manhattan.

RITUAL IN TRANSFIGURED TIME
1946, 15 min. b&w film
Distributors: Biograph Entertainment, Museum of Modern Art, Film-makers' Cooperative, Mystic Fire Video

Producer: Maya Deren
Director: Maya Deren
Choreographer: Maya Deren
Category: EXPERIMENTAL, CINEDANCE
Maya Deren, the daughter of a Russian emigré, a psychiatrist by profession, appears at first to be speaking to some invisible person as she spins wool. Three graceful, distant women dance in a circle, followed by a game between a woman and a statue made possible through re-filming.

ROAD TO THE STAMPING GROUND
1987, 58 min. color video
Distributors: Home Vision, Dance Horizons, Viewfinders, Buffalo State
Producers: Timothy Reed, Neil Mundy, RM Arts, and Polygon Pictures
Director: David Muir, for Australian Special Broadcasting Service, Hans Hulscher for NOS-TV
Choreographer: Jiri Kylian
Dance Company: Nederlands Dans Theatre
Composer: Carlos Chavez
Category: AUSTRALIA, COMPOSITION, BALLET
Dance on Camera Festival 1987 Silver Award
In this biography of a ballet from inspiration through performance, Czech choreographer Jiri Kylian is seen attending the annual gathering of five hundred aboriginal tribes on Groote Eylantdt, an island off Australia. Kylian comments on the technical and spiritual aspects of the tribal dances. Ten years later, footage of Kylian's rehearsals of the dance, inspired by the event, was intercut with flashback close-ups of the aboriginal dances.

ROAMIN' I
1980, 15 min. color film, video
Distributor: Cunningham Dance Foundation
Director: Charles Atlas
Choreographer: Merce Cunningham
Principal Dancers: Merce Cunningham, Karole Armitage, Louise Burns, Ellen Cornfield, Meg Eginton, Susan Emery, Lisa Fox, Lise Friedman, Alan Good, Catherine Kerr, Chris Komar, Robert Kovich, Joseph Lennon, Robert Remley, Jim Self
Dance Company: Merce Cunningham Dance Company
Category: MODERN, CINEDANCE
In this documentary on the filming of *Locale,* the methods and problems encountered in filming dance are illustrated.

ROBERTA
1935, 105 min. b&w film, video
Distributors: Facets, Films Inc., Swank
Producer: RKO
Director: William A. Seiter
Choreographers: Fred Astaire, Hermes Pan
Principal Dancers: Fred Astaire, Ginger Rogers
Composer: Jerome Kern
In this screen adaptation of a Broadway hit, an American football player inherits his aunt's elegant dress salon in Paris and falls in love with her assistant. Dance numbers include *Let's Begin, I Won't Dance, Smoke Gets in Your Eyes,* and *Lovely to Look At.*

ROCKING ORANGE: THREE VERSIONS
1975, 12 min. color film
Distributor: Film-makers' Cooperative

Producer: Doris Chase
Director: Doris Chase
Choreographer: Mary Staton
Dance Company: Seattle Opera Ballet
Composer: George Kleinsinger
Category: MODERN, EXPERIMENTAL
Three versions of a dance around a kinetic sculpture. The first records the dancers, the second is video synthesized, and the third is optically printed. Filmed at the Avery Court of the Wadsworth Atheneum, Hartford, Connecticut.

THE ROMANTIC BALLET
1979, 52 min. color video
Series: The Magic of Dance
Distributors: Dance Film Archive, University of Minnesota
Producers: Patricia Foy for BBC-TV and Time-Life
Director: Patricia Foy
Choreographers: Frederick Ashton, Lev Ivanov, Michel Fokine, Roland Petit
Principal Dancers: Flemming Ryberg, Mette Honningen, Margot Fonteyn, Ivan Nagy, Yoko Morishita, Roland Petit
Dance Company: Royal Danish Ballet, Royal Ballet
Composers: Frédéric Chopin, Léo Delibes, Peter Ilyich Tchaikovsky
Category: BALLET, DANCE HISTORY
Narrator: Margot Fonteyn
Discussion of choreographers-dancers Filippo Taglioni, August Bournonville and Fanny Ellsler, with excerpts from *La Sylphide*'s opening scene and Act II. The use of toe shoes through the ages is demonstrated with tales of the romantic ballerinas. Also shown, the *Waltz* from *Tales of Beatrix Potter*, the *Garland Waltz* from *Sleeping Beauty* and the *Pas de Deux* and *Finale* from *Les Sylphides*. Roland Petit performs his version of *Coppélia*.

THE ROMANTIC ERA
1987, 89 min. color video
Distributors: Kultur, Dance Horizons, Viewfinders, Corinth, Home Vision
Producer: Joseph Wishy for ABC
Director: Merrill Brockway
Choreographers: Anton Dolin, Jules Perrot
Principal Dancers: Alicia Alonso, Carla Fracci, Ghislaine Thesmar, Eva Evdokimova, Peter Schaufuss, Jorge Esquivel
Composers: Cesare Pugni, Norbert Burgmuller
Category: BALLET
Culminating with the famous ballet created for the four stars in 1945, legendary ballerinas dance *Le Grand Pas de Quatre*, *Robert the Devil*, *Les Péris*, *Natalie the Swiss Milkmaid*, and *Esmeralda*.

ROMEO AND JULIET (Bolshoi Ballet)
1954, 95 min. color film, video
Distributors: Corinth, Kultur 1202, Home Vision ROM040, Viewfinders
Director: L. Arnstam
Choreographer: Leonid Lavrovsky
Principal Dancers: Galina Ulanova, Yuri Zhdanov
Dance Company: Bolshoi Ballet
Composer: Sergei Prokofiev
Category: FULL-LENGTH BALLETS
Leonid Lavrovsky was declared the People's Artist of the U.S.S.R. on his sixtieth birthday in 1965. This performance was on the twenty-fifth anniversary of his version of Shakespeare's tragedy filmed both onstage and outdoors.

ROMEO AND JULIET (Bolshoi Ballet)
1975, 108 min. color video
Distributor: Corinth
Producer: Lothar Bock Associates, GmbH
Choreographer: Yuri Grigorovich
Principal Dancers: Natalya Bessmertnova, Mikhail Lavrovsky
Dance Company: Bolshoi Ballet
Composer: Sergei Prokofiev
Category: FULL-LENGTH BALLETS
The Russians' version of the full-length ballet based on the tragedy by William Shakespeare.

ROMEO AND JULIET (Bolshoi Ballet)
1989, 135 min. color video
Distributors: Viewfinders, Kultur, Home Vision ROM070, Corinth, Facets, Media Basics
Producers: Primetime Entertainment, NHK, Japan Arts Corporation, and Video/Film Bolshoi
Choreographers: Leonid Lavrovsky, Yuri Grigorovich
Principal Dancers: Natalya Bessmertnova, Irek Mukhamedov, Mikhail Sharkov
Dance Company: Bolshoi Ballet
Composer: Sergei Prokofiev
Category: FULL-LENGTH BALLETS
Recorded live at the Bolshoi Theatre in Moscow.

ROMEO AND JULIET (La Scala Ballet)
1982, 129 min. color video
Distributors: Corinth, Kultur 1123, Home Vision ROM020, Viewfinders, Karol, Facets, Media Basics
Producers: ITC, Rai, Teatro Alla Scala
Director: Rudolf Nureyev
Choreographer: Rudolf Nureyev
Principal Dancers: Rudolf Nureyev, Carla Fracci, Margot Fonteyn
Dance Company: La Scala Ballet Company
Composer: Sergei Prokofiev
Category: FULL-LENGTH BALLETS
Rudolf Nureyev from Russia, Carla Fracci from Italy, and Margot Fonteyn from England perform Shakespeare's tragedy on the stage of Milan's Teatro alla Scala.

ROMEO AND JULIET (Lyon Opera Ballet)
1993, 90 min. color video, laser
Distributors: Home Vision ROM120, Corinth, Facets
Director: Alexandre Tarta
Choreographer: Angelin Preljocaj
Principal Dancers: Pascale Doye, Nicolas Ducloux
Dance Company: Lyon Opera Ballet
Composer: Sergei Prokofiev
Category: FULL-LENGTH BALLETS
Dance on Camera Festival 1993 Honorable Mention
Modern stage design and costuming brings a new production of the classic tale to life, illustrating the theme of impossible love.

ROMEO AND JULIET (Royal Ballet)
1966, 124 min. color film, video
Distributors: Kultur #1183, Home Vision ROM050, Dance Horizons, Viewfinders, Karol, Facets
Producer: Royal Academy Productions
Director: Paul Czinner
Choreographer: Kenneth MacMillan
Principal Dancers: Margot Fonteyn, Rudolf Nureyev

Dance Company: Royal Ballet
Composer: Sergei Prokofiev
Category: FULL-LENGTH BALLETS
Margot Fonteyn and Rudolf Nureyev, who had defected only five years prior to this production, leave no doubts as to why their partnership is legendary.

ROMEO AND JULIET (Royal Ballet)
1984, 140 min. color video
Distributors: Viewfinders, Media Basics
Producers: BBC-TV and National Video Corporation
Directors: Colin Nears, Kenneth MacMillan
Choreographer: Kenneth MacMillan
Principal Dancers: Wayne Eagling, Alessandra Ferri
Dance Company: Royal Ballet
Composer: Sergei Prokofiev
Category: FULL-LENGTH BALLETS
This version, which premiered in 1965, was filmed live at Covent Garden just before Alessandra Ferri joined the American Ballet Theatre.

ROMEOS AND JULIETS
1990, 42 min. color video
Distributor: Rhombus International
Producers: Barbara Willis Sweete and Niv Fichman
Director: Barbara Willis Sweete
Choreographers: David Earle, James Kudelka, Marshall Pynkoski, Jeanette Zing
Composer: Sergei Prokofiev
Category: BALLET
Gemini Awards (Toronto) 1992 Best Direction, Grand Prix International Vidéo-Danse 1991 Press Prize
A musical fantasy which presents eight highly dramatic vignettes from the immortal love story, each featuring a different Romeo and Juliet. Through provocative imagery and sensual choreography, a passionate and highly original fantasy emerges.

RONDO
0 min. color film
Distributor: Modern Talking Picture Service
Producer: West Germany
Choreographer: John Neumeier
Dance Company: Hamburg Ballet
Category: BALLET
Performance choreographed by the American artist who enjoyed a long, celebrated career in Hamburg, Germany.

ROSE BLOOD
1974, 7 min. color film
Distributor: Film-makers' Cooperative
Producer: Sharon Couzin
Director: Sharon Couzin
Choreographers: Carolyn Chave Kaplan
Principal Dancers: Carolyn Chave Kaplan
Category: EXPERIMENTAL
Dance on Camera Festival 1978
A woman dances through images of flora, eyes, buildings, water, sunshine, sculpture, and through her own confusion, disintegration, and sorrow.

ROSELAND
1977, 104 min. color 35mm film
Distributor: New Yorker
Producer: Merchant Ivory

Director: James Ivory
Principal Dancers: Geraldine Page
Category: BALLROOM, FEATURES
The entangled relationships of the lonely hearts who congregate in Manhattan's dance hall, Roseland.

ROUTES OF RHYTHM WITH HARRY BELAFONTE (3 videos)
1990, 58 min. each color video
Distributor: The Cinema Guild
Directors: Howard Dratch, Eugene Rosow
Category: LATIN AMERICA, SOCIAL
Host/Narrator: Harry Belafonte
American Film and Video Festival Blue Ribbon
Afro-Cuban music, which originated five centuries ago in Africa and Spain, is traced to the contemporary sound of popular artists such as Gloria Estefan, Ruben Blades, jazz musician Dizzy Gillespie, and the rumba, mambo, cha-cha which became hot American dance crazes.

THE ROYAL BALLET
1959, 132 min. color film, video
Distributor: Viewfinders
Producers: Paramount, Paul Czinner Productions
Director: Paul Czinner
Choreographers: Konstantin Sergeyev, Lev Ivanov, Marius Petipa, Lubov Tchernickeva, Michel Fokine, Frederick Ashton, Serge Grigoriev
Principal Dancers: Margot Fonteyn, Michael Somes, Antoinette Sibley
Dance Company: Royal Ballet
Composers: Peter Ilyich Tchaikovsky, Igor Stravinsky, Hans Werner Henze
Category: BALLET COMPANIES
Forty-four cameras capture this performance of Act II of Petipa's *Swan Lake*, *The Firebird*, and Ashton's *Ondine*.

THE ROYAL DANCERS AND MUSICIANS FROM THE KINGDOM OF BHUTAN
8 min. color film, video
Distributor: Asia Society
Category: ASIA, FESTIVALS
The annual festival held in the Himalayas with the dancers preparing for and performing at the Dzong, the religious and government center.

THE ROYAL DANISH BALLET 1902–1906
1979, 14 min. b&w film
Distributor: Dance Film Archive
Producers: Dance Film Archive of the University of Rochester and Ole Brage of the Historical Archive of Danish Radio
Choreographers: August Bournonville, Poul Funk, Elizabeth Beck
Principal Dancers: Elizabeth Beck, Ellen Price, Valborg Borchsenius, Gustav Uhlendorf, Richard Jensen, Anna Agerholm
Dance Company: Royal Danish Ballet and School
Composers: V.C. Holm, F. Kuhlau, Herman Severin Lovenskjöld, Holger Simon Paulloi, Edward Helsted, Niels Gade, Giuseppe Verdi, C.C. Moller, Christophe Gluck
Category: BALLET COMPANIES, DANCE HISTORY
Nine short films mainly presenting the choreography of August Bournonville (1805–1897), filmed by the Danish Court photographer, Peter Elfelt. The dances include: *The King's Voluntary Corps on Amager* (1871); *The Elf-Hill* (1828); two versions of *La Sylphide* (1836); excerpts of

the *Tarantella* from *Napoli* (1836); the *Gypsy Dance* from *Il Trovatore* (1856); and an excerpt of *From Siberia to Moscow* (1870), a ballet for four women choreographed in 1896, restated by Elizabeth Beck in the 1970s, and set to music for the opera *Orpheus and Euridice*.

ROYAL WEDDING
1951, 93 min. color film, video
Distributors: Facets, Swank, MGM/UA
Producer: MGM
Director: Stanley Donen
Choreographer: Nick Castle
Principal Dancers: Fred Astaire, Jane Powell
Composer: Burton Lane
Category: FEATURES, MUSICALS
A brother and sister dance team goes to London to attend the royal wedding. Dance numbers include *How Could You Believe Me When I Said I Loved You, When You Know I've Been a Liar All My Life*, and *I Left My Hat in Haiti*. Highlights are Astaire's dancing on the walls and ceiling (*You're All the World To Me*) and with a hat rack.

RUBBLE DANCE LONG ISLAND CITY
1991, 20 min. color film
Distributors: Film-makers' Cooperative, Burckhardt, Rudolph
Producer: Rudolph Burckhardt
Director: Rudolph Burckhardt
Choreographer: Douglas Dunn
Principal Dancers: Douglas Dunn, Grazia della Terza, Sam Keany, Gwen Welliver, Christopher Caines, Laura Oguiza
Dance Company: Douglas Dunn and Dancers
Composer: Bill Cole
Category: MODERN, EXPERIMENTAL
Summer weekend performances in deserted lots of industrial Long Island City with the New York City midtown skyline as a backdrop.

RUDOLF NUREYEV
1991, 90 min. color video, laser
Distributors: Home Vision, Dance Horizons, Viewfinders, Corinth, Voyager, Media Basics, Laserdisc Fan Club
Producer: Patricia Foy
Director: Patricia Foy
Principal Dancers: Rudolf Nureyev, Margot Fonteyn
Category: DOCUMENTARY PORTRAITS, BALLET
Dance on Camera Festival 1993 Gold Award
The dancer's life told in his own words—and as seen in performance, in the news, and in interviews with him and close associates such as Margot Fonteyn, Ninette de Valois, and Sylvie Guillem.

RUMANIAN FOLK DANCES (11 films)
1969, 3–8 min. b&w film
Distributor: PennState
Producer: Wissen
Category: FOLK, EUROPE
Men arranged in a semi-circle dance the *Briul*, a belt dance, and the *Hodoroaga*, a limping dance accompanied by a clarinet. Gypsy music accompanies the performance of the *Feciorasca* (lad's dance) and the *Barbuncul*, a men's dance, and two women's circle dances, the *Purtata Fetelor* and the *Coconita*, from the village of Blajel. From the village of Vestem in the Sibiu district,

couples circle in a promenade for the *Hategana* dance which starts out with a slow tempo and then accelerates; the *Pe Sub Mina*; the *Invirtita* (a turning dance with three or four people holding each other by the shoulders); the *Salcioara* and *Oblii* male dances; and the *Zaluta* and *Hora Mare*. Four Saxon dances are performed by eight young couples in the yard of the old parish school at Grossau.

RUN, SISTER, RUN
1986, 39 min. color film, video
Distributor: Women Make Movies
Producer: Margie Soo Hoo Lee
Director: Margie Soo Hoo Lee
Choreographer: Cleo Robinson
Dance Company: Cleo Robinson Dance Company
Composer: Gordon Parks
Category: COLLABORATION, AFRICAN-AMERICANS
An onstage-offstage look at a collaboration between Denver-based choreographer Cleo Robinson, referred to as the Alvin Ailey of the West, and photographer-composer Gordon Parks as they work on an urban dance based on the flight of African-American activist Angela Davis.

THE RUSH DANCE COMPANY, EXCERPTS FROM *BERNARD*
1977, 10 min. b&w video
Distributor: Rush Dance Company
Producer: William Sarokin
Director: William Sarokin
Choreographer: Patrice Regnier
Dance Company: Rush Dance Company
Category: MODERN
A compilation of key segments from *Bernard*, a modern dance.

RUSSIAN BALLET: THE GLORIOUS TRADITION (3 videos)
1993, 65, 71 and 67 min. color, b&w video
Distributors: Video Artists International, Corinth, Dance Horizons, Facets, Viewfinders
Choreographers: Marius Petipa, Lev Ivanov, K. Goleisovsky, Michel Fokine, Aleksandr Gorsky
Principal Dancers: Mikhail Baryshnikov, Vladimir Vassiliev, Nadezda Gracheva, Igor Zelinsky, Ekaterina Maximova, Maya Plisetskaya, Galina Ulanova, Ludmila Semenyaka, Natalia Makarova, Yuri Soloviev, Mariana Semenova, Andrei Uvarov
Dance Company: Bolshoi Ballet
Composers: Peter Ilyich Tchaikovsky, Léon Minkus, Adolphe Adam, Sergei Prokofiev
Category: BALLET, DANCE HISTORY
Volume 1, 1971–91, presents an overview of the last two decades, beginning with footage of the young Baryshnikov and other stars in *Le Corsaire*, *The Nutcracker*, and *Swan Lake*. Volume 2, 1914–88, begins with restored archival footage of Vera Karalli dancing *The Dying Swan*, and continues with films over the years of *Swan Lake*, *La Bayadère*, *Romeo and Juliet*, *Harlequinade*, *Don Quixote*, *Faust*, and *Sleeping Beauty*. Volume 3, 1940–93, contains rare early footage of Ulanova, Plisetskaya, Makarova, Baryshnikov, and Maximova in an extended excerpt from *Gisèlle*, and Gracheva and Uvarov, two current stars, in the *Grand Pas de Deux* from *Sleeping Beauty*.

RUSSIAN FOLK SONG AND DANCE
1981, 78 min. color video
Distributors: Kultur, Viewfinders, Karol, Home Vision, Media Basics
Dance Company: Pyatnitsky Russian Folk Dance Ensemble, Siberian-Omsk Folk Chorus, Uzbekistan Dance Ensemble, Moldavia Folk Song and Dance Ensemble
Category: FOLK, EUROPE
Narrator: Tony Randall
Song, dance and instrumentalists from Ukraine, Siberia and Northern Russia, Samarkand, Central Asia and southwest Russia.

RUTH PAGE: AN AMERICAN ORIGINAL
1979, 60 min. color film, video
Distributor: Films Inc.
Producer: Nicholas Prince
Director: David Hahn
Principal Dancer: Ruth Page
Category: DOCUMENTARY PORTRAITS, CHOREOGRAPHY, AFRICAN-AMERICANS
Narrator: Celeste Holm
Ruth Page, the first choreographer to create an all-African-American and then an all-jazz ballet, commission the composer Aaron Copland, and arrange Rudolf Nureyev's United States debut, reminisces about her tours with Anna Pavlova, Serge Diaghilev, teacher-choreographer Adolph Bolm, and others.

RUTH ST. DENIS BY BARIBAULT
1950, 24 min. color film
Distributor: Dance Film Archive
Principal Dancers: Ruth St. Denis, Ted Shawn
Category: MODERN, DANCE HISTORY
Five dances by Ruth St. Denis filmed in the 1940s and early 1950s: *White Jade*, *Red and Gold Sari*, *Gregorian Chant*, *Tillers of the Soil* (with Ted Shawn), and *Incense*, choreographed in 1906, available also as a clip by itself.

RUTH ST. DENIS: TED SHAWN
1958, 30 min. b&w film
Series: Wisdom Series
Distributors: UCLA Instructional Media Library, University of Minnesota
Producer: University of Minnesota
Principal Dancers: Ruth St. Denis, Ted Shawn
Category: DANCE HISTORY, MODERN
These two pioneers of modern dance in America discuss their lives and works at Ted Shawn's farm in the Berkshires, today's setting for Jacob's Pillow. St. Denis performs *White Nautch* and *Incense*; Shawn performs his *Japanese Warrior*.

SABICAS: EL MAESTRO DE FLAMENCO
1966 (released 1996), 37 min. video
Distributor: Alegrías Productions
Producer: Creative Arts Television Archives
Dancers: Maria Alba, Sara de Luis, Miguel Angel Pataro, Orlando Romero
Category: FLAMENCO
Five guitar solos played by Sabicas, and performances of a *Siguiriya* and a *Zorongo*.

SAGARI DANCES FROM NEW GUINEA
1962, 10 min. color film (silent)
Distributor: PennState
Producer: Wissen
Category: FOLK, AUSTRALIA
Three dances, the *Lahusa*, *Tahoala*, and *Ewawala*, from the festival cycle known as *sagari* on Normanby Island, held in remembrance of the dead.

SALOME
1922, 35 min. b&w film (silent)
Distributor: Biograph Entertainment
Producer: Grapevine Productions
Director: Charles Bryant
Principal Dancers: Alla Nazimova, Mitchell Lewis
Category: MODERN, DANCE HISTORY
Set Designer: Natacha Rambova
Stylized camp with stoic slaves fanning feathers, clasping spears, sporting headresses with bouncing balls and shimmery tunics. Decor by Natacha Rambova (Mrs. Rudolph Valentino) after drawings by Aubrey Beardsley. Inspired by the play by Oscar Wilde, the veil dance is punctuated with anguished close-ups, visions, and increasingly melodramatic music.

SALSA
1988, 96 min. color video
Distributor: Swank
Producer: Cannon
Director: Boaz Davidson
Choreographer: Kenny Ortega
Principal Dancers: Bobby Rosa, Miranda Garrison
Category: FEATURES, HISPANIC
Rico has two passions: looking at himself in the mirror and salsa dancing. Rico also has a burning desire to be crowned King of Salsa at the upcoming Festival de San Juan in Los Angeles' Latino community.

SAMBA TO SLOW FOX
1988, 30 min. color video
Distributor: Wombat
Director: Maria Stratford
Category: BALLROOM, AUSTRALIA
Filmed in Australia, this witty overview of the competitive ballroom world is unusually well filmed in its close-up on details—from the sequins in the costume shot, to the elderly woman admiring her figure in the mirror, to the less than glamorous shots of the dancers in their home environment.

SANKAI JUKU
1984, 30 min. color video
Series: Alive From Off Center
Distributor: Donegon, Devillier
Dance Company: Sankai Juku
Category: BUTOH
Japan's most daring dance group perform in an abandoned London power station.

SANKOFA DANCE THEATER—A PORTRAIT
1995, 10:30 min. color video
Distributor: James Bartolomeo Films
Producer: James Bartolomeo
Director: James Bartolomeo
Choreographer: Kaura Majarral
Dance Company: Sankofa Dance Theater
Category: AFRICAN-AMERICANS, AFRICA
Dance on Camera 1995 Honorable Mention
A portrait of the Sankofa Dance Theater, a community-based program in Baltimore, Maryland which teaches traditional West African dance and drum in an urban environment.

SATIE AND SUZANNE
1995, 53 min. color film
Distributors: Bullfrog Films, Rhombus International

Producers: Niv Fishman, Daniel Iron, Jennifer Jonas
Director: Tim Southam
Choreographer: Debra Brown
Composer: Erik Satie
Category: DANCE DRAMA
In 1919, seventeen years after a brief, passionate love affair between composer Erik Satie and painter Suzanne Valadon, the former lovers meet again in a Parisian café during a flood of the river Seine. As the flood waters rise, the cast of trapped café denizens, including four exotic contortionists and a jester from the Cirque du Soleil, blend their expressive styles to the music of Satie's mystical piano works.

SATURDAY NIGHT FEVER
1977, 118 min. color film, video
Distributors: Films Inc., Paramount
Producer: Paramount
Director: John Badham
Choreographer: Lester Wilson
Principal Dancers: John Travolta, Julie Bovasso
Musicians: The Bee Gees
Category: FEATURES, SOCIAL
Brooklyn blue-collar boy-by-day, disco king-by-night. The sequel *Staying Alive*, directed by Sylvester Stallone in 1983 (also from Paramount) places Tony, now older and more ambitious, in Manhattan with the goal of conquering Broadway.

SCAPE-MATES
1972, 28 min. color film
Distributor: Electronic Arts Intermix
Director: Ed Emshwiller
Principal Dancers: Sarah Shelton, Emery Hermans
Category: EXPERIMENTAL, ANIMATION
Two dancers in a computer-animated environment by the late California-based filmmaker and painter.

THE SCENE CHANGES
1979, 52 min. color film, video
Series: The Magic of Dance
Distributors: Dance Film Archive, University of Minnesota
Producer: Patricia Foy for BBC-TV with Time-Life TV
Director: Patricia Foy
Choreographers: Lev Ivanov, Marius Petipa, Roland Petit, Glen Tetley
Principal Dancers: Natalia Makarova, Michel Denard, Fred Astaire, Lynn Seymour, Margot Fonteyn, Rudolf Nureyev, Sammy Davis, Jr., Luigi Bonino, Galina Ulanova, Virginia Johnson, Eddie Shellman
Composers: Peter Ilyich Tchaikovsky, George Gershwin, Arnold Schoenberg
Category: DANCE HISTORY, BALLET
Narrator: Margot Fonteyn
The first program in a six-part series, narrated by the late Margot Fonteyn, surveying the history of theatrical dance with excerpts from the classics (*Swan Lake*, *Sleeping Beauty*, *Le Corsaire*, and *Romeo and Juliet*) and from contemporary works (*Fascinating Rhythm*, *The Greatest*, and *Pierre Lunaire*). Sammy Davis Jr. demonstrates several styles of tap, and Fred Astaire and Rudolf Nureyev discuss their viewpoints.

SCENES FROM THE MUSIC OF CHARLES IVES
1971, 23 min. color video
Series: The Educational Performance Collection

Distributors: Dance Notation Bureau
Producer: Dance Notation Bureau
Choreographer: Anna Sokolow
Composer: Charles Ives
Category: MODERN, NOTATION
As part of the Educational Performance Collection, the Dance Notation Bureau grades this modern dance as being on an intermediate/advanced technical level, requiring an intermediary notation reading ability. Ilene Fox notated the score, which is available along with a critical text, an introductory article on labanotation, and the study and performance rights to the dance.

SCENES FROM THE WASTE LAND
1994, 46 min. color film, video
Distributors: The Kitchen
Producer: Ronit Leora
Director: Ronit Leora
Choreographers: Mariko Okamoto, Sumi Fujikage, Theresa-Chiye Speizio, Tjok Gde Arsa Artha
Category: MODERN, EXPERIMENTAL
A four-part experimental multimedia performance video which focuses on different stages of human life through the interpretation of dance.

SCHOOL FOR WIVES
1974, 28 min. color film
Distributors: Dance Film Archive
Producer: University of Wisconsin WHA-TV/21
Director: Birgit Cullberg
Choreographer: Birgit Cullberg
Principal Dancers: Mats Ek, Sighilt Pahl
Dance Company: Cullberg Ballet
Composer: Gioacchino Rossini
Category: BALLET, DANCE DRAMA
Molière's comedy told with imaginative use of chromakey(championed by a Swedish pioneer in video dance(performed by her son, Mats Ek.

SCHOOL OF AMERICAN BALLET
1973, 43 min. b&w film, video
Distributors: Brooks, Virginia
Producer: Virginia Brooks
Director: Virginia Brooks
Choreographer: George Balanchine
Principal Dancer: Fernando Bujones
Composer: Peter Ilyich Tchaikovsky
Category: BALLET, INSTRUCTIONAL
Teachers: Alexandra Danilova, Felia Doubrovska, Helene Dudin, Elise Reiman, Muriel Stuart, Antonina Tumkovsky, Helgi Tomasson, Stanley Williams
Features the school founded by George Balanchine over fifty years ago in New York City. Helgi Tomasson, the artistic director of the San Francisco Ballet, then a member of the New York City Ballet, teaches a class. Balanchine works with Madame Danilova in a rehearsal of the advanced students' workshop. Fernando Bujones performs a variation from the first act of *Swan Lake.*

SECOND CHORUS
1941, 83 min. b&w film, video
Distributor: Dance Film Archive, Facets
Director: Henry C. Potter
Choreographers: Fred Astaire, Hermes Pan
Principal Dancers: Fred Astaire, Paulette Goddard
Category: FEATURES, COMEDY
Comedy set in a college in the swing era, with duets and solos by Fred Astaire, who plays a musician aspiring to play with Artie Shaw.

SECRET OF THE WATERFALL
1983, 29 min. color video
Distributors: The Kitchen
Producer: Susan Dowling
Director: Charles Atlas
Choreographer: Douglas Dunn
Principal Dancers: Douglas Dunn, Susan Blankensop, Diane Frank, John McLaughlin, Deborah Riley, Grazia della Terza
Category: MODERN, EXPERIMENTAL
Shot in exteriors and interiors on Martha's Vineyard, the work is a collaboration of dance, video and poetry in which the language of words is intersected with the language of the body. With poetry by Reed Bye and Anne Waldman.

SEE-DO PRODUCTIONS: BALLROOM VIDEOS FOR INSTRUCTION AND COMPETITIONS (over 100 programs)
1958-present, 60–90 min. color, b&w video
Distributors: See-Do Productions
Producer: Michael Miller
Director: Michael Miller
Principal Dancers: Top ballroom dancers in the world
Category: BALLROOM, INSTRUCTIONAL
Full range of courses and demonstrations of the fox-trot, mambo, lindy, paso doble, waltz, cha-cha, samba, merengue, tango, rumba, peabody, hustle, disco. Exhibition tapes by the stars of the field and record videos of the World Professional Championships in Blackpool, England. Lectures, and world congresses of the National Association of Teachers of Dancing (NATD), which approved the only American style ballroom dance syllabus. The producer was a professional ballroom dancer who was also the photographer for Consumer Reports for thirty years. The first to assemble instructional ballroom dance films, Michael Miller also was the first in the world to introduce the samba, which he learned on his cruise ship tours for Arthur Murray to South America, and is the only American allowed to tape the annual Blackpool teaching sessions for resale purposes.

SERAMA'S MASK
5 min. color film, video
Series: World Cultures and Youth
Distributor: Coronet/MTI, Lane Education
Producers: Deepa and Paul Saltzman
Directors: Deepa and Paul Saltzman
Principal Dancer: Serama
Category: BALI
After carving a ceremonial mask, Serama, a Balinese dancer, joins his father in a masked dance to commemorate his father's retirement.

SERAPHIC DIALOGUE
1969, 25 min. color film, video
Series: Three By Martha Graham
Distributors: Pyramid, Kent State, UCLA Instructional Media Library, University of Minnesota, Viewfinders
Producer: H. Poindexter
Director: David Wilson
Choreographer: Martha Graham
Principal Dancers: Mary Hinkson, Bertram Ross, Patricia Birch, Helen McGehee, Noemi Lapzeson, Phyllis Gutelius, Takako Asakawa

Dance Company: Martha Graham Dance Company
Composer: Norman Dello Joio
Category: MODERN, DANCE HISTORY
Set Designer: Isamu Noguchi
Martha Graham's depiction of Joan of Arc at the moment of her exaltation is adapted for the camera by John Butler.

SET PIECE
1981, 9 min. color video
Distributor: Coe Film Associates
Producer: Duane Fulk
Director: Duane Fulk
Choreographer: Jeanne de Herst
Principal Dancer: Susan Watkins
Composer: Igor Stravinsky
Category: EXPERIMENTAL, MODERN
Dance on Camera Festival 1982 First in Experimental Category
A solo performed to Stravinsky's *Serenade in A* in a set resembling playground equipment.

SEVEN BRIDES FOR SEVEN BROTHERS
1954, 120 min. color film, video, laser
Distributors: MGM/UA, Swank, Home Vision, Facets
Producer: MGM
Director: Stanley Donen
Choreographers: Michael Kidd, Matt Mattox
Principal Dancers: Jacques d'Amboise, Marc Platt, Russ Tamblyn, Matt Mattox
Composer: Gene de Paul
Category: FEATURES, MUSICALS, BALLET
Academy Award
Based on a story by Stephen Vincent Benet, six rowdy Oregon farmers come to town looking for wives after their eldest brother finds a mate. A landmark dance film with choreography conceived for the screen. Dance numbers include *House-Raising Dance* and *Lonesome Polecat.*

1776
1972, 150 min. color video, laser
Distributors: Facets, Laserdisc Fan Club
Producer: Columbia
Director: Peter Hunt
Choreographer: Onna White
Composer: Sherman Edwards
Category: FEATURES, MUSICALS
Ben Franklin, Thomas Jefferson and other founding fathers and mothers in musical form.

SEVENTH SYMPHONY
1938, 32 min. b&w film
Distributor: Dance Film Archive
Choreographer: Léonide Massine
Principal Dancers: Alicia Markova, Igor Youskevitch, Frederic Franklin
Dance Company: Ballet Russe de Monte Carlo
Composer: Ludwig van Beethoven
Category: BALLET
Rehearsal by the original cast of the first three movements, *Creation, Earth,* and *Sky,* of this four-act ballet set to a piano score synchronized by Frederic Franklin.

SEVILLANAS
1991, 55 min. color film, video
Distributor: Alegrías Productions
Producer: Juan Lebrón
Director: Carlos Saura

Dancers: Matilde Coral, Merche Esmeralda, Lola Flores
Composer Paco de Lucia, Manolo Sanlucar
Category: FLAMENCO
Commissioned for the Expo 1992 held in Sevilla, this documentary covers the sweep of styles possible with this two hundred-year-old folk dance that has enjoyed great commercial success in the last ten years.

SHADES OF WIEGENLIED
199?, 3:20 min. b&w video
Distributor: DeVivo, Kerry
Director: Kerry DeVivo
Choreographer: Kerry DeVivo
Principal Dancers: Jessica Hendricks, Kerry De-Vivo
Composer: Johannes Brahms
Category: MODERN, EXPERIMENTAL
A video adaptation of a duet originally created for the stage, focusing on mysterious shadows, intimate close-ups, and intricate rhythms.

THE SHAKERS: HANDS TO WORK, HEARTS TO GOD
1985, 58 min. color video
Distributor: Direct Cinema
Producers: Ken and Amy Burns
Director: Ken Burns
Category: UNITED STATES
American Film Festival Blue Ribbon
The Shakers, a communal Christian religious sect which numbered six thousand members at the height of their success in the nineteenth-century, used devotional songs and ecstatic dancing as part of their unique beliefs.

SHAKESPEARE DANCE TRILOGY
1993, 70 min. color video
Distributors: V.I.E.W., Corinth, Media Basics
Choreographers: Nataly Rizhenko, José Limón, Victor Smirnov-Golovanov
Principal Dancers: Nikita Dogulshin, Gabriella Komleva, Svetlana Semenova, Vlastinil Garallis, Andrés Williams
Composers: Peter Ilyich Tchaikovsky, Henry Purcell
Category: BALLET, DANCE DRAMA
Three of Shakespeare's immortal dramas: *Romeo and Juliet*, *Hamlet*, and *The Moor's Pavane* (Limón's adaptation of *Othello*), are powerfully interpreted in this trilogy of one-act ballets danced by stars of the Kirov Ballet, and filmed on location at a spectacular medieval castle overlooking the sea.

SHALL WE DANCE
1937, 116 min. b&w film, video, laser
Distributors: Films Inc., Laserdisc Fan Club
Producer: RKO
Director: Mark Sandrich
Choreographer: Hermes Pan
Principal Dancers: Fred Astaire, Ginger Rogers, Harriet Hoctor
Composer: George Gershwin
Category: FEATURES, MUSICALS
A classical and a ballroom dancer pretend to be a married couple on an ocean voyage to New York. Dance numbers include *They All Laughed* and *They Can't Take That Away From Me*, and take place in an engine room (*Slap That Bass*), on a nightclub floor, on roller skates in Central Park (*Let's Call the Whole Thing Off*), and on the liner's kennel deck.

SHAPE
1972, 27 min. color video
Series: Dance as an Art Form
Distributor: Pro Arts
Producer: Chimerafilm
Director: Warren Leib
Principal Dancer: Murray Louis
Dance Company: Murray Louis Dance Company
Composer: Alwin Nikolais
Category: MODERN, INSTRUCTIONAL
Narrator: Murray Louis
Focuses on the sculptural dynamics of a body in motion, as demonstrated by dancers, athletes, actors, children, and students.

SHE STORIES
1986, 5 min. color video
Distributor: Wanner, Debra
Producer: Debra Wanner
Director: Debra Wanner
Choreographer: Debra Wanner
Category: EXPERIMENTAL, MODERN
A cast of characters—a pillow, a sheet, pajamas, a woman—interact in an autobiographical bedtime story. While the woman's face is cropped from view, a voice describes the plight of a female artist living in New York.

SHOW BOAT
1951, 108 min. color film, video, laser
Distributors: Facets, Laserdisc Fan Club, Swank, MGM/UA
Producer: MGM
Director: George Sidney
Choreographer: Robert Alton
Principal Dancers: Marge and Gower Champion
Composer: Jerome Kern
Category: FEATURES, MUSICALS
Based on the Edna Ferber novel, the third screen version of the classic Broadway show about romantic heartbreak and racial discrimination in 1870s Mississippi takes place on an old-time Mississippi River showboat. The Champions perform *I Might Fall Back On You*, and *Life Upon the Wicked Stage*. The *Cotton Blossom* opening brilliantly combines camera work, editing, staging and design.

SILK STOCKINGS
1957, 116 min. color video, laser
Distributors: Facets, Swank, MGM/UA
Producer: MGM
Director: Rouben Mamoulian
Choreographers: Hermes Pan, Eugene Loring
Principal Dancers: Cyd Charisse, Fred Astaire
Composer: Cole Porter
Category: FEATURES, MUSICALS
A musical version of *Ninotchka*, in which a female communist agent is sent to get a Russian composer back from Paris. Dance numbers include *All of You*, *The Red Blues*, *The Ritz Roll and Rock*, and *Fated to be Mated*.

SILVER FEET
1986, 51 min. color film, video
Distributor: Direct Cinema
Producers: Lee Rubenstein and Kristine Samuelson
Director: Lee Rubenstein
Dance Company: San Francisco Ballet School
Category: BALLET, CHILDREN
National Educational Film and Video Festival 1986 Fine Arts Category
Follows the rigorous training, hopes and fears of three teenage girls studying dance, and their auditions for the ballet school attached to the San Francisco Ballet Company.

SINGIN' IN THE RAIN
1952, 120 min. color film, video, laser
Distributors: MGM/UA, Swank, Facets
Producer: MGM
Directors: Gene Kelly, Stanley Donen
Choreographers: Gene Kelly, Stanley Donen
Principal Dancers: Gene Kelly, Debbie Reynolds, Donald O'Connor, Cyd Charisse
Composer: Nacio Herb Brown
Category: FEATURES, MUSICALS
Spoof of Hollywood at the dawn of the sound era with unforgettable dances in the rain, on tabletops, over sofas, on stairs, and on deserted sets. Musical and dance numbers include *Singing In the Rain*, *All I Do Is Dream of You*, *You Were Meant For Me*, *Make 'Em Laugh*, *Good Morning*, *Moses Supposes*, and *The Broadway Ballet*.

SIX METAMORPHOSES
1992, 26 min. color video
Distributor: Diamond Dance
Producers: Mark Brady and Emma Diamond
Director: Mark Brady
Choreographer: Emma Diamond
Dance Company: Diamond Dance
Composer: Benjamin Britten
Category: MODERN
Dance on Camera Festival 1993 Honorable Mention
Six short solos each depicting a Greek mythological character from the writings of Ovid: Pan, Phaeton, Niobe, Bacchus, Narcussus and Arethusa. The dances are inspired by the musical score for oboe solo by Benjamin Britten (*Six Metamorphoses after Ovid Op. 49*), in which each character undergoes a transformation, concluding the story of each in a sometimes abstract or unusual way. This piece allows the dancers the freedom to be instantly transported out of the dance studio and into sometimes unconventional and diverse settings, thus completing their metamorphoses.

SIXTEEN MILLIMETER EARRINGS
1979, 25 min. color film
Distributor: Withers, Robert
Director: Robert Withers
Choreographer: Meredith Monk
Principal Dancer: Meredith Monk
Category: MODERN, EXPERIMENTAL
A re-creation of a dance/theatre solo first performed in 1966 by Meredith Monk, the versatile composer-dancer-filmmaker who had subsequent great success with *Ellis Island* and *Book of Days*.

THE SKY'S THE LIMIT
1943, 89 min. b&w film, video
Distributors: Facets, Films Inc.
Producer: RKO
Director: Edward Griffith
Choreographer: Fred Astaire
Principal Dancers: Fred Astaire, Joan Leslie
Composer: Harold Arlen
Category: FEATURES, MUSICALS

A Flying Tiger pilot on leave in Manhattan falls in love with a news photographer. Musical numbers include *My Shining Hour, One For My Baby,* and *The Snake Dance.*

SLASK: NATIONAL FOLKLORE ENSEMBLE OF POLAND

1959, 60 min. color video
Distributor: Coe Film Associates
Producer: Michael Gelinas
Dance Company: National Folklore Ensemble of Poland
Category: FOLK, EUROPE
Folk dance, song, and traditional costumes of a touring troupe whose actions reflect the varied customs and regions of Poland.

SLEEPING BEAUTY (animated)

1959, 75 min. color video
Distributor: Buena Vista
Producer: Walt Disney
Director: Clyde Geronimi
Composer: Peter Ilyich Tchaikovsky
Category: ANIMATION, FEATURES
Disney's adaptation of Charles Perrault's tale.

SLEEPING BEAUTY (Ballet del Teatro Municipal)

1982, 120 min. color video
Distributors: Kultur 1122, Home Vision SLE020, Viewfinders, Karol
Producer: Kultur
Director: Ivan Nagy
Choreographer: Marius Petipa
Principal Dancer: Fernando Bujones
Dance Company: Ballet del Teatro Municipal
Composer: Peter Ilyich Tchaikovsky
Category: FULL-LENGTH BALLETS
Fernando Bujones performs the classic as guest artist in Chile, recorded live in 1982.

SLEEPING BEAUTY (Bolshoi Ballet)

1989, 145 min. color video
Distributors: Corinth, Home Vision, Viewfinders, Music Video Distributors
Producers: Primetime Entertainment with NHK, Japan Arts Corporation and Video/Film Bolshoi
Choreographers: Marius Petipa, Yuri Grigorovich
Principal Dancers: Nina Semizorova, Aleksei Fadeyechev, Nina Speranskaya
Dance Company: Bolshoi Ballet
Composer: Peter Ilyich Tchaikovsky
Category: FULL-LENGTH BALLETS
This three-act ballet was first performed in 1890 in the Maryinsky Theatre. Based on Charles Perrault's tale of Princess Aurora put to sleep by an evil fairy, and awakened by the kiss of a prince. Recorded in Moscow.

SLEEPING BEAUTY (Kirov Ballet)

1964, 92 min. color film, video
Distributors: Corinth, Home Vision SLE050, Kultur 1280
Producer: Corinth Films
Director: Konstantin Sergeyev
Choreographer: Marius Petipa
Principal Dancers: Alla Sizova, Natalia Makarova, Yuri Solovyov
Dance Company: Kirov Ballet
Composer: Peter Ilyich Tchaikovsky
Category: FULL-LENGTH BALLETS
The full-length classic filmed in Leningrad.

SLEEPING BEAUTY (Kirov Ballet)

1983, 147 min. color video
Distributors: Home Box Office, Music Video Distributors, Media Basics
Producers: National Video Corporation and Göstelradio
Director: Elena Macharet
Choreographers: Ivan Vsevolozhsky, Marius Petipa
Principal Dancers: Irina Kolpakova, Sergei Berezhnoi, Lubov Kunakova
Dance Company: Kirov Ballet
Composer: Peter Ilyich Tchaikovsky
Category: FULL-LENGTH BALLETS
Shot at the celebration of the Kirov's two hundredth anniversary in Leningrad, this three-act ballet, was first performed in 1890 in the Maryinsky Theatre. Based on the tale of Princess Aurora put to sleep by an evil fairy, and awakened by the kiss of a handsome prince.

SLEEPING BEAUTY (Kirov Ballet)

1989, 130 min. color video, laser
Distributors: Viewfinders, Home Vision, Facets
Producers: Pierre Morin and Beatrice Dupont
Director: Bernard Picard
Choreographer: Oleg Vinogradov
Principal Dancers: Viktor Fedotov, Larissa Lezhina, Faroukh Ruzimatov, Yulia Makhalina, Vadim Guliayev
Dance Company: Kirov Ballet
Composer: Peter Ilyich Tchaikovsky
Category: FULL-LENGTH BALLETS
The fairy tale ballet about a princess cursed by a wicked fairy, doomed to sleep for a hundred years, until awakened by the kiss of a handsome prince.

SLEEPING BEAUTY ON ICE

1987, 65 min. color video
Distributors: Kultur, Karol, Home Vision
Producer: Bernice Olenick
Principal Dancers: Robin Cousins, Rosalynn Sumners
Composer: Peter Ilyich Tchaikovsky
Category: ICE DANCE
Olympic gold and silver medalists and sixteen of the world's leading skaters in a variation of the nineteenth-century classic.

SMALL DISTANCES

1987, 14 min. color video
Distributor: Electronic Arts Intermix
Director: James Byrne
Choreographer: Victoria Marks
Category: MODERN, EXPERIMENTAL, CINEDANCE
A synthesis of dance and camera movement in which the cameraman responds to the weight and touch of the other dancers, using the camera as an extension of the body.

SNAKE DANCE TEACHER DANCE

1977–78, 18 min. color film, video
Distributor: Ile Ife Films
Producer: Bayne Williams Film Company
Choreographer: Arthur Hall
Category: AFRICA, INSTRUCTIONAL
Dance on Camera Festival 1978 Honorable Mention
West African dances, *Hail to the Chief, Sissongbukatay, Rowing Song, Tche Tche Kule, Fetish Dance, Calabash, Fanza* (a drum duet), and the Dahomey *Snake Dance,* a symbolic celebration of fertility, continuity, and longevity, as performed by the students, teachers, and administrators of the schools of Winthrop, Maine.

SOCIAL AND COMEDY DANCES

1900, 10 min. b&w film (silent)
Distributor: Dance Film Archive
Category: SOCIAL, DANCE HISTORY
Brief dance films from the turn-of-the-century showing the cakewalk and forms of "tough" dancing.

SOLO

1985, 28:31 min. color video
Distributor: Electronic Arts Intermix
Director: James Byrne
Choreographers: Wendy Morris, Maria Cheng, Marilyn Habermas-Scher, Georgia Stephens, Laurie Van Wieren
Principal Dancers: Wendy Morris, Maria Cheng, Marilyn Habermas-Scher, Georgia Stephens, Laurie Van Wieren
Composers: Victor Riley, Johann Sebastian Bach, Marilyn Haberman-Scher, Wendy Ultan, The Suburbs, Mkwaju Ensemble
Category: MODERN, EXPERIMENTAL
Five solos performed by Minneapolis women who designed and performed works expressly for the camera in sets ranging from the confinement of a small room to an expansive natural landscape. With his physical approach, James Byrne captures the intimacy of each solo in *The Members of My Party, Habitat, Vision, This Body This Place, Unnamed, Beside Herself.*

SOMETIMES IT WORKS, SOMETIMES IT DOESN'T

1983, 63 min. color video
Distributor: Cunningham Dance Foundation
Producer: Belgian Radio and Television
Directors: Chris Dercon, Stefaan Decostere
Choreographer: Merce Cunningham
Dance Company: Merce Cunningham Dance Company
Composer: John Cage
Category: MODERN, COLLABORATION
Choreographer Merce Cunningham and composer John Cage discuss at length and in separate interviews, the influence of each on the other, as well as their collaborations. Interview scenes alternate with performance footage. Concludes with *Channels/Inserts.*

SONG AND DANCE

1984, 26 min. color film, video
Distributor: The Media Guild
Producer: Thames Television
Composer: Benjamin Britten
Category: BALLET, CHILDREN
Children of the Royal Ballet School dance to Benjamin Britten's songs for children, *Friday Afternoons.*

SONG OF VENEZUELA

1983, 4 min. color video
Distributor: The Kitchen
Director: M.J. Becker
Composer: Joropo
Category: EXPERIMENTAL, BELLY DANCE
Abstraction of a belly dance shot from the side of the immobile hips.

SONGS UNWRITTEN: A TAP DANCER REMEMBERED
1988, 58 min. color video
Distributor: Wadsworth, David
Producer: David Wadsworth
Director: David Wadsworth
Principal Dancers: Leon Collins, Brenda Bufalino, James "Buster" Brown
Category: TAP, DOCUMENTARY PORTRAITS
Dance on Camera Festival 1989 Honorable Mention
A portrait of the late Boston tap dancer and Harvard professor Leon Collins, with sixteen jazz and classical pieces recorded in 1984, and historical perspectives from the 1930s to the present.

SOPHISTICATED LADIES
min. color video
Distributor: Facets
Choreographer: George Faison
Principal Dancer: Judith Jamison
Composer: Duke Ellington
Category: FEATURES, JAZZ
The Broadway musical set to thirty-four hits by Duke Ellington.

THE SORCERESS: KIRI TE KANAWA
1993, 52 min. color video
Distributor: Bullfrog Films
Producers: Niv Fichman, Piet Erkelens
Director: Barbara Willis Sweete
Choreographers: Ed Wubbe, Jeanette Zing
Dance Company: Scapino Ballet (Rotterdam), Opera Atelier (Toronto)
Composer: George Frederick Handel
Category: BALLET, OPERA
Soprano: Kiri Te Kanawa
Columbus International Film and Video Festival Bronze Plaque Award, International Film and Television Festival of New York Silver Medal
A fantasy combining operatic singing with spectacular dance, both baroque and contemporary. Having the character and shape of an archetypal fairy tale, *The Sorceress* deals with the warring forces of good and evil and the power of romantic love. The story unfolds through music, song, dance and gesture—no dialogue—and combines the striking techniques of rock video with the baroque penchant for magic and spectacle. The visuals are set to the haunting *Magic Operas* of George Frederic Handel.

THE SOUND OF MUSIC
1965, 167 min. color film, video
Distributors: Facets, Films Inc.
Producer: 20th Century Fox
Director: Robert Wise
Choreographers: Marc Breaux, DeeDee Wood
Principal Dancer: Charmian Carr
Composer: Richard Rodgers
Category: FEATURES, MUSICALS
Academy Award
A young postulant becomes governess to the seven children of the widowed Baron von Trapp and, after marrying him, all escape the Nazi invasion of their homeland by fleeing across the Alps. Musical numbers include *Do-Re-Mi*, *My Favorite Things*, and *16 Going On 17*.

SOUND OF ONE
1976, 12 min. color film
Distributor: Canyon Cinema

Principal Dancer: Bartlett, Scott
Category: EXPERIMENTAL, MARTIAL ARTS
Sinking Creek Film Festival
A solo figure executes the meditative movements of *T'ai Chi Ch'uan* against the backgrounds of a seaside cliff, forest, mountain, and inside a studio.

SOURCES OF DANCE
1984, 17 min. color film, video
Distributors: Kent State, Iowa State, University of Minnesota
Producer: The Athletic Institute
Choreographer: Lynda Davis
Category: CHOREOGRAPHY, COMPOSITION
Explores the origin of ideas for composition and the language of choreography.

SOUTH: HADO
1991, 13 min. color video
Distributor: First Run/Icarus
Director: Gaston Kahore
Category: FOLK, AFRICA
A sixty-year-old grandmother and farmer named Hado leads a group of musicians, singers and dancers in Burkina Faso, thereby helping to preserve the national heritage of music and dance.

SOUTH PACIFIC
1958, 170 min. color video
Distributor: Facets
Producer: 20th Century Fox
Director: Joshua Logan
Choreographer: LeRoy Prinz
Principal Dancer: Mitzi Gaynor
Composer: Richard Rodgers
Category: FEATURES, MUSICALS
Two romances combine to form the plot: between a Navy nurse and an older French planter on a South Sea Island, and between a Navy Lieutenant and a native girl. Musical numbers include *There is Nothing Like a Dame*, and *I'm Gonna Wash That Man Right Out Of My Hair*.

SOVIET ARMY CHORUS, BAND, AND DANCE ENSEMBLE
1981, 78 min. color video
Distributors: Kultur, Viewfinders, Karol, Home Vision
Dance Company: Soviet Army Dance Ensemble
Category: FOLK COMPANIES, EUROPE
Russian folk tunes and dances filmed on tour across the Soviet Union.

SPACE
1972, 28 min. color video
Series: Dance as an Art Form
Distributor: Pro Arts
Producer: Chimerafilm
Director: Warren Leib
Choreographer: Murray Louis
Dance Company: Murray Louis Dance Company
Composer: Alwin Nikolais
Category: MODERN, ANIMATION
Narrator: Murray Louis
Animation in addition to live action is used to give a visual picture of spaces both inside and outside the dancer.

SPACE CITY
1981, 31:30 min. color, b&w film
Distributor: Film-makers' Cooperative

Director: Robyn Brentano
Choreographer: Kenneth King
Principal Dancer: Kenneth King
Composer: William Tudor
Category: MODERN, EXPERIMENTAL
The director explains, "With the poetic logic of a dream, the soloist moves from an ancient attic through the modern city, into outer space, ending in an abstract montage of futuristic architectural planes and surfaces."

SPANISH FOLK DANCING (2 videos)
1988, 35 min. each color video
Distributors: Insight Media, Gessler
Producer: Gessler
Director: Cindy López
Category: FOLK, HISPANIC, INSTRUCTIONAL
Authentic folk dances from Spain and Latin America are performed by high school students. Volume I: The *Huaino* from Peru, *Jesucita en Chihuahua* from Mexico, and *Rado Blanquita* from Spain. Volume II: *Espunyolet* from Catalonia, *Cabillo Blanco* and *Danza de los Viejitos* from Mexico. Also included are audiocassettes, directions, and guide with cultural and costume notes.

SPARTACUS (Bolshoi Ballet)
1977, 95 and 120 min. color film, video
Distributors: Kultur, Corinth, Dance Horizons, Home Vision SPA02
Producer: Mosfilm Studios
Director: Vadim Derbenev
Choreographer: Yuri Grigorovich
Principal Dancers: Vladimir Vassiliev, Natalya Bessmertnova, Marius Liepa
Dance Company: Bolshoi Ballet
Composer: Aram Khachaturian
Category: FULL-LENGTH BALLETS
First-century B.C. Rome crackles from an insurrection led by the gladiator and slave Spartacus against the cruel general Crassus, who eventually defeats him.

SPARTACUS (Bolshoi Ballet)
1984, 128 min. color video
Distributors: Home Box Office, Home Vision SPA01, Media Basics
Producers: Göstelradio and National Video Corporation
Director: Preben Montell
Choreographer: Yuri Grigorovich
Principal Dancers: Irek Mukhamedov, Natalya Bessmertnova, Mikhail Gobovich
Dance Company: Bolshoi Ballet
Composer: Aram Khachaturian
Category: FULL-LENGTH BALLETS
Another cast for this ballet.

SPARTACUS (Bolshoi Ballet)
1990, 132 min. color video
Distributors: Viewfinders, Corinth, Media Basics
Producers: NHK, Primetime Entertainment, Video/Film Bolshoi, and Japan Arts Corporation
Director: Shuji Fujii
Choreographer: Yuri Grigorovich
Principal Dancers: Irek Mukhamedov, Aleksandr Vetrov, Ludmila Semenyaka, Maria Bilova
Dance Company: Bolshoi Ballet
Composer: Aram Khachaturian
Category: FULL-LENGTH BALLETS
Another cast for this ballet.

SPEAKING IN TONGUES
1991, 54 min. color video, laser
Series: Dance in America
Distributors: Home Vision, Dance Horizons,
    Viewfinders, Corinth
Producer: Judy Kinberg, WNET-TV
Director: Matthew Diamond
Choreographer: Paul Taylor
Dance Company: Paul Taylor Dance Company
Composer: Matthew Patton
Category: FULL-LENGTH BALLETS
Paul Taylor's dance company performs his ballet.

**SPEAKING OF DANCE: CONVERSATIONS
WITH CONTEMPORARY MASTERS OF
AMERICAN MODERN DANCE (8 videos)**
1992–94, 45–60 min. color video
Series: Speaking of Dance
Distributor: American Dance Festival Video
Director: Douglas Rosenberg
Category: DANCE HISTORY
Conversations with contemporary dance masters
    designed to preserve their history. Each piece
    contains interviews, performance and teaching
    footage, as well as remarkable stories recounted
    by the subjects about their lives in dance. Indi-
    vidual titles include: *Donald McKayle, Lucas
    Hoving, Anna Sokolow, Ethel Butler, Betty Jones,
    Talley Beatty, Daniel Nagrin* and *Erick Hawkins*.

SPECTRE OF THE ROSE
1946, 90 min. color video
Distributor: Republic Pictures
Producer: Republic Pictures
Director: Ben Hecht
Choreographer: Tamara Geva
Principal Dancers: Ivan Kirov, Viola Essen
Composer: George Antheil
Category: FEATURES, BALLET
A feature film of the murder mystery genre involv-
    ing a romance between a young ballerina and a
    principal dancer who slowly loses his mind.

SQUAREGAME VIDEO
1976, 27 min. b&w video
Distributor: Cunningham Dance Foundation
Producer: Cunningham Dance Foundation
Director: Charles Atlas
Choreographer: Merce Cunningham
Dance Company: Merce Cunningham Dance
    Company
Composer: Takehisa Kosugi
Category: MODERN, CINEDANCE
Originally conceived for eventual adaptation to
    video, *Squaregame* is a playful work of games
    involving duffle bags.

SSS
1986–89, 7 min. color film
Distributors: Film-makers' Cooperative, Canyon
    Cinema
Producer: Henry Hills
Director: Henry Hills
Principal Dancers: Sally Silvers, Pooh Kaye, Mark
    Dendy
Composers: Tom Cora, Christian Marclay, Zeena
    Parkins
Category: EXPERIMENTAL
Filmed on the streets of the pre-gentrified East
    Village in New York City, improvised move-
    ment has been painstakingly synched to music

which had been previously improvised in the
studio.

ST. FRANCIS
1938, 39 min. b&w film
Distributor: Dance Film Archive
Choreographer: Léonide Massine
Principal Dancers: Frederic Franklin, Léonide
    Massine, Nina Theilade
Dance Company: Ballet Russe de Monte Carlo
Composer: Paul Hindemith
Category: BALLET, RELIGIOUS/RITUAL
A record film conjuring up the beatific visions of
    the saint.

STANDING BY
1995, 25 min. color film
Distributor: Choreographics
Director: Wendy Rogers
Dance Company: Wendy Rogers Dance Company
Composer: Paul Dresher
Category: MODERN COMPANIES
A company portrait and a reflection on six lives
    emerge through a montage of non-narrative
    dancing, discontinuous images, music and
    sound.

STARS OF EGYPTIAN DANCE (2 videos)
1984, 85 min. each color video
Distributor: Morocco
Producer: C. V. Dinicu
Choreographers: Negwa Fouad, Mohamed Khalil,
    Soheir Zaki, Aza Sharif, Nadra Hamdi, Eman
    Sabry Wagdi, Hanan Nahed
Principal Dancers: Negwa Fouad, Soheir Zaki, Aza
    Sharif, Nadra Hamdi, Eman Sabry Wagdi,
    Hanan Nahed
Category: MIDDLE EAST
Egyptian Oriental dance's top stars at the height
    of their careers, filmed on-site during actual
    performances in Cairo, Egypt. All are now re-
    tired, as explained by narrator Morocco.

STARS OF THE RUSSIAN BALLET
1953, 80 min. b&w film, video
Distributors: Kultur, Home Vision, Viewfinders,
    Corinth
Producer: Lenfilms
Director: G. Rappaport
Choreographers: Marius Petipa, Rostislav Zakh-
    arov, Vasily Vainonen
Principal Dancers: Galina Ulanova, Natalia Dudi-
    nskaya, Konstantin Sergeyev, Maya Plisetskaya,
    Vakhtang Chabukiani, Yuri Zhdanov
Dance Company: Bolshoi Ballet
Composers: Peter Ilyich Tchaikovsky, Boris Asa-
    fiev
Category: BALLET COMPANIES
Three ballet excerpts involving love, jealousy, and
    revolution: *Swan Lake*; *The Fountain of Bakh-
    chisarai* (choreographed in 1934 by Zakharov
    after Pushkin's poem); and *The Flames of Paris*
    (choreographed by Vainonen in 1932 as a trib-
    ute to the French Revolution of 1789). With En-
    glish subtitles.

**STEEL SILK: CHAMPION ACROBATS OF
CHINA**
1992, 46 min. color video
Distributor: V.I.E.W.
Producer: Beijing Scientific and Educational Film
    Studio
Category: CIRCUS ARTS, CHINA

Champion acrobatic troupes perform innovative
    routines based on the twenty-five hundred-
    year-old tradition: *Walking the Steel Silk* (tight-
    rope dancing), *Light as the Swallows* (acrobats),
    Butterfly Resting on a Flower (foot juggling), *The
    Mastery of Movement* (tower of chairs), etc.

STEP BACK CINDY
1991, 28:30 min. color video
Distributor: Appalshop Films
Producer: Appalshop Films
Director: Anne Johnson
Category: FOLK, UNITED STATES
Interviews with traditional dancers and footage
    from performances in the mountains of south-
    west Virginia.

STEP INTO BALLET WITH WAYNE SLEEP
1994, 50 min. color video
Distributor: Dance Horizons
Category: INSTRUCTIONAL
A guide to the art of ballet by the former Royal
    Ballet star.

STEP STYLE
1980, 30 min. color film, video
Series: Movement Style and Culture
Distributor: University of California Extension
    Center
Producers: Alan Lomax, Forrestine Paulay, Irmg-
    ard Bartenieff
Directors: Alan Lomax, Forrestine Paulay, Irmg-
    ard Bartenieff
Category: ANTHROPOLOGICAL, INTERNA-
    TIONAL
CINE Golden Eagle, Dance on Camera Festival,
    Margaret Mead Film Festival, Modern Lan-
    guage Film Festival, American Film Festival
A cross-cultural study of leg and foot movements
    of dances throughout the world, and their rela-
    tion to social structures, work habits and sports.

STEPPIN'
1992, 56 min. color video
Distributor: The Cinema Guild
Producer: Jerald B. Harkness
Director: Jerald B. Harkness
Category: FOLK, UNITED STATES
A unique form of African dancing is transposed to
    the United States by students from three Indi-
    ana universities, who participate in rhythmic
    competitions of foot stomping, hand clapping,
    and cane tapping dance routines.

STEPPING OUT
1991, 108 min. color film
Distributor: Films Inc.
Producer: Paramount
Director: Lewis Gilbert
Choreographer: Danny Daniels
Principal Dancers: Liza Minnelli, Bill Irwin, Jane
    Krakowski
Composer: Peter Matz
Category: FEATURES, TAP
An out-of-work gypsy makes ends meet by teach-
    ing dance to a class of clumsy older beginners,
    molding them into a synchronized tap-dancing
    ensemble for a charity benefit.

STEPS IN A NEW DIRECTION
1994, 14 min. color video
Distributor: Leben Productions
Producer: John Leben

Director: John Leben
Choreographers: Freddie Moore, Robert Estner
Dance Company: Grand Rapids Ballet
Category: INSTRUCTIONAL, CHILDREN
Dance on Camera Festival 1994 Honorable Mention
Created as a fund-raising tool for an outreach program for "at-risk" children in Grand Rapids, the mini-documentary interviews the children and teachers and shows the dance classes taught by former Alvin Ailey Company member, Freddie Moore.

STEPS OF LIGHT
0 min. color video
Distributor: Coe Film Associates
Producer: Friends Film Productions
Category: BALLET, CHILDREN
Lithe youngsters compete for entrance into the Monte Carlo Ballet School.

STICKS, LIGHT, FIRE
1986, 16 min. color video
Series: Alive From Off Center
Distributor: Electronic Arts Intermix, In Motion Productions
Producer: Melinda Ward for KTCA-TV
Director: Skip Blumberg
Choreographer: Michael Moschen
Principal Dancer: Michael Moschen
Category: CIRCUS ARTS
The master juggler performs his feats under the direction of an artist who finds his special effects in natural accidents.

STICKS ON THE MOVE
1983, 4 min. color film, video
Distributors: Eccentric Motions, Picture Start
Producers: Pooh Kaye and Elizabeth Ross for Picture Start
Directors: Elisabeth Ross, Pooh Kaye
Composer: John Kilgore
Category: EXPERIMENTAL, COMEDY
A playful experimental film done with single shots of people chewing on, riding on, and twirling on sticks magically moving down the sidewalks of New York City.

STILL LOOKING
1989, 28 min. color film, video
Distributor: University of California Extension Center
Category: DANCE THERAPY
Therapist: Janet Adler
Dance on Camera Festival 1990 Honorable Mention
Eight women strive to move closer to the self through a practice developed by Janet Adler called Authentic Movement. This therapy relates movement to witnessing and is concerned with one's capacity to remember and tell the truth. For previous film on Adler, see *Looking For Me* under title entry.

STILT DANCERS OF LONG BOW VILLAGE
1980, 27 min. color film
Distributor: PennState
Producers: Carma Hinton and Richard Gordon
Director: Carma Hinton, Richard Gordon
Category: FOLK, CHINA
Stilt dancing, banned during the Chinese Cultural Revolution, now revived, is the main feature of this rural village pageant. Makeup and costume preparations are recorded along with villagers' reminiscences of the ban.

STILT DANCES AT KPEGBOUNI and other films from the Dan Tribe of West Africa (11 films)
1968, 4–13 min. color, b&w film
Distributor: PennState
Producer: Wissen
Director: H. Himmelheber
Category: AFRICA, ANTHROPOLOGICAL
Mask processions, dances with poisonous snakes, a Gabun viper, imitations of slowly walking frogs and many other dances from the Dan people of Ivory Coast, West Africa.

THE STONE DANCES
1988, 9 min. b&w video
Distributor: Penny Ward Video
Producer: Penny Ward
Director: Penny Ward
Choreographer: Shelley Lee
Principal Dancers: Shelley Lee, Tim Conboy, Brenda Daniels
Composer: Mary Kelley
Category: EXPERIMENTAL, CINEDANCE
This video interpretation of a twenty-five-minute multimedia work explores the theme of life continuing after death. Stills of bog people are crossed with images of a dancer's face. A woman falls back repeatedly, shown in slow-motion, followed by a duet accompanied by the sounds of chanting, stones dropping and reverberating.

THE STONE FLOWER (Bolshoi Ballet)
1990, 107 min. color video
Distributors: Corinth, Viewfinders, Media Basics
Choreographer: Yuri Grigorovich
Principal Dancers: Nikolai Dorokhov, Ludmila Semenyaka, Nina Semizorova, Yuri Vetrov
Dance Company: Bolshoi Ballet
Composer: Sergei Prokofiev
Category: FULL-LENGTH BALLETS
A record of a live performance at the historic Bolshoi Theatre in Moscow.

THE STONE FLOWER (Kirov Ballet)
1991, 112 min. color video, laser
Distributors: Dance Horizons, Home Vision, Viewfinders, Corinth
Choreographer: Yuri Grigorovich
Principal Dancers: Anna Polikarpova, Aleksandr Gulyaev, Tatiana Terekova
Dance Company: Kirov Ballet
Composer: Sergei Prokofiev
Category: FULL-LENGTH BALLETS
Ballet based on fairy tales from the Ural Mountains.

STOPPED IN HER TRACKS
1978, 6 min. color film
Distributor: Gross, Sally
Choreographer: Sally Gross
Principal Dancer: Sally Gross
Category: EXPERIMENTAL
The choreographer crawls along a stairwell in a work about perceptual distortion.

STORMY WEATHER
1943, 77 min. b&w film, video
Distributors: Facets, Films Inc.
Producer: 20th Century Fox

Director: Andrew L. Stone
Choreographers: Clarence Robinson, Nick Castle
Principal Dancers: Bill "Bojangles" Robinson, Lena Horne
Dance Company: Katherine Dunham and Her Dancers, Nicholas Brothers
Category: FEATURES, MUSICALS, AFRICAN-AMERICANS
A revue of African-American talent based lightly on the career of Bill Robinson. Dunham and dancers perform a short jungle dance to *Stormy Weather.*

STORY
1964, 20 min. b&w film, video
Distributor: Cunningham Dance Foundation
Producer: Finnish Broadcasting Company
Director: Hakki Seppala
Choreographer: Merce Cunningham
Principal Dancers: Carolyn Brown, Merce Cunningham, William Davis, Viola Farber, Deborah Hay, Barbara Lloyd, Sandra Neels, Steve Paxton, Albert Reid
Dance Company: Merce Cunningham Dance Company
Composer: Toshi Ichiyanagi
Category: MODERN
Set Designer, Costumes: Robert Rauschenberg
Helsinki's Ruotsalaisessa Teaterissa, which has a moving circular platform on the stage, gave the performers a freedom that Cunningham calls his "appetite for movement. I don't see why it has to represent something. It is what it is."

STORY
1996 10 min. color video
Distributor ARC Videodance
Producer: Jeff Bush
Choreographer: Margie Gillis
Dancer: Margie Gillis
Composer: Nico Kean
Category: MODERN
This solo is a brief reflection of innocence and loss; a dream of awakening followed by the sorrow of eternal search.

THE STORY OF VERNON AND IRENE CASTLE
1939, 94 min. b&w film, video, laser
Distributors: Films Inc., Facets
Producer: RKO
Director: Henry C. Potter
Choreographers: Fred Astaire, Hermes Pan
Principal Dancers: Fred Astaire, Ginger Rogers
Composer: Constantin Bakaleinikoff
Category: FEATURES, BALLROOM
Biography of the couple who triggered the popularity of ballroom dancing at the turn-of-the-century and influenced the style of the day. Dance numbers include: *By the Light of the Silvery Moon, Waiting for the Roger E. Lee, Too Much Mustard, Rose Room, Très Jolie, Little Brown Jug,* and *Missouri Waltz.*

STRAVINSKY
1966, 52 min. b&w film, video
Distributors: Carousel Films, Dance Film Archive
Producer: CBS News
Choreographer: George Balanchine
Principal Dancer: Maria Tallchief
Composer: Igor Stravinsky
Category: BALLET, COMPOSITION
The Russian composer Igor Stravinsky (1882–

1971) talks about his early compositions and his creative struggles. He is shown collaborating with his longtime associate, choreographer George Balanchine, conducting *Rite of Spring* in Warsaw, and being honored by Pope Paul VI.

STREETCAR: A DANCE OF DESIRE
1969, 28 min. b&w video
Distributor: Orion Enterprises
Producer: WTTW-TV/Chicago
Director: Richard Carter
Choreographer: Gus Giordano
Dance Company: Gus Giordano Dance Company
Composer: E. Berstein
Category: JAZZ, DANCE DRAMA
A dance drama inspired by Tennessee William's play (1947), focusing on the evening of Stanley's poker party. The play, which premiered in 1947, was set in New Orleans, and tells the story of Blanche Dubois, the flirtatious woman whose chances for marriage are crushed by Stanley, her disapproving brother-in-law.

STRICTLY BALLROOM
1992, 94 min. color film
Distributor: Films Inc.
Producer: Miramax
Director: Baz Luhrmann
Principal Dancers: Paul Mercurio, Antonio Vargas, Tara Morice
Composer: David Hirschfelder
Category: FEATURES, BALLROOM, FLAMENCO
Cannes Film Festival 1992 Prix de la Jeunesse, Toronto International Film Festival 1992 Audience Favorite Award
The story of a ballroom competition in which a rebellious contestant (Paul Mercurio of the Sydney Dance Company) scandalizes traditionalists by introducing new steps of his own based on flamenco traditions. Tara Morice plays the awkward wallflower who follows his lead.

STRIKE UP THE BAND
1940, 120 min. b&w video, laser
Distributors: Facets, Swank, MGM/UA
Producer: MGM
Director: Busby Berkeley
Choreographer: Busby Berkeley
Principal Dancers: Mickey Rooney, Judy Garland
Composer: Roger Edens
Category: FEATURES, MUSICALS
A nationwide radio contest showcases the youngsters of a high school band.

STRUGGLE FOR HOPE
1995, 54 min. color video
Series: Inspired by Bach
Distributor: Rhombus International
Producer: Niv Fichman
Director: Niv Fichman
Choreographer: Tamasaburo Bando
Dancer:Tamasaburo Bando
Composer: Johann Sebastian Bach
Category: COLLABORATION
US International Film and Video Festival 1996 Silver Screen Award, National Educational Media Network 1996 Gold Apple
Two celebrated artists, cellist Yo-Yo Ma and Kabuki actor Tamasaburo Bando, combine talents to create an emotionally charged dance performance to J.S. Bach's *Fifth Suite for Unaccompanied Cello* that draws its inspiration from two very distinct worlds. *Struggle for Hope* follows

Ma and Bando on this seemingly impossible collaboration. As Eastern mysticism meets Western rigor, the two rehearse and discuss the ultimate goal: a performance that enhances both traditions and transcends the cultural boundaries that naturally exist between them.

STUDIES IN NIGERIAN DANCE (2 films)
1966, 12 and 10 min. b&w film
Distributor: UCLA Instructional Media Library
Category: ANTHROPOLOGICAL, AFRICA
Three *Icough* dances performed by women of Alide village, and five dances by the Iriwge men of the Jos Plateau in Nigeria, West Africa.

A STUDY IN CHOREOGRAPHY FOR CAMERA
1945, 4 min. b&w film, video (silent)
Distributors: Museum of Modern Art, Mystic Fire Video, Biograph Entertainment, Film-makers' Cooperative
Producer: Maya Deren
Director: Maya Deren
Choreographer: Maya Deren
Principal Dancer: Talley Beatty
Category: EXPERIMENTAL, CINEDANCE
Director Maya Deren was a pioneer in exploring the ways in which the camera and the resulting footage can be manipulated to create illusions or illuminations of alternative perspectives of space and time. She tried to extend motions, heighten emotions, and play with our associative minds.

STUTTGART BALLET: THE MIRACLE LIVES
1989, 60 min. color video
Distributors: Kultur, Dance Horizons, Viewfinders, Corinth, Home Vision
Producers: Bill Boggs and Richard Baker
Director: Rolf-Dieter Zimmerman
Choreographers: John Cranko, Uwe Scholz, Jiri Kylian, Maurice Béjart
Principal Dancers: Marcia Haydee, Richard Cragun
Composers: Domenico Scarlatti, Peter Ilyich Tchaikovsky, Johannes Brahms, Sergei Prokofiev, Jacques Offenbach, Gustav Mahler, Franz Liszt, Franz Schubert, Benjamin Britten, François Poulenc
Category: BALLET COMPANIES
Dance on Camera Festival 1984
A tribute to choreographer John Cranko, who took over the Stuttgart Ballet company in 1961 and made it a world class company. The film continues with the story of the company's survival after his death. Now led by Marcia Haydee, a founding member of the German company, the Stuttgart continues to thrive and perform Cranko's many ballets.

SUE'S LEG: REMEMBERING THE THIRTIES: TWYLA THARP AND DANCERS
1976, 60 min. color video
Series: Dance in America
Distributors: PennState, Indiana University, Dance Film Archive, University of Minnesota
Producer: WNET-TV/New York
Director: Merrill Brockway
Choreographer: Twyla Tharp
Dance Company: Twyla Tharp Dance Company
Composer: Fats Waller
Category: MODERN, SOCIAL
Performance of Tharp's *Sue's Leg,* plus a collage of movie and newsreel clips from the 1930s of

dance marathons and balls as background for the choreographer's allusions. A nostalgic tribute to the spirit of another era.

THE SUGAR PLUM FAIRY VARIATION FROM THE NUTCRACKER
1941, 2:30 min. color film, video
Distributor: Dance Films Association
Producer: Dwight Godwin
Director: Dwight Godwin
Choreographer: Lev Ivanov
Principal Dancer: Alicia Markova
Composer: Peter Ilyich Tchaikovsky
Category: BALLET
Outdoor performance at Jacob's Pillow in Massachusetts.

SUITE FANTAISISTE
1982, 20 min. color video
Distributor: ARC Videodance
Producers: Jeff Bush and Celia Ipiotis
Directors: Jeff Bush, Celia Ipiotis
Choreographer: Catherine Turocy
Principal Dancer: Catherine Turocy
Category: DANCE HISTORY
Eighteenth-century life seen through the dance, poetry, and the fan language of the time. A father advises his son on the subject of women, followed by a performance of the coquettish *Follies d'Espagne* and a comic juggling dance in the *commedia dell'arte* style.

SUMMER STOCK
1950, 109 min. color film, video, laser
Distributors: Facets, Laserdisc Fan Club, Swank, MGM/UA
Producer: MGM
Director: Charles Walters
Choreographer: Nick Castle
Principal Dancers: Judy Garland, Gene Kelly
Composer: Harry Warren
Category: FEATURES, MUSICALS
With the owner's help, a farm becomes a theatre troupe's rehearsal site. Musical numbers include *You, Wonderful You,* and *Get Happy.*

SUNNY SIDE OF LIFE
1985, 58 min. color film, video
Distributor: Appalshop Films
Producer: Appalshop Films
Directors: Scott Faulkner, Anthony Slone, Jack Wright
Musicians: Home Folks, Red Clay Ramblers, John McCutcheon, Ramona Jones, Griffin Family, Charlie Osborne
Category: FOLK, UNITED STATES
History of the family of A.P. and Sara Carter, the country music pioneers who began recording the songs of the mountain people of southwest Virginia in the 1920s, and footage of the performances in The Carter Family Fold, an old-time music hall founded in 1975 in Hiltons, Virginia.

THE SUNRISE DANCE
1994, 28 min. color video, PAL
Distributors: Filmakers Library, Documentary Educational Resources
Producer: Gianfranco Norelli
Director: Gianfranco Norelli
Category: NATIVE AMERICANS, RELIGIOUS/ RITUAL
Dance on Camera Festival 1994 Honorable Mention

The *Sunrise Dance*, never before filmed, is a reaffirmation of Native American identity celebrating the role of women in Apache culture. The focus of the three-day sacred ceremony is thirteen year-old Maureen Nacho, whose initiation is accompanied by the rituals of medicine men, rites of the Sweat Lodge, and the midnight appearance of the Crown Dancers.

SUZANNE FARRELL: ELUSIVE MUSE
1996, 90 min. color film, video
Distributor: Seahorse Films
Producers: Anne Belle, Catherine Tambini
Directors: Anne Belle, Deborah Dickson
Choreographers: Wolfgang Held, Tom Hurwitz, Don Lenzer
Principal Dancers: Maurice Béjart, Jacques d'Amboise, Suzanne Farrell, Isabelle Guerin, Arthur Mitchell
Category: BALLET, DOCUMENTARY PORTRAITS
The third in a trilogy of dance films (See *Reflections of a Dancer* and *Dancing for Mr. B*), this documentary portrays the amazing career of the legendary New York City Ballet ballerina Suzanne Farrell, and also tells one of the great love stories of our time(her relationship with her mentor, choreographer George Balanchine), for whom she was the last great muse.

SWAN LAKE (American Ballet Theatre)
1980, 122 min. color video, laser
Distributors: Paramount, Home Vision SWA050, Viewfinders, Music Video Distributors, Corinth
Choreographers: Marius Petipa, Lev Ivanov
Principal Dancers: Natalia Makarova, Ivan Nagy
Dance Company: American Ballet Theatre
Composer: Peter Ilyich Tchaikovsky
Category: FULL-LENGTH BALLETS
In this four-act, classic ballet which premiered in 1877 at the Bolshoi Theatre, Prince Siegfried celebrates his twenty-first birthday by going hunting. Alone by a lakeside, he sees a swan turn into an enchanted princess who can be saved only by true love. He promises this, but is tricked by a magician who disguises his own daughter as the swan-maiden. In despair, Siegfried and the swan-maiden leap to their death.

SWAN LAKE (Bolshoi Ballet)
1957, 81 min. color film, video
Distributors: Corinth, Kultur 1197, Home Vision SWA030, Viewfinders, Facets
Director: Zoya Tulubyeva
Choreographers: Marius Petipa, Lev Ivanov
Principal Dancers: Maya Plisetskaya, Nicolai Fadeyechev
Dance Company: Bolshoi Ballet
Composer: Peter Ilyich Tchaikovsky
Category: FULL-LENGTH BALLETS
Filmed live at the Bolshoi Theatre with one of Russia's legendary ballerinas in her prime.

SWAN LAKE (Bolshoi Ballet)
1989, 128 min. color video
Distributors: Viewfinders, Karol, Corinth, Media Basics
Producers: Primetime Entertainment, NHK, Japan Arts Corporation, and Video/Film Bolshoi
Choreographers: Marius Petipa, Lev Ivanov, Yuri Grigorovich
Principal Dancers: Alla Mikhalchenko, Yuri Vasyuchenko

Dance Company: Bolshoi Ballet
Composer: Peter Ilyich Tchaikovsky
Category: FULL-LENGTH BALLETS
Recorded live at the Bolshoi Theatre in Moscow.

SWAN LAKE (Kirov Ballet)
1991, 116 min. color video, laser
Distributors: Dance Horizons, Corinth, Viewfinders, Home Vision SWA090
Choreographers: Marius Petipa, Lev Ivanov
Principal Dancers: Yulia Makhalina, Igor Zelinsky
Composer: Peter Ilyich Tchaikovsky
Category: FULL-LENGTH BALLETS
A recent production of the ballet classic.

SWAN LAKE (London Festival Ballet)
1988, 116 min. color video
Distributors: Home Vision SWA060, Dance Horizons, Viewfinders, Corinth
Producer: RM Arts
Director: Thomas Grimm
Choreographers: Marius Petipa, Natalia Makarova
Principal Dancers: Peter Schaufuss, Evelyn Hart
Dance Company: London Festival Ballet
Composer: Peter Ilyich Tchaikovsky
Category: FULL-LENGTH BALLETS
Dance on Camera Festival 1991
Full-length rendition of the classic adapted by prima ballerina Natalia Makarova.

SWAN LAKE (Royal Ballet)
1986, 137 min. color video
Distributor: Viewfinders
Producer: National Video Corporation
Director: John Michael Phillips
Choreographers: Lev Ivanov, Marius Petipa, with additions from Rudolf Nureyev and Frederick Ashton
Principal Dancers: Natalia Makarova, Anthony Dowell, Gerd Larsen
Dance Company: Royal Ballet
Composer: Peter Ilyich Tchaikovsky
Category: FULL-LENGTH BALLETS
Filmed live at Covent Garden.

SWAN LAKE (Russian State Perm Ballet)
1992, 132 min. color video
Distributors: Kultur, Viewfinders, Home Vision SWA100, Facets
Producer: Arts Core
Director: Vladimir Salimbaev
Choreographers: Aleksandr Gorsky, Lev Ivanov, Marius Petipa, Nikolai Boyarchikov
Principal Dancers: Nina Ananiashvili, Aleksei Fadeyechev
Dance Company: Russian State Perm Ballet
Composer: Peter Ilyich Tchaikovsky
Category: FULL-LENGTH BALLETS
This historic production starring two great Russian dancers, was filmed during a performance commemorating the centennial of Tchaikovsky's death.

SWAN LAKE (Vienna Opera Ballet)
1967, 107 min. color video, laser
Distributors: Home Vision SWA070, Viewfinders
Choreographer: Rudolf Nureyev
Principal Dancers: Rudolf Nureyev, Margot Fonteyn
Dance Company: Vienna State Opera Ballet
Composer: Peter Ilyich Tchaikovsky
Category: FULL-LENGTH BALLETS
Filmed during an actual 1966 performance.

THE SWAN LAKE STORY: A DANCE FANTASY
1993, 38 min. color video
Distributor: V.I.E.W.
Dance Company: Oregon State Ballet
Composer: Peter Ilyich Tchaikovsky
Category: BALLET, CHILDREN
The ballet was danced and filmed outdoors, each scene set in its natural landscape, lit by the sun and the moon, with green meadows for a stage, and the lakes, trees and mountains of the Pacific Northwest for scenery.

SWAYZE DANCING
1988, 60 min. color video
Distributor: Tapeworm
Producer: Mark Lemkin
Principal Dancers: Patrick Swayze, Patsy Swayze, Lisa Swayze, Bambi Swayze
Category: INSTRUCTIONAL, BALLROOM
Patrick Swayze, the star of *Dirty Dancing*, introduces his first teacher(his mother(along with his wife and sister, as demonstrators of Latin, swing, and ballroom techniques.

SWEET CHARITY
1969, 148 min. color video, laser
Distributors: Facets, Swank
Producer: Universal
Director: Bob Fosse
Choreographer: Bob Fosse
Principal Dancers: Shirley Maclaine, Chita Rivera, Paula Kelly, Sammy Davis Jr.
Composer: Cy Coleman
Category: FEATURES, MUSICALS
A musical revue about the romantic longings of a New York taxi dancer. Dance numbers include *Big Spender, If My Friends Could See Me Now, There's Gotta Be Something Better Than This, Rich Man's Frug, Rhythm of Life*, and *I'm a Brass Band.*

SWEPT UP
1984, 8 min. color film
Distributor: Eccentric Motions
Producer: Eccentric Motions
Director: Pooh Kaye
Choreographer: Pooh Kaye
Dance Company: Eccentric Motions
Composer: John Kilgore
Category: CHILDREN, ANIMATION
Marin County Best Children's Film
Orchestrates the riotous activities of a magical lady who turns anything she touches to graffiti—a chorus of discarded zebra-striped mattresses, a troupe of trash cans, and a couple of enraged sanitation workers.

SWING TIME
1936, 103 min. b&w film
Distributor: Films Inc.
Producer: RKO
Director: George Stevens
Choreographers: Hermes Pan, Fred Astaire
Principal Dancers: Fred Astaire, Ginger Rogers
Composer: Jerome Kern
Category: FEATURES, MUSICALS, TAP
A dancing gambler falls in love, but is engaged to another. Dance numbers include *It's Not in the Cards, Waltz in Swing Time, Bojangles of Harlem*, and *Never Gonna Dance.*

SWORD DANCE AT ÜBERLINGEN
1962, 29 min. color video
Distributor: PennState

Producer: Wissen
Category: FOLK, EUROPE
In Southern Baden, Germany, a ceremony begins with breakfast, followed by a march to the divine service and then into the town square. After the mayor has given his approval, the sword dance is performed and is followed by a maiden's dance.

LA SYLPHIDE (Paris Opera Ballet)
1971, 81 min. color video, laser
Distributors: Kultur, Home Vision, Coe Film Associates, Dance Horizons, Viewfinders, Corinth, Media Basics
Choreographer: Pierre Lacotte
Principal Dancers: Michel Dénard, Ghislaine Thesmar
Dance Company: Paris Opera Ballet
Composer: Jean Schneitzhoeffer
Category: FULL-LENGTH BALLETS
Video Review 1982 VIRA Award
Pierre Lacotte's reconstruction of Filippo Taglioni's ballet first performed in Paris in 1832 is based on Adolphe Nourrit's book on sylphs, with the original costume and set designs by Eugene Lami and P.L. Ciceri. James, about to be married, chases after an airy spirit traditionally known only to the chaste of heart, only to destroy her with a silk scarf poisoned by a vengeful friend.

LA SYLPHIDE (Royal Danish Ballet)
1989, 90 min. color laser
Distributor: Corinth
Producer: Robin Scott
Director: Thomas Grimm
Choreographer: August Bournonville
Dance Company: Royal Danish Ballet
Composer: Herman Severin Lovenskjöld
Category: FULL-LENGTH BALLETS
A recording of the performance at the Royal Theatre, Copenhagen, in October 1988.

LES SYLPHIDES (CHOPINIANA)
1987, 34 min. color video
Distributors: V.I.E.W., Karol
Producer: Soviet Film and TV
Choreographers: Yuri Grigorovich, Michel Fokine
Principal Dancers: Natalya Bessmertnova, Galina Kozlova, Irina Kholina, Alexandre Beogatyriov
Dance Company: Bolshoi Ballet
Composer: Frédéric Chopin
Category: FULL-LENGTH BALLETS
Inspired by Isadora Duncan's visit to Russia, Michel Fokine created this one-act ballet for the Bolshoi. One of the first abstract, plotless works in the Russian repertoire, it premiered in 1909 with Anna Pavlova and Vaslav Nijinsky in the leading roles.

SYLVIE GUILLEM AT WORK
1988, 53 min. color video
Distributors: Home Vision, Viewfinders, Corinth
Producers: RM Associates and La Sept
Director: André S. Labarthe
Choreographers: Marius Petipa, William Forsythe
Principal Dancer: Sylvie Guillem
Composers: Richard Strauss, Alexander Glazunov, Tom Willems
Category: BALLET, DOCUMENTARY PORTRAITS
Dance on Camera Festival 1991 Gold Award
Portrait of the young phenomenon, the *étoile* of the Paris Opera who got her start as a gymnast, with excerpts from *Raymonda*, *Four Last Songs*, *In the Middle*, and *Somewhat Elevated*.

SYMPHONIE FANTASTIQUE
1948, 51 min. b&w film
Distributor: Dance Film Archive
Choreographer: Léonide Massine
Principal Dancers: Niels Bjorn Larsen, Stanley Williams, Erik Bruhn, Mona Vangsaa, Kitshen Rolov
Dance Company: Royal Danish Ballet
Composer: Hector Berlioz
Category: BALLET
A rehearsal record of the ballet based on episodes of the life of an artist.

SYMPHONY IN D WORKSHOP
1987, 55 min. color video
Distributors: Home Vision, Viewfinders
Producer: RM Arts
Directors: Jack Bond, Hans Hulscher
Choreographer: Jiri Kylian
Dance Company: Nederlands Dans Theatre
Composer: Franz Joseph Haydn
Category: BALLET, DOCUMENTARY PORTRAITS, CHOREOGRAPHY
Dance on Camera Festival 1987 Silver Award
Jiri Kylian rehearses one of his ballets with students of the Royal Ballet School in London, and talks about his exile from Czechoslovakia and his life as a dancer and choreographer.

SYNCOPATED MELODIES
1920s, 13 min. b&w film (silent)
Distributor: Dance Film Archive
Principal Dancer: W.H. Berry
Category: SOCIAL, DANCE HISTORY
The high life in 1920s Britain with glimpses of the Charleston, the ballroom craze of the day.

SYNCOPATIONS
1988, 50 min. color film
Distributor: Rose, Kathy
Producer: Kathy Rose
Director: Kathy Rose
Principal Dancer: Kathy Rose
Composer: Charles Roth
Category: MODERN, EXPERIMENTAL
In its three-dimensional presentation, the animator-turned-filmmaker-choreographer creates a holograph effect by seeming to dance in a circle of women projected on and behind her.

SYVILLA: THEY DANCE TO HER DRUM
1979, 25 min. b&w film
Distributors: Women Make Movies, Third World Newsreel
Producer: Ayoka Chenzira
Director: Ayoka Chenzira
Choreographer: Syvilla Fort
Principal Dancers: Dyane Harvey, Syvilla Fort
Category: MODERN, DOCUMENTARY PORTRAITS
Reveals the life of Syvilla Fort, a concert dancer who became a role model to a generation of African-American dancers. Shot six months prior to her death in 1975, the film reflects the beauty of her choreography with two pieces reconstructed by Pearl Reynolds and Eugene Little and performed by Dyane Harvey, which show the virtuosity of Fort's dancing and her gifts as a teacher.

TAKE A MASTER CLASS WITH DAVID HOWARD (2 videos)
1991, 76 and 77 min. color video
Distributor: Dance Horizons
Category: INSTRUCTIONAL, BALLET
Two intermediate classes include warm-up, barre and center work

TAKE ME OUT TO THE BALL GAME
1949, 90 min. color video, laser
Distributors: Facets, Swank, MGM/UA
Producer: MGM
Director: Busby Berkeley
Choreographers: Stanley Donen, Gene Kelly
Principal Dancers: Gene Kelly, Frank Sinatra, Jules Munshin
Composer: Roger Edens
Category: FEATURES, MUSICALS
A female owner of a baseball team faces antagonism. Musical numbers include *Strictly USA*, and *O'Brien to Ryan to Goldberg*.

TAKSU: MUSIC IN THE LIFE OF BALI
1991, 24 min. color video
Distributor: University of California Extension Center
Producers: Jan Pasler, Professor of Music, University of California, San Diego
Category: BALI
Taksu, the spiritual power found in music, instruments, costumes, and dance, infuses all aspects of Balinese art and culture.

TAL FARLOW
1981, 1:30 min. b&w film
Distributor: Museum of Modern Art
Producers: Len Lye and Steven Jones
Directors: Len Lye, Steven Jones
Composer: Tal Farlow
Category: ANIMATION, JAZZ
Designs of black scratches sway to a jazz guitar solo.

THE TALES OF BEATRIX POTTER
1971, 86 min. color video
Distributors: Viewfinders, Voyager, Facets
Producer: EMI
Director: Reginald Mills
Choreographer: Frederick Ashton
Principal Dancers: Wayne Sleep, Frederick Ashton, Alexander Grant, Lesley Collier
Dance Company: Royal Ballet
Composer: John Lanchbery
Category: FULL-LENGTH BALLETS, CHILDREN
Two town mice, togged in picnic gear, waltz over the kitchen tiles and hold up their tails like trailing ball gowns in this ballet adaptation of the children's story. Granting human traits to various dancing animal characters, mice brew tea, frogs go fishing, and pigs wear smocks.

THE TALES OF HOFFMANN
1952, 118 min. color film, video, laser
Distributors: Home Vision, Corinth
Producer: London Films
Directors: Michael Powell, Emeric Pressburger
Choreographer: Frederick Ashton
Principal Dancers: Moira Shearer, Ludmilla Tcherina, Robert Helpmann, Léonide Massine
Composer: Jacques Offenbach
Category: FEATURES, BALLET
A restoration of the film inspired by the 1881 tales, in which a poet recalls his three loves—

Olympia, Giulietta and Antonia—over wine in a Nuremberg tavern, while still seeking his ideal woman.

TALKING FEET

1988, 90 min. color film, video
Distributor: Flower Films
Producers: Mike Seeger with Ruth Pershing
Director: Mike Seeger
Category: FOLK, UNITED STATES

Features the styles of oldtime Southern solo dancing (flatfoot, buck, hoedown, and rural tap dance) which are companions to old-time music and on which modern clog dancing is based. Twenty-four regional dancers are filmed on location in the Appalachian Mountains. Accompanying book available.

TALL ARCHES III

1973, 7:15 min. color film
Distributors: Film-makers' Cooperative, Doris Chase Productions
Producer: Doris Chase
Director: Doris Chase
Dance Company: Mary Staton Dance Ensemble
Composer: George Kleinsinger
Category: MODERN, EXPERIMENTAL, ART

Dances in and around three mobile arches of varying sizes. Through the use of an optical printer, Chase creates overlapping color silhouettes of the same images.

TANAGRA, USA

1996, 3 min. b&w color video
Distributor: Parkerson, Lynn
Producers: Brenda and Lynn Parkerson
Director: Brenda Parkerson
Choreographer: Isadora Duncan
Dancer: Lynn Parkerson
Composer: George Frederick Handel
Category: MODERN, EXPERIMENTAL

In an experimental collaboration between sisters, solo choreography by Isadora Duncan is set with a Florida Air Force base in the background.

TANGO

1985, 6 min. color video
Distributor: Electronic Arts Intermix
Producer: James Byrne
Director: James Byrne
Choreographer: Linda Shapiro
Dance Company: New Dance Ensemble
Composer: Jacob Gade
Category: MODERN, EXPERIMENTAL, CINEDANCE

Modern dance cut to tango rhythm, shot by a director who moves among the dancers with the camera seemingly attached to his body.

TANGO

1987, 57 min. color video
Distributors: V.I.E.W., Viewfinders, Karol
Producer: Television Suisse Romande
Director: Sandro Briner
Choreographer: Oscar Araíz
Dance Company: Geneva Grand Theatre Ballet Company
Composer: Atilio Stompone
Category: BALLET, LATIN AMERICA

Argentinian choreographer Oscar Araíz's salute to his nation's dance, the tango, integrated with ballet in a series of vignettes played by twenty-eight dancers. The war of the sexes, the struggles of the family, and the indulgence of the lovelorn, are all addressed by the tango lyrics.

TANGO! A MASTER CLASS WITH THE DINZELS

1986, 47 min. color video
Distributor: Jim Forest Videotapes
Producers: Ismael Alba, Juan José Campanella, Juan Pablo Domenech
Directors: Juan José Campanella, Juan Pablo Domenech
Principal Dancers: Rodolfo Dinzel, Gloria Dinzel
Category: SOCIAL, INSTRUCTIONAL

The basics of the Argentinian tango with performances by members of *Tango Argentino*, the smash Broadway revue, conceived and directed by Claudio Segovia and Hector Orezzoli.

TANGO: A SPECTACULAR PERFORMANCE!

1987, 57 min. color video, laser
Distributors: V.I.E.W., Viewfinders
Producer: V.I.E.W. Video
Director: Sandro Briner
Choreographer: Oscar Araíz
Dance Company: Geneva Grand Theatre Ballet Company
Category: SOCIAL

Twelve musical dance pieces that embody the music, rhythm and passion of the Argentinian tango.

TANGO BAR

1989, 90 min. color film, video
Distributor: Warner Home Video
Producers: Beco Films/Zaga Films
Director: Marcos Zurinaga
Principal Dancer: Raul Julia
Dance Company: Tango Argentino
Composers: Carlos Gardel, Astor Piazzola
Category: FEATURES, SOCIAL

Tryst between singers in a Buenos Aires café interwoven around tango sequences, old footage, and flashbacks to the romance of another era.

THE TANGO IS ALSO A HISTORY

1983, 56 min. color film, video
Distributor: First Run/Icarus
Director: Humberto Rios
Principal Dancers: Astor Piazzola, Osvaldo Pugliese
Category: LATIN AMERICA, SOCIAL
Festival Latino 1984 New York

Describes tango's role in Argentina as a chronicle of political and cultural history.

TANGOS: THE EXILE OF GARDEL

1985, 125 min. color, b&w film
Distributor: New Yorker
Director: Fernando E. Sloanas
Principal Dancers: Marie Lafôret, Philippe Leotard, Miguel Angel Sola, Marina Vlady
Composers: Astor Piazzola, Carlos Gardel
Category: FEATURES

Argentines bemoaning their political exile in Paris create a tragicomedy with music and dance in many locations, with black and white footage evocative of tango singer Carlos Gardel, who died in 1935.

TANKO BUSHI: A JAPANESE FOLK DANCE

1978, 6 min. color film
Distributor: Tempo Films
Producer: Tempo Films
Directors: Annette MacDonald, Mary Joyce
Category: FOLK, JAPAN

The Japanese coal mining dance filmed in the Bay Area of California.

TAP

1980s, 30 min. color video
Distributor: Hoctor Products
Producer: Studio Music Corporation
Category: INSTRUCTIONAL, TAP
Teachers: Danny and Jamie Hoctor

Tap routines broken down, then danced up-to-tempo.

TAP

1988, 110 min. color film, video
Distributor: Films Inc.
Producer: TriStar
Director: Nick Castle
Principal Dancers: Gregory Hines, Sammy Davis Jr.
Category: FEATURES, TAP

A dancer reconsiders trading his tap dance heritage for the easy money of stealing jewelry. A challenge dance with old timers such as Sandman Sims, Bunny Buggs, Steve Condos, Jimmy Slyde, Pat Rich, Arthur Duncan, and Harold Nicholas, is featured.

TAP ALONG WITH TOMMY (3 videos)

1980s, 120 min. each color video
Distributor: T.A.T.
Producer: Tommy Sutton
Principal Dancers: Stephanie Quinn, Tommy Sutton
Category: TAP, INSTRUCTIONAL

A visual aid to the three-volume manual demonstrating the basics and routines, with progressive levels of difficulty.

THE TAP DANCE KID

1979, 33 and 49 min. color film, video
Distributor: Learning Corporation of America
Producer: Learning Corporation of America
Director: Barbara Grant
Principal Dancers: Charles "Honi" Coles, James Pelham
Category: TAP, CHILDREN
Emmy Award, ALA Notable Children's Films

An eight-year-old boy tap dances through life, dreaming of performing on Broadway. Encouraged by his sister and tutored by his uncle, a professional dancer, but discouraged by his father, the boy finds enough drive to achieve his goal. Based on *Nobody's Family is Going to Change* by Louise Fitzhugh.

TAP DANCING FOR BEGINNERS

1981, 31 min. color video
Distributors: Kultur, Dance Horizons, Karol, Home Vision, Instructional Video
Producer: Marc Weinstein
Category: TAP, INSTRUCTIONAL
Teachers: Charles "Honi" Coles, Henry Le Tang

Tap tips from Honi Coles, master tap dancer, and Henry Le Tang, the choreographer for *Sophisticated Ladies* and teacher of such students as Eleanor Powell.

TAP DANCING: INTERMEDIATE AND ADVANCED (2 videos)

1991, 40 min. each color video
Distributor: Kultur

Producer: Put On Those Ruby Slippers
Choreographer: Charles Goddertz
Principal Dancers: Charles Goddertz, Lauren Singerman
Category: TAP, INSTRUCTIONAL
A step-by-step method for learning tap with Broadway dancer Charles Goddertz. Each video features full front/rear views, wide-angled views, demonstrations of technique, and original tap choreography.

TAPDANCIN'
1980, 58 min. color film, video
Distributor: Michael Blackwood Productions
Producer: Christian Blackwood
Director: Christian Blackwood
Principal Dancers: Bill "Bojangles" Robinson, Four Step Brothers, Cholly Atkins, The Hoofers, Charles "Honi" Coles, Nicholas Brothers, Fred Strickler, Chuck Green, Lon Chaney, James "Buster" Brown
Dance Company: Jazz Tap Ensemble, The Copasetics, Third Generation Step
Category: TAP, DANCE HISTORY
Chicago International Film Festival, Sydney Film Festival, New Directors/New Films
Everything's copasetic with this documentary on tap, featuring performances, interviews and vintage film clips.

LOS TARANTOS
1963, 81 min. color video
Distributor: Swank
Producer: Orion Enterprises
Director: Rovira-Beleta
Principal Dancers: Carmen Amaya, Sara Lezana, Antonio Gades
Category: FLAMENCO, FEATURES
A story of the love between the children of two warring gypsy families living on the outskirts of Barcelona, dancing flamenco by the sea, in bars and on streets.

TCHAIKOVSKY AND THE RUSSIANS
1972, 27 min. color video
Series: Ballet For All
Distributor: The Media Guild
Director: Nicholas Ferguson
Choreographers: Marius Petipa, Lev Ivanov
Principal Dancers: Doreen Wells, David Wall
Dance Company: Bolshoi Ballet
Composer: Peter Ilyich Tchaikovsky
Category: BALLET, COMPOSITION
A discussion of composer Peter Ilyich Tchaikovsky, comparing two Russian classical choreographers, Marius Petipa and Lev Ivanov, with a focus on Ivanov's *Swan Lake*. Excerpts also from the *Sleeping Beauty Pas de Deux* and the coda of the *Blue Bird Pas de Deux*.

TEACH ME TO DANCE
1978, 28 min. color film
Distributor: National Film Board of Canada
Producer: Vladimir Valenta
Director: Anne Wheeler
Category: CHILDREN, CANADA
Set in 1919 in Alberta, Canada, two girls, one English and the other Ukrainian, are brought together because of a mutual love of dance, but their friendship is torn apart by their community's ethnic prejudices.

TEACHING BEGINNING/ADVANCED DANCE IMPROVISATION (6 videos)
1989, 1993, 60 min. each color video
Distributor: AAHPERD
Producer: Ririe-Woodbury Dance Company
Director: Arthur Pembleton
Category: INSTRUCTIONAL, IMPROVISATION
Teachers: Shirley Ririe and Joan Woodbury
Instructional videos and workbooks on the art of improvisation.

TEAK ROOM (AUTOBIOGRAPHY OF A DANCER)
1982, 70 min. color video
Distributor: Beals, Margaret
Director: Tony Tanner
Choreographer: Margaret Beals
Principal Dancer: Margaret Beals
Composer: Gwendolyn Watson
Category: EXPERIMENTAL
Solo dance play in the form of an extended monologue, with pantomime, dance sequences, and improvisations with the audience. Tells how the artist's drive to dance arose out of an unusual childhood and created her adult lifestyle.

TEALIA
1977, 10 min. color film, video
Distributors: Phoenix, Coe Film Associates, Indiana University
Producer: Ellen Jane Kutten
Directors: George Paul Csicsery, Gordon Mueller
Choreographer: John McFall
Principal Dancers: Betty Erickson, Vane Vest
Dance Company: San Francisco Ballet
Composer: Gustav Holst
Category: BALLET, EXPERIMENTAL
Dance on Camera Festival 1978 Merit Award
Two dancers suspended in space simulate a coral-colored sea anemone with multiple arms.

TECTONIC PLATES
1992, 100 min. color video
Distributor: Bullfrog Films
Producers: Debra Hauer, Niv Fichman
Director: Peter Mettler
Choreographer: Curtis Wehrfritz
Dance Company: Theatre Repère
Composer: Michel Gosselin
Category: MODERN, EXPERIMENTAL
Figueira de Foz International Film Festival Most Innovative Film, Columbus International Film and Video Festival Chris Award
This "adaptation-integration" of the Theatre Repère stage production of Robert Leafage's *Tectonic Plates* starts from a premise in which the geology of continental drift becomes a metaphor for the evolution of human culture. As the narrative unfolds, any connection between tectonic plates and human culture seems remote—if only because geological forces operate with utter disregard for human actions.

TED SHAWN AND HIS MEN DANCERS (3 videos)
1985, 20–25 min. b&w video
Distributor: Indiana University
Producer: Jacob's Pillow Dance Festival
Choreographer: Ted Shawn
Composers: Johann Sebastian Bach, Jess Meeker
Category: MODERN, DANCE HISTORY
Jacob Pillow's reconstructions of Ted Shawn's choreography created for his all-male troupe (1933–1940) in three pieces: *The Dome,* a work in eight movements, *Kinetic Molpai,* expressing humanity's longings in strife, love, the sacred and poetic; *Labor Symphony,* a celebration of working in agriculture and industry.

TEILE DICH NACHT (Night Open Yourself)
1991, 12:30 min. color film, video
Distributor: Motion Pixels
Producer: Jean de Boysson
Director: Jean de Boysson
Choreographer: Hyonok Kim
Principal Dancer: Hyonok Kim
Composer: Isang Yun
Category: MODERN
International Video Festival of Teruel, Spain, 1991 Grand Prize, Dance on Camera Festival 1992 Gold Award
Inspired by three poems by holocaust survivor, Nelly Sachs, this expressive dance solo reveals a woman's loneliness and longing for deliverance. The piece evokes a black bird precariously balancing heaven on one wing and hell on the other.

THE TEMPLE AND THE SWAN
1995, 70 min. color video
Distributor: Kuchipudi Art Academy of Dance
Producer: Sujata Vinjamuri
Director: Vinay Dumale
Choreographers: Vempati China Satyam, Alexandria Zaherias
Dancers: Sujata, Rossana
Dance Company: Kuchipudi Art Academy of Dance
Composer: Vempati China Satyam
Category: INDIA
A wide selection of archival as well as new footage gives insights into the styles, costumes and literary traditions of the dances of India.

TENTACLE
1983, 10 min. b&w video
Distributor: ARC Videodance
Directors: Jeff Bush, Celia Ipiotis
Choreographers: Eiko and Koma
Principal Dancers: Eiko and Koma
Category: EXPERIMENTAL, MODERN
A duet conceived for close-up recording. Threads wrapping the bodies appear to be veins binding and trapping them in both combat and symbiosis.

TERPSICHORE'S CAPTIVES
1995 52 min. color video
Distributor: Borin, Anne
Producer: Efim Resnikov, Valery Sidashov
Director: Efim Resnikov
Choreographer: Ludmila Sakharova
Dancers: Natasha Balakhnecheva, Ludmila Sakharova
Dance Company: Perm Ballet School
Composer: Leonid Rossokhovaksky
Dance on Camera Festival 1996 Bronze Award, Encontros Internacionais de Cinema Document
Category: BALLET, DOCUMENTARY PORTRAITS
This documentary is based on the demanding relationship between the artistic director of the Perm Ballet School and a teenage student.

THAILAND DANCES (4 films)
1965, 6–16 min. color, b&w film
Distributor: PennState
Producer: Wissen
Category: FOLK, ASIA
Six dances of the Akha girls and boys of the Chieng Rai Province, plus a solo with a sword and scabbard. Two of the films show the dance on the New Year in Black Lahu and Lisu from the Tak Province, and another is of the dance of an acrobatic mouth organ player from Miao, Tak Province.

THAT MEANS I WANT TO GO HOME
1989, 27:23 min. color video
Distributor: Electronic Arts Intermix:
Director: James Byrne
Choreographer: Melanie Lien
Dance Company: Codanceco
Category: EXPERIMENTAL, MODERN
Multilayered montage of a homesick dance of alienation and loss of control.

THAT'S DANCING
1985, 120 min. color film, video, laser
Distributors: MGM/UA, Swank, Facets, Dance Horizons
Producer: MGM
Director: Jack Haley, Jr.
Principal Dancers: Gene Kelly, Liza Minnelli, Sammy Davis, Jr.
Category: JAZZ, TAP, BALLROOM, FEATURES
Over fifty dancers appear in this compendium of the best of dance in Hollywood musical films, including scenes from *42nd Street*, *Gold Diggers of 1935*, *The Red Shoes*, *Oklahoma*, *Sweet Charity*, *Silk Stockings*, *West Side Story*, *Fame*, and *Flashdance*.

THAT'S ENTERTAINMENT (Parts I, II and III)
1974, 1976, 1993, 133 min. each color film, video, laser
Distributors: MGM/UA, Facets, Swank (Part I), Laserdisc Fan Club (Part III)
Producer: MGM/UA
Directors: Jack Haley, Jr., Gene Kelly
Principal Dancers: Fred Astaire, Gene Kelly, Liza Minnelli, Debbie Reynolds, Donald O'Connor, Cyd Charisse, Ann Miller, Esther Williams
Category: FEATURES, TAP, JAZZ, BALLROOM
Showstoppers from over one hundred MGM musicals, comedies, and dramas woven together with new footage of Fred Astaire and Gene Kelly dancing together for the first time in thirty years.

THEATRE MEETS RITUAL
1976, 21:30 min. color film
Distributor: Film-makers' Cooperative
Principal Dancer: Eugenia Barba
Dance Company: Odin Teatret
Category: MODERN, LATIN AMERICA
Fragments of *Book of Dances* and *Come! and the Day Will Be Ours* by this European ensemble touring through Venezuela. Includes dances by the Yanomami, an Indian tribe of the Upper Orinoco, and the shaman's enactment of his tribal legend about a tortoise that killed a jaguar.

THERE'S NO BUSINESS LIKE SHOW BUSINESS
1954, 117 min. color film, video
Distributors: Facets, Films Inc.

Producer: Twentieth Century Fox
Director: Walter Lang
Choreographers: Robert Alton, Jack Cole
Principal Dancers: Donald O'Connor, Dan Dailey, Mitzi Gaynor
Composer: Irving Berlin
Category: FEATURES, MUSICALS
A story tied together by musical events and performances in the lives of a vaudeville family. Musical numbers include *There's No Business Like Show Business*, *Alexander's Ragtime Band*, *A Boy Chases a Girl*, and *Lazy*.

THEY ARE THEIR OWN GIFTS
1978, 52 min. color film, video
Distributor: Women Make Movies
Producers: Lucille Rhodes and Margaret Murphy
Choreographer: Anna Sokolow
Category: DOCUMENTARY PORTRAITS, CHOREOGRAPHY
Portraits of poet Muriel Rukeyser, painter Alice Neel, and choreographer Anna Sokolow and how they were affected by their times. Available as a trilogy or individually.

THE THIRD DAY
1994, 9 min. color video
Distributor: Wendy Woodson and Present Company
Principal Dancer: Janna Goodwin
Composer: Janna Goodwin
Category: MODERN, WOMEN
U.S. Super 8 Film and Video Festival 1995 Grand Prize Winner, German Award for Video Art 1994 Finalist, New England Film and Video Festival 1994 Director's Honorable Mention
Travels through a fast-moving series of surreal internal and external landscapes to reveal a woman's relationship with her various worlds.

THIRTY SECOND SPOTS
1982–84, 30 min. color video
Distributor: Electronic Arts Intermix
Producer: Joan Logue
Director: Joan Logue
Principal Dancers: Bill T. Jones, Arnie Zane
Category: ART, EXPERIMENTAL
Created in New York City, Paris, and San Francisco, these commercials for individual artists capture their distinctive personalities with the flair of a caricaturist.

THOUSANDS CHEER
1943, 126 min. color video, laser
Distributors: Facets, MGM/UA
Producer: MGM
Director: George Sidney
Choreographers: Gene Kelly, Stanley Donen
Principal Dancers: Gene Kelly, Judy Garland, Eleanor Powell
Category: FEATURES, MUSICALS
This elaborate World War II musical stars Kelly in an early role as a reluctant army draftee. The entertaining all-star camp show finale features a wide range of sketches and musical numbers, including a tap dance by Powell and a duet with Don Loper and Maxine Barrat based on Latino themes.

THREE DANCES
1964, 17 min. b&w film
Distributor: Friedman, Gene
Producer: Gene Friedman

Director: Gene Friedman
Choreographer: Gene Friedman
Principal Dancers: Judith Dunn, Steve Paxton, Debby Hay, Alex Hay
Category: MODERN
Three modern dances: *Public,* photographed at the Museum of Modern Art, *Party,* photographed at Judson Church in New York City, and a solo by Judith Dunn photographed in her studio.

THREE DANCES BY MARTHA CURTIS
1991, 29 min. color video
Distributor: The American Program Service/Public Television
Producers: Martha Curtis and Bruce Berryhill
Directors: Martha Curtis, Bruce Berryhill
Choreographer: Martha Curtis
Principal Dancer: Martha Curtis
Composers: Joan LaBarbara, Susan Stone, Jonathan Romeo, Cecil Hooker, Eric Heiberg, Special Fun
Category: CINEDANCE, DOCUMENTARY PORTRAITS
Dance on Camera Festival 1992 Honorable Mention
Martha Curtis, choreographer and assistant professor in the Department of Dance and Choreography at the Virginia Commonwealth University, performs three solo dances. Interwoven are interviews and behind-the-scenes shots of the video dance production in progress.

THE THREE WORLDS OF BALI
1981, 58 min. color film, video
Series: Odyssey
Distributor: Documentary Educational Resources
Producer: PBS
Director: Ira Abrams
Category: RELIGIOUS/RITUAL, BALI
On the Indonesian island of Bali, dance is one means of maintaining a balance between the demons thought to dwell in the watery underworld, and the gods in the upper world. Once a century, the entire Balinese population mobilizes for the *Eka Dasa Rudra* ceremony to transform eleven demons into beneficent spirits.

THROUGH THE VEIL
1972, 10 min. color film, video
Distributor: Glick, Stefanie
Producer: Stefanie Glick
Directors: Stefanie Glick, Tod Bresnick
Choreographer: Stefanie Glick
Principal Dancers: Stefanie Glick, Tod Bresnick
Composer: Zoltán Kodály
Category: DANCE DRAMA
Dance on Camera Festival 1993 Honorable Mention
Explores the dynamics of a traditional Jewish wedding wherein the image of the bride represents two discourses of otherness: Judaism and feminism.

TIBETAN FOLK DANCE (7 films)
1966–67, 3–6 min. color, b&w film (silent)
Distributor: PennState
Producer: Wissen
Category: FOLK, CHINA
Included are dance songs from West Tibet: *dBusg-Tsan-gZhas, mDo-stod, mDo-sMad* dances accompanied by a long-necked lute; *gSer-Gyi' Khor-Lo* song and dance accompanied by bamboo flute and lute; *KhamsgSum-dBan-'Dus-*

gZhas-Tshig and *gYag-' Krab-Pa* animal dance and dancing lute player; *Phyema leb* and *San-ge* animal dances accompanied by flute and female voice; and *bSil-IDan-Gans-Ri*, *SPu-gu'i rtsedthan* and *rGyug-rtsed* children's dances accompanied by long-necked lute and flute.

TIME
1993, 26 min. color video
Series: Dance as an Art Form
Distributor: Pro Arts
Producer: Chimerafilm
Director: Warren Leib
Choreographer: Murray Louis
Dance Company: Murray Louis Dance Company
Composer: Alwin Nikolais
Category: MODERN, INSTRUCTIONAL
Narrator: Murray Louis
For the dancer, time is the awareness of duration. Progressing from the traditional musical definition of time, the experience is broadened into other areas of time sense.

A TIME TO DANCE
1960, 29 min. b&w film, video
Series: A Time To Dance
Distributor: Indiana University
Producer: WGBH-TV/Boston
Choreographer: Marius Petipa
Principal Dancers: Melissa Hayden, Jacques d'Amboise, Daniel Nagrin
Dance Company: Jiménez-Vargas Ballet Español
Category: ART, INTERNATIONAL
Martha Myers introduces the series with paintings, sculpture and film clips of ethnic dance around the world. Examples are given of a seventeenth-century French court dance, a pas de deux performed by New York City Ballet principals from *The Nutcracker,* Spanish dance by one of the leading flamenco troupes of the day, and a solo satire from modern dancer Daniel Nagrin.

TO DREAM OF ROSES
1989, 16 min. color video
Distributor: Infinity Filmworks
Producer: Infinity/Berkshire
Director: Keith Melton
Choreographer: Lynn Taylor-Corbett
Principal Dancer: Marianna Tcherkassky
Composer: Robert Folk
Category: BALLET
Dance on Camera Festival 1991 Honorable Mention
Created for the 1990 World Exposition in Osaka, Japan, this fantasy film intercuts the dreams and reality of a prima ballerina as she falls ill during a performance.

TO MOVE IN BEAUTY: THE KABUKI TRADITION
1977, 28 min. color film
Distributor: The Japan Foundation
Producer: Broadcast Programming Center of Japan
Category: JAPAN, DANCE DRAMA
Documents the life of a group of young apprentices at the National Theatre in Tokyo, from their daily classes in recitation, music and dance to their first professional appearance.

TOP HAT
1935, 108 min. b&w film, video, laser
Distributors: Films Inc, Laserdisc Fan Club, Media Basics
Producer: RKO
Director: Mark Sandrich
Choreographers: Fred Astaire, Hermes Pan
Principal Dancers: Fred Astaire, Ginger Rogers
Composer: Irving Berlin
Category: FEATURES, MUSICALS
Mistaken identity is overcome by true love between two American dancers in London. Dance numbers include *Top Hat, White Tie and Tails, Cheek to Cheek,* and *The Piccolino.*

TOPENG BABAKAN (SOLO MASKED DANCE OF WEST JAVA)
1984, 10 min. color video
Distributor: Kallett, Jim
Producer: Jim Kallett
Directors: Jim Kallett, Mark Manoff
Principal Dancer: Sujana Arja
Category: ANTHROPOLOGICAL, ASIA
A performance in Slangit Village, West Java, Indonesia, of the Cirebon-style (West Javanese) *Topeng Babakan* dances of the Dalang Topeng (Dance Master) Sujana Arja. The dances, performed with the remarkable *Topeng* masks and with a gamelan ensemble of musicians, portray human characters based on the ancient Hindu mythological character Panji.

TORCHES OF TODAIJI
0 min. color film
Distributor: The Japan Foundation
Producer: NHK Production Services
Principal Dancer: Shoroku, Onoe
Category: DANCE DRAMA, JAPAN
In the Todaiji temple in Nara and at the religious festival of *Shunie* (which first inspired the development of Japanese performing arts), famed Kabuki actor, Onoe Shoruoku, creates a new Kabuki dance drama.

TORSE
1978, 55 min. color film
Distributor: Cunningham Dance Foundation
Producers: The New York Public Library and Museum of the Performing Arts at Lincoln Center
Director: Charles Atlas
Choreographer: Merce Cunningham
Composer: Maryanne Amacher
Category: EXPERIMENTAL, CINEDANCE
Two synchronous hour-long films to be projected simultaneously on adjacent screens. Provides a record of the dance and an approximation of the spectator's experience. The choreographer was inspired by the *I Ching,* and therefore any semblance of continuity was achieved unwittingly.

TORVILL AND DEAN: PATH TO PERFECTION
1984, 52 min. color video
Distributors: Viewfinders, Media Basics
Principal Dancers: Jayne Torvill, Christopher Dean
Category: ICE DANCE
Eight dance routines by the Olympic gold medalists ice dancers, including *Bolero.*

TOTEM
1963, 16 min. color film
Distributors: Canyon Cinema, Film-maker's Cooperative, PennState, Lane Education
Director: Ed Emshwiller
Choreographer: Alwin Nikolais
Principal Dancers: Murray Louis, Gladys Ballin
Dance Company: Alwin Nikolais Dance Company
Category: EXPERIMENTAL, CINEDANCE
Festival of Two Worlds (Spoleto, Italy) 1966
Through the experimental use of mirrors, cameras and dance, the collaborators present primordial mysteries in an exploration of optics, electronics and space.

TOUR EN L'AIR
1990, 49:30 min. color film, video
Distributor: National Film Board of Canada
Producer: George Pearson for National Film Board of Canada
Director: Grant Munro
Choreographers: Asaf Messerer, David Holmes
Principal Dancers: Anna Marie Holmes, David Holmes, Jorge Lefebvre, Alicia Alonso, Azari Plisetski
Composer: Tomaso Albinoni
Category: BALLET, DOCUMENTARY PORTRAITS
Ballet dancers David and Anna Marie Holmes rehearse, perform an excerpt from *Ballet Adagio* and take classes in Berlin, London, Lisbon, Havana, Washington D.C. and Montréal. In East Berlin, they participate in an international dance festival as the only Canadians. In Cuba, they share the stage with Alicia Alonso and Azari Plisetski. In London, they entertain friends in their apartment.

TRADITIONAL DANCES OF INDONESIA (12 films)
1990, 11–32 min. color film
Distributor: University of California Extension Center
Producer: William Heick
Category: ASIA, ANTHROPOLOGICAL
Dances of Bali (three films), Jogjakarta Central Java (three films), Surakarta Centra Java (five films), and West Sumatra (one film).

TRADITIONAL WHITSUN RITES OF THE KALUSHARS (3 films)
1969, 23–26 min. b&w film
Distributor: PennState
Producer: Wissen
Category: FOLK, EUROPE:
Romanian death game with a dance match between two groups around a flagpole. Set in Priseaca, southeast Europe.

TRAILBLAZERS OF MODERN DANCE
1977, 60 min. color film, video
Series: Dance in America
Distributors: Indiana University, University of California Extension Center, University of Minnesota
Producers: Merrill Brockway, Judy Kinberg for WNET/Channel 13
Director: Emile Ardolino
Choreographers: Frederick Ashton, Ted Shawn, Ruth St. Denis, Martha Graham, Doris Humphrey, Isadora Duncan
Principal Dancers: Annabelle Gamson, Ted Shawn, Lynn Seymour, Helen Tamiris, Ruth St. Denis, Doris Humphrey, Martha Graham, Vernon and Irene Castle, Anna Pavlova, Loie Fuller
Composers: Edward MacDowell, Johannes Brahms, Robert Schumann, Alexander Scriabin
Category: MODERN, DANCE HISTORY
Narrators: Michael Tolin, Frederick Ashton, Rosemary Harris

Dance on Camera Festival 1980 Award

Reviews the evolution of American modern dance from 1900 to the early 1930s with vintage clips and dances reconstructed for television. Includes: *Five Brahms Waltzes in the Manner of Isadora Duncan*; choreographed by Ashton; *Scriabin Études* (Duncan), *Soaring* (St. Denis and Humphrey/Schumann, reconstructed for the Joyce Trisler Dance Company by Klarna Pinska); *Polonaise* (Shawn/MacDowell, staged by Norman Walker).

THE TRAITOR

1955, 19 min. b&w film
Distributor: Dance Film Archive
Choreographer: José Limón
Principal Dancers: Lucas Hoving, José Limón
Dance Company: José Limon Company
Composer: Gunther Schuller
Category: MODERN
A modern dance portraying the betrayal of Christ by Judas.

TRANCE AND DANCE IN BALI

1951, 20 min. b&w film, video
Series: Character Formation In Different Cultures
Distributors: University of California Extension Center, University of Minnesota, PennState
Producers: Gregory Bateson and Margaret Mead
Category: BALI, DANCE DRAMA, ANTHROPOLOGICAL
Narrator: Margaret Mead
A Balinese ceremony called the *kris* dance, which plays out a drama of struggle between the death-dealing witch and the life-protecting dragon, is accompanied by comic interludes and violent trance seizures.

TRAVELING LIGHT

1995, 23 min. color video
Distributor: Palomar Pictures
Director: Morleigh Steinberg
Choreographers: Morleigh Steinberg, Roxanne Steinberg
Dancer: Roxanne Steinberg
Category: BUTOH, EXPERIMENTAL
Dance on Camera Festival 1995 Honorable Mention
The co-founder of ISO and a former member of Momix, Morleigh Steinberg creates a haunting fusion of landscapes and *Butoh.*

DAS TRIADISCHE BALLETT

1970, 30 min. color film
Distributor: Modern Talking Picture Service
Director: Hannes Winkler
Choreographer: Oskar Schlemmer
Principal Dancer: Hannes Winkler
Composer: Erich Ferstl
Category: DANCE HISTORY, BALLET
This reconstruction of Oskar Schlemmer's 1922 ballet, built around the number three as a mystical idea, demonstrates his Bauhaus philosophy of geometric forms, orders and patterns.

A TRIBUTE TO ALVIN AILEY

1990, 120 min. color video
Distributors: Home Vision, Dance Horizons, Viewfinders, Corinth, Facets
Producer: Thomas Grimm
Director: Thomas Grimm
Choreographers: Alvin Ailey, Ulysses Dove
Dance Company: Alvin Ailey American Dance Theatre
Category: MODERN, AFRICAN-AMERICANS
Host: Judith Jamison
Dance on Camera Festival 1993 Honorable Mention
Members of Ailey's dance company celebrate his memory by performing three of his works, and a special tribute choreographed by Ulysses Dove. Each piece is introduced by Judith Jamison, who was nurtured to stardom by Ailey and who is now artistic director of the company. As a choreographer, Ailey explored the African-American experience and beyond. Performances include *For Bird with Love, Witness, Memoria*, and *Episodes.*

A TRIO

1978, 10 min. b&w film (silent)
Distributor: Dance Film Archive
Director: Yvonne Rainer
Choreographer: Yvonne Rainer
Principal Dancer: Yvonne Rainer
Category: EXPERIMENTAL, MODERN
Minimalist solo made in 1965 as a rebellion against spectacle and decoration in dance.

TRIPLE DUO

1989, 16 min. color film, video
Distributor: Burchhardt, Rudolph
Producer: Rudolph Burchhardt
Choreographer: Douglas Dunn
Principal Dancers: Douglas Dunn, Grazia della Terza
Dance Company: Douglas Dunn and Dancers
Composer: Elliott Carter
Category: MODERN, EXPERIMENTAL
Shots of dancers improvising and rehearsing in a studio are intercut with those of people in the street below going about their business. We fly to Mexico as the dancers perform *Sky Eye.* Douglas Dunn and Grazia della Terza appear in the woods in an animal-like duo, and then walk through Queens on a quiet Sunday.

TRISHA AND CARMEN

1988, 13 min. color video
Distributors: Electronic Arts Intermix, Museum of Modern Art
Producer: Burt Barr
Director: Burt Barr
Choreographer: Trisha Brown
Principal Dancer: Diane Madden
Composer: Georges Bizet
Category: MODERN, DOCUMENTARY PORTRAITS
Shot in Naples where modern dance pioneer Trisha Brown, commissioned by Lina Wertmuller to choreograph the opera *Carmen*, applies makeup, intercut with a rehearsal of a duet and excerpt of the performance, which integrates the Spanish persona with Brown's individuality.

TROUT

1992, 10 min. color video
Distributor: Wendy Woodson and Present Company
Director: Wendy Woodson
Choreographer: Wendy Woodson
Principal Dancer: Peter Schmitz
Composer: Janna Goodwin
Category: MODERN
National Poetry Association Poetry Film/Video

Festival 1993 Grand Prize Winner, U.S. Super 8 Film and Video Festival 1994 Finalist
Depicts a man caught in a surreal struggle inspired by experiences with AIDS, but allowing for multiple interpretations, primarily to evoke a sense of loss and longing.

TROY GAME

1988, 39 min. color video
Distributor: Home Vision
Producer: Independent Films Producers Association
Director: Thomas Grimm
Choreographer: Robert North
Dance Company: London Contemporary Dance Theatre
Composer: Bob Downes
Category: BALLET, MODERN
Nine male dancers combine aikido exercises and acrobatics as a bow to the Greek athletic competitions. In addition to the performance, Robert Cohan warms up the company and comments on the ballet.

TURKISH BELLY DANCE (2 videos)

1989, 120 min. each color video
Distributor: Cernik, Eva
Choreographer: Tulay Karaca
Principal Dancer: Tulay Karaca
Category: MIDDLE EAST, BELLY DANCE
Filmed in Istanbul's nightclubs, studios, and Sulukule Gypsy quarter. Included on Volume I are four dances by Tulay Karaka.

TURKISH FOLK DANCES AT PRIZEN

1971, 9 min. b&w film
Distributor: PennState
Producer: Wissen
Category: FOLK, MIDDLE EAST
Folk dances filmed in southern Yugoslavia.

THE TURNING POINT

1977, 119 min. color film, video, laser
Distributors: Films Inc., CBS/Fox, Corinth
Producer: Twentieth Century Fox
Director: Herbert Ross
Choreographers: Frederick Ashton, Jean Coralli, Jules Perrot, Marius Petipa
Principal Dancers: Mikhail Baryshnikov, Leslie Browne, Antoinette Sibley, Clark Tippet, Martine van Hamel, Starr Danias, Hideo Fukagawa, Alexandra Danilova
Dance Company: American Ballet Theatre
Composers: Peter Ilyich Tchaikovsky, Sergei Prokofiev, Adolphe Adam
Category: FEATURES, BALLET
A young dancer on the verge of becoming a professional tries to skirt the pressures from her mother, a former dancer, and her godmother, a world class ballerina just past her prime, and still woo a principal dancer played by Baryshnikov. Classical excerpts include: Act II *Pas de Deux* from *Gisèlle, Blue Bird Pas de Deux* from *Sleeping Beauty*, the *White Swan Pas de Deux* from *Swan Lake*, Ashton's *Romeo and Juliet.*

TWENTY ONE WITH BILL T. JONES

1987, 15:45 min. color video
Distributor: The Kitchen
Director: Tom Bowes
Choreographer: Bill T. Jones
Composers: Brian Eno, Jerry Goodman, Etosha
Category: EXPERIMENTAL, MODERN

A man reflects on the arrest of his brother, and how it affected him as a teenager, while in college, and in Amsterdam. He alternately sits by a window, dances in an empty studio, and poses for the camera. The intercutting of the three circumstances supports the speaker's repetitive thought pattern.

TWO BAGATELLES
1962, 3 min. color film
Distributor: International Film Bureau
Producer: National Film Board of Canada
Directors: Norman McLaren, Grant Munro
Category: ANIMATION, EXPERIMENTAL
Two short divertissements: *On the Lawn,* in which a male dancer waltzes to synthetic music, and a fast march *In the Backyard,* accompanied by an old-fashioned calliope.

TWO BY LOUIS JOHNSON
1970s, 5 min. color, b&w film
Distributor: Film-makers' Cooperative
Producer: Film-makers' Cooperative
Director: Richard Preston
Choreographer: Louis Johnson
Principal Dancer: Louis Johnson
Category: EXPERIMENTAL
Two treatments of a work by Louis Johnson performed by a group dancing on a rooftop. In the second, multiple exposures create a variety of stylistic effects.

TWO ECSTATIC THEMES
1980, 13 min. color film
Distributor: Dance Film Archive
Choreographer: Doris Humphrey
Principal Dancers: Nina Watt, Carla Maxwell
Dance Company: José Limón Company
Category: MODERN
Two interpretations of a solo choreographed in 1931.

TWO FOR BALLET
1991, 57 min. color video
Distributor: The Cinema Guild
Producer: New Classic Films
Directors: John Axline, Thomas Frantz
Choreographer: Eric Hyrst
Principal Dancers: Diane Gaumond, David Kleine, David White
Dance Company: State Ballet of Oregon
Composer: Webster Young
Category: COLLABORATION, BALLET
Narrator: David Vaughan
Dance on Camera Festival 1992
Tells the story of the choreographer-composer team Eric Hyrst and Webster Young. Their method of working together is examined, and excerpts from five of their ballets are shown.

TWO TAKES ON TAP
1993, 58 min. color video
Distributor: Images
Producer: Sharon Arslanian
Director: Sharon Arslanian
Choreographers: Lynn Dally, Brenda Bufalino
Principal Dancers: Lynn Dally, Brenda Bufalino, Eddie Brown, Charles "Honi" Coles
Dance Company: Jazz Tap Ensemble
Category: TAP, CHOREOGRAPHY
Dance on Camera Festival 1993 Honorable Mention
Two virtuoso performers-choreographers discuss

their careers in tap, sharing their histories and sources of inspiration, their approaches to choreography and the creative process and their vision for the future of tap. Includes performance footage of Bufalino and Dally and also Eddie Brown, Honi Coles, the American Tap Dance Orchestra and the Jazz Tap Ensemble.

TWYLA THARP: MAKING TELEVISION DANCE
1977, 59 min. color, b&w film, video
Distributors: Phoenix, University of California Extension Center, UCLA Instructional Media Library University of Minnesota
Producer: Twyla Tharp Dance Foundation
Director: Don Mischer
Choreographer: Twyla Tharp
Principal Dancers: Twyla Tharp, Mikhail Baryshnikov
Dance Company: Twyla Tharp Dance Company
Category: MODERN, DOCUMENTARY PORTRAITS
Dance on Camera Festival 1978 Merit Award
Twyla Tharp explores the relationship between television and dance and explains her rationale behind certain exercises choreographed for the camera. Features a rehearsal with Baryshnikov of *Once More Frank* and her *Country Dances* set for five dancers.

TYMPANI
1981, 29:48 min. color video
Distributor: KTCA-TV
Producer: Kathryn Esher for Twin Cities Public TV
Director: Kathryn Esher
Choreographer: Laura Dean
Category: MODERN
A geometrically patterned dance with rhythmic stamping and prolonged spinning.

TZADDIK
1974, 30 min. color video
Distributor: Electronic Arts Intermix
Producer: Rick Hauser, WGBH Television Dance Workshop
Director: Rick Hauser
Choreographer: Eliot Feld
Principal Dancer: Eliot Feld
Dance Company: Eliot Feld Ballet
Composer: Aaron Copland
Category: BALLET, RELIGIOUS/RITUAL
Aaron Copland's trio *Vitebsk* brought back memories of childhood to choreographer Eliot Feld. In deference to those days, *Tzaddik* celebrates the joy Chassidic Jews derive from studying and performing rituals. Shot with a 250-pound camera on a crane mounted on a double-tilt cradle head, in an environment created by using *leko* patterns of Hebrew characters.

UALE, THE KNOCK-KNEED DANCE and others from Ivory Coast (8 films)
1968, 4–25 min. color, b&w film
Distributor: PennState
Producer: Wissen
Category: AFRICA, ANTHROPOLOGICAL
The Guere tribe from the Ivory Coast, West Africa perform *The Little Stool Dance* of the just-excised maidens, the *Dje, Seri,* and *Zauli* mask dances, and dances to commemorate such events as the end of war and circumcision.

THE UGLY DUCKLING
1983, 30 min. color film, video
Distributor: Phoenix
Director: Dan Bessie
Category: CHILDREN
A reworking of the fairy tale in which a bored young man, frustrated by working in the family dry goods store, finds his own kind of people(dancers and acrobats(in a parade. He joins in, discovering his own talents.

THE ULTIMATE SWAN LAKE
1984, 126 min. color video
Distributors: Kultur, Dance Horizons, Home Vision, Viewfinders
Choreographer: Yuri Grigorovich
Principal Dancers: Natalya Bessmertnova, Alexander Bogatyrev
Dance Company: Bolshoi Ballet
Composer: Peter Ilyich Tchaikovsky
Category: FULL-LENGTH BALLETS
Narrator: Gene Kelly
The full-length classic filmed in Russia is introduced by Gene Kelly, who gives a brief history of the ballet.

UNDERTOW
1988, 8 min. b&w video
Distributor: Electronic Arts Intermix
Director: James Byrne
Choreographers: Eiko and Koma
Principal Dancers: Eiko and Koma
Category: MODERN, EXPERIMENTAL
The performers appear to float through the frame, propelled by inexplicable forces in a space resembling a womb.

UNREMITTING TENDERNESS
1977, 9 min. color film
Distributors: Phoenix, Films Inc.
Producer: Bruce Elder
Director: Bruce Elder
Category: EXPERIMENTAL, CINEDANCE
An experimental film in which a dance sequence is broken down into its basic components, transformed in printing, and then rearranged in a variety of ways.

UNSETTLED DREAMS
1995, 83 min. color 35mm film, video
Distributor: A. Star Reese Production Corporation
Producers: Donald Byrd, Andrea Star Reese
Directors: Donald Byrd, Andrea Star Reese
Choreographer: Donald Byrd
Dance Company: Donald Byrd/The Group
Composer: Mio Morales
Category: FEATURES
This twist on the classic story-within-a-story has yet another wrinkle(the storyteller's dilemma as to how and whether to tell the story and the trauma of working in the arts today. Choreographer Donald Byrd plays the oppressed, depressed protagonist.

UNTITLED, ARMS
1989, 30 min. color video
Series: Alive From Off Center
Distributors: KTCA-TV, The Kitchen
Producer: KTCA-TV
Directors: John Sanborn, Mary Perillo, Isabelle Hayeur
Choreographers: Bill T. Jones, Susan Marshall
Principal Dancer: Bill T. Jones

Category: MODERN
In *Untitled,* the choreographer-dancer created a tribute to his long-time partner, Arnie Zane, who died of AIDS in 1988. Susan Marshall adapted her work *Arms,* an exploration of power relationships between men and women.

THE VALLEY OF XEBRON
1981, 15 min. color video
Distributor: Orion Enterprises
Choreographer: Gus Giordano
Principal Dancer: Gus Giordano
Category: JAZZ
Gus Giordano Jazz Dance Chicago performs to the music of Doc Severinsen and the band, Xebron.

VARIATION II
1978, 11 min. color film
Series: Doris Chase Dance Series—Three Solos
Distributors: Museum of Modern Art, Doris Chase Productions
Producer: Doris Chase for WNYC-TV
Director: Doris Chase
Principal Dancer: Sara Rudner
Composer: Joan LaBarbara
Category: MODERN, EXPERIMENTAL
Dance Film and Video Festival 1979 Merit Award
Second alteration of a three-camera shoot of a solo by Sara Rudner, formerly of Twyla Tharp's company, using tape delay, de-beaming, colorizing, and mat key.

VARIATIONS V
1966, 50 min. b&w film, video
Distributor: Cunningham Dance Foundation
Producer: Studio Hamburg, Nordeutscher Rundfunk
Director: Arne Arnborn
Choreographer: Merce Cunningham
Dance Company: Merce Cunningham Dance Company
Composer: John Cage
Category: EXPERIMENTAL, MODERN
A multimedia collaboration with twelve sound-sensitive electronic poles placed around the stage. The electronic equipment, especially designed by Bell Laboratories, translated the dancers' movements into sound altered or delayed by musicians John Cage, David Tudor, and Gordon Mumma. A montage of rehearsal footage, movie stills, and scenes retouched by Nam June Paik was projected on monitors during the performance. For his exit, Merce Cunningham rides a bicycle around the space.

VEDA SEREEM'S QUALITY OF BELLY DANCING (19 videos)
1980s, 110–120 min. color video
Distributor: Sereem, Veda
Producer: Veda Sereem
Principal Dancer: Veda Sereem
Category: BELLY DANCE, INSTRUCTIONAL
A series covering the skills for the incorporation of veils, swords, canes, basket, and zills (finger cymbals) from this teacher based in Germantown, Maryland.

VEIL TECHNIQUES IN ORIENTAL DANCE
1989, 18 min. color video
Distributors: Chandra of Damascus
Choreographer: Chandra of Damascus
Principal Dancer: Chandra of Damascus
Category: MIDDLE EAST
Demonstration of basic to advanced techniques for dancing with veils.

THE VERY EYE OF NIGHT
1959, 18 min. b&w film
Distributors: Museum of Modern Art, Mystic Fire Video, Film-makers' Cooperative
Producer: Maya Deren
Director: Maya Deren
Choreographer: Antony Tudor
Principal Dancers: Richard Englund, Richard Sandlifer, Don Freisinger, Patricia Ferrier, Bud Bready, Ginaro Gómez, Rosemary Williams, Philip Salem
Composer: Teiji Ito
Category: EXPERIMENTAL, CINEDANCE
A cine-ballet of night, filmed in the negative, creating the illusion of movement in unlimited space. The dancers resemble sleepwalkers, advancing as if planets in the night sky.

VESPUCCILAND: THE GREAT AND THE FREE
1989, 3 min. color film
Distributor: Canyon Cinema
Producer: Rock Ross
Choreographer: Rock Ross
Principal Dancers: Randy Redding, Nancy Hammer
Dance Company: Homestead Valley Dance Company
Composer: François Poulenc
Category: EXPERIMENTAL
Dance on Camera Festival 1989 Silver Award
Satire on dance trends with time-lapse photography of dancers in tunics and scarves in a backyard, going down a flight of stairs, in and out of a tent, and under an umbrella.

VIBRANT SCULPTURE FROZEN DANCE
1987, 30 min. color video
Distributor: Devi, Ritha
Producer: Ritha Devi
Principal Dancer: Ritha Devi
Category: INDIA, RELIGIOUS/RITUAL
One woman's effort to recount the legends revolving around the Sun-God, in the style of Oudra Nrutya, performed at the Temple of Konarka in Orissa, India.

VIDEO DICTIONARY OF CLASSICAL BALLET (2 videos)
1983, 270 min. color video
Distributors: Kultur, Dance Horizons, Viewfinders, Hoctor Products, Home Vision, Instructional Video
Director: Robert Beck
Principal Dancers: Georgina Parkinson, Denise Jackson, Merrill Ashley, Kevin McKenzie
Dance Company: American Ballet Theatre, New York City Ballet
Category: INSTRUCTIONAL, BALLET
VIRA Award
Index to over eight hundred variations in the Russian, French and Cecchetti styles, all numbered and explained in an accompanying booklet, with demonstrations by principals from two ballet companies.

VILLAGE DANCES OF YUGOSLAVIA
1963–82, 60 min. color film
Distributor: University of California Extension Center
Category: FOLK, EUROPE
Fifteen traditional folk dances, each originally filmed in 1963 in their natural village settings. Includes dances from Macedonia, Serbia, Slovenia, Vojvodina, and Croatia.

VISION DANCE
1982, 58:30 min. color video
Distributor: Solaris
Producer: Henry Smith for Solaris Lakota Project in association with KTCA-TV and Affiliate Artists
Director: Skip Sweeney
Choreographers: Lloyd One Star, Henry Smith
Composers: Mike Sirotta and the Ironwood Singers
Category: MODERN, NATIVE AMERICANS
Dance on Camera Festival 1983 First Prize, American Film Festival 1983 Honorable Mention, Tokyo Video Festival 1982 Special Merit Award
Shot in the Badlands and Black Hills of South Dakota in collaboration with Lakota Sioux Indians and modern dancer Henry Smith and his company. The tape is based on a dance theatre work, *Ihanbla Waktoglag Wacipi,* which means to dance one's dreams, visions, or exploits.

VIVA LAS VEGAS
1964, 86 min. color film, video, laser
Distributors: MGM/UA, Swank
Producer: MGM
Director: George Sidney
Choreographer: David Winters
Principal Dancers: Ann-Margret, Elvis Presley
Category: FEATURES, MUSICALS
The standard Elvis Presley formula is transformed into a spirited and sexy musical comedy. The costars dance together to several rock classics, including *Come On, Everybody, What'd I Say,* and Ann-Margret's dance solo routine *My Appreciation.*

VOICES OF SPRING
8 min. color film
Distributor: Modern Talking Picture Service
Producer: German Government
Principal Dancers: Students of Munich Ballet Academy
Category: BALLET, CHILDREN
Documentary on young dancers in class and performance.

VOICES OF THE ORISHAS
1993, 37 min. color video
Distributor: University of California Extension Center
Producer: Alvaro Pérez Bétancourt
Director: Alvaro Pérez Bétancourt
Choreographer: Alfredo O'Farril
Principal Dancers: Alfredo O'Farril, Daisy Romero, Julian Villa
Dance Company: Conjunto Folklórico Nacional de Cuba
Composers: Alejandro Carvajal, Lázaro Pedroso
Category: CARIBBEAN, RELIGIOUS/RITUAL
Global Africa Film Festival People's Choice Award
Documents a musical religious ceremony called the *Guemilere* in present day Cuba, where the Orishas, gods of the Yoruba religion, represent human characteristics and personalities manifested by moral and ethical symbols and attributes. The story of Shango is recreated by dancers and musicians initiated in these religious rites, with the appearance of Shango,

Oggun and Oya, deities of the Rule of Ocha (Yoruba religion), on a vacant lot in a Havana neighborhood where Santeria and Spiritism are frequently practiced.

VOODOO CHILD
1987, 5 min. color video
Distributor: Warner Home Video
Producer: Alan Douglas
Directors: Bill and Jackie Landrum
Choreographers: Bill and Jackie Landrum
Composer: Jimi Hendrix
Category: EXPERIMENTAL, MODERN, CINEDANCE
Fifteen years after a Jimi Hendrix concert was filmed, a California team choreographed a dance to his music for the camera. The dance footage was then intercut with the concert footage of the guitarist. The guitar string was symbolically used as the link between dance and music, as close-ups of Hendrix's fingers dancing on his guitar strings switch to the dancers playing under long strings.

VROTSOS VIDEOS (4 videos)
1986, 30–60 min. color video
Distributor: Taffy's By Mail
Producer: Janine Vrotsos
Category: CHILDREN, INSTRUCTIONAL
Teacher: Janine Vrotsos
A series of teaching videos: *Pre-Ballet for Fives, Sixes and Sevens* for young students, *Intermediate Ballet Class* and *Beginning/Intermediate Pointe Class* for the more advanced. Also available, *Intermediate Jazz Class* with floor stretches, barre and center.

WAKE UP CALL
1989, 8 min. color film, video
Distributor: Eccentric Motions
Producer: Pooh Kaye
Director: Pooh Kaye
Choreographer: Pooh Kaye
Composers: John Kilgore, Pooh Kaye
Category: COMEDY, ANIMATION
Boston Film/Video Foundation's Olive Jar Award
Combined live action and animation depict a young woman struggling to face the day despite her mattress sticking to her, the breakfast table wobbling, and being followed by shadows.

WALKAROUND TIME
1973, 48 min. color film, video
Distributors: Cunningham Dance Foundation, Film-makers' Cooperative
Producer: Cunningham Dance Foundation
Director: Charles Atlas
Choreographer: Merce Cunningham
Dance Company: Merce Cunningham Dance Company
Composer: David Behrman
Category: MODERN, ART
Set Designer: Jasper Johns
Homage to the work of Marcel Duchamp in concept and detail, expressing his concern with transparency by passing the dancers behind see-through vinyl inflatables.

WALKING DANCE FOR ANY NUMBER
1968, 7:30 min. b&w film
Distributor: Film-makers' Cooperative
Director: Phil Niblock
Principal Dancer: Elaine Summers

Category: EXPERIMENTAL, CINEDANCE
This experimental film focuses on a pair of legs walking down the sidewalks of a city park, making a dance within the scope of the lens, the space of the projected flat image, and the speeds of the camera. In French, Dutch and English.

WATCHING BALLET
1965, 35 min. b&w film
Distributor: Lane Education
Producer: New York State Council on the Arts and Ballet Society
Choreographer: George Balanchine
Principal Dancers: Jacques d'Amboise, Allegra Kent
Composers: Paul Hindemith, Peter Ilyich Tchaikovsky, Charles Gounod, John Philip Sousa, Hershy Kay
Category: BALLET, INSTRUCTIONAL
Jacques d'Amboise, the former New York City Ballet principal and founder of the National Dance Institute, demonstrates the basic positions and steps of ballet in different styles and combinations. Excerpts from George Balanchine's *The Nutcracker, Gounod Symphony, Stars and Stripes, Swan Lake* and *The Four Temperaments.*

WATER MOTOR
1978, 9 min. b&w film (silent)
Distributor: Dance Film Archive
Producer: Babette Mangolte
Director: Babette Mangolte
Choreographer: Trisha Brown
Principal Dancer: Trisha Brown
Category: MODERN, EXPERIMENTAL
A modern dance solo fades-in/fades-out with a quick silver middle and then is repeated in slow-motion.

THE WATER PIECES
1989, 10 min. color
Distributor: Penny Ward Video
Producer: Penny Ward
Director: Penny Ward
Choreographer: Sue Bernhard
Principal Dancer: Sue Bernhard
Composers: Dan Levitan, Glen Vélez
Category: MODERN
Dance on Camera Festival 1990 Honorable Mention
The film articulates a rhythmic language of dance, memory, and sensation.

THE WATER PIECES NO. 2
1990, 3:50 min. color video
Distributor: Penny Ward Video
Producer: Penny Ward
Director: Penny Ward
Choreographer: Sue Bernhard
Principal Dancer: Sue Bernhard
Category: MODERN, EXPERIMENTAL
Kaleidoscopic version of *The Water Pieces* involves constant movement and division, so that the body seems to fold in on itself.

WATER SPIRIT FESTIVAL
1989, 32 min. color video
Distributor: Ile Ife Films
Producer: Bayne Williams Film Company
Director: Arthur Hall
Choreographer: Arthur Hall
Composer: K. Lee

Category: CHILDREN, FESTIVALS
Recreation of a Nigerian festival by three hundred children from Lebanon, New Hampshire, who play everything from the council of elders to the river dragon.

WATER STUDY
1980, 22 min. color film
Distributor: Dance Film Archive
Choreographer: Doris Humphrey
Category: MODERN, DANCE HISTORY
The 1928 work performed by a group under the direction of Ernestine Stodelle, shown both at a distance and in close-up.

THE WAVE: ECSTATIC DANCE FOR BODY AND SOUL
1993, 35 min. color video
Distributor: Dance Horizons, Raven Recording
Producer: Nicole Ma
Director: Michelle Mahrer
Choreographer: Gabrielle Roth
Composer: Gabrielle Roth
Category: INSTRUCTIONAL
A dance workout video designed to stretch and exercise the imagination as well as the body. Uses improvisation in natural styles of movement and rhythm in order to discover the unique energy of the body in motion. Based on the movement work of Gabrielle Roth, artist, philosopher and teacher.

WAYWARD GLIMPSES
1992, 20 min. color film
Distributor: Film-makers' Cooperative
Director: Rudolph Burckhardt
Principal Dancer: Dana Reitz
Composer: Elliott Carter
Category: MODERN, WOMEN
Alice Notley reading her poem *I Work in a Whorehouse* to a surreal dance, with visits to various cities and the Maine woods, and sometimes erotic glimpses of women.

WE JIVE LIKE THIS
1993, 52 min. color video
Distributor: Filmakers Library
Producer: Cinecontact/Kinoki
Category: AFRICA
The dance, poetry, theatre and music of the South African black townships, where the performing arts flourish despite the absence of theatres or arts education.

WELCOME BACK ST. PETERSBURG: A GALA AT THE ROYAL OPERA HOUSE
1992, 118 min. color video
Distributors: Viewfinders, Corinth, Home Vision
Principal Dancers: Larissa Lezhina, Faroukh Ruzimatov, Igor Zelinsky
Dance Company: Kirov Ballet
Category: BALLET
A gala at the Royal Opera House, Covent Garden for the Kirov Opera and Ballet, celebrating the restoration of Leningrad's original name with performance excerpts by the Kirov Ballet.

THE WEST AFRICAN HERITAGE
1980, 30 min. color video
Series: Jumpstreet
Distributor: Lane Education
Dance Company: Wo'se Dance Theatre
Category: FOLK, AFRICA

Features musicians Hugh Masakela, Ahaji Bai Konte, Dembo Konte, and the Wo'se Dance Theatre from Africa.

WEST SIDE STORY
1961, 155 min. color film, video, laser
Distributors: Swank, Facets, MGM/UA, CBS/Fox
Producer: Robert Wise
Directors: Robert Wise, Jerome Robbins
Choreographer: Jerome Robbins
Principal Dancers: Rita Moreno, Eliot Feld, Russ Tamblyn
Composer: Leonard Bernstein
Category: FEATURES, MUSICALS
Academy Award
The Broadway musical about rival white and Puerto Rican gangs in New York coming to blows over an ill-fated love match. Dance numbers include *Jet Song, Dance at the Gym, America, Cool,* and *The Rumble.*

WESTBETH
1975, 32 min. b&w film, video
Distributors: Cunningham Dance Foundation, Dance Film Archive
Producer: Cunningham Dance Foundation
Director: Charles Atlas
Choreographer: Merce Cunningham
Dance Company: Merce Cunningham Dance Company
Category: MODERN, CINEDANCE
In Merce Cunningham's first collaboration with director Charles Atlas, a six-part collage was created with the knowledge that television changes our perception of time and space.

WHAT DO PINA BAUSCH AND HER DANCES DO IN WUPPERTAL?
1983, 115 min. color video
Distributor: Modern Talking Picture Service
Director: Klaus Wildenhahn
Choreographer: Pina Bausch
Dance Company: Wuppertal Dance Theatre
Composer: Peter Ilyich Tchaikovsky
Category: MODERN, CHOREOGRAPHY
The crew follows the process of creating *Bandoneon* in Wuppertal, West Germany, over a month's time. Interjected among the rehearsal footage are interviews with a factory worker who complains of the futility and flatness of her existence. Considered one of the most influential contemporary choreographers, Bauch says, in indirect response to the worker, "Everyone is looking for some kind of satisfaction which they never find." She challenges her company with daily exercises, such as expressing a symbol of freedom, or setting a trap for someone, or playing games to subdue fear.

WHAT IS NEW
1979, 52 min. color film, video
Series: The Magic of Dance
Distributors: Dance Film Archive, University of Minnesota
Producer: BBC-TV
Director: Patricia Foy
Choreographers: Grete Wiesenthal, Robert Cohan, Michel Fokine, Ruth St. Denis, Kurt Jooss
Principal Dancers: Margot Fonteyn, Mikhail Baryshnikov, Loie Fuller
Dance Company: Teatro a l'Avogaria
Dance Company: London Contemporary Dance Theatre

Composers: Johann Strauss, Bob Downes, Carl Maria von Weber
Category: BALLET, MODERN, DANCE HISTORY
Narrator: Margot Fonteyn
Includes a visit to the Parthenon in honor of Isadora Duncan's fascination with the Greeks, with a short film of Isadora dancing at a garden party; *Wine Women and Song* (Wiesenthal/Strauss); a 1906 film of Loie Fuller, *Khomsin* (Cohan/Downes); Robert North's *Troy Game;* Jooss' *The Green Table;* Fokine's *Le Spectre de la Rose;* Teatro a l'Avogaria performs *commedia dell' arte;* interview with Kyra Nijinsky about her father Vaslav Nijinsky; Ruth St. Denis excerpt.

WHAT'S REMEMBERED
1983, 20 min. color video
Series: The Educational Performance Collection
Distributor: Dance Notation Bureau
Producer: Dance Notation Bureau
Choreographer: Rachel Lampert
Composer: Louis Spohr, Jorns, Jean-Marie LeClair
Category: MODERN, NOTATION
Building on the theme of the tenuousness of relationships, the choreographer created romantic duets and frantic solos. Preparatory improvisational exercises are set and incorporated into the dance. Comes with an article on labanotation, advanced level labanotated score by Leslie Rotman, taped performance at the University of Iowa, critical text for study and performance rights to the dance.

WHITE NIGHT OF DANCE IN LENINGRAD
1987, 83 min. color video
Distributors: Kultur, Viewfinders, Corinth, Home Vision
Producers: ALAP Video, Paris/Gosteleradio
Choreographers: Oleg Vinogradov, Maurice Béjart
Principal Dancers: Faroukh Ruzimatov, Olga Chenchikova, Altynai Asylmuratova, Michael Gascard
Dance Company: Kirov Ballet, Ballet of the 20th Century
Category: BALLET
Two great dance troupes, French and Russian, join together in Leningrad's Czarist palaces, in parks and on the banks of the beautiful Volga River. It was filmed during the "white nights" when day hesitates to give way to night, and includes excerpts from *Le Sacre du Printemps, Le Corsaire, Swan Lake, Chopiniana, La Fille Mal Gardée, La Bayadère, Nôtre Faust, 1820, Conte Russe, Potemkine, Suite Grecque, Arepo, Heliogabale,* and *Le Soldat Amoureux.*

WHITE NIGHTS
1985, 135 min. color video, laser
Distributors: Films Inc., Corinth, Columbia Tristar
Producer: Columbia
Director: Taylor Hackford
Choreographers: Twyla Tharp, Mikhail Baryshnikov, Gregory Hines, Roland Petit
Principal Dancers: Mikhail Baryshnikov, Gregory Hines
Composers: Lionel Richie, Phil Collins, Johann Sebastian Bach
Category: FEATURES, TAP, BALLET
A Russian ballet defector lands in the Soviet Union as a result of a plane crash, and finds himself under the surveillance of a defector who is a Vietnam veteran and a former professional tap dancer. The film opens with an excerpt from the 1951 ballet *Le Jeune Homme et la Mort* choreographed by Petit. Throughout the film, there are solos by Baryshnikov and duets with Hines.

WIDENING GYRE
1993, 24 min. color video
Distributor: ARC Videodance
Producer: Jeff Bush
Director: Jeff Bush
Choreographer: Maureen Fleming
Principal Dancer: Maureen Fleming
Composer: David Lawson
Category: CINEDANCE, MODERN
Dance on Camera Festival 1993 Honorable Mention
A video dance in three parts, inspired by the poem *The Second Coming* by W.B. Yeats. The dance movement is woven within a sequence of spaces and images portraying the confrontation of the human body/psyche and the urban machine environment.

WILD FIELDS
1985, 12 min. color video
Distributor: ARC Videodance
Producers: Jeff Bush and Celia Ipiotis
Directors: Jeff Bush, Celia Ipiotis
Choreographer: Pooh Kaye
Category: MODERN
A group bounds playfully around a studio.

WILD GIRL FILMS
1975–81, 15 min. color video
Distributor: Eccentric Motions
Producer: Pooh Kaye
Director: Pooh Kaye
Principal Dancer: Pooh Kaye
Composers: Pooh Kaye, Jana Haimsohn
Category: MODERN
"These films reside within the realm of a primitive cinema, half way between Muybridge and Keaton."—Bruce Jenkins, *Buffalo Media Review.*

WILD SWANS IN EPITAPH AND MADHONOR
1974, 30 min. b&w film
Distributor: Beals, Margaret
Producer: Margaret Honeywell
Director: Peter Powell
Choreographer: Margaret Beals
Principal Dancer: Margaret Beals
Category: MODERN
Modern dancer Margaret Beals comments on two of her dances: *Wild Swans,* set to a suite of poems she recites, and *Madhonor,* danced in silence.

WITH MY RED FIRES
1972, 30 min. color film
Distributor: Dance Film Archive
Choreographer: Doris Humphrey
Dance Company: Connecticut College Repertory Company
Composer: Wallingford Riegger
Category: MODERN, DANCE HISTORY
The 1936 tragedy of possessive maternal love in a demagogic society, reconstructed from labanotation by Christine Clark and performed in 1972 at the American Dance Festival.

THE WIZ
1978, 133 min. color video
Distributor: Facets
Director: Sidney Lumet
Choreographer: George Faison
Principal Dancers: Michael Jackson, Richard Pryor, Lena Horne
Category: FEATURES, JAZZ, MUSICALS
Musical derived from *The Wizard of Oz* with an African-American cast.

THE WOMAN IN THE SHOE
1980s, 30 min. color video
Distributor: Hoctor Products
Choreographers: Joan Yell, Bonnie Ratzin
Category: INSTRUCTIONAL, CHILDREN
Designed for teachers planning recitals for early grade school and preschool children.

WORLD'S YOUNG BALLET
1969, 70 min. b&w film, video
Distributors: Dance Film Archive, Corinth, Home Vision, Kultur (1990 updated version)
Producer: Tsentrnauch Film Studios, Moscow
Director: Arkadi Tsineman
Choreographers: Lev Ivanov, Marius Petipa, August Bournonville, Vladimir Vassiliev, Maurice Béjart
Principal Dancers: Mikhail Baryshnikov, Peter Schaufuss, Helgi Tomasson, Vladimir Vassiliev, Azari Plisetski, Loipa Araujo, Ludmila Semenyaka, Nina Sorokina
Category: BALLET, FESTIVALS
The first Moscow International Ballet Competition in 1969, in which the young Soviet Mikhail Baryshnikov won the gold. Highlights of the competition include excerpts from *Swan Lake*, *Gisèlle*, *Flower Festival at Genzano*, *War and Peace*, *Bhakti*, and *Spartacus*.

THE WRECKER'S BALL: THREE DANCES BY PAUL TAYLOR
1996, 56 min. color video
Distributor: WNET
Producer: Judy Kinberg
Director: Matthew Diamond
Choreographer: Paul Taylor
Principal Dancers: Andrew Asnes, Rachel Berman Benz, Mary Cochran, Patrick Corbin, Hernando Cortez, Kristi Egtvedt, David Grenke, Francie Huber, Thomas Patrick
Category: MODERN
A return to the 1940s, '50s and '60s with three dances(*Company B*, *Funny Papers*, and *A Field of Grass*(et to songs by the Andrews sisters and ending with a wrecker's ball smashing into the Danceland theatre.

X-RAY EYES
1985, 14:53 min. color video
Distributor: Electronic Arts Intermix
Director: James Byrne
Choreographer: Wendy Perron
Principal Dancers: Lisa Bush, Erica Bornstein, Mary Lyman, Wendy Perron
Composers: Arto Lindsay, The Ambitious Lovers
Category: MODERN, EXPERIMENTAL
Playful, quirky movements of the dancers on a bare stage with sparse lighting are mirrored by James Byrne's angled camera, quick changes of focus, and formally composed close-ups.

XINGUANA: ABORIGINES OF SOUTH AMERICA
1971, 29 min. color film
Distributor: Lane Education
Category: ANTHROPOLOGICAL, LATIN AMERICA
Spear dances, body ornamentation and puberty rites of a tribe living by the Xingu River in Central Brazil.

YANKEE DOODLE DANDY
1942, 126 min. b&w film, video, laser
Distributors: Facets, Swank
Producer: Warner Brothers
Director: Michael Curtiz
Choreographer: LeRoy Prinz
Principal Dancer: James Cagney
Composer: George M. Cohan
Category: FEATURES, MUSICALS
A show business extravaganza about the life of the talented song-and-dance man, George M. Cohan. Musical numbers include *Give My Regards to Broadway*, *Over There*, *You're a Grand Old Flag*, and *The Yankee Doodle Boy*.

YOLANDA AND THE THIEF
1945, 109 min. color video, laser
Distributors: Facets, MGM/UA
Producer: MGM
Director: Vincente Minelli
Choreographer: Eugene Loring
Principal Dancers: Fred Astaire, Lucille Bremer
Composer: Harry Warren
Category: FEATURES, MUSICALS
An innocent young heiress falls under the "protection" of a con man. Dance numbers include *Will You Marry Me?* and *Coffee Time*.

YOU CAN DO THE HULA
1986, 45 min. color video
Distributor: Kalama Productions
Producer: Rainforest Publishing and Production Company
Director: Patty Amaral
Choreographer: Debbie Oschner
Category: HULA, INSTRUCTIONAL
Teacher: Taina Passmore
Warm-up and breathing exercises for the mind and body, history of the hula, and instructions for foot and hand movements. Concludes with a performance of a hula set to *Lehua*, a song of a lover having only the wind and stars to carry his thoughts to his beloved.

YOU WERE NEVER LOVELIER
1942, 98 min. color film, video, laser
Distributors: Facets, Films Inc., Laserdisc Fan Club
Producer: Columbia
Director: William A. Seiter
Choreographers: Fred Astaire, Val Raset
Principal Dancers: Fred Astaire, Rita Hayworth
Composer: Jerome Kern
Category: FEATURES, MUSICALS
A dancer arouses the romantic interest of an Argentinian hotel tycoon's daughter who has refused to wed. Dance numbers include *Audition Dance*, *I'm Old Fashioned*, *Shorty George*, and *You Were Never Lovelier*.

YOU'LL NEVER GET RICH
1941, 89 min. b&w film, video, laser
Distributors: Facets, Films Inc., Laserdisc Fan Club

Producer: Columbia
Director: Sidney Lanfield
Choreographer: Robert Alton
Principal Dancers: Fred Astaire, Rita Hayworth
Composer: Cole Porter
Category: FEATURES, MUSICALS
A Broadway dancer-director, in love with a girl in his show, is reunited with her at a GI army camp show. Dance numbers include *Dream Dancing*, *Astairable Rag*, and *So Near and Yet So Far*.

YOUNG AND JUST BEGINNING: PIERRE
1978, 26 min. color film, video
Distributor: Kinetic
Producer: Canadian Broadcasting Corporation
Directors: Ruth Hope, Mark Irwin
Choreographer: Barbara Forbes
Principal Dancers: Pierre Quinn, Kim Glascow, John Alleyne, Betty Oliphant, Erik Bruhn
Category: BALLET, CHILDREN
Chicago International Film Festival 1978 Gold Plaque as Best TV Documentary.
A young ballet student at Canada's National Ballet School, seen in his dance and academic classes, shares his hopes for a dance career and performs a pas de deux.

YURI GRIGOROVICH: MASTER OF THE BOLSHOI
1987, 67 min. color video
Distributors: Kultur, Viewfinders, Corinth, Dance Horizons, Home Vision
Producer: Gosteleradio
Director: Yuri Aldokin
Choreographer: Yuri Grigorovich
Principal Dancers: Vladimir Vassiliev, Marius Liepa, Boris Akimov, Natalya Bessmertnova, Ludmila Semenyaka, Nadezhda Pavlova
Dance Company: Bolshoi Ballet
Category: BALLET, DOCUMENTARY PORTRAITS
This video portrait of the Soviet choreographer and artistic director of the Bolshoi ballet features many of the Bolshoi's world famous dancers in rehearsal. It gives a unique glimpse of the choreographer, the teacher and the man. Treasures from the Soviet archives are seen here for the very first time in such ballets as *Swan Lake*, *Spartacus*, *Romeo and Juliet*, *Legend of Love*, *Ivan the Terrible*, and *The Golden Age*.

ZAJOTA AND THE BOOGIE SPIRIT
1990, 20 min. color film, video
Distributor: Filmakers Library
Producer: Ayoka Chenzira
Director: Ayoka Chenzira
Category: AFRICAN-AMERICANS, ANIMATION
Black International Cinema Berlin 1991 Best Film, National Educational Film and Video Festival 1990 Silver Apple, Columbus International Film Festival 1990, Newark Black Film Festival 1990
Incorporating African rhythms and dance, this vibrant animated film recounts the saga of African-Americans from their origins in Africa to their present life in America. The goddess Zajota watches over her people, and keeps the "boogie spirit" alive.

ZAR AND FLOORWORK
1989, 120 min. color video
Distributor: Chandra of Damascus

Producer: Chandra of Damascus
Choreographer: Chandra of Damascus
Principal Dancer: Chandra of Damascus
Category: MIDDLE EAST
A workshop on the history, rhythms and movements associated with the *zar*, a dance of exorcism and healing originating in the Middle East.

THE ZIEGFELD FOLLIES
1944, 110 min. color video, laser
Distributors: Facets, Swank, MGM/UA
Producer: MGM
Director: Vincente Minelli
Choreographer: Robert Alton
Principal Dancers: Fred Astaire, Lucille Bremer, Cyd Charisse, Gene Kelly
Composers: Harry Warren, Roger Edens, George Gershwin
Category: FEATURES, MUSICALS
Based on Florenz Ziegfeld's famous revues, the film uses the same format of unrelated songs, dances and comedy sketches. The dance numbers include *The Babbitt and the Bromide*, *Limehouse Blues*, *This Heart of Mine*, and *Bring on the Beautiful Girls*.

ZIEGFELD GIRL
1941, 131 min. b&w video, laser
Distributors: Facets, Swank, MGM/UA
Producer: MGM
Director: Robert Z. Leonard
Choreographer: Busby Berkeley
Principal Dancer: Judy Garland
Composer: Roger Edens
Category: FEATURES, MUSICALS
The working and romantic lives of Ziegfeld's chorus girls. Musical numbers include *Minnie From Trinidad*, and *You Stepped Out of a Dream*.

ZOU ZOU
1934, 92 min. b&w film, video
Distributors: Kino, Facets, Music Video Distributors
Principal Dancer: Josephine Baker
Category: FEATURES, JAZZ
The African-American comedian-dancer-singer Josephine Baker begins as an impoverished laundry woman, but quickly becomes the toast of Paris when in a twist of luck, she is allowed to take the place of a celebrated actress on opening night. This "Cinderella" story conveys Baker's comic talents and sensuality.

ZULU MEDICINE DANCES (6 films)
1965–68, 5–17 min. color film
Distributor: PennState
Producer: Wissen
Category: AFRICA, RELIGIOUS/RITUAL, ANTHROPOLOGICAL
Illustrates the procedures and treatments of bone tossing, skin scratching, inhaling, and divination dances used by medicine men of this South African tribe.

"Forbidden City, U.S.A." directed by Arthur Dong. Paul Wing, the "Chinese Fred Astaire" c. 1940s. *Photo courtesy of Arthur Dong.*

"He Makes Me Feel Like Dancing" directed by Emile Ardolino. Jacques d'Amboise teaching school children to dance. *Photo courtesy of Direct Cinema Ltd.*

"Dancing for Mr. B." directed by Anne Belle. Choreographer George Balanchine directing ballerina Merrill Ashley. *Photo courtesy of Direct Cinema Ltd.*

A · DANCE · HORIZONS · VIDEO

✦THE MEN WHO DANCED✦

THE STORY OF
TED SHAWN'S
MALE DANCERS
1933–1940

✦THE MEN WHO DANCED✦

DANCE
HORIZONS

✦THE MEN WHO DANCED✦

THE STORY OF TED SHAWN'S MALE DANCERS 1933–1940

The Men Who Danced presents the story of the first all-male dance company in the U.S. Ted Shawn's Male Dancers. It includes historic footage of the company performing in the 1930s, capturing the beauty and rigor of Shawn's choreography. Additionally, it tells the story of the founding of Jacob's Pillow, an abandoned farm that Shawn purchased to house his new company. The Pillow has become one of the most important summer schools and performance centers in the country. The video also features interviews with the surviving male dancers, including Barton Mumaw, on the occasion of the 50th reunion of the company in 1983.

Ted Shawn (1891–1972) was a pioneer of modern dance. Renowned as a dancer, choreographer, and dance writer, Shawn cofounded in 1915 the most influential modern dance troupe in America, Denishawn, along with his wife, dancer/choreographer Ruth St. Denis. The company toured the country and the world, spreading the new dance style throughout the globe. It spawned talents such as Martha Graham, Doris Humphrey, and Charles Weidman.

After breaking with St. Denis, Shawn decided to found his own company. A teaching assignment at Springfield College gave him the opportunity to train a group of dancers in his unique style. He purposely decided to limit his company to male dancers because he wanted to battle the prejudice against men pursuing a dance career. His choreography reflects his interest in the male character, drawing on themes of work and recreation from a male perspective.

The tape shows Barton Mumaw coaching Richard Cragun in his famous dance solo, "Fetish," and includes exerpts from Shawn's dances "Labor Symphony," "Polonaise," and other works.

✦

Produced and directed by Ron Honsa · © 1986 by Ron Honsa
Exclusive World Distributors:
Dance Horizons Video, Princeton Book Company, Publishers
POB 57, Pennington, NJ 08534

"The Men Who Danced: The Story of Ted Shawn's Male Dancers 1933–1940." *Cover art courtesy of Dance Horizons Video.*

A DANCE HORIZONS VIDEO

DORIS HUMPHREY
TECHNIQUE

THE CREATIVE POTENTIAL

DANCE
HORIZONS

DORIS HUMPHREY TECHNIQUE
The Creative Potential

WRITTEN, DIRECTED AND HOSTED BY ERNESTINE STODELLE
PHOTOGRAPHS BY BARBARA MORGAN

SPONSORED BY THE DORIS HUMPHREY SOCIETY

DORIS HUMPHREY
TECHNIQUE

With Four Early Humphrey Dances:

QUASI-VALSE
TWO ECSTATIC THEMES
ETUDE PATETICO
AIR FOR THE G STRING (1934) with Doris Humphrey

In this essential video for understanding the Humphrey style, Stodelle presents a series of studies illustrating falls, turns, breath rhythm, successional flow, leaps, circular swings, and leverage. She provides commentary for a clip from the 1936 silent film on the technique as well as for a sequence of photographs by Barbara Morgan. Because the technique is closely linked with choreography, the three early dances Stodelle has reconstructed serve as examples of the technique's use in composition. The video concludes with the 1934 film AIR FOR THE G STRING with Doris Humphrey performing the central role.

ERNESTINE STODELLE, member and soloist of the Doris Humphrey Concert Group and Humphrey-Weidman Company between 1929 and 1935, is a dance critic, teacher at her own Studio of Dance in Connecticut, and adjunct professor at New York University. She has recreated a number of Humphrey works, and has staged Humphrey's early choreography throughout the United States and Europe.

DORIS HUMPHREY (1895-1958) is renowned as one of the founders of modern dance.

Produced by The Doris Humphrey Society
Directed by Ernestine Stodelle
Copyright © 1992 by The Doris Humphrey Society
and Ernestine Stodelle

Cover photograph by Barbara Morgan of Doris Humphrey in Passacaglia
Cover design by Deirdre Sheean

DANCE HORIZONS VIDEO
PRINCETON BOOK COMPANY, PUBLISHERS
POB 57, PENNINGTON, NJ 08534

"Doris Humphrey Technique: The Creative Potential" directed by Ernestine Stodelle. *Cover art courtesy of Dance Horizons Video.*

"Moment of Light: The Dance of Evelyn Hart" directed by Gordon M. Reeve. *Photo courtesy of Bullfrog Films.*

"The Planets" directed by Barbara Willis Sweete. *Photo courtesy of Bullfrog Films.*

"Changing Steps" directed by Elliot Caplan and Merce Cunningham. *Photo courtesy of Cunningham Dance Foundation.*

"Image of a Dancer" directed by Bruce Nicholson. *Photo courtesy of The Cinema Guild.*

"Electric Boogie". *Photo courtesy of Filmakers Library.*

"Romeo and Juliet" directed by Paul Czinner. Margot Fonteyn and Rudolf Nureyev with the Royal Ballet. *Photo courtesy of Kultur Video.*

Bill T. Jones

Dancing to
The Promised Land

"Bill T. Jones: Dancing to the Promised Land" directed by Mischa Scorer. *Cover art courtesy of V.I.E.W. Video.*

"...The kind of performance documentary that works like a charm."
—THE NEW YORK TIMES

HI-FI STEREO

VIEW VIDEO

DANCE SERIES

"Ballroom Dancing: The International Championships." Cover art courtesy of V.I.E.W. Video.

"Steps in a New Direction" directed by John Leben. Freddie Moore and the children of Grand Rapids. *Photo courtesy of Leben Productions.*

"The Painted Princess" directed
and choreographed by Pooh Kaye.
Photo courtesy of Eccentric Motions.

"In Heaven There Is No Beer?"
directed by Les Blank.
Polka Dancers. *Photo
courtesy of Flower Films.*

"Ballet" directed by Frederick Wiseman. *Photo courtesy of Zipporah Films.*

"Making Dances: Seven Post-Modern Choreographers" directed by Michael Blackwood. *Photo courtesy of Michael Blackwood Productions.*

"Butoh: Body on the Edge of Crisis" directed by Christian Blackwood. *Photo courtesy of Michael Blackwood Productions.*

BALI BEYOND THE POSTCARD

"Bali Beyond the Postcard" directed by Peggy Stein. *Photo courtesy of Filmakers Library.*

"Terpsichore's Captives" directed by Efim Resnikov. *Photos courtesy of Efim Resnikov.*

Charles Goddertz'
TAP DANCING
ADVANCED ROUTINE
DANCE INSTRUCTIONAL

MAKING BALLET

WITH KAREN KAIN
and The National Ballet of Canada

Choreography by James Kudelka
Music by Frederic Chopin

HI-FI STEREO

VIEW
VIDEO

DANCE SERIES

"Making Ballet: Karen Kain
and the National Ballet of
Canada" directed by Anthony
Assopardi. *Cover art courtesy
of V.I.E.W. Video.*

"Syvilla: They Dance to Her Drum" directed by Ayoka
Chenzira. *Photo courtesy of Women Make Movies.*

Awards Index

THE FLAPPER STORY (SILVER PLAQUE)
GEE, OFFICER KRUPKE (SILVER PLAQUE)
NIK AND MURRAY (GOLD PLAQUE)
PICTURES AT AN EXHIBITION (1992 GOLD
   HUGO AWARD)
TAPDANCIN'
YOUNG AND JUST BEGINNING: PIERRE (1978
   GOLD PLAQUE AS BEST TV DOCUMEN-
   TARY)

**CHOICE OUTSTANDING NONPRINT MEDIA
AWARD**
DANCE MASKS: THE WORLD OF MARGARET
   SEVERN

CHRISTOPHER AWARD
HE MAKES ME FEEL LIKE DANCIN'

CINE GOLDEN EAGLE
ALWAYS FOR PLEASURE
BITTER MELONS
BUFFALO SOLDIER
THE CALL OF THE JITTERBUG (1989)
CAROLE MORISSEAU AND THE DETROIT
   CITY DANCE COMPANY (1980)
CHUCK DAVIS, DANCING THROUGH WEST
   AFRICA
CIRCLES II (1973)
THE DANCING PROPHET
DEBONAIR DANCERS (1986)
ELLIS ISLAND
THE FLAPPER STORY
LOOKING FOR ME
MEDICINE FIDDLE
MUSIC BOX
STEP STYLE

**CINEVUE INTERNATIONAL FILM FESTIVAL
   (FLORIDA)**
THE FIGHT (1994 SECOND PLACE)

**COLUMBUS INTERNATIONAL FILM AND
   VIDEO FESTIVAL**
MOMENT OF LIGHT: THE DANCE OF EVE-
   LYN HART (1993 BRONZE PLAQUE)
THE SORCERESS: KIRI TE KANAWA (BRONZE
   PLAQUE)
TECTONIC PLATES (CHRIS AWARD)
ZAJOTA AND THE BOOGIE SPIRIT (1990)

CORK 1966
NINE VARIATIONS ON A DANCE THEME

CREATIVE FILM FOUNDATION
DANCE CHROMATIC (AWARD OF EXCEP-
   TIONAL MERIT)

DANCE FILM AND VIDEO FESTIVAL
VARIATION II (1979 MERIT AWARD)

DANCE ON CAMERA FESTIVAL
¡A BAILAR! THE JOURNEY OF A LATIN
   DANCE COMPANY (1991 HONORABLE
   MENTION)
ACCENT ON THE OFFBEAT (1994 BRONZE
   AWARD)
ADZO (1994 HONORABLE MENTION)
AMERICAN BALLET THEATRE IN SAN FRAN-
   CISCO (1987 SILVER AWARD)
ANATOMY AS A MASTER IMAGE IN TRAIN-
   ING DANCERS (1989 GOLD AWARD)

AND STILL WE DANCE (1989 GOLD AWARD)
ANNUNCIATION (1977)
BALI BEYOND THE POSTCARD (1992 GOLD
   AWARD)
IL BALLARINO: THE ART OF RENAISSANCE
   DANCE (1993 HONORABLE MENTION)
BAROQUE DANCE 1675–1725 (CERTIFICATE
   OF MERIT)
BEACH BIRDS FOR CAMERA (1993 BEST OF
   SHOW)
BEDHAYA: THE SACRED DANCE (1995 HON-
   ORABLE MENTION)
BEEHIVE (1987 HONORABLE MENTION)
BEGINNINGS (1977 HONORABLE MENTION)
BILL T. JONES: DANCING TO THE PROMISED
   LAND (1994 GOLD AWARD)
BLACK AND WHITE (1986 HONORABLE MEN-
   TION)
BLUE SNAKE (GOLD AWARD)
THE BOLSHOI BALLET (1986)
BONE DREAM (1979)
BOOK OF SHADOWS (1993 HONORABLE
   MENTION)
BOYCEBALL (1992 HONORABLE MENTION)
BREAKING: STREET DANCING (1982 GOLD
   AWARD)
BRINGING TO LIGHT (1992 AWARD)
CAN YOU SEE ME FLYING? A PORTRAIT OF
   TERRY SENDGRAFF (1992 HONORABLE
   MENTION)
CELEBRATION: A HISTORY OF THE SADLER'S
   WELLS ROYAL BALLET (1990 SILVER
   AWARD)
CHANCE DANCE (1978 HONORABLE MEN-
   TION)
CHANCE ENCOUNTERS (1992 HONORABLE
   MENTION)
CHANGING STEPS (1990 GOLD AWARD)
CHARLES WEIDMAN: ON HIS OWN (1991 SIL-
   VER AWARD)
CHIANG CHING: A DANCE JOURNEY
CHILDREN WITH A DREAM (1992 HONOR-
   ABLE MENTION)
CHUCK DAVIS, DANCING THROUGH WEST
   AFRICA (1987 HONORABLE MENTION)
CIRCLES: CYCLES KATHAK DANCE (1989
   HONORABLE MENTION)
CLINIC OF STUMBLE (1978 HONORABLE
   MENTION)
THE COMPANY (1985 HONORABLE MEN-
   TION)
COUNTRY CORNERS (1978)
CRWDSPCR (1996 GOLD AWARD)
CRIME PAYS (1985)
CUNNINGHAM DANCE TECHNIQUE: ELE-
   MENTARY LEVEL (1985)
DANCE BLACK AMERICA (1985)
A DANCE FOR 15 PREGNANT WOMEN (1993
   HONORABLE MENTION)
DANCE LIKE A RIVER: ODADAA! DRUM-
   MING AND DANCING IN THE U.S (1989
   SILVER AWARD)
DANCE MASKS: THE WORLD OF MARGARET
   SEVERN
DANCE THEATRE OF HARLEM (1980 GOLD
   AWARD)
DANCE THERAPY: THE POWER OF MOVE-
   MENT
A DANCER'S GRAMMAR (1977)
DANCING FOR MR. B.: SIX BALANCHINE
   BALLERINAS (1991 AWARD)
DANCING FROM THE INSIDE OUT (1994 SIL-
   VER AWARD)

DANCING HANDS (1989 HONORABLE MEN-
   TION)
DAPHNIS AND CHLÖE (1989 GOLD AWARD)
DEBONAIR DANCERS (1987 HONORABLE
   MENTION)
DIDO AND AENEAS (1996 SILVER AWARD)
DIGITAL DANCE (1985)
DUET (1991 AWARD)
EDDIE BROWN'S "SCIENTIFIC RHYTHM"
   (1991 SILVER AWARD)
THE ELEMENTS OF DANCE (1989 GOLD
   AWARD)
L'ENFANT ET LES SORTILÈGES (1987 GOLD
   AWARD)
ESSENTIALS OF TAP TECHNIQUE (1991 SIL-
   VER AWARD)
AN EVENING WITH ALVIN AILEY AMERICAN
   DANCE THEATRE (1987 HONORABLE
   MENTION)
AN EVENING WITH KYLIAN AND THE NE-
   DERLANDS DANS THEATRE (1987 SILVER
   AWARD)
AN EVENING WITH THE BALLET RAMBERT
   (1987 HONORABLE MENTION)
EXCERPTS FROM "WITHOUT A PLACE" (1992
   AWARD)
FALLING DOWN STAIRS (1996 GOLD AWARD)
FOR DANCERS (1990 HONORABLE MEN-
   TION)
FOR THE LOVE OF DANCE (1982 AWARD)
FORBIDDEN CITY, U.S.A (1991 AWARD)
FOUR JOURNEYS INTO MYSTIC TIME (1979
   HONORS AWARD)
THE FOUR TEMPERAMENTS (1981)
FRACTURED VARIATIONS and VISUAL SHUF-
   FLE (1986)
FRANKIE MANNING'S BIRTHDAY VIDEO
   (1995 HONORABLE MENTION)
FROM SAN FRANCISCO: DANCING ON THE
   EDGE (1990 HONORABLE MENTION)
GENIUS ON THE WRONG COAST (1994 SIL-
   VER AWARD)
GISÈLLE (Ballet Nacional de Cuba) (1979)
HANYA: PORTRAIT OF A DANCE PIONEER
   (1985 GRAND PRIZE)
HELP ME TO DREAM (1993 SILVER AWARD)
HIROSHIMA (1989 GOLD AWARD)
I WILL NOT BE SAD IN THIS WORLD (1993
   SILVER AWARD)
IN HEAVEN THERE IS NO BEER? (1985)
INTRODUCTION TO DANCE MEDICINE:
   KEEPING DANCERS DANCING (1992 HON-
   ORABLE MENTION)
ISADORA DUNCAN: MOVEMENT FROM THE
   SOUL (1990 GOLD AWARD)
KA (SILVER AWARD FOR EXPERIMENTAL
   VIDEO)
KALAKSHETRA: DEVOTION TO DANCE (1986
   SILVER AWARD)
KALYIAN (1986 HONORABLE MENTION)
KARATE RAP (1989 GOLD AWARD)
KAZE-NO-KO (1985)
KING KONG IN A BLANKET (1979)
THE LADY OF THE CAMELLIAS (1988 GOLD
   AWARD)
LAURETTA: MADONNA OF THE SENIOR CIT-
   IZEN SET (1990 HONORABLE MENTION)
LEE'S FERRY (1982 HONORABLE MENTION)
THE LEGACY OF THE CHOREOGRAPHY OF
   ISADORA DUNCAN (1989 HONORABLE
   MENTION)
LIKE WIND IN MIRA'S HAIR (1993 HONOR-
   ABLE MENTION)

INTERNATIONAL EMMY AWARDS
LE DORTOIR (The Dormitory) (1991 BEST PER-
    FORMING ARTS)
FANDANGO (1992 BEST PERFORMING ARTS)

INTERNATIONAL FILM AND TELEVISION
    FESTIVAL OF NEW YORK
IMAGE OF A DANCER (SILVER MEDAL)
A MOVING PICTURE (GOLD AWARD)
POINTS IN SPACE
THE SORCERESS: KIRI TE KANAWA (SILVER
    MEDAL)

INTERNATIONAL VIDEO FESTIVAL OF
    TERUEL, SPAIN
TEILE DICH NACHT (Night Open Yourself)
    (1991 GRAND PRIZE)

KRAKOW FILM FESTIVAL
THE FIGHT (1994 GOLDEN DINOSAUR EGG)

LYON DOCUMENTARY FILM FESTIVAL
PORTRAIT OF AN ARTIST

MANNHEIM FESTIVAL
IMAGE: FLESH AND VOICE (1970)
NINE VARIATIONS ON A DANCE THEME
    (1966)

MARGARET MEAD FILM FESTIVAL
STEP STYLE

MARIN COUNTY BEST CHILDREN'S FILM
SWEPT UP

MELBOURNE FILMEX
DORIS CHASE DANCE SERIES: THREE SOLOS

MELBOURNE INTERNATIONAL FILM
    FESTIVAL
IN HEAVEN THERE IS NO BEER? (GRAND
    AWARD)

MODERN LANGUAGE FILM FESTIVAL
STEP STYLE

MONTREUX GOLDEN ROSE FESTIVAL
EVERYBODY DANCE NOW (BRONZE PRIZE)

NAFISA MAGAZINE
DELILAH'S BELLY DANCE WORKSHOP (1990,
    1991, 1992 BEST INSTRUCTIONAL VIDEO)

NATIONAL COALITION OF ARTS THERAPY
    ASSOCIATION
DANCE THERAPY: THE POWER OF MOVE-
    MENT (HONOREE)

NATIONAL COUNCIL ON FAMILY
    RELATIONS
BLACK GIRL

NATIONAL EDUCATIONAL FILM AND
    VIDEO FESTIVAL
ALICIA WAS FAINTING (SILVER APPLE)
BALI BEYOND THE POSTCARD (1992 GOLD
    APPLE)
BLACK GIRL

CHILDREN WITH A DREAM (1992 SILVER
    APPLE)
CIRCLES: CYCLES KATHAK DANCE (SILVER
    APPLE)
LE DORTOIR (The Dormitory) (1992 GOLD
    APPLE)
THE DRUMS OF WINTER (Uksuum Cauyai)
    (SILVER APPLE)
MEDICINE FIDDLE (GOLD APPLE)
MOMENT OF LIGHT: THE DANCE OF EVE-
    LYN HART (OAKLAND, 1993 BRONZE
    APPLE)
SILVER FEET (1986 FINE ARTS CATEGORY)
ZAJOTA AND THE BOOGIE SPIRIT (1990 SIL-
    VER APPLE)

NATIONAL EDUCATIONAL MEDIA
    NETWORK
STRUGGLE FOR HOPE (1996 Gold Apple)

NATIONAL POETRY ASSOCIATION POETRY
    FILM/VIDEO FESTIVAL
TROUT (1993 GRAND PRIZE)

NEW DIRECTORS/NEW FILMS
TAPDANCIN'

NEWARK BLACK FILM FESTIVAL 1990
ZAJOTA AND THE BOOGIE SPIRIT

OBIE AWARD
QUARRY

OHIO STATE AWARD
THE REHEARSAL

PARIS FESTIVAL D'AUTOMNE GRAND PRIZE
OP ODYSSEY

PBS AWARD
THE REHEARSAL

PEABODY AWARD 1992
EVERYBODY DANCE NOW

PHILADELPHIA INTERNATIONAL FILM
    FESTIVAL 1993
BOOK OF SHADOWS (1993)
THE FLAPPER STORY

PRAGUE PLAQUE D'OR
POINTS IN SPACE

PRIX GÉMEAUX 1992 BEST ARTS SPECIAL
LE DORTOIR (The Dormitory)

PRIX ITALIA
THE FIREBIRD

RAI PRIZE
AUDITION POWER: PART I, KNOWING
    WHAT IT TAKES TO BE CHOSEN and PART
    II, WORKING THE HOLLYWOOD SYSTEM
THE FIREBIRD

ROSE D'OR, SWITZERLAND
A MOVING PICTURE

SAN FRANCISCO INTERNATIONAL FILM
    FESTIVAL
BLUE SNAKE (GOLDEN GATE AWARD)
ELLIS ISLAND
ISADORA DUNCAN: MOVEMENT FROM THE
    SOUL (1989 GOLDEN GATE AWARD)
LIVE AND REMEMBER (Wo Kiksuye) (1988
    BEST OF SHOW)
NINE VARIATIONS ON A DANCE THEME
    (1966)

SCHOOL OF VISUAL ARTS
ALICIA WAS FAINTING (1994 DUSTY AWARD
    FOR BEST PICTURE, BEST DIRECTOR, BEST
    EDITOR)

SILVER CINDY-IFPA
MUSIC BOX

SINKING CREEK FILM FESTIVAL
SOUND OF ONE
MADE IN THE BRONX (JAMES BLUE DOCU-
    MENTARY AWARD)

SOCIETY FOR VISUAL ANTHROPOLOGY
AMIR: AN AFGHAN REFUGEE MUSICIAN'S
    LIFE IN PESHAWAR, PAKISTAN (1989
    AWARD OF EXCELLENCE)
CELEBRATION OF ORIGINS (AWARD OF EX-
    CELLENCE)
THE DRUMS OF WINTER (Uksuum Cauyai)
    (AWARD OF EXCELLENCE)

SORRENTO FILM FESTIVAL
FILM WITH THREE DANCERS

STEREO REVIEW
THE GOLDEN AGE (1987 VIDEO OF THE
    YEAR AWARD)

SUNDANCE SPECIAL JURY AWARD
IN HEAVEN THERE IS NO BEER?

SYDNEY FILM FESTIVAL
TAPDANCIN'

BEST 10 FILMS OF THE YEAR
ISADORA

TOKYO VIDEO FESTIVAL
VISION DANCE (1982 SPECIAL MERIT
    AWARD)

U.S. INTERNATIONAL FILM AND VIDEO
    FESTIVAL
STRUGGLE FOR HOPE (1996 Silver Screen
    Award)

TORONTO INTERNATIONAL FILM FESTIVAL
STRICTLY BALLROOM (1992 AUDIENCE FA-
    VORITE AWARD)

U.S. SUPER 8 FILM AND VIDEO FESTIVAL
TROUT (1994 FINALIST)

VENICE INTERNATIONAL FILM FESTIVAL
APPALACHIAN SPRING
CREATION OF THE WORLD: A SAMBA OPERA
  (VENICE PEOPLE'S AWARD)
A DANCER'S WORLD

VIDEO REVIEW VIRA AWARD
LA SYLPHIDE (Paris Opera Ballet)
VIDEO DICTIONARY OF CLASSICAL BALLET

VON STERNBERG PRIZE FOR MOST
  ORIGINAL FEATURE FILM
IMAGE: FLESH AND VOICE

WHITNEY ART MUSEUM SERIES
FILM WITH THREE DANCERS

WORLDFEST HOUSTON 1993
BOOK OF SHADOWS

Categories Index

OBSEQUIES FOR DECEASED REGIONAL
    CHIEFTAINS
PALM PLAY
STEP STYLE
STILT DANCES AT KPEGBOUNI
STUDIES IN NIGERIAN DANCE
TOPENG BABAKAN (SOLO MASKED DANCE
    OF WEST JAVA)
TRADITIONAL DANCES OF INDONESIA
TRANCE AND DANCE IN BALI
UALE, THE KNOCK-KNEED DANCE
XINGUANA: ABORIGINES OF SOUTH
    AMERICA
ZULU MEDICINE DANCES

ART
THE ANATOMY LESSON
ART AND MOTION
BLACK AND WHITE
BOLERO and PICTURES AT AN EXHIBITION
BRUSH AND BARRE: THE LIFE AND WORK
    OF TOULOUSE-LAUTREC IN DANCE AND
    MUSIC
CLOUD DANCE
DANCE: A REFLECTION OF OUR TIMES
DANCE CHROMATIC
LEE'S FERRY
MADE IN THE BRONX
MIRROR OF GESTURE
MONEY
THE PAINTED PRINCESS
PORTRAIT OF AN ARTIST
THE RAKE'S PROGRESS
TALL ARCHES III
THIRTY SECOND SPOTS
A TIME TO DANCE
WALKAROUND TIME

ASIA
AFGHANISTAN DANCES
AFGHANISTAN: MEN'S DANCE WITH PAN-
    TOMIMIC INTERLUDE
ASIA SOCIETY COLLECTION
ASIA SOCIETY COLLECTION
ASLI ABADI SERIES
BEDHAYA: THE SACRED DANCE
BINO-DANCE
CHINESE, KOREAN AND JAPANESE DANCE
CULTIC DANCES IN A BUDDHIST PAGODA
    NEAR HUE
DANCES OF THE SILK ROAD: AN INTRODUC-
    TION TO UZBEK AND GEORGIAN DANCE
DHANDYO
EDO: DANCE AND PANTOMIME
ISLAND OF THE RED PRAWNS
KALYIAN
KHMER COURT DANCE
KOREA: PERFORMING ARTS: THE WONDER-
    FUL WORLD OF KIM SUNG HEE
LORD OF THE DANCE/DESTROYER OF ILLU-
    SION
MA'BUGI: TRANCE OF THE TORAJA
MALAYSIAN DANCES
MAN BLONG CUSTOM
POLYNESIAN DANCES FROM THE ELLICE IS-
    LANDS
THE ROYAL DANCERS AND MUSICIANS
    FROM THE KINGDOM OF BHUTAN
THAILAND DANCES
TOPENG BABAKAN (SOLO MASKED DANCE
    OF WEST JAVA)
TRADITIONAL DANCES OF INDONESIA

AUSTRALIA
CORROBOREE: THE AUSTRALIAN BALLET
ROAD TO THE STAMPING GROUND
SAGARI DANCES FROM NEW GUINEA
SAMBA TO SLOW FOX

BALI
BALI BEYOND THE POSTCARD
BALI: ISLE OF TEMPLES
BALI MECHANIQUE
BALI: THE MASK OF RANGDA
BALI TODAY
DANCE AND TRANCE OF BALINESE CHIL-
    DREN
LEARNING TO DANCE IN BALI
MIRACLE OF BALI: A RECITAL OF MUSIC
    AND DANCING
SERAMA'S MASK
TAKSU: MUSIC IN THE LIFE OF BALI
THE THREE WORLDS OF BALI
TRANCE AND DANCE IN BALI

BALLET
ADOLESCENCE
AFTERNOON OF A FAUN
ALICE IN WONDERLAND: A DANCE FAN-
    TASY
ALICIA ALONSO: ALICIA
THE ANATOMY LESSON
ANNA KARENINA
ANTONY TUDOR
ART AND TECHNIQUE OF THE BALLET
THE ART OF THE TWENTIETH CENTURY
    BALLET
BALANCES
BALLERINA
BALLERINA: LYNN SEYMOUR
THE BALLERINAS
BALLET: A CAREER FOR BOYS
BALLET ADAGIO
BALLET CLASS
BALLET COMES TO BRITAIN
BALLET ENTERS THE WORLD STAGE
BALLET ETOILES
BALLET IN JAZZ
BALLET LEGENDS: THE KIROV'S NINEL KUR-
    GAPKINA
BALLET RUSE
BALLET STUDY FILMS
BALLET WITH EDWARD VILLELLA
THE BALLET WORKOUT
THE BALLET WORKOUT II
BALLET'S GOLDEN AGE (1830–1846)
BARYSHNIKOV AT WOLF TRAP
BARYSHNIKOV DANCES SINATRA
BARYSHNIKOV: THE DANCER AND THE
    DANCE
BECAUSE WE MUST
BEGINNINGS
THE BEGINNINGS OF TODAY
BLACK TIGHTS
BLUE SNAKE
BOB RIZZO'S BALLET CLASS FOR KIDS
BOLERO
BOLSHOI PROKOFIEV GALA
BOLSHOI SOLOISTS CLASSIQUE
BOURNONVILLE BALLET TECHNIQUE
BRITISH BALLET TODAY
BRYONY BRIND'S BALLET: THE FIRST STEPS
BUJONES IN CLASS
BUJONES: IN HIS IMAGE
CANON IN D
CAPRICCIO ESPAGNOL (Spanish Fiesta)

CARMEN (Bolshoi Ballet)
CELEBRATION OF ROCK
CHOREOGRAPHY
CHOREOGRAPHY BY BALANCHINE
CINDERELLA: A DANCE FANTASY
CLASSICAL BALLET
COPLAND PORTRAIT
COPPÉLIA: ACT II
CORROBOREE: THE AUSTRALIAN BALLET
DADDY LONGLEGS
DAISY AND HER GARDEN: A DANCE FAN-
    TASY
DANCE: A REFLECTION OF OUR TIMES
DANCE PRELUDES
DANCERS
A DANCER'S GRAMMAR
DANCING BOURNONVILLE
DANCING FOR MR. B.: SIX BALANCHINE
    BALLERINAS
DANCING THRU
DYING SWAN
THE EBB AND FLOW
ELIOT FELD: ARTISTIC DIRECTOR
L'ENFANT ET LES SORTILEGES
ENIGMA VARIATIONS
ENTR'ACTE
ERIK BRUHN: ARTIST OF THE BALLET
THE ERIK BRUHN GALA: WORLD BALLET
    COMPETITION
ESSENTIAL BALLET: RUSSIAN BALLET
FALL RIVER LEGEND
A FANTASY GARDEN BALLET CLASS: BALLET
    INSTRUCTION WITH GARDEN CREA-
    TURES FOR PRE-SCHOOLERS
FONTEYN AND NUREYEV: THE PERFECT
    PARTNERSHIP
GALA
GALINA ULANOVA
GHOST DANCES
GISELLE . . . THE MAKING OF
GODUNOV: THE WORLD TO DANCE IN
GRAND CONCERT
GREAT BALLERINA
GREAT PERFORMANCE IN DANCE
HOLIDAY OF BALLET
HOW BALLET BEGAN
HOW BALLET WAS SAVED
I AM A DANCER
I CAN DANCE: INTRODUCTION TO BALLET
    FOR CHILDREN
ILONA VERA'S BALLET CLASS
IMAGE: A DANCER
IMAGE OF A DANCER
IMMORTAL SWAN
IN A REHEARSAL ROOM
IN PRAISE OF FOLLY
INNER RHYTHM
INSTRUCTIONAL BALLET TAPES DIRECTED
    BY DOROTHY LISTER
LE JEUNE HOMME ET LA MORT
JOHN CRANKO
KAREN KAIN: BALLERINA
THE KIROV BALLET IN LONDON
KONTAKION: A SONG OF PRAISE
KYLIAN COLLECTION
LIMELIGHT
LUDMILA SEMENYAKA: BOLSHOI BALLE-
    RINA
MADEMOISELLE FIFI
THE MAGNIFICENT BEGINNING
MAKAROVA: IN A CLASS OF HER OWN
MAKAROVA RETURNS
THE MAKING OF A BALLET

CANADA
CANADIANS CAN DANCE
TEACH ME TO DANCE

CARIBBEAN
ETHNIC DANCE: ROUNDTRIP TO TRINIDAD
THE JVC/SMITHSONIAN FOLKWAYS VIDEO
   ANTHOLOGY OF MUSIC AND DANCE OF
   THE AMERICAS
VOICES OF THE ORISHAS

CHILDREN
ADOLESCENCE
AL GILBERT PRESENTS
ALICE IN WONDERLAND: A DANCE FAN-
   TASY
ALICIA WAS FAINTING
BALLET: A CAREER FOR BOYS
BLACK GIRL
BOB RIZZO'S BALLET CLASS FOR KIDS
BOB RIZZO'S JAZZ CLASS FOR KIDS
BOYCEBALL
BUILDING CHILDREN'S PERSONALITIES
   WITH CREATIVE DANCE
BUSTER COOPER WORKSHOP VIDEOS
BUSTER COOPER'S HOW TO TAP
CAN'T RUN BUT
CHAMPIONS
CHE CHE KULE: EXERCISES FOR KIDS
CHILDREN DANCE
THE CHILDREN OF THEATRE STREET
CHILDREN ON THE HILL
CHILDREN WITH A DREAM
CHILDREN'S DANCES
CINDERELLA (Berlin Comic Opera Ballet)
CINDERELLA (Bolshoi Ballet)
CINDERELLA (Bolshoi Ballet)
CINDERELLA (Lyon Opera Ballet)
CINDERELLA (Paris Opera Ballet)
CINDERELLA: A DANCE FANTASY
CREATIVE MOVEMENT: A STEP TOWARDS
   INTELLIGENCE FOR CHILDREN AGES 2–8
DAISY AND HER GARDEN: A DANCE FAN-
   TASY
DANCE AND GROW
DANCE AND TRANCE OF BALINESE CHIL-
   DREN
A DANCE FANTASY
DANCE SPACE
DANCERS IN SCHOOL
DANCING SCHOOL
DANCING THROUGH THE MAGIC EYE: A
   PORTRAIT OF VIRGINIA TANNER
DARE TO DANCE
DEAF LIKE ME
THE ELEMENTS OF DANCE
A FANTASY GARDEN BALLET CLASS: BALLET
   INSTRUCTION WITH GARDEN CREA-
   TURES FOR PRE-SCHOOLERS
FANTASY OF FEET
FIRST STEPS
FUNNY HOUSE
HE MAKES ME FEEL LIKE DANCIN'
HIP HOP SP
HOUSE OF TRES
I CAN DANCE: INTRODUCTION TO BALLET
   FOR CHILDREN
IMAGE OF A DANCER
IN PARIS PARKS
INSTRUCTIONAL BALLET TAPES DIRECTED
   BY DOROTHY LISTER
JAZZ FOR KIDZ: PROGRESSIONS AND COM-
   BINATIONS WITH BOB RIZZO

KIT'S KIDS
LITTLEST REBEL
MADE IN THE BRONX
MOVEMENT EXPLORATION: WHAT AM I
THE NUTCRACKER (American Ballet Theatre)
THE NUTCRACKER (Bolshoi Ballet)
THE NUTCRACKER (Bolshoi Ballet)
THE NUTCRACKER (Bolshoi Ballet)
THE NUTCRACKER (New York City Ballet)
THE NUTCRACKER (Paris Opera Ballet)
THE NUTCRACKER (Royal Ballet)
THE PAINTED PRINCESS
QUARRY
SILVER FEET
SONG AND DANCE
STEPS IN A NEW DIRECTION
STEPS OF LIGHT
THE SWAN LAKE STORY: A DANCE FANTASY
SWEPT UP
THE TALES OF BEATRIX POTTER
THE TAP DANCE KID
TEACH ME TO DANCE
THE UGLY DUCKLING
VOICES OF SPRING
VROTSOS VIDEOS
WATER SPIRIT FESTIVAL
THE WOMAN IN THE SHOE
YOUNG AND JUST BEGINNING: PIERRE

CHINA
ANIMAL DANCES: PHYE-MA-LEB AND SAN-
   GE
CHIANG CHING: A DANCE JOURNEY
CHINESE FOLK ARTS
DANCES OF BUDDHIST PILGRIMS
HERITAGE OF CHINESE OPERA
ON THE MOVE: THE CENTRAL BALLET OF
   CHINA
RED DETACHMENT OF WOMEN
STEEL SILK: CHAMPION ACROBATS OF
   CHINA
STILT DANCERS OF LONG BOW VILLAGE
TIBETAN FOLK DANCE

CHOREOGRAPHY
ANNA SOKOLOW, CHOREOGRAPHER
ANTONY TUDOR
ARTISTS OF THE DANCE
THE BALANCHINE ESSAYS: ARABESQUE
BART COOK: CHOREOGRAPHER
BEYOND ROUTINE
BEYOND THE MAINSTREAM: POSTMODERN
   DANCERS
BILL T. JONES: DANCING TO THE PROMISED
   LAND
A CHOREOGRAPHER AT WORK: JOHN
   BUTLER
CHOREOGRAPHY
DANCE: FOUR PIONEERS
DANCE: IN SEARCH OF "LOVERS"
DANCE: NEW DIRECTIONS
DANCE: NEW YORK CITY BALLET
DANCING BOURNONVILLE
DAVID GORDON: PANEL
EIGHT GREAT STEPS TO CHOREOGRAPHY
GLEN TETLEY: PORTRAIT OF THE CHORE-
   OGRAPHER
GREAT PERFORMANCE IN DANCE
HANYA: PORTRAIT OF A DANCE PIONEER
INNER RHYTHM
JOHN CRANKO
THE LEGACY OF THE CHOREOGRAPHY OF
   ISADORA DUNCAN

MAKING DANCES: SEVEN POSTMODERN
   CHOREOGRAPHERS
MEREDITH MONK
MODERN DANCE: CHOREOGRAPHY AND
   THE SOURCE
MODERN DANCE: CREATIVE IMAGINATION
   AND CHOREOGRAPHY
MURRAY LOUIS IN CONCERT: VOLUME I,
   DANCE SOLOS
NIJINSKA: A LEGEND IN DANCE
THE PENNSYLVANIA BALLET: DA MUMMY,
   NYET MUMMY
REPETITIONS
RUTH PAGE: AN AMERICAN ORIGINAL
SOURCES OF DANCE
SYMPHONY IN D WORKSHOP
THEY ARE THEIR OWN GIFTS
TWO TAKES ON TAP
WHAT DO PINA BAUSCH AND HER DANCES
   DO IN WUPPERTAL?

CINEDANCE
AIRDANCE and LANDINGS
BALLET ADAGIO
BEACH BIRDS FOR CAMERA
BLUE STUDIO: FIVE SEGMENTS
CAN'T RUN BUT
CHANNELS/INSERTS
COAST ZONE
DANCE ON VIDEO: AN INTRODUCTION TO
   VIDEOTAPING DANCE
DANCE OUTLINE
DIALOGUE FOR CAMERAMAN AND DANCER
DIONYSUS
THE DUTCH NATIONAL BALLET
ENTROPY: REVERSE TO OMEGA
THE EYE HEARS, THE EAR SEES
FANDANGO
FOUR MOVES IN SPACE: A VIDEODANCE
   SUITE
FRACTIONS I
FRACTURED VARIATIONS and VISUAL
   SHUFFLE
FRAGMENTS: MAT/GLASS
FROM AN ISLAND SUMMER
IMAGES IN DISTRACTED TIME
IMPROVISATION
IN PARIS PARKS
INSIDE EYES
IOWA BLIZZARD '73
KEI TAKEI
LOCALE
LOOK! WE HAVE COME THROUGH
LUMINAIRE
MAYA DEREN: EXPERIMENTAL FILMS
MEDIATION ON VIOLENCE
MERCE BY MERCE BY PAIK
A MOMENT IN LOVE
A MOVING PICTURE
NINE VARIATIONS ON A DANCE THEME
THE OFFICIAL DOCTRINE
PAS DE DEUX
LA PROMENADE
RITUAL IN TRANSFIGURED TIME
ROAMIN' I
SMALL DISTANCES
SQUAREGAME VIDEO
THE STONE DANCES
A STUDY IN CHOREOGRAPHY FOR CAMERA
TANGO
THREE DANCES BY MARTHA CURTIS
TORSE
TOTEM

SPEAKING OF DANCE: CONVERSATIONS
   WITH CONTEMPORARY MASTERS OF
   AMERICAN MODERN DANCE
SUITE FANTAISISTE
SYNCOPATED MELODIES
TAPDANCIN'
TED SHAWN AND HIS MEN DANCERS
TRAILBLAZERS OF MODERN DANCE
DAS TRIADISCHE BALLETT
WATER STUDY
WHAT IS NEW
WITH MY RED FIRES

DANCE THERAPY
AMICI DANCE
BEST OF ALL A DANCER
BILL T. JONES: STILL-HERE WITH BILL
   MOYERS
BIRDS OF A FEATHER
BODY TALK: EIGHT MOVEMENT THERAPIES
COME DANCE WITH ME
THE CONQUEST OF EMPTINESS
DANCE THERAPY: THE POWER OF MOVE-
   MENT
DANCING FREE
DEBONAIR DANCERS
INTRODUCTION TO DANCE MEDICINE:
   KEEPING DANCERS DANCING
JUST FOR ME
KING KONG IN A BLANKET
LOOKING FOR ME
LOWER EXTREMITY DANCE MEDICINE: OR-
   THOPEDIC EXAMINATION WITH DR. WIL-
   LIAM HAMILTON
MOVING TOWARD HEALTH
MOVING TRUE
POSITIVE MOTION
STILL LOOKING

DISABILITIES
AMICI DANCE
BEST OF ALL A DANCER
CAN YOU SEE ME FLYING? A PORTRAIT OF
   TERRY SENDGRAFF
DANCING FROM THE INSIDE OUT
THE DANCING MAN: PEG LEG BATES
DEAF LIKE ME
DEBONAIR DANCERS
FUNDAMENTAL DANCE SIGNS
INTRODUCTION TO DANCE MEDICINE:
   KEEPING DANCERS DANCING
LOWER EXTREMITY DANCE MEDICINE: OR-
   THOPEDIC EXAMINATION WITH DR. WIL-
   LIAM HAMILTON

DOCUMENTARY PORTRAITS
THE ACHIEVERS: KATHERINE DUNHAM
ALICIA ALONSO: ALICIA
AMIR: AN AFGHAN REFUGEE MUSICIAN'S
   LIFE IN PESHAWAR, PAKISTAN
ANNA SOKOLOW, CHOREOGRAPHER
ANTONY TUDOR
ART AND DANCE
BALLERINA
BALLERINA: LYNN SEYMOUR
BALLET LEGENDS: THE KIROV'S NINEL KUR-
   GAPKINA
BALLET WITH EDWARD VILLELLA
BARBARA MORGAN: EVERYTHING IS
   DANCING
BART COOK: CHOREOGRAPHER
BARYSHNIKOV: THE DANCER AND THE
   DANCE

BEYOND THE MAINSTREAM: POSTMODERN
   DANCERS
BILL T. JONES: DANCING TO THE PROMISED
   LAND
BLUE SNAKE
BORN FOR HARD LUCK: PEG LEG SAM
   JACKSON
CAGE/CUNNINGHAM
CAN YOU SEE ME FLYING? A PORTRAIT OF
   TERRY SENDGRAFF
CARMEN (Bolshoi Ballet)
A CERTAIN AGE
CHARLES WEIDMAN: ON HIS OWN
CHIANG CHING: A DANCE JOURNEY
THE DANCE
DANCE AND MYTH: THE WORLD OF JEAN
   ERDMAN
DANCE: ANNA SOKOLOW'S *ROOMS*
DANCE BLACK AMERICA
DANCE IN AMERICA
DANCE MASKS: THE WORLD OF MARGARET
   SEVERN
THE DANCER
DANCING FOR MR. B.: SIX BALANCHINE
   BALLERINAS
DANCING GIRLS OF LAHORE
THE DANCING PROPHET
THE DANCING PROPHET
DANCING'S ALL OF YOU
DENISHAWN: THE BIRTH OF MODERN
   DANCE
DOLLY, LOTTE, AND MARIA
ELECTRIC BOOGIE
ELIOT FELD: ARTISTIC DIRECTOR
ERICK HAWKINS' AMERICA
ERIK BRUHN: ARTIST OF THE BALLET
THE EYE HEARS, THE EAR SEES
FALLING DOWN STAIRS
FONTEYN AND NUREYEV: THE PERFECT
   PARTNERSHIP
FORBIDDEN CITY, U.S.A
FULL CIRCLE: THE WORK OF DORIS CHASE
GALINA ULANOVA
GENIUS ON THE WRONG COAST
GERD BOHNER
GLEN TETLEY: PORTRAIT OF THE CHORE-
   OGRAPHER
GODUNOV: THE WORLD TO DANCE IN
HANYA: PORTRAIT OF A DANCE PIONEER
I AM A DANCER
IMAGE: A DANCER
IN A JAZZ WAY: A PORTRAIT OF MURA
   DEHN
IN CONCERT: PROFILE OF GUS GIORDANO
   JAZZ DANCE CHICAGO
INVOCATION: MAYA DEREN
JAZZ HOOFER: BABY LAURENCE
JEAN ERDMAN: OUT OF CHAOS, AMOR
JEAN-LOUIS BARRAULT: A MAN OF THE
   THEATRE
JOHN CRANKO
JOHN LINDQUIST: PHOTOGRAPHER OF
   DANCE
KAREN KAIN: BALLERINA
KATHERINE DUNHAM
THE LAST DANCING ISADORABLE
LAURETTA: MADONNA OF THE SENIOR CIT-
   IZEN SET
A LIFE IN TWO WORLDS: TAMASABURO
   BANDO
LUDMILA SEMENYAKA: BOLSHOI BALLE-
   RINA
MAKAROVA: IN A CLASS OF HER OWN

MAKAROVA RETURNS
MAN WHO DANCES: EDWARD VILLELLA
THE MARGOT FONTEYN STORY
MARTHA CLARKE: LIGHT AND DARK
MARTHA GRAHAM: THE DANCER RE-
   VEALED
MARY WIGMAN: MY LIFE IS DANCE
MARY WIGMAN: 1886–1973: *WHEN THE FIRE
   DANCES BETWEEN THE TWO POLES*
MERCE CUNNINGHAM AND COMPANY
MILDRED: THE FIRST 90 YEARS
MOMENT OF LIGHT: THE DANCE OF EVE-
   LYN HART
NATASHA
NIK AND MURRAY
NINA ANANIASHVILI AND INTERNATIONAL
   STARS
NO MAPS ON MY TAPS
OUT OF THE LIMELIGHT, HOME IN THE
   RAIN
PAUL TAYLOR AND COMPANY: AN ARTIST
   AND HIS WORK
PAVLOVA: A TRIBUTE TO A LEGENDARY
   BALLERINA
PETER MARTINS: A DANCER
PLISETSKAYA DANCES
A POEM OF DANCES ALSO KNOWN AS PLI-
   SETSKAYA: CARMEN
PORTRAIT OF AN ARTIST
PROCESSION: CONTEMPORARY DIREC-
   TIONS IN AMERICAN DANCE
RECKIN' SHOP "LIVE FROM BROOKLYN"
REFLECTIONS OF A DANCER: ALEXANDRA
   DANILOVA, PRIMA BALLERINA ASSOLUTA
REMEMBERING THELMA
REPETITIONS
RHYTHMETRON: THE DANCE THEATRE OF
   HARLEM WITH ARTHUR MITCHELL
RUDOLF NUREYEV
RUTH PAGE: AN AMERICAN ORIGINAL
SONGS UNWRITTEN: A TAP DANCER RE-
   MEMBERED
SUZANNE FARRELL: ELUSIVE MUSE
SYLVIE GUILLEM AT WORK
SYLVILLA: THEY DANCE TO HER DRUM
SYMPHONY IN D WORKSHOP
TERPSICHORE'S CAPTIVES
THEY ARE THEIR OWN GIFTS
THREE DANCES BY MARTHA CURTIS
TOUR EN L'AIR
TRISHA AND CARMEN
TWYLA THARP: MAKING TELEVISION
   DANCE
YURI GRIGOROVICH: MASTER OF THE BOL-
   SHOI

EUROPE
ALBANIAN COUNTRY FOLKDANCES
ALL THE BEST FROM RUSSIA
ANASTENARIA
BALLADE
BALLET COMES TO BRITAIN
BRITISH BALLET TODAY
DISCOVERING RUSSIAN FOLK MUSIC
DISCOVERING THE MUSIC OF THE MIDDLE
   AGES
GERMAN FOLK DANCES
LAMBACHEN and STEINHAUSER LANDLER
THE JVC/SMITHSONIAN FOLKWAYS VIDEO
   ANTHOLOGY OF MUSIC AND DANCE OF
   EUROPE
MUNICH COOPERS' DANCE

OTHER VOICES, OTHER SONGS: THE ARME-
NIANS
OTHER VOICES, OTHER SONGS: THE
GREEKS
RADL AND HATSCHO FROM JIHLAVA
RUMANIAN FOLK DANCES
RUSSIAN FOLK SONG AND DANCE
SLASK: NATIONAL FOLKLORE ENSEMBLE OF
POLAND
SOVIET ARMY CHORUS, BAND, AND DANCE
ENSEMBLE
SWORD DANCE AT ÜBERLINGEN
TRADITIONAL WHITSUN RITES OF THE KA-
LUSHARS
VILLAGE DANCES OF YUGOSLAVIA

EXPERIMENTAL
ACCUMULATION WITH TALKING PLUS
WATER MOTOR
ALMIRA 38
AMPHIBIAN
ANGEL OF TIME
ANIMA
ANNUNCIATION
ANTIGONE/RITES OF PASSION
ART OF MEMORY
AS SEEN ON TV
ASHES, MIST AND WIND BLOWN DUST
BALLET MECHANIQUE
BALLET ROBOTIQUE
BARBARA IS A VISION OF LOVELINESS
BESIDE HERSELF
BLACK AND WHITE
THE BLACK BOOTS
BLUE STUDIO: FIVE SEGMENTS
BOLERO and PICTURES AT AN EXHIBITION
BONE DREAM
BOOK OF SHADOWS
BRANCHES
BREAK
BRUSH AND BARRE: THE LIFE AND WORK
OF TOULOUSE-LAUTREC IN DANCE AND
MUSIC
BULLFIGHT
THE CATHERINE WHEEL
CAUGHT
CERBERUS
A CHAIRY TALE
CHANCE DANCE
CHANNELS/INSERTS
CHOICE CHANCE WOMAN DANCE
CHRYSALIS
CIRCLES I
CIRCLES II
CLINIC OF STUMBLE
CLOUD DANCE
COLOR IN DANCE
THE CONCERT
CUP/SAUCER/TWO DANCERS/RADIO
DANCE CHROMATIC
DANCE ELEVEN
DANCE FIVE
DANCE FOUR
DANCE FRAME
DANCE IN THE SUN
DANCE NINE
DANCE OF DARKNESS
DANCE SEVEN
DANCE TEN
DANCE THREE
DANCER FOR THE CORONATION
DANCING HANDS
DERVISH

DIALOGUE FOR CAMERAMAN AND DANCER
DIGITAL DANCE
DIONYSUS
DORIS CHASE DANCE SERIES: FOUR SOLOS
DORIS CHASE DANCE SERIES: THREE SOLOS
DUNE DANCE
ELEMENT
ELEMENT
ELLIS ISLAND
ENCOUNTER
ENDANCE
ETUDE IN FREE
EXCERPTS FROM "WITHOUT A PLACE"
FIELDS
FILM WITH THREE DANCERS
FOOTAGE
FOR THE SPIDER WOMAN
FOUR JOURNEYS INTO MYSTIC TIME
FOUR MOVES IN SPACE: A VIDEODANCE
SUITE
FRACTURED VARIATIONS and VISUAL
SHUFFLE
FROM AN ISLAND SUMMER
GEOGRAPHY AND METABOLISM
HAIL THE NEW PURITAN
HELICAL WIND
HERALD'S ROUND
HERE AND NOW WITH WATCHERS
HIROSHIMA
HOW DO YOU FEEL, EMPEROR'S NEW
CLOTHES, ROCKER
I WILL NOT BE SAD IN THIS WORLD
IMAGE: FLESH AND VOICE
IN THE BLINK OF AN EYE . . . (AMPHIBIAN
DREAMS) IF I COULD FLY I WOULD FLY
INDEX
INSIDE THE HOUSE OF FLOATING PAPER
INTROSPECTION
IT DOESN'T WAIT
JAZZ DANCE
JONATHAN AND THE ROCKER
JUMP
KA
KALAHARI
KINETIC COLOR IN DANCE
LAMBETH WALK: NAZI STYLE
LAMENT
LEE'S FERRY
LIES
LIGHT, PART 5
LIKE WIND IN MIRA'S HAIR
LIVE VIDEO DANCE
LODELA
LOOK! WE HAVE COME THROUGH
LOVERS FRAGMENTS
LUMIA I and II: THE DESIGN OF DANCE
LUMINAIRE
MALAMBO DEL SOL
MASS
MAYA DEREN: EXPERIMENTAL FILMS
MEDIATION ON VIOLENCE
MEHANG SUSAH
MERCE BY MERCE BY PAIK
MESHES OF THE AFTERNOON
MIXED DOUBLE
A MOMENT IN LOVE
MONEY
MOON
MOON GATES: THREE VERSIONS
MOTHER AND CHILD/50
MUSIC BOX
NARCISSUS
NEW YORK POST WAVE

NINE VARIATIONS ON A DANCE THEME
NOCTURNAE
THE OFFICIAL DOCTRINE
ONCE AGAIN
THE ONE I SEE
ONEIRO: IN THE SHADOW OF ISADORA
OP ODYSSEY
PARADES AND CHANGES
PARAFANGO
PARCELLE DE CIEL
PARIS
PAS DE DEUX
PERIL OF ANGELS
PILOBOLUS AND JOAN
PLANES, TRAINS, AUTOMOBILES
PRIVATE PERFORMANCE
PURE REMAINS
RITUAL IN TRANSFIGURED TIME
ROCKING ORANGE: THREE VERSIONS
ROSE BLOOD
RUBBLE DANCE LONG ISLAND CITY
SCAPE-MATES
SCENES FROM THE WASTE LAND
SECRET OF THE WATERFALL
SET PIECE
SHADES OF WIEGENLIED
SHE STORIES
SIXTEEN MILLIMETER EARRINGS
SMALL DISTANCES
SOLO
SONG OF VENEZUELA
SOUND OF ONE
SPACE CITY
SSS
STICKS ON THE MOVE
THE STONE DANCES
STOPPED IN HER TRACKS
A STUDY IN CHOREOGRAPHY FOR CAMERA
SYNCOPATIONS
TALL ARCHES III
TANAGRA, USA
TANGO
TEAK ROOM (AUTOBIOGRAPHY OF A
DANCER)
TEALIA
TECTONIC PLATES
TENTACLE
THAT MEANS I WANT TO GO HOME
THIRTY SECOND SPOTS
TORSE
TOTEM
TRAVELING LIGHT
A TRIO
TRIPLE DUO
TWENTY ONE WITH BILL T. JONES
TWO BAGATELLES
TWO BY LOUIS JOHNSON
UNDERTOW
UNREMITTING TENDERNESS
VARIATION II
VARIATIONS V
THE VERY EYE OF NIGHT
VESPUCCILAND: THE GREAT AND THE FREE
VOODOO CHILD
WALKING DANCE FOR ANY NUMBER
WATER MOTOR
THE WATER PIECES NO. 2
X-RAY EYES

FEATURES
ALL THAT JAZZ
AN AMERICAN IN PARIS
EL AMOR BRUJO

ANCHORS AWEIGH
ANITA: DANCES OF VICE
ANNA KARENINA
ANNIE
¡AY, CARMELA!
BABES IN ARMS
BABES ON BROADWAY
LE BAL
THE BALLERINAS
THE BAND WAGON
THE BARKLEYS OF BROADWAY
BATHING BEAUTY
THE BELLE OF NEW YORK
BLACK TIGHTS
BLOOD WEDDING
BODY ROCK
BORN TO DANCE
BREAKIN'
BRIGADOON
BROADWAY MELODY OF 1936
BROADWAY MELODY OF 1938
BROADWAY MELODY OF 1940
BYE BYE BIRDIE
CABARET
CAN-CAN
CAREFREE
CARMEN
CAROUSEL
A CHORUS LINE
THE COTTON CLUB
COVER GIRL
DADDY LONGLEGS
DAMES
A DAMSEL IN DISTRESS
THE DANCER
DANCERS
DEEP IN MY HEART
DIRTY DANCING
DU BARRY WAS A LADY
EASTER PARADE
FAME
FANTASIA
FASHIONS OF 1934
FIDDLER ON THE ROOF
FLAMENCO
FLASHDANCE
FLYING DOWN TO RIO
FOLLOW THE FLEET
FOOTLIGHT PARADE
FOOTLOOSE
FOR ME AND MY GAL
42ND STREET
FRENCH CANCAN
FUNNY FACE
FUNNY GIRL
THE GANG'S ALL HERE
THE GAY DIVORCEE
GOLD DIGGERS OF 1933
GOLD DIGGERS OF 1935
THE GOLDWYN FOLLIES
GREASE
HAIR
HALF A SIXPENCE
THE HARVEY GIRLS
HELLO DOLLY
HOLIDAY INN
HOLLYWOOD CLOWNS
INVITATION TO THE DANCE
ISADORA
ISADORA DUNCAN, THE BIGGEST DANCER
   IN THE WORLD
IT'S ALWAYS FAIR WEATHER
JUPITER'S DARLING

THE KING AND I
KISS ME KATE
LET'S DANCE
LIMELIGHT
LITTLEST REBEL
LOVELY TO LOOK AT
MEET ME IN ST. LOUIS
THE MUSIC MAN
MY FAIR LADY
THE NEXT STEP
NIJINSKY
OKLAHOMA!
OLIVER!
ON THE TOWN
ON YOUR TOES
THE PIRATE
PRINCESS TAM TAM
THE RED SHOES
THE REHEARSAL: A ROCK BALLET
ROSELAND
ROYAL WEDDING
SALSA
SATURDAY NIGHT FEVER
SECOND CHORUS
SEVEN BRIDES FOR SEVEN BROTHERS
1776
SHALL WE DANCE
SHOW BOAT
SILK STOCKINGS
SINGIN' IN THE RAIN
THE SKY'S THE LIMIT
SLEEPING BEAUTY (animated)
SOPHISTICATED LADIES
THE SOUND OF MUSIC
SOUTH PACIFIC
SPECTRE OF THE ROSE
STEPPING OUT
STORMY WEATHER
THE STORY OF VERNON AND IRENE CASTLE
STRICTLY BALLROOM
STRIKE UP THE BAND
SUMMER STOCK
SWEET CHARITY
SWING TIME
TAKE ME OUT TO THE BALL GAME
THE TALES OF HOFFMANN
TANGO BAR
TANGOS, THE EXILE OF GARDEL
TAP
LOS TARANTOS
THAT'S DANCING
THAT'S ENTERTAINMENT
THERE'S NO BUSINESS LIKE SHOW BUSINESS
THOUSANDS CHEER
TOP HAT
THE TURNING POINT
UNSETTLED DREAMS
VIVA LAS VEGAS
WEST SIDE STORY
WHITE NIGHTS
THE WIZ
YANKEE DOODLE DANDY
YOLANDA AND THE THIEF
YOU WERE NEVER LOVELIER
YOU'LL NEVER GET RICH
THE ZIEGFELD FOLLIES
ZIEGFELD GIRL
ZOU ZOU

FESTIVALS
AND STILL WE DANCE
DAMBIO FESTIVAL DANCE FROM CENTRAL
   SUDAN
DANCE FESTIVAL: MAKIRITARE

THE ERIK BRUHN GALA: WORLD BALLET
   COMPETITION
FESTIVAL IN COMMEMORATION OF THE
   DEAD
FESTIVAL OF THE DANCE
FOLKMOOT USA
GBAGBA MASK DANCE AT ASOUAKRO
HOLIDAY OF BALLET
KING KAMEHAMEHA HULA COMPETITION:
   14th AND 15th ANNUAL
THE MAGANA BAPTISTE SIXTH ANNUAL
   BELLY DANCE FESTIVAL
MAKAHIKI FESTIVAL
THE MARRAKESH FOLK FESTIVAL AND
   MORE!
MOIMO FESTIVAL DANCE FROM CENTRAL
   SUDAN
MUSIC, DANCE AND FESTIVAL AMONG THE
   WAIAPI INDIANS OF BRAZIL
NATIONAL FOLK FESTIVAL
NIGHT ON THE SEA OF GALILEE: ISRAEL
   FOLK DANCE FESTIVAL
NSAMBO DANCE FESTIVAL AT ISANGI
THE ROYAL DANCERS AND MUSICIANS
   FROM THE KINGDOM OF BHUTAN
WATER SPIRIT FESTIVAL
WORLD'S YOUNG BALLET

FLAMENCO
EL AMOR BRUJO
¡AY, CARMELA!
BLOOD WEDDING
CARMEN
COMPLETE FLAMENCO DANCE TECHNIQUE
FLAMENCO
FLAMENCO AT 5:15
FLAMENCO GITANO
FLAMENCOS DE LA LUZ
THE LOVERS OF TERUEL
SABICAS: EL MAESTRO DE FLAMENCO
SEVILLANAS
STRICTLY BALLROOM
LOS TARANTOS

FOLK
AFGHANISTAN DANCES
AFGHANISTAN: MEN'S DANCE WITH PAN-
   TOMIMIC INTERLUDE
AFRICA DANCES
AFRICAN MUSICIANS
ALBANIAN COUNTRY FOLKDANCES
ALL THE BEST FROM RUSSIA
AND STILL WE DANCE
ANIMAL DANCES: PHYE-MA-LEB AND SAN-
   GE
APPALACHIAN JOURNEY
ARAB DANCES FROM CENTRAL SUDAN
ARABIAN DANCES
ASIA SOCIETY COLLECTION
ASIA SOCIETY COLLECTION
ASLI ABADI SERIES
AWA ODORI
BALLADE
BALLET FOLKLÓRICO NACIONAL DE
   MÉXICO
BANGUZA TIMBILA
BINO-DANCE
BUCKDANCER
CANADIANS CAN DANCE
CARNIVAL OF RHYTHM
CHILDREN'S DANCES
CHINESE FOLK ARTS
CHINESE, KOREAN AND JAPANESE DANCE

THE CACHUCHA
CAPRICCIO ESPAGNOL (Spanish Fiesta)
CAVALCADE OF DANCE
DANZAS REGIONALES ESPAÑOLAS
FLAMENCO
FLAMENCO GITANO
INTERNATIONAL STYLE LATIN DANCING
JOSÉ GRECO: IN PERFORMANCE
MACHITO: A LATIN JAZZ LEGACY
SALSA
SPANISH FOLK DANCING

HULA
CHARMAINE'S HAWAIIAN/TAHITIAN VIDEO
   PEARLS
EVERYTHING YOU SHOULD KNOW ABOUT
   HAWAIIAN/TAHITIAN HULA
KING KAMEHAMEHA HULA COMPETITION:
   14th AND 15th ANNUAL
KUMU HULA: KEEPERS OF A CULTURE
MAKAHIKI FESTIVAL
YOU CAN DO THE HULA

ICE DANCE
ICE SKATING SHOWCASE: GREAT ROUTINES
   OF THE 1980S
MAGIC MEMORIES ON ICE
THE PLANETS
SLEEPING BEAUTY ON ICE
TORVILL AND DEAN: PATH TO PERFECTION

IMPROVISATION
THE ART OF BODY MOVEMENT
CHRYSALIS
DELILAH & SIROCCO . . . LIVE & WILD!
DUNE DANCE
GOLDBERG VARIATIONS
IMPROVISATION TO BANSURI FLUTE AND
   SEASCAPES
IMPROVISATIONS TO CHOPIN
IMPULSES
MOTION
MOVING PASTURES
POLYNESIAN DANCES FROM THE ELLICE IS-
   LANDS
TEACHING BEGINNING/ADVANCED DANCE
   IMPROVISATION

INDIA
ADRIENNE CHERIE INTERPRETS DANCES OF
   INDIA
CIRCLES: CYCLES KATHAK DANCE
DANCES OF INDIA: KATHAKALI
THE DELHI WAY
DISCOVERING THE MUSIC OF INDIA
HELEN: QUEEN OF THE NAUTCH GIRLS
INDIA CABARET
INDIA: HAUNTING PASSAGE
KALAKSHETRA: DEVOTION TO DANCE
KATHAK
MIRROR OF GESTURE
THE TEMPLE AND THE SWAN
VIBRANT SCULPTURE FROZEN DANCE

INSTRUCTIONAL
ADRIENNE CHERIE INTERPRETS DANCES OF
   INDIA
AL GILBERT PRESENTS
AMERICAN BALLROOM DANCING
ANATOMY AS A MASTER IMAGE IN TRAIN-
   ING DANCERS
ARGENTINE TANGO

ART AND MOTION
ART AND TECHNIQUE OF THE BALLET
THE ART OF BODY MOVEMENT
ASPECTS OF SYMMETRY
AUDITION POWER: PART I, KNOWING
   WHAT IT TAKES TO BE CHOSEN and PART
   II, WORKING THE HOLLYWOOD SYSTEM
IL BALLARINO: THE ART OF RENAISSANCE
   DANCE
BALLET CLASS
BALLET STUDY FILMS
THE BALLET WORKOUT
THE BALLET WORKOUT II
BALLROOM DANCING
BASIC PRINCIPLES OF POINTE/PARTNERING
BEGINNINGS
BELLY DANCE! MAGICAL MOTION
BELLY DANCE: SLOW MOVES; BELLY DANCE:
   FAST MOVES
BEYOND ROUTINE
BOB RIZZO'S BALLET CLASS FOR KIDS
BOB RIZZO'S 50 TURNS AND JUMPS
BOB RIZZO'S JAZZ CLASS FOR KIDS
THE BODY AS AN INSTRUMENT
BONNIE BIRD DEMONSTRATES GRAHAM
   TECHNIQUE
BOURNONVILLE BALLET TECHNIQUE
BROADWAY TAP
BRYONY BRIND'S BALLET: THE FIRST STEPS
BUILDING CHILDREN'S PERSONALITIES
   WITH CREATIVE DANCE
BUJONES IN CLASS
BUSTER COOPER WORKSHOP VIDEOS
BUSTER COOPER'S HOW TO TAP
THE CAROLINA SHAG
CHARMAINE'S HAWAIIAN/TAHITIAN VIDEO
   PEARLS
CHE CHE KULE: EXERCISES FOR KIDS
CHILDREN DANCE
CHILDREN WITH A DREAM
CHRISTY LANE'S LINE DANCING
CLASSICAL BALLET
THE COMPANY
COMPLETE FLAMENCO DANCE TECHNIQUE
CONTEMPORARY DANCE TRAINING
COSTUMING: SKIRT AND ACCESSORIES
CREATIVE MOVEMENT: A STEP TOWARDS
   INTELLIGENCE FOR CHILDREN AGES 2–8
CUNNINGHAM DANCE TECHNIQUE: ELE-
   MENTARY LEVEL
CUNNINGHAM DANCE TECHNIQUE: INTER-
   MEDIATE LEVEL
DANCE AND GROW
DANCE BABY DANCE
DANCE CLASS WITH SERENA
DANCE DESIGN: MOTION
DANCE DESIGN: SHAPING
DANCE DESIGN: SPACE
THE DANCE EXPERIENCE
DANCE IMAGING
THE DANCE INSTRUMENT
DANCE ON VIDEO: AN INTRODUCTION TO
   VIDEOTAPING DANCE
DANCE TO THE MUSIC
A DANCER'S GRAMMAR
DANCERS IN SCHOOL
DANCING THROUGH THE MAGIC EYE: A
   PORTRAIT OF VIRGINIA TANNER
DARE TO DANCE
DEBBIE DEE TAP TECHNIQUE
DEBONAIR DANCERS
DELILAH'S BELLY DANCE WORKSHOP
DELILAH'S COSTUME WORKSHOP

DISCOVERING YOUR EXPRESSIVE BODY
   WITH PEGGY HACKNEY
ECHOES OF JAZZ
EDDIE BROWN'S "SCIENTIFIC RHYTHM"
EIGHT GREAT STEPS TO CHOREOGRAPHY
THE ELEMENTS OF DANCE
THE ENDURING ESSENCE: THE TECHNIQUE
   AND CHOREOGRAPHY OF ISADORA DUN-
   CAN, REMEMBERED AND RECON-
   STRUCTED BY GEMZE DE LAPPE
ESSENTIALS OF TAP TECHNIQUE
EVERYTHING YOU SHOULD KNOW ABOUT
   HAWAIIAN/TAHITIAN HULA
A FANTASY GARDEN BALLET CLASS: BALLET
   INSTRUCTION WITH GARDEN CREA-
   TURES FOR PRE-SCHOOLERS
FANTASY OF FEET
FIRST STEPS
FLAMENCO AT 5:15
FLAMENCOS DE LA LUZ
FOUR DANCE CLASSES IN EGYPT
FRANK HATCHETT: INSPIRATION
FRANK HATCHETT PRESENTS SIZZLIN' HOT
   JAZZ
FRED ASTAIRE LEARN TO DANCE
FRENCH FOLK DANCING
FUNDAMENTAL DANCE SIGNS
GAMEEL GAMAL (Oh! Beautiful Dancer)
GERMAN FOLK DANCES
HAVE A FLING WITH DANCE
HE MAKES ME FEEL LIKE DANCIN'
HOW TO IMPROVE YOUR BALLET TECH-
   NIQUE/PIROUETTES/POINTE TECHNIQUE
   WITH RONI MAHLER
HOW TO MOVE BETTER
HUMPHREY TECHNIQUE
I CAN DANCE: INTRODUCTION TO BALLET
   FOR CHILDREN
I HATE TO EXERCISE, I LOVE TO TAP
ILONA VERA'S BALLET CLASS
INSTRUCTIONAL BALLET TAPES DIRECTED
   BY DOROTHY LISTER
INTENSIVE COURSE IN ELEMENTARY LABA-
   NOTATION)
INTERNATIONAL STYLE LATIN DANCING
INTERNATIONAL STYLE MODERN DANCING
INTRODUCTION TO BALLROOM DANCING
AN INTRODUCTION TO BELLY DANCE
IROQUOIS SOCIAL DANCE I AND II
ISADORA DUNCAN: TECHNIQUE AND CHO-
   REOGRAPHY
ISADORA DUNCAN: TECHNIQUE AND REP-
   ERTORY
JAZZ
JAZZ DANCE CLASS 1989
JAZZ DANCE CLASS WITH GUS GIORDANO
JAZZ DANCE WITH CHRISTY LANE
JAZZ FOR KIDZ: PROGRESSIONS AND COM-
   BINATIONS WITH BOB RIZZO
JAZZ JAZZ JAZZ
JITTERBUG: BEGINNERS! and JITTERBUG 2:
   INTERMEDIATE
JUST FOR FUN
KALAKSHETRA: DEVOTION TO DANCE
KATHY'S DANCE
KEMOKO SANO TEACHES AFRICAN DANCE
   FROM THE REPUBLIC OF GUINEA
KICKER DANCIN' TEXAS STYLE: HOW TO DO
   THE TOP TEN COUNTRY AND WESTERN
   DANCES LIKE A TEXAS COWBOY
KIT'S KIDS
LEARN HOW TO DANCE

LESTER HORTON TECHNIQUE: THE WARM UP
LINDY VIDEOTAPES
LUIGI
MIDEASTERN DANCE: AN INTRODUCTION TO BELLY DANCE
MIME TECHNIQUE: PART I
MOVEMENT EXPLORATION: WHAT AM I
MOVEMENT IN CLASSIC DANCE: THE PELVIC AREA
OLD TIME DANCES
AN ORIGINAL BILL ROBINSON VIDEO
AN ORIGINAL JULIA MAYER VIDEO
PARTNERING FOR THE THEATRE ARTS
POINTE BY POINT
PREPARING TO DANCE
THE PRINCE OF BROADWAY
RHYTHM 'N RED SHOES
SCHOOL OF AMERICAN BALLET
SEE-DO PRODUCTIONS: BALLROOM VIDEOS FOR INSTRUCTION AND COMPETITIONS
SHAPE
SNAKE DANCE TEACHER DANCE
SPANISH FOLK DANCING
STEP INTO BALLET WITH WAYNE SLEEP
STEPS IN A NEW DIRECTION
SWAYZE DANCING
TAKE A MASTER CLASS WITH DAVID HOWARD
TANGO! A MASTER CLASS WITH THE DINZELS
TAP
TAP ALONG WITH TOMMY
TAP DANCING FOR BEGINNERS
TAP DANCING: INTERMEDIATE AND ADVANCED
TEACHING BEGINNING/ADVANCED DANCE IMPROVISATION
TIME
VEDA SEREEM'S QUALITY OF BELLY DANCING
VIDEO DICTIONARY OF CLASSICAL BALLET
VROTSOS VIDEOS
WATCHING BALLET
THE WAVE: ECSTATIC DANCE FOR BODY AND SOUL
THE WOMAN IN THE SHOE
YOU CAN DO THE HULA

INTERNATIONAL
DANCES OF THE WORLD
DANCING
ETHNIC DANCE AROUND THE WORLD
LACHO DROM
NATIONAL FOLK FESTIVAL
STEP STYLE
A TIME TO DANCE

JAPAN
AWA ODORI
BUTOH: BODY ON THE EDGE OF CRISIS
COURT DANCE: TAIHEIRAKU and ETENRAKU
GAGAKU "BAIRO" IN TWO STYLES
INVITATION TO KABUKI
JAPAN: THE FROZEN MOMENT
KABUKI: CLASSIC THEATRE OF JAPAN
KAZE-NO-KO
A LIFE IN TWO WORLDS: TAMASABURO BANDO
NOH DRAMA
THE ONDEKO-ZA IN SADO
TANKO BUSHI: A JAPANESE FOLK DANCE

TO MOVE IN BEAUTY: THE KABUKI TRADITION
TORCHES OF TODAIJI

JAZZ
ALL THAT JAZZ
BALLET IN JAZZ
BOB RIZZO'S JAZZ CLASS FOR KIDS
BREAKIN'
CALL OF THE DRUM: NAPOLEONIC DANCES
CELEBRATION OF ROCK
DANCE BABY DANCE
THE DANCE EXPERIENCE
DANCE TO THE MUSIC
DANCE TO THE MUSIC
A DANCE TRIBUTE TO MICHAEL JORDAN
ECHOES OF JAZZ
FLASHDANCE
FOOTLOOSE
FRANK HATCHETT: INSPIRATION
FRANK HATCHETT PRESENTS SIZZLIN' HOT JAZZ
HAVE A FLING WITH DANCE
IN A JAZZ WAY: A PORTRAIT OF MURA DEHN
IN CONCERT: PROFILE OF GUS GIORDANO JAZZ DANCE CHICAGO
JAZZ
JAZZ DANCE CLASS 1989
JAZZ DANCE CLASS WITH GUS GIORDANO
THE JAZZ DANCE JIGSAW
JAZZ DANCE WITH CHRISTY LANE
JAZZ FOR KIDZ: PROGRESSIONS AND COMBINATIONS WITH BOB RIZZO
JAZZ JAZZ JAZZ
JAZZ PARADES: FEET DON'T FAIL ME NOW
JUST FOR FUN
KIT'S KIDS
LUIGI
MACHITO: A LATIN JAZZ LEGACY
MILT AND HONI
MUSIC BOX
NAGRIN VIDEOTAPE LIBRARY OF DANCE
THE NEXT STEP
NOT FOR LOVE ALONE
PRINCESS TAM TAM
RAG TO ROCK TO DISCO
REALITY OF A DREAMER: RIVER NORTH DANCE COMPANY
REQUIEM FOR A SLAVE
RHYTHM 'N RED SHOES
SOPHISTICATED LADIES
STREETCAR: A DANCE OF DESIRE
TAL FARLOW
THAT'S DANCING
THAT'S ENTERTAINMENT
THE VALLEY OF XEBRON
THE WIZ
ZOU ZOU

LATIN AMERICA
ARUANA MASKED DANCES
BAHIA: AFRICA IN THE AMERICAS
BALLET FOLKLÓRICO NACIONAL DE MÉXICO
BERIMBAU
CARNIVAL OF RHYTHM
CREATION OF THE WORLD: A SAMBA OPERA
DANCE FESTIVAL: MAKIRITARE
DISCOVERING THE MUSIC OF LATIN AMERICA
FOLKLÓRICO
GHOST DANCES
HARVEST DANCES

HIP HOP SP
THE JVC/SMITHSONIAN FOLKWAYS VIDEO ANTHOLOGY OF MUSIC AND DANCE OF THE AMERICAS
MEXICAN DANCES
MUSIC, DANCE AND FESTIVAL AMONG THE WAIAPI INDIANS OF BRAZIL
THE MUSIC OF THE DEVIL, THE BEAR AND THE CONDOR
ORISUN OMI (THE WELL): PROLOGUE TO THE YORUBA CYCLE
PALENQUE: UN CANTO
ROUTES OF RHYTHM WITH HARRY BELAFONTE
TANGO
THE TANGO IS ALSO A HISTORY
THEATRE MEETS RITUAL
XINGUANA: ABORIGINES OF SOUTH AMERICA

MARTIAL ARTS
BERIMBAU
CERBERUS
KALYIAN
KARATE RAP
SOUND OF ONE

MIDDLE EAST
ANCIENT ART OF BELLY DANCING
ARAB DANCES FROM CENTRAL SUDAN
ARABIAN DANCES
BASIC SWORD
DANCE IMAGING
DELILAH & SIROCCO . . . LIVE & WILD!
DISCOVERING THE MUSIC OF THE MIDDLE EAST
EVA AS DANCER
FAN TECHNIQUES FOR ORIENTAL DANCE
FOUR DANCE CLASSES IN EGYPT
IBRAHIM FARRAH PRESENTS RARE GLIMPSES: DANCES FROM THE MIDDLE EAST, VOLUME I
LIFTING THE VEIL OF TIME
A LITTLE FOR MY HEART AND A LITTLE FOR MY GOD: A MUSLIM WOMEN'S ORCHESTRA
MOROCCO AND THE CASBAH DANCE EXPERIENCE
MOROCCO, BODY AND SOUL
THE NATIONAL FOLK TROUPE OF EGYPT (FIRQUA KAWMIYYA)
NIGHT ON THE SEA OF GALILEE: ISRAEL FOLK DANCE FESTIVAL
REAL EGYPTIAN FOLK
STARS OF EGYPTIAN DANCE
TURKISH BELLY DANCE
TURKISH FOLK DANCES AT PRIZEN
VEIL TECHNIQUES IN ORIENTAL DANCE
ZAR AND FLOORWORK

MODERN
ACCUMULATION WITH TALKING PLUS WATER MOTOR
ACROBATS OF GOD
ADVENTURES IN ASSIMILATION
AILEY DANCES
AIR FOR THE G STRING
AIRDANCE and LANDINGS
AIRWAVES
ALMIRA 38
ALVIN AILEY: MEMORIES AND VISIONS
AMPHIBIAN
ANTIGONE/RITES OF PASSION

YOU WERE NEVER LOVELIER
YOU'LL NEVER GET RICH
THE ZIEGFELD FOLLIES
ZIEGFELD GIRL

NATIVE AMERICANS
ALWAYS FOR PLEASURE
AMERICAN INDIAN SOCIAL DANCING
BARBARA MORGAN: EVERYTHING IS
    DANCING
BEAR DANCE
CIRCLE OF THE SUN
CROOKED BEAK OF HEAVEN
THE CROW/SHOSHONE SUNDANCE
DANZANTE
DISCOVERING AMERICAN INDIAN MUSIC
DREAM DANCES OF THE KASHIA POMO:
    THE BOLE-MARU RELIGIOUS WOMEN'S
    DANCES
THE DRUMMAKER
HAA SHAGOON
HOPI KACHINAS
HUPA INDIAN WHITE DEERSKIN DANCE
IN THE LAND OF THE WAR CANOES
INDIANS OF THE PLAINS, SUNDANCE CERE-
    MONY
IROQUOIS SOCIAL DANCE I AND II
ITAM HAKIM ITOPIIT (We Someone, the Hopi)
KASHIA MEN'S DANCES: SOUTHWESTERN
    POMO INDIANS
LIVE AND REMEMBER (Wo Kiksuye)
LONGEST TRAIL
MEDICINE FIDDLE
MESQUAKIE
NAVAJO NIGHT DANCES
POW WOW!
THE SUNRISE DANCE
VISION DANCE

NATURE
BEEHIVE
DANCES OF MEXICO: ANIMAL ORIGINS
INDICATIONS OF DISTANCE AND DIREC-
    TION IN THE HONEYBEE: ROUND AND
    WAGGLE DANCE

NIGHTCLUB
CABARET
CAN-CAN
COVER GIRL
FORBIDDEN CITY, U.S.A
FRENCH CAN-CAN
GAITÉ PARISIENNE
GAITÉ PARISIENNE
THE GOLDEN AGE
HELEN: QUEEN OF THE NAUTCH GIRLS
INDIA CABARET
PARISIAN FOLLIES

NOTATION
CHILDREN ON THE HILL
FALLING OFF THE BACK PORCH
INTENSIVE COURSE IN ELEMENTARY LABA-
    NOTATION
NOT FOR LOVE ALONE
SCENES FROM THE MUSIC OF CHARLES IVES
WHAT'S REMEMBERED

OPERA
HERITAGE OF CHINESE OPERA
THE SORCERESS: KIRI TE KANAWA

PANTOMIME
ART OF SILENCE: PANTOMIMES WITH MAR-
    CEL MARCEAU
BALLET ENTERS THE WORLD STAGE
DEAF LIKE ME
DOLLY, LOTTE, AND MARIA
EDO: DANCE AND PANTOMIME
HOLLYWOOD CLOWNS
JEAN-LOUIS BARRAULT: A MAN OF THE
    THEATRE
JEAN-LOUIS BARRAULT: THE BODY SPEAKS
KAZE-NO-KO
LIES
MARCEAU ON MIME
MARCEL MARCEAU OU L'ART DU MIME
THE MIME
THE MIME OF MARCEL MARCEAU
MIME TECHNIQUE: PART I
PANTOMIMES
REINCATNATED

RELIGIOUS/RITUAL
AFRICAN CARVING: A DOGON KANAGA
    MASK
AFRICAN RELIGIOUS AND RITUAL DANCES
ANASTENARIA
BALI: ISLE OF TEMPLES
BALI: THE MASK OF RANGDA
BEDHAYA: THE SACRED DANCE
BEHIND THE MASK
BELL DANCE FOR THE CONJURATION OF
    THE SACRED BUSH COW
CIRCUMCISION
CULTIC DANCES IN A BUDDHIST PAGODA
    NEAR HUE
DANCES AND RITES AFTER THE DEATH OF A
    TRIBAL CHIEF
DANZANTE
DREAM DANCES OF THE KASHIA POMO:
    THE BOLE-MARU RELIGIOUS WOMEN'S
    DANCES
FESTIVAL IN COMMEMORATION OF THE
    DEAD
JESUS, SON OF MAN
KONTAKION: A SONG OF PRAISE
LORD OF THE DANCE/DESTROYER OF ILLU-
    SION
MA'BUGI: TRANCE OF THE TORAJA
MAGDALENE
MAN BLONG CUSTOM
MOURNING CELEBRATIONS FROM ETHI-
    OPIA
MOURNING DANCES FROM CHAD
OBSEQUIES FOR DECEASED REGIONAL
    CHIEFTAINS
PRAISE HOUSE
ST. FRANCIS
THE SUNRISE DANCE
THE THREE WORLDS OF BALI
TZADDIK
VIBRANT SCULPTURE FROZEN DANCE
VOICES OF THE ORISHAS
ZULU MEDICINE DANCES

SOCIAL
¡A BAILAR! THE JOURNEY OF A LATIN
    DANCE COMPANY
ARGENTINE TANGO
LE BAL
THE CALL OF THE JITTERBUG
THE CAROLINA SHAG

CREATION OF THE WORLD: A SAMBA OPERA
DELI COMMEDIA
DIRTY DANCING
ELECTRIC BOOGIE
THE FLAPPER STORY
FRANKIE MANNING'S BIRTHDAY VIDEO
FRED ASTAIRE LEARN TO DANCE
IN HEAVEN THERE IS NO BEER?
JITTERBUG: BEGINNERS! and JITTERBUG 2:
    INTERMEDIATE
JITTERING JITTERBUGS
LINDY VIDEOTAPES
OLD TIME DANCES
ROUTES OF RHYTHM WITH HARRY BELA-
    FONTE
SATURDAY NIGHT FEVER
SOCIAL AND COMEDY DANCES
SUE'S LEG: REMEMBERING THE THIRTIES:
    TWYLA THARP AND DANCERS
SYNCOPATED MELODIES
TANGO! A MASTER CLASS WITH THE DIN-
    ZELS
TANGO: A SPECTACULAR PERFORMANCE!
TANGO BAR
THE TANGO IS ALSO A HISTORY

TAP
THE BELLE OF NEW YORK
BROADWAY MELODY OF 1936
BROADWAY MELODY OF 1938
BROADWAY MELODY OF 1940
BROADWAY TAP
BUSTER COOPER'S HOW TO TAP
THE COTTON CLUB
A DAMSEL IN DISTRESS
THE DANCE EXPERIENCE
DANCE TO THE MUSIC
THE DANCING MAN: PEG LEG BATES
DANCING THRU
DANCING'S ALL OF YOU
DEBBIE DEE TAP TECHNIQUE
ECHOES OF JAZZ
EDDIE BROWN'S "SCIENTIFIC RHYTHM"
ESSENTIALS OF TAP TECHNIQUE
FLYING DOWN TO RIO
FOLLOW THE FLEET
FOR DANCERS
THE GAY DIVORCEE
HONI COLES, THE CLASS ACT OF TAP
I HATE TO EXERCISE, I LOVE TO TAP
JAZZ HOOFER: BABY LAURENCE
LET'S SCUFFLE
LITTLEST REBEL
MASTERS OF TAP
MILT AND HONI
NO MAPS ON MY TAPS
AN ORIGINAL BILL ROBINSON VIDEO
AN ORIGINAL JULIA MAYER VIDEO
THE PRINCE OF BROADWAY
PUTTIN' ON THE RITZ
SONGS UNWRITTEN: A TAP DANCER RE-
    MEMBERED
STEPPING OUT
SWING TIME
TAP
TAP
TAP ALONG WITH TOMMY
THE TAP DANCE KID
TAP DANCING FOR BEGINNERS
TAP DANCING: INTERMEDIATE AND AD-
    VANCED

Choreographers Index

ABBOTT, TOM
FIDDLER ON THE ROOF

ADDY, YACUB
DANCE LIKE A RIVER: ODADAA! DRUM-
MING AND DANCING IN THE U.S.

ADOMINAS, SANDRA
ANNUNCIATION

AILEY, ALVIN
AILEY DANCES
ALVIN AILEY: MEMORIES AND VISIONS
AMERICAN BALLET THEATRE: A CLOSE-UP
IN TIME
DANCE BLACK AMERICA
AN EVENING WITH ALVIN AILEY AMERICAN
DANCE THEATRE1295. A TRIBUTE TO
ALVIN AILEY

AKILOV, ISAKAR
AN INTRODUCTION TO UZBEK DANCE

ALEKSIDZE, GEORGIY
MEDEA

ALEXANDER, ROD
CAROUSEL

ALONSO, ALBERTO
ALICIA ALONSO: ALICIA
CARMEN (Bolshoi Ballet)
A POEM OF DANCES ALSO KNOWN AS PLI-
SETSKAYA: CARMEN

ALONSO, ALICIA
GISÈLLE (Ballet Nacional de Cuba)

ALSTON, RICHARD
PULCINELLA/SOLDAT

ALTON, ROBERT
THE BARKLEYS OF BROADWAY
BATHING BEAUTY
THE BELLE OF NEW YORK
EASTER PARADE
THE HARVEY GIRLS
THE PIRATE
SHOW BOAT
THERE'S NO BUSINESS LIKE SHOW BUSINESS
YOU'LL NEVER GET RICH
THE ZIEGFELD FOLLIES

ALVEBERG, KJERSTI
ASHES, MIST AND WIND BLOWN DUST

AMAGATSU, USHIO
BUTOH: BODY ON THE EDGE OF CRISIS

ANASTOS, PETER
BALLET RUSE

ANDERSON, JOHN MURRAY
BATHING BEAUTY

ANWAR, ANDREA
BRINGING TO LIGHT

ARAÍZ, OSCAR
TANGO
TANGO: A SPECTACULAR PERFORMANCE!

ARBEAU
LE GRATIE D'AMORE (The Graces of Love)

ARBUS, LOREEN
ARGENTINE TANGO

ARGENTINITA
CAPRICCIO ESPAGNOL (Spanish Fiesta)

ARMITAGE, KAROLE
FROM AN ISLAND SUMMER
PARAFANGO

ARPINO, GERALD
ATTITUDES IN DANCE
DANCE: ROBERT JOFFREY BALLET

ARTHA, TJOK GDE ARSA
SCENES FROM THE WASTE LAND

ASHIKAWA, YOKO
BUTOH: BODY ON THE EDGE OF CRISIS

ASHTON, FREDERICK
BALLERINA: LYNN SEYMOUR
BALLET
BALLET FAVORITES
BRITISH BALLET TODAY
CELEBRATION: A HISTORY OF THE SADLER'S
WELLS ROYAL BALLET
CURTAIN UP
ENIGMA VARIATIONS
AN EVENING WITH THE ROYAL BALLET
LA FILLE MAL GARDÉE (Royal Ballet)
FONTEYN AND NUREYEV: THE PERFECT
PARTNERSHIP
I AM A DANCER
THE MAGNIFICENT BEGINNING
NATASHA
OUT OF THE LIMELIGHT, HOME IN THE
RAIN
THE ROMANTIC BALLET
THE ROYAL BALLET
THE TALES OF BEATRIX POTTER
THE TALES OF HOFFMANN
TRAILBLAZERS OF MODERN DANCE
THE TURNING POINT

ASTAIRE, FRED
THE BAND WAGON
THE BARKLEYS OF BROADWAY

BROADWAY MELODY OF 1940
DADDY LONGLEGS
A DAMSEL IN DISTRESS
EASTER PARADE
FLYING DOWN TO RIO
FOLLOW THE FLEET
FUNNY FACE
THE GAY DIVORCEE
HOLIDAY INN
ROBERTA
SECOND CHORUS
THE SKY'S THE LIMIT
THE STORY OF VERNON AND IRENE CASTLE
SWING TIME
TOP HAT
YOU WERE NEVER LOVELIER

ATKINS, CHOLLY
EVERYBODY DANCE NOW

BALANCHINE, GEORGE
AMERICAN BALLET THEATRE AT THE MET
THE BALANCHINE ESSAYS: ARABESQUE
BALLET WITH EDWARD VILLELLA
CHOREOGRAPHY BY BALANCHINE
DANCE: NEW YORK CITY BALLET
DANCE THEATRE OF HARLEM
DAVIDSBÜNDLERTANZE
THE EBB AND FLOW
THE FOUR TEMPERAMENTS
THE GOLDWYN FOLLIES
HE MAKES ME FEEL LIKE DANCIN'
MAN WHO DANCES: EDWARD VILLELLA
NATASHA
THE NUTCRACKER (New York City Ballet)
ON YOUR TOES
PETER MARTINS: A DANCER
SCHOOL OF AMERICAN BALLET
STRAVINSKY
WATCHING BALLET

BANDO, TAMASABURO
STRUGGLE FOR HOPE

BANGOURA, HAMIDOU
AFRICA DANCES

BARYSHNIKOV, MIKHAIL
BALLET FAVORITES
DANCERS
DON QUIXOTE (American Ballet Theatre)
THE NUTCRACKER (American Ballet Theatre)
WHITE NIGHTS

BAUSCH, PINA
WHAT DO PINA BAUSCH AND HER DANCES
DO IN WUPPERTAL?

BEALS, MARGARET
MOVING PASTURES
RAGAS FOR SWAMI SATCHIDANANDA

TEAK ROOM (AUTOBIOGRAPHY OF A
    DANCER)
WILD SWANS IN EPITAPH AND MADHONOR

BEATTY, TALLEY
AN EVENING WITH ALVIN AILEY AMERICAN
    DANCE THEATRE

BECK, ELIZABETH
THE ROYAL DANISH BALLET 1902–1906

BECK, HANS
DANCING BOURNONVILLE

BÉJART, MAURICE
THE ART OF THE TWENTIETH CENTURY
    BALLET
BOLERO
BUJONES: IN HIS IMAGE
NATASHA
STUTTGART BALLET: THE MIRACLE LIVES
WHITE NIGHT OF DANCE IN LENINGRAD
WORLD'S YOUNG BALLET

BELILOVE, LORI
ONEIRO: IN THE SHADOW OF ISADORA

BERGER, ROBERT
GEE, OFFICER KRUPKE

BERGSOHN, ISA
ADOLESCENCE OF BALLET

BERKELEY, BUSBY
AMERICAN MUSICALS: FAMOUS PRODUC-
    TION NUMBERS
BABES IN ARMS
BABES ON BROADWAY
DAMES
FASHIONS OF 1934
FOOTLIGHT PARADE
42ND STREET
THE GANG'S ALL HERE
GOLD DIGGERS OF 1933
GOLD DIGGERS OF 1935
STRIKE UP THE BAND
ZIEGFELD GIRL

BERNHARD, SUE
THE WATER PIECES
THE WATER PIECES NO. 2

BERNSTEIN, BONNIE
DANCING FREE

BETTIS, VALERIE
THE DESPERATE HEART
GREAT PERFORMANCE IN DANCE

BILLINGS, JACK
DANCING THRU

BIRCH, PATRICIA
GREASE

BIRRINGER, JOHANNES
LOVERS FRAGMENTS

BLAIR, DAVID
AMERICAN BALLET THEATRE: A CLOSE-UP
    IN TIME
GISÈLLE (American Ballet Theatre)

BORGATTA, MIA
MEHANG SUSAH

BORLIN, JEAN
ENTR'ACTE

BOURNONVILLE, AUGUST
BALLET ENTERS THE WORLD STAGE
BOURNONVILLE BALLET TECHNIQUE
DANCING BOURNONVILLE
HOW BALLET BEGAN
I AM A DANCER
THE KIROV BALLET: CLASSIC BALLET NIGHT
NAPOLI
NINA ANANIASHVILI AND INTERNATIONAL
    STARS
THE ROYAL DANISH BALLET 1902–1906
LA SYLPHIDE (Royal Danish Ballet)
WORLD'S YOUNG BALLET

BOYARCHIKOV, NIKOLAI
SWAN LAKE (Russian State Perm Ballet)

BOYCE, JOHANNA
RETRACING STEPS: AMERICAN DANCE
    SINCE POSTMODERNISM

BRADLEY, LARRY
BOYCEBALL

BREAUX, MARC
THE SOUND OF MUSIC

BRIDGMAN, ART
A DANCE FOR 15 PREGNANT WOMEN

BRIGGS, BUNNY
NO MAPS ON MY TAPS

BROMBERG, ELLEN
DANCING ON THE EDGE
FROM SAN FRANCISCO: DANCING ON THE
    EDGE

BROWN, DEBRA
SATIE AND SUZANNE

BROWN, TRISHA
ACCUMULATION WITH TALKING PLUS
    WATER MOTOR
AEROS
BEYOND THE MAINSTREAM: POSTMODERN
    DANCERS
MAKING DANCES: SEVEN POSTMODERN
    CHOREOGRAPHERS
TRISHA AND CARMEN
WATER MOTOR

BRUCE, CHRISTOPHER
AN EVENING WITH THE BALLET RAMBERT
GHOST DANCES

BRUHN, ERIK
BOLD STEPS

BUFALINO, BRENDA
ESSENTIALS OF TAP TECHNIQUE
TWO TAKES ON TAP

BUIRGE, SUSAN
PARCELLE DE CIEL

BURRILL, JENNY
ANGEL OF TIME

BUTLER, JOHN
A CHOREOGRAPHER AT WORK: JOHN
    BUTLER
ECHOES OF JAZZ

BYRD, DONALD
THE NEXT STEP
UNSETTLED DREAMS

CAROSO
IL BALLARINO: THE ART OF RENAISSANCE
    DANCE
LE GRATIE D'AMORE (The Graces of Love)

CARSON, MICHAEL A.
HELP ME TO DREAM

CARTER, ALAN
THE DANCE

CARTER, WILLIAM
IN A REHEARSAL ROOM

CARTWRIGHT, HILARY
PAVLOVA: A TRIBUTE TO A LEGENDARY
    BALLERINA

CASTLE, GENE
I HATE TO EXERCISE, I LOVE TO TAP

CASTLE, NICK
ROYAL WEDDING
STORMY WEATHER
SUMMER STOCK

CECCHETTI, ENRICO
BALLET STUDY FILMS
COPPÉLIA: ACT II
CURTAIN UP

CERNIK, EVA
DANCE IMAGING

CHABUKIANI, VAKHTANG
LA BAYADÈRE (Kirov Ballet)
PLISETSKAYA DANCES

CHAMBERS, BRENDA
MALAMBO DEL SOL

CHAMPION, GOWER
JUPITER'S DARLING

CHAMPIONS, THE
CHAMPIONS

CHANDRA OF DAMASCUS
BASIC SWORD
FAN TECHNIQUES FOR ORIENTAL DANCE
VEIL TECHNIQUES IN ORIENTAL DANCE
ZAR AND FLOORWORK

DE VALOIS, NINETTE
BALLET COMES TO BRITAIN
CHECKMATE
THE RAKE'S PROGRESS

DEAN, LAURA
BEYOND THE MAINSTREAM: POSTMODERN
    DANCERS
BILLBOARDS
TYMPANI

DECOUFLE, PHILIPPE
JUMP

DELANGHE, GAY
ALMIRA 38

DELILAH
DANCE DELILAH, DANCE!
DANCE TO THE GREAT MOTHER
DELILAH & SIROCCO . . . LIVE & WILD!
DELILAH'S BELLY DANCE WORKSHOP
DELILAH'S COSTUME WORKSHOP

DEREN, MAYA
MEDIATION ON VIOLENCE
MESHES OF THE AFTERNOON
RITUAL IN TRANSFIGURED TIME
A STUDY IN CHOREOGRAPHY FOR CAMERA

DESROSIERS, ROBERT
BLUE SNAKE
INNER RHYTHM
RAVEL

DEVI, RUKMINI
KALAKSHETRA: DEVOTION TO DANCE

DEVIVO, KERRY
PLANES, TRAINS, AUTOMOBILES
PURE REMAINS
SHADES OF WIEGENLIED

DIAMOND, EMMA
SIX METAMORPHOSES

DIBIA, I WAYAN
BODY TJAK

DINIZULU, NINA
DINIZULU AND HIS AFRICAN DRUMMERS,
    DANCERS AND SINGERS

DITCHBURN, ANN
A MOVING PICTURE

DOLIN, ANTON
THE KIROV BALLET: CLASSIC BALLET NIGHT
PAS DE QUATRE and THE CHARIOTEER
THE ROMANTIC ERA

DONAHUE, JACK
BATHING BEAUTY

DONEN, STANLEY
ANCHORS AWEIGH
COVER GIRL
IT'S ALWAYS FAIR WEATHER
ON THE TOWN

SINGIN' IN THE RAIN
TAKE ME OUT TO THE BALL GAME
THOUSANDS CHEER

DOVE, ULYSSES
A TRIBUTE TO ALVIN AILEY

DOW, SHERRY ZUNKER
REALITY OF A DREAMER: RIVER NORTH
    DANCE COMPANY

DRIVER, SENTA
DANCE PRELUDES

DUDLEY, JANE
HARMONICA BREAKDOWN

DUNAS, WILLIAM
FEATHERS

DUNCAN, ISADORA
THE ENDURING ESSENCE: THE TECHNIQUE
    AND CHOREOGRAPHY OF ISADORA DUN-
    CAN, REMEMBERED AND RECON-
    STRUCTED BY GEMZE DE LAPPE
INVENTION IN DANCE
ISADORA DUNCAN: MOVEMENT FROM THE
    SOUL
ISADORA DUNCAN: TECHNIQUE AND CHO-
    REOGRAPHY
ISADORA DUNCAN: TECHNIQUE AND REP-
    ERTORY
THE LEGACY OF THE CHOREOGRAPHY OF
    ISADORA DUNCAN
TANAGRA, USA
TRAILBLAZERS OF MODERN DANCE

DUNCAN, MARIA-THERESA
THE LAST DANCING ISADORABLE

DUNHAM, KATHERINE
CARNIVAL OF RHYTHM
THE DANCE

DUNN, DOUGLAS
DANCE: NEW DIRECTIONS
MAKING DANCES: SEVEN POSTMODERN
    CHOREOGRAPHERS
RUBBLE DANCE LONG ISLAND CITY
SECRET OF THE WATERFALL
TRIPLE DUO

DUNN, JUDITH
INDEX
THE OFFICIAL DOCTRINE

DURANG, JOHN
THE EBB AND FLOW

EARLE, DAVID
RAVEL
ROMEOS AND JULIETS

ECKERT, RINDE
DANCING ON THE EDGE
FROM SAN FRANCISCO: DANCING ON THE
    EDGE

EIKO AND KOMA
BONE DREAM
LAMENT

TENTACLE
UNDERTOW

ELIZARIEV, V
NINA ANANIASHVILI AND INTERNATIONAL
    STARS

ELKINS, DOUG
IT DOESN'T WAIT

ENGLUND, SORELLA
ORFEUS AND JULIE

ERDMAN, JEAN
DANCE AND MYTH: THE WORLD OF JEAN
    ERDMAN
JEAN ERDMAN: OUT OF CHAOS, *AMOR*

ESTNER, ROBERT
STEPS IN A NEW DIRECTION

EVANS, DERRICK
REALITY OF A DREAMER: RIVER NORTH
    DANCE COMPANY

FAGAN, GARTH
GRIOT NEW YORK

FAISON, GEORGE
SOPHISTICATED LADIES
THE WIZ

FALCO, LOUIS
FAME

FARLEY, GINGER
REALITY OF A DREAMER: RIVER NORTH
    DANCE COMPANY

FARRAH, IBRAHIM
IBRAHIM FARRAH PRESENTS RARE
    GLIMPSES: DANCES FROM THE MIDDLE
    EAST, VOLUME I

FASINO, CINZIA
MAGDALENE

FELD, ELIOT
ELIOT FELD: ARTISTIC DIRECTOR
TZADDIK

FELIX, SEYMOUR
AMERICAN MUSICALS: FAMOUS PRODUC-
    TION NUMBERS
COVER GIRL

FENLEY, MOLISSA
GEOGRAPHY AND METABOLISM
RETRACING STEPS: AMERICAN DANCE
    SINCE POSTMODERNISM

FERGUSON, KATHRYN
DANCES FROM THE CASBAH
MIDEASTERN DANCE: AN INTRODUCTION
    TO BELLY DANCE

FISHER, ELLEN
DANCING HANDS

FLEMING, MAUREEN
MOTHER AND CHILD/50
WIDENING GYRE

FOKINE, MICHEL
AMERICAN BALLET THEATRE: A CLOSE-UP
   IN TIME
AMERICAN BALLET THEATRE AT THE MET
THE BALLERINAS
BALLET STUDY FILMS
BARYSHNIKOV AT WOLF TRAP
THE BEGINNINGS OF TODAY
BOLSHOI: DIVERTISSEMENTS
BOLSHOI SOLOISTS CLASSIQUE
CARMEN (Bolshoi Ballet)
DYING SWAN
AN EVENING WITH THE ROYAL BALLET
GALINA ULANOVA
IMMORTAL SWAN
MARGOT FONTEYN IN LES SYLPHIDES
THE MARYINSKY BALLET
NATASHA
NIJINSKY
NINA ANANIASHVILI AND INTERNATIONAL
   STARS
PARIS DANCES DIAGHILEV
PAVLOVA: A TRIBUTE TO A LEGENDARY
   BALLERINA
REFLECTIONS OF A DANCER: ALEXANDRA
   DANILOVA, PRIMA BALLERINA ASSOLUTA
THE ROMANTIC BALLET
THE ROYAL BALLET
RUSSIAN BALLET, THE GLORIOUS TRADI-
   TION
LES SYLPHIDES (CHOPINIANA)
WHAT IS NEW

FORBES, BARBARA
YOUNG AND JUST BEGINNING: PIERRE

FORSYTHE, WILLIAM
SYLVIE GUILLEM AT WORK

FORT, SYVILLA
SYVILLA: THEY DANCE TO HER DRUM

FOSSE, BOB
ALL THAT JAZZ
CABARET
KISS ME KATE
SWEET CHARITY

FOUAD, NEGWA
STARS OF EGYPTIAN DANCE

FOWLER, LINDA
BRUSH AND BARRE: THE LIFE AND WORK
   OF TOULOUSE-LAUTREC IN DANCE AND
   MUSIC

FRANKLIN, FREDERIC
CREOLE GISÈLLE

FREEDMAN, LAURIE
KA

FRIEDMAN, GENE
INDEX
THE OFFICIAL DOCTRINE
THREE DANCES

FUJIKAGE, SUMI
SCENES FROM THE WASTE LAND

FULLER, LARRY
ON YOUR TOES . . . THE MAKING OF

FUNK, POUL
THE ROYAL DANISH BALLET 1902–1906

FUNNY HOUSE
FUNNY HOUSE

GADES, ANTONIO
EL AMOR BRUJO
BLOOD WEDDING
CARMEN

GAINES, WILL
MASTERS OF TAP

GALANTE, MARCUS
PRIVATE PERFORMANCE

GAMAL, NADIA
IBRAHIM FARRAH PRESENTS RARE
   GLIMPSES: DANCES FROM THE MIDDLE
   EAST, VOLUME I

GARDEL, MAXIMILLIEN
THE MAGNIFICENT BEGINNING

GARRARD, MIMI
MIMI GARRARD DANCE THEATRE

GENNARO
NATASHA

GEVA, TAMARA
SPECTRE OF THE ROSE

GIL, CHRIS
DANCING THRU

GILLIS, MARGIE
STORY

GIORDANO, GUS
CALL OF THE DRUM: NAPOLEONIC DANCES
CELEBRATION OF ROCK
A DANCE TRIBUTE TO MICHAEL JORDAN
IN CONCERT: PROFILE OF GUS GIORDANO
   JAZZ DANCE CHICAGO
JAZZ DANCE CLASS WITH GUS GIORDANO
MUSIC BOX
THE REHEARSAL
STREETCAR: A DANCE OF DESIRE
THE VALLEY OF XEBRON

GIOVSKY, VICTOR
NINA ANANIASHVILI AND INTERNATIONAL
   STARS

GLADSTEIN, DEBORAH
HELICAL WIND
KALAHARI

GLICK, STEFANIE
THROUGH THE VEIL

GODDERTZ, CHARLES
TAP DANCING: INTERMEDIATE AND AD-
   VANCED

GOLEISOVSKY, K.
RUSSIAN BALLET, THE GLORIOUS TRADI-
   TION

GONCALVES, JULIE
DANCER REHEARSING

GOODE, JOE
DANCING ON THE EDGE
EXCERPTS FROM "WITHOUT A PLACE"
FROM SAN FRANCISCO: DANCING ON THE
   EDGE

GORDON, DAVID
BEYOND THE MAINSTREAM: POSTMODERN
   DANCERS
DAVID GORDON: PANEL
MAKING DANCES: SEVEN POSTMODERN
   CHOREOGRAPHERS

GORSKY, ALEKSANDR
BALLET FAVORITES
DON QUIXOTE (Kirov Ballet)
DON QUIXOTE (Russian State Perm Ballet)
NINA ANANIASHVILI AND INTERNATIONAL
   STARS
PLISETSKAYA DANCES
RAYMONDA (Bolshoi Ballet)
RUSSIAN BALLET, THE GLORIOUS TRADI-
   TION
SWAN LAKE (Russian State Perm Ballet)

GOULD, DAVE
AMERICAN MUSICALS: FAMOUS PRODUC-
   TION NUMBERS
BORN TO DANCE
BROADWAY MELODY OF 1936
BROADWAY MELODY OF 1938
FLYING DOWN TO RIO
THE GAY DIVORCEE

GRAHAM, MALLORY
RHYTHM 'N RED SHOES

GRAHAM, MARTHA
ACROBATS OF GOD
APPALACHIAN SPRING
CLYTEMNESTRA
CORTEGE OF EAGLES
DANCE: FOUR PIONEERS
A DANCER'S WORLD
FESTIVAL OF THE DANCE
FLUTE OF KRISHNA
LAMENTATION
THE MARTHA GRAHAM DANCE COMPANY
MARTHA GRAHAM: THE DANCER RE-
   VEALED
MARTHA GRAHAM: THREE CONTEMPO-
   RARY CLASSICS
NIGHT JOURNEY
SERAPHIC DIALOGUE
TRAILBLAZERS OF MODERN DANCE

GRAVES, JAMALE
EVERYBODY DANCE NOW

GRAY, DARYL
BEYOND ROUTINE
EIGHT GREAT STEPS TO CHOREOGRAPHY

GREEN, CHUCK
MASTERS OF TAP
NO MAPS ON MY TAPS

GREENFIELD, AMY
ANTIGONE/RITES OF PASSION
DERVISH
DIALOGUE FOR CAMERAMAN AND DANCER
ELEMENT
ENCOUNTER
FOUR SOLOS FOR FOUR WOMEN
FRAGMENTS: MAT/GLASS

GREGORY, MICHAEL SCOTT
KARATE RAP

GRIGORIEV, SERGE
THE ROYAL BALLET

GRIGOROVICH, YURI
BOLSHOI: DIVERTISSEMENTS
BOLSHOI PROKOFIEV GALA
GISÈLLE (Bolshoi Ballet)
GISÈLLE (Bolshoi Ballet)
THE GOLDEN AGE
IVAN THE TERRIBLE (Bolshoi Ballet)
IVAN THE TERRIBLE (Bolshoi Ballet)
THE NUTCRACKER (Bolshoi Ballet)
THE NUTCRACKER (Bolshoi Ballet)
RAYMONDA (Bolshoi Ballet)
ROMEO AND JULIET (Bolshoi Ballet)
ROMEO AND JULIET (Bolshoi Ballet)
SLEEPING BEAUTY (Bolshoi Ballet)
SPARTACUS (Bolshoi Ballet)
SPARTACUS (Bolshoi Ballet)
SPARTACUS (Bolshoi Ballet)
THE STONE FLOWER (Bolshoi Ballet)
THE STONE FLOWER (Kirov Ballet)
SWAN LAKE (Bolshoi Ballet)
LES SYLPHIDES (CHOPINIANA)
THE ULTIMATE SWAN LAKE
YURI GRIGOROVICH: MASTER OF THE BOL-
   SHOI

GROSS, SALLY
BLACK AND WHITE
LEE'S FERRY
STOPPED IN HER TRACKS

HABERMAS-SCHER, MARILYN
SOLO

HADLEY, SUSAN
FIELDS

HAFT, NINA
DANCING FROM THE INSIDE OUT

HALL, ARTHUR
CHE CHE KULE: EXERCISES FOR KIDS
OBATALA
ORISUN OMI (THE WELL): PROLOGUE TO
   THE YORUBA CYCLE

SNAKE DANCE TEACHER DANCE
WATER SPIRIT FESTIVAL

HALL, PAUL
PAUL'S PIECE OF SKY

HALPRIN, ANNA
POSITIVE MOTION

HAMDI, NADRA
STARS OF EGYPTIAN DANCE

HAMMER, VALERIE
OP ODYSSEY

HANAN
STARS OF EGYPTIAN DANCE

HARRIS, RENNIE
P FUNK

HARTMAN, RUSTY
BEST OF ALL A DANCER

HAUSER, MATTHEW M.
ADZO

HAWKINS, ERICK
ERICK HAWKINS' AMERICA

HAYDEE, MARCIA
GISELLE . . . THE MAKING OF

HAYWOOD, CLAIRE
ARTISTS OF THE DANCE

HELD, WOLFGANG
SUZANNE FARRELL: ELUSIVE MUSE

HELPMANN, ROBERT
CELEBRATION: A HISTORY OF THE SADLER'S
   WELLS ROYAL BALLET
THE RED SHOES

HERRMAN, BIRGITTA
EARTHMATTERS

HESS, SALLY
DANCING HANDS

HEYN-CUBACUB, JAN
KALYIAN

HIJIKATA, TATSUMI
BUTOH: BODY ON THE EDGE OF CRISIS

HINES, GREGORY
THE COTTON CLUB
WHITE NIGHTS

HINES, MAURICE
THE COTTON CLUB

HOLDER, GEOFFREY
DANCE THEATRE OF HARLEM
ETHNIC DANCE: ROUNDTRIP TO TRINIDAD

HOLLANDER, JONATHAN
DANCE TEN
DORIS CHASE DANCE SERIES: THREE SOLOS
JONATHAN AND THE ROCKER

HOLM, ESKE
MIXED DOUBLE
ORFEUS AND JULIE

HOLM, HANYA
DANCE: FOUR PIONEERS
HANYA: PORTRAIT OF A DANCE PIONEER

HOLMES, DAVID
BALLET ADAGIO
TOUR EN L'AIR

HORNADAY, JEFFREY
A CHORUS LINE
FLASHDANCE

HORTON, LESTER
DANCE THEATRE OF HARLEM
DANCE THEATRE OF HARLEM
GENIUS ON THE WRONG COAST
LESTER HORTON TECHNIQUE: THE WARM
   UP

HOYER, DORE
THE DANCE

HUMPHREY, DORIS
AIR FOR THE G STRING
DANCE: FOUR PIONEERS
THE DANCE WORKS OF DORIS HUMPHREY:
   WITH MY RED FIRES AND NEW DANCE
DAY ON EARTH
FESTIVAL OF THE DANCE
HUMPHREY TECHNIQUE
LAMENT
NEW DANCE: RECORD FILM
TRAILBLAZERS OF MODERN DANCE
TWO ECSTATIC THEMES
WATER STUDY
WITH MY RED FIRES

HURWITZ, TOM
SUZANNE FARRELL: ELUSIVE MUSE

HYRST, ERIC
TWO FOR BALLET

IPIOTIS, CELIA
DANCE ON VIDEO: AN INTRODUCTION TO
   VIDEOTAPING DANCE
FOUR MOVES IN SPACE: A VIDEODANCE
   SUITE
IMAGES IN DISTRACTED TIME

IVANOV, LEV
AMERICAN BALLET THEATRE: A CLOSE-UP
   IN TIME
ART AND TECHNIQUE OF THE BALLET
THE BALLERINAS
BALLET: A CAREER FOR BOYS
BALLET FAVORITES
BALLET STUDY FILMS
CLASSICAL BALLET
COPPÉLIA: ACT II
MODERN BALLET
NINA ANANIASHVILI AND INTERNATIONAL
   STARS
THE NUTCRACKER (American Ballet Theatre)
THE NUTCRACKER (Royal Ballet)
PLISETSKAYA DANCES
THE ROMANTIC BALLET

LLOYD ONE STAR
VISION DANCE

LOCKETZ, JAN MARCE
ANIMA

LORING, EUGENE
COPLAND PORTRAIT
DEEP IN MY HEART
FUNNY FACE
SILK STOCKINGS
YOLANDA AND THE THIEF

LOUIS, MURRAY
THE BODY AS AN INSTRUMENT
MOTION
MURRAY LOUIS IN CONCERT: VOLUME I,
    DANCE SOLOS
NIK AND MURRAY
SPACE
TIME

LOWE, MELISSA
THE BALLET WORKOUT
THE BALLET WORKOUT II
CREATIVE MOVEMENT: A STEP TOWARDS
    INTELLIGENCE FOR CHILDREN AGES 2–8

LOZANO, SILVIA
BALLET FOLKLORICO NACIONAL DE
    MEXICO

LUBOVITCH, LAR
BALLERINA: LYNN SEYMOUR
BOLERO and PICTURES AT AN EXHIBITION
FANDANGO
THE PLANETS

LUIGI
LUIGI

LYNN, GILLIAN
HALF A SIXPENCE

MACÍAS, RAUL
MEXICAN DANCES

MACMILLAN, KENNETH
AMERICAN BALLET THEATRE AT THE MET
AMERICAN BALLET THEATRE IN SAN FRAN-
    CISCO
BALLERINA: LYNN SEYMOUR
BALLET FAVORITES
BRITISH BALLET TODAY
CELEBRATION: A HISTORY OF THE SADLER'S
    WELLS ROYAL BALLET
CURTAIN UP
HOW BALLET BEGAN
MANON
MAYERLING
NATASHA
NIJINSKY
THE PRINCE OF THE PAGODAS
ROMEO AND JULIET (Royal Ballet)
ROMEO AND JULIET (Royal Ballet)

MAJARRAL, KAURA
SANKOFA DANCE THEATER—A PORTRAIT

MAHEU, GILLES
LE DORTOIR (The Dormitory)

MAKAROVA, NATALIA
AMERICAN BALLET THEATRE AT THE MET
LA BAYADÈRE (Royal Ballet)
SWAN LAKE (London Festival Ballet)

MANN, SARA SHELTON
LIKE WIND IN MIRA'S HAIR

MARIN, MAGUY
CINDERELLA (Lyon Opera Ballet)

MARKO, IVAN
JESUS, SON OF MAN

MARKS, VICTORIA
INSIDE EYES
SMALL DISTANCES

MARO, AKAJI
BUTOH: BODY ON THE EDGE OF CRISIS

MARSHALL, SUSAN
UNTITLED, ARMS

MARTEL, DIANE
HOUSE OF TRES
RETRACING STEPS: AMERICAN DANCE
    SINCE POSTMODERNISM

MARTINS, PETER
ACCENT ON THE OFFBEAT
PETER MARTINS: A DANCER

MASON, VIRGINIA
HALF A SIXPENCE

MASSINE, LÉONIDE
THE BALLERINAS
BALLET COMES TO BRITAIN
CAPRICCIO ESPAGNOL (Spanish Fiesta)
GAITÉ PARISIENNE
GAITÉ PARISIENNE
GREAT PERFORMANCE IN DANCE
THE RED SHOES
SEVENTH SYMPHONY
ST. FRANCIS
SYMPHONIE FANTASTIQUE

MATTOX, MATT
SEVEN BRIDES FOR SEVEN BROTHERS

MAZUR, THAÏS
DANCING FROM THE INSIDE OUT

MCDONALD, BOBBI
AMERICAN BALLROOM DANCING

MCFALL, JOHN
TEALIA

MCINTYRE, DIANNE
ETUDE IN FREE

MCKAYLE, DONALD
ECHOES OF JAZZ

MELANCON, MURIEL
NOCTURNAE

MERANTE, LOUIS
CLASSICAL BALLET

MESSERER, ASAF
BALLET ADAGIO
TOUR EN L'AIR

MILLER, BUZZ
NOT FOR LOVE ALONE

MITCHELL, ARTHUR
DANCE THEATRE OF HARLEM
DANCE THEATRE OF HARLEM
RHYTHMETRON: THE DANCE THEATRE OF
    HARLEM WITH ARTHUR MITCHELL

MOISEYEV, IGOR
MOISEYEV DANCE COMPANY: A GALA EVE-
    NING

MONK, MEREDITH
BOOK OF DAYS
ELLIS ISLAND
MAKING DANCES: SEVEN POSTMODERN
    CHOREOGRAPHERS
MEREDITH MONK
PARIS
QUARRY
SIXTEEN MILLIMETER EARRINGS

MOORE, CHARLES
DANCE BLACK AMERICA

MOORE, FREDDIE
STEPS IN A NEW DIRECTION

MORCA, TÉO
COMPLETE FLAMENCO DANCE TECHNIQUE

MORELAND, BARRY
KONTAKION: A SONG OF PRAISE

MORGAN, DAVID
BEST OF ALL A DANCER

MORISSEAU, CAROLE
BUFFALO SOLDIER
CAROLE MORISSEAU AND THE DETROIT
    CITY DANCE COMPANY

MOROCCO
MOROCCO AND THE CASBAH DANCE EXPE-
    RIENCE

MORRIS, MARK
THE HARD NUT

MORRIS, WENDY
SOLO

MOSCHEN, MICHAEL
IN MOTION WITH MICHAEL MOSCHEN
STICKS, LIGHT, FIRE

MOSS, RICHARD DEAN
ADVENTURES IN ASSIMILATION

MOULTON, CHARLES
BILLBOARDS
FRACTURED VARIATIONS and VISUAL
    SHUFFLE
LUMINAIRE
NEW DANCE

MURPHEY, CLAUDIA
CRIME PAYS
DIGITAL DANCE

DON QUIXOTE (Australian Ballet)
DON QUIXOTE (Kirov Ballet)
DON QUIXOTE (Russian State Perm Ballet)
THE EBB AND FLOW
AN EVENING WITH THE ROYAL BALLET
FONTEYN AND NUREYEV: THE PERFECT
   PARTNERSHIP
GISÈLLE (Ballet Teatro Municipal of Rio de Ja-
   neiro)
GISÈLLE (Bolshoi Ballet)
GODUNOV: THE WORLD TO DANCE IN
GRAND CONCERT
GREAT BALLERINA
GREAT PERFORMANCE IN DANCE
HOW BALLET BEGAN
I AM A DANCER
IMMORTAL SWAN
THE KIROV BALLET: CLASSIC BALLET NIGHT
KIROV SOLOISTS: INVITATION TO THE
   DANCE
LUDMILA SEMENYAKA: BOLSHOI BALLE-
   RINA
THE MAGIC OF THE BOLSHOI BALLET
THE MAGIC OF THE KIROV BALLET
THE MARYINSKY BALLET
MODERN BALLET
NINA ANANIASHVILI AND INTERNATIONAL
   STARS
THE PARIS OPERA BALLET: SEVEN BALLETS
THE PARIS OPERA BALLET: SIX BALLETS
PAS DE DEUX
PAVLOVA: A TRIBUTE TO A LEGENDARY
   BALLERINA
PLISETSKAYA DANCES
RAYMONDA (Bolshoi Ballet)
RAYMONDA (Bolshoi Ballet)
REFLECTIONS OF A DANCER: ALEXANDRA
   DANILOVA, PRIMA BALLERINA ASSOLUTA
THE ROYAL BALLET
RUSSIAN BALLET, THE GLORIOUS TRADI-
   TION
THE SCENE CHANGES
SLEEPING BEAUTY (Ballet del Teatro Municipal)
SLEEPING BEAUTY (Bolshoi Ballet)
SLEEPING BEAUTY (Kirov Ballet)
SLEEPING BEAUTY (Kirov Ballet)
STARS OF THE RUSSIAN BALLET
SWAN LAKE (American Ballet Theatre)
SWAN LAKE (Bolshoi Ballet)
SWAN LAKE (Bolshoi Ballet)
SWAN LAKE (Kirov Ballet)
SWAN LAKE (London Festival Ballet)
SWAN LAKE (Royal Ballet)
SWAN LAKE (Russian State Perm Ballet)
SYLVIE GUILLEM AT WORK
TCHAIKOVSKY AND THE RUSSIANS
A TIME TO DANCE
THE TURNING POINT
WORLD'S YOUNG BALLET

PETIT, ROLAND
BLACK TIGHTS
THE BLUE ANGEL
CARMEN (Ballet National de Marseille)
DADDY LONGLEGS
IN PRAISE OF FOLLY
LE JEUNE HOMME ET LA MORT
KAREN KAIN: BALLERINA
KIROV SOLOISTS: INVITATION TO THE
   DANCE
THE MAGNIFICENT BEGINNING
MAKAROVA: IN A CLASS OF HER OWN
NATASHA

PUSS IN BOOTS
THE ROMANTIC BALLET
THE SCENE CHANGES
WHITE NIGHTS

PETRONIO, STEPHEN
RETRACING STEPS: AMERICAN DANCE
   SINCE POSTMODERNISM

PHILLIPS, ARLENE
ANNIE

PINNOCK, THOMAS
THE LURE AND THE LORE

PLISETSKAYA, MAYA
ANNA KARENINA

PONOMARYOV, VLADIMIR
LA BAYADÈRE (Kirov Ballet)

PORTILLO, ALBERTO
¡AY, CARMELA!

POSIN, KATHY
KATHY'S DANCE

PRELJOCAJ, ANGELIN
ROMEO AND JULIET (Lyon Opera Ballet)

PRINZ, LEROY
SOUTH PACIFIC
YANKEE DOODLE DANDY

PUCCI, PETER
BILLBOARDS

PYNKOSKI, MARSHALL
ROMEOS AND JULIETS

RADUNSKY, ALEXANDER
THE LITTLE HUMPBACKED HORSE

RAINER, YVONNE
BEYOND THE MAINSTREAM: POSTMODERN
   DANCERS
A TRIO

RAMSEY, KEVIN
ESSENTIALS OF TAP TECHNIQUE

RANDAZZO, PETER
DANCE CLASS

RASET, VAL
YOU WERE NEVER LOVELIER

RATZIN, BONNIE
THE WOMAN IN THE SHOE

RECONSTRUCTED BY JULIA SUTTON
IL BALLARINO: THE ART OF RENAISSANCE
   DANCE

REGNIER, PATRICE
FIRST SOLO
RABL
THE RUSH DANCE COMPANY, EXCERPTS
   FROM *BERNARD*

REID, REX
CORROBOREE: THE AUSTRALIAN BALLET

REITZ, DANA
AIRWAVES
ONCE AGAIN

RIZHENKO, NATALY
SHAKESPEARE DANCE TRILOGY

ROBBINS, JEROME
FIDDLER ON THE ROOF
THE KING AND I
PETER MARTINS: A DANCER
WEST SIDE STORY

ROBEL, DAVID
DADDY LONGLEGS

ROBINSON, BILL "BOJANGLES"
LET'S SCUFFLE
AN ORIGINAL BILL ROBINSON VIDEO

ROBINSON, CLARENCE
STORMY WEATHER

ROBINSON, CLEO
RUN, SISTER, RUN

ROSS, HERBERT
DANCE: A REFLECTION OF OUR TIMES
FUNNY GIRL

ROSS, ROCK
VESPUCCILAND: THE GREAT AND THE FREE

ROTH, GABRIELLE
THE WAVE: ECSTATIC DANCE FOR BODY
   AND SOUL

ROUSSEVE, DAVID
PULL YOUR HEAD TO THE MOON

RUDNER, SARA
DANCE FRAME
DANCE OUTLINE
DORIS CHASE DANCE SERIES: THREE SOLOS
MAKING DANCES: SEVEN POSTMODERN
   CHOREOGRAPHERS

RUUD, TOMM
BALANCES

SABRY, NAHED
STARS OF EGYPTIAN DANCE

SAINT LÉON, ARTHUR
BARYSHNIKOV AT WOLF TRAP
BEGINNINGS
COPPÉLIA (Ballets de San Juan)
GREAT PERFORMANCE IN DANCE
HOW BALLET WAS SAVED
THE KIROV BALLET: CLASSIC BALLET NIGHT
THE MARYINSKY BALLET
PLISETSKAYA DANCES

DANCE THREE
DORIS CHASE DANCE SERIES: THREE SOLOS
IMPROVISATION
LIGHT, PART 5

TALIAFERRO, CLAY
FALLING OFF THE BACK PORCH

TAMIRIS, HELEN
HELEN TAMIRIS IN NEGRO SPIRITUALS

TANAKA, MIN
BUTOH: BODY ON THE EDGE OF CRISIS

TARANDA, GEDEMINAS
RAYMONDA (Bolshoi Ballet)

TARDIF, DANIELLE
LE DORTOIR (The Dormitory)

TAYLOR, PAUL
AMERICAN BALLET THEATRE IN SAN FRAN-
   CISCO
JUNCTION
PAUL TAYLOR AND COMPANY: AN ARTIST
   AND HIS WORK
THE PAUL TAYLOR DANCE COMPANY
SPEAKING IN TONGUES
THE WRECKER'S BALL: THREE DANCES BY
   PAUL TAYLOR

TAYLOR-CORBETT, LYNN
AMERICAN BALLET THEATRE IN SAN FRAN-
   CISCO
FOOTLOOSE
TO DREAM OF ROSES

TCHERNICKEVA, LUBOV
THE ROYAL BALLET

TERRY, KEITH
BODY TJAK
DANCING HANDS

TETLEY, GLEN
THE ANATOMY LESSON
BOLD STEPS
DANCE: IN SEARCH OF "LOVERS"
THE FIREBIRD
GLEN TETLEY: PORTRAIT OF THE CHORE-
   OGRAPHER
I AM A DANCER
THE SCENE CHANGES

THARP, TWYLA
BARYSHNIKOV DANCES SINATRA
THE CATHERINE WHEEL
HAIR
SUE'S LEG: REMEMBERING THE THIRTIES:
   TWYLA THARP AND DANCERS
TWYLA THARP: MAKING TELEVISION
   DANCE
WHITE NIGHTS

THEODORE, LEE
LIVING AMERICAN THEATER DANCE

TIMOFEEV, V.
KIROV SOLOISTS: INVITATION TO THE
   DANCE

TIMOFEYEVA, NINA
BOLSHOI SOLOISTS CLASSIQUE

TOLEDANO, ALBERTO
ARGENTINE TANGO

TOMLINSON, KELLOM
THE ART OF DANCING: AN INTRODUCTION
   TO BAROQUE DANCE

TORRES, EDDIE
¡A BAILAR! THE JOURNEY OF A LATIN
   DANCE COMPANY

TOWERS, DEIRDRE
MALAMBO DEL SOL

TUDOR, ANTONY
AMERICAN BALLET THEATRE: A CLOSE-UP
   IN TIME
AMERICAN BALLET THEATRE IN SAN FRAN-
   CISCO
ANTONY TUDOR
MODERN BALLET
THE VERY EYE OF NIGHT

TURGANBAEVA, MUKARRAM
AN INTRODUCTION TO UZBEK DANCE

TURGELEV, NURDEN
MORNING STAR (CHOLPON)

TUROCY, CATHERINE
THE ART OF DANCING: AN INTRODUCTION
   TO BAROQUE DANCE
SUITE FANTAISISTE

VAGANOVA, AGRIPPINA
THE KIROV BALLET: CLASSIC BALLET NIGHT
KIROV SOLOISTS: INVITATION TO THE
   DANCE
MOMENT OF LIGHT: THE DANCE OF EVE-
   LYN HART
PLISETSKAYA DANCES

VAINONEN, VASILY
STARS OF THE RUSSIAN BALLET

VALK, ACHMED
ENTROPY: REVERSE TO OMEGA

VAN DANTZIG, RUDI
THE DUTCH NATIONAL BALLET
THE MAKING OF A BALLET
MOMENT OF LIGHT: THE DANCE OF EVE-
   LYN HART

VAN MANEN, HANS
THE DUTCH NATIONAL BALLET

VAN SCHAYK, TOER
THE DUTCH NATIONAL BALLET

VAN TUYL, MARIAN
CLINIC OF STUMBLE

VAN WIEREN, LAURIE
SOLO

VASSILIEV, VLADIMIR
ANYUTA
CARMEN (Bolshoi Ballet)

MACBETH
A POEM OF DANCES ALSO KNOWN AS PLI-
   SETSKAYA: CARMEN
WORLD'S YOUNG BALLET

VINOGRADOV, OLEG
COPPÉLIA (Kirov Ballet)
THE KIROV BALLET IN LONDON
THE MARYINSKY BALLET
SLEEPING BEAUTY (Kirov Ballet)
WHITE NIGHT OF DANCE IN LENINGRAD

VSEVOLOZHSKY, IVAN
SLEEPING BEAUTY (Kirov Ballet)

WAGDI, EMAN
STARS OF EGYPTIAN DANCE

WAGMAN, VERA
HIGH NOON

WALKER, NORMAN
ATTITUDES IN DANCE
JOHN LINDQUIST: PHOTOGRAPHER OF
   DANCE

WALTERS, CHARLES
DU BARRY WAS A LADY
MEET ME IN ST. LOUIS

WANNER, DEBRA
SHE STORIES

WAQUARI, YUKIO
BUTOH: BODY ON THE EDGE OF CRISIS

WEAVER, JOHN
HOW BALLET BEGAN

WEHRFRITZ, CURTIS
TECTONIC PLATES

WEIDMAN, CHARLES
CHARLES WEIDMAN: ON HIS OWN
DANCE: FOUR PIONEERS
FESTIVAL OF THE DANCE
FLICKERS
NEW DANCE: RECORD FILM

WEISS, RICHARD
DANCE PRELUDES

WHITE, ONNA
BYE BYE BIRDIE
THE MUSIC MAN
OLIVER!
1776

WIESENTHAL, GRETE
WHAT IS NEW

WIGMAN, MARY
THE DANCE
MARY WIGMAN: FOUR SOLOS
MARY WIGMAN: MY LIFE IS DANCE

Composers Index

BERLIOZ, HECTOR
SYMPHONIE FANTASTIQUE

BERNSTEIN, LEONARD
GEE, OFFICER KRUPKE
ON THE TOWN
WEST SIDE STORY

BERSTEIN, E.
STREETCAR: A DANCE OF DESIRE

BIBALO, ANTONIO
ASHES, MIST AND WIND BLOWN DUST

BIZET, GEORGES
ALICIA ALONSO: ALICIA
BALLET ROBOTIQUE
BLACK TIGHTS
CARMEN
CARMEN (Ballet National de Marseille)
CARMEN (Bolshoi Ballet)
EIGHT GREAT STEPS TO CHOREOGRAPHY
KAREN KAIN: BALLERINA
NATASHA
A POEM OF DANCES ALSO KNOWN AS PLI-
    SETSKAYA: CARMEN
TRISHA AND CARMEN

BLACKBURN, MAURICE
A PHANTASY

BLISS, SIR ARTHUR
CHECKMATE

BOCK, JERRY
FIDDLER ON THE ROOF

BOLCOMB, WILLIAM
DANCE TEN
DORIS CHASE DANCE SERIES: THREE SOLOS
JONATHAN AND THE ROCKER

BORDEN, DAVID
CHOICE CHANCE WOMAN DANCE

BOYCE, WILLIAM
BOYCEBALL

BRAHMS, JOHANNES
CHARLES WEIDMAN: ON HIS OWN
ELIOT FELD: ARTISTIC DIRECTOR
THE LEGACY OF THE CHOREOGRAPHY OF
    ISADORA DUNCAN
SHADES OF WIEGENLIED
STUTTGART BALLET: THE MIRACLE LIVES
TRAILBLAZERS OF MODERN DANCE

BRANCA, GLENN
ANTIGONE/RITES OF PASSION

BREGLIA, EVE-MARIE
LA PROMENADE

BRITTEN, BENJAMIN
FOR DANCERS
THE PRINCE OF THE PAGODAS
SIX METAMORPHOSES
SONG AND DANCE
STUTTGART BALLET: THE MIRACLE LIVES

BROWN, NACIO HERB
BROADWAY MELODY OF 1936
BROADWAY MELODY OF 1938
SINGIN' IN THE RAIN

BRUDER, LOU
THE BLUE ANGEL

BUCHEN, BILL
FRACTURED VARIATIONS and VISUAL
    SHUFFLE

BURGMULLER, NORBERT
KIROV SOLOISTS: INVITATION TO THE
    DANCE
THE ROMANTIC ERA

BURWELL, CARTER
RABL

BUSH, KATE
A MOVING PICTURE

BYRNE, DAVID
THE CATHERINE WHEEL

CAGE, JOHN
BEACH BIRDS FOR CAMERA
CAGE/CUNNINGHAM
CHANGING STEPS
THE COLLABORATORS: CAGE, CUNNING-
    HAM, RAUSCHENBERG
DANCE AND MYTH: THE WORLD OF JEAN
    ERDMAN
EVENT FOR TELEVISION
MERCE BY MERCE BY PAIK
MERCE CUNNINGHAM
NOT FOR LOVE ALONE
POINTS IN SPACE
SOMETIMES IT WORKS, SOMETIMES IT
    DOESN'T
VARIATIONS V

CAHN, SAMMY
ANCHORS AWEIGH

CARTER, ELLIOTT
TRIPLE DUO
WAYWARD GLIMPSES

CARVAJAL, ALEJANDRO
VOICES OF THE ORISHAS

CHAPLIN, CHARLES
LIMELIGHT

CHARNIN, MARTIN
HE MAKES ME FEEL LIKE DANCIN'

CHAUSSON, ERNEST
AMERICAN BALLET THEATRE IN SAN FRAN-
    CISCO

CHAVEZ, CARLOS
KYLIAN COLLECTION
ROAD TO THE STAMPING GROUND

CHOPIN, FRÉDÉRIC
ADOLESCENCE
AMERICAN BALLET THEATRE: A CLOSE-UP
    IN TIME

AMERICAN BALLET THEATRE AT THE MET
THE BALLERINAS
BALLET RUSE
BALLET STUDY FILMS
BECAUSE WE MUST
THE BEGINNINGS OF TODAY
BOLSHOI: DIVERTISSEMENTS
AN EVENING WITH THE ROYAL BALLET
GALINA ULANOVA
HIGH NOON
IMMORTAL SWAN
IMPROVISATIONS TO CHOPIN
ISADORA DUNCAN: MOVEMENT FROM THE
    SOUL
ISADORA DUNCAN: TECHNIQUE AND CHO-
    REOGRAPHY
ISADORA DUNCAN: TECHNIQUE AND REP-
    ERTORY
THE LADY OF THE CAMELLIAS
MAKING BALLET: KAREN KAIN AND THE
    NATIONAL BALLET OF CANADA
MARGOT FONTEYN IN LES SYLPHIDES
THE MARYINSKY BALLET
NATASHA
THE ROMANTIC BALLET
LES SYLPHIDES (CHOPINIANA)

CLARIDA, BOB
IT DOESN'T WAIT

CLARKE, HARRY AKST-GRANT
THE COTTON CLUB

CLAYTON, MERRY
DIRTY DANCING

COHAN, GEORGE M
YANKEE DOODLE DANDY

COHEN, FREDERICK
THE DANCE

COHEN, LEONARD
A MOVING PICTURE

COLE, BILL
RUBBLE DANCE LONG ISLAND CITY

COLEMAN, CY
SWEET CHARITY

COLLINS, PHIL
WHITE NIGHTS

COLTRANE, ALICE
AILEY DANCES
AN EVENING WITH ALVIN AILEY AMERICAN
    DANCE THEATRE

CONSTANT, MARIUS
BLACK TIGHTS
IN PRAISE OF FOLLY

COPLAND, AARON
AMERICAN BALLET THEATRE: A CLOSE-UP
    IN TIME
APPALACHIAN SPRING
DAY ON EARTH
MARTHA GRAHAM, AN AMERICAN ORIGI-
    NAL IN PERFORMANCE

THE MARTHA GRAHAM DANCE COMPANY
OUR TOWN: THE MAKING OF A BALLET
TZADDIK

CORA, TOM
SSS

CORBIN, DOUG
BALLET CLASS

COWELL, HENRY
DANCE AND MYTH: THE WORLD OF JEAN
ERDMAN

CREAMER, HENRY
ALL THAT JAZZ

CUNNINGHAM, DAVID
RETRACING STEPS: AMERICAN DANCE
SINCE POSTMODERNISM

CZERNY, KARL
AMERICAN BALLET THEATRE: A CLOSE-UP
IN TIME
BOLD STEPS

DA LUCIA, PACO
CARMEN

DAMASE, JEAN MICHEL
BLACK TIGHTS

DAVENPORT, LANOUE
IN PARIS PARKS

DAVIS, KENNY
HANYA: PORTRAIT OF A DANCE PIONEER

DAVIS, PETER MAXWELL
KONTAKION: A SONG OF PRAISE

DE FALLA, MANUEL
EL AMOR BRUJO

DE LUCA, PACO
SEVILLANAS

DE PAUL, GENE
SEVEN BRIDES FOR SEVEN BROTHERS
DEAD CAN DANCE
 MAGDALENE

DEBUSSY, CLAUDE
AFTERNOON OF A FAUN
BALLET COMES TO BRITAIN
DANCE AND MYTH: THE WORLD OF JEAN
ERDMAN
AN EVENING WITH KYLIAN AND THE NE-
DERLANDS DANS THEATRE
FALLING OFF THE BACK PORCH
KYLIAN COLLECTION
NIJINSKY
PARIS DANCES DIAGHILEV

DELDEVEZ, EDWARD
CELEBRATION: A HISTORY OF THE SADLER'S
WELLS ROYAL BALLET

DELIBES, LÉO
AMERICAN BALLET THEATRE AT THE MET
THE BALLERINAS

BALLET STUDY FILMS
BEGINNINGS
CLASSICAL BALLET
COPPÉLIA (Ballets de San Juan)
COPPÉLIA (Kirov Ballet)
COPPÉLIA: ACT II
LE CORSAIRE
CURTAIN UP
GREAT PERFORMANCE IN DANCE
HOW BALLET BEGAN
HOW BALLET WAS SAVED
PAVLOVA: A TRIBUTE TO A LEGENDARY
BALLERINA
THE ROMANTIC BALLET

DELIUS, FREDERICK
MODERN BALLET

DELLO JOIO, NORMAN
THE LANGUAGE OF DANCE
SERAPHIC DIALOGUE

DENICOLA, JOHN
DIRTY DANCING

DESYLVA, BUDDY
AMERICAN MUSICALS: FAMOUS PRODUC-
TION NUMBERS

DIAMOND, DAVID
ERICK HAWKINS' AMERICA

DIENG, AIYB
LIFE IN THE DUST: FRAGMENTS OF AFRICAN
VOYAGES

DIXON, BILL
INDEX

DMITRI
HOUSE OF TRES

DOME
BECAUSE WE MUST

DOWNES, BOB
DANCE THEATRE OF HARLEM
TROY GAME
WHAT IS NEW

DRESHER, PAUL
STANDING BY

DREWS, STEVE
CHOICE CHANCE WOMAN DANCE

DRIGO, RICCARDO
BALLET LEGENDS: THE KIROV'S NINEL KUR-
GAPKINA
THE KIROV BALLET: CLASSIC BALLET NIGHT
LUDMILA SEMENYAKA: BOLSHOI BALLE-
RINA
THE MAGIC OF THE KIROV BALLET
THE MARYINSKY BALLET
PAVLOVA: A TRIBUTE TO A LEGENDARY
BALLERINA

DUGGAN, MARK
NEMETON

DUKAS, PAUL
FANTASIA

EASDALE, BRIAN
THE RED SHOES

EDENS, ROGER
STRIKE UP THE BAND
TAKE ME OUT TO THE BALL GAME
THE ZIEGFELD FOLLIES
ZIEGFELD GIRL

EDWARDS, SHERMAN
1776

EIGEN, ERIC
DANCE FOUR

EL-DABH, HALIM
CLYTEMNESTRA

ELGAR, EDWARD
ENIGMA VARIATIONS
OUT OF THE LIMELIGHT, HOME IN THE
RAIN

ELLINGTON, DUKE
AILEY DANCES
AMERICAN BALLET THEATRE: A CLOSE-UP
IN TIME
THE COTTON CLUB
ECHOES OF JAZZ
MILT AND HONI
SOPHISTICATED LADIES

ENO, BRIAN
TWENTY ONE WITH BILL T. JONES

ETOSHA
TWENTY ONE WITH BILL T. JONES

FAIN, SAMMY
FOOTLIGHT PARADE

FARLOW, TAL
TAL FARLOW

FASINO, CINZIA
NOCTURNAE

FAURÉ, GABRIEL
CHOREOGRAPHY BY BALANCHINE
ELEGY

FERNANDEZ BARROSO, SERGIO
PLASMASIS

FERSTL, ERICH
DAS TRIADISCHE BALLETT

FLORIAN, MICHEL
DUET

FLYNN, STEVEN
DANCE DELILAH, DANCE!
DELILAH'S BELLY DANCE WORKSHOP
DELILAH'S COSTUME WORKSHOP

FOLK, ROBERT
TO DREAM OF ROSES

FRANCK, CÉSAR
BALLET

FRANK MAYA
DANCING HANDS

FRANZ, SIEGFRIED
BALLET IN JAZZ

FREEDMAN, HARRY
BOLD STEPS

FRIEDMAN, JOAN
CHOICE CHANCE WOMAN DANCE

FRIPP, ROBERT
CAUGHT

GABICHVADZE, REVAZ
MEDEA

GADE, JACOB
TANGO

GADE, NIELS
NAPOLI
THE ROYAL DANISH BALLET 1902–1906

GAGNON, ANDRÉ
A MOVING PICTURE

GALAS, DIAMANDA
ANTIGONE/RITES OF PASSION

GALASSO, MICHAEL
CLOUD DANCE

GARDEL, CARLOS
TANGO BAR
TANGOS, THE EXILE OF GARDEL

GASPARIAN, DJIVAN
I WILL NOT BE SAD IN THIS WORLD

GAVRILIN, VALERY
ANYUTA

GERSHWIN, GEORGE
AN AMERICAN IN PARIS
BOLSHOI SOLOISTS CLASSIQUE
A DAMSEL IN DISTRESS
FUNNY FACE
THE GOLDWYN FOLLIES
THE SCENE CHANGES
SHALL WE DANCE
THE ZIEGFELD FOLLIES

GEYRA, DAVID
KA

GIBSON, JOHN
FRACTIONS I

GILBERT, PHILIP
LIFE IN THE DUST: FRAGMENTS OF AFRICAN
    VOYAGES

GIORDANO, GUS
CELEBRATION OF ROCK

GLAZUNOV, ALEXANDER
BARYSHNIKOV DANCES SINATRA
CARMEN (Bolshoi Ballet)
THE MAGIC OF THE KIROV BALLET
PLISETSKAYA DANCES
A POEM OF DANCES ALSO KNOWN AS PLI-
    SETSKAYA: CARMEN
RAYMONDA (Bolshoi Ballet)
RAYMONDA (Bolshoi Ballet)
SYLVIE GUILLEM AT WORK

GLINKA, MIKHAIL IVANOVICH
THE BOLSHOI BALLET: GALINA ULANOVA
THE PERSISTENT IMAGE and VALSE

GLUCK, CHRISTOPH
ISADORA DUNCAN: MOVEMENT FROM THE
    SOUL
THE ROYAL DANISH BALLET 1902–1906

GOLDSTEIN, MALCOM
BRANCHES

GOODE, JOE
EXCERPTS FROM "WITHOUT A PLACE"

GOODMAN, JERRY
TWENTY ONE WITH BILL T. JONES

GOODWIN, JANNA
THE THIRD DAY
TROUT

GORDON, CRAIG
THE BAUHAUS DANCES OF OSKAR SCHLEM-
    MER: A RECONSTRUCTION

GORDON, GAVIN
BALLET COMES TO BRITAIN
THE RAKE'S PROGRESS

GORDON, PETER
RETRACING STEPS: AMERICAN DANCE
    SINCE POSTMODERNISM

GORE, MICHAEL
FAME

GOSPEL AND BLUES
AN EVENING WITH ALVIN AILEY AMERICAN
    DANCE THEATRE

GOSSELIN, MICHEL
TECTONIC PLATES

GOTTSCHALK, LOUIS
AMERICAN BALLET THEATRE IN SAN FRAN-
    CISCO
THE BLACK BOOTS
DANCE: NEW YORK CITY BALLET

GOULD, MORTON
BOLD STEPS
DANCE THEATRE OF HARLEM
FALL RIVER LEGEND

GOUNOD, CHARLES
THE BOLSHOI BALLET: GALINA ULANOVA
WATCHING BALLET

GRAVEL, GAËTAN
LE DORTOIR (The Dormitory)

GRAY, MARK
DANCING FROM THE INSIDE OUT

GRAYSON, GLENN
ENTROPY: REVERSE TO OMEGA

GREEN, JOHNNY
BATHING BEAUTY

GRIEG, EDVARD
DANCE THEATRE OF HARLEM
THE PARIS OPERA BALLET: SEVEN BALLETS

HAASE, GARY
BLACK AND WHITE

HABERMAN-SCHER, MARILYN
SOLO

HACKLEMANN, JAY SCOTT
ADRIENNE CHERIE INTERPRETS DANCES OF
    INDIA

HAIMSOHN, JANA
WILD GIRL FILMS

HALL, DARYL
CRIME PAYS

HAMILTON, JUDITH
DANCE THEATRE OF HARLEM
DANCE THEATRE OF HARLEM

HAMLISCH, MARVIN
A CHORUS LINE

HANDEL, GEORGE FREDERICK
AMERICAN BALLET THEATRE IN SAN FRAN-
    CISCO
THE SORCERESS: KIRI TE KANAWA
TANAGRA, USA

HARRIS, ROY
CHARLES WEIDMAN: ON HIS OWN

HARRISON, LOUIS
DANCE AND MYTH: THE WORLD OF JEAN
    ERDMAN
DANCE CHROMATIC
DANCE: ROBERT JOFFREY BALLET

HASSAN, AHMED
BLUE SNAKE
INNER RHYTHM

HAUSER, MATTHEW M.
ADZO

HAYDN, FRANZ JOSEPH
BARYSHNIKOV DANCES SINATRA
KYLIAN COLLECTION

KODÁLY, ZÓLTAN
LAMENTATION
THE MARTHA GRAHAM DANCE COMPANY
THROUGH THE VEIL

KOSUGI, TAKEHISA
LOCALE
MERCE CUNNINGHAM
SQUAREGAME VIDEO

KOTOKO, OGUN
ORISUN OMI (THE WELL): PROLOGUE TO
    THE YORUBA CYCLE

KREISLER, FRITZ
PAVLOVA: A TRIBUTE TO A LEGENDARY
    BALLERINA

KREUTZFELDT, STIG
MIXED DOUBLE

KUHLAU, F.
THE ROYAL DANISH BALLET 1902–1906

KYRKOSTAS, MARK
MOROCCO AND THE CASBAH DANCE EXPE-
    RIENCE

LABARBARA, JOAN
DANCE FRAME
DANCE OUTLINE
DORIS CHASE DANCE SERIES: THREE SOLOS
THREE DANCES BY MARTHA CURTIS
VARIATION II

LADERMAN, EZRA
DANCE AND MYTH: THE WORLD OF JEAN
    ERDMAN

LAJARTE, THEODORE
MADEMOISELLE FIFI

LAL, CHATUR
A CHAIRY TALE

LALO, EDOUARD
RADHA

LAMARR, RAMAL
BELLY DANCE! MAGICAL MOTION

LAMB, JOSEPH
BARYSHNIKOV DANCES SINATRA

LANCHBERY, JOHN
THE TALES OF BEATRIX POTTER

LANDOWSKI, MARCEL
THE ANATOMY LESSON

LANDRY, RICHARD
AEROS

LANE, BURTON
BABES ON BROADWAY
JUPITER'S DARLING
ROYAL WEDDING

LANG, JOHN
BLUE SNAKE
INNER RHYTHM

LANZALACO, MAURIZIO
NOCTURNAE

LAPIDUS, JOELLEN
ANNUNCIATION

LAWSON, DAVID
MOTHER AND CHILD/50
WIDENING GYRE

LECLAIR, JEAN-MARIE
WHAT'S REMEMBERED

LEE, K.
WATER SPIRIT FESTIVAL

LÉHAR, FRANZ
THE MERRY WIDOW

LEIBER, JERRY
ALL THAT JAZZ

LEMOS, PAUL
ANTIGONE/RITES OF PASSION

LEROY, A.
BESIDE HERSELF
CHANCE ENCOUNTERS
RETRACING STEPS: AMERICAN DANCE
    SINCE POSTMODERNISM

LESTER, EUGENE
CORTEGE OF EAGLES

LEVITAN, DAN
THE WATER PIECES

LEWIS, GRAHAM
BECAUSE WE MUST
BREAK

LINDSAY, ARTO
X-RAY EYES

LINTON, DAVID
RETRACING STEPS: AMERICAN DANCE
    SINCE POSTMODERNISM

LISZT, FRANZ
THE DUTCH NATIONAL BALLET
I AM A DANCER
JESUS, SON OF MAN
MAYERLING
OUT OF THE LIMELIGHT, HOME IN THE
    RAIN
STUTTGART BALLET: THE MIRACLE LIVES

LLOYD, NORMAN
BULLFIGHT
LAMENT
A MOMENT IN LOVE

LOESSER, FRANK
LET'S DANCE

LOEWE, FREDERICK
BRIGADOON
MY FAIR LADY

LONGWORTH, ERIC
LODELA

LOTRING, WAYAN
BALI MECHANIQUE

LOVE, RON
MADE IN THE BRONX

LOVENSKJÖLD, HERMAN SEVERIN
BALLET ENTERS THE WORLD STAGE
I AM A DANCER
LA SYLPHIDE (Royal Danish Ballet)

LULLY, JEAN
HOW BALLET BEGAN

LUMBYE
NAPOLI

MACDERMOT, GALT
HAIR

MACDOWELL, EDWARD
TRAILBLAZERS OF MODERN DANCE

MAHAFFEY, MIKE
DANCE FOUR
OP ODYSSEY

MAHLER, GUSTAV
THE ART OF THE TWENTIETH CENTURY
    BALLET
ELIOT FELD: ARTISTIC DIRECTOR
STUTTGART BALLET: THE MIRACLE LIVES

MANN, BARRY
ALL THAT JAZZ

MANNO, JESSE
PURE REMAINS

MARCER, T.
DANCE: ROBERT JOFFREY BALLET

MARCLAY, CHRISTIAN
SSS

MARKHAM, SHELLEY
I HATE TO EXERCISE, I LOVE TO TAP

MARKOWITZ, DONALD
DIRTY DANCING

MARQUETTI, ANDRE
LOVERS FRAGMENTS

MARSALIS, WYNTON
ACCENT ON THE OFFBEAT
GRIOT NEW YORK

MARSHALL, INGRAM
NEW YORK POST WAVE

MARTEL, DIANE
RETRACING STEPS: AMERICAN DANCE
    SINCE POSTMODERNISM

PAGANINI, NICCOLO
ADOLESCENCE

PARKER, CHARLIE
JAZZ HOOFER: BABY LAURENCE

PARKINS, ZEENA
SSS

PARKS, GORDON
RUN, SISTER, RUN

PARRISH, MAN
BEEHIVE

PATTON, MATTHEW
SPEAKING IN TONGUES

PAULI, HOLGER SIMON
NAPOLI
THE ROYAL DANISH BALLET 1902–1906

PEARCE, JUDITH
IMPROVISATION TO BANSURI FLUTE AND
    SEASCAPES

PEDROSO, LÁZARO
VOICES OF THE ORISHAS

PIAZZOLA, ASTOR
TANGO BAR
TANGOS, THE EXILE OF GARDEL

PICKET, LENNY
RETRACING STEPS: AMERICAN DANCE
    SINCE POSTMODERNISM

PORTER, COLE
BORN TO DANCE
BROADWAY MELODY OF 1940
CAN-CAN
DU BARRY WAS A LADY
THE GAY DIVORCEE
KISS ME KATE
THE PIRATE
SILK STOCKINGS
YOU'LL NEVER GET RICH

POULENC, FRANÇOIS
BALLET COMES TO BRITAIN
STUTTGART BALLET: THE MIRACLE LIVES
VESPUCCILAND: THE GREAT AND THE FREE

PREVIN, ANDRÉ
INVITATION TO THE DANCE
IT'S ALWAYS FAIR WEATHER

PREVITE, FRANKE
DIRTY DANCING
PRINCE
BILLBOARDS

PROKOFIEV, SERGEI
AMERICAN BALLET THEATRE AT THE MET
AMERICAN BALLET THEATRE IN SAN FRAN-
    CISCO
BALLERINA
BALLERINA: LYNN SEYMOUR
BALLET FAVORITES

THE BOLSHOI BALLET
BOLSHOI PROKOFIEV GALA
CINDERELLA (Berlin Comic Opera Ballet)
CINDERELLA (Bolshoi Ballet)
CINDERELLA (Bolshoi Ballet)
CINDERELLA (Lyon Opera Ballet)
CINDERELLA (Paris Opera Ballet)
CINDERELLA: A DANCE FANTASY
FONTEYN AND NUREYEV: THE PERFECT
    PARTNERSHIP
GALINA ULANOVA
GRAND CONCERT
IVAN THE TERRIBLE (Bolshoi Ballet)
IVAN THE TERRIBLE (Bolshoi Ballet)
KAREN KAIN: BALLERINA
MOMENT OF LIGHT: THE DANCE OF EVE-
    LYN HART
NATASHA
THE PERSISTENT IMAGE and VALSE
PLISETSKAYA DANCES
ROMEO AND JULIET (Bolshoi Ballet)
ROMEO AND JULIET (Bolshoi Ballet)
ROMEO AND JULIET (Bolshoi Ballet)
ROMEO AND JULIET (La Scala Ballet)
ROMEO AND JULIET (Lyon Opera Ballet)
ROMEO AND JULIET (Royal Ballet)
ROMEO AND JULIET (Royal Ballet)
ROMEOS AND JULIETS
RUSSIAN BALLET, THE GLORIOUS TRADI-
    TION
THE STONE FLOWER (Bolshoi Ballet)
THE STONE FLOWER (Kirov Ballet)
STUTTGART BALLET: THE MIRACLE LIVES
THE TURNING POINT

PUBLIC ENEMY
PULL YOUR HEAD TO THE MOON

PUENTE, TITO
¡A BAILAR! THE JOURNEY OF A LATIN
    DANCE COMPANY

PUGNI, CESARE
ALICIA ALONSO: ALICIA
THE BALLERINAS
THE KIROV BALLET: CLASSIC BALLET NIGHT
KIROV SOLOISTS: INVITATION TO THE
    DANCE
THE MARYINSKY BALLET
MOMENT OF LIGHT: THE DANCE OF EVE-
    LYN HART
PAS DE QUATRE and THE CHARIOTEER
THE ROMANTIC ERA

PURCELL, HENRY
DIDO AND AENEAS
THE MAGNIFICENT BEGINNING
MOOR'S PAVANE (VARIATIONS ON THE
    THEME OF OTHELLO)
PARCELLE DE CIEL
SHAKESPEARE DANCE TRILOGY

QUINN, J. MARK
REQUIEM FOR A SLAVE

RACHMANINOV, SERGEI
THE BOLSHOI BALLET
THE BOLSHOI BALLET: GALINA ULANOVA

RANSTRÖM, TURE
MISS JULIE

RAUCHWERGHER, MIKHAIL
MORNING STAR (CHOLPON)

RAVEL, MAURICE
THE ART OF THE TWENTIETH CENTURY
    BALLET
ATTITUDES IN DANCE
BOLERO
BOLERO and PICTURES AT AN EXHIBITION
THE BOLSHOI BALLET
CHOREOGRAPHY BY BALANCHINE
DAPHNIS AND CHLÖE
L'ENFANT ET LES SORTILÈGES
FANDANGO
ONEIRO: IN THE SHADOW OF ISADORA
RAVEL

REBEL
THE MAGNIFICENT BEGINNING
REALITY OF A DREAMER: RIVER NORTH
    DANCE COMPANY

REX, T.
BECAUSE WE MUST

RICHIE, LIONEL
WHITE NIGHTS

RICHTER, PAT
DELI COMMEDIA

RIEGGER, WALLINGFORD
THE DANCE WORKS OF DORIS HUMPHREY:
    WITH MY RED FIRES AND *NEW DANCE*
FESTIVAL OF THE DANCE
NEW DANCE: RECORD FILM
WITH MY RED FIRES

RIETI, VITTORIO
ATTITUDES IN DANCE

RILEY, VICTOR
SOLO

RIMSKY-KORSAKOV, NIKOLAI
CAPRICCIO ESPAGNOL (Spanish Fiesta)
INVITATION TO THE DANCE
NIJINSKY

RIVERA, MIGUEL
FLAMENCOS DE LA LUZ

ROBERTS, HOWARD
ALVIN AILEY: MEMORIES AND VISIONS

ROBERTS, MEGAN
FOR DANCERS

ROBINSON, MCNEIL
NINE VARIATIONS ON A DANCE THEME

RODGERS, RICHARD
BABES IN ARMS
BALI MECHANIQUE
CAROUSEL
THE KING AND I

OKLAHOMA!
ON YOUR TOES
ON YOUR TOES . . . THE MAKIN OF
THE SOUND OF MUSIC
SOUTH PACIFIC

ROMBERG, SIGMUND
DEEP IN MY HEART

ROMEO, JONATHAN
THREE DANCES BY MARTHA CURTIS

ROSENSTOCK, MILTON
DANCE THEATRE OF HARLEM

ROSSINI, GIOACCHINO
BALLET COMES TO BRITAIN
BART COOK: CHOREOGRAPHER
NAPOLI
SCHOOL FOR WIVES

ROSSOKHOVAKSKY, LEONID
TERPSICHORE'S CAPTIVES

ROTH, CHARLES
SYNCOPATIONS

ROTH, GABRIELLE
THE WAVE: ECSTATIC DANCE FOR BODY
AND SOUL

RUSSELL, LEON
ALVIN AILEY: MEMORIES AND VISIONS

RUTHERFORD, NORMAN
LIKE WIND IN MIRA'S HAIR
POSITIVE MOTION

SACHDEV, G.S.
IMPROVISATION TO BANSURI FLUTE AND
SEASCAPES
MOVING PASTURES

SAINT-SAËNS, CAMILLE
THE BOLSHOI BALLET: GALINA ULANOVA
BOLSHOI SOLOISTS CLASSIQUE
CARMEN (Bolshoi Ballet)
DYING SWAN
IMMORTAL SWAN
NATASHA
THE PARIS OPERA BALLET: SEVEN BALLETS
PAVLOVA: A TRIBUTE TO A LEGENDARY
BALLERINA

SAINTE MARIE, BUFFY
A MOVING PICTURE

SAKAMOTO, RYUICHI
RETRACING STEPS: AMERICAN DANCE
SINCE POSTMODERNISM

SANLUCAR, MANOLO
SEVILLANAS

SANO, KEMOKO
KEMOKO SANO TEACHES AFRICAN DANCE
FROM THE REPUBLIC OF GUINEA

SATIE, ERIK
ENTR'ACTE
SATIE AND SUZANNE

SATYAM, VEMPATI CHINA
THE TEMPLE AND THE SWAN

SCARLATTI, DOMENICO
STUTTGART BALLET: THE MIRACLE LIVES

SCHAEFER, R. MURRAY
CARNIVAL OF SHADOWS

SCHNEITZHOEFFER, JEAN
LA SYLPHIDE (Paris Opera Ballet)

SCHOENBERG, ARNOLD
AMERICAN BALLET THEATRE: A CLOSE-UP
IN TIME
KYLIAN COLLECTION
MODERN BALLET
THE SCENE CHANGES

SCHUBERT, FRANZ
ADOLESCENCE
DANCE THEATRE OF HARLEM
FANTASIA
ISADORA DUNCAN: MOVEMENT FROM THE
SOUL
ISADORA DUNCAN: TECHNIQUE AND CHO-
REOGRAPHY
ISADORA DUNCAN: TECHNIQUE AND REP-
ERTORY
STUTTGART BALLET: THE MIRACLE LIVES

SCHULLER, GÜNTHER
ECHOES OF JAZZ
THE TRAITOR

SCHUMAN, WILLIAM
MARTHA GRAHAM, AN AMERICAN ORIGI-
NAL IN PERFORMANCE
MODERN BALLET
NIGHT JOURNEY

SCHUMANN, ROBERT
DAVIDSBÜNDLERTANZE
NIJINSKY
TRAILBLAZERS OF MODERN DANCE

SCHWARTZ, ARTHUR
THE BAND WAGON

SCIORTINI, PATRICIA
ALVIN AILEY: MEMORIES AND VISIONS

SCRIABIN, ALEXANDER
BALLERINA: LYNN SEYMOUR
ISADORA DUNCAN: MOVEMENT FROM THE
SOUL
ISADORA DUNCAN: TECHNIQUE AND CHO-
REOGRAPHY
NOT FOR LOVE ALONE
TRAILBLAZERS OF MODERN DANCE

SENTES, JOHN
THE HIGHWAYMAN

SHANKAR, RAVI
A CHAIRY TALE
INDIA: HAUNTING PASSAGE
RAGAS FOR SWAMI SATCHIDANANDA

SHARP, ELLIOTT
ANTIGONE/RITES OF PASSION

SHCHEDRIN, RODION
ANNA KARENINA
CARMEN (Bolshoi Ballet)
THE LITTLE HUMPBACKED HORSE

SHOSTAKOVICH, DMITRI
BALLET LEGENDS: THE KIROV'S NINEL KUR-
GAPKINA
BRITISH BALLET TODAY
THE GOLDEN AGE
THE PARIS OPERA BALLET: SIX BALLETS
THE PENNSYLVANIA BALLET: DA MUMMY,
NYET MUMMY

SIBELIUS, JEAN
THE PARIS OPERA BALLET: SEVEN BALLETS

SIMON, PAUL
CAN'T RUN BUT

SIMONE, NINA
FOUR WOMEN

SIMOPOULOS, NANA
ALICIA WAS FAINTING

SIROCCO
DANCE TO THE GREAT MOTHER
DELILAH & SIROCCO . . . LIVE & WILD!

SIROTTA, MICHAEL
LIFE IN THE DUST: FRAGMENTS OF AFRICAN
VOYAGES
VISION DANCE

SMITH, WILLIAM O.
CIRCLES II

SOUSA, JOHN PHILIP
WATCHING BALLET

SOWASH, BRADLEY
FIELDS

SPECIAL FUN
THREE DANCES BY MARTHA CURTIS

SPIEGEL, LAURIE
DANCE ELEVEN
DORIS CHASE DANCE SERIES: FOUR SOLOS
INVISIBLE DANCE

SPOHR, LOUIS
WHAT'S REMEMBERED

STANFORD, LYNN
BALLET CLASS

STOBART, PAUL
BRYONY BRIND'S BALLET: THE FIRST STEPS

STOCKDALE, GARY
FORBIDDEN CITY, U.S.A

STOCKHAUSEN, KARLHEINZ
I AM A DANCER

STOLLER, MIKE
ALL THAT JAZZ

STOMPONE, ATILIO
TANGO

STONE, SUSAN
THREE DANCES BY MARTHA CURTIS

STRAUSS, JOHANN
BALLET LEGENDS: THE KIROV'S NINEL KUR-
    GAPKINA
GREAT PERFORMANCE IN DANCE
ISADORA DUNCAN: MOVEMENT FROM THE
    SOUL
ISADORA DUNCAN: TECHNIQUE AND REP-
    ERTORY
WHAT IS NEW

STRAUSS, RICHARD
EIGHT GREAT STEPS TO CHOREOGRAPHY
JOSEPH'S LEGENDE
SYLVIE GUILLEM AT WORK

STRAVINSKY, IGOR
BALLET
BALLET WITH EDWARD VILLELLA
THE BEGINNINGS OF TODAY
CHOREOGRAPHY BY BALANCHINE
DANCE: NEW YORK CITY BALLET
THE EBB AND FLOW
AN EVENING WITH KYLIAN AND THE NE-
    DERLANDS DANS THEATRE
FANTASIA
THE FIREBIRD
THE MARYINSKY BALLET
NIJINSKY
PARIS DANCES DIAGHILEV
PETER MARTINS: A DANCER
PULCINELLA/SOLDAT
THE ROYAL BALLET
SET PIECE
STRAVINSKY

STROUSE, CHARLES
ANNIE
BYE BYE BIRDIE

STYNE, JULE
ANCHORS AWEIGH
FUNNY GIRL

SUBOTNIK, MORTON
CIRCLES I

THE SUBURBS
SOLO

SURINACH, CARLOS
ACROBATS OF GOD
PAUL TAYLOR AND COMPANY: AN ARTIST
    AND HIS WORK

SWAYZE, PATRICK
DIRTY DANCING

TAKEMITSU, TORU
AN EVENING WITH KYLIAN AND THE NE-
    DERLANDS DANS THEATRE

TATUM, ART
JAZZ HOOFER: BABY LAURENCE

TCHAIKOVSKY, PETER ILYICH
ALICIA ALONSO: ALICIA
AMERICAN BALLET THEATRE: A CLOSE-UP
    IN TIME
AMERICAN BALLET THEATRE IN SAN FRAN-
    CISCO
ART AND TECHNIQUE OF THE BALLET
BACKSTAGE AT THE KIROV
THE BALLERINAS
BALLET
BALLET: A CAREER FOR BOYS
BALLET FAVORITES
BALLET LEGENDS: THE KIROV'S NINEL KUR-
    GAPKINA
BALLET ROBOTIQUE
BALLET RUSE
BALLET STUDY FILMS
BEAUTY AND THE BEAST
THE BEGINNINGS OF TODAY
BOLD STEPS
THE BOLSHOI BALLET: GALINA ULANOVA
BOLSHOI: DIVERTISSEMENTS
BOLSHOI SOLOISTS CLASSIQUE
CLASSICAL BALLET
DANCE: NEW YORK CITY BALLET
ESSENTIAL BALLET: RUSSIAN BALLET
AN EVENING WITH THE ROYAL BALLET
FANTASIA
FONTEYN AND NUREYEV: THE PERFECT
    PARTNERSHIP
GRAND CONCERT
GREAT BALLERINA
GREAT PERFORMANCE IN DANCE
THE HARD NUT
HOW BALLET BEGAN
I AM A DANCER
THE LEGACY OF THE CHOREOGRAPHY OF
    ISADORA DUNCAN
LUDMILA SEMENYAKA: BOLSHOI BALLE-
    RINA
THE MAGIC OF THE KIROV BALLET
MAKAROVA RETURNS
THE MARGOT FONTEYN STORY
MODERN BALLET
THE NUTCRACKER (American Ballet Theatre)
THE NUTCRACKER (Bolshoi Ballet)
THE NUTCRACKER (Bolshoi Ballet)
THE NUTCRACKER (New York City Ballet)
THE NUTCRACKER (Paris Opera Ballet)
THE NUTCRACKER (Royal Ballet)
ONEGIN
THE PARIS OPERA BALLET: SEVEN BALLETS
THE PARIS OPERA BALLET: SIX BALLETS
PAVLOVA: A TRIBUTE TO A LEGENDARY
    BALLERINA
PETER MARTINS: A DANCER
PLISETSKAYA DANCES
A POEM OF DANCES ALSO KNOWN AS PLI-
    SETSKAYA: CARMEN
PUSS IN BOOTS
THE ROMANTIC BALLET
THE ROYAL BALLET
RUSSIAN BALLET, THE GLORIOUS TRADI-
    TION
THE SCENE CHANGES
SCHOOL OF AMERICAN BALLET
SHAKESPEARE DANCE TRILOGY
SLEEPING BEAUTY (animated)
SLEEPING BEAUTY (Ballet del Teatro Municipal)
SLEEPING BEAUTY (Bolshoi Ballet)

SLEEPING BEAUTY (Kirov Ballet)
SLEEPING BEAUTY (Kirov Ballet)
SLEEPING BEAUTY (Kirov Ballet)
SLEEPING BEAUTY ON ICE
STARS OF THE RUSSIAN BALLET
STUTTGART BALLET: THE MIRACLE LIVES
THE SUGAR PLUM FAIRY VARIATION FROM
    THE NUTCRACKER
SWAN LAKE (American Ballet Theatre)
SWAN LAKE (Bolshoi Ballet)
SWAN LAKE (Bolshoi Ballet)
SWAN LAKE (Kirov Ballet)
SWAN LAKE (London Festival Ballet)
SWAN LAKE (Royal Ballet)
SWAN LAKE (Russian State Perm Ballet)
SWAN LAKE (Vienna Opera Ballet)
THE SWAN LAKE STORY: A DANCE FANTASY
TCHAIKOVSKY AND THE RUSSIANS
THE TURNING POINT
THE ULTIMATE SWAN LAKE
WATCHING BALLET
WHAT DO PINA BAUSCH AND HER DANCES
    DO IN WÜPPERTAL?

TCHEREPNINE, NICHOLAS
REFLECTIONS OF A DANCER: ALEXANDRA
    DANILOVA, PRIMA BALLERINA ASSOLUTA

TELSON, BOB
LIES

TERRY, BRAD
KING KONG IN A BLANKET

TERRY, SONNY
HARMONICA BREAKDOWN

THEODORAKIS, MIKIS
THE LOVERS OF TERUEL

THOMPSON, TIMOTHY
DANCE FIVE
JONATHAN AND THE ROCKER

THOMSON, VIRGIL
ERICK HAWKINS' AMERICA

TKACHENKO, IGON
THE BLACK BOOTS

TUCKER, GREGORY
CLINIC OF STUMBLE

TUDOR, DAVID
CHANNELS/INSERTS
EVENT FOR TELEVISION
RAINFOREST

TUDOR, WILLIAM
SPACE CITY

TYRANNY, "BLUE" GENE
ENDANCE

UAKTI
ANIMA

ULTAN, WENDY
SOLO

VALERA, MANUEL
THE PARIS OPERA BALLET: SIX BALLETS

VAN TIEGHEM, DAVID
ANTIGONE/RITES OF PASSION
IN MOTION WITH MICHAEL MOSCHEN

Dancers Index

ABDUL, PAULA
EVERYBODY DANCE NOW

ABDUSILOV, S.
MORNING STAR (CHOLPON)

ABDYEV, REJEN
LA BAYADÈRE (Kirov Ballet)

ACCARDI, DONATELLA
HIGH NOON

ADAIR, TOM
FALL RIVER LEGEND

ADAMS, CAROLYN
JUNCTION

ADAMS, DAVID
BALLET STUDY FILMS

ADAMS, DIANA
INVITATION TO THE DANCE

ADOMINAS, SANDRA
ANNUNCIATION

AFANASKOV, VITALI
THE KIROV BALLET: CLASSIC BALLET NIGHT

AGERHOLM, ANNA
THE ROYAL DANISH BALLET 1902–1906

AILEY, ALVIN
DANCE BLACK AMERICA
GENIUS ON THE WRONG COAST

AKIMOV, BORIS
IVAN THE TERRIBLE (Bolshoi Ballet)
YURI GRIGOROVICH: MASTER OF THE BOL-
    SHOI

ALBA, MARIA
SABICAS: EL MAESTRO DE FLAMENCO

ALBERT, EDDIE
ON YOUR TOES

ALBERTSON, MARGARET
MOON

ALDOUS, LUCETTE
DON QUIXOTE (Australian Ballet)

ALFARO, NANCY
I WILL NOT BE SAD IN THIS WORLD

ALHANKO, ANNELI
THE DANCER

ALLEMANN, SABINE
ONEGIN

ALLEN, GRACIE
A DAMSEL IN DISTRESS

ALLEYNE, JOHN
YOUNG AND JUST BEGINNING: PIERRE

ALLISON, NANCY
DANCE AND MYTH: THE WORLD OF JEAN
    ERDMAN

ALONSO, ALICIA
ALICIA ALONSO: ALICIA
GISÈLLE (Ballet Nacional de Cuba)
A PORTRAIT OF GISÈLLE
THE ROMANTIC ERA
TOUR EN L'AIR

ALONSO, FERNANDO
GISÈLLE (Ballet Nacional de Cuba)

ALWAY, KENDALL
THE PAINTED PRINCESS

AMAYA, CARMEN
LOS TARANTOS

AMINA, TAIA
GAMEEL GAMAL (Oh! Beautiful Dancer)

ANANIASHVILI, NINA
BOLSHOI: DIVERTISSEMENTS
DON QUIXOTE (Russian State Perm Ballet)
ESSENTIAL BALLET: RUSSIAN BALLET
NINA ANANIASHVILI AND INTERNATIONAL
    STARS
SWAN LAKE (Russian State Perm Ballet)

ANDERSON, CYNTHIA
DANCE ELEVEN
DORIS CHASE DANCE SERIES: FOUR SOLOS

ANDERSON, DAVID
BEAUTY AND THE BEAST

ANDERSON, IB
DANCING BOURNONVILLE
DAVIDSBÜNDLERTANZE

ANDREW, THOMAS
GREAT PERFORMANCE IN DANCE

ANN-MARGRET
BYE BYE BIRDIE
VIVA LAS VEGAS

ANWAR, ANDREA
BRINGING TO LIGHT

APONTE, CHRISTOPHER
IMAGE: A DANCER

ARAUJO, LOIPA
WORLD'S YOUNG BALLET

ARBUS, LOREEN
ARGENTINE TANGO

ARGENTINITA
GREAT PERFORMANCE IN DANCE

ARJA, SUJANA
TOPENG BABAKAN (SOLO MASKED DANCE
    OF WEST JAVA)

ARKHIPOVA, NATALYA
BOLSHOI PROKOFIEV GALA
THE NUTCRACKER (Bolshoi Ballet)

ARMITAGE, KAROLE
FRACTIONS I
FROM AN ISLAND SUMMER
MERCE CUNNINGHAM
PARAFANGO
ROAMIN' I

ARNOLD, BECKY
CHOICE CHANCE WOMAN DANCE

ARROYAVE, ROSEMARIE
RAVEL

ARSLANIAN, SHARON
THE ENDURING ESSENCE: THE TECHNIQUE
    AND CHOREOGRAPHY OF ISADORA DUN-
    CAN, REMEMBERED AND RECON-
    STRUCTED BY GEMZE DE LAPPE

ASAKAWA, TAKAKO
ACROBATS OF GOD
CORTEGE OF EAGLES
THE MARTHA GRAHAM DANCE COMPANY
MARTHA GRAHAM: THREE CONTEMPO-
    RARY CLASSICS
SERAPHIC DIALOGUE

ASHLEY, MERRILL
THE BALANCHINE ESSAYS: ARABESQUE
CHOREOGRAPHY BY BALANCHINE
DANCING FOR MR. B.: SIX BALANCHINE
    BALLERINAS
THE FOUR TEMPERAMENTS
VIDEO DICTIONARY OF CLASSICAL BALLET

ASHMOLE, DAVID
CURTAIN UP

ASHTON, FREDERICK
THE MARGOT FONTEYN STORY
THE TALES OF BEATRIX POTTER

ASTAFIEV, ALEKSANDR
DON QUIXOTE (Russian State Perm Ballet)

ASTAIRE, FRED
AMERICAN MUSICALS: FAMOUS PRODUC-
    TION NUMBERS
THE BAND WAGON
THE BARKLEYS OF BROADWAY
THE BELLE OF NEW YORK
BROADWAY MELODY OF 1940
CAREFREE
DADDY LONGLEGS
A DAMSEL IN DISTRESS
EASTER PARADE
FLYING DOWN TO RIO
FOLLOW THE FLEET
FUNNY FACE
THE GAY DIVORCEE
HOLIDAY INN
LET'S DANCE
ROBERTA
ROYAL WEDDING
THE SCENE CHANGES
SECOND CHORUS
SHALL WE DANCE
SILK STOCKINGS
THE SKY'S THE LIMIT
THE STORY OF VERNON AND IRENE CASTLE
SWING TIME
THAT'S ENTERTAINMENT
TOP HAT
YOLANDA AND THE THIEF
YOU WERE NEVER LOVLIER
YOU'LL NEVER GET RICH
THE ZIEGFELD FOLLIES

ASYLMURATOVA, ALTYNAI
BACKSTAGE AT THE KIROV
LA BAYADÈRE (Royal Ballet)
LE CORSAIRE
THE KIROV BALLET IN LONDON
THE LENINGRAD LEGEND
THE MARYINSKY BALLET
WHITE NIGHT OF DANCE IN LENINGRAD

ATHENOES, CLEO
AIR FOR THE G STRING

ATKINS, CHOLLY
TAPDANCIN'

ATLAS, CHARLES
DUNE DANCE

AUGUSTYN, FRANK
KAREN KAIN: BALLERINA
ONEGIN
PAVLOVA: A TRIBUTE TO A LEGENDARY
    BALLERINA

AVIOTTE, PIERRE
THE BLUE ANGEL

AYUPOVA, ZHANNA
NINA ANANIASHVILI AND INTERNATIONAL
    STARS

AZA, MARÍA ELENA
THE HIGHWAYMAN

AZIZA
PULL YOUR HEAD TO THE MOON

BABALIS, MIA
FANDANGO

BACON, FAITH
FAN AND BUBBLE DANCES

BACON, KEVIN
FOOTLOOSE

BADILLO, MANUEL
FLAMENCOS DE LA LUZ

BAEZA, RAMÓN
THE FIGHT

BAILEY, CARL
BUFFALO SOLDIER

BAKER, JOSEPHINE
PARISIAN FOLLIES
PRINCESS TAM TAM
ZOU ZOU

BALAKHNECHEVA, NATASHA
TERPSICHORE'S CAPTIVES

BALLIN, GLADYS
TOTEM

BALZAROVA, MARTA
DAISY AND HER GARDEN: A DANCE FAN-
    TASY

BAMBERGER, JÜRGEN
I WILL NOT BE SAD IN THIS WORLD

BANDO, TAMASABURO
A LIFE IN TWO WORLDS: TAMASABURO
    BANDO
STRUGGLE FOR HOPE

BANGOURA, HAMIDOU
AFRICA DANCES

BAPTISTE, DEVI ANANDA
THE MAGANA BAPTISTE SIXTH ANNUAL
    BELLY DANCE FESTIVAL

BARBA, EUGENIA
THEATRE MEETS RITUAL

BARBEE, VICTOR
DON QUIXOTE (American Ballet Theatre)

BARBIERI, MARGARET
BALLET ENTERS THE WORLD STAGE
THE CACHUCHA
CURTAIN UP
HOW BALLET WAS SAVED

BARSNESS, ERIC
BREAK

BARTHO, CATHRINA
EARLY DANCE FILMS 1894–1912

BARTLETT, SCOTT
SOUND OF ONE

BARYSHNIKOV, MIKHAIL
AMERICAN BALLET THEATRE AT THE MET
BALLET FAVORITES
BARYSHNIKOV AT WOLF TRAP
BARYSHNIKOV DANCES SINATRA
BARYSHNIKOV: THE DANCER AND THE
    DANCE
BOLD STEPS
CARMEN (Ballet National de Marseille)
DANCE SPACE
DANCERS
DON QUIXOTE (American Ballet Theatre)
THE EBB AND FLOW
GISÈLLE (American Ballet Theatre)
THE NUTCRACKER (American Ballet Theatre)
RUSSIAN BALLET, THE GLORIOUS TRADI-
    TION
THE TURNING POINT
TWYLA THARP: MAKING TELEVISION
    DANCE
WHAT IS NEW
WHITE NIGHTS
WORLD'S YOUNG BALLET

BATENHORST, CHRISTOPHER
MASS

BAUER, ZONNI
ANIMA

BAUMANN, KARL
PICTURES AT AN EXHIBITION

BAXTER, JOHN R.
INTROSPECTION

BEALS, JENNIFER
FLASHDANCE

BEALS, MARGARET
THE DESPERATE HEART
IMPULSES
MOVING PASTURES
RAGAS FOR SWAMI SATCHIDANANDA
TEAK ROOM (AUTOBIOGRAPHY OF A
    DANCER)
WILD SWANS IN EPITAPH AND MADHONOR

BEATTY, TALLEY
CARNIVAL OF RHYTHM
MAYA DEREN: EXPERIMENTAL FILMS
THE NEW DANCE GROUP GALA CONCERT
A STUDY IN CHOREOGRAPHY FOR CAMERA

BECK, ELIZABETH
THE ROYAL DANISH BALLET 1902–1906

BEER, HENRY
MASS

BEISHENALIYEVA, BIBISARA
MORNING STAR (CHOLPON)

BÉJART, MAURICE
SUZANNE FARRELL: ELUSIVE MUSE

BELARBI, KADER
MOMENT OF LIGHT: THE DANCE OF EVE-
    LYN HART

BROWN, JAMES
EVERYBODY DANCE NOW

BROWN, JAMES "BUSTER"
SONGS UNWRITTEN: A TAP DANCER RE-
MEMBERED
TAPDANCIN'

BROWN, KING RASTUS
JAZZ HOOFER: BABY LAURENCE

BROWN, RONALD
AILEY DANCES

BROWN, TRISHA
ACCUMULATION WITH TALKING PLUS
WATER MOTOR
BEYOND THE MAINSTREAM: POSTMODERN
DANCERS
THE JUDSON PROJECT TAPES
MAKING DANCES: SEVEN POSTMODERN
CHOREOGRAPHERS
WATER MOTOR

BROWNE, LESLIE
NIJINSKY
THE TURNING POINT

BRUCE, CHRISTOPHER
BALLET COMES TO BRITAIN

BRUHN, ERIK
BOLD STEPS
DANCING BOURNONVILLE
ERIK BRUHN: ARTIST OF THE BALLET
GISÈLLE (American Ballet Theatre)
SYMPHONIE FANTASTIQUE
YOUNG AND JUST BEGINNING: PIERRE

BRYANS, RUDY
KAREN KAIN: BALLERINA

BUBBLES, JOHN
JAZZ HOOFER: BABY LAURENCE

BUCKLEY, TIMOTHY
ENDANCE

BUFALINO, BRENDA
ESSENTIALS OF TAP TECHNIQUE
SONGS UNWRITTEN: A TAP DANCER RE-
MEMBERED
TWO TAKES ON TAP

BUJONES, FERNANDO
AMERICAN BALLET THEATRE AT THE MET
AMERICAN BALLET THEATRE IN SAN FRAN-
CISCO
BUJONES IN CLASS
BUJONES: IN HIS IMAGE
COPPÉLIA (Ballets de San Juan)
GISÈLLE (Ballet Teatro Municipal of Rio de Ja-
neiro)
SCHOOL OF AMERICAN BALLET
SLEEPING BEAUTY (Ballet del Teatro Municipal)

BURGE, GREGG
A CHORUS LINE

BURNITT, ELIZABETH
EXCERPTS FROM "WITHOUT A PLACE"

BURNS, DONNIE
BALLROOM DANCING: THE INTERNA-
TIONAL CHAMPIONSHIPS

BURNS, GEORGE
A DAMSEL IN DISTRESS

BURNS, LOUISE
FOR DANCERS
FRACTIONS I
MERCE CUNNINGHAM
ROAMIN' I

BURRILL, JENNY
ANGEL OF TIME

BUSH, LISA
X-RAY EYES

BUSSELL, DARCEY
MAYERLING
THE PRINCE OF THE PAGODAS

BUTLER, JOHN
ECHOES OF JAZZ

CAGNEY, JAMES
FOOTLIGHT PARADE
YANKEE DOODLE DANDY

CAHAN, CORA
ATTITUDES IN DANCE

CAINES, CHRISTOPHER
RUBBLE DANCE LONG ISLAND CITY

CAMERON, SANDRA
PARTNERS

CANNER, BARBARA
ANIMA

CAPPELETTI, JIM
PICTURES AT AN EXHIBITION

CAPUCILLI, TERESE
MARTHA GRAHAM: THREE CONTEMPO-
RARY CLASSICS

CARBERRY, DEIRDRE
BARYSHNIKOV DANCES SINATRA

CARLSON, CAROLYN
CHOICE CHANCE WOMAN DANCE
FILM WITH THREE DANCERS
IMAGE: FLESH AND VOICE

CARLYLE, THOM
ADOLESCENCE OF BALLET

CARMINES, AL
THE JUDSON PROJECT TAPES

CARNEY, CHRISTOPHER
PULCINELLA/SOLDAT

CARON, LESLIE
AN AMERICAN IN PARIS
DADDY LONGLEGS

CARPENTER, KEVIN
OUR TOWN: THE MAKING OF A BALLET

CARR, CHARMIAN
THE SOUND OF MUSIC

CARRAFA, JOHN
KING KONG IN A BLANKET

CARRENO, LÁZARO
PLASMASIS

CARSON, MICHAEL A.
HELP ME TO DREAM

CARTER, ALAN
THE RED SHOES

CASTAÑÓN, ANA MARÍA
COPPÉLIA (Ballets de San Juan)

CASTLE, VERNON AND IRENE
GREAT PERFORMANCE IN DANCE
TRAILBLAZERS OF MODERN DANCE

CAU, JEAN
IN PRAISE OF FOLLY

CERF, A.
CHARLESTON

CERNIK, EVA
DANCE IMAGING
EVA AS DANCER

CHABUKIANI, VAKHTANG
CLASSIC KIROV PERFORMANCES
STARS OF THE RUSSIAN BALLET

CHAGRIN, JULIAN
THE CONCERT

CHAMBERS, MICHAEL
BREAKIN'

CHAMPION, MARGE AND GOWER
JUPITER'S DARLING
LOVELY TO LOOK AT
SHOW BOAT

CHANDRA OF DAMASCUS
BASIC SWORD
FAN TECHNIQUES FOR ORIENTAL DANCE
VEIL TECHNIQUES IN ORIENTAL DANCE
ZAR AND FLOORWORK
CHANEY, LON
TAPDANCIN'

CHAPLIN, CHARLIE
HOLLYWOOD CLOWNS

CHAPMAN, WES
BALLET

CHARISSE, CYD
THE BAND WAGON
BLACK TIGHTS
BRIGADOON
DEEP IN MY HEART

CURTIS, MARTHA
THREE DANCES BY MARTHA CURTIS

CUTRI, ALISON
CUNNINGHAM DANCE TECHNIQUE: ELE-
MENTARY LEVEL

D'ABBRACCI, NINA
ANIMA

D'AMBOISE, CHARLOTTE
KARATE RAP

D'AMBOISE, JACQUES
CAROUSEL
DANCE: NEW YORK CITY BALLET
DANCE SPACE
DANCING
DAVIDSBÜNDLERTANZE
SEVEN BRIDES FOR SEVEN BROTHERS
SUZANNE FARRELL: ELUSIVE MUSE
A TIME TO DANCE
WATCHING BALLET

D'ANGELO, ANN MARIE
PAVLOVA: A TRIBUTE TO A LEGENDARY
BALLERINA

D'ARTURO, ELEANOR
AMERICAN BALLET THEATRE: A CLOSE-UP
IN TIME

DABNEY, STEPHANIE
DANCE THEATRE OF HARLEM

DAILEY, DAN
IT'S ALWAYS FAIR WEATHER
THERE'S NO BUSINESS LIKE SHOW BUSINESS

DALE, GROVER
ECHOES OF JAZZ

DALLY, LYNN
TWO TAKES ON TAP

DANIAS, STARR
THE TURNING POINT

DANIELIAN, LEON
GAITÉ PARISIENNE

DANIELS, BRENDA
THE STONE DANCES

DANILOVA, ALEXANDRA
CAPRICCIO ESPAGNOL (Spanish Fiesta)
GAITÉ PARISIENNE
GREAT PERFORMANCE IN DANCE
MADEMOISELLE FIFI
REFLECTIONS OF A DANCER: ALEXANDRA
DANILOVA, PRIMA BALLERINA ASSOLUTA
THE TURNING POINT

DAVIES, BILL
PARTNERS

DAVIS, CHUCK
MADE IN THE BRONX

DAVIS, JR., SAMMY
THE SCENE CHANGES
SWEET CHARITY

TAP
THAT'S DANCING

DAVIS, LYNDA
DANCE DESIGN: MOTION
DANCE DESIGN: SHAPING
DANCE DESIGN: SPACE
THE DANCE INSTRUMENT
HOW TO MOVE BETTER

DAVIS, WILLIAM
STORY

DE FRUTOS, JAVIER
L'ARMARI
THE FIGHT

DE JONG, BETTIE
JUNCTION
NINE VARIATIONS ON A DANCE THEME

DE KEERSMAEKER, ANNE TERESA
REPETITIONS

DE LA BYE, WILLY
THE ANATOMY LESSON

DE LA PEÑA, GEORGE
THE MERRY WIDOW
NIJINSKY

DE LA REZA, MICHELE
PERIL OF ANGELS

DE LAPPE, GEMZE
THE ENDURING ESSENCE: THE TECHNIQUE
AND CHOREOGRAPHY OF ISADORA DUN-
CAN, REMEMBERED
AND RECONSTRUCTED BY GEMZE DE LAPPE
ISADORA DUNCAN: TECHNIQUE AND CHO-
REOGRAPHY

DE LAVALLADE, CARMEN
A CHOREOGRAPHER AT WORK: JOHN
BUTLER
DANCE: IN SEARCH OF "LOVERS"
ETHNIC DANCE: ROUNDTRIP TO TRINIDAD
GENIUS ON THE WRONG COAST

DE LUIS, SARA
SABICAS: EL MAESTRO DE FLAMENCO

DE MARCO, JOHN
LIGHT, PART 5

DE ROSA, FRANCESCA
LE BAL

DE RUBI, ESBART DANSIRE
THE EBB AND FLOW

DE ST. CROIX, BRUCE
DUNE DANCE

DE VALOIS, NINETTE
FONTEYN AND NUREYEV: THE PERFECT
PARTNERSHIP
THE MARGOT FONTEYN STORY

DE VULPIAN, CLAUDE
THE PARIS OPERA BALLET: SIX BALLETS

DEAN, CHRISTOPHER
TORVILL AND DEAN: PATH TO PERFECTION

DEANE, ALLYSON
BALANCES

DECOUFLE, PHILIPPE
PARAFANGO

DEE, DEBBIE
DEBBIE DEE TAP TECHNIQUE

DEHN, MURA
IN A JAZZ WAY: A PORTRAIT OF MURA
DEHN

DEL RIO, DOLORES
FLYING DOWN TO RIO

DEL SOL, LAURA
CARMEN

DEL VECCHIO, SUZANNA
A DANCE ORIENTAL EXTRAVAGANZA

DELANGHE, GAY
ALMIRA 38
DORIS CHASE DANCE SERIES: FOUR SOLOS
JAZZ DANCE

DELILAH
DANCE DELILAH, DANCE!
DANCE TO THE GREAT MOTHER
DELILAH & SIROCCO . . . LIVE & WILD!
DELILAH'S BELLY DANCE WORKSHOP
DELILAH'S COSTUME WORKSHOP

DELLA TERZA, GRAZIA
RUBBLE DANCE LONG ISLAND CITY
SECRET OF THE WATERFALL
TRIPLE DUO

DENDY, MARK
SSS

DEREN, MAYA
MESHES OF THE AFTERNOON

DESOTO, EDWARD
EMPEROR JONES

DESROSIERS, ROBERT
A MOVING PICTURE

DETRICH, TAMAS
GISELLE . . . THE MAKING OF

DEVI, RITHA
VIBRANT SCULPTURE FROZEN DANCE

DEVIVO, KERRY
SHADES OF WIEGENLIED

DIAMOND, JILL
CUNNINGHAM DANCE TECHNIQUE: ELE-
MENTARY LEVEL

EMERY, SUSAN
ROAMIN' I

EMETS, VALERI
THE KIROV BALLET: CLASSIC BALLET NIGHT

ENGLUND, RICHARD
THE VERY EYE OF NIGHT

ENGLUND, SORELLA
MIXED DOUBLE
ORFEUS AND JULIE

ERDMAN, JEAN
JEAN ERDMAN: OUT OF CHAOS, *AMOR*
THE NEW DANCE GROUP GALA CONCERT

ERICKSON, BETTY
TEALIA

ESMERALDA, MERCHE
SEVILLANAS

ESQUIVEL, JORGE
THE ROMANTIC ERA

ESSEN, VIOLA
SPECTRE OF THE ROSE

EVANS, ALBERT
ACCENT ON THE OFFBEAT

EVDOKIMOVA, EVA
THE ROMANTIC ERA

EVERETT, TIMMY
THE MUSIC MAN

EVTEEVA, ELENA
THE KIROV BALLET; CLASSIC BALLET NIGHT

FADEYECHEV, ALEKSEI
DON QUIXOTE (Russian State Perm Ballet)
MACBETH
NINA ANANIASHVILI AND INTERNATIONAL
   STARS
SLEEPING BEAUTY (Bolshoi Ballet)
SWAN LAKE (Russian State Perm Ballet)

FADEYECHEV, NIKOLAI
THE BOLSHOI BALLET: GALINA ULANOVA
CARMEN (Bolshoi Ballet)
A POEM OF DANCES ALSO KNOWN AS PLI-
   SETSKAYA: CARMEN
SWAN LAKE (Bolshoi Ballet)

FAIRWEATHER, GAYNOR
BALLROOM DANCING: THE INTERNA-
   TIONAL CHAMPIONSHIPS

FALCO, LOUIS
DIONYSUS

FARBER, VIOLA
STORY

FARRELL, SUZANNE
CHOREOGRAPHY BY BALANCHINE
DANCE: NEW YORK CITY BALLET

DAVIDSBÜNDLERTANZE
THE FOUR TEMPERAMENTS
PETER MARTINS: A DANCER
SUZANNE FARRELL: ELUSIVE MUSE

FATIMA
IBRAHIM FARRAH PRESENTS RARE
   GLIMPSES: DANCES FROM THE MIDDLE
   EAST, VOLUME I

FAYE, DENISE
THE NEXT STEP

FEDOTOV, VIKTOR
SLEEPING BEAUTY (Kirov Ballet)

FELD, ELIOT
ELIOT FELD: ARTISTIC DIRECTOR
TZADDIK
WEST SIDE STORY

FENLEY, MOLISSA
RETRACING STEPS: AMERICAN DANCE
   SINCE POSTMODERNISM

FENSTER, NANCY
DANCE CHROMATIC

FERGUSON, KATHRYN
DANCES FROM THE CASBAH
AN INTRODUCTION TO BELLY DANCE
MIDEASTERN DANCE: AN INTRODUCTION
   TO BELLY DANCE

FERRAGUT, MABEL
MAGDALENE

FERRI, ALESSANDRA
BALLET
BALLET FAVORITES
DANCERS
ROMEO AND JULIET (Royal Ballet)

FERRIER, PATRICIA
THE VERY EYE OF NIGHT

FINE, MICHAEL
L'ARMARI

FLAVIN, TIM
NATASHA

FLEMING, MAUREEN
MOTHER AND CHILD/50
WIDENING GYRE

FLIER, JAAP
THE ANATOMY LESSON

FLORES, LOLA
SEVILLANAS

FOKINE, VERA
DYING SWAN

FOLDI, ERZSEBET
ALL THAT JAZZ

FONSECA, PETER
BALLET CLASS

FONTEYN, MARGOT
THE EBB AND FLOW
AN EVENING WITH THE ROYAL BALLET

FONTEYN AND NUREYEV: THE PERFECT
   PARTNERSHIP
I AM A DANCER
MARGOT FONTEYN IN LES SYLPHIDES
THE MARGOT FONTEYN STORY
OUT OF THE LIMELIGHT, HOME IN THE
   RAIN
THE ROMANTIC BALLET
ROMEO AND JULIET (La Scala Ballet)
ROMEO AND JULIET (Royal Ballet)
THE ROYAL BALLET
RUDOLF NUREYEV
THE SCENE CHANGES
SWAN LAKE (Vienna Opera Ballet)
WHAT IS NEW

FOREST, JIM
AMERICAN BALLROOM DANCING
INTERNATIONAL STYLE MODERN DANCING

FORT, SYVILLA
CARNIVAL OF RHYTHM
SYVILLA: THEY DANCE TO HER DRUM

FORTI, SIMONE
THE JUDSON PROJECT TAPES

FORTUNE, SANDRA
ARTISTS OF THE DANCE

FOSSE, BOB
KISS ME KATE

FOSTER, JULIA
HALF A SIXPENCE

FOUAD, NEGWA
STARS OF EGYPTIAN DANCE
FOUR STEP BROTHERS
TAPDANCIN'

FOX, LISA
FRACTIONS I
ROAMIN' I

FRACCI, CARLA
THE BALLERINAS
ERIK BRUHN: ARTIST OF THE BALLET
GISÈLLE (American Ballet Theatre)
I AM A DANCER
NIJINSKY
A PORTRAIT OF GISÈLLE
THE ROMANTIC ERA
ROMEO AND JULIET (La Scala Ballet)

FRANCA, CELIA
BOLD STEPS

FRANCIS, JANET
HOW BALLET WAS SAVED

FRANK, DIANE
SECRET OF THE WATERFALL

FRANKLIN, BONNIE
I HATE TO EXERCISE, I LOVE TO TAP

FRANKLIN, FREDERIC
CAPRICCIO ESPAGNOL (Spanish Fiesta)
GAITÉ PARISIENNE

KYLIAN, JIRI
DANCING

LA FOSSE, ROBERT
BARYSHNIKOV DANCES SONATRA

LAFÔRET, MARIE
TANGOS, THE EXILE OF GARDEL

LAFORTUNE, SYLVAIN
FANDANGO
NARCISSUS

LAING, HUGH
ANTONY TUDOR
MODERN BALLET

LAMAS, LORENZO
BODY ROCK

LAMBERT, GARY
PULCINELLA/SOLDAT

LAMY, MARTINE
THE ERIK BRUHN GALA: WORLD BALLET
COMPETITION

LANDBORN, ADAIR
ADOLESCENCE OF BALLET

LANDERS, AUDREY
A CHORUS LINE

LANE, JENNIFER
ELEMENT

LANGLAND, PAUL
I WILL NOT BE SAD IN THIS WORLD

LANGSNER, NANCY
CUNNINGHAM DANCE TECHNIQUE: ELE-
MENTARY LEVEL

LANSBURY, ANGELA
THE HARVEY GIRLS

LAPZESON, NOEMI
SERAPHIC DIALOGUE

LARKIN, ED
COUNTRY CORNERS

LAROSE, PETER
MASS

LARSEN, GERD
GISÈLLE (Bavarian State Ballet)
SWAN LAKE (Royal Ballet)

LARSEN, NIELS BJORN
SWAN LAKE (Royal Ballet)
SYMPHONIE FANTASTIQUE

LARSON, KAILE
PLANES, TRAINS, AUTOMOBILES

LAST, BRENDA
BALLET COMES TO BRITAIN

LATHROP, DOROTHY
AIR FOR THE G STRING

LAUREL AND HARDY
HOLLYWOOD CLOWNS

LAURENCE, BABY
JAZZ HOOFER: BABY LAURENCE

LAVROVSKY, MIKHAIL
BOLSHOI SOLOISTS CLASSIQUE
GISÈLLE (Bolshoi Ballet)
GRAND CONCERT
LUDMILA SEMENYAKA: BOLSHOI BALLE-
RINA
ROMEO AND JULIET (Bolshoi Ballet)

LAZARUS, SUSAN
CHOICE CHANCE WOMAN DANCE

LEAVENS, THEODORA
ANCIENT ART OF BELLY DANCING

LEDIAKH, GENNADI
CINDERELLA (Bolshoi Ballet)
CINDERELLA (Bolshoi Ballet)

LEE, MARY ANN
DANCING THROUGH THE MAGIC EYE: A
PORTRAIT OF VIRGINIA TANNER

LEE, SHELLEY
THE STONE DANCES

LEFEBVRE, JORGE
TOUR EN L'AIR

LEGRIS, MANUEL
MOMENT OF LIGHT: THE DANCE OF EVE-
LYN HART
THE PARIS OPERA BALLET: SEVEN BALLETS

LEIGH, JANET
BYE BYE BIRDIE

LELAND, SARA
DAVIDSBÜNDLERTANZE

LELAPPE, GEMZE
THE KING AND I

LENNON, JOSEPH
ROAMIN' I

LEOTARD, PHILIPPE
TANGOS, THE EXILE OF GARDEL

LEPESHINSKAYA, OLGA
GRAND CONCERT

LESLIE, JOAN
THE SKY'S THE LIMIT

LEST, BRENDA
BRITISH BALLET TODAY

LESTER, MARK
OLIVER!

LEVIEN, JULIA
ISADORA DUNCAN: TECHNIQUE AND CHO-
REOGRAPHY

THE LEGACY OF THE CHOREOGRAPHY OF
ISADORA DUNCAN

LEWIS, DANIEL
DANCE PRELUDES

LEWIS, MITCHELL
SALOME

LEWIS, TOM
LINDY VIDEOTAPES

LEWITSKY, BELLA
DANCERS IN SCHOOL
GENIUS ON THE WRONG COAST

LEWKOWICZ, BONNIE
DANCING FROM THE INSIDE OUT

LEZANA, SARA
LOS TARANTOS

LEZHINA, LARISSA
ESSENTIAL BALLET: RUSSIAN BALLET
THE MARYINSKY BALLET
SLEEPING BEAUTY (Kirov Ballet)
WELCOME BACK ST. PETERSBURG: A GALA
AT THE ROYAL OPERA HOUSE

LI, GEORGE
CLASSICAL BALLET

LIEPA, ANDRIS
ESSENTIAL BALLET: RUSSIAN BALLET
HOLIDAY OF BALLET
LUDMILA SEMENYAKA: BOLSHOI BALLE-
RINA
NINA ANANIASHVILI AND INTERNATIONAL
STARS

LIEPA, MARIUS
SPARTACUS (Bolshoi Ballet)
YURI GRIGOROVICH: MASTER OF THE BOL-
SHOI

LIMÓN, JOSÉ
DANCE PRELUDES
LAMENT
THE LANGUAGE OF DANCE
MOOR'S PAVANE (VARIATIONS ON THE
THEME OF OTHELLO)
THE TRAITOR

LINKE, SUSANNA
MARY WIGMAN: MY LIFE IS DANCE

LINN, BAMBI
A CHOREOGRAPHER AT WORK: JOHN
BUTLER

LIPPE, JANIS
ANCIENT ART OF BELLY DANCING

LISKA, IVAN
THE LADY OF THE CAMELLIAS
LITTLE EGYPT
ANCIENT ART OF BELLY DANCING

MASLOW, SOPHIE
THE NEW DANCE GROUP GALA CONCERT

MASON, MONICA
GISÈLLE (Bavarian State Ballet)

MASON, TERESA
BALLROOM DANCING

MASSENBERG, CAROL
FAME

MASSINE, LÉONIDE
CAPRICCIO ESPAGNOL (Spanish Fiesta)
GAITÉ PARISIENNE
THE RED SHOES
ST. FRANCIS
THE TALES OF HOFFMANN

MATEO, DIANE
HIGH NOON

MATTOX, MATT
SEVEN BRIDES FOR SEVEN BROTHERS

MAULE, MICHAEL
BALLET STUDY FILMS
MADEMOISELLE FIFI

MAURA, CARMEN
¡AY, CARMELA!

MAURIN, ELISABETH
THE NUTCRACKER (Paris Opera Ballet)

MAXIMOVA, EKATERINA
ANYUTA
THE BOLSHOI BALLET
CINDERELLA (Bolshoi Ballet)
CINDERELLA (Bolshoi Ballet)
THE MAGIC OF THE BOLSHOI BALLET
THE NUTCRACKER (Bolshoi Ballet)
THE NUTCRACKER (Bolshoi Ballet)
RUSSIAN BALLET, THE GLORIOUS TRADI-
    TION

MAXWELL, CARLA
TWO ECSTATIC THEMES

MAYER, JULIA
AN ORIGINAL BILL ROBINSON VIDEO
AN ORIGINAL JULIA MAYER VIDEO

MCBRIDE, PATRICIA
BALLET WITH EDWARD VILLELLA
CHOREOGRAPHY BY BALANCHINE
DANCE: NEW YORK CITY BALLET
MAN WHO DANCES: EDWARD VILLELLA
THE MERRY WIDOW
PAS DE DEUX
A PORTRAIT OF GISÈLLE

MCDERMOTT, JOAN
PILOBOLUS AND JOAN

MCDONALD, BOBBI
AMERICAN BALLROOM DANCING

MCDONALD, GENE
A DANCER'S WORLD

MCDONALD, RAY
BABES ON BROADWAY

MCDOWELL, JOHN HERBERT
THE JUDSON PROJECT TAPES

MCGEHEE, HELEN
ACROBATS OF GOD
APPALACHIAN SPRING

A DANCER'S WORLD
SERAPHIC DIALOGUE

MCGOLDRICK, LARISSA
CUNNINGHAM DANCE TECHNIQUE: INTER-
    MEDIATE LEVEL

MCGOWAN, CHARLES
A CHORUS LINE

MCINTYRE, DIANNE
ETUDE IN FREE

MCINTYRE, GERRY
THE NEXT STEP

MCKAYLE, DONALD
THE NEW DANCE GROUP GALA CONCERT

MCKENZIE, KEVIN
AMERICAN BALLET THEATRE IN SAN FRAN-
    CISCO
THE ERIK BRUHN GALA: WORLD BALLET
    COMPETITION
VIDEO DICTIONARY OF CLASSICAL BALLET

MCKERROW, AMANDA
AMERICAN BALLET THEATRE AT THE MET
HOLIDAY OF BALLET
PAVLOVA: A TRIBUTE TO A LEGENDARY
    BALLERINA

MCLAINE, SHIRLEY
CAN-CAN

MCLAUGHLIN, JOHN
SECRET OF THE WATERFALL

MEADE, CHARLIE
LINDY VIDEOTAPES

MEI LING, JACK
FORBIDDEN CITY, U.S.A

MERCIER, MARGARET
BALLERINA
THE EYE HEARS, THE EAR SEES
PAS DE DEUX

MERCURIO, PAUL
STRICTLY BALLROOM

MEYER, LYNDA
BEAUTY AND THE BEAST

MEZENTSEVA, GALINA
BACKSTAGE AT THE KIROV
BALLET FAVORITES
THE CHILDREN OF THEATRE STREET
GISÈLLE (Kirov Ballet)
THE KIROV BALLET: CLASSIC BALLET NIGHT

MICHIKO
THE KING AND I

MIERE MOKE, BONIFACE
LIFE IN THE DUST: FRAGMENTS OF AFRICAN
    VOYAGES

MIKHALCHENKO, ALLA
SWAN LAKE (Bolshoi Ballet)

MILADOVA, MILADA
GAITÉ PARISIENNE

MILLER, ANN
DEEP IN MY HEART
EASTER PARADE
KISS ME KATE
LOVELY TO LOOK AT
ON THE TOWN
THAT'S ENTERTAINMENT

MILLER, BUZZ
ECHOES OF JAZZ

MINNELLI, LIZA
CABARET
STEPPING OUT
THAT'S DANCING
THAT'S ENTERTAINMENT

MIRANDA, CARMEN
THE GANG'S ALL HERE

MIRK, SHONACH
THE ART OF THE TWENTIETH CENTURY
    BALLET

MITCHELL, ARTHUR
DANCE: NEW YORK CITY BALLET
RHYTHMETRON: THE DANCE THEATRE OF
    HARLEM WITH ARTHUR MITCHELL
SUZANNE FARRELL: ELUSIVE MUSE

MITCHELL, JAMES
INTROSPECTION
OKLAHOMA!

MITCHELL, MIKE
IROQUOIS SOCIAL DANCE I AND II

MOHONGA, THÉRÈSE
LIFE IN THE DUST: FRAGMENTS OF AFRICAN
    VOYAGES

MOISEYEVA, OLGA
BACKSTAGE AT THE KIROV

MONK, MEREDITH
MAKING DANCES: SEVEN POSTMODERN
    CHOREOGRAPHERS
MEREDITH MONK
PARIS
QUARRY
SIXTEEN MILLIMETER EARRINGS

MONTAGUE, OWEN
THE ERIK BRUHN GALA: WORLD BALLET
    COMPETITION

MONTE, ELISA
THE MARTHA GRAHAM DANCE COMPANY

MOORE, ANNABELLE
BEFORE HOLLYWOOD: TURN OF THE CEN-
    TURY FILM FROM AMERICAN ARCHIVES
EARLY DANCE FILMS 1894–1912

O'BRIEN, MARGARET
MEET ME IN ST. LOUIS

O'CONNOR, DENNIS
CAVE
CUNNINGHAM DANCE TECHNIQUE: INTER-
    MEDIATE LEVEL
LA PROMENADE

O'CONNOR, DONALD
SINGIN' IN THE RAIN
THAT'S ENTERTAINMENT
THERE'S NO BUSINESS LIKE SHOW BUSINESS

O'FARRIL, ALFREDO
VOICES OF THE ORISHAS

O'NEIL, ROB
ANIMA

OBERFELDER-RIEHM, JODY
CHANCE ENCOUNTERS
DUET

ODO, CHRIS
LIFE IN THE DUST: FRAGMENTS OF AFRICAN
    VOYAGES

OGUIZA, LAURA
RUBBLE DANCE LONG ISLAND CITY

OHNO, KAZUO
DANCE OF DARKNESS

OKUYAMA, YUKIE
CUNNINGHAM DANCE TECHNIQUE: INTER-
    MEDIATE LEVEL

OLGUI
A DANCE ORIENTAL EXTRAVAGANZA

OLIPHANT, BETTY
YOUNG AND JUST BEGINNING: PIERRE

OLIVÉ-BELLÉS, NÚRIA
ALICIA WAS FAINTING

ONE STAR, LLOYD
LIVE AND REMEMBER (Wo Kiksuye)

ORCUTT, EDITH
HUMPHREY TECHNIQUE

ORSER, BRIAN
THE PLANETS

OSGOOD, BETH
CLINIC OF STUMBLE

OSIPENKO, ALLA
THE BOLSHOI BALLET

OTTO, MARINA
THE JOY OF BACH

OWENS, R.
BALLET IN JAZZ

PÁJARES, ANDRÉS
¡AY, CARMELA!

P'ANSORI
ASIA SOCIETY COLLECTION

PAGE, GERALDINE
ROSELAND

PAGE, RUTH
RUTH PAGE: AN AMERICAN ORIGINAL

PAHL, SIGHILT
SCHOOL FOR WIVES

PALMER, LELAND
ALL THAT JAZZ

PANKOVA, YELENA
LE CORSAIRE

PAREDES, MARCOS
AMERICAN BALLET THEATRE: A CLOSE-UP
    IN TIME

PARISI, SUSAN
JITTERBUG: BEGINNERS! and JITTERBUG 2:
    INTERMEDIATE

PARK, WAIMEA FALLS
MAKAHIKI FESTIVAL

PARKER, SPENCER
HOW BALLET WAS SAVED

PARKERSON, LYNN
TANAGRA, USA

PARKINSON, GEORGINA
VIDEO DICTIONARY OF CLASSICAL BALLET

PARSONS, DAVID
CAUGHT

PASSLOFF, AILEEN
THE JUDSON PROJECT TAPES

PATARO, MIGUEL ANGEL
SABICAS: EL MAESTRO DE FLAMENCO

PATE, MALDWYN
LIGHT, PART 5

PAVLOVA, ANNA
THE BEGINNINGS OF TODAY
CLASSIC KIROV PERFORMANCES
GREAT PERFORMANCE IN DANCE
IMMORTAL SWAN
TRAILBLAZERS OF MODERN DANCE

PAVLOVA, NADEZHDA
YURI GRIGOROVICH: MASTER OF THE BOL-
    SHOI

PAVLOVA, NADIA
THE NUTCRACKER (Bolshoi Ballet)

PAXTON, STEVE
BEYOND THE MAINSTREAM: POSTMODERN
    DANCERS

GOLDBERG VARIATIONS
THE JUDSON PROJECT TAPES
STORY
THREE DANCES

PEASLEY, COLIN
DON QUIXOTE (Australian Ballet)

PELHAM, JAMES
THE TAP DANCE KID

PELL, IRIS
FOR DANCERS

PENDLETON, MOSES
PILOBOLUS DANCE THEATRE

PENNEY, JENNIFER
MANON

PÉREZ DE GUZMÁN, PILAR
FLAMENCOS DE LA LUZ

PERRIER, CHARLES
IL BALLARINO: THE ART OF RENAISSANCE
    DANCE
EARLY DANCE

PERRON, SARAH
LA PROMENADE

PERRON, WENDY
RETRACING STEPS: AMERICAN DANCE
    SINCE POSTMODERNISM
X-RAY EYES

PERRY, RONALD
DANCE THEATRE OF HARLEM

PERRYMAN, STANLEY
DANCE THEATRE OF HARLEM

PETIT, ROLAND
BLACK TIGHTS
THE BLUE ANGEL
KAREN KAIN: BALLERINA
THE MAGNIFICENT BEGINNING
MAKAROVA: IN A CLASS OF HER OWN
THE ROMANTIC BALLET

PETRONIO, STEPHEN
RETRACING STEPS: AMERICAN DANCE
    SINCE POSTMODERNISM

PETROVNA, SONIA
ADOLESCENCE

PIAZZOLA, ASTOR
THE TANGO IS ALSO A HISTORY

PICKLES, VIVIEN
ISADORA DUNCAN, THE BIGGEST DANCER
    IN THE WORLD

PILAFIAN, CHRISTOPHER
FRACTURED VARIATIONS and VISUAL
    SHUFFLE

REYNOLDS, MARJORIE
HOLIDAY INN

RHODES, LAWRENCE
ATTITUDES IN DANCE
A DANCER'S GRAMMAR

RICHARD, NATHALIE
PARAFANGO

RICHE, NICOLAS
NINA ANANIASHVILI AND INTERNATIONAL
   STARS

RILEY, DEBORAH
SECRET OF THE WATERFALL

RINPOCHE, TRULSHIG
LORD OF THE DANCE/DESTROYER OF ILLU-
   SION

RIRIE, SHIRLEY
THE COMPANY

RITTER, LLOYD
HOW DO YOU FEEL, EMPEROR'S NEW
   CLOTHES, ROCKER

RIVERA, CHITA
SWEET CHARITY

RIVERA, MIGUEL
CERBERUS

ROACH, FRANCIS
LUIGI

ROBERTSON, CURTIS
ALICIA WAS FAINTING

ROBINSON, BILL "BOJANGLES"
JAZZ HOOFER: BABY LAURENCE
LET'S SCUFFLE
LITTLEST REBEL
STORMY WEATHER
TAPDANCIN'

RODRIGUEZ, BEATRÍZ
AS SEEN ON TV

RODRIQUEZ, SONIA
THE PLANETS

ROE, DAVID
THE PAINTED PRINCESS

ROGERS, GINGER
AMERICAN MUSICALS: FAMOUS PRODUC-
   TION NUMBERS
THE BARKLEYS OF BROADWAY
CAREFREE
FLYING DOWN TO RIO
FOLLOW THE FLEET
THE GAY DIVORCEE
GOLD DIGGERS OF 1933
ROBERTA
SHALL WE DANCE
THE STORY OF VERNON AND IRENE CASTLE

SWING TIME
TOP HAT

ROGERS, WENDY
DUNE DANCE

ROLES, RITA
REQUIEM FOR A SLAVE

ROLOV, KITSHEN
SYMPHONIE FANTASTIQUE

ROMERO, DAISY
VOICES OF THE ORISHAS

ROMERO, ORLANDO
SABICAS: EL MAESTRO DE FLAMENCO

ROONEY, MICKEY
BABES IN ARMS
BABES ON BROADWAY
STRIKE UP THE BAND

ROSA, BOBBY
SALSA

ROSE, JULIA
THE NUTCRACKER (Royal Ballet)

ROSE, KATHY
PRIMITIVE MOVERS
SYNCOPATIONS

ROSE, SUSAN
FOR DANCERS

ROSS, BERTRAM
ACROBATS OF GOD
ANTIGONE/RITES OF PASSION
APPALACHIAN SPRING
CORTEGE OF EAGLES
A DANCER'S WORLD
NIGHT JOURNEY
SERAPHIC DIALOGUE

ROSS, ROBERT
FLUTE OF KRISHNA
ROSSANA
THE TEMPLE AND THE SWAN

ROUDENKO, LUBOV
GAITE PARISIENNE

ROUSSEVE, DAVID
DANCE AND MYTH: THE WORLD OF JEAN
   ERDMAN
PULL YOUR HEAD TO THE MOON

ROUSSEVE, GENEVIEVE
PULL YOUR HEAD TO THE MOON

ROY, MELINDA
ACCENT ON THE OFFBEAT

RUBIN, HYLA
AIR FOR THE G STRING

RUDNER, SARA
DANCE FRAME
DANCE OUTLINE

DORIS CHASE DANCE SERIES: THREE SOLOS
DUNE DANCE
MAKING DANCES: SEVEN POSTMODERN
   CHOREOGRAPHERS
VARIATION II

RUEFF, STEPHEN
BREAK

RUENNE, PATRICIA
BRITISH BALLET TODAY

RUSANOV, PETER
COPPÉLIA (Kirov Ballet)

RUSSELL, DARCEY
LA BAYADÈRE (Royal Ballet)

RUZIMATOV, FAROUKH
LE CORSAIRE
DON QUIXOTE (Kirov Ballet)
ESSENTIAL BALLET: RUSSIAN BALLET
THE KIROV BALLET IN LONDON
THE LENINGRAD LEGEND
THE MAGIC OF THE KIROV BALLET
THE MARYINSKY BALLET
NINA ANANIASHVILI AND INTERNATIONAL
   STARS
SLEEPING BEAUTY (Kirov Ballet)
WELCOME BACK ST. PETERSBURG: A GALA
   AT THE ROYAL OPERA HOUSE
WHITE NIGHT OF DANCE IN LENINGRAD

RYBERG, FLEMMING
THE ROMANTIC BALLET

RYDELL, BOBBY
BYE BYE BIRDIE

SABIN, EVELYN
FLUTE OF KRISHNA

SABRY, NAHED
STARS OF EGYPTIAN DANCE

SADDLER, DONALD
RADHA

SAKAMOTO, NANCY
MOON

SAKHAROVA, LUDMILA
TERPSICHORE'S CAPTIVES

SALEM, PHILIP
THE VERY EYE OF NIGHT

SALIBA, PAUL
DAPHNIS AND CHLÖE

SAMSOVA, GALINA
BALLERINA: LYNN SEYMOUR

SANASARDO, PAUL
A MOMENT IN LOVE

SANDLIFER, RICHARD
THE VERY EYE OF NIGHT

SANTOS, LEE
FRED ASTAIRE LEARN TO DANCE

SKELTON, RED
BATHING BEAUTY

SLEEP, WAYNE
THE EBB AND FLOW
THE TALES OF BEATRIX POTTER

SMALL, NEVA
FIDDLER ON THE ROOF

SMITH, HENRY
CERBERUS
FRAGMENTS OF VOYAGES IN AFRICA

SMITH, JUDITH
DANCING FROM THE INSIDE OUT

SMITH, LINDA
DANCING THROUGH THE MAGIC EYE: A
　　PORTRAIT OF VIRGINIA TANNER

SMITH, LOIS
BALLET STUDY FILMS

SMITH, LOWELL
CREOLE GISÈLLE

SOKOLOW, ANNA
ANNA SOKOLOW, CHOREOGRAPHER
BULLFIGHT
DANCE: ANNA SOKOLOW'S ROOMS
THE NEW DANCE GROUP GALA CONCERT

SOLA, MIGUEL ANGEL
TANGOS, THE EXILE OF GARDEL

SOLEAU, WILLIAM
DANCE PRELUDES

SOLEK, WALT
IN HEAVEN THERE IS NO BEER?

SOLOMONS, GUS
DANCE NINE
DORIS CHASE DANCE SERIES: FOUR SOLOS

SOLOVYOV, YURI
RUSSIAN BALLET, THE GLORIOUS TRADI-
　　TION
SLEEPING BEAUTY (Kirov Ballet)

SOMES, MICHAEL
I AM A DANCER
MARGOT FONTEYN IN LES SYLPHIDES
OUT OF THE LIMELIGHT, HOME IN THE
　　RAIN
THE ROYAL BALLET

SOROKINA, NINA
WORLD'S YOUNG BALLET

SOTO, JOCK
ACCENT ON THE OFFBEAT

SPARLING, PETER
DAY ON EARTH
HERALD'S ROUND
THE MARTHA GRAHAM DANCE COMPANY

SPEARS, WARREN
BUFFALO SOLDIER

SPERANSKAYA, NINA
SLEEPING BEAUTY (Bolshoi Ballet)

SPESSIVTZEVA, OLGA
A PORTRAIT OF GISÈLLE

SPICER, BETH
MAGDALENE

ST. DENIS, RUTH
DANCE OF THE AGES/ON THE SHORE
THE DANCING PROPHET
INVENTION IN DANCE
RADHA
RUTH ST. DENIS BY BARIBAULT
RUTH ST. DENIS: TED SHAWN
TRAILBLAZERS OF MODERN DANCE

STAFFORD, ANTHONY
RABL

STARBUCH, JAMES
GAITE PARISIENNE

STEELE, TOMMY
HALF A SIXPENCE

STEINBERG, ROXANNE
TRAVELING LIGHT

STEPHENS, GEORGIA
SOLO

STERN, REBECCA
PICTURES AT AN EXHIBITION

STEVENSON, EARNE
ANIMA

STODELL, ERNESTINE H.
AIR FOR THE G STRING

STREB, ELIZABETH
AIRDANCE and LANDINGS
AMPHIBIAN
COLLECTED WORKS OF ELIZABETH STREB
IN THE BLINK OF AN EYE . . . (AMPHIBIAN
　　DREAMS) IF I COULD FLY I WOULD FLY
MASS

STREISAND, BARBRA
FUNNY GIRL
HELLO DOLLY

STRICKLER, FRED
FOR DANCERS
TAPDANCIN'

STROM, MARY ELLEN
DANCE EX MACHINA

STRUCHKOVA, RAISA
THE BOLSHOI BALLET
THE BOLSHOI BALLET: GALINA ULANOVA
CINDERELLA (Bolshoi Ballet)
CINDERELLA (Bolshoi Ballet)

STURR, JIMMY
IN HEAVEN THERE IS NO BEER?

SUJATA
THE TEMPLE AND THE SWAN

SUMMERS, ELAINE
THE JUDSON PROJECT TAPES
WALKING DANCE FOR ANY NUMBER

SUMNERS, ROSALYNN
SLEEPING BEAUTY ON ICE

SUN, DOTTIE
FORBIDDEN CITY, U.S.A

SUN, OCK LEE
ASIA SOCIETY COLLECTION

SURASENA
ASIA SOCIETY COLLECTION

SUTHERLAND, PAUL
ATTITUDES IN DANCE

SUTTON, TOMMY
TAP ALONG WITH TOMMY

SWAYZE, BAMBI, LISA AND PATSY
SWAYZE DANCING

SWAYZE, PATRICK
DIRTY DANCING
SWAYZE DANCING

SYKES-DIETZE, BARBARA
KALYIAN

SYMONS, OLIVER
HOW BALLET WAS SAVED

TAIA
GAMEEL GAMAL (Oh! Beautiful Dancer)

TAKEI, KEI
DANCE FIVE
DANCE THREE
DORIS CHASE DANCE SERIES: THREE SOLOS
IMPROVISATION
LIGHT, PART 5

TALIAFERRO, CLAY
DANCE DESIGN: MOTION
DANCE DESIGN: SHAPING
DANCE DESIGN: SPACE
THE DANCE INSTRUMENT
EMPEROR JONES

TALLCHIEF, MARIA
CLASSICAL BALLET
DANCING FOR MR. B.: SIX BALANCHINE
　　BALLERINAS
STRAVINSKY

TAMBLYN, RUSS
SEVEN BRIDES FOR SEVEN BROTHERS
WEST SIDE STORY

TAMIRIS, HELEN
HELEN TAMIRIS IN NEGRO SPIRITUALS
TRAILBLAZERS OF MODERN DANCE

UHLENDORF, GUSTAV
THE ROYAL DANISH BALLET 1902–1906

ULANOVA, GALINA
THE BOLSHOI BALLET: GALINA ULANOVA
CLASSIC KIROV PERFORMANCES
DANCING THRU
GALINA ULANOVA
GRAND CONCERT
GREAT BALLERINA
THE MAGIC OF THE BOLSHOI BALLET
A PORTRAIT OF GISÈLLE
ROMEO AND JULIET (Bolshoi Ballet)
RUSSIAN BALLET, THE GLORIOUS TRADI-
    TION
THE SCENE CHANGES
STARS OF THE RUSSIAN BALLET

USHER, GRAHAM
THE BEGINNINGS OF TODAY

UVAROV, ANDREY
RUSSIAN BALLET, THE GLORIOUS TRADI-
    TION

VACANTI, SUZANNE
FLUTE OF KRISHNA

VAMOS, YOURI
JOHN LINDQUIST: PHOTOGRAPHER OF
    DANCE

VAN, BOBBY
KISS ME KATE

VAN DYKE, DICK
BYE BYE BIRDIE

VAN HAMEL, MARTINE
AMERICAN BALLET THEATRE AT THE MET
GISÈLLE (American Ballet Theatre)
THE TURNING POINT

VAN MANEN, HANS
BLACK TIGHTS

VAN WIEREN, LAURIE
SOLO

VANGSAA, MONA
SYMPHONIE FANTASTIQUE

VARGAS, ANTONIO
STRICTLY BALLROOM

VARJAN, KRIS
CERBERUS
LIFE IN THE DUST: FRAGMENTS OF AFRICAN
    VOYAGES

VASSILIEV, VLADIMIR
ANYUTA
THE BALLERINAS
THE LITTLE HUMPBACKED HORSE
THE MAGIC OF THE BOLSHOI BALLET
THE NUTCRACKER (Bolshoi Ballet)
THE NUTCRACKER (Bolshoi Ballet)
PLISETSKAYA DANCES
RUSSIAN BALLET, THE GLORIOUS TRADI-
    TION
SPARTACUS (Bolshoi Ballet)

WORLD'S YOUNG BALLET
YURI GRIGOROVICH: MASTER OF THE BOL-
    SHOI

VASYUCHENKO, YURI
BOLSHOI PROKOFIEV GALA
GISÈLLE (Bolshoi Ballet)
RAYMONDA (Bolshoi Ballet)
SWAN LAKE (Bolshoi Ballet)

VELOZ, YOLANDA
CAVALCADE OF DANCE

VERA-ELLEN
THE BELLE OF NEW YORK
ON THE TOWN

VEREEN, BEN
ALL THAT JAZZ

VERRY, PIERRE
ART OF SILENCE: PANTOMIMES WITH MAR-
    CEL MARCEAU

VEST, VANE
TEALIA

VETROV, ALEKSANDR
BOLSHOI PROKOFIEV GALA
SPARTACUS (Bolshoi Ballet)

VETROV, YURI
THE NUTCRACKER (Bolshoi Ballet)
THE STONE FLOWER (Bolshoi Ballet)

VILLA, JULIAN
VOICES OF THE ORISHAS

VILLELLA, EDWARD
BALLET WITH EDWARD VILLELLA
DANCE: NEW YORK CITY BALLET
MAN WHO DANCES: EDWARD VILLELLA

VILUMSEN, ARNE
NAPOLI

VINOGRADOV, OLEG
BACKSTAGE AT THE KIROV

VLADIMIROFF, PIERRE
IMMORTAL SWAN

VLADIMIROV, YURI
ANNA KARENINA
IVAN THE TERRIBLE (Bolshoi Ballet)

VLADY, MARINA
TANGOS, THE EXILE OF GARDEL

VON AROLDINGEN, KARIN
DAVIDSBÜNDLERTANZE

WAGDI, EMAN
STARS OF EGYPTIAN DANCE

WAGONER, DAN
JUNCTION

WALKER, NORMAN
ATTITUDES IN DANCE

WALL, DAVID
BALLERINA: LYNN SEYMOUR
BALLET COMES TO BRITAIN

THE MAGNIFICENT BEGINNING
TCHAIKOVSKY AND THE RUSSIANS

WALSEMANN, ANNE
NEW YORK POST WAVE

WALTER, KIM
DAPHNIS AND CHLÖE

WALTON, ELIZABETH
JUNCTION

WAN-KYUNG, CHO
CHINESE, KOREAN AND JAPANESE DANCE

WANVEN, SUE
BAROQUE DANCE 1675–1725

WARREN, CHARMAINE
PULL YOUR HEAD TO THE MOON

WARREN, VINCENT
THE EYE HEARS, THE EAR SEES
PAS DE DEUX

WASHINGTON, ENO
DANCE ON THE WIND

WATKINS, SUSAN
SET PIECE

WATT, NINA
TWO ECSTATIC THEMES

WATTS, HEATHER
ACCENT ON THE OFFBEAT
DAVIDSBÜNDLERTANZE
PETER MARTINS: A DANCER

WEBB, KYLE
JITTERBUG: BEGINNERS! and JITTERBUG 2:
    INTERMEDIATE

WEIDMAN, CHARLES
CHARLES WEIDMAN: ON HIS OWN
THE NEW DANCE GROUP GALA CONCERT

WEISS, RICHARD
DANCE PRELUDES

WEISS, ROBERT
CHOREOGRAPHY BY BALANCHINE
THE FOUR TEMPERAMENTS

WEKSLER, TERI
BEEHIVE

WELLIVER, GWEN
RUBBLE DANCE LONG ISLAND CITY

WELLS, DOREEN
TCHAIKOVSKY AND THE RUSSIANS

WHELAN, WENDY
ACCENT ON THE OFFBEAT
THE NUTCRACKER (New York City Ballet)

WHITE, ANNE
THE PENNSYLVANIA BALLET: DA MUMMY,
    NYET MUMMY

Dance Companies Index

BILL T JONES/ARNIE ZANE DANCE
    COMPANY
BILL T JONES: DANCING TO THE PROMISED
    LAND
BILL T JONES: STILLHERE WITH BILL
    MOYERS

THE BODY ROCK CREW
BODY ROCK

BOLSHOI BALLET
ALL THE BEST FROM RUSSIA
ANNA KARENINA
ANYUTA
THE BOLSHOI BALLET
THE BOLSHOI BALLET: GALINA ULANOVA
BOLSHOI: DIVERTISSEMENTS
BOLSHOI PROKOFIEV GALA
BOLSHOI SOLOISTS CLASSIQUE
CARMEN (Bolshoi Ballet)
CINDERELLA (Bolshoi Ballet)
CINDERELLA (Bolshoi Ballet)
GALINA ULANOVA
GISÈLLE (Bolshoi Ballet)
GISÈLLE (Bolshoi Ballet)
THE GOLDEN AGE
IVAN THE TERRIBLE (Bolshoi Ballet)
IVAN THE TERRIBLE (Bolshoi Ballet)
THE LITTLE HUMPBACKED HORSE
LUDMILA SEMENYAKA: BOLSHOI BALLE-
    RINA
MACBETH
THE MAGIC OF THE BOLSHOI BALLET
NINA ANANIASHVILI AND INTERNATIONAL
    STARS
THE NUTCRACKER (Bolshoi Ballet)
THE NUTCRACKER (Bolshoi Ballet)
THE NUTCRACKER (Bolshoi Ballet)
PLISETSKAYA DANCES
A POEM OF DANCES ALSO KNOWN AS PLI-
    SETSKAYA: CARMEN
RAYMONDA (Bolshoi Ballet)
RAYMONDA (Bolshoi Ballet)
ROMEO AND JULIET (Bolshoi Ballet)
ROMEO AND JULIET (Bolshoi Ballet)
ROMEO AND JULIET (Bolshoi Ballet)
RUSSIAN BALLET, THE GLORIOUS TRADI-
    TION
SLEEPING BEAUTY (Bolshoi Ballet)
SPARTACUS (Bolshoi Ballet)
SPARTACUS (Bolshoi Ballet)
SPARTACUS (Bolshoi Ballet)
STARS OF THE RUSSIAN BALLET
THE STONE FLOWER (Bolshoi Ballet)
SWAN LAKE (Bolshoi Ballet)
SWAN LAKE (Bolshoi Ballet)
LES SYLPHIDES (CHOPINIANA)
TCHAIKOVSKY AND THE RUSSIANS
THE ULTIMATE SWAN LAKE
YURI GRIGOROVICH: MASTER OF THE BOL-
    SHOI

BUTLER IRISH DANCERS
CANADIANS CAN DANCE

BYAKKO-SHA
BUTOH: BODY ON THE EDGE OF CRISIS
DANCE OF DARKNESS

CARBONE 14
LE DORTOIR (The Dormitory)

CENTRAL BALLET OF CHINA
ON THE MOVE: THE CENTRAL BALLET OF
    CHINA

CENTRAL PENNSYLVANIA YOUTH BALLET
CHILDREN WITH A DREAM

THE CHAMPIONS
CHAMPIONS

CHARLES MOORE DANCE THEATRE
DANCE BLACK AMERICA

CHUCK DAVIS DANCE COMPANY
DANCE BLACK AMERICA

CLAN NA GAEL
DANCES OF THE WORLD

CLEO ROBINSON DANCE COMPANY
RUN, SISTER, RUN

CODANCECO
THAT MEANS I WANT TO GO HOME

COMPANIA FOLKLÓRICA LAS MESAS DE
    CAYEY
DANCES OF THE WORLD

CONJUNTO FOLKLÓRICO NACIONAL DE
    CUBA
VOICES OF THE ORISHAS

CONNECTICUT COLLEGE REPERTORY
    COMPANY
NEW DANCE: RECORD FILM
WITH MY RED FIRES

CONTRABAND
LIKE WIND IN MIRA'S HAIR

THE COPASETICS
TAPDANCIN'

CULLBERG BALLET
SCHOOL FOR WIVES

CZECH TELEVISION ARTS COMPANY
DAISY AND HER GARDEN: A DANCE FAN-
    TASY

DAI RAKUDA KAN
BUTOH: BODY ON THE EDGE OF CRISIS
DANCE OF DARKNESS

DANCE ACADEMY OF PEKING
THE MAGNIFICENT BEGINNING

DANCE THEATRE OF HARLEM
CREOLE GISÈLLE
DANCE THEATRE OF HARLEM
DANCE THEATRE OF HARLEM
LOWER EXTREMITY DANCE MEDICINE: OR-
    THOPEDIC EXAMINATION WITH DR WIL-
    LIAM HAMILTON
RHYTHMETRON: THE DANCE THEATRE OF
    HARLEM WITH ARTHUR MITCHELL

DANCER'S WORKSHOP COMPANY
PROCESSION: CONTEMPORARY DIREC-
    TIONS IN AMERICAN DANCE

DANUBE SWABIAN YOUTH
CANADIANS CAN DANCE

DANZA AZTECA DE ANAHUAC
DANZANTE

DAVID WOODBERRY DANCE COMPANY
INVISIBLE DANCE

DETROIT CITY DANCE COMPANY
BUFFALO SOLDIER
CAROLE MORISSEAU AND THE DETROIT
    CITY DANCE COMPANY

DIAMOND DANCE
SIX METAMORPHOSES

DINIZULU AND HIS AFRICAN DRUMMERS,
    DANCERS AND SINGERS
DINIZULU AND HIS AFRICAN DRUMMERS,
    DANCERS AND SINGERS

DON COSSACK DANCERS
ALL THE BEST FROM RUSSIA

DON REDLICH DANCE COMPANY
HANYA: PORTRAIT OF A DANCE PIONEER

DONALD BYRD/THE GROUP
UNSETTLED DREAMS

DOUGLAS DUNN AND DANCERS
RUBBLE DANCE LONG ISLAND CITY
TRIPLE DUO

DUNHAM, KATHERINE AND HER DANCERS
STORMY WEATHER

DÜSSELDORF BALLET
NINA ANANIASHVILI AND INTERNATIONAL
    STARS

DUTCH NATIONAL BALLET
THE DUTCH NATIONAL BALLET
THE MAKING OF A BALLET

ECCENTRIC MOTIONS
THE PAINTED PRINCESS
SWEPT UP

ELECTRIC CURRENT DANCE COMPANY
DECLARATION OF INDEPENDENCE

ELIOT FELD BALLET
TZADDIK

ERICK HAWKINS DANCE COMPANY
ERICK HAWKINS
ERICK HAWKINS' AMERICA

ESTONIAN FOLK GROUP
CANADIANS CAN DANCE

FOLKLÓRICO GAUTEQUE BALLET
DANCES OF THE WORLD

FUNNY HOUSE CO-OP
FUNNY HOUSE

GARDEN STATE BALLET
BALLET RUSE

GARTH FAGAN'S BUCKET DANCE THEATRE
DANCE BLACK AMERICA
GRIOT NEW YORK

LONDON CONTEMPORARY DANCE THEATRE
KONTAKION: A SONG OF PRAISE
TROY GAME
WHAT IS NEW

LONDON FESTIVAL BALLET
SWAN LAKE (London Festival Ballet)

LYON OPERA BALLET
CINDERELLA (Lyon Opera Ballet)
ROMEO AND JULIET (Lyon Opera Ballet)

MACEDONIAN FOLKLORISTS
CANADIANS CAN DANCE

MAGNIFICENT FORCE
DANCE BLACK AMERICA

MAHMOUD REDA TROUPE
REAL EGYPTIAN FOLK

MAIJUKU
BUTOH: BODY ON THE EDGE OF CRISIS

MALY
ANYUTA

MAMA LU PARKS' JAZZ DANCERS
DANCE BLACK AMERICA

MANDALA FOLK DANCE COMPANY
OTHER VOICES, OTHER SONGS: THE
GREEKS

MARCUS SCHULKIND DANCE COMPANY
THE BLACK BOOTS

MARIN BALLET
IMAGE OF A DANCER

MARK MORRIS DANCE GROUP
DIDO AND AENEAS
FALLING DOWN STAIRS
THE HARD NUT

MARTHA GRAHAM DANCE COMPANY
ACROBATS OF GOD
APPALACHIAN SPRING
CLYTEMNESTRA
CORTEGE OF EAGLES
A DANCER'S WORLD
THE MARTHA GRAHAM DANCE COMPANY
MARTHA GRAHAM: THREE CONTEMPO-
RARY CLASSICS
NIGHT JOURNEY
SERAPHIC DIALOGUE

MARY STATON DANCE ENSEMBLE
CIRCLES II
FULL CIRCLE: THE WORK OF DORIS CHASE
MOON GATES: THREE VERSIONS
TALL ARCHES III

**MARYINSKY BALLET (FORMERLY THE
KIROV)**
THE MARYINSKY BALLET

MERCE CUNNINGHAM DANCE COMPANY
BEACH BIRDS FOR CAMERA
CAGE/CUNNINGHAM

CHANGING STEPS
CHANNELS/INSERTS
COAST ZONE
THE COLLABORATORS: CAGE, CUNNING-
HAM, RAUSCHENBERG
CRWDSPCR
DELI COMMEDIA
FRACTIONS I
MERCE CUNNINGHAM AND COMPANY
POINTS IN SPACE
RAINFOREST
ROAMIN' I
SOMETIMES IT WORKS, SOMETIMES IT
DOESN'T
SQUAREGAME VIDEO
STORY
VARIATIONS V
WALKAROUND TIME
WESTBETH

MERVEILLES D'AFRIQUE
KEMOKO SANO TEACHES AFRICAN DANCE
FROM THE REPUBLIC OF GUINEA

METROPOLITAN OPERA BALLET
THE GOLDWYN FOLLIES

MICHAEL CLARK COMPANY
BECAUSE WE MUST

MIMI GARRARD DANCE THEATRE
MIMI GARRARD DANCE THEATRE

MOISEYEV DANCE COMPANY
MOISEYEV DANCE COMPANY: A GALA EVE-
NING

**MOLDAVIA FOLK SONG AND DANCE
ENSEMBLE**
RUSSIAN FOLK SONG AND DANCE

MOMIX
BOLERO and PICTURES AT AN EXHIBITION
PICTURES AT AN EXHIBITION

**MONKSEATON DANCERS OF NEWCASTLE-
UPON-TYNE**
DANCES OF THE WORLD

**MOROCCO AND THE CASBAH DANCE
EXPERIENCE**
MOROCCO AND THE CASBAH DANCE EXPE-
RIENCE

MOULTON ENSEMBLE
NEW DANCE

MOVING EARTH COMPANY
KEI TAKEI

MURRAY LOUIS DANCE COMPANY
THE BODY AS AN INSTRUMENT
SHAPE
SPACE
TIME

MUTEKI-SHA
BUTOH: BODY ON THE EDGE OF CRISIS

NATIONAL BALLET OF CANADA
BLUE SNAKE
BOLD STEPS
THE ERIK BRUHN GALA: WORLD BALLET
COMPETITION
FOR THE LOVE OF DANCE
GALA
MAKING BALLET: KAREN KAIN AND THE
NATIONAL BALLET OF CANADA
A MOVING PICTURE
ONEGIN

NATIONAL CULTURAL TROUPE
MALAYSIAN DANCES

**NATIONAL FOLKLORE ENSEMBLE OF
POLAND**
SLASK: NATIONAL FOLKLORE ENSEMBLE OF
POLAND

NEDERLANDS DANS THEATRE
THE ANATOMY LESSON
L'ENFANT ET LES SORTILEGES
AN EVENING WITH KYLIAN AND THE NE-
DERLANDS DANS THEATRE
KYLIAN COLLECTION
ROAD TO THE STAMPING GROUND
SYMPHONY IN D WORKSHOP

NETHERLANDS FOLKLORE CIRCLE
CANADIANS CAN DANCE

NEW DANCE ENSEMBLE
TANGO

NEW JERSEY CENTER DANCE COLLECTIVE
DENISHAWN: THE BIRTH OF MODERN
DANCE

NEW YORK CITY BALLET
ACCENT ON THE OFFBEAT
THE BALANCHINE ESSAYS: ARABESQUE
BALLET: A CAREER FOR BOYS
BALLET WITH EDWARD VILLELLA
BEGINNINGS
CHOREOGRAPHY BY BALANCHINE
DANCE: NEW YORK CITY BALLET
DANCING FOR MR B : SIX BALANCHINE BAL-
LERINAS
DAVIDSBÜNDLERTANZE
THE FOUR TEMPERAMENTS
LOWER EXTREMITY DANCE MEDICINE: OR-
THOPEDIC EXAMINATION WITH DR WIL-
LIAM HAMILTON
THE MERRY WIDOW
NINA ANANIASHVILI AND INTERNATIONAL
STARS
THE NUTCRACKER (New York City Ballet)
VIDEO DICTIONARY OF CLASSICAL BALLET

NEW YORK NEGRO BALLET
REMEMBERING THELMA

NICHOLAS BROTHERS
STORMY WEATHER

NORMAN MAEN DANCERS
NATASHA

OAKLAND BALLET
ISADORA DUNCAN: MOVEMENT FROM THE
SOUL
NIJINSKA: A LEGEND IN DANCE

LA SCALA BALLET COMPANY
ROMEO AND JULIET (La Scala Ballet)

SCAPINO BALLET, ROTTERDAM
THE SORCERESS: KIRI TE KANAWA

SCHOOL OF AMERICAN BALLET
CANON IN D

SEATTLE OPERA BALLET
ROCKING ORANGE: THREE VERSIONS

SIBERIAN-OMSK FOLK CHORUS
RUSSIAN FOLK SONG AND DANCE

SLOVENIA NAGELI GROUP
CANADIANS CAN DANCE

SOLARIS DANCE THEATRE
FRAGMENTS OF VOYAGES IN AFRICA

SOUTHERN APPALACHIAN CLOGGERS
FULL OF LIFE A-DANCIN'

SOVIET ARMY DANCE ENSEMBLE
SOVIET ARMY CHORUS, BAND, AND DANCE
ENSEMBLE

STATE BALLET OF OREGON
TWO FOR BALLET

STEP SISTERS
A DANCE ORIENTAL EXTRAVAGANZA

STUTTGART BALLET
GISELLE . . . THE MAKING OF
JOHN CRANKO
ON YOUR TOES . . . THE MAKING OF

SURAKARTA COURT DANCERS
BEDHAYA: THE SACRED DANCE

SYDNEY DANCE COMPANY
DAPHNIS AND CHLÖE

TANEO WAKAYAMA AND COMPANY
EDO: DANCE AND PANTOMIME

TANGO ARGENTINO
TANGO BAR

TARANTELLA ITALIAN DANCERS
CANADIANS CAN DANCE

TEATRO A L'AVOGARIA DANCE COMPANY
WHAT IS NEW

**TED SHAWN AND THE MEMBERS OF HIS
ORIGINAL TROUPE**
THE MEN WHO DANCED: THE STORY OF
TED SHAWN'S MALE DANCERS 1933–1940

THEATRE REPERE
TECTONIC PLATES

THIRD GENERATION STEP
TAPDANCIN'

TIRTA SARI
BALI MECHANIQUE

TORONTO DANCE THEATRE
DANCE CLASS
FOR THE LOVE OF DANCE
RAVEL

TRISHA BROWN COMPANY
AEROS

TWYLA THARP DANCE COMPANY
THE CATHERINE WHEEL
HAIR
SUE'S LEG: REMEMBERING THE THIRTIES:
TWYLA THARP AND DANCERS
TWYLA THARP: MAKING TELEVISION
DANCE

**UNIVERSITY OF CALIFORNIA AT LOS
ANGELES DANCE COMPANY**
FOUR JOURNEYS INTO MYSTIC TIME

URBAN BUSH WOMEN
PRAISE HOUSE

UZBEKISTAN DANCE ENSEMBLE
RUSSIAN FOLK SONG AND DANCE

V'LA L'BON VENT ENSEMBLE
CANADIANS CAN DANCE

VIENNA STATE OPERA BALLET
JOSEPH'S LEGENDE
SWAN LAKE (Vienna Opera Ballet)

WENDY ROGERS DANCE GROUP
STANDING BY

WILLIAM "BUNGO" HINTON ENSEMBLE
MOKO JUMBIE: TRADITIONAL STILT
WALKERS

WINNIPEG BALLET
FOR THE LOVE OF DANCE

**WINNIPEG CONTEMPORARY DANCE
COMPANY**
FOR THE LOVE OF DANCE
GALA

WO'SE DANCE THEATRE
THE WEST AFRICAN HERITAGE

WUPPERTAL DANCE THEATRE
WHAT DO PINA BAUSCH AND HER DANCES
DO IN WUPPERTAL?

XANADU DANCERS
DANCES FROM THE CASBAH

JIMÉNEZ-VARGAS BALLET ESPAÑOL
A TIME TO DANCE

YVES MUSARD AND VADANCERS
LA PROMENADE

Directors Index

ABERLE, VIOLA
ANTONY TUDOR

ABRAMS, IRA
THE THREE WORLDS OF BALI

ADDY, YACUB
DANCE LIKE A RIVER: ODADAA! DRUM-
MING AND DANCING IN THE U.S

AKESTER, MIKE
THE MUSIC OF THE DEVIL, THE BEAR AND
THE CONDOR

ALDOKIN, YURI
YURI GRIGOROVICH: MASTER OF THE BOL-
SHOI

ALLAN, HAVELOCK
AN EVENING WITH THE ROYAL BALLET

ALLISON, NANCY
DANCE AND MYTH: THE WORLD OF JEAN
ERDMAN

ALPER, JOHN
LIVING AMERICAN THEATER DANCE

ALTMANN, KARIN
BALLERINA: LYNN SEYMOUR

AMARAL, PATTY
YOU CAN DO THE HULA

AMATO, MEG
THE JAZZ DANCE JIGSAW

ANDERSON, GERD
ANTONY TUDOR

ANDERSON, REID
ONEGIN

ANDRÉ, MARIE
REPETITIONS

ARCHIBALD, JAMES
ENIGMA VARIATIONS

ARDOLINO, EMILE
CLYTEMNESTRA
DANCE IN AMERICA (over 75 titles)
DIRTY DANCING
HE MAKES ME FEEL LIKE DANCIN'
THE NUTCRACKER (New York City Ballet)
THE PAUL TAYLOR DANCE COMPANY
PILOBOLUS DANCE THEATRE
TRAILBLAZERS OF MODERN DANCE

ARLEDGE, SARA KATHRYN
INTROSPECTION

ARNBORN, ARNE
VARIATIONS V

ARNSTAM, L
ROMEO AND JULIET (Bolshoi Ballet)

ARSLANIAN, SHARON
EDDIE BROWN'S "SCIENTIFIC RHYTHM"
THE ENDURING ESSENCE: THE TECHNIQUE
AND CHOREOGRAPHY OF ISADORA DUN-
CAN, REMEMBERED AND RECON-
STRUCTED BY GEMZE DE LAPPE
TWO TAKES ON TAP

ASCH, PATSY AND TIMOTHY
CELEBRATION OF ORIGINS

ASQUITH, ANTHONY
AN EVENING WITH THE ROYAL BALLET

ASSOPARDI, ANTHONY
MAKING BALLET: KAREN KAIN AND THE
NATIONAL BALLET OF CANADA

ATLAS, CHARLES
AS SEEN ON TV
BECAUSE WE MUST
BLUE STUDIO: FIVE SEGMENTS
CHANNELS/INSERTS
COAST ZONE
FRACTIONS I
FROM AN ISLAND SUMMER
HAIL THE NEW PURITAN
JUMP
LOCALE
MERCE BY MERCE BY PAIK
PARAFANGO
ROAMIN' I
SECRET OF THE WATERFALL
SQUAREGAME VIDEO
TORSE
WALKAROUND TIME
WESTBETH

ATTENBOROUGH, RICHARD
A CHORUS LINE

AVERY, CAROLINE
DANCER FOR THE CORONATION

AVILDSEN, JOHN
DANCE SPACE

AXLINE, JOHN
TWO FOR BALLET

BACON, LLOYD
AMERICAN MUSICALS: FAMOUS PRODUC-
TION NUMBERS

FOOTLIGHT PARADE
42ND STREET

BADHAM, JOHN
SATURDAY NIGHT FEVER

BAILEY, DEREK
LA BAYADÈRE (Royal Ballet)
BILLBOARDS
DAPHNIS AND CHLÖE
THE LENINGRAD LEGEND
MAKAROVA: IN A CLASS OF HER OWN
MAKAROVA RETURNS
NATASHA
THE PRINCE OF THE PAGODAS

BAILY, JOHN
AMIR: AN AFGHAN REFUGEE MUSICIAN'S
LIFE IN PESHAWAR, PAKISTAN

BAKER, BRUCE
THE DANCING PROPHET

BALASH, MURIEL
JEAN-LOUIS BARRAULT: A MAN OF THE
THEATRE
JEAN-LOUIS BARRAULT: THE BODY SPEAKS
A PORTRAIT OF GISÈLLE

BARNES, JOHN
ART OF SILENCE: PANTOMIMES WITH MAR-
CEL MARCEAU
CULTIC DANCES IN A BUDDHIST PAGODA
NEAR HUE

BARR, BURT
AEROS
TRISHA AND CARMEN

BARTENIEFF, IRMGARD
PALM PLAY
STEP STYLE

BARTOLOMEO, JAMES
SANKOFA DANCE THEATER—A PORTRAIT

BATESON, GREGORY
LEARNING TO DANCE IN BALI

BAYLAUCQ, PHILIPPE
LODELA

BECK, ROBERT
VIDEO DICTIONARY OF CLASSICAL BALLET

BECKER, M.J
SONG OF VENEZUELA

BEEMAN, ANDREA
BRINGING TO LIGHT

BELINSKY, ALEXANDER
ANYUTA

BELLE, ANNE
DANCING FOR MR. B.: SIX BALANCHINE
BALLERINAS

REFLECTIONS OF A DANCER: ALEXANDRA
DANILOVA, PRIMA BALLERINA ASSOLUTA
SUZANNE FARRELL: ELUSIVE MUSE

BENNETT, YUDI
THE POINT IS

BERGSOHN, HAL
ADOLESCENCE OF BALLET
EARLY DANCE

BERKELEY, BUSBY
AMERICAN MUSICALS: FAMOUS PRODUC-
TION NUMBERS
BABES IN ARMS
BABES ON BROADWAY
FOR ME AND MY GAL
THE GANG'S ALL HERE
GOLD DIGGERS OF 1935
STRIKE UP THE BAND
TAKE ME OUT TO THE BALL GAME

BERKOWITZ, DAN
DANCE AND MYTH: THE WORLD OF JEAN
ERDMAN

BERRYHILL, BRUCE
THREE DANCES BY MARTHA CURTIS

BESSIE, DAN
THE UGLY DUCKLING

BIRRINGER, JOHANNES
LOVERS FRAGMENTS

BISHOP, JOHN
KHMER COURT DANCE
NEW ENGLAND DANCES

BLACKWOOD, CHRISTIAN
BUTOH: BODY ON THE EDGE OF CRISIS
ELIOT FELD: ARTISTIC DIRECTOR
NIK AND MURRAY
TAPDANCIN'

BLACKWOOD, MICHAEL
ELIOT FELD: ARTISTIC DIRECTOR
GLEN TETLEY: PORTRAIT OF THE CHORE-
OGRAPHER
MAKING DANCES: SEVEN POSTMODERN
CHOREOGRAPHERS
RETRACING STEPS: AMERICAN DANCE
SINCE POSTMODERNISM

BLANK, LES
ALWAYS FOR PLEASURE
IN HEAVEN THERE IS NO BEER?

BLECHMAN, MARCUS
HELEN TAMIRIS IN NEGRO SPIRITUALS

BLUMBERG, SKIP
BODY TJAK
CHAMPIONS
DANCING HANDS
DINIZULU AND HIS AFRICAN DRUMMERS,
DANCERS AND SINGERS
DREAM DANCES OF THE KASHIA POMO:
THE BOLE-MARU RELIGIOUS WOMEN'S
DANCES

ESSENTIALS OF TAP TECHNIQUE
IN MOTION WITH MICHAEL MOSCHEN
MICHAEL MOSCHEN
NEW DANCE
STICKS, LIGHT, FIRE

BOND, JACK
SYMPHONY IN D WORKSHOP

BOOTHE, POWER
BESIDE HERSELF
MOON

BOULTENHOUSE, CHARLES
DIONYSUS

BOWES, TOM
TWENTY ONE WITH BILL T. JONES

BOXELL, TIM
DANCING ON THE EDGE
FROM SAN FRANCISCO: DANCING ON THE
EDGE
LIKE WIND IN MIRA'S HAIR

BOZZE, MARÍA RAQUEL
PALENQUE: UN CANTO

BRADY, MARK
SIX METAMORPHOSES

BREED, JACK
HOPI KACHINAS

BRENTANO, ROBYN
CLOUD DANCE
SPACE CITY

BRESNICK, TOD
THROUGH THE VEIL

BREVAR, RICHARD
KAZE-NO-KO

BREWER, GIOVANNI
BAHIA: AFRICA IN THE AMERICAS

BREWER, MICHAEL
BAHIA: AFRICA IN THE AMERICAS

BRINER, SANDRO
TANGO
TANGO: A SPECTACULAR PERFORMANCE!

BROCK, NORRIS
DANCE THERAPY: THE POWER OF MOVE-
MENT

BROCKMAN, SUSAN
LEE'S FERRY

BROCKWAY, MERRILL
ATTITUDES IN DANCE
BEYOND THE MAINSTREAM: POSTMODERN
DANCERS
CHOREOGRAPHY BY BALANCHINE
DANCE IN AMERICA (over 75 titles)
DANCE THEATRE OF HARLEM
DAVIDSBÜNDLERTANZE

EVENT FOR TELEVISION
THE FOUR TEMPERAMENTS
THE MARTHA GRAHAM DANCE COMPANY
ON THE MOVE: THE CENTRAL BALLET OF
CHINA
THE ROMANTIC ERA
SUE'S LEG: REMEMBERING THE THIRTIES:
TWYLA THARP AND DANCERS

BRODSKY, ROBERT P
JOHN LINDQUIST: PHOTOGRAPHER OF
DANCE

BROOKS, VIRGINIA
CANON IN D
CHARLES WEIDMAN: ON HIS OWN
ISADORA DUNCAN: TECHNIQUE AND CHO-
REOGRAPHY
SCHOOL OF AMERICAN BALLET

BROWN, CAROLYN
DUNE DANCE

BRYANT, CHARLES
SALOME

BURCKHARDT, RUDOLPH
JUNCTION
RUBBLE DANCE LONG ISLAND CITY
WAYWARD GLIMPSES

BURNS, KEN
THE SHAKERS: HANDS TO WORK, HEARTS
TO GOD

BUSH, JEFF
THE ART OF DANCING: AN INTRODUCTION
TO BAROQUE DANCE
BONE DREAM
DANCE ON VIDEO: AN INTRODUCTION TO
VIDEOTAPING DANCE
ETUDE IN FREE
FOUR MOVES IN SPACE: A VIDEODANCE
SUITE
IMAGES IN DISTRACTED TIME
SUITE FANTAISISTE
TENTACLE
WIDENING GYRE
WILD FIELDS

BUTLER, DAVID
AMERICAN MUSICALS: FAMOUS PRODUC-
TION NUMBERS
LITTLEST REBEL

BUTOMAN, V
BALLET LEGENDS: THE KIROV'S NINEL KUR-
GAPKINA

BYRD, DONALD
UNSETTLED DREAMS

BYRNE, JAMES
FIELDS
INSIDE EYES
LAMENT
SMALL DISTANCES
SOLO
TANGO
THAT MEANS I WANT TO GO HOME

DAVIDSON, BOAZ
SALSA

DE BOE, GÉRARD
AFRICAN MUSICIANS

DE BOYSSON, JEAN
LAURETTA: MADONNA OF THE SENIOR CIT-
    IZEN SET
LA PROMENADE
TEILE DICH NACHT (Night Open Yourself)

DE FIGUEIREDO, VERA
CREATION OF THE WORLD: A SAMBA OPERA

DE NONNO, TONY
DANCING'S ALL OF YOU

DECOSTERE, STEFAAN
SOMETIMES IT WORKS, SOMETIMES IT
    DOESN'T

DEL RUTH, ROY
BORN TO DANCE
BROADWAY MELODY OF 1936
BROADWAY MELODY OF 1938
DU BARRY WAS A LADY

DELILAH
DELILAH & SIROCCO . . . LIVE & WILD!

DEMME, JONATHAN
ACCUMULATION WITH TALKING PLUS
    WATER MOTOR

DERBENEV, VADIM
CARMEN (Bolshoi Ballet)
A POEM OF DANCES ALSO KNOWN AS PLI-
    SETSKAYA: CARMEN
SPARTACUS (Bolshoi Ballet)

DERCON, CHRIS
SOMETIMES IT WORKS, SOMETIMES IT
    DOESN'T

DEREN, MAYA
MAYA DEREN: EXPERIMENTAL FILMS
MEDIATION ON VIOLENCE
MESHES OF THE AFTERNOON
RITUAL IN TRANSFIGURED TIME
A STUDY IN CHOREOGRAPHY FOR CAMERA
THE VERY EYE OF NIGHT

DESMOND, JANE
CHUCK DAVIS, DANCING THROUGH WEST
    AFRICA

DEVIVO, KERRY
PLANES, TRAINS, AUTOMOBILES
PURE REMAINS
SHADES OF WIEGENLIED

DIAMOND, DENNIS
DANCE PRELUDES

DIAMOND, MATTHEW
SPEAKING IN TONGUES
THE WRECKER'S BALL: THREE DANCES BY
    PAUL TAYLOR

DIAMONDSTEIN, GERALDINE
CHILDREN DANCE

DICKSON, W.K.L
BEFORE HOLLYWOOD: TURN OF THE CEN-
    TURY FILM FROM AMERICAN ARCHIVES

DIETERLE, WILLIAM
FASHIONS OF 1934

DOMENECH, JUAN PABLO
TANGO! A MASTER CLASS WITH THE DIN-
    ZELS

DONATELLI, GARY
BALLET CLASS

DONEN, STANLEY
DEEP IN MY HEART
FUNNY FACE
IT'S ALWAYS FAIR WEATHER
ON THE TOWN
ROYAL WEDDING
SEVEN BRIDES FOR SEVEN BROTHERS
SINGIN' IN THE RAIN

DONG, ARTHUR
FORBIDDEN CITY, U.S.A

DORNHELM, ROBERT
THE CHILDREN OF THEATRE STREET

DRATCH, HOWARD
ROUTES OF RHYTHM WITH HARRY BELA-
    FONTE

DUBIN, CHARLES S.
DANCE: FOUR PIONEERS
DANCE: NEW YORK CITY BALLET
DANCE: ROBERT JOFFREY BALLET
ECHOES OF JAZZ

DUBOULAY, CHRISTINE
THE PERSISTENT IMAGE and VALSE

DUMALE, VINAY
THE TEMPLE AND THE SWAN

DUNLOP, GEOFF
MERCE CUNNINGHAM

EHRNVALL, TORBJÖRN
AN EVENING WITH KYLIAN AND THE NE-
    DERLANDS DANS THEATRE

ELDER, BRUCE
BARBARA IS A VISION OF LOVELINESS
LOOK! WE HAVE COME THROUGH
UNREMITTING TENDERNESS

ELDER, SARA
THE DRUMS OF WINTER (Uksuum Cauyai)

ELISOFON, ELIOT
AFRICAN CARVING: A DOGON KANAGA
    MASK

ELLIS, RICHARD
THE PERSISTENT IMAGE and VALSE

EMSHWILLER, ED
CHOICE CHANCE WOMAN DANCE
CHRYSALIS
DANCE CHROMATIC
FILM WITH THREE DANCERS
IMAGE: FLESH AND VOICE
PILOBOLUS AND JOAN
SCAPE-MATES
TOTEM

ENRIGHT, RAY
DAMES
ON YOUR TOES

EPSTEIN, MARCELO
ANNUNCIATION
BODY ROCK

ERSKINE, MAREN
BEGINNINGS

ERSKINE, REED
BEGINNINGS

ESHER, KATHRYN
BREAK
PARIS
TYMPANI

ETTINGER, CLIFFORD
CHINESE, KOREAN AND JAPANESE DANCE

FABER, CHRISTIAN
THE NEXT STEP

FALK, JANNIKE
ASHES, MIST AND WIND BLOWN DUST

FANSHEL, SUSAN
MADE IN THE BRONX

FASINO, CINZIA
MAGDALENE
NOCTURNAE

FAULKNER, SCOTT
SUNNY SIDE OF LIFE

FEINBERG, NINA
A DANCER'S GRAMMAR

FEJOS, PAUL
DANCE CONTEST IN ESIRA

FERGUSON, DON
BOOK OF SHADOWS

FERGUSON, NICHOLAS
BALLET COMES TO BRITAIN
BALLET ENTERS THE WORLD STAGE
THE BEGINNINGS OF TODAY
BRITISH BALLET TODAY
HOW BALLET BEGAN
HOW BALLET WAS SAVED
TCHAIKOVSKY AND THE RUSSIANS

FICHMAN, NIV
BLUE SNAKE
INNER RHYTHM
STRUGGLE FOR HOPE

FIORE, ROBERT
FULL OF LIFE A-DANCIN'

FITZGERALD, KIT
BART COOK: CHOREOGRAPHER
LIVE VIDEO DANCE

FLYNN, STEVEN
DANCE TO THE GREAT MOTHER
DELILAH & SIROCCO . . . LIVE & WILD!
DELILAH'S COSTUME WORKSHOP

FORGENCY, VLADIMIR
ADOLESCENCE

FORMAN, MILOS
HAIR

FOSSE, BOB
ALL THAT JAZZ
CABARET
SWEET CHARITY

FOY, PATRICIA
THE EBB AND FLOW
THE MARGOT FONTEYN STORY
OUT OF THE LIMELIGHT, HOME IN THE
   RAIN
THE ROMANTIC BALLET
RUDOLF NUREYEV
THE SCENE CHANGES
WHAT IS NEW

FRANKEL, CYRIL
BOLD STEPS

FRANTZ, THOMAS
TWO FOR BALLET

FREELAND, THORNTON
AMERICAN MUSICALS: FAMOUS PRODUC-
   TION NUMBERS
FLYING DOWN TO RIO

FRIEDMAN, GENE
INDEX
THE OFFICIAL DOCTRINE
THREE DANCES

FROEMKE, SUSAN
ACCENT ON THE OFFBEAT

FRUCHTMAN, MILTON A.
RHYTHMETRON: THE DANCE THEATRE OF
   HARLEM WITH ARTHUR MITCHELL

FUJII, SHUJI
GISÈLLE (Bolshoi Ballet)
SPARTACUS (Bolshoi Ballet)

FULK, DUANE
SET PIECE

GAJDA, JAROSLAV
BALLROOM DANCING: THE INTERNA-
   TIONAL CHAMPIONSHIPS

GARDNER, ROBERT
DEEP HEARTS

GATLIF, TONY
LACHO DROM

GEAREY, DAVE
AIRWAVES
BRANCHES
FOOTAGE
ONCE AGAIN

GEISEL, DAVE
DANCE: ANNA SOKOLOW'S *ROOMS*

GELB, PETER
ACCENT ON THE OFFBEAT

GELLER, DANIEL
ISADORA DUNCAN: MOVEMENT FROM THE
   SOUL

GENINI, IZZA
MOROCCO, BODY AND SOUL

GERONIMI, CLYDE
SLEEPING BEAUTY (animated)

GHERTLER, LOUISE
IN A JAZZ WAY: A PORTRAIT OF MURA
   DEHN

GIBSON, KEAN
A CELEBRATION OF LIFE: DANCES OF THE
   AFRICAN-GUYANESE

GIGLIOTTI, DAVIDSON
FIRST SOLO

GILBERT, LEWIS
STEPPING OUT

GILBERT, SUE
A DANCE FANTASY

GIRARD, FRANÇOIS
LE DORTOIR (The Dormitory)

GLICK, STEFANIE
THROUGH THE VEIL

GLUSHANOK, PETER
APPALACHIAN SPRING
A DANCER'S WORLD
MARTHA GRAHAM, AN AMERICAN ORIGI-
   NAL IN PERFORMANCE

GOBERMAN, JOHN
GISÈLLE (American Ballet Theatre)

GODWIN, DWIGHT
DAY ON EARTH
RADHA
THE SUGAR PLUM FAIRY VARIATION FROM
   THE NUTCRACKER

GOLDFINE, DAYNA
ISADORA DUNCAN: MOVEMENT FROM THE
   SOUL

GOLDONI, LELIA
GENIUS ON THE WRONG COAST

GOLDSMITH, SILVIANNA
ANGEL OF TIME
ONEIRO: IN THE SHADOW OF ISADORA

GORDON, DAVID
DAVID GORDON: PANEL

GORDON, RICHARD
STILT DANCERS OF LONG BOW VILLAGE

GOTTLIEB, ROBERT
CIRCLES: CYCLES KATHAK DANCE

GOULD, JOHN
MARCEAU ON MIME

GOULET, PIERRE MARIE
BALLADE

GRANT, BARBARA
THE TAP DANCE KID

GRAY, LAUREL
AN INTRODUCTION TO UZBEK DANCE

GREEN, WHITNEY
BALANCES

GREENAWAY, PETER
MEREDITH MONK

GREENE, SHERRY
LEARN HOW TO DANCE

GREENFIELD, AMY
ANTIGONE/RITES OF PASSION
DERVISH
DIALOGUE FOR CAMERAMAN AND DANCER
ELEMENT
ENCOUNTER
FOUR SOLOS FOR FOUR WOMEN
FRAGMENTS: MAT/GLASS

GREVILLE, EDMOND
PRINCESS TAM TAM

GRIFFITH, EDWARD
THE SKY'S THE LIMIT

GRIGOROVICH, YURI
THE NUTCRACKER (Bolshoi Ballet)
THE NUTCRACKER (Bolshoi Ballet)

GRIMM, THOMAS
CREOLE GISÈLLE
DANCE IN AMERICA (over 75 titles)
DANCE THEATRE OF HARLEM
AN EVENING WITH ALVIN AILEY AMERICAN
   DANCE THEATRE
AN EVENING WITH THE BALLET RAMBERT
THE FIREBIRD
MARTHA GRAHAM: THREE CONTEMPO-
   RARY CLASSICS
THE MARYINSKY BALLET
SWAN LAKE (London Festival Ballet)
LA SYLPHIDE (Royal Danish Ballet)

A TRIBUTE TO ALVIN AILEY
TROY GAME

GROSSMAN, KAREN
CHILDREN WITH A DREAM

GRUNSTEIN, MIGUEL
DANZANTE

HACKFORD, TAYLOR
WHITE NIGHTS

HAHN, DAVID
IN A REHEARSAL ROOM
RUTH PAGE: AN AMERICAN ORIGINAL

HAIMES, TED
FIRST STEPS

HALDANE, DON
ALL THE BEST FROM RUSSIA

HALEY, JR., JACK
THAT'S DANCING
THAT'S ENTERTAINMENT

HALL, ARTHUR
ORISUN OMI (THE WELL): PROLOGUE TO
   THE YORUBA CYCLE
WATER SPIRIT FESTIVAL

HALLIS, RON
BANGUZA TIMBILA

HALPRIN, ANNA
PARADES AND CHANGES

HAMMID, ALEXANDER
MARTHA GRAHAM, AN AMERICAN ORIGI-
   NAL IN PERFORMANCE
NIGHT JOURNEY

HANCOCK, BILL
JAZZ HOOFER: BABY LAURENCE

HANDLEY, ROBERT
BUFFALO SOLDIER

HARAMIS, PETER
ANASTENARIA

HARDY, ROBIN
INDIA: HAUNTING PASSAGE

HARKNESS, JERALD B.
STEPPIN'

HARMAYN, SHANTY
BEDHAYA: THE SACRED DANCE

HARNETT, DANIEL
DECLARATION OF INDEPENDENCE

HARRIS, HILARY
NINE VARIATIONS ON A DANCE THEME

HARRIS, JUSTIN
DARE TO DANCE

HART, DEREK
BACKSTAGE AT THE KIROV

HARTLEY, ELDA
BALI: THE MASK OF RANGDA
BALI TODAY

HARVEY, HAROLD
KOREA: PERFORMING ARTS: THE WONDER-
   FUL WORLD OF KIM SUNG HEE

HARWOOD, GERALD
MIDEASTERN DANCE: AN INTRODUCTION
   TO BELLY DANCE

HAUSER, MATTHEW M.
ADZO

HAUSER, RICK
TZADDIK

HAYEUR, ISABELLE
UNTITLED, ARMS

HÉBERT, BERNAR
PICTURES AT AN EXHIBITION

HECHT, BEN
SPECTRE OF THE ROSE

HEGEDUS, CHRIS
DANCE BLACK AMERICA

HEISE, WILLIAM
BEFORE HOLLYWOOD: TURN OF THE CEN-
   TURY FILM FROM AMERICAN ARCHIVES

HENKE, GABRIELE
ON YOUR TOES . . . THE MAKING OF

HENSON, JOAN
DANCE CLASS

HEUS, RICHARD
BEST OF ALL A DANCER

HILLS, HENRY
BALI MECHANIQUE
LITTLE LIEUTENANT
MONEY
SSS

HILMER, DAVE
I HATE TO EXERCISE, I LOVE TO TAP

HIMMELHEBER, H.
ACROBATIC DANCE OF THE SNAKE
   MAIDENS
ASHANTI DANCE ADJEMLE AT KOUADJIKRO
DANCE OF THE BUSHCLEARING SOCIETY
   "GUA"
GOLI MASK DANCE
STILT DANCES AT KPEGBOUNI

HINTON, CARMA
STILT DANCERS OF LONG BOW VILLAGE

HIRSH, HY
CLINIC OF STUMBLE

HOFFMAN, MATT
REALITY OF A DREAMER: RIVER NORTH
   DANCE COMPANY

HOLSTEN, GLEN
EARTHMATTERS
HELP ME TO DREAM
P FUNK

HOLUB, JOHANNES
IL BALLARINO: THE ART OF RENAISSANCE
   DANCE
THE NEW DANCE GROUP GALA CONCERT

HOPE, RUTH
YOUNG AND JUST BEGINNING: PIERRE

HORN, ANDREW
CLOUD DANCE

HOWE, JOHN
CANADIANS CAN DANCE

HULSCHER, HANS
L'ENFANT ET LES SORTILEGES
AN EVENING WITH KYLIAN AND THE NE-
   DERLANDS DANS THEATRE
ROAD TO THE STAMPING GROUND
SYMPHONY IN D WORKSHOP

HUNT, PETER
1776

HURWITZ, TOM
HARMONICA BREAKDOWN

HUSTON, JOHN
ANNIE

IPIOTIS, CELIA
THE ART OF DANCING: AN INTRODUCTION
   TO BAROQUE DANCE
BONE DREAM
DANCE AND MYTH: THE WORLD OF JEAN
   ERDMAN
DANCE ON VIDEO: AN INTRODUCTION TO
   VIDEOTAPING DANCE
ETUDE IN FREE
HERALD'S ROUND
SUITE FANTAISISTE
TENTACLE
WILD FIELDS

IRWIN, MARK
YOUNG AND JUST BEGINNING: PIERRE

ITTLESON, JOHN
HANYA: PORTRAIT OF A DANCE PIONEER

IVORY, JAMES
THE DELHI WAY
ROSELAND

JACK, DEL
AUDITION POWER: PART I, KNOWING
   WHAT IT TAKES TO BE CHOSEN and PART
   II, WORKING THE HOLLYWOOD SYSTEM

JACQUOT, BENOÎT
MERCE CUNNINGHAM AND COMPANY

JAFFE, PATRICIA
REINCATNATED

JAMES, ASHLEY
AND STILL WE DANCE

JESSEN, VICTOR
GAITÉ PARISIENNE

LEVIEN, JULIA
ISADORA DUNCAN: TECHNIQUE AND REPERTORY

LIEBERMAN, ROBERT H.
BOYCEBALL

LIEFF, JUDITH
NEMETON

LIESENDAHL, HEINZ
THE NUTCRACKER (American Ballet Theatre)

LIGHT, DONNA
MALAMBO DEL SOL

LIN, TED
PAS DE DEUX

LIPPE, STEWART
THE ANATOMY LESSON
ANCIENT ART OF BELLY DANCING
MIME TECHNIQUE: PART I

LIPPERT, RICK ALLEN
BALLROOM DANCING

LIPSKIS, PETER
DANCE MASKS: THE WORLD OF MARGARET SEVERN

LOCKETZ, JAN MARCE
ANIMA

LOCKYER, BOB
PULCINELLA/SOLDAT

LOFTON, GREG
POINTE BY POINT

LOGAN, JOSHUA
SOUTH PACIFIC

LOGUE, JOAN
THIRTY SECOND SPOTS

LOMAX, ALAN
DANCE AND HUMAN HISTORY
PALM PLAY
STEP STYLE

LÓPEZ, CINDY
GERMAN FOLK DANCES
SPANISH FOLK DANCING

LOW, COLIN
CIRCLE OF THE SUN

LOWRY, MARK
PARIS

LUCIER, MARY
AMPHIBIAN
IN THE BLINK OF AN EYE . . . (AMPHIBIAN DREAMS) IF I COULD FLY I WOULD FLY
MASS

LUHRMANN, BAZ
STRICTLY BALLROOM

LUMET, SIDNEY
THE WIZ

LUTZ, JURGEN
A MOVING PICTURE

LYE, LEN
TAL FARLOW

LYNE, ADRIAN
FLASHDANCE

LÉGER, FERNAND
BALLET MECHANIQUE

MACALUSO, SUSAN
INTRODUCTION TO DANCE MEDICINE: KEEPING DANCERS DANCING
LOWER EXTREMITY DANCE MEDICINE: ORTHOPEDIC EXAMINATION WITH DR. WILLIAM HAMILTON

MACDONALD, ANNETTE
DANCES OF MEXICO: ANIMAL ORIGINS
MARY WIGMAN: 1886–1973: *WHEN THE FIRE DANCES BETWEEN THE TWO POLES*
TANKO BUSHI: A JAPANESE FOLK DANCE

MACHARET, ELENA
BALLET FAVORITES
LA BAYADÈRE (Kirov Ballet)
SLEEPING BEAUTY (Kirov Ballet)

MACIEK ALBRECHT
HIROSHIMA

MACK, EARL
THE CHILDREN OF THEATRE STREET

MACMILLAN, KENNETH
ROMEO AND JULIET (Royal Ballet)

MAHRER, MICHELLE
THE WAVE: ECSTATIC DANCE FOR BODY AND SOUL

MAMOULIAN, ROUBEN
SILK STOCKINGS

MANGOLTE, BABETTE
WATER MOTOR

MANNING, NICK
AMERICAN INDIAN SOCIAL DANCING
IROQUOIS SOCIAL DANCE I AND II

MANOFF, MARK
TOPENG BABAKAN (SOLO MASKED DANCE OF WEST JAVA)

MANTELL-SEIDEL, ANDREA
ISADORA DUNCAN: TECHNIQUE AND REPERTORY

MARKLE, GREG
FRENCH FOLK DANCING

MARSHALL, GEORGE
THE GOLDWYN FOLLIES

MARSHALL, JOHN
BITTER MELONS
N/UM TCHAI: THE CEREMONIAL DANCE OF THE !KUNG BUSHMEN

MARTEL, DIANE
HOUSE OF TRES
RECKIN' SHOP "LIVE FROM BROOKLYN"

MARTI, WALTER
FLAMENCO

MARX, SUE
CAROLE MORISSEAU AND THE DETROIT CITY DANCE COMPANY

MASAYESVA JR., VICTOR
ITAM HAKIM ITOPIIT (We Someone, the Hopi)

MASON, EDWARD A.
GEE, OFFICER KRUPKE

MASON HAUSER, NANCY
HANYA: PORTRAIT OF A DANCE PIONEER

MATH, STUART
FRANKIE MANNING'S BIRTHDAY VIDEO

MAYER, ANTHONY
KALAKSHETRA: DEVOTION TO DANCE

MCCALL, DEBRA
THE BAUHAUS DANCES OF OSKAR SCHLEMMER: A RECONSTRUCTION

MCCARTY, MARK
PROCESSION: CONTEMPORARY DIRECTIONS IN AMERICAN DANCE

MCCONKEY, LAWRENCE
KUMU HULA: KEEPERS OF A CULTURE

MCKENNIREY, MICHAEL
FOR THE LOVE OF DANCE
GALA

MCLAREN, NORMAN
BALLET ADAGIO
A CHAIRY TALE
DANCE SQUARED
NARCISSUS
PAS DE DEUX
A PHANTASY
TWO BAGATELLES

MCLEOD, NORMAN Z.
LET'S DANCE

MCPHEDRAN, PHILIP
KAREN KAIN: BALLERINA

MEKAS, JONAS
CUP/SAUCER/TWO DANCERS/RADIO
HERE AND NOW WITH WATCHERS

PAVIOT, P.
MARCEL MARCEAU OU L'ART DU MIME

PEMBLETON, ARTHUR
TEACHING BEGINNING/ADVANCED DANCE
  IMPROVISATION

PENNEBAKER, D.A.
DANCE BLACK AMERICA
DANCERS IN SCHOOL
RAINFOREST

PENNEY, EDMUND
THE DANCING PROPHET

PERILLO, MARY
DANCE EX MACHINA
ENDANCE
FRACTURED VARIATIONS and VISUAL
  SHUFFLE
GEOGRAPHY AND METABOLISM
UNTITLED, ARMS

PETERSON, SIDNEY
CLINIC OF STUMBLE

PETIT, ROLAND
IN PRAISE OF FOLLY
LE JEUNE HOMME ET LA MORT

PHILLIPS, JOHN MICHAEL
SWAN LAKE (Royal Ballet)

PICARD, BERNARD
SLEEPING BEAUTY (Kirov Ballet)

PIÑEDA BARNET, ENRIQUE
GISÈLLE (Ballet Nacional de Cuba)

POTTER, HENRY C.
SECOND CHORUS
THE STORY OF VERNON AND IRENE CASTLE

POWELL, MICHAEL
THE RED SHOES
THE TALES OF HOFFMANN

POWELL, PETER
IMPULSES
WILD SWANS IN EPITAPH AND MADHONOR

PREISS, JEFF
HOUSE OF TRES

PRESSBURGER, EMERIC
THE RED SHOES
THE TALES OF HOFFMANN

PRESTON, RICHARD
TWO BY LOUIS JOHNSON

PREVOTS, NAIMA
CHILDREN DANCE

PRINDEL, KAREN
REQUIEM FOR A SLAVE

PÉREZ BÉTANCOURT, ALVARO
VOICES OF THE ORISHAS

RAINER, YVONNE
A TRIO

RALOV, KIRSTEN
NAPOLI

RAPPAPORT, G.
STARS OF THE RUSSIAN BALLET

REED, CAROL
OLIVER!

REED, PETER
THE ONE I SEE

REESE, ANDREA STAR
UNSETTLED DREAMS

REEVE, GORDON M.
MOMENT OF LIGHT: THE DANCE OF EVE-
  LYN HART

REINHARD, HANS
BALLET IN JAZZ

REISZ, KAROL
ISADORA

RENOIR, JEAN
CHARLESTON
FRENCH CAN-CAN

RESNIKOV, EFIM
TERPSICHORE'S CAPTIVES

REUTERSWARD, MANS
CINDERELLA (Lyon Opera Ballet)
MISS JULIE

RHODES, LUCILLE
ANNA SOKOLOW, CHOREOGRAPHER

RIOS, HUMBERTO
THE TANGO IS ALSO A HISTORY

RIRIE, SHIRLEY
THE ELEMENTS OF DANCE

ROBBINS, JEROME
WEST SIDE STORY

ROBINSON, JAMES F.
JAZZ DANCE CLASS WITH GUS GIORDANO
MUSIC BOX

ROGERS, BOB
BALLET ROBOTIQUE

ROGERS, WENDY
STANDING BY

ROLAND, ERIC
KUMU HULA: KEEPERS OF A CULTURE

ROMANO, ROBERTO
CAUGHT
IMPROVISATION TO BANSURI FLUTE AND
  SEASCAPES

ROSE, KATHY
PRIMITIVE MOVERS
SYNCOPATIONS

ROSEN, BOB
ELLIS ISLAND

ROSEN, PETER
GODUNOV: THE WORLD TO DANCE IN

ROSENBERG, DOUGLAS
SPEAKING OF DANCE: CONVERSATIONS
  WITH CONTEMPORARY MASTERS OF
  AMERICAN MODERN DANCE

ROSOW, EUGENE
ROUTES OF RHYTHM WITH HARRY BELA-
  FONTE

ROSS, ELISABETH
STICKS ON THE MOVE

ROSS, HERBERT
DANCERS
FOOTLOOSE
NIJINSKY
THE TURNING POINT

ROSS, NAN
KING KONG IN A BLANKET

ROSS, TANA
THE CALL OF THE JITTERBUG

ROULEAU, RAYMOND
THE LOVERS OF TERUEL

ROVIRA-BELETA
LOS TARANTOS

ROWE, ALEXANDER
CINDERELLA (Bolshoi Ballet)
CINDERELLA (Bolshoi Ballet)

ROWLEY, BILL
IOWA BLIZZARD '73

ROY, MERVYN
GOLD DIGGERS OF 1933
LOVELY TO LOOK AT

RUBENSTEIN, LEE
SILVER FEET

RUSSELL, KEN
ISADORA DUNCAN, THE BIGGEST DANCER
  IN THE WORLD

SAARMA, RAMAKANTHA
AFRICA DANCES

SALIMBAEV, VLADIMIR
DON QUIXOTE (Russian State Perm Ballet)
SWAN LAKE (Russian State Perm Ballet)

SALTZMAN, DEEPA AND PAUL
SERAMA'S MASK

SANBORN, JOHN
DANCE EX MACHINA
ENDANCE

STEINBERG, CAROL
COLLECTED WORKS OF ELIZABETH STREB

STEINBERG, MORLEIGH
TRAVELING LIGHT

STERN, PEGGY
BALI BEYOND THE POSTCARD

STEVENS, GEORGE
A DAMSEL IN DISTRESS
SWING TIME

STOCKTON, PHIL
MOVEMENT IN CLASSIC DANCE: THE PEL-
VIC AREA

STODELL, JIM
CHANCE DANCE

STODELLE, ERNESTINE
DORIS HUMPHREY TECHNIQUE: THE CRE-
ATIVE POTENTIAL

STONE, ANDREW L.
STORMY WEATHER

STRAITON, JOHN
ANIMALS IN MOTION

STRATE, WALTER V.
LAMENT
MOOR'S PAVANE (VARIATIONS ON THE
THEME OF OTHELLO)

STRATFORD, MARIA
SAMBA TO SLOW FOX

STROYEVA, VERA
GRAND CONCERT

SUGGS, JEANNE
LESTER HORTON TECHNIQUE: THE WARM
UP

SUMMA, VICTOR
RAG TO ROCK TO DISCO

SUTTON, JULIA
IL BALLARINO: THE ART OF RENAISSANCE
DANCE

SWEENEY, SKIP
CERBERUS
VISION DANCE

SWEETE, BARBARA WILLIS
CARNIVAL OF SHADOWS
DIDO AND AENEAS
FALLING DOWN STAIRS
FANDANGO
THE PLANETS
ROMEOS AND JULIETS
THE SORCERESS: KIRI TE KANAWA

SWENSON, JAMES
HONI COLES, THE CLASS ACT OF TAP

SYKES-DIETZE, BARBARA
KALYIAN

SZOBOSZLAY, PETER
DANCING SCHOOL

TALBOT, TONY
BERIMBAU

TAMBINI, CATHERINE
SUZANNE FARRELL: ELUSIVE MUSE

TANASESCU, GINO
DANCING ON THE EDGE
FROM SAN FRANCISCO: DANCING ON THE
EDGE

TANNER, TONY
TEAK ROOM (AUTOBIOGRAPHY OF A
DANCER)

TARTA, ALEXANDRE
ROMEO AND JULIET (Lyon Opera Ballet)

TATGE, CATHERINE
MARTHA GRAHAM: THE DANCER RE-
VEALED

TAUROG, NORMAN
BROADWAY MELODY OF 1940

TEGEDER, ULRICH
MARY WIGMAN: MY LIFE IS DANCE

THARP, TWYLA
THE CATHERINE WHEEL

TIKHOMIROV, ROMAN
MORNING STAR (CHOLPON)

TIKHONOV, NIKITA
BOLSHOI PROKOFIEV GALA

TIRANOFF, LOUISE
ARTISTS OF THE DANCE
MILT AND HONI

TRACEY, ANDREW
THE CHOPI TIMBILA DANCE
MGODO WA MBANGUZI

TSINEMAN, ARKADI
WORLD'S YOUNG BALLET

TULUBYEVA, ZOYA
THE LITTLE HUMPBACKED HORSE
SWAN LAKE (Bolshoi Ballet)

TUPPER, LOUIS
JUST FOR ME

VALK, ACHMED
ENTROPY: REVERSE TO OMEGA

VALKENBERG, PAUL
EDO: DANCE AND PANTOMIME

VANOVER-FELDMAN, HARMONY
A DANCE FOR 15 PREGNANT WOMEN

VASSILIEV, VLADIMIR
MACBETH

VASULKA, WOODY
ART OF MEMORY

VELÉZ, EDIN
DANCE OF DARKNESS

VERDIN, WALTER
GOLDBERG VARIATIONS

VERNON, JOHN
BALLET FAVORITES
BOLSHOI: DIVERTISSEMENTS
LA FILLE MAL GARDÉE (Royal Ballet)

VIDOR, CHARLES
COVER GIRL

VON PRAUNHEIM, ROSA
ANITA: DANCES OF VICE

VUOLLE, ERIC
BALLET RUSE

WADSWORTH, DAVID
SONGS UNWRITTEN: A TAP DANCER RE-
MEMBERED

WAGMAN, VERA
HIGH NOON

WALTERS, CHARLES
THE BARKLEYS OF BROADWAY
THE BELLE OF NEW YORK
EASTER PARADE
SUMMER STOCK

WANNER, DEBRA
SHE STORIES

WARD, PENNY
THE LEGACY OF THE CHOREOGRAPHY OF
ISADORA DUNCAN
MEHANG SUSAH
THE STONE DANCES
THE WATER PIECES
THE WATER PIECES NO. 2

WATKINSON, JOHN
BRYONY BRIND'S BALLET: THE FIRST STEPS

WEIDMAN, HEINRICH
THE DANCE

WEINER, HAL
BLACK GIRL

WEINER, MARILYN
BLACK GIRL

WEINSTEIN, LARRY
RAVEL

WHEELER, ANNE
TEACH ME TO DANCE

WILCKEN, MARK
DANCER REHEARSING

WILDENHAHN, KLAUS
WHAT DO PINA BAUSCH AND HER DANCES
DO IN WUPPERTAL?

Excerpts Index

CAN, REMEMBERED AND RECON-
STRUCTED BY GEMZE DE LAPPE

LA BAMBA
MEXICAN DANCES

BAMBOU
THE PARIS OPERA BALLET: SEVEN BALLETS

BANDA
ETHNIC DANCE: ROUNDTRIP TO TRINIDAD

BANDONEON
WHAT DO PINA BAUSCH AND HER DANCES
DO IN WUPPERTAL?

BARBER'S ADAGIO
THE MARYINSKY BALLET

BARBUNCUL
RUMANIAN FOLK DANCES

BARDJAT
DANCES FROM DJAYA

BARONG-RANGDA
BALI: THE MASK OF RANGDA

BASIC STRATEGIES
RETRACING STEPS: AMERICAN DANCE
SINCE POSTMODERNISM

LA BASTRINQUE
FRENCH FOLK DANCING

BATUCADA
CARNIVAL OF RHYTHM

LA BAYADÈRE
BOLD STEPS
BOLSHOI: DIVERTISSEMENTS
BUJONES: IN HIS IMAGE
CLASSIC KIROV PERFORMANCES
THE MAGIC OF THE KIROV BALLET
RUSSIAN BALLET, THE GLORIOUS TRADI-
TION
WHITE NIGHT OF DANCE IN LENINGRAD

LE BEAU DANUBE
GREAT PERFORMANCE IN DANCE

BEGIN THE BEGUINE
NATASHA

BELE
ETHNIC DANCE: ROUNDTRIP TO TRINIDAD

THE BELOVED
DANCE THEATRE OF HARLEM
DANCE THEATRE OF HARLEM

BERNARD
THE RUSH DANCE COMPANY, EXCERPTS
FROM *BERNARD*

BESIDE HERSELF
SOLO

BHAKTI
WORLD'S YOUNG BALLET

LES BICHES
BALLET COMES TO BRITAIN
NIJINSKA: A LEGEND IN DANCE

BIDJERUA
RECREATIONAL DANCES FROM CENTRAL
SUDAN

BIGHEAD
KASHIA MEN'S DANCES: SOUTHWESTERN
POMO INDIANS

BILLY THE KID
COPLAND PORTRAIT

BIOSFERA
RHYTHMETRON: THE DANCE THEATRE OF
HARLEM WITH ARTHUR MITCHELL

THE BLACK DRESS
FROM SAN FRANCISCO: DANCING ON THE
EDGE

BLACK LAKE
ERICK HAWKINS' AMERICA

THE BLACK SWAN
ARTISTS OF THE DANCE

BLESSED SPIRITS
THE ENDURING ESSENCE: THE TECHNIQUE
AND CHOREOGRAPHY OF ISADORA DUN-
CAN, REMEMBERED AND RECON-
STRUCTED BY GEMZE DE LAPPE

BLUE BIRD
BALLET STUDY FILMS

CLASSICAL BALLET
TCHAIKOVSKY AND THE RUSSIANS

THE BLUE DANUBE
ISADORA DUNCAN: MOVEMENT FROM THE
SOUL

BLUE SNAKE
INNER RHYTHM

BLUE STUDIO
MERCE BY MERCE BY PAIK

BLUES SUITE
ALVIN AILEY: MEMORIES AND VISIONS

BODA TARASCA
BALLET FOLKLÓRICO NACIONAL DE
MÉXICO

BOLERO
THE BOLSHOI BALLET
TORVILL AND DEAN: PATH TO PERFECTION

BOOK OF DANCES
THEATRE MEETS RITUAL

LA BOULANGÈRE
FRENCH FOLK DANCING

BOUTIQUE FANTASQUE
BALLET COMES TO BRITAIN

BOXES
MODERN DANCE: CHOREOGRAPHY AND
THE SOURCE

LE BRANLE À SIX
FRENCH FOLK DANCING

LE BRANLE DU QUÉRCY
FRENCH FOLK DANCING

BRIUL
RUMANIAN FOLK DANCES

BROTHER JACKASS
RETRACING STEPS: AMERICAN DANCE
SINCE POSTMODERNISM

BUGAKU
DANCE THEATRE OF HARLEM

CABILLO BLANCO
SPANISH FOLK DANCING

LA CACHUCA
THE BALLERINAS

CAKEWALK
DANCE BLACK AMERICA

CALABASH
SNAKE DANCE TEACHER DANCE

CALCIUM LIGHT NIGHT
PETER MARTINS: A DANCER

CALIFORNIA POPPY
IMMORTAL SWAN

LE CAMARGO
THE MAGNIFICENT BEGINNING

CANON IN D
IN A REHEARSAL ROOM

THE CANTEEN KEEPER
THE KIROV BALLET: CLASSIC BALLET NIGHT

CAPRICHOS
DANCE: A REFLECTION OF OUR TIMES

CARMEN
ALICIA ALONSO: ALICIA
BLACK TIGHTS
CARMEN (Bolshoi Ballet)
KAREN KAIN: BALLERINA
THE MAGNIFICENT BEGINNING

NATASHA
A POEM OF DANCES ALSO KNOWN AS PLI-
SETSKAYA: CARMEN

CARNIVAL DE VENISE
KIROV SOLOISTS: INVITATION TO THE
DANCE

EL CARRETERO
MEXICAN DANCES

CASTELLANA
JOSÉ GRECO: IN PERFORMANCE

LA CATHÉDRALE ENGLOUTIE
AN EVENING WITH KYLIAN AND THE NE-
DERLANDS DANS THEATRE

GOOD THING GONE
IMAGES IN DISTRACTED TIME

GOUNOD SYMPHONY
WATCHING BALLET

GOURD DANCE
POW WOW!

GRANADA
JOSÉ GRECO: IN PERFORMANCE

GRAND PAS CLASSIQUE
THE PARIS OPERA BALLET: SEVEN BALLETS

GRAND PAS DE QUATRE
ALICIA ALONSO: ALICIA
THE ROMANTIC ERA

GRASS DANCE
INDIANS OF THE PLAINS, SUNDANCE CERE-
   MONY

GREAT GALLOPING GOTTSCHALK
AMERICAN BALLET THEATRE IN SAN FRAN-
   CISCO

THE GREATEST
THE SCENE CHANGES

THE GREEN TABLE
THE DANCE
WHAT IS NEW

GREENSLEEVES DUET
MODERN DANCE: CHOREOGRAPHY AND
   THE SOURCE

GREGORIAN CHANT
RUTH ST. DENIS BY BARIBAULT

GUISTINO
THE SORCERESS: KIRI TE KANAWA

GUM BOOT RHYTHM DANCE
DINIZULU AND HIS AFRICAN DRUMMERS,
   DANCERS AND SINGERS

GYPSY MAZURKA
ISADORA DUNCAN: MOVEMENT FROM THE
   SOUL

GYPSY SCENE AND DANCE
CAPRICCIO ESPAGNOL (Spanish Fiesta)

HABITAT
SOLO

HAIL TO THE CHIEF
SNAKE DANCE TEACHER DANCE

HAMADRYAD
DANCE AND MYTH: THE WORLD OF JEAN
   ERDMAN

HAMLET
SHAKESPEARE DANCE TRILOGY

THE HAND POWER DANCE
DREAM DANCES OF THE KASHIA POMO:
   THE BOLE-MARU RELIGIOUS WOMEN'S
   DANCES

HARLEQUINADE
BALLET LEGENDS: THE KIROV'S NINEL KUR-
   GAPKINA
RUSSIAN BALLET, THE GLORIOUS TRADI-
   TION

HATEGANA
RUMANIAN FOLK DANCES

HELIOGABALE
WHITE NIGHT OF DANCE IN LENINGRAD

HERE WE COME
BOLD STEPS

HERETIC
MARTHA GRAHAM: THE DANCER RE-
   VEALED

HIDDEN RITES
ALVIN AILEY: MEMORIES AND VISIONS

HODOROAGA
RUMANIAN FOLK DANCES

THE HOLBERG SUITE
DANCE THEATRE OF HARLEM

HOLZER DUETT . . . TRUISMS
RETRACING STEPS: AMERICAN DANCE
   SINCE POSTMODERNISM

HORE MARE
RUMANIAN FOLK DANCES

HOT TAMALES
IN CONCERT: PROFILE OF GUS GIORDANO
   JAZZ DANCE CHICAGO

HOUSE OF THE RISING SUN
ALVIN AILEY: MEMORIES AND VISIONS

HOVERING
CAN YOU SEE ME FLYING? A PORTRAIT OF
   TERRY SENDGRAFF

LA HUASTECA
BALLET FOLKLÓRICO NACIONAL DE
   MÉXICO

HURRAH!
ERICK HAWKINS' AMERICA

THE ICE SKATERS
THE PARIS OPERA BALLET: SIX BALLETS

IMPROVISATION
IMPROVISATION TO BANSURI FLUTE AND
   SEASCAPES

IN THE BACKYARD
TWO BAGATELLES

IN THE MIDDLE
SYLVIE GUILLEM AT WORK

INCENSE
DENISHAWN: THE BIRTH OF MODERN
   DANCE
RUTH ST. DENIS BY BARIBAULT
RUTH ST. DENIS: TED SHAWN

INCUBUS
DANCE: ROBERT JOFFREY BALLET

INDIANA
EDDIE BROWN'S "SCIENTIFIC RHYTHM"

LOS INDIOS
CARNIVAL OF RHYTHM

INITIATION
FOUR JOURNEYS INTO MYSTIC TIME

INTERMEZZO
ELIOT FELD: ARTISTIC DIRECTOR

INTIMATE LETTERS
BALLERINA: LYNN SEYMOUR

INTIMATE PAGES
AN EVENING WITH THE BALLET RAMBERT

INVIRTITA
RUMANIAN FOLK DANCES

INVITATION TO THE DANCE
IMMORTAL SWAN

INVOCATION TO IGUNNU
AFRICAN RELIGIOUS AND RITUAL DANCES

IVAN THE TERRIBLE
BOLSHOI PROKOFIEV GALA
YURI GRIGOROVICH: MASTER OF THE BOL-
   SHOI

JAPANESE WARRIOR
RUTH ST. DENIS: TED SHAWN

JARABE MIXTECO
BALLET FOLKLÓRICO NACIONAL DE
   MÉXICO

JAROBE TAPATICO
MEXICAN DANCES

JARDIN AUX LILAS
AMERICAN BALLET THEATRE IN SAN FRAN-
   CISCO
ANTONY TUDOR
MODERN BALLET

MARKITENKA
THE MARYINSKY BALLET

MARRIAGE DANCE
DREAM DANCES OF THE KASHIA POMO:
THE BOLE-MARU RELIGIOUS WOMEN'S
DANCES

MARY LOU'S MASS
ALVIN AILEY: MEMORIES AND VISIONS

THE MATRIARCH
CELEBRATION OF ROCK

MATSUKAZE
JAPAN: THE FROZEN MOMENT

THE MATTER
BEYOND THE MAINSTREAM: POSTMODERN
DANCERS

MAXIXE
CAVALCADE OF DANCE

MAZURKA FOR TWO
ISADORA DUNCAN: TECHNIQUE AND CHO-
REOGRAPHY

MEADOWLARK
ELIOT FELD: ARTISTIC DIRECTOR

MEDITATION
DANCE: NEW YORK CITY BALLET

MELLOW TONE
EDDIE BROWN'S "SCIENTIFIC RHYTHM"

THE MEMBERS OF MY PARTY
SOLO

MEMORIA
A TRIBUTE TO ALVIN AILEY

MERCE AND MARCEL
MERCE BY MERCE BY PAIK

A MERRY MOURNING
BLACK TIGHTS

MILITARY MARCH
ISADORA DUNCAN: MOVEMENT FROM THE
SOUL

MINUET D'OMPHALLE
THE ART OF DANCING: AN INTRODUCTION
TO BAROQUE DANCE

MINUTIAE
THE COLLABORATORS: CAGE, CUNNING-
HAM, RAUSCHENBERG
EVENT FOR TELEVISION

MISSING PERSONS
DANCE PRELUDES

MOBILE
BALANCES

MODERN DANCES
MAKING DANCES: SEVEN POST-MODERN
CHOREOGRAPHERS

MOLDAVIAN SUITE
MOISEYEV DANCE COMPANY: A GALA EVE-
NING

MOLLY'S NOT DEAD
PILOBOLUS DANCE THEATRE

MOMIX
PILOBOLUS DANCE THEATRE

A MONTH IN THE COUNTRY
NATASHA

MOODS
NINA ANANIASHVILI AND INTERNATIONAL
STARS

THE MOON
DANCE AND MYTH: THE WORLD OF JEAN
ERDMAN

THE MOOR'S PAVANE
SHAKESPEARE DANCE TRILOGY

THE MOTHER
THE ENDURING ESSENCE: THE TECHNIQUE
AND CHOREOGRAPHY OF ISADORA DUN-
CAN, REMEMBERED AND RECON-
STRUCTED BY GEMZE DE LAPPE
ISADORA DUNCAN: MOVEMENT FROM THE
SOUL
ISADORA DUNCAN: TECHNIQUE AND CHO-
REOGRAPHY

MOTHERLESS CHILD
DANCE ON VIDEO: AN INTRODUCTION TO
VIDEOTAPING DANCE

MOTHERLESS CHILD IV
IMAGES IN DISTRACTED TIME

MOURNER'S BENCH
THE NEW DANCE GROUP GALA CONCERT

MOVING PICTURES
RETRACING STEPS: AMERICAN DANCE
SINCE POSTMODERNISM

MUSTERIUM
FOUR JOURNEYS INTO MYSTIC TIME

MUSUME DOJOJI
KABUKI: CLASSIC THEATRE OF JAPAN
A LIFE IN TWO WORLDS: TAMASABURO
BANDO

MUTU DODI
MOURNING DANCES FROM CHAD

NAPA
DANCES FROM DJAYA

NAPOLI
THE ROYAL DANISH BALLET 1902–1906

NARCISSUS
ISADORA DUNCAN: MOVEMENT FROM THE
SOUL

NATALIE THE SWISS MILKMAID
THE ROMANTIC ERA

LA NEGRA
MEXICAN DANCES

THE NEGRO SPEAKS OF RIVERS
THE NEW DANCE GROUP GALA CONCERT

NEW DANCE
THE DANCE WORKS OF DORIS HUMPHREY:
WITH MY RED FIRES AND NEW DANCE
FESTIVAL OF THE DANCE

NEW ORLEANS 1900
ECHOES OF JAZZ

NIGHT CREATURES
AILEY DANCES

NIGHT JOURNEY
A DANCER'S WORLD
MARTHA GRAHAM: THE DANCER RE-
VEALED

LES NOCES
NIJINSKA: A LEGEND IN DANCE
PARIS DANCES DIAGHILEV

NOCTURNES
IMPROVISATIONS TO CHOPIN

EL NORTE
BALLET FOLKLÓRICO NACIONAL DE
MÉXICO

NÔTRE DAME DE PARIS
KIROV SOLOISTS: INVITATION TO THE
DANCE

NÔTRE FAUST
WHITE NIGHT OF DANCE IN LENINGRAD

NOUMENON
INVENTION IN DANCE

NUGARAFOLK
ARAB DANCES FROM CENTRAL SUDAN

LA NUIT
THE BEGINNINGS OF TODAY
IMMORTAL SWAN

THE NUTCRACKER
BALLET FAVORITES
CLASSIC KIROV PERFORMANCES
ESSENTIAL BALLET: RUSSIAN BALLET
LUDMILA SEMENYAKA: BOLSHOI BALLE-
RINA
RUSSIAN BALLET, THE GLORIOUS TRADI-
TION
A TIME TO DANCE
WATCHING BALLET

OBLII
RUMANIAN FOLK DANCES

OISEAUX EXOTIQUES
BOLD STEPS

OLD CITY QUADRILLE
MOISEYEV DANCE COMPANY: A GALA EVE-
NING

PRODIGAL SON
CHOREOGRAPHY BY BALANCHINE

PROUST REMEMBERED
NATASHA

PUBLIC
THREE DANCES

PURTATA FETELOR
RUMANIAN FOLK DANCES

PUSH COMES TO SHOVE
BARYSHNIKOV DANCES SINATRA

QUARRY
MEREDITH MONK

QUARTET
MERCE CUNNINGHAM AND COMPANY

LOS QUETZALES
BALLET FOLKLÓRICO NACIONAL DE
   MÉXICO

RADHA
INVENTION IN DANCE

RADO BLANQUITA
SPANISH FOLK DANCING

RAINBOW 'ROUND MY SHOULDER
THE NEW DANCE GROUP GALA CONCERT

RAINFOREST
EVENT FOR TELEVISION

THE RAKE'S PROGRESS
BALLET COMES TO BRITAIN

RAMAYANA
INDIA: HAUNTING PASSAGE

RAYMONDA
CARMEN (Bolshoi Ballet)
CLASSIC KIROV PERFORMANCES
THE MAGIC OF THE KIROV BALLET
NINA ANANIASHVILI AND INTERNATIONAL
   STARS
PLISETSKAYA DANCES
A POEM OF DANCES ALSO KNOWN AS PLI-
   SETSKAYA: CARMEN
SYLVIE GUILLEM AT WORK

REACHES
DANCE PRELUDES

RED AND GOLD SARI
RUTH ST. DENIS BY BARIBAULT

THE REHEARSAL CONTINUES
IN CONCERT: PROFILE OF GUS GIORDANO
   JAZZ DANCE CHICAGO

RELACHE
ENTR'ACTE

REVELATIONS
AILEY DANCES
ALVIN AILEY: MEMORIES AND VISIONS

**AN EVENING WITH ALVIN AILEY AMERICAN
DANCE THEATRE**

REVOLT OF THE FLESH
BUTOH: BODY ON THE EDGE OF CRISIS

THE REVOLUTIONARY ETUDE
ISADORA DUNCAN: MOVEMENT FROM THE
   SOUL
ISADORA DUNCAN: TECHNIQUE AND CHO-
   REOGRAPHY

RHYTHMETRON
RHYTHMETRON: THE DANCE THEATRE OF
   HARLEM WITH ARTHUR MITCHELL

RIA JALISCIENCE
BALLET FOLKLÓRICO NACIONAL DE
   MÉXICO

RITES DE PASSAGE
KATHERINE DUNHAM

RITUAL FIRE DANCE
AFRICAN RELIGIOUS AND RITUAL DANCES

THE RIVER
AMERICAN BALLET THEATRE: A CLOSE-UP
   IN TIME

RIXE
THE PARIS OPERA BALLET: SEVEN BALLETS

ROADRUNNERS
MERCE CUNNINGHAM AND COMPANY

ROBERT THE DEVIL
THE ROMANTIC ERA

RODEO
AMERICAN BALLET THEATRE: A CLOSE-UP
   IN TIME

ROMEO AND JULIET
AMERICAN BALLET THEATRE IN SAN FRAN-
   CISCO
ANTONY TUDOR
BALLERINA: LYNN SEYMOUR
BALLET FAVORITES
BOLSHOI PROKOFIEV GALA
CLASSIC KIROV PERFORMANCES
FONTEYN AND NUREYEV: THE PERFECT
   PARTNERSHIP
GALINA ULANOVA
GRAND CONCERT
KAREN KAIN: BALLERINA
THE MAGIC OF THE BOLSHOI BALLET
MODERN BALLET
MOMENT OF LIGHT: THE DANCE OF EVE-
   LYN HART
NATASHA
PLISETSKAYA DANCES
RUSSIAN BALLET, THE GLORIOUS TRADI-
   TION
THE SCENE CHANGES
SHAKESPEARE DANCE TRILOGY
THE TURNING POINT
YURI GRIGOROVICH: MASTER OF THE BOL-
   SHOI

ROOMS
ANNA SOKOLOW, CHOREOGRAPHER
DANCE: ANNA SOKOLOW'S *ROOMS*

ROWING SONG
SNAKE DANCE TEACHER DANCE

RUBIES
BALLET WITH EDWARD VILLELLA
MAN WHO DANCES: EDWARD VILLELLA

RUNES
THE PAUL TAYLOR DANCE COMPANY

RUSLAN AND LUDMILA
CLASSIC KIROV PERFORMANCES

LE SACRE DU PRINTEMPS
BALLET
WHITE NIGHT OF DANCE IN LENINGRAD

SAINT FERREUL
FRENCH FOLK DANCING

SALCIOARA
RUMANIAN FOLK DANCES

SALUT D'AMOUR
OUT OF THE LIMELIGHT, HOME IN THE
   RAIN

SCARF DANCE
CHINESE, KOREAN AND JAPANESE DANCE

SCHOOL FOR BIRD PEOPLE
NIK AND MURRAY

SCHUBERT WALTZES
DENISHAWN: THE BIRTH OF MODERN
   DANCE

SCORPIO
CELEBRATION OF ROCK

SCRAMBLE
EVENT FOR TELEVISION
MERCE CUNNINGHAM AND COMPANY

SCRIABIN ETUDES
TRAILBLAZERS OF MODERN DANCE

SEA SHADOW
ATTITUDES IN DANCE

SEARCHING
THE ONE I SEE

SEASCAPES
IMPROVISATION TO BANSURI FLUTE AND
   SEASCAPES

SECOND HAND ROSE
DECLARATION OF INDEPENDENCE

SECOND SIGHT
RETRACING STEPS: AMERICAN DANCE
   SINCE POSTMODERNISM

Series Titles Index

A TIME TO DANCE
A CHOREOGRAPHER AT WORK: JOHN
  BUTLER
CLASSICAL BALLET
DANCE: A REFLECTION OF OUR TIMES
ETHNIC DANCE: ROUNDTRIP TO TRINIDAD
GREAT PERFORMANCE IN DANCE
INVENTION IN DANCE
THE LANGUAGE OF DANCE
MODERN BALLET
A TIME TO DANCE

TOOLS FOR CHOREOGRAPHY
BEYOND ROUTINE
EIGHT GREAT STEPS TO CHOREOGRAPHY

TRIBAL EYE
BEHIND THE MASK
CROOKED BEAK OF HEAVEN
MAN BLONG CUSTOM

USA DANCE SERIES
DANCE: ANNA SOKOLOW'S *ROOMS*
DANCE: FOUR PIONEERS
DANCE: IN SEARCH OF "LOVERS";
DANCE: NEW YORK CITY BALLET
DANCE: ROBERT JOFFREY BALLET
ECHOES OF JAZZ

WISDOM SERIES
RUTH ST. DENIS: TED SHAWN

WORLD CULTURES AND YOUTH
SERAMA'S MASK

WORLD THEATRE SERIES
INDIA: HAUNTING PASSAGE
JAPAN: THE FROZEN MOMENT

Directory of Distributors

A. STAR REESE PRODUCTION COMPANY
303 Greenwich Street #6D
New York, NY 10013
(212) 227-6223

AAHPERD (AMERICAN ALLIANCE FOR
HEALTH, PHYSICAL EDUCATION,
RECREATION AND DANCE)
1900 Association Drive
Reston, VA 22091
(703) 476-3400 (800) 321-0789

ABC SPORTS
P.O. Box 2284
South Burlington, VT 05407
(800) 422-2827

ACA ENTERPRISES
P.O. Box 58
Altadena, CA 91003
(213) 681-8059

AIMS MEDIA
9710 DeSoto Avenue
Chatsworth, CA 91311-4409
(800) 367-2467 FAX (818) 341-6700

ALEGRIAS PRODUCTIONS
666 West End Avenue, 14J
New York, NY 10025
(212) 874-5772

ALIENNATION COMPANY
1341 West Foster
Chicago, IL 60640
(312) 275-3480

AMERICAN DANCE FESTIVAL VIDEO
2355 University Avenue, Suite P
Madison, WI 53705
(608) 231-1969 FAX (608) 231-1954

AMERICAN DANCE GUILD
31 West 21 Street, 3rd Floor
New York, NY 10010
(212) 627-3790

THE AMERICAN FEDERATION OF ARTS
41 East 65th Street
New York, NY 10021
(212) 988-7700 FAX (212) 861-2487

THE AMERICAN PROGRAM SERVICE
PUBLIC TELEVISION
120 Boylston Street
Boston, MA 02116
(617) 338-4455

APPALSHOP FILMS
306 Madison Street
Whitesburg, KY 41858
(606) 633-0108 (800) 545-SHOP
FAX (606) 633-1009

ARC VIDEODANCE
150 Fifth Avenue, Room 324
New York, NY 10011
(212) 206-6492/627-2838

ARTHUR CANTOR, INC.
1501 Broadway, Suite 403
New York, NY 10036
(212) 391-2650 (800) 237-3801
FAX (212) 391-2677

THE ASIA SOCIETY
Performing Arts Department 725 Park Avenue
New York, NY 10021-5088
(212) 288-6400 FAX (212) 517-8315

AUDIENCE PLANNERS, INC.
5341 Derry Avenue
Agoura Hills, CA 91301
(818) 865-1233 FAX (818) 865-1327

BACKALLEY PRODUCTIONS
P.O. Box 105
Arcata, CA 95521
(707) 822-5678

BAM PRODUCTIONS
375 Mt. Auburn Street
Cambridge, MA 02138
(617) 491-5791 FAX (617) 578-8804

BARDSLEY, KAY
6305 South Geneva Circle
Englewood, CO 80111-5437
(303) 850-5441 FAX (303) 850-5442

BARR FILMS
12801 Schabarum Avenue
P.O. Box 7878 Irwindale, CA 91706-7878
(818) 338-7878 (800) 234-7878

BASTET PRODUCTIONS
P.O. Box 77029
Tucson, AZ 85703
(602) 293-8088 FAX (602) 293-8088

BATIUCHOK, MARGARET
238 East 14th Street
New York, NY 10003
(212) 598-0154

BEALS, MARGARET
228 West Broadway
New York, NY 10013
(212) 431-3869

BEAM PRODUCTIONS
32 Cooper Square
New York, NY 10003
(212) 677-1756

BEEMAN, ANDREA
431 East 6th Street
New York, NY 10009
(212) 995-1247

BEST FILM AND VIDEO CORPORATION
108 New South Road
Hicksville, NY 11801-5223
(800) 527-2189 (516) 931-6969

BIOGRAPH ENTERTAINMENT
2 Depot Plaza, Suite 202-B
Bedford Hills, NY 10507
(914) 242-9838 (800) 346-3144
FAX (914) 242-9854

BORIN, ANNE
60 West 66th Street
New York, NY 10023
(212) 362-3412

BOXELL FILM PRODUCTION
P.O. Box 77274
San Francisco, CA 94107

BRODSKY & TREADWAY
P.O. Box 335
Rowley, MA 01969
(617) 666-3372

BROOKS, VIRGINIA
460 Riverside Drive
New York, NY 10027
(212) 222-9887

BUENA VISTA HOME VIDEO (WALT DISNEY)
3900 West Alameda
Burbank CA 91505
(818) 567-5000 FAX (818) 567-6464

BUFFALO STATE COLLEGE
Film and Video Center
E.H. Butler Library 180
1300 Elmwood Avenue
Buffalo, NY 14222-1095
(716) 878-6682 FAX (716) 878-3163
(Rentals Only)

BULLFROG FILMS
P.O. Box 149
Oley, PA 19547
(215) 779-8226 (800) 543-FROG
FAX (215) 370-1978

BURCKHARDT, RUDOLPH
50 West 29th Street, #5E
New York, NY 10001
(212) 679-5519

BUSTER COOPER DANCE VIDEOS
3046-A Forest Lane
Dallas, TX 75234
(214) 385-8729

BUTTERFLY VIDEO
P.O. Box 184-91C
Antrim, NH 03440
(603) 588-2105 FAX (603) 588-3205

CADIGAN, KATIE
357 Vincent Drive
Mountain View, CA 94041

CANYON CINEMA COOPERTIVE
2325 Third Street, Suite 338
San Francisco, CA 94107
(415) 626-2255

CAROUSEL FILMS
260 Fifth Avenue, Suite 405
New York, NY 10001
(212) 683-1660 (800) 683-1660
FAX (212) 683-1662

CBS/FOX VIDEO
2121 Avenue of the Stars
Los Angeles, CA 90067
(800) 800-2369

CENTRE COMMUNICATIONS
1800 30th Street, Suite 207
Boulder, CO 80301
(303) 444-1166 (800) 886-1166
FAX (303) 444-1168

CERNIK, EVA
419 South Sherman Street, Dept. C
Denver, CO 80209
(303) 573-7610

CHANDRA OF DAMASCUS MIDDLE EAST
DANCE CENTER
6706 North West 18th Avenue
Gainesville, FL 32605
(352) 332-9080

CHARMAINE
862 Pangola Drive
North Ft. Myers, FL 33903

CHOREOGRAPHICS
1187 Shattuck AvenueBerkeley, CA 94707
(510) 524-9254

THE CINEMA GUILD
1697 Broadway, Suite 506
New York, NY 10019-5904
(212) 246-5522 (800) 723-5522
FAX (212) 246-5525

CIRCUIT THEATRE, INC.
635 Carroll Street
Brooklyn, NY 11215
(718) 638-4878

CLEARWATER PRODUCTIONS
P.O. Box 517 Ansonia Station
New York, NY 10023
(800) 769-8510 FAX (212) 362-2754

COE FILM ASSOCIATES, INC.
65 East 96th Street
New York, NY 10128
(212) 831-5355 FAX (212) 996-6728

COLUMBIA TRISTAR HOME VIDEO
Culver City, CA 91505-4627
(310) 280-8000 FAX (310) 972-0937

CONSULATE GENERAL OF THE
NETHERLANDS
Press and Cultural Section
1 Rockefeller Plaza, 11th Floor
New York, NY 10020
(212) 246-1429

CORINTH VIDEO
34 Gansevoort Street
New York, NY 10014
(212) 463-0305 (800) 221-4720
FAX (212) 929-0010

CORONET/MTI FILM AND VIDEO
P.O. Box 2649
Columbus, OH 432165
(800) 321-3106 FAX (614) 771-6372

CREATIVE ARTS REHABILITATION CENTER
251 West 51st Street
New York, NY 10019

CROSSCURRENT MEDIA/NAATA
346 Ninth Street
San Fancisco, CA 94130
(415) 552-9550

CUNNINGHAM DANCE FOUNDATION
55 Bethune Street
New York, NY 10014
(212) 255-3130 (FAX (212) 633-2453

DANCE FILM ARCHIVE
University of Rochester
Rochester, NY 14627
(716) 275-5236 FAX (716) 271-1616

DANCE FILMS ASSOCIATION, INC.
31 West 21st Street, 3rd Floor
New York, NY 10010
(212) 727-0764 FAX (212) 675-9657

DANCE HORIZONS VIDEO
Princeton Book Company Publishers
12 West Delaware Avenue
Pennington, NJ 08534-0057
(609) 737-8177 (800) 220-7149
FAX (609) 737-1869

DANCE MEDICINE EDUCATION FUND, INC.
P.O Box 572
Jackson Heights, NY 11372
(718) 426-8606 FAX (718) 426-1405

DANCE NOTATION BUREAU
33 West 21st Street, 3rd Floor
New York, NY 10010
(212) 807-7899

DANCE ON VIDEO
620 East 81st Terrace
Kansas City, MO 64131-2123
(816) 333-7935

DANCE REP INC.
73 Fifth Avenue
New York, NY 10003
(212) 242-0088

DANCING VIDEO
5637 Rosalind Avenue
El Cerrito, CA 94530
(510) 658-0377/235-8730

DE NONNO PIX
7119 Shore Road
Brooklyn, NY 11209
(718) 745-3937

DEBORAH GLADSTEIN AND SAM KANTER
484 West 43rd Street, #16A
New York, NY 10036
(212) 563-2972

DEBRA ZALKIND TALKING DANCE
FOUNDATION
187 Buena Vista Drive
Ringwood, NJ 07452
(201) 839-0137

DEVI, RITHA
330 East 85th Street, Apt. #C
New York, NY 10028
(212) 988-7697

DEVIVO, KERRY
41 Brookside Avenue
Putnam Valley, NY 10579
(914) 528-9203

DIAMOND DANCE
2350 Broadway, #234
New York, NY 10024
(212) 877-0851

DIRECT CINEMA, LTD.
P.O. Box 10003
Santa Monica, CA 90410-9003
(310) 636-8200 (800) 525-0000
FAX (310) 636-8228

DOCUMENTARY EDUCATIONAL RESOURCES
101 Morse Street
Watertown, MA 02172
(617) 926-0491 (800) 569-6621
FAX (617) 926-9519

DONEGAN, DEVILLIER
4401 Connecticut Avenue NW
Washington, DC 20005
(202) 686-3980

DORIS CHASE PRODUCTIONS
222 West 23rd Street
New York, NY 10011
(212) 929-7285

DUSTER FILMS
1155 Hacienda Place, #305
West Hollywood, CA 90069
(213) 650-5820

DUSTY NELSON PICTURES
2598 Smith Grade
Santa Cruz, CA 95060
(408) 426-0565

ECCENTRIC MOTIONS
99 Vandam Street
New York, NY 10013
(212) 691-9522

ECHO PRODUCTIONS
308 West 4th Street
New York, NY 10014
(212) 645-7536

ECLIPSE PRODUCTIONS
135 St. Pauls Avenue
Staten Island, NY 10301
(718) 727-5593

ELECTRONIC ARTS INTERMIX
536 Broadway, 9th Floor
New York, NY 10012
(212) 966-4605 FAX (212) 941-6118

EMBASSY OF MALAYSIA
2401 Massachusetts Avenue NW
Washington, DC 20008
(202) 328-2700

ENCYCLOPAEDIA BRITANNICA
EDUCATIONAL CORPORATION (EBEC)
310 South Michigan Avenue
Chicago, IL 60604
(312) 347-7000 (FAX (312) 347-7903
(800) 621-3900/554-9862

FACETS VIDEO
1517 West Fullerton Avenue
Chicago, IL 60614
(312) 281-9075 (800) 331-6197
FAX (312) 929-5437

FACSEA (FRENCH AMERICAN CULTURAL
SERVICES AND EDUCATIONAL AID)
972 Fifth Avenue
New York, NY 10021
(212) 439-1471 (800) WFRENCH

FARRAH, IBRAHIM
1 Sherman Square, Suite 22F
New York, NY 10023
(212) 595-2843

FILMAKERS LIBRARY
124 East 40th Street
New York, NY 10016
(212) 808-4980 FAX (212) 808-4983

FILM-MAKERS' COOPERATIVE
175 Lexington Avenue
New York, NY 10016
(212) 889-3820 FAX (212) 808-4983

FILMOPOLIS
320 Wiltshire Boulevard #206
Santa Monica, CA 90401
(310) 914-1776 FAX (310) 914-1777

FILMS FOR THE HUMANITIES AND
· SCIENCES
P.O. Box 2053
Princeton, NJ 08543-2053
(800) 257-5126 (609) 275-1400
FAX (609) 275-3767

FILMS INC.
5547 North Ravenswood Avenue
Chicago, IL 60640-1199
(800) 323-4222 X42
(800) 223-6246 (Northeast)
(800) 343-0416 (video division)
(914) 667-0800 (NY collect)
(312) 878-2600 X42 (IL collect)
FAX (312) 878-0416

FIRST RUN/ICARUS FILMS
153 Waverly Place
New York, NY 10014
(212) 727-1711 (800) 876-1710
FAX (212) 989-7649

FLOWER FILMS
10341 San Pablo Avenue
El Cerrito, CA 94530
(510) 525-0942 (800) 572-7618
FAX (510) 525-1204

FOLKMOOT USA
P.O. Box 658
Waynesville, NC 28786
(704) 452-2997

FOREFRONT FILMS
507 17th Street
Brooklyn, NY 11217
(718) 832-3395 FAX (718) 832-4951

FRAMELINE
346 Ninth Street
San Francisco, CA 94103
(415) 703-8650

FRANCISCAN COMMUNICATIONS
1229 South Santee Street
Los Angeles, CA 90015-2566
(800) 989-3600 (213) 746-2916
FAX (213) 747-9126

FREEDMAN, LAURIE
18 LaDue Road
Hopewell Junction, NY 12533
(914) 897-3914

FRIEDMAN, GENE
P.O. Box 275
Wainscott, NY 11975
(516) 537-0178

GESSLER PUBLISHING COMPANY, INC.
10 East Church Avenue
Roanoke, VA 24011
(540) 342-7172 (800) 456-5825

GLICK, STEFANIE
688 President Street
Brooklyn, NY 11215
(718) 399-8994

GOTHAM CITY FILMWORKS
425 Riverside Drive, #6H
New York, NY 10025

GREEN MOUNTAIN CINE WORKS, INC.
53 Hamilton Avenue
Staten Island, NY 10301
(718) 981-0120

GREEN RIVER ROAD
P.O. Box 7835
Van Nuys, CA 91409
(818) 786-0778

GREY DAWN PRODUCTIONS
3538 East Spruce Street
Seattle, WA 98122
(800) 400-2036

GROSS, SALLY
463 West Street
New York, NY 10014
(212) 691-1283

HAL BERGSOHN ASSOCIATES
3512 North Brookhaven Lane
Tucson, AZ 85712
(602) 795-5644

HARNETT, DANIEL
6 Bleecker Street
New York, NY 10012

HARTLEY FILM FOUNDATION
Cat Rock Road
Cos Cob, CT 06807
(203) 869-1818 (800) 937-1819
FAX (203) 869-1905

HIGH FREQUENCY WAVELENGTHS
500 Riverside Drive Suite 16E
New York, NY 10027
(212) 222-7204

HIGH TIDE DANCE, INC.
65 Greene Street
New York, NY 10012
(212) 925-5024

HMS MEDIA
2257 Ridge Avenue
Evanston, IL 60201
(847) 491-1933

HOCTOR PRODUCTS FOR EDUCATION
P.O. Box 38
Waldwick, NJ 07463
(201) 652-7767 FAX (201) 652-2599

HOME BOX OFFICE HOME VIDEO (HBO)
1100 Avenue of the Americas
New York, NY 10036
(212) 512-7400

HOME VISION
P.O. Box 800
Concord, MA 01742
Consumers (800) 262-8600
Retailers (800) 826-3456
Institutions (800) 343-4312

ILE IFE FILMS
754 Mount Ephraim Road
Searsport, ME 04974
(207) 548-2445

IMAGES VIDEO PRODUCTION COMPANY
11 Massasoit Street
Northhampton, MA 01060
(413) 585-5755

IN MOTION PRODUCTIONS
373 Broadway, E3
New York, NY 10013
(212) 431-8480 FAX (212) 431-8603

INDIANA UNIVERSITY
Center for Media and Teaching Resources
Bloomington, IN 47405-5901
(812) 855-8087 (800) 552-8620
FAX (812) 855-8404

INFINITY FILMWORKS
3626 Regal Place
Los Angeles, CA 90068
(213) 851-7788 FAX (213) 851-2612

INSIGHT MEDIA
2162 Broadway
New York, NY 10024
(212) 721-6316 FAX (212) 799-5309

INSTRUCTIONAL VIDEO
727 O Street
Lincoln, NE 68508
(800) 228-0164

INTERAMA
301 West 53rd Street, Suite 19E
New York, NY 10019
(212) 977-4830 FAX (212) 581-6582

INTERNATIONAL FILM BUREAU, INC.
332 South Michigan Avenue
Chicago, IL 60604-4382
(312) 427-4545 FAX (312) 427-4550

IOWA STATE UNIVERSITY
Media Resources Center
121 Pearson Hall
Ames, IA 50011-2203
(515) 294-1540 (800) 447-0060
FAX (515) 294-8089
(Rentals only)

JAMES BARTOLOMEO FILMS
187 Plymouth Street #2R
Brooklyn, NY 11201
(718) 694-0986

THE JAPAN FOUNDATION
152 West 57th Street
New York, NY 10019
(212) 489-0299

JIM FOREST VIDEOTAPES
Takoma Park, MD 20912
(301) 593-8933

JULIE MILLER PRODUCTIONS
4231 23rd STreet
San Francisco, CA 94114
(415) 824-2361

KAHREEN AND KIRA
Kismet Dancers of Miami
1089 NE 104th Street
Miami Shores, FL 33138
(305) 754-0258

KALAMA PRODUCTIONS, INC.
76 North King Street #202
Honolulu, HI 96817-5157
(808) 536-5050

KALLETT, JIM
1232 Pacific Avenue
San Francisco, CA 94109
(415) 771-0450

KAROL VIDEO
P.O. Box 7600Wilkes-Barre, PA 18773-7600
(800) 526-4773 FAX (717) 822-8226

KENT STATE UNIVERSITY
Audio Visual Services
330 Library Building
Kent, OH 44242-0001
(216) 672-3456 (800) 338-5718
FAX (216) 672-3463
(Rentals only)

KINEPED PRODUCTIONS
82 Washington Place, #1E
New York, NY 10011
(212) 473-4818

KINETIC FILM ENTERPRISES, LTD.
255 Delaware Avenue, Suite 340
Buffalo, NY 14202
(716) 856-7631(800) 466-7631
FAX (716) 856-7631

KINO ON VIDEO
333 West 39th Street, Suite 503
New York, NY 10018
(212) 629-6880 (800) 562-3330
FAX (212) 714-0871

THE KITCHEN CENTER FOR VIDEO, MUSIC
AND DANCE
512 West 19th Street
New York, NY 10011
(212) 255-5793 FAX (212) 645-4258

KQED-TV INC.
2601 Mariposa Street
San Francisco, CA 94110
(415) 864-2000 FAX (415) 553-2380

KTCA-TV
Video Services Department
172 East 4th Street
St. Paul, MN 55101
(612) 229-1356/1252
FAX (612) 229-1282

KUCHIPUDI ART ACADEMY OF DANCE
13109 Mason Bend Lane
Creve Coeur, MO 63141
(314) 878-2861

KULTUR VIDEO
195 Highway 36
West Long Branch, NJ 07764
(908) 229-2343 (800) 4-KULTUR
FAX (908) 229-0066

LANE EDUCATION SERVICE DISTRICT
Continuing Education Film and Video Library,
    P.O. Box 2680
Eugene, OR 97402-0374
(541) 689-6500 X220
FAX (541) 688-4015

LASERDISC FAN CLUB, INC.
1058 East 230th Street
Carson, CA 90745
(800) 801-DISC FAX (310) 952-3000

LEARNING CORPORATION OF AMERICA
c/o Coronet/MTI
108 Wilmot Road
Deerfield, IL 60015
(708)940-1260 (800) 621-2131
FAX (708) 940-3600

LEBEN PRODUCTIONS
450 Culver/Box 8
Saugatuck, MI 49453
(616) 857-4780

LIEFF, JUDITH
227 West 11th Street
New York, NY 10014
(212) 929-6878

LOCKETZ, JAN MARCE
Ayers Road
Locust Valley, NY 11560
(516) 676-3228

LOUISE TIRANOFF PRODUCTIONS
488 14th Street
Brooklyn, NY 11215
(718) 788-6403

MAGANA BAPTISTE ROYAL ACADEMY
Seacliff Center of Yoga, Health, and Belly Dance
730 Euclid Avenue
San Francisco, CA 94118
(415) 387-6833

MAGICAL MOTION ENTERPRISES
12228 Venice Boulevard, Suite 402
Los Angeles, CA 90066
(310) 521-8123

MASTERVISION, INC.
969 Park Avenue
New York, NY 10028
(212) 879-0448 FAX (212) 744-3560

MAYER, JULIA
601 61st Avenue North
Myrtle Beach, SC 29577

MCA/UNIVERSAL HOME VIDEO
70 Universal City Plaza
University City, CA 91608-9955
(818) 777-1000 FAX (818) 733-0226

MEDIA BASICS VIDEO
Lighthouse Square
705 Boston Post Road
Guilford, CT 06437
(203) 458-2505 (800) 542-2505
FAX (203-458-9816

THE MEDIA GUILD
11722 Sorrento Valley Road
San Diego, CA 92121
(619) 755-9191 (800) 886-9191
FAX (619) 755-4931

METTLER STUDIOS
Tucson Creative Dance Center
3131 North Cherry Avenue
Tucson, AZ 85719
(602) 327-7453

MEYER, SYBIL
3130 College Avenue, #4
Berkeley, CA 94705
(415) 658-0636

MGM/UNITED ARTISTS HOME VIDEO
2500 Broadway
Santa Monica, CA 90404
(310) 449-3000

MICHAEL BLACKWOOD PRODUCTIONS,
INC.
251 West 57th Street
New York, NY 10019
(212) 247-4710 FAX (212) 247-4713

MIMI GARRARD DANCE THEATRE
155 Wooster Street
New York, NY 10012
(212) 674-6868

MODERN TALKING PICTURE SERVICE
381 Park Avenue South New York, NY 10016
(212) 696-9065 (800) 243-6877
FAX (212) 696-9065
Free film and video loans.

MOORE, FRANK
45 Crosby Street
New York, NY 10012
(212) 925-4875

MORCA FOUNDATION
1349 Franklin Street
Bellingham, WA 98225
(206) 676-1864

MOROCCO
320 West 15th Street
New York, NY 10011
(212) 727-8326 FAX (212) 463-7116

MOTION PIXELS
c/o David Bryan
150 St. Marks Place
Brooklyn, NY 11217
(718) 636-8720

MOVING VISIONS PRODUCTIONS
37 Edwards Street
North Haven, CT 06511

MULTICULTURAL MEDIA
RR3 Box 6655 Granger Road
Barre, VT 05641
(802) 223-1294 (800) 550-9675
FAX (802) 229-1834

MURPHEY, CLAUDIA
4000 Tunlaw Road NW, #809
Washington, DC 20007

MUSEUM AT LARGE
20 West 22nd Street
New York, NY 10011
(212) 691-3220

MUSEUM OF MODERN ART
Circulating Film Library
11 West 53rd Street
New York, NY 10019
(212) 708-9530 FAX (212) 708-9531

MUSIC VIDEO DISTRIBUTORS
P.O. Box 1128
Norristown, PA 19404
(800) 888-0486 FAX (610) 650-9102

MYSTIC FIRE VIDEO, INC.
P.O. Box 422, Prince Street Station
New York, NY 10012
(212) 941-0999 (800) 292-9001
FAX (212) 941-1443

NAGRIN, DANIEL
208 East 14th Street
Tempe, AZ 85281
(602) 968-4063

NATIONAL ARCHIVES
8601 Adelphi Road
College Park, MD 20740
(301) 713-7060

NATIONAL FILM BOARD OF CANADA
1251 Avenue of the Americas
New York, NY 10020-1173
(212) 586-5131 FAX (212) 596-1779

NATIONAL TECHNICAL INFORMATION
SERVICE (NTIS)
U.S. Department of Commerce
5285 Port Royal RoadSpringfield, VA 22161
(703) 487-4650 (800) 788-6282
FAX (703) 487-4009
Formerly the National Audiovisual Center.
Central distribution and information source for
av materials produced by the U.S. government.

NEW DAY FILMS
22D Hollywood Avenue
Ho-Ho-Kus, NJ 07423
(201) 652-6590 FAX (201) 652-1973

NEW LINE HOME VIDEO
116 North Robertson Boulevard
Los Angeles, CA 90048
(310) 967-6679 FAX (310) 854-0602

NEW YORKER FILMS
16 West 61st Street
New York, NY 10023
(212) 247-6110 (800) 447-0196
FAX (212) 582-4697

OLIVE-BELLES, NURIA
712 Washington Street, #4B
New York, NY 10014(212) 691-3538
FAX (212) 647-0788

ORION ENTERPRISES
c/o Jazz Dance World Congress
614 Davis Street
Evanston, IL 60201
(847) 866-9443/251-4434

OVERFOOT, INC.
234 East 4th Street
New York, NY 10009
(212) 777-6227

PACIFIC ARTS VIDEO
11858 LaGrange
Los Angeles, CA 90025
(310) 820-0991 (800) 538-5856
FAX (310) 826-4779

PALOMAR PICTURES
5657 Wiltshire Boulevard, 5th floor
Los Angeles, CA 90036
(213) 525-2900 FAX (213) 525-2912

PARAMOUNT HOME VIDEO
5555 Melrose Avenue
Los Angeles, CA 90038-3197(213) 956-5000

PARKERSON, LYNN
1601 Third Avenue #18J
New York, NY 10128
(212) 876-4961

PBS VIDEO
1320 Braddock Place
Alexandria, VA 22314-1698
(800) 424-7963/328-7271
(703) 739-5000/5383
FAX (703) 739-0775

PENNEBAKER ASSOCIATES, INC.
262 West 91st Street
New York, NY 10024
(212) 496-9195

PENNSTATE (PENNSYLVANIA STATE
UNIVERSITY)
Audio Visual Services
Special Services Building
1127 Fox Hill Road
University Park, PA 16803-1824
(814) 865-6314 (800) 826-0132
FAX (814) 863-2574

PENNY WARD VIDEO
5 Rivington Street #4
New York, NY 10002
(212) 228-1427

PENTACLE
104 Franklin Street
New York, NY 10013
(212) 226-2000

PHOENIX FILMS AND VIDEO
2349 Chaffee Drive
St. Louis, MO 63146
(314) 569-0211 FAX (314) 569-2834

PICTURE START
1727 West Catalpa
Chicago, IL 60640
(800) 528-TAPE

PING CHONG AND COMPANY
47 Great Jones Street
New York, NY 10012
(212) 529-1557 FAX (212) 529-1703

PRO ARTS INTERNATIONAL
Nikolais/Louis Dance
611 Broadway Suite 221
New York, NY 10012
(212) 420-0700 FAX (212) 420-0770

PYRAMID FILM AND VIDEO
Box 1048, 2801 Colorado Avenue
Santa Monica, CA 90406
(310) 828-7577 (800) 421-2304
FAX (310) 453-9083

RAVEN RECORDING
744 Broad Street, #1815
Newark, NJ 07102
(201) 642-7942

REPUBLIC PICTURES HOME VIDEO
5700 Wiltshire Boulevard #525 North
Los Angeles, CA 90036
(213) 965-6900 FAX (213) 965-6963

RHAPSODY FILMS, INC.
P.O. Box 179
New York, NY 10014
(212) 243-0152 FAX (212) 645-9250

RHOMBUS INTERNATIONAL, INC.
489 King Street West, Suite 102
Toronto, Ontario, Canada M5V 1L3
(416) 971-7856 FAX (416) 971-9647

RIRIE-WOODBURY DANCE COMPANY
50 West 200 Southt
Salt Lake City, UT 84101
(801) 328-1062

ROMANO, ROBERTO
317 West 93rd Street
New York, NY 10025

ROSE, KATHY
10 Stuyvesant Oval 6F
New York, NY 10009
(212) 353-9891

RUSH DANCE COMPANY
392 Broadway
New York, NY 10019
(212) 431-7051

SAMURAI STUDIOS, INC.
160 Washington Spring Road
Palisades, NY 10964
(914) 359-5330

SANO VIDEOS
P.O. Box 442
Scarsdale, NY 10583
(212) 486-9519

SCHULZ, LARRY
c/o Sandra Cameron Dance Center
439 Lafayette Street
New York, NY 10003
(212) 674-0505

SEAHORSE FILMS
12 Harrison Street
New York, NY 10013
(212) 226-0294 FAX (212) 219-8582

SEARCHLIGHT FILMS
30 Berry Street
San Francisco, CA 94123
(415) 543-1254

SEE-DO PRODUCTIONS
P.O. Box 135
Croton-on-Hudson, NY 10520
(914) 271-3806 FAX same

SEREEM, VEDA
20130 Larkspur Court
Germantown, MD 20874

SERENA STUDIOS, INC.
201 West 54th Street
New York, NY 10019
(212) 247-1051

SERPENTINE PRODUCTIONS
4822 St. Elmo Avenue
Bethesda, MD 20814
(301) 654-2224 FAX (301) 229-0621

SHIMIN, TANIA
437 Reed Court
Goleta, CA 93117
(805) 685-5580

SOLARIS
264 West 19th Street
New York, NY 10011
(212) 741-0778 FAX (212) 242-2201

ST. ANN'S SCHOOL
129 Pierrepont Street
Brooklyn, NY 11201(718) 522-1660

STANFORD UNIVERSITY DOCUMENTARY
FILM AND VIDEO PROGRAM
3862 23rd Street
San Francisco, CA 94114
(415) 206-9424

STEPPING TONES RECORDS AND
VIDEOTAPES, LTD.
P.O. Box 35236
Los Angeles, CA 90035
(213) 737-4007

THE STUTZ COMPANY
2600 Tenth Street
Berkeley, CA 94710-2586
(510) 644-2200 FAX (510) 644-2230

SUMMERS, ELAINE
1622 Laurel Street
Sarasota, FL 34236
(941) 952-0599

SWANK MOTION PICTURES
350 Vanderbilt Motor Parkway
Hauppauge, NY 11787
(800) 876-3344
(516) 434-1560 collect
910 Riverside Drive
Elmhurst, IL 60126
(800) 876-3330
(708) 833-0061 collect
201 South Jefferson Avenue
St. Louis, MO 63103
(800) 876-5577
(314) 534-6300 collect

TAFFY'S BY MAIL
701 Beta Drive
Cleveland, OH 44143
(216) 461-3360 FAX (216) 461-9787
Mail-order house with retail stores
across the country

TANGUERO PRODUCTIONS
5351 Corteen Place
North Hollywood, CA 91607
(818) 506-0780

TAPEWORM VIDEO DISTRIBUTORS
27833 Avenue Hopkins, Unit 6
Valencia, CA 91355(805) 257-4904 (800) 367-
8437
FAX (805) 257-4820

T.A.T. INC.
3189 Weslock Circle
Decatur, GA 30034

TEMPO FILMS
1800 Robin Whipple Way
Belmont, CA 94002
(415) 595-1359 (408) 248-6517

TERRA NOVA FILMS, INC.
9848 South Winchester Avenue
Chicago, IL 60643
(312) 881-8491 (800) 779-8491
FAX (312) 881-3368

THIRD WORLD NEWSREEL
335 West 38th Street, 5th floor
New York, NY 10018
(212) 947-9277 FAX (212) 549-6417

THUNDEROUS PRODUCTIONS
1328 Broadway, Suite 956
New York, NY 10001
(212) 695-4250

TOM DAVENPORT FILMS
11324 Pearlstone Lane
Delaplane, VA 20144
(540) 592-3701 FAX (540) 592-3717

TREMAINE DANCE CONVENTIONS
14531 Hamlin Street, #104
Van Nuys, CA 91411
(818) 988-8006 FAX (818) 988-7314

UCLA INSTRUCTIONAL MEDIA CENTER
University of California at Los Angeles
46 Powell Library
Los Angeles, CA 90095-1517
(310) 825-0755 FAX (310) 206-5392

UNITED NATIONS VISUAL MATERIALS
LIBRARY
Department of Public Information
Room S-0808
New York, NY 10017
(212) 963-7318/19
FAX (212) 963-1658

UNIVERSITY OF CALIFORNIA EXTENSION
CENTER FOR MEDIA AND INDEPENDENT
LEARNING
2000 Center Street, 4th floor
Berkeley, CA 94704
(510) 642-0460 FAX (510) 643-9271

UNIVERSITY OF MINNESOTA
University Film and Video
1313 Fifth Street SE, Suite 108
Minneapolis, MN 55414
(612) 627-4270 (800) 847-8251
FAX (612) 627-4280
(Rentals only)

UROBOROS, INC.
325 East 21 Street, Suite 22
New York, NY 10010
(212) 475-5310

UZBEK DANCE AND CULTURE SOCIETY
P.O. Box 65195
Washington, DC 20035-5195
(301) 585-1105 FAX: same

VALK, ACHMED
1743 Fairchile Avenue
Manhattan, KS 66502-4037

VESTRON
c/o Live Home Video
15400 Sherman Way, P.O. Box 10124
Van Nuys, CA 91410-0124
(818) 988-5060

VIDEO ARTISTS INTERNATIONAL
109 Wheeler Avenue
Pleasantville, NY 10570
(914) 769-3691 (800) 477-7146

VIDEO D PRODUCTIONS
29 West 21st Street
New York, NY 10010
(212) 242-3345

V.I.E.W. VIDEO (VIDEO INTERNATIONAL
ENTERTAINMENT WORLD)
34 East 23rd Street
New York, NY 10010
(212) 674-5550 (800) 843-9843
FAX (212) 979-0266

VIEWFINDERS, INC.
P.O. Box 1665
Evanston, IL 60204
(708) 869-0602 (800) 342-3342
FAX (708) 869-1710

VIRGINIA TANNER CREATIVE DANCE
CENTER
University of Utah
1215 Annex Building
Salt Lake City, UT 84112
(801) 581-7374

VISION VIDEO
2030 Wentz Church Road
Worchester, PA 19490
(215) 584-1893 800 523-0226
FAX (215) 584-4610

VISIONARY DANCE PRODUCTIONS
P.O. Box 30797
Seattle, WA 98103
(206) 632-2353

VOYAGER VIDEO
P.O. Box 1122
Darien, CT 06820-1122
(800) 786-9248 FAX (203) 655-1486

VPI (VIDEFILM PRODUCERS
INTERNATIONAL)
8899 Beverly Boulevard #909
Los Angeles, CA 90048
(310) 550-7588 FAX (310) 550-1009

WADSWORTH, DAVID
P.O. Box 28128
Philadelphia, PA 19131
(215) 878-4482

WAGMAN, VERA
550 Grand Street, #2G
New York, NY 10002
(212) 260-3552

WANNER, DEBRA
121 First Avenue
New York, NY 10003
(212) 473-5495

WARNER HOME VIDEO
4000 Warner Boulevard
Burbank, CA 91522
(818) 954-6000

WARNERVISION ENTERTAINMENT
80 Fitness Quest Plaza
Canton, Ohio 44750
(800) 321-9236

WENDY WOODSON AND PRESENT
COMPANY
340 South Pleasant Street
Amherst, MA 01002
(413) 256-0948

WHYY-TV 12
150 North Sixth Street
Philadelphia, PA 19106
(215) 351-1200 (215) 351-0398

WIMM PRODUCTIONS
327 East 34th Street, #4D
New York, NY 10016
(212) 684-1548

WITHERS, ROBERT
202 West 80th Street, #5W
New York, NY 10024
(212) 873-1353

WNET
P.O. Box 2284
South Burlington, VT 05407
(800) 336-1917 FAX (802) 864-9846

WOMBAT PRODUCTIONS
250 West 57th Street, Suite 2421
New York, NY 10019
(212) 315-2502 (800) 542-5552
FAX (212) 582-0585

WOMEN MAKE MOVIES
426 Broadway, Suite 500
New York, NY 10013
(212) 925-0606 FAX (212) 925-2052

XENON
P.O. Box 1440
Santa Monica, CA 90406
(310) 451-5510

ZIPPORAH FILMS
1 Richdale Avenue, Unit #4
Cambridge, MA 02140
(617) 576-3603 FAX (617) 864-8006

Resources for Dance on Camera (United States)

AMERICAN DANCE FESTIVAL ARCHIVES
DANCING FOR THE CAMERA FESTIVAL
Box 90772
Durham, NC 27710-0772
(919) 684-6402 FAX (919) 684-5459
Sponsors America's foremost modern dance festival, held annually in June and July, with performances, workshops, symposiums; maintains an archival collection including film and video documentation of its activities dating back to the 1930s, with access to the collection by appointment only. Also sponsors an annual international festival of film video dance, soliciting entries in three categories—Choreography for the Camera, Documentary, and Experimental—for juried public screenings.

THE AMERICAN FEDERATION OF ARTS
41 East 65th Street
New York, NY 10021(212) 988-7700 FAX (212) 861-2487
Organizes art, film and video exhibitions that travel throughout the United States and abroad.

CONSULATES GENERAL
Sources for free loan of dance films and videos about individual countries; located mainly in Washington, DC and New York, NY.

DANCE COLLECTION
The New York Public Library Performing Arts Research Center at Lincoln Center
111 Amsterdam Avenue
New York, NY 10023
(212) 870-1657 FAX (212) 787-3852
In-house viewing of over 9,000 dance films and videotapes for research and scholarly use only; telephone and letter reference service for inquiries on all aspects of dance film and video.

DANCE FILMS ASSOCIATION, INC.
31 West 21st Street, 3rd floor
New York, NY 10010
(212) 727-0764
Provides rental and on-site viewing of selected dance films and videos, information and equipment services; compiles *Dance on Camera* catalog; publishes bi-monthly *Dance on Camera News*; sponsors annual Dance on Camera Festival.

DANCE NOTATION BUREAU LIBRARY
31 West 21st Street, 3rd Floor
New York, NY 10010
(212) 807-7899 FAX (212) 675-9657
Provides films and videos of dances which have notated dance scores, often rough rehearsal or performance recordings which can be used for pre-reconstruction viewing; available for rental by members.

DANCE THEATRE OF HARLEM LIBRARY/ ARCHIVES
466 West 152nd StreetNew York, NY 10031
(212) 690-2800 FAX (212) 690-8736

Videotapes focused on Dance Theatre of Harlem, also ballet technique and other dance styles; non-circulating.

DANCE VIDEO CENTER
P.O Box 292244
Los Angeles, CA 90029
(818) 244-6485

DOCUMENTARY EDUCATIONAL RESOURCES
101 Morse Street, Department AM
Watertown, MA 02172
(617) 926-0491 (800) 569-6621
FAX (617) 926-9519
Specializes in ethnographic films and videos, including the subject of dance, available as footage and by database for exhibits and instructional needs.

DONNELL MEDIA CENTER
The New York Public Library
20 West 53rd Street
New York, NY 10019
(212) 621-0611Film and video loan; study center for viewing films by appointment.

GOETHE HOUSE NEW YORK
German Cultural Center
1014 Fifth Avenue
New York, NY 10028
(212) 439-8700
Library has a selection of videos on German dance and dance theatre.

HARVARD THEATRE COLLECTION
Harvard College Library
Harvard University
Cambridge, MA 02138
(617) 495-2445 FAX (617) 495-1376
Archives and footage of major dance figures.

HISTORICAL DANCE FOUNDATION
31 Union Square West, Suite 15D
New York, NY 10003
(212) 255-5545 FAX (212) 366-4979
Classes in and choreography for renaissance, baroque, and nineteenth century social dance.

INSTITUTE OF THE AMERICAN MUSICAL
121 North Detroit Street
Los Angeles, CA 90036

INTERNATIONAL TAP ASSOCIATION
Colorado Dance Festival
Box 356
Boulder, CO 80306
(303) 442-7666
Tap dance stock footage.

JACOB'S PILLOW DANCE FESTIVAL ARCHIVES
P.O. Box 287
Lee, MA 01238

(413) 637-1322 FAX (413) 243-4744
Archival footage of Ted Shawn and his company, Ruth St. Denis, and the Denishawn era.

JOHN F. KENNEDY CENTER
The Performing Arts Library
Washington, DC 20566
(202) 707-6245
Focus of materials is on performances given in the Center, including some videotapes.

JOSE LIMON DANCE FOUNDATION ARCHIVES
611 Broadway, 9th Floor
New York, NY 10012
(212) 777-3353
Archival footage of the choreography of Jose Limon and Doris Humphrey; for on-site viewing by appointment.

LABAN/BARTENIEFF INSTITUTE OF MOVEMENT STUDIES
11 East 4th Street
New York, NY 10003
(212) 477-4299 FAX (212) 477-3702
Over 600 non-circulating videotapes.

THE LIBRARY OF CONGRESS
Motion Picture, Broadcasting, and Recorded Sound Division, Rm. 338
James Madison Memorial Building
Washington, DC 20540
(202) 707-5000
Access to researchers by appointment for viewing of all copyrighted films and videotapes; holds many special collections such Martha Graham's and Bob Fosse's (see essay by David Parker on "Dance on Film and Video at The Library of Congress").

THE MARIN COUNTY FESTIVAL OF DANCE
1320 Grand Avenue
San Rafael, CA 94901
(415) 454-7796 x119/453-6705 x24
Seeks entries of works merging the art forms of film/video and movement, including dances specifically created for film/video.

METROPOLITAN MUSEUM OF ART DANCE INDEX
Metropolitan Museum of Art
1000 Fifth Avenue
New York, NY 10028
(212) 879-5500, x3572
Catalog of images of sculptures, paintings, objects from the Museum's collection relating to dance.

MUSEUM OF MODERN ART
11 West 53rd Street
New York, NY 10019
(212) 708-9614
Study center for viewing films open by appointment.

MUSEUM OF TELEVISION AND RADIO
25 West 52nd Street
New York, NY 10019
(212) 621-6600
Television programs produced from 1939 to the
present available for study on the premises.

NEW YORK CITY BALLET
Education Department
70 Lincoln Center
New York, NY 10023
(212) 595-2154
Provides educational programs called "Storytelling Through Dance" to New York metropoli-
tan-area schools.

PBS VIDEOFINDERS
425 East Colorado
Glendale, CA 91205
(800) 328-7271
Phone information service on the distributors for
feature films or programs produced by Public
Broadcasting Service.

THE PROGRAM FOR ART ON FILM
c/o Pratt Institute School of Information and Library Science
200 Willoughby Avenue
Brooklyn, NY 11205
(718) 399-4206 FAX (718) 399-4207
Compiles *Art on Screen Database,* a computer
index to more than 23,000 productions on fine
and visual arts, including dance; publishes *Art
on Screen on CD-ROM* (G.K. Hall/ Macmillan).

SAN FRANCISCO PERFORMING ARTS LIBRARY AND MUSEUM
399 Grove Street
San Francisco, CA 94102
(415) 255-4800 FAX (415) 255-1913
Videos of local dance performances including the
San Francisco Ethnic Dance Festival and some
commercial dance tapes, for on-site viewing.

THE SCHOMBURG CENTER FOR RESEARCH IN BLACK CULTURE
Moving Images and Recorded Sound
515 Lenox AvenueNew York, NY 10027
(212) 491-2236
Films, videos, oral histories of leading African
American figures such as Katherine Dunham,
Alvin Ailey, Pearl Primus, Talley Beatty; viewing
and/or listening by appointment. Copies of the
Ernie Smith Collection of films on African
American dance may be viewed.

STERN'S PERFORMING ARTS DIRECTORY
33 West 60th Street
New York, NY 10023
(212) 245-8937
Annual international guide to dance companies,
performers, managers, and festivals.

THE TWYLA THARP ARCHIVE
Jerome Lawrence and Robert E. Lee Theatre Research Institute Library
Ohio State University
1430 Lincoln Tower
1800 Cannon Drive

Columbus, OH 43210-1230
(614) 292-6614 FAX (614) 292-3222Archival footage of Twyla Tharp, her company and other
companies and artist with whom she has
worked; includes videotapes of rehearsals and
performances available for viewing by appointment only; also archival footage of Robert Post.

UCLA FILM AND TELEVISION ARCHIVE
Research and Study Center
46 Powell Library, Box 951517
Los Angeles, CA 90024-1517
(310) 206-5388 FAX (310) 206-5392
Archival collection holding a variety of films and
television programs on the subject of dance.
Available by appointment for on-site viewing
for research and study.

VIDEODA
Lisa Nelson
P.O. Box 22
East Charleston, VT 05833
Rental and sales of videotaped documents and ed-
ited narrative histories of contact improvisa-
tion, made by the originators of the form.

THE WPA FILM LIBRARY
5525 West 159th Street
Oak Forest, IL 60452
(708) 535-1540 (800) 777-2223
FAX (708) 535-1541
Sells stock footage to producers, including the
subject of dance (e.g. *Black Bottom in Paris,*
1927 and *Underwater Charleston,* 1926).

International Resources for Dance on Camera

ARTS COUNCIL FILMS
14, Great Peter Street
London SW1 P3NQ, England
(44-71) 973-6454/6581
FAX (44-71) 973-6590
Distributor.

ARTS PUBLISHING INTERNATIONAL
International Arts Manager Magazine
4 Assam Street
London E17 QS, England
(44-71) 247-0066
FAX (44-71) 247-6868
Annual performing arts directory for Europe; lists ministries of culture, funding agencies, national organizations, resource centers, dance companies, competitions, etc.

CANADIAN FILMMAKERS DISTRIBUTION CENTRE
67A Portland Street
Toronto, Ontario M5V 2M9, Canada
(416) 593-1808 FAX (416) 593-8661
Distributor.

CANADIAN FILMMAKERS DISTRIBUTION WEST
402 West Pender Street, #606
Vancouver, BC V6B 1T6, Canada
(604) 684-3014
Distributor.

CANAL DANSA
Travessia Sant Antoni
No. 6, pral 1/08012
Barcelona, Spain
TEL/FAX (34) 34-160957
International bi-annual festival which began in 1987, three weeks long, featuring dance videos.

CENTRE GEORGES POMPIDOU
25, rue du Renard
75191 Paris, France
(33-1) 44-78-12-33
FAX (33-1) 44-78-13-00
Library and museum which sponsors film programs and festivals; in-house viewing of collection of dance films and videos.

CINEMATHEQUE DE LA DANSE
29, rue du Colisee
75008 Paris, France
(33-1) 45-53-21-86
FAX (33-1) 42-56-08-55
Collection of stills, films, and videos.

THE DANCE MUSEUM
Laboratoriegatan 10
115 27 Stockholm, Sweden
(46-8) 678512

Archive, exhibit, research center; maintains the UNESCO Dance and Video Collection.

DON FEATHERSTONE PRODUCTIONS
7134 Bennett Street
Bondi NSW 2026, Australia
(61-2) 386-1469
Producer of Michelle Mahrer films such as *The Black Swan: Meryl Tankard Choreographer*, distributed by RM Arts.

FILM AUSTRALIA
Eton Road
Lindfield NSW 2070, Australia
(61-2) 413-8777 FAX (61-2) 416-5672
Distributor.

FUNDACION ANDALUZA DE FLAMENCO
Palacio Pemartin
Plaza de San Juan, 1
11403 Jerez, Spain
Archive of stills, films and videos of flamenco artists, founded 1988.

GRAND PRIX INTERNATIONAL VIDEO-DANSE
30 Boulevard Gambetta
06130 Grasse, France
(33) 93-40-19-50
FAX (33) 93-36-55-84
Annual international competition for dance on video; houses library of entries for on-site viewing.

IMZ (INTERNATIONALES MUSIKZENTRUM WIEN)
Lothringerstrasse 20
A-1030 Vienna, Austria
(43-1) 7130777-17
FAX (43-1) 7130777-17 or 21
Sponsors Dance Screen world competition for dance video; compiles database of performing arts programs.

INTERNATIONAL FESTIVAL OF FILMS ON ART
640 Rue St. Paul Ouest, Bureau 406
Montreal (Quebec) Canada H3C 1L9
(514) 874-1637 FAX (514) 874-9929
Festival du Film sur l'Art (FIFA) promotes all types of art on film, with dance as one of the 26 categories screened in Montreal.

ISRAEL DANCE LIBRARY
Beit Ariela
25 Shaul Hamelech Boulevard
P.O. Box 33235
Tel-Aviv 61221, Israel
Collection includes over 800 hours of films and videotapes.

J.C.S.
206 Jaffa Street
Jerusalem, Israel 91131
(972-2) 701777Distributor.

KUNSTE ACADEMY IN BERLIN DANCE ARCHIVE
Gottschedstrasse Postfach 1453
0-7010 Leipzig, Germany
(49-41) 209628
Collection includes over 800 films on such topics as German folk dance, dancers, and children's dance.

NATIONAL FILM AND TELEVISION ARCHIVE
British Film Institute
21 Stephen Street
London W1P 2LN, England
(44-71) 255-1444
FAX (44-71) 580-7503
Collection of films, videotapes, television programs and stills, from the beginning of cinema to the present day, includes thousands of dance titles, many Hollywood musicals and documentaries from other countries.

NATIONAL VIDEO CORPORATION ARTS INTERNATIONAL
46 Great Marlborough Street
London, WIR 5DE England
(44-71) 434-9571
FAX (44-71) 434-9700
Distributor.

THE PLACE DANCE SERVICES
17 Dukes Road
London, WC1H 9AB
(44-71) 1-388-5407
FAX (44-71) 1-383-2003
Holds Dance on Screen, an annual festival of screenings of international dance films, talks, and workshops for choreographers, dancers and filmmakers.

RHOMBUS INTERNATIONAL, INC.
489 King Street West, Suite 102
Toronto, Ontario, Canada M5V 1L3
(416) 971-7856 FAX (416) 971-9647
Distributor.

RM ARTS
46 Great Malborough Street
London W1V 1DB, England
(44-71) 439-2637 FAX (44-71) 439-2316
Distributor.

SK STIFTUNG KULTUR
Videotanz im Mediapark 7
50670 Koln, Germany
(49-221) 226-2906
FAX (49-221) 226-3410
Supports videodance with an international dance film series called TANZ-Gerschichetn (DANCE Histories), Dance Film Night, the German Videodance Prize, Dance Videotheque, and publi-

cation of monographs on dance history and cassettes of dance films.

STATENS FILMCENTRAL
Vestergade 27
Copenhagen K, Denmark DK-1456
(45-1) 33-13-26-86
Distributor.

TANZ PERFORMANCE KOLN
Melchiorstrasse 3
D-50670 Koln, Germany
(49-221) 722133 FAX (49-221) 7392030
Organizes an international festival on dance film and new media called Pictures of (e)Motion.

TERCER FESTIVAL INTERNATIONAL DE VIDEO DANZA DE BUENOS AIRES
Centro Cultural Ricardo Rojas
Av. Corrientes 2038, 2º piso
    (1045) Capital Federal, Argentina

(541) 951-6060 FAX (541) 522-0597
Dance video festival featuring three categories: Video Dance as an Art Form, Dance Documentaries, and Dance on Screen and Live (mixed media).

VIDEOGRAPHE, INC.
4550 Garnier Street
Montreal, Quebec, Canada H2J 3S6
(514) 521-2116
Distributor.

YORK UNIVERSITY
Sound and Moving Image Library
4700 Keele Street
North York, Ontario M3J 1P3 Canada
(416) 736-2100
Includes many films and videos on dance and dance related topics.

WISSEN (INSTITUTE FOR WISSENSCHAFTLICHEN FILMS)
Nonnenstieg 72
Gottingen, West Germany BRD D-3400
(49) 0551-21034
Producer.

For a more complete list of dance resources (libraries, archives, organizations, associations, publishers, bookstores, reference sources, serials, abstracts, indexes, etc.), see Mary S. Bopp's *Research in Dance: A Guide to Resources*, New York: G.K. Hall & Company, 1994.

About the Editor

Louise Spain is Associate Professor and Director of Media Services in the Library Media Resources Center of LaGuardia Community College, The City University of New York. She is also President of the Board of Directors of Dance Films Association.